Encyclopedia of
American Indian History

Encyclopedia of
American Indian History

VOLUME III

Bruce E. Johansen
Barry M. Pritzker

EDITORS

A B C ⬤ C L I O
Santa Barbara, California • Denver, Colorado • Oxford, England

Cataloging-in-Publication Data is on file with the Library of Congress

ISBN: 978-1-85109-817-0   ebook: 978-1-85109-818-7

12 11 10 09 08   1 2 3 4 5 6 7 8

Production Editor: Vicki Moran
Editorial Assistant: Sara Springer
Production Manager: Don Schmidt
Media Editor: John Whithers
Media Resources Coordinator: Ellen Brenna Dougherty
Media Resources Manager: Caroline Price
File Manager: Paula Gerard

ABC-CLIO, Inc.
130 Cremona Drive, P.O. Box 1911
Santa Barbara, California 93116-1911

This book is also available on the World Wide Web as an ebook. Visit http://www.abc-clio.com for details.

This book is printed on acid-free paper. ∞

Manufactured in the United States of America

For our families,
and for future generations

Bruce E. Johansen
Barry M. Pritzker

Contents

Volume III

Introduction, xiii

People and Groups in American Indian History

Primary Source Documents

Introduction

A BOOK CAN BE A TIME MACHINE, opening a window on the unquestioned judgments and assumptions of authors in other times. Many of these have been delivered with a sense of European-American self-congratulation. Consider John D. Hicks, who, in *The Federal Union: A History of the United States to 1865* (1937) opens a 700-page tome with the words "The civilization that grew up in the United States . . ." implying that nothing worth the name occurred before Columbus planted European seeds here (Hicks, 1937, 1). Paragraph two begins: "America before the time of Columbus had developed no great civilizations of its own" (Hicks, 1937, 1). This text states authoritatively that the Mayas, Aztecs, and Incas could not match "the best that Europe had to offer" (Hicks, 1937, 1), despite the fact that accounts of the Cortez invasion expressed a sense of awe at the Aztecs' capital city Tenochtitlan when they first saw it. In the same paragraph, Hicks develops reasons why he believes that Europeans surpassed America's "primitive civilization": "racial traits may account in part for this failure, but the importance of the environment cannot be overlooked" (Hicks, 1937, 1).

No time and no people speak with a single voice, however. So while Hicks' assumptions of racial superiority remind us of Richard Henry Pratt's advertising slogan for the boarding schools he built ("Kill the Indian, Save the Man") even Pratt's and Hicks' time were informed by other voices that asserted enduring value to Native American peoples and cultures. While Pratt's slogan is sometimes interpreted as an endorsement of genocide in our time, to him it was friendly advice to peoples whom he assumed would die culturally as well as genetically if they held fast to cultures that he considered out of date in a modern world. Multicultural ideas that inform public discourse (as well as census reports) in our time had precedents in Pratt's and Hicks' time. The majority society was just not listening. Consider Walt Whitman, for example, during 1883, as Pratt was fashioning his campaign to save Indians by killing their cultures:

As to our aboriginal or Indian population . . . I know it seems to be agreed that they must gradually dwindle as time rolls on, and in a few generations more leave only a reminiscence, a blank. But I am not at all clear about that. As America . . . develops, adapts, entwines, faithfully identifies its own—are we to see it cheerfully accepting using all the contributions of foreign lands from the whole outside globe—and then rejecting the only ones distinctly its own? (Moquin, 1973, 5–6).

One newspaper, the *Omaha World-Herald*, sent a native woman, Susette LaFlesche (an Omaha), to describe the aftermath of the Wounded Knee massacre. She was married to Thomas Tibbles. Together, a decade earlier, they had roused their city of Omaha in anger over the torturous treatment suffered by the Ponca Standing Bear and his band. Exiled in Indian Territory from their homeland along the Niobrara River (in northernmost Nebraska), the Poncas had escaped and walked home, stopping in the city, their feet bleeding in the snow, so hungry that they had chewed on their moccasins. General George Crook volunteered to be the defendant in a legal case that established the Poncas' right to return home.

History is full of surprises. The same year that Hicks' book was published, Matthew W. Stirling, chief and later director of the American Bureau of Ethnology for thirty years (1928–1958), stated in *National Geographic* that the Albany Plan of Union (1754) was fundamentally shaped by the Iroquois Confederacy through Benjamin Franklin (Stirling, 1937). Such an idea is hardly universally accepted, even in our time. For one, Steven Pinker, in *The Blank Slate*, asserted that the same idea was flimsy enough to dismiss without explanation in two words: "1960s granola" (Pinker, 2002, 298).

Historically, we stand with Whitman and Stirling. *The Encyclopedia of American Indian History* attempts to redress assumptions that any single culture is superior to any other. American Indian voices were available to historians in the 1930s; it was, after

all, a time of major Native rights assertion under the Indian Reorganization Act, but many non-Native historians seemed not to be listening. The writings of Dr. Charles A. Eastman (or, to use his Dakota name, Ohiyesa) and Luther Standing Bear were widely published, among many others. Major nineteenth-century feminists (Elizabeth Cady Stanton and Matilda Joslyn Gage, to name two) had acknowledged their debt to Native matriarchal societies. Still, one can hardly imagine Hicks having any use for an encyclopedia entry titled "American Indian Contributions to the World."

We start with six essays, written by our co-editors and members of our editorial board, which focus on the themes that dominate particular eras in American Indian history. So, for example, if a reader wants to find out why the Trail of Tears migration happened when it did, s/he would find that context covered in the essay dealing with the period from 1800 to 1850. The late Vine Deloria, Jr. once advised non-Indian scholars to study the history of topics of contemporary importance to Native peoples, and a section of the encyclopedia addresses those issues that are prominent both in the history of Native peoples and in Native societies today. These entries range from archaeology and pre-contact Native history to topics like gaming and water rights, which are still so relevant. Subsequent sections deal with the most important events of American Indian history, aspects of Native cultures that have had ramifications in history, Native interactions with non-Indian governments, and the roles of both individuals and groups in American Indian history. One of the most important sections of the encyclopedia, the histories of particular Native nations, is absolutely vital to the stories we're seeking to have told and deserves to be highlighted. Also, primary sources from throughout American Indian history are presented so that readers can get a flavor of how different people viewed these events as they happened.

The occupancy of most of North America by Europeans on a sustained basis is less than 200 years old—four consecutive human lives then, less than three now. Thus, the importance of American Indian history to the recent history of all peoples on this continent is clear. The history is written in what we call our homeland—many of our cities, half the constituent states in the federal union that calls itself the United States, bear names that have Native roots.

If there is one thing we've learned from trying to organize and do justice to such a vast and important subject, it is that there is no way to present this material that is perfect for everyone. Different people learn best in different ways. However, we've endeavored to be as clear as possible, making the large number of materials and resources as easy to locate and use as possible. An encyclopedia is not a cast-iron product, but a collection of many contributors' work. In our case, this is a mixture of Native and non-Native voices. Selection of subject matter is subject to judgment, and interpretation, and will be reviewed—something or someone is included, someone or something else is ignored, or given short shrift. We can say only that we have done our best.

Bruce E. Johansen and Barry M. Pritzker, Editors
Steven L. Danver, Project Editor

References and Further Reading

Hicks, John D. *The Federal Union: A History of the United States to 1865.* 1937. Boston: Houghton-Mifflin.

Moquin, Wayne. *Great Documents in American Indian History.* 1973. New York: Praeger.

Pinker, Steven. *The Blank Slate: The Modern Denial of Human Nature.* 2002. New York: Viking (Penguin Putnam).

Pritzker, Barry M. *Native America Today: A Guide to Community Politics and Culture.* 1999. Santa Barbara, CA: ABC-CLIO.

Stirling, Matthew W. "America's First Settlers, the Indians." *National Geographic* 72:5 (1937), cited in Bruce E. Johansen, comp. *Native America and the Evolution of Democracy: A Supplementary Bibliography.* 1999, 140. Westport, CT: Greenwood.

Encyclopedia of
American Indian History

People and Groups in American Indian History

Aboriginal Peoples Television Network

"History would have been told differently if our reporters had been there." Or so claims the aboriginal Peoples Television Network (APTN), Canada's first and only aboriginal television network, established in 1999. The journey from concept to active broadcaster was, however, long and at times arduous.

In the late 1960s, aboriginal opposition to proposed changes to federal legislation aimed at terminating Canadian Indian special status manifested itself in the form of political organizations. In an attempt to keep aboriginal people nationwide informed of political events, several organizations established newsletters, many of which developed into larger monthly and weekly newspapers. An aboriginal print media industry slowly developed that eventually expanded to include small, community-based aboriginal-owned radio stations. During the early 1990s, however, significant cutbacks to federal funding nearly crippled the industry. While a number of publications survived, national statistics showed newspaper readership numbers to be waning while television viewers to be increasing significantly. Federal aboriginal officials soon began to promote the creation of a national aboriginal television network in an attempt to stabilize the national aboriginal communications program.

A small northern aboriginal television network, Television Northern Canada (TVNC), which began broadcasting northern and aboriginal programming from the Yukon to northern Labrador in 1991, was the catalyst that fueled the national aboriginal television network debate. A federal survey followed in 1998 that showed two-thirds of all Canadians supporting the idea of a national aboriginal television network, even if it meant displacing available services. Additional surveys demonstrated that Canadians were willing to pay an additional 15 percent for their monthly cable bill to receive an aboriginal television network. Canadian public support combined with strong lobbying by aboriginal communities, producers, and a variety of organizations led the

Canadian Radio-Television Telecommunications Commission (CRTC) to announce in February 1999 that the APTN would receive a national broadcast license.

The Aboriginal Peoples Television Network (APTN), Canada's first national aboriginal television network dedicated to Native programming, was launched on September 1, 1999. With programming for and about aboriginal people, APTN was developed to provide aboriginal producers, directors, actors, writers, and media professionals the opportunity to create innovative and relevant programming for national viewers reflecting Canada's diverse aboriginal cultures, both contemporary and historic. APTN offers a window into these worlds through a variety of programming, including dramas, entertainment specials, documentaries, news magazines, children's series, cooking shows, and education programs.

As APTN has grown, so has its audience. What was an upstart national television network with a limited market has evolved into an important entertainment, news, and educational choice delivered to more than 9 million households in Canada. Seventy percent of APTN programming originates in Canada, with more than half of the programs broadcast in English, 15 percent in French, and one-quarter in a variety of aboriginal languages including Inuktitut, Cree, Inuinaqtuun, Ojibway, Inuvialuktun, Mohawk, Dene, Gwich'in and Miqma'aq, Slavey, Dogrib, Chipweyan, and Tlingit. Nearly half of its programming is APTN-specific and cannot be seen on other networks. APTN airs 70 percent Canadian content with the remaining 30 percent of the schedule devoted to broadcasting indigenous programming from Australia, New Zealand, Central and South America, and the United States. Perhaps most notably, the majority of APTN programming originates with independent aboriginal producers from across the country and around the world, with the exception of news and live events. Network revenues are derived predominantly from subscriber fees and advertising proceeds. Employees of aboriginal descent comprise three-quarters of the APTN staff.

APTN has become more important than people realized following its inaugural 1999 broadcast. Recent data indicate that there are 500 aboriginal producers and broadcasters operating from a limited pool of money and that the communications system needs an influx of $10 million (Belanger, Newhouse, and Fitzmaurice, 2005). Without this funding, most of these broadcasters could be off the air in less than a year. With statistics showing that APTN viewing numbers have grown from weekly totals of 900,000 in 1999 to over 1,750,000 in 2003, APTN could become the main source of aboriginal news and entertainment in Canada in the near future.

Yale D. Belanger

See also Canada, Indian Policies of; Language and Language Renewal.

References and Further Reading

Aboriginal Peoples Television Network (APTN). "APTN Viewing Audience Continues to Grow." Available at: http://aptn.ca:8080/Whats_New/whatsnew_html. Accessed March 27, 2005.

Baltruschat, Doris. 2004. "Television and Canada's Aboriginal Communities: Seeking Opportunities Through Traditional Storytelling and Digital Technologies." *Canadian Journal of Communications* 29: 47–59.

Belanger, Yale, David Newhouse, and Kevin Fitzmaurice. 2005. *Creating a Seat at the Table: Aboriginal Programming at Canadian Heritage.* Gatineau, QC: Canadian Heritage.

Akwesasne Freedom School

The history of Native America would not be complete without mention of decades of forced assimilation through education in which speaking one's Native tongue was forbidden. Native students were often sent to boarding schools far from their homes, resulting in Native language decline and loss over a number of generations. However, across the nation, tribes have been making efforts at language revitalization and cultural reclamation, including the Mohawks of Akwesasne ("land where the partridge drums").

Beginning in 1979, an unprecedented effort to take control of their children's education began on the Akwesasne Mohawk Reservation with the establishment of the Akwesasne Freedom School (AFS). The Akwesasne Reservation, also known as the St. Regis Mohawk Indian Reservation, is located in northern New York and straddles the Canadian international border extending into Quebec and Ontario. The Mohawks are one of the five original members of the Haudenosaunee (People of the Longhouse) or Iroquois Confederacy, which also includes the Oneida, Onondaga, Cayuga, and Seneca.

AFS was started in 1979 by a group of traditional Mohawk parents and community members who were concerned with the lack of cultural teaching and Mohawk language in public schools. AFS was dedicated to raising children in a traditional manner and to regaining what little remained of the Mohawk language. At its beginning, AFS held classes in makeshift classrooms during a two-year-long encampment. Conflict over tribal and state jurisdiction created division among the residents of Akwesasne, and families in the encampment decided not to send their children to public schools. Instead, they took responsibility for their children's education into their own hands. Parents, who had been forbidden to speak Mohawk in their own schooling, transformed themselves into teachers and carpenters building a grassroots community-based school.

Today, this pre-K through eight independent school is known for its language immersion program, conducting instruction in the Kanienkéha (Mohawk) language for grades pre-K through six. The school adopted a total immersion approach in 1985 in hopes of speeding up the process of developing language fluency. Students are placed in a transition program during seventh and eighth grades when English-dominant instruction prepares them to enter an off-reservation public high school. The school operates on a year-round, six-weeks-on/two-weeks-off basis and enrolls approximately sixty-five students. The schedule allows students to follow the natural seasonal cycle and helps ensure they are using the language on a year-round basis. Parents continue to play an integral role in the school's operation, sharing responsibilities from construction and cleaning to curriculum development.

The curriculum is based on the Ohén:ton Karíwahtékwen ("Words That Come Before All Else"), also known as the Thanksgiving Address, which pays respect to all living things. Students begin and end each day with its recitation while reading, writing, math, science, and history revolve around its teachings. Using art, song, and traditional stories, teachers instill values of respect, peace, and community. Community gardens and walks through nearby woods provide a natural environment for learning about traditional medicine plants and human relationships with the natural world. Students have the opportunity to attend traditional Longhouse ceremonies throughout the year as part of the curriculum. Originally a housing structure for extended families that went out of use in the nineteenth century, the Longhouse today refers to the traditional ceremonial place of the Haudenosaunee.

The school's goals are to ground students in their culture while teaching skills and knowledge necessary in the non-Native world. In 2002, AFS students were awarded the President's Environmental Youth Award for a wetland restoration project. Some alumni were awarded a place with the high school National Honor Society while others achieved valedictorian status. A sense of Mohawk identity, culture, and language provides a solid foundation for academic achievement.

AFS is independent of state and federal funding and relies primarily on support from the Akwesasne Mohawk Board of Education, private foundations, donations, and fund-raisers. An annual quilt auction is the largest fund-raising event for the school, and handmade donated quilts bring in thousands of dollars.

In 1986 toxic chemicals from a nearby industrial plant were found in the school wells. While bottled water helped the problem temporarily, a massive campaign to build a new school has been underway for the past several years. Partially completed, inadequate funding temporarily halted the project. However, AFS continues to work toward the goal of finishing its new building and toward supporting and encouraging Mohawk children to learn their roles and responsibilities as Haudenosaunees.

Louellyn White

See also Assimilation; Education; Identity; Language and Language Renewal.

Reference and Further Reading

Akwesasne Freedom School. Available at: http://www.potsdam.edu/EDUC/Akwesasn/AFS.html. Accessed February 23, 2005).

Akwesasne Notes

Started during American Indian activism's modern reassertion in the late 1960s, *Akwesasne Notes* became one of the foremost Native-owned editorial voices for Native American rights in the United States and Canada. In a trade where advertising pays most of the bills, it carried nearly none. At a time when newspapers have come to resemble poor cousins of television, it rarely published in color, relying instead on pages dense with text. In a media world of megacorporations, *Akwesasne Notes* operated on a shoestring budget, rarely paying contributors or

editors and fiercely maintaining its editorial independence.

Akwesasne Notes was first begun as a compilation of news on topics of concern to Native Americans. In December 1968, the idea for such a journal was born around the kitchen table of Ernie (Kaientaronkwen) Benedict at Akwesasne. The first editor of the newspaper was Jerry Gambill, a non-Native Canadian, who was given the Mohawk name Rarihokwats. Gambill was employed as a community assistance worker in the Canadian Department of Indian Affairs when he first traveled to Akwesasne. He was fired from his government job in 1967 but remained at Akwesasne, living on Cornwall Island.

Akwesasne Notes's coverage has included a reunion of Native peoples who took part in the occupation of Alcatraz Island, reports on a heated intellectual debate over whether the Iroquois Great Law helped inspire the U.S. Constitution, a report from indigenous peoples in Australia contributed by a Mohawk family who visited there, the latest plans for coal mining on the Hopi Reservation, and an account of negotiations between Nicaraguan Native peoples and the U.S. government. Other articles reported on the repression of Tibetan Natives by the Chinese government and the organization of U.S. chapters of the Green Party. *Akwesasne Notes* has also described Native American resistance to the destruction of Brazil's rain forests, detailed accounts of human rights violations in Guatemala, reported trade agreements between American Indian tribes and Third World nations, discussed a proposed world constitution, and editorially supported Greenpeace.

Akwesasne Notes's circulation averaged about 10,000 copies per issue during the 1970s. Most subscribers received the paper by mail. The publication had a geographic reach that few newspapers could match, with copies being mailed to indigenous people and their supporters around the world.

As a voice of Akwesasne's traditional council of chiefs, the newspaper's content reflected its global approach to issues involving indigenous rights, but the focus of its coverage remained the Haudenosaunee ("People of the Longhouse"), the confederation of Indian nations that the French called the Iroquois and the English the Six Nations. To read *Notes*, one had to lay aside any notions of the noble savage, because its pages freely reported on internal dissension and occasional murder and fraud, providing graphic descriptions of the abysmal living conditions on many reservations.

On January 9, 1988, a firebomb razed the newspaper's offices during gambling-related violence at Akwesasne. Installed in a new office with donated equipment gathered from a worldwide network of supporters, *Akwesasne Notes* didn't miss a bimonthly issue after it sustained $200,000 in uninsured losses from the midwinter fire. The fire gutted the Nation House that had been the newspaper's home for much of the previous two decades. In its first editorial after the fire (Spring 1988), the editors wrote: "Our offices were torched by those amongst us here at Akwesasne who oppose our reporting on the conflicts that are plaguing the Haudenosaunee [Iroquois] nations. . . . With the gambling, the cigarette smuggling, the violence . . . it is understandable why those criminal elements amongst us are opposed to a free press disseminating information about the illegal and immoral activities around us . . . They almost succeeded in putting us out of business . . . but we will survive" ("How It Is with Us," 1988, 2).

In 1991, following ongoing gambling-related turmoil at Akwesasne, the newspaper stopped publishing. It resumed in early 1995 in a glossy magazine format. For almost two years, the magazine provided a showcase for Native American issues and artwork. Unable to support the expenses of such a format, the publication reverted to a tabloid newspaper format in 1997, then again ceased publication. During almost three decades of publication, *Akwesasne Notes* incubated the talents of a number of notable Native American journalists and scholars, among them Jose Barreiro, editor of *Native Americas* magazine; John C. Mohawk, Seneca professor of Native American Studies at the State University of New York (Buffalo); and Doug George-Kanentiio, Mohawk activist and freelance writer.

Bruce E. Johansen

See also Mohawk, John C.
References and Further Reading
"How It Is with Us." 1988. *Akwesasne Notes*, 2 (Spring).
Johansen, Bruce E. 1993. *Life and Death in Mohawk Country*. Golden, CO: North American Press/Fulcrum.

Alaska Native Brotherhood

Twelve Alaskan Indian men who were former students of the Sitka Industrial Training School and the Carlisle Indian School formed the Alaska Native Brotherhood (ANB) on November 5, 1912, in Juneau,

Alaska. Initially, membership was restricted to English-speaking, Christian Indians who pledged abstinence from alcohol. The ANB focused its energies on promoting Native solidarity, achieving U.S. citizenship, abolishing racial prejudice, and securing economic equality through the recognition of Indian land title and mineral rights, as well as the preservation of salmon stocks. The ANB promoted citizenship through good hygiene, punctuality, and regular school attendance, in addition to wearing Western dress, securing gainful and regular employment, using English as the primary language, and living in self-contained housing units apart from other Indians. The ANB embraced three central goals: (1) to force the recognition of the citizenship rights for the Natives of southeast Alaska; (2) to provide proper education for Native children; and (3) to abolish customs regarded by non-Natives as barbaric and uncivilized.

Comprised mainly of Tlingit and Haida men, the ANB was patterned after the non-Native fraternal organization known as the Arctic Brotherhood, a formal fishing union that strenuously lobbied the U.S. government for Alaskan congressional representation. Local ANB chapters called "camps" were located in various Native communities, guided by a central organizational and communications hub known as the Grand Camp that kept ANB delegates in regular contact and informed of political occurrences. Members held an annual convention of all the camps each November. Despite its nonsectarian approach, the ANB officers maintained a close relationship with the Presbyterian Sheldon Jackson school. By advocating the civilization and assimilation doctrine promoted by the federal government, the ANB's leaders embraced a political philosophy that was antithetical to traditional Tlingit and Haida political culture. Nevertheless, by the mid-1920s, nearly every Native community in southeast Alaska had a local camp of either the ANB or the Alaska Native Sisterhood (established 1915). Further, the members of most Native communities openly cooperated with the Brotherhood and the Sisterhood.

The U.S. government during this period considered Native people to be wards of the state. This prompted ANB leaders to fight for citizenship and its attendant rights. As the ANB grew in popularity, its leaders became increasingly convinced of the organization's influence over Alaskan politics. In 1921, ANB representative William Paul attempted to convince officials in Washington to prohibit fish traps from narrow bays and channels in Alaska.

Although Paul's request was ignored, his appearance informed federal officials that the ANB was the political voice for Native Alaskans. The ANB continued lobbying federal officials to grant Indians full citizenship status, and, in 1924, the U.S. government acquiesced, subsequently passing the Indian Citizenship Act. Following the ANB's attainment of Alaskan Indian enfranchisement, the Brotherhood attempted to extend its influence by subsequently working with both Native and non-Native labor leaders, eventually establishing itself as an influential labor union and bargaining agent. By the mid-1920s, the ANB represented Native Alaskans in both political and labor matters. Buoyed by support resulting from the distribution of the ANB journal, the *Alaska Fisherman* (established 1924), the ANB would remain an influential bargaining agent and labor force into the 1940s. Toward the end of the 1920s, ANB leaders denounced as discriminatory a recent announcement by the federal government that a single school system would be established for Native Americans. In 1929, William Paul successfully argued in court that Native parents had the right to send their children to the school of their choice. The attempt to dispose of separate Indian schools and to compel the federal government to recognize Native people as citizens was an ANB strategy designed to wrest from government control the direction of their lives. The ANB also announced its intention in 1929 to recover Tlingit land by joining forces with the Haidas to pursue a land claim settlement against the U.S. government. The ANB refined its political strategy at each of its subsequent five annual conventions, while persistently lobbying federal officials for change. The U.S. government eventually gave in and passed the Tlingit and Haida Jurisdictional Act of 15 June 1935, enabling the Tlingits and Haidas to initiate their land claim against the government and the U.S. Court of Claims.

By 1935, there were twenty-two camps with 2,200 members out of a total population of 6,000 Tlingit and Haida (Drucker, 1958). Significant community-based support notwithstanding, the Brotherhood was denied control of the land claims suit. Instead, the Department of the Interior supervised the creation of the Tlingit-Haida Central Council to pursue the land claim. For the first time in two decades, a proposed ANB strategy had failed. During this period, the ANB returned to the Tlingit heritage they had suppressed since the organization's inception in 1912. Both the Tlingit language and the potlatch were reintegrated into the ANB philosophy.

The following year, the federal government extended the Indian Reorganization Act (IRA) to Alaska (1936), enabling the formation of tribal governments at the village level. The ANB supported the IRA, a popular move that further strengthened its political resolve.

As the ANB grew in popularity, the Brotherhood became involved in issues beyond labor activism and its desire to ensure Native incorporation. In 1929, an ANB Grand Officer was refused access to the main level of a movie theater in Juneau. Informed that he would have to sit in the Native section of the balcony, he brought his complaint to the ANB. A similar event occurred a few years later when a group of Natives caused damage to an ice-cream parlor after being refused admission. The goal was to have their case heard publicly in court. Following these two high-profile events, the ANB aggressively lobbied the Alaska Territorial Legislature for change, and, in 1946, an antidiscrimination law was passed. Despite claiming these impressive political accomplishments, the ANB created the Tlingit-Haida Central Council (THCC) in the 1940s. The THCC was the legal organization established by the ANB to pursue the land claim, since anyone in Alaska could join the ANB. Despite the separate mandates (the ANB specialized in community activism, while the THCC took over more formal governmental duties), the two organizations continued to work together and share leadership at many levels.

The ANB continued in the wake of diminished political influence, and by the 1950s it could claim the financial stability that helped it remain free of political coercion. Financial success also meant that the ANB could spend $50,000 to construct a new building at Hoonah in time for its 1952 convention. Organizational funding was largely generated through membership fees; each member contributed $10 to join and paid an annual $12 fee (Drucker, 1958). The Grand Camp directed half of this money to the Grand Treasurer. The money raised was used for a variety of other purposes, which included hiring a lawyer to defend a Native man convicted of violating fishing laws in the early 1950s.

The 1960s was a tumultuous period for Native people in Alaska and, in particular, the ANB. Having long been usurped by the Tlingit-Haida Central Council as the governing body of the Tlingit and Haida people, the land claim filed in the 1930s that the ANB had hoped to resolve was finalized in 1968 with an award to the Tlingits and Haidas of $7.5 million. This opened the door for the Alaska Native

Claims Settlement Act (ANSCA) in 1971, which transferred approximately one-ninth of Alaska's land plus $962.5 million in compensation to Native interests, thereby resolving all land claims previously brought against the state. Even though it was part of the original movement to support Alaska land claims and despite the fact that the ANB was one of the constituent organizations of the Alaska Federated Natives (AFN), it was largely shut out of these discussions. The ANB was further excluded from AFN operations following a reorganization in the mid-1970s. They nevertheless continued to hold annual meetings each November and delegates continued to pass resolutions that the Grand Camp took to state and federal officials. In October 2005, the ANB held its ninety-second annual convention, in Juneau.

As of 2005, the ANB was restructuring. Now visible online (ANB, n.d.), the organization Web site proudly lists ANB accomplishments, which include desegregation of Alaska schools, securing the Native franchise and relief for elderly Natives, supporting implementation of the IRA in Alaska, and bringing hospitals to Native people in Alaska. This is an impressive list to be sure, although most of these events occurred prior to the 1950s. The group is also refashioning its constitution, its manual of ceremonies, and its rules of order and official handbook. Criticism has been leveled at the ANB for becoming overly intricate, suggesting organizational inertia. Further, complaints persist that the ANB is slow to develop and circulate and to act on resolutions. Nevertheless, the ANB persists into the twenty-first century.

Yale D. Belanger

See also Alaska Native Claims Settlement Act; Land, Identity and Ownership of, Land Rights.

References and Further Reading

Alaska Native Brotherhood (ANB). No date. Available at: http://www.anbgrandcamp.org/. Accessed January 15, 2007.

Drucker, Phillip. 1958. *The Native Brotherhoods: Modern Intertribal Organizations on the Northwest Coast.* Bureau of Ethnology Bulletin, No. 168. Washington, DC: Smithsonian Institution.

Haycox, Stephen. 1989. "Alaska Native Brotherhood Convention: Sites and Grand Officers, 1912–1959." *Alaska History* 4, no. 2: 38–47.

Milburn, Maureen. 1987. "The Politics of Possession: Louis Shortridge and the Tlingit Collections at the University of Pennsylvania Museum." Ph.D. dissertation, University of British Columbia.

Thornton, Thomas. 2002. "From Clan to Kwáan to Corporation: The Continuing Complex Evolution of Tlingit Political Organization." *Wicazo Sa Review* 17, no. 2: 167–194.

All Indian Pueblo Council

The All Indian Pueblo Council (AIPC) is a representative, pantribal body composed of the governors of the nineteen New Mexico pueblos. As a consortium, the AIPC is empowered by and through each of the pueblo governors and tribal councils to act on behalf of all the member pueblos on matters that affect numerous member tribes, such as legal, economic, political, social, and environmental issues. The AIPC does not have governmental authority over the pueblos. Rather, each pueblo governs and usually advocates for itself in most matters, with the AIPC often coordinating pueblo efforts on issues concerning land rights, water rights, education, and religious and cultural issues.

Many Pueblo people assert that the roots of the AIPC extend back to the 1680 Pueblo Revolt, when leaders of many Pueblo groups met to organize resistance to the Spanish occupation, taxation, and religious repression. Although there is ample evidence from Pueblo leaders that a pantribal council met periodically throughout their history, the modern AIPC was formed in 1922 when numerous Pueblo leaders, along with Indian activist John Collier, called a meeting to formulate a strategy to deal with the threat posed by a bill sponsored by New Mexico senator Holm Bursum to Pueblo land and water rights, and, by extension, to their entire way of life. Successful in their efforts against the Bursum Bill, the group established a precedent for cooperative action to influence government policy that would continue to guide the AIPC.

Much of its early activity during the 1920s and 1930s was concerned with land rights, in particular learning how to deal with the federal government through Collier's tutelage (Collier served as Commissioner of Indian Affairs during the Roosevelt administration). Pueblo leaders learned how to organize and affect federal and state decisions that impacted both their tribal sovereignty and their land and water rights in the legislative, bureaucratic, and judicial realms. The AIPC was successful in advocating for the establishment of the Pueblo Lands Board to settle the countless claims arising from the presence of non-Indian squatters on lands promised to the Pueblos through the Treaty of Guadalupe Hidalgo's guarantees of the Spanish land grants.

However, local concerns were never far from the minds of the Pueblo leaders who actually made up the council. After World War II, AIPC members concentrated on improving the day-to-day existence of the Pueblo peoples. Much of this work had to do with spurring the Office of Indian Affairs both to take action on long-term issues and to deal effectively with ad hoc emergencies. Martin Vigil, the AIPC chairman for much of the postwar period, thought that the AIPC should be a forum for dealing with issues concerning the relationship between the Pueblos and the state and federal governments, particularly with regard to land and water rights.

In contrast with the American Indian Movement and other Red Power groups of the 1960s and 1970s, the AIPC kept its focus on issues of local importance, although many of these issues, such as water rights, had national implications. Education, which had always been important to the AIPC, also took on a new emphasis during these years. In its modern guise, the AIPC has concentrated more on issues of preserving Pueblo cultures through the operation of the Indian Pueblo Cultural Center and the Institute for Pueblo Indian Studies in Albuquerque, and on the operation of education and alcohol/addiction programs. However, it has served and continues to serve a vital role in protecting and even expanding the Pueblos' land base and water rights over much of the twentieth century. Its example shows that successful, coordinated action can be taken to protect tribal self-determination over land and water resources.

Steven L. Danver

See also Collier, John; Education; Land, Identity and Ownership of, Land Rights; Pan-Indianism; Pueblo Revolt.

References and Further Reading

DuMars, Charles T., et al. 1984. *Pueblo Indian Water Rights: Struggle for a Precious Resource.* Tucson: University of Arizona Press.

Philp, Kenneth R. 1981. *John Collier's Crusade for Indian Reform, 1920–1954.* Tucson: University of Arizona Press.

Sando, Joe S. 1992. *Pueblo Nations: Eight Centuries of Pueblo History.* Santa Fe, NM: Clear Light Publishers.

Sando, Joe S. 1998. *Pueblo Profiles: Cultural Identity Through Centuries of Change.* Santa Fe, NM: Clear Light Publishers.

American Indian Higher Education Consortium

The American Indian Higher Education Consortium (AIHEC) was founded in 1972 by the presidents of the six oldest tribally controlled community colleges in America to lobby for American Indian Higher Education initiatives. Their mission was, and still is, to further the ability of Indian students to realize their academic potential and to foster Indian self-determination. AIHEC's Web page says that its mission:

> . . . identifies four objectives: maintain commonly standards of quality in American Indian education; support the development of new tribally controlled colleges; promote and assist in the development of legislation to support American Indian higher education; and encourage greater participation by American Indians in the development of higher education policy . . .

AIHEC now represents more than thirty colleges and universities in the United States and one in Canada. The consortium works to locate and maintain funding through the Tribally Controlled College or University Assistance Act and other government sources. Tribal colleges and universities do not usually qualify for state or local funds, due to their trust relationship with the federal government and their location on land held in trust (AIHEC, 2006, 1).

AIHEC was instrumental in securing legislation by executive order, No. 13021 issued by President Bill Clinton on October 19, 1996 and also signed by President George W. Bush on July 3, 2002 (No. 13270). These executive orders guarantee the support of various federal agencies and departments for tribal colleges. AIHEC and the presidents of the tribal colleges spent three years working to secure the initial executive order (Executive Orders 13021 and 13270, n.d., 1). In 1994, a research initiative was created by the AIHEC board of directors as a joint effort between the AIHEC and the American Indian College Fund. The initiative's goal is to conduct research and to create and maintain a database to track "Tribal college enrollment, budgets, curricula, facilities, services and student outcome" (Database, 1994, 1). Another aspect of the research initiative is to improve each college's research abilities. The AIHEC board of directors has identified this research initiative as being a top priority, second only to securing

and maintaining financial and legislative support for tribal colleges (Research Abilities, n.d.).

The AIHEC also acts as a clearinghouse for tribal colleges, government agencies, and the general public. AIHEC supports the *Tribal College Journal* (*TCJ*), providing the advisory board a voice, while granting editorial independence, "so it [is] not a typical in-house publication." After twelve years in publication, *TCJ* now prints more than 11,000 copies of its quarterly journal (*TCJ*, n.d.).

The American Indian Higher Education Consortium may be reached at:

AIHEC
121 Oronoco Street, Alexandria, VA
22314 (703) 838–0400

The *Tribal College Journal* can be reached at:

Tribal College Journal of American Indian
Higher Education Consortium
PO Box 720, Mancos, CO 81328
(970) 533–9170

Daniel R. Gibbs

See also Boarding Schools, United States and
    Canada; Education and Social Control; Indian
    Self-Determination and Education Assistance
    Act; Education; Tribal Colleges.

References and Further Readings

American Indian Higher Education Consortium
    (AIHEC). No date. http://www.aihec.org/
    (Accessed January 15, 2007).
Database. 1994. Available at: http://www.aihec
    .org/research.html.
Executive Orders 13021 and 13270. No date.
    Available at: http://www.aihec.org/
    PolicyComponents.html 2006, 1.
Research Abilities. No date. Available at: http://
    www.aihec.org/research.html.
Tribal College Journal (TCJ). No date. Available at:
    http://www.tribalcollegejournal.org/about/hi
    story.html. Accessed January 15, 2007.

American Indian Movement

The American Indian Movement (AIM) was founded in 1968 by a group of Anishinabe that included Dennis Banks, Mary Jane Wilson, George Mitchell, and Pat Ballanger. Modeling itself after the Black Panther Party, AIM initially gained credibility

by forming street patrols to quell police violence routinely visited on the Indian community in Minneapolis. Over the next few years, service programs similar to those of the Panthers were established, including alternative schools, a multimedia news service, legal and health clinics, low-cost housing initiatives, and job-placement assistance.

In 1969 a group calling itself Indians of All Tribes (IAT) seized and occupied the abandoned federal prison on Alcatraz Island in San Francisco Bay. Visiting Alcatraz in late 1969, Dennis Banks recruited a young Santee Sioux, John Trudell, who served as AIM's primary spokesperson from 1970 to 1979. Russell Means, a reservation-born, urban-raised Oglala Lakota, was also recruited. Means, a brilliant media strategist, conceived of and led the occupation of Mount Rushmore in the fall of 1970 and organized AIM's seizure of the *Mayflower* replica at Plymouth, Massachusetts, on Thanksgiving Day, 1971.

By 1971, AIM was focusing on land and treaty issues, with an increased emphasis on reservation life. The group rapidly gained credibility, dramatically increasing the size and diversity of its membership. By late 1972, by unofficial count, forty-three AIM chapters had been started in the United States and another half-dozen in Canada. AIM soon had solid alliances with the Crusade for Justice, a Denver-based Chicano organization headed by Rodolfo "Corky" Gonzales, the Los Angeles–based Brown Berets and Chicano Moratorium, Jesse Jackson's Operation Push in Chicago, the Puerto Rican Young Lords Party in New York, and the remnants of the Black Panther Party in Oakland, California. Euro-American activists supported AIM through organizations such as Venceremos and Vietnam Veterans Against the War (VVAW), and Cherokee activist/artist Jimmie Durham organized a network of Native American Support Committees (NASCs) that spanned the continent. An international dimension was added by AIM's relationship with the All-African People's Revolutionary Party, headed by Stokely Carmichael (Kwame Turé).

For several years AIM pursued a strategy of forcing highly visible confrontations with federal, state, and local authorities. The 1971 takeover of unused military facilities at Fort Lawton, near Seattle, resulted in the construction of an American Indian cultural institution on the site, The Daybreak Star Center. Confrontations in Oklahoma and Minnesota led to the establishment of Native-controlled schools. In Denver, AIM actions produced improved health care for Native people.

Members of the American Indian Movement (AIM) beat a drum in support of their cause during the 1973 occupation of Wounded Knee, South Dakota. AIM's flag is displayed behind the group. (Corbis/Bettman-UPI)

It was, however, in the small town of Gordon, Nebraska, just south of the Pine Ridge Reservation, that AIM consolidated its reputation among Native peoples. There, Raymond Yellow Thunder, a middle-aged Oglala, had been tortured and murdered by two local residents, Melvin and Leslie Hare, in January 1972. As was routine in those days, local authorities refused to respond and Yellow Thunder's family appealed to AIM. Russell Means led more than one thousand Indians and supporters into Gordon, announcing that AIM had come to put Gordon on the map, adding that if the Hares weren't charged with murder within seventy-two hours, they would come back to take it *off* the map. Shortly thereafter, the Hare brothers became the first whites in Nebraska history to be prosecuted, convicted, and imprisoned for killing an Indian.

As a result of this unprecedented victory, AIM gained the widespread respect of traditionalists,

who were beginning to view the movement as a modern warriors' society dedicated to defending the people. Hundreds of younger members were attracted by the movement's confrontational politics, which released them from a lifelong sense of disempowerment. Soon, displays of "Indianness" such as braids, ribbon shirts, and chokers joined bumper stickers reading "Indian and Proud" as standard fashion statements wherever Native people gathered. The shame of being born into oppression had been cast off in Indian country.

Trail of Broken Treaties

The Trail of Broken Treaties ended with the most spectacular of AIM's confrontations, in which the Bureau of Indian Affairs' Washington, D.C. headquarters was occupied. By 1972 the organization had been embraced by Leonard Crow Dog, a Brûlé Lakota traditionalist from the Rosebud Reservation, adjoining Pine Ridge. He became the movement's spiritual leader and after his 1972 Sun Dance, it was agreed that AIM should carry the struggle forward into a new phase by organizing delegations from as many peoples as possible to converge on Washington, D.C. AIM's intent was to force President Richard M. Nixon, then running for reelection, to publicly acknowledge and pledge corrective action concerning the U.S. government's long-standing pattern of violating treaties with American Indians, usurping their governments, and expropriating their lands and resources. As a result of such policies and practices, Native people had long been the most impoverished population group identified in the U.S. Census. In 1972, for example, annual per-capita income on the Pine Ridge Reservation was barely $1,200, unemployment hovered at about 90 percent, and male life expectancy averaged 44.6 years.

Arrangements were made with federal authorities for planned demonstrations and ceremonies, as well as for food and housing for the participants. When officials reneged, several hundred protesters occupied the BIA headquarters, conducting daily press conferences and refusing to leave until Nixon personally agreed to respond to each demand in the demonstrators' twenty-point program. Nixon agreed—another promise that would be broken— and the occupiers withdrew, taking large numbers of BIA files with them. Over the next several months, the files were copied, the originals returned to the BIA, and duplicates distributed to the peoples whose assets and affairs were affected. Among many other

programs that provoked Indian peoples' rage, the BIA files revealed an involuntary sterilization program secretly run by the BIA's Indian Health Service (IHS). Eventually it was estimated that, between 1970 and 1975, approximately 40 percent of all American Indian women of childbearing age had been sterilized, a disclosure that forced the relocation of IHS to the Department of Health, Education and Welfare (now Health and Human Services).

BIA documents also revealed fraudulent governmental activity with respect to assets managed in trust by the BIA as a result of the plenary power asserted by the United States over Indian affairs since 1903. Under BIA-negotiated leases, American Indians were receiving, on average, about 10 percent of the royalties they would have received on the open market. Armed with this information, many Native people were able to force changes in the administration of their lands and resources, although trust funds still unaccounted for by the BIA total well over a $100 billion.

Rather than responding to the issues raised by the Trail of Broken Treaties, the Nixon administration launched a campaign to discredit AIM and whatever information it might disseminate. Sensational stories were planted in the press, falsely claiming that AIM "vandals" had done more physical damage to the Capitol than anyone since the British in 1812. The federally funded National Tribal Chairmen's Association denounced AIM leaders as irresponsible revolutionaries without a Native constituency. In the meantime, the FBI was instructed to target and politically neutralize the movement.

Wounded Knee Siege

As AIM members returned home in triumph, Russell Means found himself barred from the Pine Ridge Reservation—despite the fact that he was an enrolled tribal member and owned land there—by thugs working for recently installed Pine Ridge President Dick Wilson. Wilson had been given federal funds to establish a paramilitary group that came to be known as the Guardians of the Oglala Nation (GOONs). The GOONs, who overlapped considerably with the BIA police, were used to terrorize Wilson's opponents. In response, the Oglala Sioux Civil Rights Organization (OSCRO), headed by Pedro Bissonette, was organized to impeach Wilson.

In January 1973 Dennis Banks called for AIM members to gather in Rapid City to begin a major civil rights campaign. Upon arrival, they learned

that Wesley Bad Heart Bull, a young Oglala, had been stabbed to death in the nearby town of Buffalo Gap. As in the Yellow Thunder case, local police refused to bring charges and the victim's mother asked for AIM's help. This time, however, the authorities were prepared when the AIM contingent arrived in Custer, South Dakota. First, an anonymous caller caused the *Rapid City Journal* to announce that the demonstration had been canceled, so the turnout was low. The Indians were then met by a combined force of local, county, and state police tactical units, overseen by FBI observers. In the ensuing struggle, the Custer County Courthouse and the local chamber of commerce building were set ablaze and most of the Indians, including Russell Means, Dennis Banks, and Bad Heart Bull's mother Sarah were subsequently arrested on charges of riot and arson. The trials dragged on for years and resulted in convictions of most of the defendants. Sarah Bad Heart Bull was sentenced to serve a year in jail, while her son's killer never spent a day behind bars.

In the meantime, impeachment efforts on Pine Ridge had been thwarted. OSCRO had obtained more signatures for Wilson's removal than the number of votes by which he was elected, but the BIA—having first brought in a sixty-man Special Operations Group (SOG) of U.S. marshals to "maintain order"—allowed Wilson to preside over his own impeachment. Under these conditions, Wilson was retained in office by a fourteen-to-zero vote of the tribal council and immediately proclaimed a reservation-wide ban on all political meetings. Unable to resolve their grievances through any sort of conventional due process, the elders of the traditional Oglala leadership asked AIM to intervene.

On February 27, 1973, it was decided that a press conference would be held the following day to expose what was happening on Pine Ridge. A symbolic site was chosen—the mass grave of some 350 Lakotas massacred by the U.S. Army at Wounded Knee in 1890. About 150 AIM members immediately went to the tiny hamlet to prepare, while others began notifying the media. At dawn, those inside Wounded Knee realized that, overnight, Wilson's GOONs had set up roadblocks that both prevented press access and sealed in the AIM organizers. SOG reinforcements and FBI personnel soon arrived and by the following day, two "consultants"—actually special warfare experts—had been dispatched by Nixon's military advisor, General Alexander Haig.

The seventy-one-day Siege of Wounded Knee had begun. Unprepared for an armed confrontation or a protracted occupation, the AIM contingent obtained weapons from a local trading post and quickly improvised defensive "bunkers." Supporters soon worked out a way to smuggle in food, clothing, arms, and ammunition through the federal lines. By March 7, nearly 300 marshals and more than 100 FBI agents were deployed on Pine Ridge, supported by about 250 BIA police, most of them SWAT team members from other reservations, some 150 GOONs and about an equal number of non-Indian vigilantes. State and local police in the five surrounding states intercepted anyone suspected of heading for Wounded Knee, arresting some 1,200 persons over the next two months.

General Haig's "consultants" arranged for the provision of military equipment, ranging from armored personnel carriers to M-79 grenade launchers; an elite rapid deployment force stood by for an airborne assault; and the Strategic Air Command conducted aerial reconnaissance. More flares illuminated the perimeter at night than were used by U.S. forces in Vietnam during any year of the war. All told, a half-million rounds were fired into the perimeter during the siege, killing Frank Clearwater, an Apache, and Buddy Lamont, an Oglala, and wounding many others. In addition, Wilson's GOONs are believed to have murdered as many as thirteen people captured while attempting to slip in. When sheer government firepower failed to stop supplies from reaching the encampment, the grass was burned off for a half-mile in all directions.

The confrontation ended only when federal officials agreed to conduct a full investigation of the Wilson regime and to meet with traditional Oglala leaders concerning U.S. violations of the 1868 Fort Laramie Treaty, the document that officially defines U.S.–Lakota relations. Again, the agreement was violated by the authorities, but AIM's purpose had been accomplished. By the end of the siege on May 7, 1973, the conditions on Pine Ridge, and in Indian Country generally, had been the focus of international attention for over two months.

Within the year, AIM would translate this attention into the establishment of its diplomatic arm, the International Indian Treaty Council (IITC). Directed by NASC's Jimmie Durham, the IITC's mandate was to bring the issue of indigenous rights to the United Nations. By 1977, it was the first Native American organization to attain formal United

Nations consultative status. Durham was instrumental in organizing the "Indian Summer in Geneva," a conference that led to the establishment in 1982 of the UN Working Group on Indigenous Populations. The Working Group provided a regular forum for reporting violations of Native rights and for drafting a Universal Declaration of Rights of Indigenous Peoples for adoption by the UN General Assembly. It has become a major international forum for indigenous peoples around the world, and the Draft Declaration, completed in 1993, is under review by the UN Commission on Human Rights.

AIM Trials

In May 1973, however, these international developments lay in the future. AIM's priority was to survive the 185 indictments its members faced following the siege of Wounded Knee. In February 1974 Russell Means and Dennis Banks went to trial, charged with everything from criminal conspiracy and kidnapping to car theft and assaulting federal officers. Prosecutors were unscrupulous, even introducing the testimony of an "eyewitness" who had been in California during the siege. After more than eight months, Judge Fred J. Nichol dismissed all charges, noting that the waters of justice had been "polluted" (his word) by governmental misconduct, and that "[t]he FBI has stooped to a new low" (Johansen and Maestas, 1979, 91).

Later it was revealed the FBI had an infiltrator in the defense team throughout the trial. By the end of 1974, the government had obtained only five minor convictions after having prosecuted forty cases. The Wounded Knee Legal Defense/Offense Committee (WKLDOC), created by attorneys Ken Tilson and Beverly Axelrod, challenged U.S. jurisdiction over the remaining cases as violating the 1868 treaty. Judge Warren Urbom ruled, in effect, that, while this would once have been true, the United States had so long and regularly violated the treaty that its legal force had been eroded. The Justice Department dismissed fifty pending cases, but twenty "leadership trials" dragged on for another year. Spiritual leader Leonard Crow Dog, Oklahoma AIM leader Carter Camp, and Stan Holder, who headed security at Wounded Knee, were convicted of interfering with a group of marshals who had attempted to enter the AIM perimeter disguised as postal inspectors. Ultimately, federal prosecutors obtained only fifteen guilty verdicts, none for substantial offenses.

It later became apparent that the government had not gone to court expecting a better conviction rate. Rather, its strategy was one of political neutralization, using pretextual arrests to keep the activists tied up in court, their organization bankrupted by bail and legal costs. This continued, albeit on a more selective basis. Russell Means, for example, faced one charge after another for years. He was even tried for murder in 1976, despite the fact that his alleged victim stated repeatedly before he died that Means was *not* one of the assailants. Acquitted in each case, the apparently endless proceedings eventually exhausted Means's patience. His refusal, as well as that of other AIM members, to rise for the judge in Sarah Bad Heart Bull's 1974 trial resulted in a courtroom brawl and Means's only felony conviction, for which he was sentenced to four years under a South Dakota statute that had never before been used and was repealed while he was in prison.

Dennis Banks was convicted on the Custer charges in July 1975. Facing a fifteen-year sentence, he became a fugitive. California Governor Jerry Brown granted him sanctuary, citing South Dakota Attorney General William Janklow's statement that "the way to deal with AIM leaders is to put a bullet between their eyes." Janklow had campaigned on a pledge to "put the AIM leaders either in jail or under it" (Churchill and Vander Wall, 2002, 345–346).

In 1982 Brown was succeeded by George Deukmejian, and Banks again went underground, surfacing on the Onondaga Reservation in upstate New York. Finally, in September 1984, after obtaining assurances of safety from Janklow, who had since become governor of South Dakota, Banks surrendered and served thirteen months.

In the meantime, in November 1975, Banks, his wife Kamook, and AIM members Kenny Loud Hawk and Russell Redner were charged with federal explosives and firearms violations. The case was dismissed for lack of evidence in 1976, reinstated in 1980, and again dismissed in 1983, this time because the government had violated the defendants' right to a speedy trial. In January 1986 the U.S. Supreme Court reinstated the charges, and six months later the case was again thrown out on the basis of additional prosecutorial misconduct. The Justice Department sought reinstatement yet again and, in late 1988, a weary Dennis Banks entered a pro forma guilty plea in exchange for a suspended sentence and the dropping of charges against his codefendants.

In another case, Los Angeles AIM members Paul "Skyhorse" Durant and Richard "Mohawk"

Billings were accused of the torture and murder of a cab driver. Local officials had arrested the likely culprits within hours of the slaying and were preparing charges when the FBI apparently convinced them to immunize the accused as state's witnesses and to charge Skyhorse and Mohawk instead. When the case finally came to trial it became obvious that the state's evidence was either meaningless or crudely fabricated. Finally a primary witness admitted that he had killed the victim, and Skyhorse and Mohawk were acquitted. By then, however, they had been imprisoned for nearly four years and AIM's reputation in California was irreparably damaged.

Summing up this ongoing legal travesty, WKL-DOC attorney William Kunstler observed, "the purpose of the trials [was] to break the spirit of the American Indian Movement by tying up its leaders and supporters in court and forcing [it] to spend huge amounts of money, time and talent to keep [its] people out of jail, instead of building an organization that can work effectively for the Indian people" (Matthiessen, 1991, 193–194). Black Panther Party attorney Charles Garry noted that this approach was identical to that used by the FBI in its efforts to destroy the Panthers' political effectiveness between 1969 and 1971.

Reign of Terror on Pine Ridge

During the siege, Dick Wilson proclaimed that AIM would die at Wounded Knee. In a less dramatic manner this was confirmed by a 1973 FBI document entitled "Paramilitary Operations in Indian Country." Even before the U.S. marshals were withdrawn from Wounded Knee, the GOONs were appearing with new, fully automatic M-16 rifles and state-of-the-art military communications equipment. Years later, GOON leader Duane Brewer admitted that the FBI had secretly funneled weapons, munitions, and equipment to them. The FBI claims it only provided the BIA police with such lethal paraphernalia, but it was common knowledge that approximately two-thirds of the reservation police doubled as GOONs.

Between March 1973 and March 1976, at least sixty-nine AIM members and supporters were murdered on or near Pine Ridge, giving the reservation a murder rate *eight times* that of Detroit, then considered the "murder capital of the United States" (Johansen and Maestas, 1979, 83). One of the first fatalities was OSCRO leader Pedro Bissonette, shot point-blank in the chest with a 12-gauge shotgun after being stopped at a police roadblock in October

1973 and then was left to bleed to death. In March 1975, Bissonette's apolitical sister-in-law Jeanette was also shot to death. According to Brewer, she had been mistaken for Ellen Moves Camp, a prominent Pine Ridge activist. AIM supporter Jim Little was severely beaten in September 1975 and died while the ambulance took an hour to come the two miles from the BIA hospital. In January 1976, attorney Byron DeSersa, a Wilson opponent, was shot and left to bleed to death in a ditch. Numerous witnesses identified the assailants—all known GOONs—but FBI personnel on the scene arrested no one but one witness, an elderly Cheyenne named Guy Dull Knife, whom the agents accused of becoming "abusive" when they failed to act.

As the death toll rose, approximately 340 additional AIM members and supporters on Pine Ridge were subjected to serious physical assaults, including attempts on their lives. In March 1975, the home of seventy-year-old Matthew King, an assistant to Chief Fools Crow and an uncle of Russell Means, was riddled by gunfire. Two nights later, Fools Crow's house was burned to the ground. Tribal council member Severt Young Bear's home was shot at so often that he "lost track" of the number of instances. In June, Means was shot in the back by a BIA police officer, who claimed that Means was engaging in "rowdy behavior." The following November, a BIA officer opened fire on the home of AIM supporter Chester Stone, wounding Stone, his wife, and two small children.

AIM and its supporters continued to seek due-process remedies. In 1974 Russell Means opposed Wilson in the elections for tribal president. Means won the primary by a wide margin but ostensibly lost the runoff by an even larger number of votes. The Denver office of the Justice Department's Civil Rights Division found evidence of massive fraud, but nonetheless Wilson remained in office. Criminal investigation of the Wilson regime had been a central demand of the Wounded Knee standoff, and in 1975 the General Accounting Office finally completed an audit. It concluded that Wilson could not account for more than $300,000 in federal highway funds, but no charges were ever filed.

Many, perhaps most, of the crimes committed against AIM and its supporters were committed by the BIA police who were not likely to investigate themselves. George O'Clock, special agent in charge of the FBI's Rapid City Resident Agency, which had primary jurisdiction over the reservation, explained that he was too "short of manpower" to investigate

the homicides, attempted homicides, or assaults against AIM. During this same period, however, O'Clock had sufficient resources to create more than 316,000 investigative documents on the victims of this violence.

In July 1975 Denver Civil Rights Division investigators returned to Pine Ridge and concluded that the Wilson regime, with the complicity of federal authorities, had visited a "reign of terror" on reservation residents for over two years. Their recommendation for resumption of a congressional inquiry into FBI operations on Pine Ridge, which had just been "indefinitely postponed," was ignored. In 1987, GOON leader Duane Brewer confirmed that, for all practical purposes, the GOONs had operated as a death squad, coordinated by the FBI in much the same way that the Central Intelligence Agency used paramilitary organizations in Latin America. The reign of terror on Pine Ridge was not law enforcement gone awry so much as an exercise in counterinsurgency warfare by domestic police agencies. The FBI, it appears, was escalating the illegal counterintelligence operations, or COINTELPROs revealed in the 1975 Senate Select Committee's *Report on Intelligence Activities and the Rights of Americans,* that the Bureau had conducted to "disrupt, destabilize and destroy" the Black Panther Party and other activist organizations.

Despite all of these efforts, the FBI had not succeeded in destroying the American Indian Movement. AIM security had organized armed defensive clusters around the reservation and the GOONs began to back off. An opportunity to eliminate the resistance altogether presented itself on June 26, 1975, when two FBI agents, Ronald Williams and Jack Coler, approached a Northwest AIM encampment on the property of Harry and Cecelia Jumping Bull, elderly traditionalists living a few miles south of the town of Oglala. Ostensibly the agents were serving a (nonexistent) warrant for the arrest of seventeen-year-old Jimmy Eagle, accused of stealing a pair of used cowboy boots. In fact, they stopped close to the Northwest AIM camp and opened fire. Receiving heavy return fire, the two agents were soon fatally shot as they radioed frantically for backup. Despite the reservation's remote location, the requested help began to arrive almost immediately. The FBI later claimed that roughly 150 BIA SWAT personnel were "coincidentally" in the area for an unrelated training exercise, and before the end of the day FBI SWAT teams based in Quantico, Virginia, Minneapolis, Chicago, Denver, and elsewhere

were on the scene. Governor Janklow managed to arrive with a group of local vigilantes while the firefight was still in progress. Apparently the FBI had hoped to quickly overrun the AIM encampment at the Jumping Bull compound, then send in an overwhelming force to eliminate AIM positions across the reservation. However, when AIM responded strongly, both BIA and FBI units took up blocking positions rather than mounting an attack. Coler and Williams were thus abandoned and all of the "insurgents" escaped, with the exception of Joe Stuntz Killsright, an AIM member from Coeur d'Alene, Idaho, killed by a sniper at long range.

The FBI immediately barred the press from the scene, then "explained" publicly that the agents had been "lured" into an "ambush" by "AIM guerillas." The government spokesperson, flown in from Washington, D.C., for the occasion, even provided reporters with what were supposed to be one of the agents' last words before he was "viciously executed." None of this was factual, but headlines across the country depicted AIM as killers and the FBI sent in 400 agents, complete with combat fatigues, M-16s, armored personnel carriers, and Huey helicopters. For two months they conducted Vietnam-style "sweeps" through the reservation, kicking in doors and mounting "air assaults" on the properties of known AIM members on both Pine Ridge and Rosebud.

As AIM was being pounded into disarray, Dick Wilson went to Washington to sign preliminary documents transferring title of the Sheep Mountain Gunnery Range to the Interior Department's National Park Service. This area, the northwestern eighth of the reservation, was ostensibly to be incorporated into the Badlands National Monument, but the Interior Department had known for some time that it contained large deposits of uranium intermixed with molybdenum. Eventually the Oglalas recovered the surface lands involved, but not the subsurface mineral rights.

The FBI still needed to hold someone accountable for the deaths of Coler and Williams, and it also wanted to prevent AIM from effectively regrouping. To these ends it began the RESMURS (Reservation Murders) investigation, an acronym applied only to the deaths of the agents, not to the scores of still unsolved Indian homicides. Although the FBI knew that a number of local Oglalas were involved, it targeted Bob Robideau, Dino Butler, and Leonard Peltier, "outsiders" perceived to be the backbone of Northwest AIM.

Butler and Robideau were captured in the summer of 1975 and tried in Cedar Rapids, Iowa, in June 1976. At trial, the government's credibility was undermined by its reliance on transparently false witnesses, and the all-white jury returned verdicts of not guilty on all counts. The jury noted that Butler and Robideau had acted in self-defense, doing "only what any reasonable person would do, under the circumstances" that had been created on Pine Ridge (Churchill, 2003, 280).

Meanwhile, Peltier had escaped to a traditional Cree community in Alberta, Canada. Arrested in February 1976, he was extradited to the United States, primarily on the basis of a fraudulent "eyewitness affidavit" prepared by the FBI. This flagrant violation of the U.S.–Canada extradition treaty was later exposed, prompting the Canadian parliament to consider canceling the treaty altogether. Peltier was still fighting extradition during the Butler and Robideau trials and thus was tried separately upon his return.

Determined not to repeat the "mistakes" of its first trial, the Justice Department had Peltier's case moved to North Dakota, where it found district judge Paul Benson willing to narrowly restrict the evidence to the events of June 26, 1975. This precluded the introduction of the Cedar Rapids trial record and, more generally, any explanation of the reign of terror prevailing at the time of the firefight. Prosecutors then argued a "lone gunman" theory, completely contradicting the evidence they had introduced against Butler and Robideau. Based on the introduction of much fabricated evidence, the jury quickly found Peltier guilty of double homicide and on June 1, 1977, Judge Benson sentenced Peltier to two consecutive life sentences.

The Eighth Circuit Court of Appeals acknowledged more than thirty reversible errors, but allowed Peltier's conviction to stand. Shortly thereafter, William Webster, the chief judge of the circuit court, became director of the FBI, but both the Eighth Circuit and the Supreme Court denied review. Despite ongoing appeals based on additional evidence of governmental misconduct and on prosecutor Lynn Crooks' 1987 acknowledgment that he "really has no idea who shot those agents," Leonard Peltier remains in prison in 2007, routinely denied parole because he refuses to "accept responsibility" for the deaths of the agents. Petitions for his release have been signed by more than 14 million people internationally, and Amnesty International has declared Peltier a "prisoner of conscience." In January 2001, President Bill Clinton was on the verge of signing a long-promised commutation of Peltier's sentence when FBI agents mounted highly publicized protests and Clinton backed down. Peltier thus remains in prison, not for any crime he has committed, but as a symbol of the federal government's arbitrary ability to repress indigenous peoples' legitimate aspirations to liberation.

The Ongoing Struggle

By the late 1970s AIM was in serious decline. Its reputation suffered as a result of rumors, which may have had some substance, that in February 1976 AIM members had murdered one of their own, a Mi'kmaq named Anna Mae Pictou Aquash, who had been "bad-jacketed" (a standard COINTELPRO tactic) as an infiltrator. In 2005, the case was revived by federal prosecutors, apparently as part of a wider effort to discredit activist organizations of the 1960s and 1970s. One former AIM member, Arlo Looking Cloud, was tried and convicted; another, John Graham, is fighting extradition from Canada; and it appears that indictments will be brought against several others.

In 1979, shortly after his wife, three children, and mother-in-law were murdered on the Duck Valley Reservation in Nevada, John Trudell, the only remaining "national" AIM officer, resigned and announced that all comparable positions had been abolished.

In 1978 Dennis Banks organized The Longest Walk, a march from San Francisco to Washington, D.C., to protest pending legislation to repeal all treaties with American Indians. The bills were subsequently defeated, in part due to this action but more fundamentally because U.S. claims to the legitimacy of the occupation of Indian lands are based largely on those same treaties. Banks, too, has "retired" from AIM, although he continues to coordinate walks and runs to draw attention to Native issues.

During 1979 Jimmie Durham and IITC associate director Paul Chaat Smith resigned as well, citing the organization's increasingly close ties to the governments of Cuba and other socialist countries. During the mid-1980s the IITC incorporated and replaced its council of traditional elders with a handpicked board, which immediately aligned itself with Nicaragua's Sandinista government, thereby helping quash the right of the indigenous people in Nicaragua to self-determination. This splintered what was left of AIM. The Treaty Council continues

to exist, without a discernible base of grassroots support and functioning essentially as an appendage of the statist entities it was created to oppose.

Russell Means during 1981 led the seizure of an 880-acre tract in the Black Hills National Forest. Named Yellow Thunder Camp, the site was continuously occupied until 1985 while AIM took the battle to court. It won a landmark decision, with District Judge Robert O'Brien ruling that the Lakotas, and thus other Indians, were entitled to view entire geographic areas as sacred sites and to enjoy use and, in certain instances, occupancy rights. This was soon nullified, however, by the Supreme Court's 1988 decision in the "G-O Road" case, *Lyng v. Northwest Indian Cemetery Protective Association.*

Means and Colorado AIM leader Glenn Morris organized a broad coalition of local organizations to protest the annual Columbus Day parade in Denver during the early 1990s. In the summer of 1992, a jury not only acquitted Means, Morris, and two other Colorado AIM members of violating the First Amendment rights of the Columbus Day organizers, but stated that the city of Denver had violated international law by issuing a permit for the parade. This led to the cancellation of an extravagant 1992 celebration of the quincentennial of Columbus's "discovery of America." By 2000 such celebrations of genocide had reemerged, and again protestors led by Colorado AIM were acquitted. In 2002, over 240 people were arrested and charged with disrupting the parade; after losing yet another jury trial, Denver officials were forced to drop charges against all remaining defendants.

AIM's Denver victories in the early 1990s stimulated activities in chapters across the country, and even this modest resurgence illustrated that the FBI was still anxious to neutralize the movement. In a bizarre twist, a barrage of notices were issued by an entity calling itself the National American Indian Movement, claiming that the Colorado chapter was fraudulent, that its leadership consisted of "white men masquerading as Indians" and "probable police agents," and that the entire group had therefore been "summarily expelled" from AIM. It turned out that "National AIM" was actually a Minnesota-based nonprofit corporation with no membership of its own, subsisting on corporate and federal funding. Nonetheless, the confusion it generated negated any potential for a genuine AIM revitalization.

Despite the generally successful neutralization of the movement, AIM was instrumental in transforming the circumstances of Native life in ways that may prove irreversible. A sense of pride was instilled among people long oppressed; Indian issues were forced into public consciousness for the first time in many generations; and the movement illustrated that gains could be made by direct confrontation. This understanding is reflected in the armed confrontations undertaken by Mohawks at Oka, near Montreal, and elsewhere, confrontations over land issues that continue in 2006 in places such as Caledonia, Ontario. The militant struggles of the 1970s have laid the groundwork for a future that certainly looks brighter than it did for Indian people two generations ago.

Ward Churchill

See also Aquash, Anna Mae Pictou; Banks, Dennis; Identity; Means, Russell; Oakes, Richard; Occupation of Alcatraz Island; Pan-Indianism; Peltier, Leonard; Pine Ridge Political Murders; Red Power Movement; Trail of Broken Treaties; Wilson, Richard; Wounded Knee, South Dakota, Massacre at.

References and Further Reading

Anderson, Robert, et al. 1974. *Voices from Wounded Knee.* Rooseveltown, NY: Akwesasne Notes.

Brown, Dee. 1970. *Bury My Heart at Wounded Knee: An Indian History of the American West.* New York: Holt, Rinehart, and Winston.

Burnette, Robert, with John Koster. 1974. *The Road to Wounded Knee.* New York: Bantam.

Churchill, Ward. 1996. "Death Squads in the United States: Confessions of a Government Terrorist." In *From a Native Son: Selected Essays in Indigenism, 1985–1995,* 231–270. Boston: South End Press.

Churchill, Ward. 2003. "The Bloody Wake of Alcatraz: Repression of the American Indian Movement During the 1970s." In *Perversions of Justice: Indigenous Peoples and Angloamerican Law.* Edited by Ward Churchill, 263–302. San Francisco: City Lights.

Churchill, Ward, and Jim Vanderwall. 2002. *Agents of Repression: The FBI's Secret Wars Against the Black Panther Party and the American Indian Movement.* Classics edition. Boston: South End Press.

Churchill, Ward, and Jim Vanderwall. 2002. *The COINTELPRO Papers: Documents from the FBI's Secret Wars Against Dissent in the United States.* Classics ed. Boston: South End Press.

Deloria, Vine, Jr. 1974. *Behind the Trail of Broken Treaties: An Indian Declaration of Independence.* New York: Delta Books.

Dillingham, Brint. 1977. "Indian Women and IHA Sterilization Practices." *American Indian Journal* 3 (January): 1.

Johansen, Bruce, and Roberto Maestas. 1979. *Wasi'chu: The Continuing Indian Wars.* New York: Monthly Review Press.

Johnson, Troy, Joane Nagel, and Duane Champaign, eds. 1997. *American Indian Activism: Alcatraz to the Longest Walk.* Urbana: University of Illinois Press.

Matthiessen, Peter. 1991. *In the Spirit of Crazy Horse: The Story of Leonard Peltier,* 2nd ed. New York: Viking.

Means, Russell, with Marvin J. Wolf. 1995. *Where White Men Fear to Tread: The Autobiography of Russell Means.* New York: St. Martin's Press.

Sayer, John William. 1997. *Ghost Dancing the Law: The Wounded Knee Trials.* Cambridge, MA: Harvard University Press.

Smith, Paul Chaat, and Robert Allen Warrior. 1996. *Like a Hurricane: The American Indian Movement from Alcatraz to Wounded Knee.* New York: New Press.

Weyler, Rex. 1992. *Blood of the Land: The U.S. Government and Corporate War Against the American Indian Movement,* 2nd ed. Philadelphia, PA: New Society Publishers.

Anderson, Wallace Mad Bear

A medicine man and prophet, Wallace Mad Bear Anderson also was a noted Native American rights activist during the 1950s and 1960s. During his lifetime, he led national and international efforts for the recognition of the sovereignty of Indian nations.

Anderson, a member of the Tuscarora nation, was born on November 9, 1927, in Buffalo, New York. Called Mad Bear by his grandmother because of his temper, he grew up on the Tuscarora Indian Reservation, near Niagara Falls. As a young man, he enlisted in the U.S. Navy. After he returned from service, Anderson applied for a loan under the GI Bill to build a house on the reservation. When the loan was denied, Anderson's belief that he was discriminated against because of his race prompted him to become an activist for Native American rights.

In 1957, Anderson led Iroquois protests against state income taxes. The demonstrations culminated in a march to the Massena, New York, state courthouse, where several hundred protestors burned summonses for their unpaid taxes. The following year, Anderson became a key figure in the Tuscarora Reservoir Protest. After the Power Authority of the State of New York seized 1,383 acres of the Tus-carora Reservation to build a reservoir that would flood the land, Tuscarora men, women, and children joined forces to resist the taking of their land. Anderson and others blocked surveyors from entering the reservation and deflated workers' tires. When approximately 100 state troopers threatened to enter the reservation, the demonstrators laid in the road to block their trucks. Despite the efforts of the Tuscaroras, the U.S. Supreme Court ruled in *Federal Power Commission v. Tuscarora Indian Nation* (1960) that the taking of the land was legal, and the reservoir was eventually built.

In March 1959, Anderson aided in a revolt of Iroquois at the Six Nations Reserve in Brantford, Ontario. After the Iroquois declared their sovereignty, twelve Royal Canadian Mounted Police invaded the reservation's council house, but the Iroquois forced them to leave. That same month, Anderson attempted a citizen's arrest of Commissioner of Indian Affairs Glenn Emmons, whom some Native Americans, resentful of the federal termination policy, had accused of misconduct in office. Emmons avoided Anderson but later resigned.

After receiving an invitation from revolutionary leader Fidel Castro, Anderson led a delegation of Native Americans to Cuba in July 1959. Members of the Six Nations and the Miccosukee of Florida agreed to recognize the sovereignty of Cuba in exchange for Cuba's recognition of their own sovereignty. Indian sovereignty was an important issue for Anderson; he once stated that his main purpose in life was to help the Indian people regain sovereignty, rather than be absorbed by a society that he regarded as "sick."

Anderson founded the North American Indian Unity Caravan in 1967 to encourage the activism that was growing among Native Americans nationwide. Later that year, he delivered to Congress messages from 133 tribes that did not want their reservations to be terminated, which helped to defeat one of the final termination bills. Anderson toured the nation with his caravan for the following six years, but he paused to plan and participate in the Alcatraz Occupation in 1969. In 1975, he was the national director of the Indian Nationalist Movement of North America.

Anderson's work as a medicine man was featured in the book *Rolling Thunder* (1974) by Doug Boyd. In discussing his concept of good medicine, Anderson also articulates the philosophy behind his individual activism.

Wallace Mad Bear Anderson arguing with a toll collector in New York. (Corbis/Bettman)

See also Red Power Movement; Tribal Sovereignty.
References and Further Reading
Boyd, Doug. 1994. *Mad Bear: Spirit, Healing, and the Sacred in the Life of Native American Medicine Man.* New York: Simon & Schuster.
Olson, James S., Mark Baxter, Jason M. Tetzloff, and Darren Pierson. 1997. *Encyclopedia of American Indian Civil Rights.* Westport, CT: Greenwood Press.
Roleff, Tamara, ed. 1998. *Native American Rights.* San Diego, CA: Greenhaven Press.

Anishinabe Algonquin National Council

The Council (also called the Algonquin Anishinabeg Nation Tribal Council) is a political unit representing seven Algonquin communities located in the Ottawa River watershed. Six of the communities are located in the Outaouais and Abitibi-Témiscamingue regions of the province of Quebec: la Première Nation Abitibiwinni (Pikogan, population 800), Eagle Village First Nation–Kipawa (Temiscaming, population 650), Kitcisakik First Nation (Val d'Or, population 386), Kitigan Zibi Anishin-

abeg (Maniwaki, population 2500), La Nation Anishnabe de Lac Simon (Lac Simon, population 1200), and Long Point First Nation (Winneway River, population 650). The seventh community is located in the district of Cochrane in the province of Ontario: Wahgoshig First Nation (Matheson, population 250). Of all the communities, Kitigan Zibi is the closest to Ottawa.

In 1989, Algonquin communities in western Quebec, including those just listed, submitted a formal and comprehensive land claim to Canada's Department of Indian and Northern Affairs regarding lands in the Ottawa River watershed. In light of research conducted by these communities, the federal government agreed to pursue land claims negotiations with the Algonquin of western Quebec. In 1992, representatives of Abitibiwinni, Eagle Village, Lac Simon, Long Point, and Kitigan Zibi Anishinabeg met to form the Algonquin Anishinabeg Nation Tribal Council specifically to facilitate the land claims process. Although the initial meeting was hosted by the Kitcisakik First Nation, the Council decided to operate out of Kitigan Zibi since it was only eighty-four miles north of Ottawa.

The areas claimed by the Algonquin Anishinabeg Nation Tribal Council cover a large area, although not all nations' claims are equal in size. The smallest is Eagle Village at 21.49 hectares. The largest is Kitigan Zibi at 18,437 hectares.

The Council initially focused strictly on politics. Its office in Kitigan Zibi had only two staff members, who were both involved in the land claims process. In 1996, however, the Council hired an architect, a human resources advisor, and an engineer to offer expanded services to the member communities. In 1999, Kitcisakik First Nation joined the Tribal Council. The following year, Wahgoshig First Nation also became a member, although its participation was limited to political issues. That same year, the Minister for Indian and Northern Affairs proposed that the Algonquin Chiefs conduct a scooping-out exercise, whose purpose was to determine if sufficient common ground existed to begin negotiations with the potential for success within a reasonable time frame.

Kipawa, Kitcisakik, Kitigan Zibi, Pikogan, Lac Simon, and Long Point–Winneway initially agreed to this exercise, beginning the scooping-out exercise in February 2001. Kitigan Zibi later pulled out of this collaboration and conducted its own scooping-out exercise. In October 2002, Kitigan Zibi and Lac Simon requested the beginning of negotiations. As of 2006, the Algonquin nation as a whole had yet to decide if there will be issues of overlapping claims that could affect negotiations.

The Anishinabe Algonquin National Council has two current priorities. The first is the advancement and protection of aboriginal rights. The second is the provision of advisory and technical services to member communities. To accomplish these priorities, the Council has embarked on a training plan to develop the skills of its members, including training courses on basic management skills.

The Council is governed by a board of directors, composed of the chiefs from the member communities as well as representatives for elders, women, and youth. All of these representatives are elected by the people.

In 2004, the Council Office expanded its staff by hiring an information officer and an economic development officer. That same year, perhaps in an effort to launch land claims negotiations, the Long Point First Nation presented a resolution to the Assembly of First Nations, asking support for its natural resources permit system. The resolution also called on the federal and Quebec governments to respect the permit system.

During the 2005 federal election campaign, Gilles Duceppe, leader of the Bloc Quebecois Party, drew attention to the poor living conditions that existed in Kitcisakik First Nation and called for the federal government to proceed with the construction of a new town. Since the community is not covered under the Indian Act, however, and the negotiation process had yet to begin as of 2006, it is not clear which government is responsible for assisting the community.

The Anishinabe Algonquin National Council maintains an informative Web site, and the Department of Indian and Northern Affairs keeps a regularly updated report of land claims issues on its Web site.

Elizabeth Sneyd

References and Further Reading
Algonquin Anishinabeg Nation Tribal Council. No date. "The History of the Algonquin Anishinabeg Nation Tribal Council." Available at: http://www.anishinabenation.ca/eng/history_en.htm. Accessed August 30, 2006.
Algonquin Anishinabeg Nation Tribal Council. No date. "History of the Algonquin Nation." Available at: http://www.anishinabenation.ca/eng/alg_history_en.htm. Accessed August 30, 2006.

Anishinabe Algonquin National Council. No date. Available at: http://www.anishinabenation.ca. Accessed January 15, 2007.

Assembly of First Nations. 2004. "Resolution 80: Support for the Long Point First Nation Natural Resources Permit Policy." Moved by Chief Steve Mathias (Long Point First Nation), Seconded by Chief Dwight Sutherland (Taykwa Tagamou/New Post, Ontario). Assembly of First Nations Annual General Assembly, July 20–22. Charlottetown, PEI. Available at: http://www.afn.ca/article.asp?id=453. Accessed August 30, 2006.

CBC News. 2005. "Duceppe Vows to Help Isolated Algonquin Community." December 11. Available at: http://www.cbc.ca/story/canadavotes2006/national/2005/12/11/duceppe-Kitcisakik051211.html. Accessed August 30 2006.

Department of Indian and Northern Affairs. Updated. Report of Land Claims Issues. Available at: http://www.ainc-inac.ca. Accessed January 15, 2007.

Reserve of Eagle Village First Nation–Kipawa. No date. Available at: http://www.ainc-inac.gc.ca/qc/gui/kipawa_e.html. Accessed January 15, 2007.

Reserve of Kitigan Zibi. No date. Available at: http://www.ainc-inac.gc.ca/qc/gui/Kitigan_e.html. Accessed January 15, 2007.

Reserve of Lac Simon. No date. Available at: http://www.ainc-inac.gc.ca/qc/gui/Lac_Simon_e.html. Accessed January 15, 2007.

Reserve of Pikogan (La Première Nation Abitibiwinni). No date. Available at: http://www.ainc-inac.gc.ca/qc/gui/abitibiwinni_e.html. Accessed August 30, 2006.

Settlement of Kitcisakik First Nation. No date. Available at: http://www.ainc-inac.gc.ca/qc/gui/Kitcisakik_e.html. Accessed January 15, 2007.

Settlement of Winneway (Long Point First Nation). No date. Available at: http://www.ainc-inac.gc.ca/qc/gui/Long_Point_e.html. Accessed January 15, 2007.

Apess, William

Author of the first published American Indian autobiography, *A Son of the Forest,* and a leader in the Mashpee Revolt, William Apess (Pequot) was born in Colrain, Massachusetts, on January 31, 1798. His father, William, reportedly a descendent of the Wampanoag King Philip, was Pequot and white, and his mother, Candace, was perhaps African American and Pequot, and probably a slave.

Apess's Pequot ancestors had been nearly eliminated in 1637, when the Pilgrims, Puritans, and other tribes with which they had allied burned the Mystic River Pequot fort, killing seven hundred men, women, and children. Survivors were largely sold into slavery in the West Indies. A few, like Apess's family, persisted on the fringes in southeastern Connecticut, eking out livings as domestics and day laborers. Some report that Apess's father was a shoemaker; others suggest both of Apess's parents were basketmakers. What is certain is that Apess's world was one carved out of the leftovers of genocide and colonialism.

Apess's early years were spent in extreme poverty, hunger, and abuse at the hands of his alcoholic grandparents, with whom he and his siblings had been left. After being nearly beaten to death by his grandmother, Apess was "bound out" at the age of five. The Furmans, the white family with whom he was first indentured, allowed him an education for at least part of the year between the ages of six and eleven. This was the only formal education he received. He was subsequently sold to two wealthy families before running away in April of 1813, from the William Williamses of New York, who forbade his attending Methodist camp meetings. Apess had studied the teaching of John Calvin, repopularized during the Second Great Awakening—humans, all miserable sinners, could be saved only by God's grace. He was later drawn to the Methodists, who taught that Christ was the savior of all mankind, brethren in their belief and in His love.

Apess enlisted as a drummer in the War of 1812 and developed a problem with alcohol, later working for a while in Canada, trying to quit drinking. Around 1816–1817, Apess returned to Connecticut. Despite his lengthy separation from his people, Apess conceived of himself as Pequot. He was baptized in December 1818. In 1821, he married Mary Wood of Salem, Connecticut, a mixed-blood formerly bound servant and fellow Methodist. They had two daughters and a son. Apess was ordained as a Protestant Methodist minister between 1829 and 1830.

Published in 1829, his *A Son of the Forest* recounts his early life in a manner that might seem dispassionate to some readers given the circumstances. It is, in one sense, a Christian conversion narrative, making it appealing to a white audience marveling

at the novelty of an Indian writer and giving faith to Natives and African Americans, who might be "saved" and "civilized." However, *A Son of the Forest* sharply indicts whites for colonialism and for bringing alcohol and poverty to his people and other tribes. Apess also published in 1831 *The Increase of the Kingdom of Christ: A Sermon,* along with an appendix entitled "The Indians: The Ten Lost Tribes." Apess followed this with the publication of his *The Experiences of Five Christian Indians of the Pequot Tribe* in 1833, the first edition of which included his "An Indian's Looking-Glass for the White Man," an essay denouncing white Christian hypocrisy.

As an itinerant preacher, Apess met the Mashpee. His actions on their behalf, including serving jail time, were some of the earliest intertribal activist efforts on behalf of tribal sovereignty. During the Mashpee revolt, he wrote and published a list of Indian complaints regarding the whites entitled *Indian Nullification of the Unconstitutional Laws of Massachusetts, Relative to the Mashpee Tribe; or, the Pretended Riot Explained* (1835). He gave his popular "Eulogy on King Philip" in Boston during 1836. Apess's death in 1839 may have been a result of his continuing struggle with alcohol.

Kimberly Roppolo

See also Pequot War.
References and Further Reading
Hirschfelder, Arlene, and Paulette Molin, eds. 2000. *Encyclopedia of Native American Religions,* updated ed. New York: Facts on File.
Malinowski, Sharon, ed. 1995. *Notable Native Americans.* Detroit, MI: Gale Research.
Malinowski, Sharon, and Simon Glickman, eds. 1996. *Native North American Biography.* Vol. 1. New York: UXL.
O'Connell, Barry. 1996. "Apess, William." In *Encyclopedia of North American Indians: Native American History, Culture, and Life from Paleo-Indians to the Present.* Edited by Frederick E. Hoxie, 30–31. Boston: HoughtonMifflin.

Aquash, Anna Mae Pictou

One of the leading women of the American Indian Movement in the early 1970s, Anna Mae Pictou Aquash was a stanch advocate for American Indian rights. In spite of her many endeavors as an activist, however, she is often remembered for her untimely and mysterious murder on the Pine Ridge Reservation in South Dakota.

Born to Mi'kmaq parents on March 27, 1945, near Shubenacadie, Nova Scotia, Anna Mae, along with her two older sisters and younger brother, spent much of her youth in poverty in Pictou Landing, a Mi'kmaq reserve in Nova Scotia. Her father practiced traditional craftwork and instilled into his stepdaughter a sense of her heritage and culture until his death in 1956. Her mother then abandoned her children to marry another man. Anna Mae's insecure family life, combined with the racial taunts she received from her non-Indian schoolmates, had a detrimental effect on her grades. She attended Milford High School but dropped out at the end of the ninth grade.

In 1962, Anna Mae journeyed to Maine to work the potato and berry harvest, then moved to Boston, Massachusetts, with Jake Maloney, another Mi'kmaq. She secured a job at the Elvin Selow sewing factory while Jake opened a karate school. In June 1964, the couple had their first child, Denise, followed by Deborah, seventeen months later. Desiring to raise their daughters in a more traditional setting, the family moved to New Brunswick, where they formally married at Richibucto and settled onto a Mi'kmaq reserve.

In 1969, the couple's marriage ended, and Anna Mae returned to her job at the sewing factory while volunteering at the Boston Indian Council—an organization that she had helped to create. Among other things, the Council strove to aid the city's Indian population avoid alcohol abuse, a problem with which Anna Mae struggled herself in the aftermath of her marital difficulties. In November 1970, Anna Mae participated in the American Indian Movement's national day of mourning at the 350th anniversary celebration of the arrival of the Pilgrims in Plymouth, Massachusetts. Her interest in Indian activism piqued as she listened enthusiastically to Russell Means's oratory. Quitting her factory job, Anna Mae moved to Bar Harbor, Maine, and worked as a teacher in the Teaching and Research in Bicultural Education School Project (TRIBES) until its funding expired. In 1971, she returned with her daughters to Boston and entered the New Careers program at Wheelock College. She began teaching at the experimental Ruggles Street Day Care in the district of Roxbury—a predominantly black community in the city. Offered a scholarship to Brandeis University, she chose instead to continue her work with urban Indians and helped initiate the Boston Indian Council's job placement

program with the General Motors Plant in Framingham, Massachusetts.

During her time in Boston, Anna Mae met and established a relationship with Nogeeshik Aquash, an Ojibwa artist from Walpole Island in Ontario, Canada. The two traveled to Washington, D.C., with members of the Boston Indian Council to participate in the final stage of the Trail of Broken Treaties. In March 1973, she and Nogeeshik left for the Pine Ridge Reservation in South Dakota to help the besieged Indian activists at Wounded Knee. There, Anna Mae smuggled supplies past the government roadblocks at night and aided in the construction of protective bunkers for the beleaguered Indians. On April 12, Wallace Black Elk married Anna Mae and Nogeeshik in a traditional Lakota ceremony. Thirteen days later, the Aquashes were detained and released by the FBI as they attempted to leave Wounded Knee. Returning first to Boston in an unsuccessful attempt to start an AIM survival school in the city, the couple then moved to Ontario to set up a display of Indian art and culture at the National Arts Centre. The exhibit spawned an interest in traditional Mi'kmaq ribbon shirts, and Anna Mae foresaw the sale of these colorful shirts as a fund-raising enterprise for AIM.

With the conclusion of her exhibit in May 1974, Anna Mae, now separated from her husband, moved to the Minneapolis–St. Paul area, where she made ribbon shirts and worked for the Red School House, the AIM survival school in St. Paul, and for AIM's central office in Minneapolis. There, she became closely associated with Dennis Banks and soon became a national AIM leader in her own right. In the fall, she traveled to Los Angeles to aid in the establishment of an AIM office on the West Coast. In January 1975, she along with fellow workers from the Los Angeles office, Dino Butler and his future wife Nilak (Kelly Jean McCormick), journeyed to Gresham, Wisconsin, to aid the Menominee Warrior Society in their short-lived takeover of an unused abbey—hoping to convert the building into an Indian health center. After departing Gresham, she organized a benefit concert in St. Paul for AIM survival schools before moving briefly to Rosebud, South Dakota, and then to Oglala on the Pine Ridge Reservation near Tent City—the AIM encampment on the property of the Jumping Bull family. AIM members were there in reaction to growing tensions on the reservation between Pine Ridge tribal chairman Dick Wilson and Lakota traditionalists. Anna Mae became involved in community work with local women and began to develop plans for a comprehensive cultural history of the Indian peoples of North America.

In early June 1975, Anna Mae accompanied her compatriots at Tent City to the annual AIM convention in Farmington, New Mexico. Upon their return to Pine Ridge, the activists were involved in a June 26 shoot-out on the Jumping Bull property with two FBI agents. Both agents died, along with one member of AIM. The reservation immediately became the focus of a massive manhunt as the FBI attempted to apprehend the individuals responsible for the death of their agents. As far as the government was concerned, Anna Mae's presence implicated her as either a suspect in or a witness to the incident. Finally located on the Rosebud Reservation at the home of AIM's spiritual leader, Leonard Crow Dog, she was charged on September 5 with unlawful possession of explosives and firearms and taken to Pierre, South Dakota. Released on bond, Anna Mae chose to flee rather than stay and face trial. Recaptured by the FBI on November 14 on the Port Madison Reservation in Washington, she returned to South Dakota to stand trial on the Rosebud charges. Released again prior to the day of her trial, Anna Mae left her Pierre motel room on the evening of November 24 and went into hiding in Colorado.

On February 24, 1976, a rancher discovered Anna Mae's decomposed and frozen body in a ravine near Wanblee, South Dakota. Unable to identify the body, the pathologist removed her hands for possible later identification and ruled that exposure was the cause of death. On March 3, Jane Doe was buried in the cemetery at the Holy Rosary Mission (Red Cloud Indian School) at Pine Ridge. That same day, the FBI lab identified the severed hands as belonging to Anna Mae Aquash. Her family asked for a second autopsy and had the body exhumed on March 10. An independent pathologist discovered that she had been murdered—shot in the back of the head at close range with a .32-caliber weapon. Four days later, her body was reburied at the Wallace Little Ranch in Oglala, where it remained for twenty-eight years. On June 21, 2004, Anna Mae's family returned her remains to the Mi'kmaq reserve in Nova Scotia.

What happened to Anna Mae following her November 24 flight from Pierre until her death in December 1975 (or possibly early January 1976) is conjecture. There is compelling evidence that she fled to Denver and was there kidnapped and taken to South Dakota by some members of AIM who

falsely suspected her of being an FBI informant. She was subsequently killed, according to this theory, to rid the organization of a government spy. Although approached several times in the past by the FBI in hopes of employing her services, Anna Mae openly denied any allegations that she was on the FBI's payroll. The FBI also stated that there was no truth to the assertions. Other members of AIM believe she was killed by a faction of the organization who believed she could identify those responsible for the June 26 deaths of the two FBI agents on the Jumping Bull property. Arlo Looking Cloud was convicted of the murder in 1974.

Alan C. Downs

See also American Indian Movement; Peltier, Leonard; Pine Ridge Political Murders.
References and Further Reading
Brand, Johanna, 1993. *Life and Death of Anna Mae Aquash.* Toronto, ON: Lorimer.
Matthiessen, Peter. 1991. *In the Spirit of Crazy Horse.* New York: Penguin.

Assembly of First Nations

The Assembly of First Nations (AFN) was established in 1982 as Canada's national organization representing the First Nations' political interests. Following the Canadian government's announcement that it had initiated the Constitutional repatriation process, the National Indian Brotherhood (NIB), the Native Council of Canada (NCC), and the Inuit Committee on National Issues were invited to participate in the 1978 deliberations. By the time of the nation's adoption of self-governance in 1982, however, the NIB, once considered Canada's premier First Nations political organization, had imploded from internal dissension. Emerging from the organizational debris was the Assembly of First Nations (AFN).

The evolution of the AFN can be traced to the establishment of the National Indian Council (NIC) in 1961. This organization was created to represent Canadian First Nations groups, including status Indians, nonstatus Indians, Inuit, and the Métis. However, the conflicting interests of the various First Nations groups led the NIC to split into two unaffiliated organizations in 1968: The NIB was formed to represent status Indians, while the Métis established the Canadian Métis Society. The NIB emerged prior to the federal government's 1969 white paper policy, which called for the assimilation of all the First Nations peoples into Canadian society and the elimination of the mention of Indians from the Canadian Constitution. Following the white paper's release, however, the NIB aggressively and successfully lobbied Parliament to rescind the unpopular policy proposal.

For the next thirteen years, the NIB's organizational structure remained unchanged. This became a cause of friction, due primarily to the fact that NIB members were appointed, not elected. Complaints asserting that the NIB was not accountable to the chiefs were politically destabilizing. Unsure that the NIB could effectively represent their interests, 300 status Indians and First Nations chiefs arrived in London, England, in 1979, in an attempt to halt the repatriation of the Constitution, causing even greater dissension among First Nations leaders. First Nations confidence in the NIB failed after a number of questionable moves by its founder, Del Riley, which were followed by calls for organizational reform. The discussion of organizational restructuring focused on the need to create a body that was representative and accountable to First Nations community leaders. It was at this point that the NIB began the transition which led to the formation in 1982 of the AFN. The AFN was an organization open to the chiefs representing all of the status Indian bands in Canada, as opposed to being an organization of regional representatives. The new structure permitted First Nations leaders to formulate and administer AFN policies.

In response to the First Nations' lobbying efforts, Canada revised its Constitution in 1982 and recognized aboriginal rights. The Constitution recognized the Métis, Inuit, status Indians, and nonstatus Indians of Canada as aboriginal people, while also affirming "existing aboriginal and treaty rights." From 1983–1987, the AFN met with the provincial premiers at four First Ministers Conferences in an attempt to define aboriginal self-government. The AFN also began working closely with other prominent lobbying groups and organizations, such as the United Nations, in an attempt to convince Canada to uphold the spirit and intent of treaties. By the mid-1980s, the AFN had become an influential contributor to the ongoing Constitutional debates, as well as a critic of the U.S.–Canada Free Trade Agreement and other proposed legislative changes and issues affecting Canada's First Nations. AFN resistance helped scuttle the Meech Lake Accord in 1990, which proposed Constitutional amendments that recognized Quebec's distinct society while simultaneously ignoring distinct First Nations societies. This, in turn,

Assembly of First Nations Chief Phil Fontaine (left) smokes from a pipe offered by Elder Fred Kelly in a ceremony marking an announcement regarding Indian Residential Schools. (Jim Young/Reuters/Corbis)

resulted in the federal government's openly consulting with First Nations leaders prior to drafting the Charlottetown Accord in 1992, which was rejected by Canadians in a national referendum in 1992. Had the Accord been successful, aboriginal self-government would have been realized, significantly augmenting the First Nations' political influence.

Throughout the 1990s, the AFN continued working with the federal government while zealously lobbying for the formal recognition of aboriginal self-government and the expansion of aboriginal rights. Once again, in 2001, the Canadian government put proposed changes to legislation on the agenda. Without consulting First Nations leaders, federal officials in 2001 proposed legislative changes known as the First Nations Governance Initiative (FNGI) that many AFN delegates considered analogous to the termination policy embodied in the 1969 white paper policy. After years of AFN-led resis-

tance, the Liberal government in 2004 rescinded its unpopular initiative.

Yale D. Belanger

See also Canada, Indian Policies of; Constitution Act; Department of Indian Affairs and Northern Development; Indian Act; Royal Commission on Aboriginal Peoples.

References and Further Reading

Gibbins, Roger, and J. Rick Ponting. 1980. *Out of Irrelevance: A Socio-Political Introduction to Indian Affairs in Canada*. Toronto, ON: Butterworths.

Richardson, Boyce. 1989. *Drumbeat: Anger and Renewal in Indian Country*. Toronto, ON: Summerhill Press.

Sanders, Douglas. 1983. "The Indian Lobby." In *And No One Cheered. Federalism: Democracy and the Constitution Act*. Edited by Keith Banting and Richard Simeon, 301–333. Toronto, ON: Methuen.

Banderas, Juan de la Cruz

Juan Banderas was a noted Yaqui Indian war leader of the early nineteenth century. After receiving visions in 1825, Banderas attempted to unite the Indian nations of northwestern Mexico under the banner of the Virgin of Guadalupe and the last great Aztec emperor, Moctezuma II. Although Banderas successfully challenged Mexican dominance for seven years between 1825 and 1832, local forces captured and executed the Yaqui leader in January 1833. Thereafter Banderas became a powerful symbol of Yaqui resistance to foreign domination.

Banderas was born Juan Ignacio Jusacamea in the Yaqui town Rahum, possibly from the family line that included Muni, leader of the Yaqui Rebellion of 1740. In Rahum, Banderas held the important post of flag bearer in the town military organization. Following Mexican independence from Spain in 1821, Banderas rose to prominence, leading resistance to state land and political policies aimed at integrating the Yaquis into the Mexican nation. In particular, the western state of Occidente (modern Sonora and Sinaloa) attempted to impose taxes on the Yaquis, survey their lands, and integrate Indian towns into the local municipal system. Upon arrest for resisting state programs, Banderas reported having visions summoning him to establish an independent Indian nation-state. In several proclamations, the Yaqui leader invoked the protection of the patron saint and symbol of Mexican independence, the Virgin of Guadalupe, and expressed a desire to restore the sovereignty of the last great Aztec emperor, Moctezuma II. A man of great organizational and oratory skill, Banderas invited all the Indian nations of Sonora and Sinaloa to join the rebellion, although he garnered strong support only from the Yaqui, Mayo, and Opata nations.

From 1825 to 1827, Banderas's forces restored Indian control over much of the state of Occidente. With between 2,000 and 3,000 fighters armed largely with bows and arrows, Indian units enjoyed several military victories over the disorganized state forces. Banderas excelled at guerilla tactics, engaging in strikes on lonely outposts, and then retreating to local Indian towns or mountain ranges. Combined Yaqui, Mayo, and Opata units forced panicked Mexicans to consolidate in the larger towns of Guaymas and Alamos, and prompted local non-Indians to relocate the capital from El Fuerte south to Cosalá, Sinaloa. Defeated in 1827, Banderas accepted a pardon. His resistance, however, forced the Occidente government to acknowledge the Yaqui leader's position as commander general of his nation, a concession to the preindependence system. Although Banderas invoked European and indigenous religious symbols, the messianic appeal of his movement was likely overridden by more concrete political and strategic concerns among his followers.

By 1831, a new series of state laws aimed at colonizing Yaqui territory and incorporating their towns into the local municipal structure sparked a second Banderas rebellion. That year, the Yaqui commander allied with Opata Indian leader Dolores Gutiérrez and gained immediate success. Having several thousand warriors in their command, Banderas and Gutiérrez enjoyed support among the Opata and Lower Pima peoples in northern Occidente and the Yaqui and Mayo peoples in the south of the state. For approximately two years rebel forces swept the countryside, attacking isolated ranches and mines, burning farms and houses, profaning churches, and killing settlers. Banderas's military success ended in December 1832, however, when his troops met defeat at Soyopa, Sonora. The revolt crushed, in January 1833 Banderas, Gutiérrez, and eleven others were executed. Thereafter, Banderas's main rival, Juan María Jusacamea, succeeded him as captain general and accommodated Mexican nationalist policies. Banderas's articulated goals of an independent Indian state did not die with him, however. His movement ushered in intermittent warfare between Yaquis and Mexicans that would continue through the Mexican Revolution. In light of Yaqui resistance, nineteenth-century Mexican officials never fully succeeded in their aims of integrating the Yaqui towns into the local municipal system, collecting taxes, or alienating Yaqui lands.

Contemporaries and later observers have debated the significance of Juan Banderas and his movement. Mexicans of the time viewed him simply as a military strongman, leading a bandit movement for personal reward. Twentieth-century anthropologist Edward Holland Spicer places Banderas squarely within a longer tradition of Yaqui resistance to European encroachment. Historian Evelyn Hu-DeHart credits him with beginning the Yaquis' century-long guerilla war against the more powerful Mexican nation-state. To modern Yaquis, Banderas holds an exalted place: a militant torchbearer of the independent spirit of their people.

Mark Edwin Miller

See also Assimilation; Tribal Sovereignty.
References and Further Reading
Hu-DeHart, Evelyn. 1984. *Yaqui Resistance and
    Survival: The Struggle for Land and Autonomy,
    1821–1910*. Madison: University of Wisconsin
    Press.
Spicer, Edward H. 1980. *The Yaquis: A Cultural
    History*. Tucson: University of Arizona Press.

Banks, Dennis

From the 1960s to the present, Dennis Banks has been a prominent Native American activist, educator, and advocate for Indian rights. He is most famous for his activities as cofounder of the American Indian Movement (AIM) and leader in the historic standoff between the FBI and AIM at Wounded Knee, South Dakota. While he has attracted great political controversy, he is widely loved by traditional indigenous elders and Native rights supporters from around the world.

Born in 1937 on the Leech Lake Reservation in Minnesota, Banks's Ojibwa grandparents raised him to have traditional cultural values. He recalled what happened when he returned home as a boy and announced that he had killed a porcupine, his first success as a hunter. When asked to show his grandparents the porcupine, he confessed that he left it deep in the forest. To teach him an important lesson in life—not to kill any living creature indiscriminately—he was instructed to go back into the dark forest and recover the porcupine. He then was taught the proper way to pray over the animal, asking for forgiveness and promising to use every part of the animal for a good purpose. He cleaned it, cooked the meat, and saved all the quills to be used as decorations for quillwork clothing and birchbark boxes. The experience profoundly changed his worldview at an early age.

His life was seriously disrupted when U.S. government officials took him from his family. They forced him to attend a government boarding school, where he was subjected to a repressive assimilation program. At the age of seventeen, Banks enlisted in the U.S. Air Force and shipped off to Japan. He fell in love with the Japanese people and married a Japanese woman.

When banks left the Air Force, he was shipped back to the United States and found himself in the Indian slums of Minneapolis, Minnesota. He was arrested and sent to prison for stealing groceries to feed his growing family. Here he decided to educate himself, becoming immersed in the study of federal Indian affairs. He learned of the existence of more than 300 broken treaties. Reading in the U.S. Constitution (Article VI) that "treaties are to be judged the supreme law of the land," Banks discovered a legal basis for the defense of Indian rights. Upon his release, he and a number of other Indians, including Russell Means and Vernon and Clyde Bellecourt, founded the American Indian Movement.

In 1972, Banks helped organize a march on Washington, D.C., called the Trail of Broken Treaties. The group arrived at the Bureau of Indian Affairs and demanded that past broken treaties be honored. When a positive response was not received, AIM entered and occupied the BIA building. They raised their AIM flag, barricaded the doors, and called the media. President Richard M. Nixon called for additional snipers to protect the White House and asked the FBI to intervene. After the Iroquois chiefs arrived, a settlement was negotiated. Banks and the AIM members left the BIA building and caravanned in parade of old "rez cars" back to the Lakota reservation in Pine Ridge, South Dakota. The Lakota medicine men, Frank Fools Crow and Leonard Crow Dog, conducted ceremonies.

On February 27, 1973, Dennis Banks and 200 people, including AIM members and their Lakota supporters, found themselves surrounded by FBI agents, U.S. marshals, BIA police officers, and the notorious goon squad of the Pine Ridge tribal council. They had been invited onto the reservation by tribal elders for protection against the terrorism fostered by tribal president Richard "Dick" Wilson. The confrontation quickly turned into an armed standoff. The FBI brought in superior firepower and armored personnel carriers designed for wartime combat. Banks called the Iroquois chiefs, the Muskogee medicine man Philip Deere, and other tribal leaders for support. The armed siege made national news, as TV cameras lined up to record the "last battle of the Indian wars." The standoff lasted seventy-one days, ending, after the deaths of two Indian men, with the signing of a "peace pact" that soon was added to the list of broken treaties.

Dennis Banks was given sanctuary from federal prosecution by California Governor Jerry Brown. Having earned an associates of arts degree at Davis University, Banks went on to serve as chancellor of Deganawidah-Quetzalcoatl (D-Q) University, developing educational programs while organizing in 1978 a new and larger march from Alcatraz Island to Washington, D.C, called the Longest Walk. Modeled

causes, and he remains active as a substance abuse counselor, lecturer, and elder.

Gregory Schaaf

See also American Indian Movement; Peltier, Leonard; Pine Ridge Political Murders; Trail of Broken Treaties; Wilson, Richard; Occupation of Wounded Knee.

References and Further Reading

Banks, Dennis, and Richard Erdoes. 2004. *Ojibwa Warrior: Dennis Banks and the Rise of the American Indian Movement.* Norman: University of Oklahoma Press.

Deloria, Vine, Jr. [1974] 1985. *Behind the Trail of Broken Treaties.* Austin: University of Texas Press.

Dennis Banks, an Ojibwa, was a co-founder of the American Indian Movement. (Bettman/Corbis)

Bearskin, Leaford

Leaford Bearskin (b. 1921) was elected in 1983 as Chief of the Wyandotte Nation, known since the 1500s in American history as part of the Hurons, as well as the Keepers of the Council Fire for the Old Northwest (Delaware) Confederacy. In this capacity, he led the Wyandotte into the twenty-first century after a long career as a military officer and civilian employee of the U.S. Air Force. Among his accomplishments as chief, Bearskin helped the tribe achieve economic self-sufficiency with several business ventures that have benefited both the tribe and local communities. Through his leadership, the Wyandotte have enhanced health care, education, nutrition services, employment opportunities, and emergency services for tribal members. Magnified by his history as a bomber pilot in World War II, an airlift squadron commander during the Berlin Blockade of 1948, and an air base group commander, Bearskin also initiated several Veterans' Day events in northeastern Oklahoma and established a Wyandotte Color Guard to represent the tribe at nationwide events.

Bearskin was born in a log cabin on 140 acres of allotment land along Sycamore Creek in the hills northeast of Wyandotte, Oklahoma, where he attended public school. The family lost the land after his older brother was stricken with polio. Bearskin's parents borrowed money from the local bank to get medication. Subsequently, a land speculator came through town and bought several mortgages from the bank, including the Bearskins', and then foreclosed on them.

After graduating from high school, Bearskin wanted to attend college but he lacked the financial

after Martin Luther King's civil-rights marches, the event's purpose, ultimately successful, was to halt proposed legislation to abrogate Indian treaties.

Taking refuge on the Onondaga nation after Governor Brown left office, Banks eventually surrendered to authorities and served eighteen months in a South Dakota prison. After his release, he worked as a substance abuse counselor on the Pine Ridge Reservation. Banks went on to work successfully for strict legislation to protect Indian graves against desecration. He published his autobiography, *Sacred Soul,* in 1988.

Dennis Banks led the ultimately unsuccessful 1996 drive for executive clemency for the political prisoner, Leonard Peltier. He has performed in movies and has released CDs of original and traditional music. He continues to lead sacred runs around the world in support of various Native

means to do so. Since he also harbored a secret desire to fly an airplane, Bearskin joined the Army Air Corps in 1941. Assigned to an air base in Alaska after the Japanese bombed Pearl Harbor, Bearskin applied for flight school when the Corps revised the minimum requirements for pilot training to a high school diploma. Thus began a highly distinguished career in which Bearskin was awarded such military honors as the Distinguished Flying Cross, the Asiatic Campaign Medal (with four major battle stars), the National Defense Medal, the United Nations Service Medal, and the Air Force Longevity Service Award (with three bronze oak-leaf clusters). After numerous outstanding efficiency ratings and many commendations, Bearskin retired from the Air Force in 1960. Following his retirement, Bearskin spent another twenty years working for the Air Force as a civil servant in the areas of missile weapons systems, logistics, and headquarters operations.

Beginning with his election as chief in 1983, Bearskin has made voluminous contributions to the Wyandotte nation and the surrounding communities of northeastern Oklahoma. Bearskin rewrote the tribal constitution, obtained a grant for the tribe's first economic development project (the Wyandotte convenience store complex), and returned the Wyandotte nation offices to tribal land. He also led a $5.7-million settlement with the U.S. government of Wyandotte land claims in Ohio. Additional tribal programs Bearskin instituted include a senior citizens nutrition program, a food delivery program to local shut-ins, the construction of a tribal social activities center, the creation of a tribal library, and the establishment of a health clinic also available to non-Indian members of the community on a space-available basis. Educationally, the Wyandotte Turtle Tots preschool was recognized as the best preschool in the United States in 1995 and 1996 by the U.S. Department of Education.

Also impacting communities nearby, such as Wyandotte, Fairland, and Miami, Oklahoma, Bearskin oversaw the creation of a cemetery for anyone in the area, Indian or non-Indian, who needed a place to be buried. Under his watch, the Wyandotte nation also made significant enhancements to local public services. The tribe helped the city of Wyandotte create twenty-four-hour law enforcement, helping cut down on crime in the area. The tribe also supports the city's fire department, emergency medical services, and flood management control, and it supervises and funds several regional transportation projects, building or improving roads and

bridges to benefit the whole of Ottawa County. Chief Bearskin also ensured that the tribe's wellness center is available to the entire community. Nationally, Bearskin oversaw the tribe's purchase of six technical schools across the United States that teach highly employable vocational subjects such as court reporting, medical records maintenance, and other skills.

Chief Bearskin instigated the establishment of a Wyandotte Cultural Center, and he directed a cultural committee to revive an annual powwow that had not occurred since the early 1960s. Since its rebeginning in 1991, the annual intertribal event draws up to 4,000 people to the Wyandotte nation in early September and has a dramatic impact on the service-oriented businesses of the area. Chief Bearskin also instituted a Wyandotte language program that is ongoing, and throughout his career traveled extensively speaking about the Wyandottes, their lifeways, and concerns. In 2005, Bearskin led the Wyandotte nation in establishing a gaming complex in Wyandotte County, Kansas.

Hugh W. Foley, Jr.

See also Economic Development.
References and Further Reading
Bearskin, Leaford. 1998. Interview by author, October 18.
Wyandotte Nation of Oklahoma. "Chief Leaford Bearskin." Available at: http://www.wyandotte-nation.org. Accessed May 24, 2005.

Black Elk

Black Elk, a Lakota spiritual leader, came of age during the late nineteenth century, as European encroachment reached his homeland. His views of Native life at that time reached large audiences beginning in the early twentieth century through the books of John Neihardt, the best-known of which is *Black Elk Speaks*. Black Elk is therefore known as a traditional spiritual leader, although he also spent much of his later life as a Catholic.

Black Elk was eleven years old in the summer of 1874 when, by his account (published in *Black Elk Speaks*), an expedition under General George Armstrong Custer invaded the *Paha Sapa* ("hills that are black"), land sacred to the Lakota. The Black Hills had been guaranteed to the Lakota "in perpetuity" by the Fort Laramie Treaty of 1868. Custer's expedition was on a geological mission, not a military one.

Custer was looking for gold. He found it, and in his wake several thousand gold seekers poured into the Black Hills, ignoring the treaty.

In the words of Black Elk, the Lakota and Cheyenne "painted their faces black"—went to war—to regain the Black Hills. The result was Custer's Last Stand in 1876. In his memoir, Black Elk told Neihardt that he was a young warrior who participated in the battle of the Little Bighorn. Young Black Elk tried to take the first scalp, but the soldier under Black Elk's hatchet proved to have an unusually tough scalp, so Black Elk shot him.

The Seventh Calvary initiated a battle that the Lakota Chief Kill Eagle likened to a hurricane or to bees swarming out of a hive. Completely surrounded and cut off from reinforcements stationed only nine miles away, Custer's force was cut to ribbons during one furious, bloody hour on a battleground that nearly disappeared under a huge cloud of dust. The battle provoked momentary joy among the Sioux and Cheyennes, who for decades had watched their hunting ranges curtailed by what Black Elk characterized as the gnawing flood of the Wasi'chu (literally "takers of the fat," used to characterize the invaders).

After the Wounded Knee massacre, Black Elk watched his people, once the mounted lords of the Plains, become hungry, impoverished prisoners, pent up on thirteen government reservations. In 1886, when he was twenty-three years of age, Black Elk joined Buffalo Bill's Wild West Show. After a tour of large cities on the eastern seaboard, the troupe traveled to England.

The first three decades of Black Elk's life are chronicled in Neihardt's book-length poem Black Elk Speaks, first published in 1932; much of the same period was covered in Joseph Epes Brown's The Sacred Pipe: Black Elk's Account of the Seven Rites of the Oglala Sioux. The final words in Dee Brown's Bury My Heart at Wounded Knee (1970) come from Black Elk: "It was a beautiful dream . . . The nation's hoop is broken and scattered. There is no center anymore, and the sacred tree is dead."

Another book, Michael Steltenkamp's Black Elk: Holy Man of the Oglala (1993), describes Black Elk's final years as a Roman Catholic missionary. Steltenkamp, who is a Jesuit himself (as well as an anthropologist), said he learned of Black Elk's conversion from Lucy Looks Twice, Black Elk's only surviving child, who died in 1978. The Catholic Church also sent Black Elk on fund-raising trips to cities such as New York, Boston, Chicago, Washington, D.C., and Omaha. In 1934, shortly after publication of Black Elk Speaks, Black Elk complained that Neihardt hadn't said enough about his life as a Catholic. Black Elk added that his family was all baptized. All his children and grandchildren belonged to the Catholic Church, he asserted.

During his later years, Black Elk combined Catholic missionary work with occasional showmanship at South Dakota tourist attractions that capitalized on his image as a Lakota holy man. Steltenkamp wrote that Black Elk sensed no contradictions in mixing the two interpretations of the "great mystery." Black Elk died in 1950. He is said to have believed that lights in the sky would accompany his death. The night Black Elk died, the Pine Ridge area experienced an intense and unusually bright meteor shower.

Bruce E. Johansen

See also Missionaries, French Jesuit.
References and Further Reading
Black Elk. 1973. The Sacred Pipe. Edited by Joseph Epes Brown. New York: Penguin.
Brown, Dee. 1970. Bury My Heart at Wounded Knee. New York: Holt, Rinehart, and Winston.
Nabokov, Peter. 1991. Native American Testimony. New York: Viking.
Neihardt, Hilda. 1995. Black Elk & Flaming Rainbow: Personal Memories of the Lakota Holy Man. Lincoln: University of Nebraska Press.
Neihardt, John. Black Elk Speaks. 1932. Lincoln: University of Nebraska Press.
Rice, Julian. Black Elk's Story. 1991. Albuquerque: University of New Mexico Press.

Blackfeet Confederacy

The Blackfeet claim modern-day central Montana, southern Alberta, and western Saskatchewan to be their homeland. Recent archaeological discoveries confirm these claims while demonstrating thousands of years of Blackfeet territorial occupation. Four distinctive political groups comprised the Blackfeet Confederacy: the Piikunis, North Piikunis, Kainais, and Siksikas. The imposition of the U.S.–Canadian border in the nineteenth century split the members of the Blackfeet Confederacy, leaving six bands in Canada and one in the United States. In the United States, the Piikunis reside on a reservation in Montana, while in Canada, where they are known as the Blackfoot, three reserve communities in southern Alberta are home to the Kanais, the North Piikunis, and the Siksikas.

The name "Blackfeet" is an English term originally used to describe the people who dyed their moccasins black. The Blackfeet were organized into small bands typically no larger than twenty or thirty people. The bands were self-governing and self-sufficient entities that occupied demarcated territories for their exclusive use and benefit. They fended off anyone who broached their sovereignty, be it American whiskey traders or other nations, such as the Crees from the east or the Shoshones from the south. Prior to their acquisition of horses in the mideighteenth century, the Blackfeet traversed their territory on foot. During this period known as the "dog days," characterized by limited mobility, dogs were the beasts of burden and hooked up to travois to haul teepees and other heavier materials. While the small band sizes were militarily limiting, they made hunting buffalo effective. This resulted in the creation of highly refined techniques for hunting buffalo, the animal the Blackfeet were most dependent on spiritually and materially.

The introduction of the horse in the early eighteenth century was a technological revolution of sorts, permitting the development of more efficient hunting techniques. The Blackfeet were able to travel farther east on horseback, a development that led also to their acquiring guns from the French. This had the effect of positioning the Blackfeet as the preeminent military power in the northwestern region of the Great Plains. A period of rapid and aggressive territorial expansion followed, as the Blackfeet pushed the Shoshones to the southwestern corner of Montana while forcing the Flatheads and Kootenais across the Continental Divide. Northern movement led the Blackfeet to effectively displace the Crees from those territories. By the end of the eighteenth century, the Blackfeet controlled a significant portion of the Montana territory, extending into modern Alberta and western Saskatchewan. The explorers Lewis and Clark confirm these results, claiming that, as of 1806, the Piikunis controlled all of north-central Montana. With an estimated population of 15,000, an ample source of raw materials in the form of buffalo to maintain their traditional economy, and a well-known reputation as fierce warriors, the Blackfeet controlled this extensive region well into the mid-nineteenth century despite the appearance of British officials and the U.S. cavalry seeking to expand their territorial claims.

From 1840 to 1860, the Blackfeet Confederacy bands became distinctive political entities occupying specific territories. For instance, the Kainais, North Piikunis, and Siksikas remained north of the international boundary, whereas the Piikunis lived south of the border. In 1851, following the signing of the Treaty of Fort Laramie, the U.S. government identified the Piikunis as one of the tribes authorized to use the vast Montana territory north of the Missouri River and east of the Continental Divide, even though they were not directly involved in the treaty negotiations. This nevertheless did not end cross-cultural hostilities. Colonel E. M. Baker almost killed Heavy Runner's entire band, the majority of who were women and children, in a surprise attack in January 1870. The Baker Massacre was revenge for the murder of a prominent settler named Malcolm Clark. In all, 173 Blackfeet died and an additional 140 were taken prisoner. This, in turn, led to a reduction of the overall Blackfeet reserve in 1873 and 1874.

In Canada, the Kainais, the North Piikunis, and the Siksikas signed Treaty 7 with representatives of the British crown and the Canadian government in 1877. Despite their poor experience treating with the U.S. government, Canadian success in removing whiskey traders from southern Alberta convinced Blackfeet leaders to negotiate with the crown. In return for annuities, the promise from federal officials to protect the buffalo, and the establishment of protected reserves, the Kainais, North Piikunis, and Siksikas agreed to cede more than 25,000 square miles of their territory to the Canadian government. The Piikuni remained south of the international boundary, contained on their reservation north of the Missouri and Marias Rivers. The loss of the buffalo by the early 1880s led to a desperate situation in Canada and the United States, however. In the United States, Blackfeet leaders were forced to sell a portion of their land, which broke up the contiguous Blackfeet Reservation. The Blackfoot (which is the accepted designation for these bands living in Canada) north of the border found themselves increasingly confined to their reserves, as they became more dependent on government rations and Indian agent generosity for their survival. Later, pressure from the U.S. government led the Blackfeet to surrender a scenic portion of their reservation, land that eventually became part of Glacier National Park.

Indian agents on both sides of the forty-ninth parallel argued that farming and ranching were key to Blackfeet self-sufficiency. As part of Treaty 7, the crown provided farming implements and minimal training to aspiring Blackfoot farmers. In addition to farming, the U.S. government permitted the Black-

feet the right to allot lands to individual families on the reservation, and within a year construction on a large irrigation project began. By the early 1920s, however, the Blackfeet's economy had all but collapsed, with an estimated two-thirds of tribal members reliant on federal handouts. Similarly, in Canada, Blackfoot bands faced tough economic times, due in part to federal efforts to dispossess Indians of the reserves through the illegal leasing and allocation of land to Great War veterans as a reward for their efforts in the European theater. In response, Kainai war veteran Mike Mountain Horse organized two political conferences, in 1924 and 1925, to bring an end to the illegal leasing of reserve lands and to lobby the government for a renewed political relationship. Although little came of the conferences, most Blackfoot leaders continued to resist the leasing of reserve lands. In particular, Kainai Chief Shot Both Sides became a vocal proponent of protecting his people's territorial autonomy and, in the 1920s, initiated a moratorium on leasing reserve land.

The Blackfeet in Montana reorganized according to the provisions of the 1934 Indian Reorganization Act (IRA), the land allotment process was terminated, the sale of reservation lands to non-Indians was halted, and a number of vocational training programs were implemented. In Canada, Blackfoot leaders reacted to the federal government's policy of benign neglect by forming the Indian Association of Alberta (IAA) in 1939. A strictly regional organization that concerned itself with Alberta Indian issues, the IAA promoted equality without endorsing Indian assimilation. It was concerned with drawing the public's attention to social issues on reserves while never losing sight of protecting the Alberta treaties. It continued as a lobby group until the 1970s.

By the 1960s, the Blackfeet, both in the United States and Canada, began to witness better economic times. The Blackfeet in Montana began receiving petroleum royalties, followed by the construction of a pencil factory in 1972. Although still under the threat of termination from the U.S. government, the Blackfeet boast an enrollment of 15,560, of which 8,560 are off-reservation and 7,000 are on-reservation. The Blackfoot in Canada are separated into three main reserve communities: Kainais, Piikunis, and Siksikas. Kainais have a population of more than 9,000, while the Piikunis and Siksikas have a total registered population of 3,375 and 5,922, respectively. The Kainais have a small industrial base, receive royalties on water rights and mineral extraction, and maintain active farming and ranching industries. The Siksikas First Nation receives natural resource royalties and engage in agriculture and ranching, while benefiting from tourism. They also hold exclusive land rights to one of Canada's fastest growing economic sectors. The Piikunis are engaged in petroleum exploration, agriculture and ranching, as well as tourism.

The connection between the Blackfeet of Montana and the Blackfoot of Canada remains close, with friends and family regularly crossing the international boundary to visit and work. The Sun Dance celebration remains a central event and various religious societies still meet, entailing cross-border travel.

Yale D. Belanger

See also Canada, Indian Policies of; Confederacies; Economic Development; Welch, James.

References and Further Reading

Bastien, Betty. 2004. *Blackfoot Ways of Knowing: The World View of the Siksikaitsitapi.* Calgary, AB: University of Calgary Press.

Bear Robe, Andrew. 1996. "The Historical, Legal and Current Basis for Siksika Nation Governance, Including Its Future Possibilities Within Canada." In *For Seven Generations: An Information Legacy of the Royal Commission on Aboriginal Peoples.* [CD-ROM] Ottawa, ON: Canada Communications Group.

Belanger, Yale D. 2005. "'An All Round Indian Affair': The Native Gatherings at Macleod, 1924 & 1925." *Alberta History* 53, no. 3: 13–23.

Dempsey, Hugh. 1972. *Crowfoot: Chief of the Blackfeet.* Edmonton, AB: Hurtig Publishers.

Meijer-Drees, Laurie. 2002. *The Indian Association of Alberta: A History of Political Action.* Vancouver: University of British Columbia Press.

Rosier, Paul C. 2001. *Rebirth of the Blackfeet Nation, 1912–1954.* Lincoln: University of Nebraska Press.

Treaty 7 Elders and Tribal Council, with Walter Hildebrant, Sarah Carter, and Dorothy First Rider. 1996. *The True Spirit and Intent of Treaty 7.* Kingston, ON, and Montreal, QC: McGill-Queen's University Press.

Black Hawk

Black Hawk (Makataimeshekiakiak) was a distinguished warrior in the War of 1812 and an inveterate foe of American expansion. Two decades later, he waged the last Indian war in the Old Northwest to curb white encroachment of his homeland.

Black Hawk was a chief of the Thunder Clan of the Sauk and Fox. (Library of Congress)

Black Hawk was born about 1767, a member of the Thunder Clan of the Sauk and Fox, and grew up at Saukenuk in northeastern Illinois. He joined his first war party at the age of fifteen and fought in successive wars and raids against the neighboring Osages and Cherokees. A chief since 1788, Black Hawk resented American interference in Indian affairs and became stridently pro-British in outlook. This sentiment conflicted directly with most tribal elders, who were friendly toward the United States and received gifts and annuities in return.

By 1804, Black Hawk's dislike turned to hatred when Indiana territorial Governor William Henry Harrison persuaded several Sauk and Fox chiefs to sell most of their peoples' land east of the Mississippi River. Black Hawk refused to sign the treaty and remained at his village of Saukenuk. When the War of 1812 erupted eight years later, his warrior band joined Tecumseh's pan-tribal alliance in their struggle against the whites. Real Indian unity proved fleeting, however. Despite Black Hawk's

best efforts, the Sauk and Fox nation split into the British band under himself and a pro-American faction allied to Chief Keokuk.

Black Hawk fought and helped defeat General James Winchester at the Battle of Frenchtown in January 1813 and subsequently attended the unsuccessful siege of Fort Meigs that May. When British forces failed to dislodge Major George Croghan from Fort Stephenson in August 1813, however, he grew disillusioned and withdrew to his homeland for the winter. Black Hawk reentered the fray in July 1814 when his warriors ambushed and defeated a detachment of the First U.S. Infantry on Campbell's Island in the Mississippi River.

In September, Black Hawk enjoyed similar success when he drove off an expedition under Major Zachary Taylor at Rock River, Illinois. Black Hawk was therefore very upset with his British allies when they signed a peace treaty and abandoned all their western conquests to the United States. Throughout the spring of 1815, he raided several settlements near Fort Howard, Missouri, in protest. His warriors defeated a pursuing party of rangers at the Battle of the Sinkhole in June 1815, the final skirmish of the War of 1812. The following year, Black Hawk sullenly concluded a peace treaty with the United States and was the last war chief to do so.

For the next twenty years, Black Hawk lived in an uneasy truce with his white neighbors at Saukenuk, but by 1829 the Illinois state government applied pressure on the Indians to migrate. When the old chief refused, Governor John Reynolds called out the militia in June 1831 to evict them by force. Bloodshed was averted, however, when the Sauk and Fox tribe slipped quietly across the Mississippi River into Iowa and endured an uncomfortable winter there. Black Hawk had come under the influence of White Cloud, a Winnebago prophet, who urged action against the whites, and Black Hawk decided to reclaim his ancestral home. On April 5, 1832, the tribe, numbering 1,400 men, women, and children, crossed back into Illinois for the stated purpose of occupying Saukenuk. It was hoped hostilities could be avoided.

The Americans reacted by summoning the troops of General Henry Atkinson and Colonel Henry Dodge, who immediately marched against them. The Indians, having received no pledge of assistance from the neighboring Winnebago and Potawatomi tribes, decided the odds were too steep and tried to surrender. When two of their peace envoys were killed by Illinois militia, the Battle of

Stillman's Run erupted on May 14, 1832, and Black Hawk was again victorious. The Indians then reached the Mississippi River and prepared to cross. They were in the act of building rafts when they were attacked by the steamboat *Warrior* on August 1, 1832.

Again, the Indians tried to signal their surrender, to no avail. After inflicting considerable losses, the steamboat withdrew because of lack of fuel, just as Atkinson's column arrived. An intense battle ensued in which 150 Native Americans were slain and a similar number captured. Several survivors made their way across to the west bank of the Mississippi, where they were immediately attacked by Sioux Indian war parties. Black Hawk was eventually captured and taken east by Lieutenant Jefferson Davis to meet with President Andrew Jackson. After several months of confinement at Fort Monroe, Virginia, he was released in the custody of rival chief, Keokuk.

Back in Iowa, Black Hawk dictated his memoirs, a stinging indictment against European-American injustice, to Indian agent Antonine LeClaire. When published in 1833, the book became a national best seller. Black Hawk continued living quietly for another five years and died in Keokuk's village on October 3, 1838. His defeat signaled the collapse of Native American resistance to white expansion east of the Mississippi.

See also Black Hawk's War; Harrison, William Henry.

References and Further Reading

Armstrong, Perry A. 1887. *The Sauks and the Black Hawk War.* Springfield, IL: H. W. Rokker.

Eckert, Allan W. 1988. *Twilight of Empire: A Narrative.* Boston: Little, Brown and Company.

Hagen, William T. 1958. *The Sac and Fox Indians.* Norman: University of Oklahoma Press.

Jackson, Donald, ed. 1964. *Black Hawk: An Autobiography.* Urbana: University of Illinois Press.

Nichols, Roger L. 1992. *Black Hawk and the Warrior's Path.* Wheeling, IL: Harlan Davidson.

Stark, William F. 1984. *Along the Black Hawk Trail.* Sheboygan, WI: Zimmerman Press.

Thayer, Crawford B. 1981. *Hunting a Shadow: The Search for Black Hawk.* Privately published.

Black Kettle

Perhaps the most famous Southern Cheyenne leader during the mid-1800s was the peace advocate Black Kettle (Moketavato). His rise in power came when the Cheyenne people turned to more centralized authority as the threat of American encroachment increased. While some Cheyenne leaders and warrior societies chose aggression, Black Kettle preferred to guide the Cheyennes through the violence of the 1860s that defined Cheyenne–American government relations by peaceful resolutions. Despite suffering horrific atrocities by the American military, being opposed and even ostracized by his own people, and being betrayed and vilified by white leaders, Black Kettle endorsed peace—even until his own violent death—as the answer to the threatening destruction of the Cheyennes.

Few biographical details are known about Black Kettle, especially of his earlier years. The famed trader George Bent, who married Black Kettle's niece, provides some information. According to Bent, Black Kettle was the son of Swift Hawk Lying Down (who never was a chief), who was of the Sutaio tribe (a kindred people to the Cheyennes and a portion of whom were incorporated into the tribe during the 1700s and became one of the tribe's divisions) and who was a good warrior. Cheyenne historian George Bird Grinnell suggests that Black Kettle even carried Medicine Arrows into battle against the Delaware in 1853. When exactly Black Kettle became a chief is uncertain, but he is known to have become *the* principal chief by 1860. That same year historical evidence identifies the Cheyenne leader with the name Black Kettle, the name for which he is most known. Black Kettle lived on the vast territory of the southern Plains, a region guaranteed the tribe under the Fort Laramie Treaty of 1851. The Pike's Peak gold rush of 1859, however, created a flood of white migration to Colorado, bringing with it intrusion on Cheyenne lands and hostilities between the two cultures.

The U.S. government sought to resolve the situation by forcing a new treaty on the Cheyennes in 1861 (Treaty of Fort Wise) that would cede all tribal lands save a small reservation (the Sand Creek reservation) in southeastern Colorado. Black Kettle supported the treaty, fearing an even worse outcome if he did not, and then he struggled to see the Cheyennes kept their part of the agreements. The lack of agricultural success and hunting at the Sand Creek Reservation, along with epidemic diseases, created a dismal situation for the Cheyennes. Young men began to leave the reservation and prey on nearby settlers and passing wagon trains. Tensions escalated between the two cultures, especially after federal troops left the West to fight the Civil War.

Black Kettle continued to press for harmonious relations, especially for his band, but Coloradans refused the peace.

Coloradans desired a world cleansed of Native peoples, and leading that charge were men like Colonel John M. Chivington, commander of the Third Colorado Volunteers. Without warning, Chivington's troops attacked Black Kettle's encampment on Sand Creek in southeastern Colorado on November 29, 1864, in spite of Black Kettle's efforts to secure peace. The attack left about 200 of Black Kettle's Cheyennes, many women and children, slaughtered by Chivington's men, who then sexually mutilated, scalped, and took body parts as trophies of their conquest.

Black Kettle miraculously escaped the massacre at Sand Creek. More remarkably, he continued to be an advocate for peace even as other Cheyennes pursued violent retribution throughout the southern Plains. Eventually, Black Kettle and other Indian leaders achieved an uneasy truce with the government and agreed to a new reservation in Kansas. Not all Cheyennes approved. Many ignored the agreements and continued ranging over their ancestral lands. Federal negotiators again sought to remove the Cheyennes, this time to two smaller reservations in Indian Territory (today's Oklahoma). Black Kettle was among the chiefs who signed this treaty, the Medicine Lodge Treaty of 1867. The federal government, however, failed to uphold its agreements by not giving the Cheyennes all the promised supplies. As a result, many Cheyennes left the reservations to hunt, roam, and raid. Some attacked white settlements, leading to a full-scale American military response. In 1868, General Philip Sheridan orchestrated a wintertime total war campaign against any southern Plains tribes not found at the agencies. The newly formed Seventh Cavalry led by George Armstrong Custer was selected to take the lead.

On the frozen morning of November 27, 1868, almost four years to the day since the Sand Creek Massacre, Custer's command attacked Black Kettle's Cheyenne camp on the Washita River, well within the boundaries of the Cheyenne Reservation. During the initial attack, both Black Kettle and his wife were shot down. In that moment the Cheyennes lost one of its greatest leaders. In a matter of months the old Cheyenne way of life was lost as well.

S. Matthew DeSpain

See also Genocide; Sand Creek Massacre.

References and Further Reading
Greene, Jerome A. 2004. *Washita: The U.S. Army and the Southern Cheyennes, 1867–1869*. Norman: University of Oklahoma Press.
Hatch, Thom. 2004. *Black Kettle: The Cheyenne Chief Who Sought Peace but Found War*. Hoboken, NJ: John Wiley & Sons.

Boas, Franz

Franz Boas was an influential social philosopher and anthropologist. He is remembered today largely because of his application of the scientific method to the study of human society and his resulting rejection of the notion of racial hierarchy.

Boas was born in Germany in 1858. He completed a Ph.D. in physics but later became interested in studying human geography. In 1887, Boas immigrated to New York City. A year later, he accepted his first teaching position, and in 1896 he was hired by Columbia University, where he taught anthropology for more than forty years. He died in 1942. Boas was an impolitic, unyielding academician dedicated to the pursuit of knowledge and truth (at least as he defined it). Because he was an unconventional thinker who was frank in his assessment of others' work, the early part of Boas's academic career was marred by friction, frequent job changes, and occasional periods of unemployment.

Boas was a highly productive writer and researcher. During the most productive eighteen years of his career, he published more than sixty journal articles, a monograph, and two academic papers. Boas wrote and published both popular and scientific articles, but the bulk of his published work consists of ethnographic data that he gathered and recorded during his anthropological fieldwork in tribal communities. These data include myths, songs, linguistic information, descriptions of rituals, and physical measurements, such as head size and height.

Although Boas was in many ways ahead of his peers, he was still a product of the Victorian era (1837–1901) in which he grew up. For example, early in his career, Boas participated in now discredited research, such as attempting to gauge a people's intelligence based on their average head size. A common criticism of Boas's work is that he emphasized the gathering and recording of ethnographic data over its analysis. To a certain extent, this emphasis can be explained as an attempt to catalogue and preserve for future generations what Boas and his contemporaries perceived to be vanishing cultures. Another explanation might be an unwillingness and/or inability to see Native perspectives.

In addition to his work as a scholar and educator, for many years Boas curated museum exhibits. When Boas began his museum work, artifacts were customarily arranged in groups of similar items—for example, weapons, pottery, tools. Typically, the artifacts also were organized to create an appearance of evolutionary development. Thus, a stone arrowhead from North America would be placed beside a Viking age iron spear point, which would lie next to a steel Bowie knife, and so forth. Boas revolutionized this type of museum exhibit by rearranging the displays, grouping objects from a single tribe and placing the artifacts of neighboring tribes in close proximity. This new exhibit style eventually transformed museum displays around the world.

At the time that anthropology was gaining strength as an academic discipline, social theory had not yet separated the concepts of culture, race, and nationality. The prevalent view was that people from each region of the world had a certain "temperament," or personality, that was the result of factors such as climate, diet, religion, language, and physical traits. According to this view, nations, or races, could be grouped into a hierarchy, or pyramid, with one's own group at the top and other races at the bottom. Among Europeans and European-Americans, a common belief was that Caucasians surpassed all other human groups in intelligence, physique, and social development. This belief was used to justify such racially motivated policies as slavery, the removal of Native Americans from their lands, and the European fascist movements that led to World War II. While some of the most prominent early American anthropologists used anthropology to perpetuate the racially deterministic beliefs of the day, Boas did just the opposite.

Boas applied the scientific method he had learned in his study of physics to the study of human society. This led him to reject the theory of racial hierarchy and instead to theorize that differences among societies did not indicate that one group was superior or inferior to another, but rather that each group was uniquely well adapted to fulfill its members' needs and ensure their collective survival. Boas's scholarship and ideas were widely disseminated and came eventually to affect the views of the larger society, ultimately helping to break the monolithic Victorian worldview into the separate

Franz Boas was an influential social philosopher and anthropologist. (Library of Congress)

concepts of race, culture, and language that characterize how we view the world today.

Amy L. Propps

See also Bureau of American Ethnology.
References and Further Reading
Boas, Franz. 1963. *The Mind of Primitive Man.* Toronto, ON: Collier-Macmillan Canada.
Hyatt, Marshall. 1990. *Franz Boas: Social Activist.* Westport, CT: Greenwood Press.

Bonnin, Gertrude Simmons

Gertrude Bonnin (Yankton Dakota, 1876–1938), whose Native name was Zitkala-sa, provided a written window on Sioux life at the juncture of the Native American and Anglo-American worlds. Born the year of the Custer Battle, she died on the

Throughout her life pan-Indian activist and writer Gertrude Bonnin fought for Native American self-determination and the preservation of Indian culture. (Library of Congress)

eve of World War II. Bonnin was one of several prominent literary figures to come out of the boarding schools, whose engines of assimilation produced strident critiques of their methods (and of Anglo-American society generally) by the likes of Luther Standing Bear, George Eastman, and Bonnin, among others.

"This is a story," wrote Ruth Spack, in *America's Second Tongue: American Indian Education and the Ownership of English, 1860–1900* "of language and how people used it to further their own political and cultural agendas" (2002, 7). Thus, Bonnin and other Native American students took control of English as a means of expression even as they were forced to speak it to the exclusion of their Native tongues. This was not always the kind of assimilation that their Anglo-American teachers had anticipated.

Bonnin distrusted most non-Indians, but early sought a formal education against her mother's wishes, eventually attending the Boston Conserva-

tory of Music. Her articles and poetry were published in large-circulation magazines, such as her "Red Man's Helper" in the June 1900 edition of *The Atlantic Monthly.* One of Bonnin's books, the autobiographical *American Indian Stories* (1921), described her changing perceptions of the Euro-American world and her gradual acceptance of Christianity. She also authored *Old Indian Legends* (1901), among other titles.

Bonnin returned to the Carlisle Industrial School as a teacher and developed a curriculum for boarding school education from a Native perspective (which was rejected). She also edited *American Indian Magazine,* a publication of the Society of American Indians. She was among a number of very literate American Indian activists in her time who valued printed media (non-Indian outlets as well as their own) to advocate for change. Bonnin's autobiographical essays, including "Impressions of an Indian Childhood," "School Days of an Indian Girl," and "An Indian Teacher Among Indians," enraged Richard Henry Pratt, founder of the boarding school system, even as he used her reputation as an example of how Native American children were helped by the schools (Katanski, 2005, 17).

Bonnin intensely resented the use of her work to support theories of social evolution; at one point, she wrote, "No one can dispute my own impressions and bitterness" (Katanski, 2005, 29). Amelia V. Katanski, in *Learning to Write "Indian,"* characterizes much of Bonnin's work as "images of angry, pain-filled students, whose plight challenged white educators' justifications of the boarding schools" (2005, 166). However, she recognized the compromises between tradition and non-Native change that so affected her life, as in the first sentence of "Impressions of an Indian Childhood," in which she described living with her mother in a tepee made not of buffalo hides, but canvas (Katanski, 2005, 116).

With Eastman, Bonnin was a founder of the Society of American Indians, an early pan-Indian advocacy organization in the 1920s. She also was known for her talent on the violin. Bonnin investigated the swindling of Indians in Oklahoma by settlers who swarmed into the area after the discovery of oil, and she advised the government's Meriam Commission in the late 1920s. Bonnin remained active in Indian affairs until she died in 1938.

Bruce E. Johansen

See also Society of American Indians.

References and Further Reading
Katanski, Amelia V. 2005. *Learning to Write "Indian:"
The Boarding School Experience and American
Indian Literature.* Norman: University of
Oklahoma Press.
Spack, Ruth. 2002. *America's Second Tongue: American
Indian Education and the Ownership of English,
1860–1900.* Lincoln: University of Nebraska
Press.

Brant, Joseph

Joseph Brant was an influential Mohawk leader whose lasting achievement was the establishment of the Six Nations Grand River Reservation in southern Ontario. An active ally of the British during the American Revolution, he was known for conducting military raids against New York State colonists. After the war, his allegiance to the British was rewarded with a reserve of several hundred square miles along the Grand River, held in trust by the British crown. The final ten years of his life were marked by frustration with British authorities, however, who often blocked his attempts to sell portions of the land to raise sorely needed money for his people. Very well educated for a frontiersman, Brant helped to translate a bilingual Mohawk–English prayer book, and kept up an extensive political correspondence for much of his life. His Mohawk name, Thayendanegea (pronounced Tai-yen-da-nay-geh), has been variously translated as "He Places Two Bets" or "Two Sticks of Wood Bound Together."

The records of Brant's youth are obscure, but both of his principal biographers agree that he was born of humble origins. Little is known of his parents, Margaret and Peter (Tehonwaghkwanger-aghkwa). John Norton, a close friend of Brant's, wrote that they may have been captured Canadian Wyandots adopted by the Mohawks near the Bay of Quinte. Because Margaret was certainly not from sachem lineage, her son's political future was limited. Joseph was probably born on a hunting trip in Haudenosaunee (Six Nations, or Iroquois) territory in Ohio during 1743. Over the next ten years, Margaret went though three husbands, had more children (Molly was from her second husband), and lived in the town of Canajoharie on the Mohawk River. Her third husband was a well connected Mohawk sachem named Brant Canagaraduncka.

Because Joseph's new father-in-law was a sachem, Sir William Johnson's courtship of his half sister, Molly, made political sense for the rising

Mohawk chief Joseph Brant, also known as Thayendanega, was a significant Native American leader during the American Revolution. Brant allied himself with the British against the American colonists. (National Archives and Records Administration)

British Indian superintendent. Johnson wished to keep the Mohawks as strong allies, and he took fifteen-year-old Brant on raids and battles against the French in 1758, although Brant did not see much action until the siege of Fort Niagara in 1759.

When the Reverend Eleazar Wheelock wrote to Johnson seeking bright young candidates for his Indian school in Lebanon, Connecticut, Johnson sent Brant in 1761. In addition to learning basic skills in English literacy, Brant developed friendships with many of the missionaries trained at Wheelock's school, such as Samuel Kirkland. In 1763, Pontiac's rebellion broke out, however, and Brant was summoned home by his mother. Brant was asked to recruit warriors to discipline Pontiac's Shawnees and Delawares who were waging war against the

British. While on a recruiting trip along the Susquehanna River, Brant met Neggen Aoghyatonghere, or Peggy, whom he eventually married in 1765. They had two children, Isaac and Christina, and lived a comfortable life in Canajoharie, with Brant working as an interpreter for William Johnson, and then his successor Guy Johnson, for seventy pounds a year. After Peggy died of tuberculosis in 1771, Brant married her half sister Susanna in 1773.

As war with the colonies loomed in 1775, Brant went to England with his superior, Guy Johnson, who was seeking appointment as Indian superintendent. During his eight-month stay, Brant met George III, attended parties, and was generally well liked for his pledges of fidelity to the crown.

Although the British initially resisted employing Indians in warfare, by 1777 Brant was asked by Guy Johnson to recruit the members of the Six Nations for action. For the next several years, Captain Brant headed small groups of Indians and frontier Loyalists to harass upstate New York towns. Brant commanded several noteworthy raids on Oriskany, Cherry Valley, and German Flats, even burning his friend Samuel Kirkland's church at Oneida. Thomas Campbell, in his 1806 poem, "Gertrude of Wyoming," blamed "the Monster Brant" for the massacre of 227 people at Wyoming, New York, even though Brant was not present.

Following General Sullivan's march through central New York in 1779, Brant conducted many successful raids in 1780 and 1781, but the pro-British Indians were largely forced to hunker down at Fort Niagara for the remainder of the war. Brant's second wife, Susanna, died there, also of tuberculosis. Shortly afterward, however, Brant met Catharine Adonwentishon, daughter of George Croghan and a Mohawk woman. At thirty-six years of age, Brant married her and he also became lifelong friends with her half brother, the sachem Henry Tekarihoga.

When the war ended in 1783, the British made no provisions for their Indian allies, and, as a result, they were afraid that the Indians might turn on them. Although Brant remained an ostensible supporter of the British for the next twenty years, he began also to support pan-Indian unity as a means to counteract the intrigues of British and American politics. At an important postwar council at Sandusky, Ohio, in 1783, Brant recommended that all the Indian nations act as one body in the future. The British General Frederick Haldimand, trying to placate the Mohawks, arranged in October 1784 to award them several hundred square miles of land along the Grand River as recompense for the lands they had lost in New York.

Brant was grateful to Haldimand but the political betrayal by the British had lasting consequences. Just after the war, Brant went again to England to request financial restitution on behalf of the Mohawks for what they lost in the war and to inquire about the delay in his Indian department pension. Although he was finally successful on both counts, he was insulted that Indian requests were so slowly acted on.

The second half of Brant's life saw him trying simultaneously to heal the disagreements between the various Indian nations and to obtain Indian ownership of Grand River. As a result, he was sometimes perceived as unscrupulous. In actuality, however, it was the British and the Americans who drove these intrigues. To his credit, Brant frequently made trips to Ohio and Detroit, telling the Indians not to rely on the British for military aid. He told the Haudenosaunee living in New York, who began to court the favor of the United States after 1790, that they should not rely on American favors. By August 1793, when the Miami and Shawnee rebellions were at their peak of success, Brant urged the western Indians to accept a compromise borderline with the United States at the Muskingum River, but other British agents successfully quashed his peace proposal. From the Americans' point of view, however, the collapse of the August 1793 negotiations was due to Brant.

At the same time that Brant was unsuccessfully trying to get the western and Haudenosaunee Indians to work together, he also was involved in numerous Haudenosaunee land sales. Although Brant was probably guilty of accepting bribes at the largest New York sales—the 1788 Phelps-Gorham Purchase and the 1797 Treaty of Big Tree—even most of the whites who attended were directly bribed or had some financial stake in the sale. Bribed or not, most of these land sales should be evaluated in light of the crushing poverty that the Haudenosaunee began to experience in the 1790s.

Indian poverty was the primary motive behind the final act of Brant's life, the sale of large portions of the Grand River lands to his business associates (Johnson, 1964; Kelsay, 1984). Haldimand gave the land to the Six Nations in trust in 1784. By 1797, however, Brant was petitioning the trustees to give the Indians the land in fee simple, allowing them the

right to make sales. British authorities, who saw Indian populations on the border as useful political tools, declined. Over the course of the next ten years, Brant became enraged by the delaying tactics of the British Indian Superintendent William Claus and Canada's Lieutenant Governor Peter Russell. In 1804, Brant secretly sent his friend, John Norton, an adopted Mohawk of Scottish ancestry, to go over Russell's head and lobby English authorities directly. When the Six Nation sachems heard that Norton was advertising himself as a Mohawk chief on a mission they knew nothing about, they met in 1805 and stripped Brant of his authority. Although Brant was eventually reinstated by his Grand River constituents, he died on November 24, 1807, before he cleared title on the land.

The principal biographies of Brant have different strengths. The first, by William Leete Stone, is extraordinarily thorough regarding his Revolutionary activities and politics. Stone benefited from correspondence with many people who knew Brant well. Even today, Stone's biography remains a rich source of primary documents and speeches not reprinted in later works on Brant. Curiously, however, Stone spends only twenty pages on the final decade of Brant's life. Isabel Kelsay's modern biography, which corrects Stone's omission, is very well footnoted and an excellent research tool for scholars. Charles Johnson's collection provides a detailed and comprehensive overview of Brant's financial dealings at Grand River.

Granville Ganter

See also French and Indian War; Johnson, William.
References and Further Reading
Johnson, Charles M., ed. 1964. *The Valley of the Six Nations: A Collection of Documents on the Indians of the Grand River.* Toronto, ON: Champlain Society.
Kelsay, Isabel. 1984. *Joseph Brant, 1743–1807: Man of Two Worlds.* Syracuse, NY: Syracuse University Press.
McCallum, James Dow, ed. 1932. *The Letters of Eleazar Wheelock's Indians.* Hanover, NH: Dartmouth College Publications,
Norton, John. 1970. *Journal of Major John Norton.* Edited by Carl F. Klinck and James J. Talman. Toronto, ON: Champlain Society.
Stone, William Leete. 1838. *Life of Joseph Brant— Thayendanegea, Including the Indian Wars of the American Revolution.* 2 volumes. New York: George Dearborn and Co.

Campbell, Ben Nighthorse

Ben Nighthorse Campbell was elected four times to the U.S. House of Representatives from Colorado, beginning in 1986. In 1993, he became the only modern-day Native American to serve in the United States Senate, serving two terms until 2005. At the same time, Campbell also was a member of the traditional Council of 44 in his Northern Cheyenne homeland in Montana.

Campbell's mother, Mary Vierra, was a Portuguese immigrant who arrived in the United States at the age of six. The Vierra family settled in a large Portuguese community near Sacramento, California. When Vierra contracted tuberculosis, she met Albert Campbell, a Northern Cheyenne, at a hospital where he was being treated for alcoholism. The couple later married. Campbell was born April 13, 1933, in Auburn, California. During Campbell's childhood, his father continued to have problems with alcohol, often leaving the family for months at a time. Campbell's mother also continued to experience health problems with tuberculosis. At home, often no one was available to care for Campbell or his younger sister, Alberta. As a result, the young Campbell spent much of his youth in the streets, getting into trouble.

By age ten, Campbell had spent five years in Sacramento's St. Patrick's Catholic Orphanage. He attended Placer High School but dropped out in 1951 to join the U.S. Air Force and served in the Korean War. He was discharged from the Air Force in 1953 with the rank of Airman Second Class, as well as the Korean Service Medal and the Air Medal.

Returning to the United States, Campbell earned a bachelor of arts in physical education and fine arts at California State University (San Jose), graduating in 1957. Campbell also became a championship competitor in judo. He won the U.S. collegiate championship in his weight class three times and took a gold medal at the 1963 Pan American Games. Campbell also attended Tokyo's Meiji University between 1960 and 1964, majoring in Japanese culture. In 1964, he represented the United States as captain of the judo team at the 1964 Tokyo Olympic Games. Campbell was chosen to carry the American flag during the closing ceremonies after swimmer Don Schollander was unable to attend. In 1974, Campbell authored a judo training manual, *Championship Judo Training Drills.*

In 1983, Campbell became the second Native American to be elected to Colorado's legislature,

Ben Nighthorse Campbell, former Colorado congressman and Northern Cheyenne. (Peter Turnley/Corbis)

where he served until his election to the U.S. House of Representatives in 1986. He served in the House from 1987 to 1993, after which he was elected to the U.S. Senate, becoming the first Native American in more than sixty years—since Charles Curtis—to serve in the Senate. In 1995, he switched from the Democratic to the Republican party.

Campbell was reelected to the Senate in 1998 and served from January 3, 1993, to January 3, 2005, during which time he chaired the Committee on Indian Affairs. Campbell declined to run for reelection to the Senate in 2004. His Senate seat was won by Democrat Ken Salazar in the November 2004 election.

Senator Campbell had more freestanding Senate legislation passed into law (twelve public laws) than any other member of the 106th Congress. Senator Campbell consistently fought to balance the federal budget through spending cuts, to reduce the tax rate on American families, and to impose strict account-

ability for all federal spending. He was a recognized leader in public lands and natural resources policy. In the 106th Session of Congress he alone sponsored legislation that created the Sand Creek Massacre National Historic Site, the Black Canyon of the Gunnison National Park, and the Colorado Ute Settlement Act Amendments of 2000.

An advocate of zero-tolerance for illegal drug use legislation, Senator Campbell secured funding to combat drug trafficking through the creation of the Rocky Mountain High Intensity Drug Trafficking Area. The program coordinates federal, state, and local law enforcement agencies efforts to combat the manufacture and distribution of illegal drugs such as methamphetamine.

Campbell has been married to the former Linda Price for more than thirty-five years. He is the father of two children, Colin Campbell and Shanan Longfellow, and grandfather to Luke and Saylor Longfellow and Lauren Campbell. The family shares

many activities, including riding motorcycles. He has been a rancher and a horse trainer in his adopted hometown of Ignacio, Colorado, and long has maintained a jewelry design business.

Bruce E. Johansen

Suggestions for Further Reading

Henry, Christopher, and W. David Baird. 1994. *Ben Nighthorse Campbell: Cheyenne Chief and U.S. Senator.* New York: Chelsea House Publishers.

Campbell, Ben Nighthorse. "Biographical Directory of the United States Congress." Available at: http://bioguide.congress.gov/scripts/biodisplay.pl?index=C00007. Accessed June 26, 2006.

This url contains the text: http://www.infoplease.com/biography/us/congress/campbell-ben-nighthorse.html

Campbell, Ben Nighthorse. 2004. In *Native Americans in Sports.* Edited by C. Richard King. Armonk, NY: M. E. Sharpe.

Canassatego

As tadadaho (speaker) of the Haudensaunee (Iroquois) Confederacy during the mideighteenth century, Canassatego played an important role in frontier diplomacy, notably educating Benjamin Franklin and other Anglo-American colonial leaders regarding the value of the Haudenosaunee (Iroquois) Confederacy as a political model.

In 1742, Pennsylvania officials met with Iroquois sachems in council at Lancaster to secure an Iroquois alliance against the threat of French encroachment. At this council, Canassatego spoke to Pennsylvania officials on behalf of the Six Nations. He confirmed the League of Friendship that existed between the two parties and stated that "We are bound by the strictest leagues to watch for each other's preservation" (Colden, 1902, 2: 18).

Two years later, Canassatego would go beyond pledging friendship to the English colonists. At a 1744 treaty council also in Lancaster, Pennsylvania, the great Iroquois chief advised the assembled colonial governors on Iroquois concepts of unity, telling them, "Our wise forefathers established Union and Amity between the Five Nations. This has made us formidable; this has given us great Weight and Authority with our neighboring Nations. We are a powerful Confederacy; and by your observing the same methods, our wise forefathers have taken, you will acquire such Strength and power. Therefore whatever befalls you, never fall out with one another" (Van Doren and Boyd, 1938, 75).

The preacher Richard Peters provided this description of Canassatego at Lancaster: "a tall, well-made man," with "a very full chest and brawny limbs, a manly countenance, with a good-natired [sic] smile. He was about sixty years of age, very active, strong, and had a surprising liveliness in his speech" (Boyd, 1942, 244–245). Dressed in a scarlet coat and a fine, gold-laced hat, Canassatego is described by historical observers such as Peters as possessing an awesome presence that turned heads whenever he walked into a room.

Shortly after he advised colonial leaders to form a federal union at the 1744 Lancaster Treaty Council, Canassatego also became a British literary figure, the hero of John Shebbeare's *Lydia, or, Filial Piety,* published in 1755. The real Canassatego had died in 1750. With the flowery eloquence prized by romantic novelists of his time, Shebbeare portrayed Canassatego as something more than human—something more, even, than the noble savage that was so popular in Enlightenment Europe. Having saved the life of a helpless English maiden from the designs of a predatory English ship captain en route to England, Canassatego, once in England, became judge and jury for all that was contradictory and corrupt in mideighteenth-century England.

While Shebbeare described his work as history and himself as an historian, *Lydia* is obviously a story that many people today would call historical fiction, with an emphasis on fiction. Canassatego never visited Europe. While not an historical account per se, *Lydia* is another example of how images of American Indians and their societies were used in counterpoint to Europe's. Borrowing the eyes of Canassatego to needle the corruptions of English civilization, Shebbeare assures his readers that the Iroquois sachem is qualified for the job. Not only were the Iroquois known throughout the Western world for their valor and military prowess, but, according to Shebbeare, "Nor, in the milder parts of legislative knowledge, are their souls deficient. Elocution, reason, truth, and probity are not less the characteristics of this people's knowledge" (Shebbeare, 1755, Act 1: 34).

Shebbeare seemed to have researched the real Canassatego's life relatively well. At the Lancaster Treaty Council of 1744, in addition to advising the colonists to form a federated union on an Iroquois model, Canassatego worried about the increasing

dependence of his people on European manufactured goods. In *Lydia*, Shebbeare has Canassatego complaining that many Native Americans have become dependent on European manufactures: "What are we but slaves, who traverse the wide Woods of America in search of furs and skins" (Shebbeare, 1755, Act 1: 11)

Disembarking in England, Shebbeare's Canassatego meets with a rude sight: a ragged collection of dwellings "little better than the Huts of Indians" and men rising from the bowels of the earth, dirty, broken, and degraded. Asking his hosts for an explanation, Canassatego is told that the men have been digging coal. The Iroquois sachem inquires whether everyone in England digs coal for a living and reflects that he is beginning to understand why so many English have fled to America.

Subsequent encounters do little to warm Canassatego to English life and government. The sachem's hosts are forced to confess that England has a class structure and that some labor for the benefit of others: "He asked if England were not a free country," wrote Shebbeare, "where all were destined to the same employment, or if the Great Spirit had made two species of men, one inferior to the other, and the lesser destined to the service of the greater? How can it be reconciled that Creatures born of the same land, in the same Form, and endowed with the same Faculties, should be doomed to this inhuman labour whilst others live at ease?" (Shebbeare, 1755, Act 2: 7).

Bruce E. Johansen

See also Democracy and Native American Images among Europeans; Franklin, Benjamin, Native American Influences; Haudenosaunee Confederacy, Political System.

References and Further Reading

Boyd, Julian. [1942] 1981. "Dr. Franklin: Friend of the Indian." In *Meet Dr. Franklin*. Edited by Roy N. Lokken. Philadelphia, PA: Franklin Institute.

Colden, Cadwallader. 1902. *History of the Five Nations*. New York: New Amsterdam Book Company.

Grinde, Donald A., Jr., and Bruce E. Johansen. 1991. *Exemplar of Liberty: Native America and the Evolution of Democracy*. Los Angeles, CA: UCLA American Indian Studies Center.

Shebbeare, John. [1755] 1974. *Lydia, or Filial Piety*. New York: Garland Publishing.

Van Doren, Carl, and Julian P. Boyd, eds. 1938. *Indian Treaties Printed by Benjamin Franklin 1736–1762*. Philadelphia: Historical Society of Pennsylvania.

Canonicus

The name of Canonicus (ca. 1562–1647), also called Cananacus, Conanicus, and various other variations, might be a Latin derivation of Qunnoune (Drake, 1880, 118). He was the sachem of the Narragansetts, a native North American nation established in what is today Rhode Island. Although "he never fully trusted the English" (Hodge, 1912, I, 202), mostly because of their aggressive ways, Canonicus always remained friendly to them. He gave Roger Williams the tract of land where Providence, Rhode Island, now stands. Long after his death, he was still remembered as a great sachem, as evidenced by the U.S. Navy naming four ships after him. He should not be confused with Canonchet, a later Narragansett sachem.

The earliest Narragansett sachem that the English had heard about was Tashtasick, who is sometimes referred to as Canonicus's father. But the tradition also reports that Wessonsuoum and Keneschoo, his son and daughter, were the parents of Canonicus (Drake, 1880, 118). He spent his life in a village called Narragansett, north of what is now Kingston, Rhode Island. Following the two-sachem rule, the Narragansetts had Canonicus as their home sachem, while Miantonomo, his nephew, dealt with other matters, such as war parties.

Unlike other nearby nations, the Narragansetts largely avoided the diseases that devastated New England's native population in 1617–1619. This situation strengthened Canonicus's power and authority, in part because numerous refugees from other nations joined his people. Although he fought the Wampanoags, Canonicus remained at peace with his English neighbors. In the spring of 1636, after he escaped from Massachusetts, Roger Williams went to the Narragansett country. Tradition reports that he was greeted by Canonicus with the words, "What cheer, nétop [my friend]" (Simmons, 1978, 194). They soon established a good relationship and Canonicus later gave some land to Williams, who was involved in the diplomatic efforts to stop the Narragansett war against the Wampanoags. It was also under Williams's influence that Canonicus decided, in 1637, to help the Puritans and their Mohegan allies in their war against the Pequots.

After the Pequot nation's dispersal following that devastating war, Mohegans and Narragansetts agreed to a treaty that would erase old enmities. It was broken in 1643 when Sequasson, an allied sachem, was attacked by Uncas, sachem of the Mohegans. Miantonomo asked the English if he

could retaliate and their answer was that they would not intervene. Unfortunately, he was captured by Uncas in a raid soon after. Despite the £40 ransom sent by Canonicus, Uncas handed Miantonomo over to the English, who sentenced him to death secretly under Uncas's rule. The Narragansetts sought revenge for the disrespect of the ransom custom.

On April 19, 1644, after having been under Puritan pressure for a long time, the Narragansetts surrendered themselves and their lands voluntarily to King Charles I for protection. Canonicus refused to explain his decision, and suffered a loss of esteem among his people as a result.

Canonicus signed a surrender treaty on August 28, 1645, in which he acknowledged various misdeeds, as he agreed to cede the Pequot country (Simmons, 1978, 92). Canonicus never regained his full authority. He died on June 4, 1647, at the age of roughly eighty-five (Drake, 1880, 119).

Philippe Charland

See also Pequot War; Williams, Roger.
References and Further Reading
Drake, Samuel. 1880. *Drake's Indians of North America.* New York: Hurst and Company.
Hodge, Frederick Webb, ed.1912. *Handbook of North American Indians.* Vols. 1 and 2: *North of Mexico.* Washington, DC: U.S. Government Printing Office.
Simmons, William S. 1978. "Narragansett." In *Handbook of North American Indians.* Vol. 15: *Northeast.* Edited by Bruce G. Trigger, 190–197. Washington, DC: Smithsonian Institution.

Captain Jack

Kintpuash (Modoc, ca. 1837–1873), later called Captain Jack by Anglo-American colonists of California, played a major role as a leader in the Modoc War of 1872–1873. Born at the Wa'chamshwash village on the Lower Lost River near the California–Oregon border, Kintpuash's father was ambushed and slain by whites during the Ben Wright Massacre of 1846. Little is known of his life before age twenty-five. We do know that his Modoc name, Kintpuash, meant "he has water brash [psoriasis]."

The Modocs had little contact with the immigrants until the advent of the 1849 California Gold Rush. Around this time, Kintpuash acquired the nickname Captain Jack because he wore a uniform coat with brass buttons that had been given to him

Captain Jack, aka Kintpuash, a Modoc leader, was a key leader in the Modoc war. (Library of Congress)

by a U.S. Army officer. Although the Modocs opposed Anglo-American expansion into their lands, Captain Jack counseled peace and encouraged trade with the settlers living near Eureka, California, during the 1840s. He had taken two wives by this time.

The Gold Rush intensified tensions and hostilities in the 1850s until Schonchin John, a Modoc chief, signed a treaty removing his band to a reservation in Oregon in 1864. The area was also the traditional homeland of the Klamaths, however, who resented the Modoc intrusion. Realizing that the land in Oregon was insufficient, Captain Jack and his followers returned to California and requested a reservation there. The federal and state authorities denied their request.

Settlers soon began to insist on the forced removal of Modocs. On November 28, 1872, forces invaded Captain Jack's camp and coerced him into consenting to removal. As tensions mounted at the

meeting, violence broke out. Scarfaced Charley, a Modoc leader angered by the Army's behavior, refused to give up his gun, and shots were fired during the ensuing struggle. When the fighting stopped, eight soldiers and fifteen Modocs were dead.

Fearing reprisals, the Modocs under Captain Jack fled to the Lava Beds nearby, believing that they would be safe there. However, this was not to be the case. Hooker Jim and his Modocs, encamped on the other side of the Lost River, were attacked by settlers, and, while retreating to the Lava Beds, they killed twelve whites in revenge. Within this hostile environment, the Modoc leaders, Captain Jack, Schonchin John, and Hooker Jim prepared for an attack in the vast, largely inaccessible volcanic area. But Captain Jack still counseled peace and negotiation, arguing that the government would ultimately win. However, more militant factions under Hooker Jim and Schonchin John outvoted him.

On January 13, 1873, troops moved into the Lava Beds to quell the Modoc uprising. On February 28, Captain Jack's cousin, Winema (married to a white man named Frank Riddle), and a peace delegation began talks with the rebellious Modocs. Hooker Jim and Schonchin John believed Captain Jack to be a coward for consenting to the talks, so they insisted that Captain Jack kill General Edward S. Canby, the head of the delegation. The Modoc militants also believed that American resolve would be damaged by the death of Canby.

Reluctantly, Captain Jack agreed to their terms only if the Modocs were refused amnesty and a return to their California homeland. At a meeting on April 11, Captain Jack shot Canby. The Reverend Eleazar Thomas was also killed, and Albert Meachum, the Indian superintendent, was severely wounded. Winema and her husband managed to escape with the remaining members of the peace party. Quickly, the government fielded more troops and heavier weapons.

The rugged lava rock terrain worked to the Modocs' advantage at first, but dissension among the Modoc leaders and harsh conditions weakened their position. Captain Jack surrendered in late May. After a military trial with Hooker Jim testifying for the prosecution, Captain Jack, Boston Charley, Black Jim, and Schonchin John were hanged on October 3, 1873. Since the administration of President Ulysses S. Grant had instituted a Peace Policy toward Indians, the American people were stunned by the uprising and the consequent inhumanity and insensitivity of the pursuit and hanging of the Modocs.

In the final analysis, white prejudice, Indian betrayal, greed, and an opportunistic press made a deplorable situation far worse. Employing more than a thousand soldiers to fight a Modoc force that never numbered more than fifty-three, the Army incurred losses of seven officers, thirty-nine soldiers, two scouts, and sixteen civilians. The Modoc dead numbered eleven women and seven men. An enormous human and financial cost was endured to capture and remove 155 Modocs to Indian Territory.

A melodrama entitled "Captain Jack" was staged for a brief time in 1873 but it failed to fully capitalize on the tragic bloodletting. A second group of grisly entrepreneurs were more successful. On the day after Captain Jack's execution, robbers excavated his grave, embalmed his body and put it on display in a carnival sideshow that toured profitably across many Eastern cities.

In 1909, fifty-one of the Oklahoma Modocs were permitted to return to their reservation in Oregon.

Bruce E. Johansen

See also California Indians, Genocide of; Hooker Jim.

References and Further Reading

Hagen, Olaf T. No date. "Modoc War Correspondence and Documents, 1865–1878." May 1942. Typescript, Office of Archeology and Historic Preservation, National Park Service. [Approximately 1,780 pages of documents selected from records in the National Archives, War Department, Presidio of San Francisco, University of California (Berkeley) Library, and the Applegate Collection.]

McCarthy, Michael. No date. "Journal of Michael McCarthy." Library of Congress. http://www.cr.nps.gov/history/online_books/labe/biblio.htm.

Miller, Colonel William Haven. No date. "Incidents of the Modoc War." [Narrative made available to Dr. Ron Rickey by Miller's grandson, Captain Charles F. Humphrey, Vallejo, California. Miller was a second lieutenant in Troop F, First Cavalry, during the Modoc War.]

Carson, Christopher "Kit"

One of the most controversial figures in the history of the American West, Christopher "Kit" Carson (1809–1868) has been lauded as a great frontiersman and hero by some, and condemned as a mass murderer by others. The chief point of contention is his role in the last great Navajo war, which led to the forced relocation of roughly 8.000 Navajos from their

traditional homeland to the wastelands of Bosque Redondo in eastern New Mexico. For the Navajo, this trek is known simply as the Long Walk, and its memory is alive and well—and painful—in their oral tradition.

Kit Carson was born on Christmas Eve, 1809, in Madison County, Kentucky. As a boy, he dreamed of heading west to the great Rocky Mountains where he hoped to carve out a niche for himself. In 1826, young Kit took off for Santa Fe and soon became a mountain man and fur trapper. He eventually found employment as a hunter at Bent's Fort in southeastern Colorado and earned a reputation as a reliable and experienced frontiersman. In the mid-1840s, Carson served as a guide to John C. Frémont, who was exploring the Rocky Mountain West for the U.S. government. Frémont recorded and subsequently published an account of his travels. The charismatic and rugged Carson was a central character in the report and soon gained notoriety and fame throughout the land. His reputation was further enhanced by his role in the Bear Flag Revolt during the Mexican–American War.

Between 1854 and 1861, Carson was Indian agent to the Utes, with whom he developed a positive rapport. When the Civil War broke out, Carson took a commission as colonel in the First New Mexico Volunteers. He fought off invading Texans in the Battle of Valverde and helped in expunging the Confederates from the New Mexico Territory. In 1863, Carson was reassigned and ordered to fight the Mescalero Apaches who were raiding the settlements of encroaching whites. The famed mountain man successfully brokered an agreement with the Indians, leading to their relocation near the watchful eye of Fort Sumner. Next, General James H. Carleton commanded Carson to conduct a campaign against the Navajos in eastern Arizona and western New Mexico. Hoping to return home to his family in Taos, a reluctant Carson nevertheless took the commission.

Though Carson was hesitant to wage war on the Navajo, he was relentless in carrying out his assigned duty. He launched an all-out assault against his adversaries, who quickly realized that they had to conduct a guerrilla-like war against Carson's formidable army. The Navajo hoped to disrupt the invaders by making quick lightning strikes before retreating back into the canyons and mesas spread across their homeland. Carson was not discouraged. If he could not fight them head-on, he would carry out a protracted war of attrition by

Scout Christopher "Kit" Carson was renowned as a frontiersman, but also has a controversial legacy for his treatment of Native Americans. (Library of Congress)

destroying their crops and livestock and burning their homes and possessions. His scorched-earth strategy worked. The Navajos, on the run, were forced deep into Cañon de Chelly. As winter set in, the fugitives had no food or shelter; many starved or succumbed to the elements. Finally, in January 1864, most of the Navajos surrendered, accepting Carson's terms and their removal to Bosque Redondo. Carson was not present during the Long Walk to eastern New Mexico, but his roundup led directly to it. Like the Trail of Tears, the death and despair that marked the forced trek and the Navajos' confinement at Bosque Redondo were compounded by the psychological impact of being torn away from their homeland.

After his campaign against the Navajo, Carson went on to lead 1,000 troops, accompanied by Ute and Apache scouts, in an assault on the Kiowa and Comanche of the Great Plains. Soon, however, Carson's health began to decline, and he returned home to his family in Taos, New Mexico. On May 25, 1868, Kit Carson died.

Carson's reputation only grew after his untimely death. In the late nineteenth century he became the subject of countless dime novels. These sensationalist and, more often than not, fictitious books portrayed Carson as a near superhero. Though he was still celebrated, this pulp Kit Carson was a fearless Indian killer and scalper, rather than the trusty mountain man and guide described in John Fremont's report. In the 1960s and 1970s, Carson's image was further revamped. With the mounting Indian activism of the era, Kit was targeted for his role in the Indian wars and, more specifically, the campaign against the Navajo. Today, Carson remains a point of contention between scholars, who hope to restore his legendary status as an American icon and Western hero, and the Navajos, who can never forget the tears and suffering that he brought to their ancestors.

Bradley Shreve

See also Forced Marches; Long Walk.
Refereces and Further Reading
Gordon-McCutchan, R. C., ed. 1996. *Kit Carson: Indian Fighter or Indian Killer?* Boulder: University Press of Colorado.
Hutton, Paul. 2006. "Why Is This Man Forgotten?" *True West* 53, no. 2: 24–32.
Trafzer, Clifford E. 1982. *The Kit Carson Campaign: The Last Great Navajo War.* Norman: University of Oklahoma Press.

Casas, Bartolome de las

The first Catholic priest ordained in the New World (1512), Bartolome de las Casas is considered by many, along with Antonio de Montesinos and Juan Quevado, to be among the first Indian rights activists. His *The Devastation of the Indies: A Brief Account*, first published in 1552, chronicles Spanish depredations and was translated almost immediately following its publication into every major European language. Though its original audience was intended to be Charles V of the Holy Roman Empire and Charles I of Spain, to whom de las Casas appealed to end these atrocities, it was later used by other European powers in attempts to discredit Spain's colonial claims. It caused a major public outcry, both against the conquistadors and soldiers as well as against de las Casas himself for exposing them.

Las Casas was born in Seville, Spain, in 1484, the son of merchant Pedro de las Casas who had made enough money to finance his son's study of Latin. Pedro and three of his brothers were on Columbus's second voyage. Of their time there, scholars only know that Pedro was given an Indian youth as a slave, whom he subsequently bestowed on his son. Bartolome gave the boy back to Spanish authorities so that he might return home. In 1502, at the age of eighteen, de las Casas himself journeyed to the Indies with Nicolas de Ovando's twenty-five hundred soldiers. After returning to Europe to be ordained as a deacon in Rome, he returned, meeting such figures as Hernán Cortéz and Pedro de Alvarado, some of the most notorious leaders of the invasion. De las Casas went with Diego de Velasquez and Panfilo de Narvaz as a chaplain during the invasion and genocide in Cuba, where soldiers engaged in horrific slaughter while Columbus lay ill. De las Casas was rewarded, along with the others, with Indians and land for his service as a priest just as the soldiers were for their "work." In 1514, de las Casas shocked his parish by preaching against Spanish behavior toward the Indians.

Thus, Las Casas began a crusade that would gradually grow until he was granted an audience with the king in 1520, both to testify regarding his views and to defend himself in regard to the charges pressed against him by other Spanish colonists. Charles ruled in de las Casas's favor, agreeing that the time for military conquest was over and that Natives could be converted and saved according to peaceful means along with a nonviolent agricultural colonization. However, this did not change the actual conditions. De las Casas returned to the New World later that year to start a missionary community in Venezuela that he planned to be self-sustaining, but it failed due to the propagandizing of his enemies, which caused an Indian uprising. He became a Dominican monk, writing his plan for peaceful conversion in his *The Only Method of Attracting Everyone to the True Religion*. He also began in the monastery *Apology for the History of the Indies* and *The History of the Indies*.

Finally, in 1537, Pope Paul III issued a bull according human status to American Indians; as humans, they had the right to have their lives and property protected under church law. King Charles also backed an enterprise by de las Casas and the Dominican order to put the plan proposed in *The Only Method* to work in missions in Guatemala. The king issued his New Laws in 1542, making Indian slavery illegal and outlawing the inheritance of

land and slaves (known as *encomiendas*) given in the earlier years of colonization. In Spain at the time, de las Casas had contributed to the passage of the New Laws, reading part of his *Devastation* to the court.

The Devastation of the Indies: A Brief Account is a plea for human rights. The Spaniards, arriving on slow wooden ships, distant from home and king, were free to do anything they pleased in violation of morality and law. Their actions, in part, stem from Spain's similar experiences under Moorish dominance for centuries. Papal bulls had also given permission to invade the lands and enslave the people "in the name of Christ" and justified war with resisting populations. De las Casas, as a Christian Spaniard, cannot tolerate the evils being perpetuated by his fellow Spaniards in the name of his God. De las Casas testifies to the poverty, humility, and peacefulness of the inhabitants of Hispaniola, which was shortly reduced from his estimate of 3 million to 200 in less than fifty years at the hands of the Spaniards. He adds that Cuba, San Juan, and Jamaica, along with numerous other small islands, had been almost entirely depopulated and devastated.

De las Casas recounts horrors that may even exceed those of the German Holocaust of the Jews. Part of the legacy of the Spanish is a program of genocide in the Americas that killed an estimated 100 million over the last 500 years (Stannard, 1992, 150–151). Certainly, even with 6 million Jews killed during World War II, the holocaust in the Americas has outdone it in numbers and scope. The Spaniards killed not only Indians in combat, but also the elderly and the children, pregnant women and those in childbirth, not just "stabbing and dismembering them but cutting them to pieces as if dealing with sheep in the slaughter house" (de las Casas, 1992, 33). The Spaniards wagered over who could cut an Indian in two with one pass of the sword, cut off an Indian's head most efficiently, or empty his belly of bowels the quickest. De las Casas reports infants being taken from their mothers, thrown off cliffs or into rivers, smashing their heads against the rocks. He indicates that other Indians were put to death by hanging them from gallows with their toes dangling above the ground, a blaze lit beneath them to honor "the memory of Our Redeemer and His twelve Apostles" (de las Casas, 1992, 34), their tongues depressed with sticks to suppress their screams as they slowly cooked to death.

Bartolome de las Casas (1474–1566), a Spanish historian, and the earliest European crusader for human rights in the New World. (Bettman/Corbis)

He also reports on the practice of "dogging," that is, of hunting, typically Indian children, but also adults, for sport and amusement and for the purpose of feeding the Spaniards' war dogs. He reports the rape of Indian women for the purpose of increasing her sale value as a pregnant slave and for the purpose of degrading the men. Michele de Cuneo, an Italian nobleman who accompanied Columbus on his second voyage:

> While I was in the boat I captured a very beautiful Carib woman, whom the said Lord Admiral gave to me, and with whom, having taken her into my cabin, she being naked according to their custom, I conceived desire to take pleasure. I wanted to put my desire into execution but she did not want it and treated me with her finger nails in such a manner that I wished I had never begun. But seeing that . . . I

took a rope and thrashed her well, for which she raised such unheard of screams that you would not have believed your ears. Finally we came to an agreement in such manner that I can tell you she seemed to have been brought up in a school of harlots (Quoted in Stannard, 1992, 84).

De las Casas also relates the horrors experienced by the survivors in Spanish slavery, many of whom died in transport being brought from other areas of the New World once the population of the earliest contact was devastated. Throughout the area of the Americas invaded by the Spanish, de las Casas cites the deaths of numerous others, many of them children, through malnutrition and starvation, abuse, overwork, disease, and suicide. Some Spaniards practiced cannibalism by choice and forced the Indians they enslaved to engage in it as well. Children were sometimes killed to save them from the slow, tortuous death of enslavement that often began before the age of three. De las Casas details Spanish atrocities against the Aztecs brought by Cortes and throughout the Americas, all in the name of gold more than God, also indicting Germans for similar behavior, though they were in the Americas in fewer numbers. De las Casas died in July 1556 and was buried in the chapel of the convent of Our Lady of Atocha in Madrid, regretting he had not been able to do more.

Kimberly Roppolo

See also Democracy and Native American Images Among Europeans; Spanish Influence.
References and Further Reading
Champagne, Duane, ed. 1994. *The Native North American Almanac.* Detroit, MI: Gale Research.
de las Casas, Bartolome. 1992. *The Devastation of the Indies: A Brief Account.* Translated by Herma Briffault. Baltimore, MD: Johns Hopkins University Press.
Donovan, Bill. 1992. "Introduction." In *The Devastation of the Indies: A Brief Account.* By Bartolome de las Casas. Translated by Herma Briffault, 1–25. Baltimore, MD: Johns Hopkins University Press.
Hoxie, Frederick E., ed. 1996. *Encyclopedia of North American Indians: Native American History, Culture, and Life from Paleo-Indians to the Present.* Boston: Houghton-Mifflin.
Stannard, David E. 1992. *American Holocaust: The Conquest of the New World.* New York: Oxford University Press.

Catlin, George

George Catlin (1796–1872) was born July 26, 1796, at Wilkes-Barre, Pennsylvania. He died December 23, 1872, at Jersey City, New Jersey. Catlin married Clara Gregory in 1828 and had four children: Elizabeth, Clara, Louise, and George, Jr. Catlin was a self-taught artist who painted in the American Romantic tradition. He is famous for his paintings, sketches, and artifact collection of Plains Indian life. He is less well-known for his landscape and miniature paintings as well as his Central American, South American, and Pacific Coast Indian paintings. Along with his artwork, Catlin published books about Plains Indian life, as well as his experiences while living among the Indians and traveling in Europe. Catlin also promoted justice for the Indian. Like others in the 1830s and 1840s, Catlin advocated that a large reservation be established for the remnants of the "Indian race." Catlin's work and Indian Gallery, displayed in Europe for over thirty years, helped establish the Plains Indian as the "typical" North American Indian in popular imagination.

Catlin's mother, Polly Sutton, survived the 1778 Wyoming Valley Massacre. His father, Putnam Catlin, was a lawyer and landowner as well as Revolutionary War veteran. Growing up in the Susquehanna Valley, New York, Catlin collected Indian curiosities and formed a brief friendship with an Oneida family—On-O-Gong-way, his wife, and daughter—who camped on the family farm.

While largely homeschooled, Catlin did attend the Classical Academy in Wilkes-Barre and the Gould and Reeve Law School in Connecticut. Upon graduation from law school in 1818, Catlin worked as a lawyer until 1820, when he decided to become an artist. His initial endeavors were miniatures of locals and some oil-on-canvas paintings of notables, such as Sam Houston. In 1827, Catlin expanded his repertoire by painting Niagara Falls, as well as the Erie and Welland Canals. It was during his efforts to establish his artistic career that Catlin met a delegation of western chiefs, in Philadelphia, who were heading to Washington for treaty negotiations. This meeting gave Catlin the impetus to travel to the West to paint the last remaining "uncivilized" Indians.

During 1830, Catlin arrived in St. Louis, where he became a protégé of General William Clark. From 1831 to 1836, Catlin visited and painted various Plains nations, such as the Pawnees, Otos, Kansas, Poncas, Assiniboines, Ricarees, Dakota, Mandans, Blackfeet, Crows, the Five Civilized Tribes, Osages,

Comanches, Picts, Kiowas, and Wicos, as well as the Ojibwas of Minnesota. In 1837, Catlin opened his Indian Gallery in New York City. Catlin offered to sell his collection of approximately 500 paintings and thousands of artifacts to the U.S. federal government, which declined his offer. Afterward, he transported the collection to England in 1839. On February 1, 1840, he opened the gallery at the Egyptian Hall, Piccadilly, which drew thousands, including commoners and royalty. As interest in the display waned, Catlin utilized showmanship to keep the crowds coming. Initially employing English cockneys to play Indians, Catlin hired a group of Canadian Ojibwas and later a group of Iowas to recreate aspects of their culture for entertainment and education. Realizing that England was tiring of the exhibition, Catlin moved the entire gallery, including the Iowas, to Paris with great fanfare. Tragedy soon resulted. Catlin's wife, son, and four of the Iowas died in France of disease. After hiring Ojibwa performers, eight became ill with smallpox which resulted in two deaths shortly after reaching Belgium. The remainder were hospitalized in Brussels at Catlin's expense. The direct result of these misfortunes forced Catlin to mortgage his collection, which was sold to cover debts. His daughters were taken in by wealthy in-laws.

During the 1850s, Catlin set out to paint the Indians of Central and South America, as well those along the West Coast of the United States. He eventually completed 600 new Indian paintings. In 1871 Catlin returned to New York to display his work. Unable to secure funds, he accepted free living space at the Smithsonian Institution, where he lived in poverty until his death in Jersey City in 1872.

Catlin's paintings, sketches, and writings are a wonderful resource on Plains Indian culture at its pinnacle. Significant collections of his work are located at the Smithsonian Institute and the American Museum of Natural History.

Catlin is also credited as the first Euro-American to visit the stone quarries near present-day Pipestone, Minnesota. The soft red stone, used to make sacred pipes, is known as Catlinite.

Karl S. Hele

See also Democracy and Native American Images among Europeans.
References and Further Reading
Catlin, George. 1842. *Letters and Notes on the Manners, Customs, and Condition of the North American Indians*. London: Tilt and Bogue.

Catlin, George. 1848. *A Descriptive Catalogue of Catlin's Indian Collection*. London: G. Catlin.
Catlin, George. 1848. *Illustrations of the Manners, Customs and Condition of the North American Indians: In a Series of Letters and Notes Written During Eight Years of Travel and Adventure among the Wildest and Most Remarkable Tribes Now Existing*. London: H.G. Bohn.
Catlin, George. 1852. *Adventures of the Ojibbeway and Ioway Indians in England, France, and Belgium: Being Notes of Eight Years' Travels and Residence in Europe with His North American Indian Collection*. London: G. Catlin.
Catlin, George. 1867. *Last Rambles Amongst the Indians of the Rocky Mountains and the Andes*. Edinburgh: Gall and Inglis.
Catlin, George. 1867. *O-kee-pa: A Religious Ceremony, and Other Customs of the Mandans*. London: Trubner & Company.
Catlin, George. 1875. *Life Among the Indians*. London: Edinburgh: Gall and Inglis.
Dippie, Brian W. 1990. *Catlin and His Contemporaries: The Politics of Patronage*. Lincoln: University of Nebraska Press.
Ewers, John C., ed. 1993. *George Catlin's "Indian Gallery": Views of the American West*. Richmond: Virginia Museum of Fine Arts.
Flavin, Francis. 2002. "The Adventurer-Artists of the Nineteenth Century and the Image of the American Indian." *Indiana Magazine of History* 98, no. 1: 1–29.
Millichap, Joseph R. 1977. "George Catlin." *American History Illustrated* 12, no. 5: 4–9, 43–48.
Von Tungeln, Annie Laurie. 1974. "Catlin, Painter of Indians." *Americas* 26, no. 6/7: 15–21.

Cherokee Phoenix and Indian Advocate

By the 1820s, the Cherokees were an immensely literate people, possessing a written constitution that emulated that of the United States, a written language (developed by Sequoyah), and a bilingual newspaper, *The Cherokee Phoenix and Indian Advocate*. *The Cherokee Phoenix*, the first Native American newspaper, is still published today. During the years before the Trail of Tears (beginning in 1838), the newspaper acted as an official organ of the Cherokees' government and as a key institution in the battle against removal.

Sequoyah's written Cherokee language was introduced in 1821, after twelve years of experimentation. He developed the language with an eye to its social and political uses, making it easy to learn

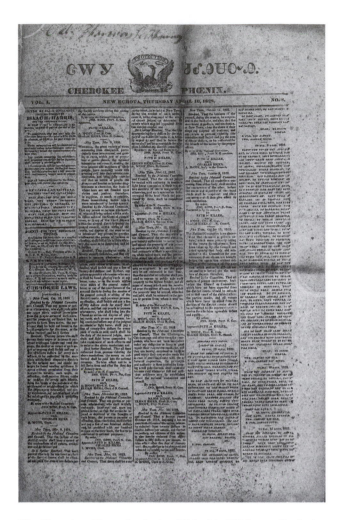

The Cherokee Phoenix, *first published in 1828, was the first Native American newspaper. (Library of Congress)*

(many Cherokee acquired it in two weeks) and to use in the preparation of documents, including newspapers.

In 1828, the Cherokee Tribal Council initiated a weekly newspaper, printing bilingual editions in Cherokee and English.

The missionary Samuel Worcester, whose name became affixed to what is perhaps the best-known case in American Indian law (*Worcester v. Georgia*, 1832), was a community activist among the Cherokees. Worcester collaborated with Stephen Foreman on a translation of *The Bible* into Cherokee, and, with aid from the American Board of Commissioners for Foreign Missions, he worked to procure type fonts and a press for the *Cherokee Phoenix*. Worcester played a role in having type cast in Sequoyah's symbols, hiring a printer, and choosing Elias Boudinot as the newspaper's first editor.

When *The Cherokee Phoenix* began publishing at New Echota on February 21, 1828, Worcester also was a major editorial force. The newspaper quickly acquired an international circulation but also experienced financial problems due, in part, to Boudinot's salary of $300 a year, a relatively high wage at the time. A number of prominent Cherokees, including John Ross, Stand Watie, and John Ridge, spoke on behalf of the newspaper to raise money for what they regarded as an important voice in crucial times.

By 1832, however, Boudinot, Ridge, and others split with Ross as they began to support removal. Ross at first asked them to curtail their editorials in favor of removal. When they refused, he forced Boudinot's resignation. Charles Hicks, Ross's brother-in-law, then became editor. Hicks was strongly opposed to removal, but he restricted his views to editorials. The newspaper continued to publish views on both sides of the issue, including letters from Boudinot.

The Cherokee Phoenix continued to publish as pressure for removal grew. It shared news reports with a hundred other newspapers, but shortages of ink and the illnesses of printers and editors caused publication to become erratic. Georgia officials made obvious their desire to close the paper.

Financial problems persisted; on May 31, 1834, the paper ceased publication when the Cherokee Nation ran out of money as the federal government reneged on treaty obligations. When money again became available, the newspaper's staff planned a move to Red Clay, Tennessee, out of concern that the Georgia Guard would prevent its publication at New Echota. However, "Hours before the move, Elias Boudinot's brother, Stand Watie, joined the Guard in a raid on the offices of the Phoenix. They dumped the soft lead type on the ground and stamped it into the red Georgia clay with their feet, effectively silencing the voice of the Cherokee Nation. Watie and the Guard then removed the press and set fire to the building" (Worthy, n.d.).

The newspaper was revived after the Cherokees' forced march to Indian Territory, now Oklahoma. The original site of the newspaper's office in New Echota became a tourist attraction when a state park opened in the area in 1962. Today, the newspaper may be read in Cherokee and English on the Internet.

Bruce E. Johansen

See also Ross, John; Sequoyah; Watie, Stand.

References and Further Reading

Anderson, William L., ed. 1991. *Cherokee Removal: Before and After*. Athens: University of Georgia Press.

Cherokee Phoenix. Newspaper of the Cherokee Nation of Oklahoma. Available at: http://www .cherokeephoenix.org/. Accessed April 9, 2006.

McLoughlin, William G. 1993. *After the Trail of Tears: The Cherokees' Struggle for Sovereignty, 1839–1880*. Chapel Hill: University of North Carolina Press.

Worthy, Larry. No date. "About North Carolina." *Cherokee Phoenix (and Indian Advocate)*. Available at: http://ngeorgia.com/history/phoenix.html. Accessed April 9, 2006.

Clark, George Rogers

George Rogers Clark (1752–1818) enjoyed a brief burst of fame between 1778 and 1782, due to his exploits in Illinois and Ohio during the Revolutionary War. By 1782, however, his fragile reputation was on the wane, and ten years later he was in full disgrace.

The second son of John and Ann Rogers Clark—his younger brother, William, accompanied Meriwether Lewis on the Lewis and Clark Expedition—George Rogers grew up in Virginia, where his parents first owned a small farm near Charlottesville, before inheriting a four-hundred-acre plantation in Caroline County. Despite this seeming prosperity, the family was neither elevated nor educated. With only a minimal period at a private school at age eleven, Clark remained essentially illiterate his entire life, causing him problems in later military positions that required frequent and comprehensible paperwork.

The way up the economic ladder in Clark's Virginia led through Indian Country: Up-and-comers surveyed, inevitably Native American land, for the purpose of speculation. In 1772, at age twenty, George left on his first surveying mission. After involving himself in 1774 in Lord Dunmore's War—a blatantly illegal attempt to seize Ohio—Clark formally took up surveying in 1775 as a deputy surveyor of Kentucky, a "colony" of Virginia already carved out of Native lands. Clark earned a small wage but garnered a living through land speculation (Indian Historical Bureau, 2; James, 1: 9, 28).

In 1776, as war heated up with England along the seacoast—and with Native America in "the west" for control of land—Clark led a delegation to Virginia, securing 500 pounds of gunpowder for Kentucky "defense." Thereby called to the attention of Patrick Henry, then governor of Virginia, Clark was secretly commissioned to seize, if he could, western territories in Illinois from the purported control of the British before Virginia's rival, Pennsylvania, could manage the same feat. The resultant and daring Illinois campaigns of 1777–1779 are, today, the lynchpins of Clark's fame, although his murderous depredations against the Shawnees of Ohio in 1780 and 1782 were at least as famous among his contemporaries.

Avoiding Vincennes at first, because the British Fort Sackville was garrisoned there, Clark sneaked up at night on Kaskaskia, Illinois, a French settlement that was not expecting trouble, taking it on July 4, 1778, deeply frightening the inhabitants. The next day, Clark hiked over to Cahokia, demanding and receiving it as well. That October, Clark likewise seized Vincennes with ease, although he promptly lost it with equal ease in December to British Lieutenant Governor Henry Hamilton. After a cold February march back to Vincennes, Clark reseized the town and its fort in March 1779. These "victories" look more impressive on paper than they did on the ground, for, in truth, the French inhabitants of Illinois rolled quickly with the punches, placating whichever commander held the upper hand at the moment. Furthermore, neither Clark nor Hamilton was in any position to raise the armies for a real contest. Clark had, at most, 175 men, and Hamilton, but thirty-nine, after his seventy-five French militiamen defected ("Account . . . ," 1908, 492, 502; Barnhart, 1951, 149, 181; Clark, 1966, 518, 528).

Throughout his time in Illinois, Clark deliberately terrorized the French settlers, the Illinois Native Americans, and the British, boasting later of his policy of terror (Clark, 1966, 475, 479, 481). In retaking Fort Sackville in 1779, he staged horrifying tortures, including the live, slow scalping of a party of Natives taken prisoner as its members entered Vincennes without knowing of recent events. These atrocities were performed in full view of the besieged small garrison of Fort Sackville, specifically to effect its immediate surrender. A horrified Hamilton (reviled by the Americans as "the famous Hair Buyer General") left a vivid description of a blood-covered Clark sluicing off the gore while boasting of his escapade to the now captive British officer ("Account . . . ," 1908, 501; Barnhart,

Colonel George Rogers Clark confers with Native Americans at Cahokia in the Illinois Territory. The group surrendered to Clark and his men in 1778, and Clark continued with his successful attempt to acquire, without conflict, immense tracts of land for the United States. (National Archives and Records Administration)

1951, 182–183; Clark, 1966, 534, 541; Mann, 2005, 114–116).

Establishing Fort Jefferson on a flood plain at the confluence of the Mississippi and Ohio Rivers (only to abandon it in 1780) Clark headed back to Kentucky to raise an August attack on the Shawnees in Ohio, then clearly Native American territory. Clark was frankly racist in his attitudes, admitting that he awaited but a "sufficient excuse to put all the Indians & partisans to death" (ISHL, 1903, 144) and viewed their "extirpation" (Barnhart, 1951, 189) as his "divine" mission (Clark, 1996, 539). Taking 1,000 men (against 300 Native defenders), Clark ploughed into Shawnee lands, destroying around 1,000 acres of crops and all the housing he could find, including Old (also called Little) Chillicothe and three Piqua clan towns on the Big Miami River, his men plundering towns, murdering and mutilating straggling Natives, and pulling bodies out of graves to scalp for state bounties. As a quickly combined "Union" force (a pan-Native alliance in Ohio) bore down on him, Clark beat a hasty retreat home (Mann, 2005, 124–127).

By the end of 1780, Clark was so acclaimed in the back settlements that George Washington handed him the all-important campaign to roust the British from their western headquarters in Detroit. Due to a fraught rivalry that erupted into a recruiting and supplying competition with Colonel Daniel Brodhead, commander of the Western Department headquartered at Fort Pitt, Clark was unable to raise enough men for the effort or to keep those he had raised from deserting. Setting out in a scattered way from Fort Henry (Wheeling, West Virginia) on July 20, 1781, by the end of August, Clark's troops had been entirely defeated by the Ohio Union (Mann, 2005, 143–146).

Clark was placed in the military command of Kentucky in 1781, where he failed not only to support outlying posts but also to report back to Virginia, whose governor, Benjamin Harrison, blamed the problem on Clark's raging alcoholism (ISHL, 1926, 132), but which was equally the fault of Clark's illiteracy. Consequent of his failures, the massive August 19, 1782, defeat of the Kentucky militia by the Ohio Union at Blue Licks was blamed on Clark. Partially to regain his prestige and partially to make one last grab at Ohio before a signed Treaty of Paris prohibited continued invasion, Clark led a second, unauthorized invasion of Shawnee lands in November 1782, attacking and looting an evacuated Chillicothe (modern-day Piqua), along with Willistown, Pigeon Town, two Piqua clan towns, and a British trading post. He destroyed 10,000 bushels of corn, the Shawnees' entire winter supply (Mann, 2005, 174–179).

After the Revolution, in recognition of his military services, Clark was "paid" 8,059 acres of Native land in Ohio and 73,962 acres of Chickasaw land farther west (Lutz, 1969, 250, 251–252). He also was tapped as an Indian agent during the U.S. attempt to seize Ohio by treaty (thus to remit all congressional land warrants issued as soldiers' pay during the Revolution). In 1786, Clark negotiated a strong-armed treaty with the Shawnees, which was immediately repudiated, and then led an attack on the Wabash Miami nations.

Clark's star was, however, decidedly declining; Virginia held him personally liable for paying war supply debts it claimed he had incorrectly managed. (In fact, Clark had properly submitted receipts, as he had always claimed.) As Clark struggled with these woes, James Wilkinson, a Spanish double agent, conspired to depose him from his position as Indian agent, subsequently taking over Clark's post. Now in serious trouble, Clark tried some skullduggery of his own, in a scheme to create a Spanish colony in Mississippi. Continuing his new career as a foreign agent, Clark attempted in 1793 to drag the United States into Franco-Anglo hostilities. He died in Louisville in 1799, his reputation in tatters.

Barbara Alice Mann

See also American Revolution, Native American Participation.

References and Further Reading

"Account of the Expedition of Lieut. Gov. Hamilton." 1908. *Reports of the Pioneer Society of the State of Michigan,* 2nd ed. Vol. 9. Lansing, MI: Wynkoop Hallenbeck Crawford Company, State Printers.

Barnhart, John D., ed. 1951. *Henry Hamilton and George Rogers Clark in the American Revolution, with the Unpublished Journal of Lieut. Gov. Henry Hamilton.* Crawfordsville, IN: R. E. Banta.

Carstens, Kenneth C. 2004. *The Life of George Rogers Clark, 1752–1818: Triumps and Tragedies.* Edited by Nancy Son Carstens. Westport, CT: Praeger.

Clark, George Rogers. [1791] 1966. *Clark's Memoir,* from English's *Conquest of the Country.* Ann Arbor, MI: Readex Microprint.

Fisher, James. 1996. "A Forgotten Hero Remembered, Revered, and Revised: The Legacy and Ordeal of George Rogers Clark." *Indiana Magazine of History* 92 (June) 109–132.

"Geo: Rogers Clark to Gov: Harrison." 1968. *Calendar of Virginia State Papers and Other Manuscripts,.* Vol. 3: 1875–1893. Millwood, NY: Kraus Reprint.

Henry, Patrick, and George Rogers Clark. 1974. "The Secret Orders." In *The Secret Orders & "Great Things Have Been Done by a Few Men . . . ."* Indianapolis: Indiana Historical Society.

Illinois State Historical Library (ISHL). 1903. *Collections of the Illinois State Historical Library.* Vol. 8. Springfield: Illinois State Historical Library.

Illinois State Historical Library (ISHL). 1926. *Collections of the Illinois State Historical Library.* Vol. 19. Springfield: Illinois State Historical Library.

Indiana Historical Bureau. 2005. "George Rogers Clark Biography." March 1. Available at: http://www.statelib.lib.in.us/www/ihb/resources/grcbio.html. Accessed March 4, 2005.

James, Alton, ed. [1912] 1972. *George Rogers Clark Papers.* 2 volumes. New York: AMS Press.

Johnson, Allen, and Dumas Malone, eds. 1958. *Dictionary of American Biography,* 62–63. 20 volumes. New York: Charles Scribner's Sons.

Lutz, Paul V. 1969. "Fact and Myth Concerning George Rogers Clark's Grant of Land at Paducah, Kentucky." *Register of the Kentucky Historical Society* 67, no. 3: 248–253.

Mann, Barbara Alice. 2005. *George Washington's War on Native America, 1779–1782.* Westport, CT: Praeger.

Cochise

Often thought of as the greatest of Apache leaders, Cochise was born between 1800 and 1813 somewhere in the Chiricahua Mountains of southeastern Arizona (Sweeney, 1991, 6). Not much is known of his early life, but historians have written (Sweeney, 1991, 14) that at about age fifteen the young man had been physically and mentally prepared for the first of the four raids he undertook as a novice warrior. Raiding was as necessary to the Apache people as breathing. Survival depended on raiding, as did the quality and skills of the leader.

The young Chiricahua Apache learned all the rituals associated with raiding. He came to understand the special language spoken by the raiders, why he and his people had to travel by night, where waterholes were, and how to avoid the many taboos that adversely affected a raid's success. After four grueling trips under the watchful eyes of experienced warriors, his conduct satisfied the men, and he was accepted as one of them.

Cochise married at least three times. With his second wife, Dostehseh, the daughter of the powerful Mimbres Apache chief, Mangas Coloradas, he fathered two sons: Taza and Naiche. Taza never married and died an untimely death in Washington, D.C., as he sought peace after his father's demise. Naiche, born about 1856, was the last leader of the free Chiricahua Apaches and became Geronimo's colleague. Theirs was a cooperative relationship: Geronimo deferred to Naiche in all matters other than warfare and healing; Naiche reciprocated similarly when it came to warring.

Cochise was a complex individual whose great intelligence has never been disputed. For years he outsmarted and outfought the most competent Indian fighters the U.S. Army sent after him. He has

A master of hit-and-run tactics, Cochise became one of the best-known Native American warriors in the Southwest. Cochise was a predecessor of Geronimo, leading the Chiricahua Apache during the 1860s and early 1870s. (Bettman/Corbis)

been called a military genius and a master of guerrilla warfare who struck, killed, and got away. Over a period of slightly more than a decade, with as few as 300 widely dispersed warriors, he eluded thousands of American soldiers. At the same time, Cochise was a compassionate man, a philosopher and an orator. He practiced truth and loyalty, and he had supreme respect for his word. When given, he kept it under all conditions and circumstances. Cochise was also a teacher, instructing his warriors in the ways of battle, including how to cover their hair with grass and twigs and crawl inch by inch until they were inside the camp of the enemy. He showed the men how to roll their bodies in the thick gray dust of the trail and then crouch in shallow gullies or behind gray boulders to wait patiently for an opportunity to strike.

A peaceful person by nature, Cochise sincerely believed in the brotherhood of man, had a code of honor, and conducted himself as a statesman even as he saw white settlers take over much of his people's land. His physical presence was imposing. The manager of a stagecoach station recalled Cochise as "about six feet tall and straight as an arrow, built from the ground up as perfect as any man could be" (Stockel, 1989, 3). One writer described him as being "straight as a yucca stalk. Wiry and muscular, he walked proudly, as befitted a hereditary chieftain . . . His dark face was dominated by a fine aquiline nose. His intelligent black eyes were deep-set, and the skin was drawn taut over very high cheek-bones, and sharply jutting jaws. His dignity, his simple courtesy, his fierce, eagle-sharp eyes, all proclaimed the proud, brave warrior" (Stockel, 1989, 3).

By 1831, Apache relations with Mexico had deteriorated sharply. Unable to defeat the Indians under Cochise's leadership with regular troops, Mexican officials hired mercenaries and scalp hunters to exterminate the group. Infamous massacres occurred in 1837 and 1846 (Thrapp, 1991, 290), years when more than 175 Chiricahuas were killed, possibly including Cochise's father; his hatred of the enemy grew considerably after that. In 1856, Cochise became the principal war leader of the Chokonen (Chiricahuan) band after the death of its chief, Miguel Narbona, and constantly led brutal and bloody warfare battles against Mexican enemies.

Tragic circumstances led to hostilities between the Chiricahua Apaches and the United States. On January 27, 1861, unknown Indians ran off cattle from the Patagonia, Arizona, ranch of John Ward and seized his wife's twelve-year old son, Felix. Ward reported the event to Lieutenant Colonel Pitcairn Morrison, Seventh Infantry, who ordered Lieutenant George Bascom, a recent West Point graduate, and fifty-four infantrymen to find the boy (Sweeney, 1991, 148).

Encamped near Cochise and his peaceful group, Bascom sent word that he wanted to meet. Not suspecting treachery, Cochise cooperated and set out with family members to the officer's camp. Inside his tent, Bascom accused Cochise of kidnapping the child and stealing Ward's livestock. Insulted beyond belief, Cochise denied both actions but offered to try to get the boy back. Bascom's strategy was to hold Cochise captive until his followers returned the child, but Cochise recognized the trap, jumped to his feet, pulled a knife, slashed

open a hole in the tent and escaped. Fifty shots were fired at him as he fled. His brother, two nephews, and two others couldn't get away. Cochise never forgot the lesson: Under the disguise of friendship, he had been tricked and nearly imprisoned by those he trusted.

The next day, Cochise and others approached the Army camp waving a white flag of truce. Their intention was to lure Bascom out of his tent and take him hostage to trade later for the relatives. "Tell the boy soldier I have Americans to trade for my people," Cochise said (Arnold, 1951, 7). When the plan failed, Cochise sacked a mail station, captured three white men, killed and burned eight other men, and held several hostages. He contacted the Army again and offered to exchange his collection of captives for his relatives. Bascom refused, killed Cochise's family, and the Apache wars started. Cochise's fury then knew no bounds (Thrapp, 1967, 18).

In June 1862, Cochise participated in the Battle of Apache Pass. Believing that the troops, under command of Brigadier General James Carleton, had come to punish them (the soldiers were actually on their way eastward to drive Confederate forces back to Texas), the Apaches prepared an ambush that failed when two mountain howitzers lobbed several shells at them (Sweeney, 1991, 198–200). Even though the Indians retreated this time, in the eyes of the American government they had become the principal stumbling block to white settlement and, importantly, to establishing business enterprises, such as a railroad, in southeastern Arizona.

Tom Jeffords, a government mail contractor, risked his life by riding into the Dragoon Mountains in search of Cochise. His mission was to convince the Apache to allow his mail carriers through without killing them. Jeffords later told an historian:

Cochise had killed fourteen men in my employ. I made up my mind that I wanted to see him. I located his camp . . . went into his camp alone, fully armed. I told him I was there to talk with him personally and that I wanted to leave my arms in his possession . . . to be returned to me when I was ready to leave, which would probably be in a couple of days (Sonnichsen, 1991, 13).

Impressed by Jeffords' bravery, Cochise honored the request to let the mail riders live as they crossed his territory, and remarkably the two men became close friends for the rest of their lives.

In 1863, the Americans murdered Mangas Coloradas (Sweeney, 1998, 455–465), Cochise's father-in-law, causing great grief and creating an even stronger desire for revenge against all enemies, Mexican or American. Twelve years and 5,000 deaths later, President Ulysses S. Grant sent General Oliver O. Howard to the southwest to explore peace with Cochise through a treaty.

At the conclusion of the lengthy talks, Cochise and Howard agreed on three main points: the site of a reservation in southeastern Arizona, adequate food and clothing to be furnished by the government, and the appointment of Tom Jeffords as their agent at the new site. Cochise promised a truce that would keep the roads open without danger (Sweeney, 1991, 363) and that would allow settlers and others, such as miners and merchants, to enter southern Arizona safely. He kept his word.

Cochise became progressively ill and died on June 8, 1874, two years after being placed on the reservation. Agent Jeffords was unable to keep some of the Chiricahuas from resuming their former ways; so in 1876 the government, after much ado, abolished the reservation. Cochise's followers were marched to San Carlos, Arizona, a desolate spot. Intolerable at best, this site was one of the motivating factors that caused earlier problems to reemerge, resulting in continuing hostilities between the government and the Chiricahua Apaches that continued until Geronimo's final surrender in September 1886.

H. Henrietta Stockel

See also Apache Wars; Mangas Coloradas.
References and Further Reading
Arnold, Elliot. 1951. "Cochise—Greatest of the Apaches." *Arizona Quarterly,* 7, no.1 (Spring): 7.
Sonnichsen, C. L. 1991. "Cochise & Jeffords." *Arizona Highways* (November): 13–15.
Stockel, H. Henrietta. 1989. "Cochise: Greatest of the Apaches." Unpublished paper written for Mescalero Apache Chief Wendel Chino.
Sweeney, Edwin R. 1991. *Cochise: Chiricahua Apache Chief.* Norman: University of Oklahoma Press.
Sweeney, Edwin R. 1998. *Mangas Coloradas: Chief of the Chiricahua Apaches.* Norman: University of Oklahoma Press.
Thrapp, Dan L. 1967. *The Conquest of Apacheria.* Norman: University of Oklahoma Press.
Thrapp, Dan L. 1978. "Cochise." *Arizona Highways* (October): 38–46.
Thrapp, Dan L. 1991. *Encyclopedia of Frontier Biography: I.* Lincoln: University of Nebraska Press.

Cody, William Frederick

William "Buffalo Bill" Cody (1846–1917) lived during a time of significant change on the Great Plains. Non-Natives were settling the West in great numbers, the stagecoach and the Pony Express made daily trips across the country, and the railroad was cutting through Indian lands. One of the Indians' primary sources of food, the buffalo, was being hunted to extinction. As a boy, Cody herded cattle, rode for the Pony Express, and drove the stagecoach. As a young man, he killed buffalo for the railroad men. The latter half of the nineteenth century saw many major Indian wars in the West, and William Cody played an important part as a civilian scout for the Army during much of this time. He later recruited many Indians for his famous Wild West Show.

William Frederick Cody was born on February 26, 1846, in Scott County, Iowa. He was one of eight children and a son of Isaac and Mary Ann (Laycock) Cody. The family moved to Kansas in 1853 and Cody's father died in 1857. At eleven years of age, Cody decided to find work to support his mother and siblings. He pursued a job with Majors and Russell (later Russell, Majors, and Waddell), a freighting firm in Leavenworth, Kansas. He was first hired as a messenger boy and later helped to herd oxen. He claimed to have shot his first Indian while returning to Fort Kearney in Nebraska with a group of bullwackers (ox team drivers). He was heralded the "youngest Indian slayer of the Plains."

During this time he met James "Wild Bill" Hickok. They would remain good friends until Hickok's death in 1876. In 1859, Russell, Majors, and Waddell started the Pony Express, and Cody was hired as a rider. He rode for the company on and off until it went out of business in October 1861. In 1862, he joined the Ninth Kansas Volunteer Cavalry as a civilian guide and scout. He later became one of the Red Legged Scouts (the name coming from the red leggings they wore), an informal (some say vigilante) militia acting on the side of the Union. In 1863, he joined the Seventh Kansas Cavalry, also as a civilian scout. He married Louisa Maude Frederici on March 6, 1866. They first settled in Salt Creek Valley, Kansas. During their marriage they had four children: Arta born in 1866, Kit Carson (named after the famed Kit Carson) in 1870, Orra in 1872, and Irma in 1883. After a failed attempt at running a hotel, Cody returned to scouting. It was during this time that he met George Armstrong Custer.

In 1867, with a partner, Cody tried his hand at establishing a town near Fort Hays in anticipation of the coming of the railroad. Named Rome, it flourished until the Kansas Pacific Railroad established a town nearby and Rome slowly declined. Cody was then hired to kill buffalo for the workmen who were building the railroad. They required twelve buffalo daily to feed the employees. He claims to have killed 4,280 buffalo in eighteen months, and it was at this time that Cody was christened "Buffalo Bill." His job hunting buffalo ended in the spring of 1868 when the building of the track was done.

Cody immediately returned to scouting. In 1869 he was appointed chief of scouts for the Fifth Cavalry that was going up against the Dog Soldiers, a band of Cheyennes. On July 11, 1869, General Eugene A. Carr, Major Frank North, three companies of the Fifth Cavalry, and two companies of Pawnee soldiers, with William Cody as chief scout, surprised the Dog Soldiers' encamped near the South Platte River at Summit Springs, Colorado. This battle is significant because it broke the back of the Dog Soldiers and virtually ended their raids on the Colorado settlers. Cody claims to have killed many Indians during his career as a scout. One of these, Chief Tall Bull, he claims to have ambushed and killed for his horse in 1869 at Summit Springs. Another, Chief Yellow Hair (also called Yellow Hand), he killed in 1876 at War Bonnet Creek (Hat Creek) and then claimed to have cried, "The first scalp for Custer." In 1872, Cody won the Medal of Honor for gallantry in action on April 26, 1872, in the battle at Loup Fork on the Platte River in Nebraska. In the fall of 1872 he was elected to represent the Twenty-Sixth District in the legislature of Nebraska, thus adding the title "Honorable" to his name.

During this time, Cody was being urged by a friend to represent himself on stage. He declined at first but eventually agreed and started on his career as a performer. In 1873, he organized his own theatrical company known as the Buffalo Bill Combination, which included Wild Bill Hickok that first season. Cody moved his family to Rochester, New York, to be closer to the show. In April 1876, his only son died of scarlet fever. Heartbroken, Cody closed the show early and returned to scouting for the Fifth Cavalry. Shortly thereafter, he received word that General George Custer had been killed in the Battle of Little Bighorn. In 1877, Cody went into the cattle business with his friend, Major Frank North. Cody's ranch was near North Platte in

Nebraska, and in 1878 his family moved from Rochester to settle there.

In 1883, Cody started a new venture, which he called Buffalo Bill's Wild West Show. In it he depicted all of the history that he had experienced during his life on the Plains: the buffalo hunt, the first settlers, the Pony Express, the Deadwood stage, the wagon trains, the soldiers and scouts, and the Indians. It was highly successful in the United States, and in 1887 he took his show to England where he played before the Queen. He made several more trips to London and other European cities.

Cody returned from one of his European tours in November 1890 to find continuing warfare in Sioux Country. Because of his intimate knowledge of the Badlands of North Dakota, he was immediately summoned to Chicago by General Nelson Miles. He was also asked, because of his prior friendship with Sitting Bull, to go to him and try to quell the imminent uprising. Before Cody could reach Sitting Bull, however, the order was rescinded by President Benjamin Harrison. Sitting Bull was killed on December 15, 1890. On December 29, 1890, the massacre occurred at Wounded Knee, at which Miniconjou Chief Big Foot and about 300 Indian men, women, and children were killed by U.S. soldiers. Shortly thereafter, Cody negotiated with the government to take 100 Indians, including prisoners from Wounded Knee, to tour with his show.

Buffalo Bill's Wild West Show ran from 1883 to 1913. For the most part it was a great success. Nevertheless, due primarily to an extravagant lifestyle that included numerous affairs and much drinking, William "Buffalo Bill" Cody ended up penniless and bankrupt. Cody died on January 10, 1917, while visiting his sister in Colorado. His wife Louisa died in 1921. They are buried together on Lookout Mountain in Colorado.

In his second autobiography (published after his death), Cody expresses his sentiments about Indians:

> I . . . hope that the dealings of this Government of ours with the Indians will always be just and fair. They were the inheritors of the land that we live in. They were not capable of developing it, or of really appreciating its possibilities, but they owned it when the White Man came, and the White Man took it away from them. It was natural that they should resist. It was natural that they employed the

William "Buffalo Bill" Cody was a scout and showman. (Library of Congress)

only means of warfare known to them against those whom they regarded as usurpers. It was our business, as scouts, to be continually on the warpath against them when they committed depredations. But no scout ever hated the Indians in general.

Gayle Yiotis

See also Black Elk; Sitting Bull.

References and Further Reading

Blackstone, Sarah J. 1954. *Buckskins, Bullets, and Business: A History of Buffalo Bill's Wild West.* Westport, CT: Greenwood Press.

Bridger, Bobby. 2002. *Buffalo Bill and Sitting Bull: Inventing the Wild West.* Austin: University of Texas Press.

Carter, Robert A. 2000. *Buffalo Bill Cody: The Man Behind the Legend.* New York: John Wiley & Sons.

Cody, William F. [1879] 1978. *The Life of Hon. William F. Cody: Known as Buffalo Bill: The Famous Hunter, Scout, and Guide. An Autobiography.* Foreword by Don Russell. Lincoln: University of Nebraska Press.

Cody, William F. 1920. *An Autobiography of Buffalo Bill (Colonel W.F. Cody).* New York: Cosmopolitan Book.

Russell, Don. 1960. *The Lives and Legends of Buffalo Bill.* Norman: University of Oklahoma Press.

Wetmore, Helen Cody. 1899. *Last of the Great Scouts: The Life Story of Col. William F. Cody "Buffalo Bill" as Told by His Sister Helen Cody Wetmore.* Duluth, MN: Duluth Printing Services.

Yost, Nellie Irene Snyder. 1979. *Buffalo Bill, His Family, Friends, Fame, Failures, and Fortunes.* Chicago: Sage Books.

Cohen, Felix

Felix Cohen (1907–1953) was the author of the *Handbook of Federal Indian Law* (1942), a basic reference book in its field for decades. Cohen also served as associate solicitor of the Interior Department, and chaired the Department's Board of Appeals. He played an instrumental role in drafting the legal infrastructure of the Indian Claims Commission, founded in 1946. Cohen was especially active in securing for American Indians the right to vote and receive social security benefits.

In addition to the *Handbook of Federal Indian Law,* Cohen also authored a number of other books, including *Ethical Systems and Legal Ideals* (1933) and *Combating Totalitarian Propaganda: A Legal Appraisal* (1944). Elegant of speech, erudite of pen, and possessing a humane heart, Cohen sailed headlong into the political gauntlet that had once favored allotment and in his time sought termination of Native American nations as collective bodies.

Cohen was born in New York City and earned an AB degree in 1926 (summa cum laude) from City College, where, as a student, he edited *The Campus,* a student newspaper. Cohen earned a Ph.D. from Harvard in 1929 and an LLB from Columbia Law School in 1931. He was the son of Morris Raphael Cohen, a legal philosopher, writer, and professor at City College. The younger Cohen became well-known in the field of law well beyond cases concerning American Indians. In 1951, he coauthored a textbook, *Readings in Jurisprudence and Legal Philosophy,* with his father. The book contained the usual descriptions of European legal precedents, from Aristotle to the English Common Law, but also included a chapter titled "Law and Anthropology," which described the legal traditions of tribal peoples in North America, including the Sioux and Cheyenne.

Cohen also was a student of Native American societies and a social critic. On one occasion, Cohen compared the Native American influence on immigrants from Europe to the ways in which the Greeks had shaped Roman culture: "When the Roman legions conquered Greece, Roman historians wrote with as little imagination as did the European historians who have written of the white man's conquest of America. What the Roman historians did not see was that captive Greece would take captive conquering Rome [with] Greek science [and] Greek philosophy . . ." (Cohen, 1952, 180).

Cohen wrote that American historians had too often paid attention to military victories and changing land boundaries, while failing to see that in agriculture, government, sport, education, and our views of nature and of other people, the first Americans also had helped shape their battlefield conquerors. American historians have seen America mainly as an imitation of Europe, Cohen asserted. In his view, the real epic of America is the yet unfinished story of the Americanization of the white man.

It is likely that Cohen honed his definition of these ideas through his friendship with Mohawk culture bearer Ray Fadden of Onchiota, New York. For many years in the 1940s, Cohen had a cabin at Buck Pond, within walking distance of the Fadden home. John Kahionhes Fadden, Ray's son, recalled his father and Cohen walking in the woods and having long conversations.

Cohen resigned from government service in 1948 to practice American Indian law in the New York City–Washington, D.C., firm of Riegelman, Stasser, Schwartz, and Spiegelberg. Cohen often represented the interests of the Montana Blackfeet, Oglala Sioux, All-Pueblo Council, and San Carlos Apaches. Cohen also served as a visiting professor of law at Yale University and City College. He also taught at Rutgers Law School and the New School for Social Research.

Cohen died of cancer October 19, 1953, at his home in New York City. At his funeral, which was held in Washington, D.C., pallbearers included Felix Frankfurter, an associate justice of the United States Supreme Court; Senator Hubert H. Humphrey; John Collier, former commissioner of Indian Affairs; and Oliver LaFarge, author and president of the Association on American Indian Affairs.

Bruce E. Johansen

References and Further Reading

Cohen, Felix. 1952. "Americanizing the White Man." *The American Scholar* 21, no. 2: 171–191.

Cohen, Felix. 1960. *The Legal Conscience: Selected Papers of Felix S. Cohen.* Edited by Lucy Kramer Cohen. New Haven, CT: Yale University Press.

Collier, John

John Collier (1884–1968), an idealistic reformer, became commissioner of Indian affairs in 1933 during the Democratic Franklin Delano Roosevelt administration. The Indian Reorganization Act (IRA), passed by Congress in 1934, was his creation and the centerpiece of the Indian New Deal. The IRA ended the disastrous allotment policy that had dispossessed Native tribes of tens of millions of acres of reservation lands. Yet the Indian New Deal left a mixed heritage with respect to the aspirations of many American Indians. Never completely successful, it was criticized and underfunded by its detractors in Congress, and even opposed by many Indian nations and tribes. The legacy of Collier's Indian reform program poses some interesting questions: How did Collier become a passionate admirer of Indian culture and an advocate of cultural pluralism, and how successful was his program of Indian reform? His biography may provide answers to these questions.

John Collier was born in Atlanta, Georgia, in 1884. His father was a lawyer and banker who went on to become mayor of Atlanta. His mother, a New Englander, instilled in her son a love of literature and nature. The family eventually fell on hard times, and both parents died when Collier was a teenager. As a youth he began regular restorative trips to the southern Appalachian Mountains, and a love of the outdoors continued throughout his life. His later interest in folk cultures began during these outings. Collier entered Columbia University in 1902 and later studied at Woods Hole Marine Laboratory in Massachusetts. He soon turned from the study of biology to an interest in social issues. According to Collier's biographer, Kenneth R. Philp, a book by the Russian anarchist, Prince Peter Kropotkin, *Mutual Aid,* caught the young man's imagination and began his interest in the community life of precapitalist societies. It was a harbinger of his later interest in American Indians.

Upon leaving college, he at first took a job as a newspaper reporter. By 1907, however, he had become a reform social worker who for the next twelve years devoted himself to the welfare of European immigrants on Manhattan Island. In this endeavor he shared the interests of early American sociologists in the problems of immigration and urbanization. They, like Collier, believed that the machine age had undermined the old sense of community found in preindustrial societies and left the individual isolated. Crime and social problems were the result.

Collier became civic secretary for the People's Institute, an immigrant betterment organization, and editor of the Institute's bulletin. The Institute sponsored regular forums on relevant social issues for Jewish and Italian immigrants, along with the establishment of school community centers. Collier was a vigorous opponent of the Americanization policy that pressured immigrants to give up their native languages and cultures.

By 1912, Collier had become a frequenter of Mabel Dodge's weekly salons in New York City where leading intellectuals of the day gathered to share radical ideas. Dodge was to play a pivotal role in Collier's entry into American Indian advocacy a few years later. As a writer, poet, lecturer, and social reformer, Collier continued his social activism, establishing a training school for community workers and becoming editor of the publication of the National Community Center Conference. In 1916, when funding for the New York operations dried up and political difficulties arose, he moved with his family to Los Angeles, California, to become the director of the state's adult education program. After taking up the new work, he lectured extensively and established public forums similar to those of the People's Institute. His two main themes were the cooperative movement and the "Bolshevik experiment" of the Russian Revolution, both of which he admired. Collier's radical social work roots were to cause him problems later as Commissioner of Indian Affairs when he lobbied Congress for an Indian New Deal.

By the beginning of the twentieth century, Anglo-America had been persuaded that Indians were a vanishing race; therefore, the assimilation of the survivors through Americanization and Christianization was made to seem a task of philanthropy. In reality, American Indians had passed the nadir of their population decline and were no longer "vanishing," either physically or culturally. It was at this juncture that the missionary-oriented Indian Rights Association called on the Indian Office to place a ban on Indian ceremonial dancing.

John Collier was the U.S. Indian Affairs Commissioner from 1933 to 1945. (Library of Congress)

In the early 1920s, Indian commissioner Charles H. Burke banned Indian religious dances, and Secretary of the Interior Albert Fall sponsored legislation that would legitimize the seizure of 60,000 acres of Pueblo lands and the individualization of tribal economic assets.

In 1920, Collier interrupted a wilderness trip to Mexico to visit the Taos pueblo in New Mexico at the urging of his old friend Mabel Dodge. For two years he resided at the pueblo where he and others from the art community gathered around the fireplace in Mabel Dodge's home to discuss the meaning of Indian life. He came away determined that Pueblo culture, and Indian life in general, must be preserved. After his stay at Taos, Collier returned to California to accept a lecturer position at San Francisco State College.

A strong believer in cultural pluralism, Collier took up the protest from the Pueblos against the persecution by the Office of Indian Affairs and its Christian "reformers." The controversy over the Pueblo land grants, part of the larger struggle aimed at stopping reservation land dispossession and pauperization stemming from the 1887 General Allotment Act, led to the founding of the American Indian Defense Association (AIDA) by Collier in May 1923. The political agitation by the AIDA, along with the 2-million-member General Federation of Women's Clubs and the Indian Rights Association, led to the resignation of Secretary of the Interior Albert Fall from the Harding administration.

The year 1928 saw the issuance of the government's *The Problem of Indian Administration*, better known as the Meriam Report. For Collier it con-

firmed the horrible legacy of the allotment policy and the fact that major reform was needed in Indian administration. When Franklin D. Roosevelt was elected in 1932, the new president chose Harold Ickes as his Secretary of the Interior. Ickes was a Chicago progressive and former director of the American Indian Defense Association. Collier was then tapped to become the new commissioner of Indian affairs.

By 1934, the new commissioner had drafted a bill that became the framework for the Indian Reorganization Act. It was rough sailing for Collier, however, and Congress ended up dropping key provisions from the bill and amending others. The section of Title II having to do with promoting Indian arts, crafts, skills, and traditions was deleted by Congress, as was the section in Title III having to do with land alienation and the Indian heirship problem. Title IV, dealing with law and order, was dropped entirely. Not to be outdone, Collier launched his Indian New Deal anyway through a series of administrative reforms and edicts to the Office of Indian Affairs. A singular feature of the Indian New Deal was the exclusion of Christian missionaries from the Collier administration and the inclusion of anthropologists in their place. This represented a policy shift from cultural assimilation to cultural pluralism.

The new commissioner's critics, including a number of Indian tribes and reservation superintendents, viewed self-government under the IRA with suspicion, as socialistic and un-American. Collier, on the other hand, proposed that Indian tribes become chartered corporations with the powers of a community or county, a form of limited self-government. The new tribal councils would act as advisory bodies to the Secretary of the Interior. The IRA self-government provisions were seen by Collier as a form of indirect rule by the federal government and a progressive advance in U.S. Indian policy. By the 1920s and 1930s the European powers had come to favor this form of colonial administration since direct rule, especially by the French, had been such an abysmal failure. From today's perspective, Collier's reform may be criticized as a form of neocolonialism, but, taken in the context of the times, his ideas resulted in a progressive shift in federal Indian policy.

Despite the accomplishments of the IRA, World War II drained funds from the reform program and turned Congress and the country to other priorities. Discouraged, Collier resigned on January 10, 1945,

after twelve years as the head of Indian affairs. For the next twenty-three years he continued an active public life. During his tenure as commissioner, Collier helped found the first pan-American conference on Indian life held at Patzcuaro, Mexico, in the spring of 1940. He headed up a National Indian Institute in 1943 that undertook an important Indian personality research study, founded the Institute of Ethnic Affairs in 1945, and took an active interest in America's newly acquired trusteeships in the Pacific after the war. He published a major work in 1947, *Indians of the Americas,* which was used in anthropology courses for many years. In the same year he became professor of sociology and anthropology at the City College of New York, a position he retained until 1955. His memoir, *From Every Zenith,* came out in 1960, and he died at his Taos residence in 1968 at the age of eighty-four.

How should one evaluate the Collier legacy? In the first place, the IRA resulted in only a partial and imperfect restoration of Indian sovereignty. Furthermore, for all his democratic idealism, Collier's administrative style as commissioner has been criticized as authoritarian and paternalistic. In some cases he manipulated tribal elections to favor IRA acceptance. He also imposed Anglo-American model constitutions and charters on traditionally oriented tribes that undercut the political leadership of chiefs and the old band and treaty councils. The Navajo Nation never forgave him for the ruthlessness of his pursuit of the livestock reduction program on their reservation. The Lakota and some other tribes with allotted lands split into factions as a result of the IRA, the bitter legacy of which manifested itself in the occupation of Wounded Knee on the Pine Ridge Reservation in 1973.

It may be that religious freedom was his most lasting accomplishment. In his memoirs Collier depicts ceremonial tribal dances as the core of Indian religion. "Through the dances are united body and soul, and self with the community, and self and tribe with nature and with God." Upon taking office as commissioner he immediately reversed the old Bureau policy of religious persecution by issuing Circular No. 2970, "Indian Religious Freedom and Indian Culture." He also issued an order curtailing missionary activity on the reservations. Yet the issue of Indian religious freedom was excluded from the Indian Reorganization Act. Religious persecution continued in less obvious ways and was not specifically addressed by Congress until the passage of the

American Indian Religious Freedom Act in 1978 and the Native American Graves Protection and Repatriation Act in 1990. The repatriation of human remains is still not resolved, and the question of sacred lands has scarcely been addressed by public policy.

Steve Talbot

See also Assimilation; Bureau of Indian Affairs: Establishing the Existence of an Indian Tribe; Indian Reorganization Act; Meriam Report.
References and Further Reading
Collier, John. 1963. *From Every Zenith.* Denver, CO: Sage Books.
Kelly, Laurence C. 1996. "Indian New Deal." *Native America in the Twentieth Century: An Encyclopedia.* Edited by Mary B. Davis, 218–220. New York: Garland Publishing.
Philp, Kenneth R. 1977. *John Collier's Crusade for Indian Reform: 1920–1954.* Tucson: University of Arizona Press.
Stefon, Frederick J. 1983–1984. "The Indians' Zarathustra: An Investigation into the Philosophical Roots of John Collier's New Deal Educational and Administrative Policies." *The Journal of Ethnic Studies* Part I: 11, no. 5 (Fall 1983): 1–28; Part II: 11, no. 4 (Winter 1984): 29–45.

Coon Come, Matthew

As president of the Canadian Assembly of First Nations and as grand chief of the nine Cree councils, Matthew Coon Come (b. 1956) has become one of the late twentieth century's major Canadian Native leaders, especially in the campaign to halt exploitation of the James Bay region by Hydro-Quebec.

Coon Come was born in 1956 in a hut along the Mistissini trapline that his parents worked in northern Quebec. This was a seasonal encampment for the Crees, where they hunted and fished near James Bay. Coon Come didn't see a non-Native until he was six years of age. The first non-Native he saw was the Indian Affairs agent who arrived by float plane to take him to a residential school. Coon Come attended residential schools in Moose Factory, La Tuque, and Hull. He later studied political science, law, economics, and native studies at Trent and McGill Universities.

Coon Come's Cree elders recognized him as a natural leader. He was asked to coordinate inland Cree communities' negotiations with Canada that enabled the James Bay Crees to escape the Indian Act and gain the first ever aboriginal self-government legislation in Canada. Coon Come also served two terms as chief of the Mistissini First Nation, helping to acquire for his community a new arena, an adult education center, a bank, new administrative offices, new health facilities, and major improvements to its housing and community infrastructure.

Coon Come married Maryann Matoush in 1976; they later had three daughters and two sons. At age twenty-one, Coon Come became deputy chief for the Cree Nation of Northern Quebec. Later, he became the grand chief for roughly 12,000 Crees. He was a vocal opponent on behalf of aboriginal peoples in the province during the Quebec separation movement. He later became grand chief of the Crees' Grand Council in Quebec as a whole. He was first elected as grand chief of the Grand Council of the Crees and chairman of the Cree Regional Authority in 1987. Coon Come soon became known throughout Canada for his efforts to end federal policies that favored the abolition of aboriginal peoples' human rights and legal self-determination.

Coon Come was reelected by the James Bay Cree People through four successive terms as grand chief, during which he became known for his international work to protect aboriginal peoples' traditional ways of life. Coon Come brought these issues to the 1992 Earth Summit in Brazil, when he formed a coalition with other indigenous peoples and environmental organizations to defend the traditional use of Native lands worldwide.

During the early 1990s, Coon Come fought Hydro-Quebec's James Bay II proposal to dam eight major rivers that flow into James Bay in northern Quebec, at a cost of up to $170 billion, to provide electricity for urban Canada as well as several states in the U.S. Northeast. The area is virtually unknown to most Euro-Americans but has been home for thousands of years to roughly 10,000 Crees, many of whom would be forced from their homelands by flooding and toxic contamination.

Coon Come's Crees also had opposed construction of James Bay I, completed in 1985, which dammed or diverted five large rivers and flooded 4,000 square miles of forest. Rotting vegetation in the area had released about 184 million tons of carbon dioxide and methane gas into the atmosphere by 1990, possibly accelerating global warming around the world and saddling Quebec electric rate payers with a debt of $3,500 per person. Rotting vegetation also caused an acceleration of microbial activity that converts elemental mercury in submerged glacial rock to toxic methyl mercury, which rapidly diffused throughout the food chain. Methyl

mercury poisoning can cause loss of vision, numbness of limbs, uncontrollable shaking, and chronic neurological disease. By 1990, some Cree elders had twenty times the level of methyl mercury in their bodies that the World Health Organization considers safe. A 1984 survey of people residing in Chisasibi showed that 64 percent of its people had elevated levels of this toxin in their bodies. The Quebec government responded to these findings by telling the Crees not to eat fish, one of their main sources of protein.

The flooding also caused one-quarter of the Crees' caribou herds, about 12,000 animals, to drown in the first phase of the project. However, the human problems brought on by James Bay I were not limited to the flooding of forestland and increasing discharge of toxins. The arrival of many non-Natives, drawn by large-scale construction projects (including road building), was linked by Coon-Come and other Cree leaders with rising levels of substance abuse, violence, and suicide in their communities. All of these changes contribute to the breakdown of traditional family patterns and ways of making a living.

Coon Come and the Crees enlisted international support in their ultimately unsuccessful legal battle against the first phase of the James Bay project. In their efforts to stop the second phase, the Crees forged alliances with environmental groups around the world, with special emphasis on the Northeastern United States, where a large proportion of the project's power would be sold. In 1993, New York State dealt a grievous blow to the project by withdrawing from agreements to purchase power from Hydro-Quebec.

The James Bay projects, as previously planned, were not single dams across single rivers that flood valleys between mountains. They were massive earth-moving projects across an area as large as the state of Oregon. According to Coon Come:

> A project of this kind involves the destruction and rearrangement of a vast landscape, literally reshaping the geography of the land. This is what I want you to understand: it is not a dam. *It is a terrible and vast reduction of our entire world.* It is the assignment of vast territories to a permanent and final flood. The burial of trees, valleys, animals, and even the graves [of the Crees] beneath tons of contaminated soil. All of this serves only one purpose: the generation of more electricity to get more revenue and more

temporary jobs and to gain political power [emphasis added] (Coon Come, 1992, 82).

In 1994, Coon Come was awarded the Goldman Environmental Prize for his activism against the James Bay projects. It carries a $60,000 stipend. In November of that year, Hydro-Quebec announced that it was shelving the second phase of the James Bay project indefinitely, a major victory for the Crees. The project later was revived, but in a scaled-down form to accommodate the Crees.

Bruce E. Johansen

See also Assembly of First Nations; Canada, Indian Policies of; Department of Indian Affairs and Northern Development; Environment and Pollution; Hazardous Waste; James Bay and Northern Quebec Agreement; Water Rights.

References and Further Reading

Bigert, Claus. 1995. "A People Called Empty." In *Amazon of the North: James Bay Revisited.* By Rainer Wittenborn and Claus Biegert. Unpaginated program for show (August 4–September 5), Santa Fe Center for Contemporary Arts.

"Canadian Indians Paddle to New York City to Protest Quebec Power Plant." 1990. *Syracuse Post-Standard,* April 5: A-2.

Coone Come, Matthew. 1992. "A Vast Reduction. . . ." In *Our People, Our Land: Perspectives on Common Ground.* Edited by Kurt Russo. Bellingham, WA: The Florence R. Kluckhohn Center.

Gorrie, P. 1990. "The James Bay Power Project—The Environmental Cost of Reshaping the Geography of Northern Quebec." *Canadian Geographic* (February–March): 20–31.

Cooper, James Fenimore

The twelfth of the thirteen children of Elizabeth Fenimore and William Cooper, the Father of American Literature was born James Cooper (1789–1851) in Burlington, New Jersey, on September 15, 1789. He added Fenimore to his name in 1826, as his literary career was taking off.

When James was one year old, his father William, a land speculator, moved the family to a large tract of land around Otsego Lake in upstate New York. Although the Iroquois were not actually done using the land themselves, this land transfer is usually presented as a sale, because the Iroquois had been too devastated by U.S. genocidal attacks during

James Fenimore Cooper authored the classic Last of the Mohicans, *among many other works. (Library of Congress)*

the American Revolution to put up a struggle. His land deed in hand, William next set up Cooperstown, with himself as its local gentry, becoming a Federalist judge. The backwood setting around Cooperstown was to serve Fenimore's pen well in his famous Leatherstocking Tales. Critics regard *The Pioneers* (1823), with its unethical Judge Temple and townlet of Templeton, as Cooper's borrowing from his family history, while the generous Elizabeth Temple is often regarded as a tribute to Fenimore's beloved elder sister, Hannah, who died at twenty-three after falling from her horse.

Cooper's youth was troubled. He was obviously bright, but his passionate and forthright nature, which was to anger those around him throughout his life, kept him from following an easy path. He spent time in a boarding school in Albany before entering Yale College in 1803, where he lasted only until 1805, when he was summarily expelled for blowing up a fellow student's door. For his grand finale, he planned to run away to sea in 1806, but his father's pretensions would not allow a son of his to become an ordinary sailor. Instead, William purchased a commission for Fenimore in the fledgling

U.S. Navy, a career from which Fenimore drew heavily in his sea novels.

In 1810, Cooper met Susan Augusta De Lancey, a child of wealth from Westchester, New York, falling in love with alacrity and marrying by year's end. Between 1811 and 1824, the (from all accounts) happy couple produced five daughters—Elizabeth (1811), Susan Augusta (1813), Caroline Martha (1815), Ann Charlotte (1817), and Maria Francis (1819)—as well as two sons—Fenimore (1821) and Paul (1824)—of whom Elizabeth and Fenimore died as toddlers.

Within five months of marriage, Fenimore resigned his naval commission, on the plea of marriage, but the dates of the marriage (New Year's Day in 1811) and resignation (May 6, 1811) struck Fenimore's enemies as suspicious, especially in light of the De Lancey family's Tory stand during the American Revolution. By mid-1811, the War of 1812 was obviously looming with England, so Cooper's enemies darkly charged him with cowardice, disloyalty, and/or desertion, but the death of William Cooper in 1809, as well as Susan's champagne tastes, probably factored the most heavily into the decision.

Far from authoring books, the young Fenimore anticipated life as a wealthy country squire, after inheriting the family estate following the early and unexpected deaths of *all* of his elder brothers. This turn of events was only superficially fortunate. William had left the estate in deep legal trouble over the true ownership of the land (which was then being contested by other settlers, not the Iroquois). In addition, the War of 1812 caused a major economic depression in the United States, deflating the value of the estate even more significantly. On top of that, Cooper not only inherited the family estate, but also the responsibility of caring for the now widowed families of his deceased brothers. Clearly, he needed to find a source of income.

At first, in 1819, he attempted to invest in whaling, financing a ship, *The Union,* but after soaking up Cooper's investment, the venture failed to produce much revenue. By 1820, Cooper was nearly desperate. He knew he needed to scare up a regular source of income, so he was on the lookout for opportunities, although it is unlikely that writing crossed his mind. In fact, family stories claim that he loathed and avoided writing chores.

A charming family legend has Cooper's career as an author starting on a dare. In those days before videos, Ipods, televisions, or radios, families read aloud to each other for entertainment. With his wife

lying on the couch, feeling unwell, Cooper began reading a new book to her. After the first couple of chapters, Fenimore threw the book down in disgust, declaring, "I could write you a better book than that myself!" His wife erupted in laughter at the thought of a man whom wild elephants could not drag to the writing desk composing a whole book. Always passionately stubborn, especially when challenged, Fenimore stuck by his declaration until he had no choice but to put up or shut up; so he put up, immediately writing the opening chapters of his first novel, *Precaution* (1820). A rather dreadful imitation of his favorite authors, Jane Austen, Sir Walter Scott, and Amelia Opie, *Precaution* soon slid into obscurity, but Fenimore's new career had been born.

Cooper's writing improved dramatically once he began writing according to his own lights, not someone else's. His next novel, *The Spy: A Tale of the Neutral Ground* (1821), established patterns he was to use thereafter. Harvey Birch, his protagonist, was a man of marginal social status and lowly calling, for at the time spying was despised as unworthy. The novel was set during the American Revolution and ran violently about in the backwoods while posing large political questions. Here was Cooper's material in spades: warfare, political illegitimacy, lower-class actors, thrills, chills, and a lot of violence. The novel was a blockbuster of sorts, held up as proving to Europe that Americans could produce world-class literature. While praising Cooper's efforts, W. H. Gardiner, a literary reviewer for the *North American Review*, famously urged Cooper in 1822 to turn his talents to the "howling wilderness" and "the long struggle of civilization, encroaching on the dominion of barbarism" (Gardiner, 1822, 254–255).

Seeing the possibilities, Cooper immediately took this advice, but he did not rush headlong into his topic without research. For a while, he cast about, looking for a good source on Native North America. Two contenders came to his attention. First, there was John Heckewelder, the Moravian missionary who had been adopted by and lived with the Lenápes for forty-nine years, counting many as close friends. Heckewelder had produced *History, Manners, and Customs*, along with many other writings, both published and unpublished. He is still regarded as the best primary source for his place, time, and topic of all early Indian ethnographers. Second, there was General Lewis Cass, known to Ohio Native oral tradition as The Butcher and to his settler contemporaries as a man who wanted to be president. As part of orchestrating his political ambitions, he had pro-

duced a pamphlet on Natives, *Inquiries*, that was really no more than a racist creed viciously promoting genocide. Cass has since fallen into the deep oblivion he deserves.

At first, as Cooper confessed to his bookseller, Charles Wiley, that he felt as bewildered by the choice between the open-minded, Native-boosting Heckewelder and the racist murderer Cass as "an ass between two locks of hay," adding that Cass "condemns all that his rival praises, and praises all that his rival condemns" (Cooper, 1959, xxv). However, studying both sources and drawing on his own sense of political justice, Fenimore soon realized that Heckewelder was the informed author of the two.

Using Heckewelder while slighting Cass was a step that Cass never forgave or forgot. Writing anonymously for the conservative *North American Review*, Cass did his best to smear Cooper's *and* Heckewelder's reputations. Unfortunately, since Cass's reviews are easily pulled up today, most literary critics still read them, without also reading (or often even knowing) the entire history of Cooper's choice or that he was politically attacked for it. Literally, to the end of his life, Cooper defended his choice of Heckewelder, praising him in the 1850 preface to his collected Leatherstocking Tales as "ardent" and "benevolent" (Cooper, 1982, x). Also, literally to the end of his life, Cooper was hounded and attacked by political enemies, Cass among the number with his coterie in tow, including Henry Rowe Schoolcraft, whose racist and fraudulent "studies" Cass promoted over Heckewelder's.

Using Heckewelder's ethnographic information, Cooper created his most famous works, the five so-called Leatherstocking Tales: *The Pioneers* (1823), *The Last of the Mohicans* (1826), *The Prairie* (1827), *The Pathfinder* (1840), and *The Deerslayer* (1841). Ironically (since he was very class conscious), the Leatherstocking Tales powerfully feature Hawkeye, or Natty Bumppo, a natural man living on the far fringes of settler society whose closest friends were Lenápes and whose standards of morality were far above those of the undoubtedly white cohorts around him. Although the racist attitudes that permeated Cooper's milieu dribbled in around the edges, Cooper broke ranks with settler expectations of "savages" to present humanized Native Americans, whom he showed as deserving of civil and land rights. At the time, his thematic commentaries on race and class sat on the liberal end of the political scale, angering conservatives and hawks.

In addition to his "Indian stories" (which include some not in the Leatherstocking Tales series), Cooper added lively sea adventures to the pantheon of American fiction, including *The Pilot* (1823), *Red Rover* (1828), *The Water Witch* (1830), and *The Sea Lions* (1849). In his time, these were as celebrated as his Leatherstocking Tales. Never one to suffer yokels gladly, Cooper also bitingly satirized American provincialism, managing to offend, and quite deeply, many in his American audience with such offerings as *The Monikins* (1935), about a country of monkeys trying to imitate British culture. The damage was not ameliorated by his forays into didactic writing with such painful offerings as *The American Democrat* (1838), in which he unwittingly contradicted the libertarian values of his own novels, and *A Letter to His Countrymen* (1834), which dispensed with satire in favor of diatribe against rusticity. In a less bitter mood, Cooper penned naval histories of some worth.

All of this writing was accomplished in a boggling supernova of creativity that few today could match, even using computers. Cooper pumped out books, sometimes two a year, covering a wealth of subjects. Between 1820 and 1850, he produced thirty-six novels, sixteen nonfiction works, a volume's worth of reviews, countless letters, and journals. The youth who detested writing was long gone.

In 1826, as his name and fame were rising, Cooper took his wife and children for a seven-year sojourn in Europe. European, especially French, readers held Cooper in high esteem, so that, even after his enemies and his own sharp commentary had nicked his reputation at home, it continued to fly high in Europe. The Coopers toured extensively, polishing their manners to a sheen that was taken for arrogance once they came back home.

Upon returning to the United States in 1833, Cooper saw, and ferociously criticized, the sudden drop in the elegance of the customs and manners around him. As critics flailed away at him over this new affront, he also launched two one-man crusades: one to force ethics and standards of truth on American journalism, whose political right was libeling him with breathtaking abandon; the other to force his New York neighbors to respect his property rights, which they were violating flagrantly in a de facto seizure of his land. Cooper was a veritable dynamo in these causes, ultimately winning all of his lawsuits (seventeen by one count).

The victory was Pyrrhic, however, in that it cost Cooper financially just when he could least afford it.

By this point, Cooper was almost entirely dependent on royalties to keep him solvent, and the sales of his books were falling, with the international depression of 1837 driving them down as much as the shameless attacks by his political enemies. However, not even his enemies could entirely destroy the general public's appreciation of his adventure yarns. Cooper's book sales in the 1840s roughly matched those of the 1820s; so while his finances limped, they never crashed.

Cooper died on September 14, 1851, in Cooperstown, hailed on both sides of the Atlantic as America's premier author. Although his critical reputation took a nosedive in the late nineteenth and early twentieth centuries, a new generation of critics at the beginning of the twenty-first century is beginning to appreciate the intricately layered and often surprisingly progressive commentaries, especially on race relations, lacing his best novels.

Barbara Alice Mann

See also Democracy and Native American Images Among Europeans.

References and Further Reading

Beard, James Franklin, ed. 1960–1968. *The Letters and Journals of James Fenimore Cooper.* 6 volumes. Cambridge, MA: Belknap/Harvard University Press.

Cass, Lewis. 1821. *Inquiries Respecting the History, Traditions, Languages, Manners, Customs, Religion, &c. of the Indians, Living Within the United States.* Detroit, MI: Sheldon and Reed.

Clavel, Maurice. 1938. *Fenimore Cooper: Sa Vie et son oeuvre: La Jeunesse.* Aix-en-Provence: Universitaire de Provence.

Cooper, James Fenimore. [1823] 1959. "Letter to Mr. Charles Wiley, Bookseller." Reproduced in *The Pioneers,* xxv–xxvii. New York: Rinehard & Company.

Cooper, James Fenimore. [1841, 1850] 1982. "Preface to the Leatherstocking Tales." Reproduced in *The Deerslayer, or The First Warpath,* x. New York: Bantam.

Cooper, James Fenimore [grandson], ed. 1922. *Correspondence of James Fenimore Cooper.* 2 volumes. New Haven, CT: Yale University Press.

Cooper, Susan Fenimore [daughter]. 1861. *Pages and Pictures from the Writings of James Fenimore Cooper.* New York: W. A. Townsend.

Gardiner, W. H. 1822. "Article XII." *North American Review* 15 (July): 250–282.

Grossman, James. [1949] 1967. *James Fenimore Cooper: A Biographical and Critical Study.* Stanford, CA: Stanford University Press.

Heckewelder, John. [1820] 1971. *History, Manners, and Customs of the Indian Nations Who Once Inhabited Pennsylvania and Neighboring States.* First American Frontier Series. New York: Arno Press and New York Times.

James Fenimore Cooper Society. Available at: http://external.oneonta.edu/cooper/index.html. Accessed January 16, 2007.

Mann, Barbara A. 1997. "Forbidden Ground: Racial Politics and Hidden Identity in James Fenimore Cooper's Leather-Stocking Tales." Ph.D. dissertation, University of Toledo.

McWilliams, John P. 1972. *Political Justice in a Republic: James Fenimore Cooper's America.* Berkeley: University of California Press.

Long, Robert Emmet. 1990. *James Fenimore Cooper.* New York: Continuum International Publishing Group.

Spiller, Robert E., and Philip C. Blackburn. [1934] 1968. *A Descriptive Bibliography of the Writings of James Fenimore Cooper.* New York: Burt Franklin.

Taylor, Alan. 1995. *William Cooper's Town: Power and Persuasion on the Frontier of the Early American Republic.* New York: Alfred A. Knopf.

Copway, George

Born a Mississuaga-Ojibwa in 1818 near the Trent River in upper Canada (Ontario), George Copway (Kahgegagahbowh) died in Lac-des-Deux-Montagnes (Oka), Quebec, in 1869. Copway worked as an interpreter, teacher, and preacher for the Methodists, as well as an author, lecturer, herbal doctor, Union Army recruiter, and Catholic convert. He is best remembered for his autobiographical and historical work on the Ojibwas as well as numerous writings that appeared in newspapers throughout Canada and the United States.

By his own account, Copway lived a traditional life with his parents until they encountered Methodist missionaries. He enrolled at the Rice Lake School and in 1830 his dying mother convinced Copway to convert to Methodism. After his 1831 conversion, his teacher James Evans convinced Copway by 1834 to work among the Lake Superior Ojibwas under the auspices of the American Episcopal Methodist Church. He served at these missions until 1838, at which time he was permitted to enroll in the Ebenezer Manual Labor School in Illinois. After graduating in 1839, Copway returned to Canada and married Elizabeth Howell, a white woman, in 1840. The couple spent from 1840 to 1842 working at Methodist missions in Wisconsin and Minnesota.

Although not born in the United States, George Copway, also known as Kahgegagahbowh (He Who Stands Forever, or Stands Fast) spent much of his life there as an early Indian missionary and writer. (Library of Congress)

From 1842 to 1846, Copway worked for the Wesleyan Methodist Canadian Conference in Canada West (Ontario). In 1846 Copway was briefly imprisoned and expelled from the church after being accused of embezzlement by the Rice Lake and Saugeen Indian bands.

In 1847 he moved to the United States, where his autobiography was published and he entered the lecture circuit. During his lectures, Copway spoke of his conversion and the Indian's plight as well as advocating the creation of an Indian state on the northeast side of the Missouri River. This territory, called Kahgega after himself, was submitted to Congress but was never discussed. In 1850 and 1851, he published three more books, a newspaper titled *Copway's American Indian,* and an epic poem, *The Ojibway Conquest.* (The poem actually was written by

Julius Clark.) Copway's literary and speaking career brought him into contact with historian Francis Parkman, ethnologists Lewis Henry Morgan and Henry Rowe Schoolcraft, as well as authors Henry W. Longfellow, James Fenimore Cooper, and Washington Irving. His fame brought Copway to the 1850 World Peace Conference in Frankfurt Germany, although by this point it was becoming obvious that his lecture career was winding down. It was during this time 1849–1850 that Copway lost three of four children to disease.

By the late 1850s, the New York papers advertised his lectures, but a brief arrest for not paying his rental of a hall indicated that he was having difficulty making a living. He volunteered in 1858 to convince the remaining Florida Seminoles to relocate to Indian Territory in Oklahoma. By 1864, Copway worked as a Union Army recruiter in Canada, where he managed to enlist a few Indians. In 1867, Copway surfaced in Detroit working as an Indian healer. The following year, Copway's wife Elizabeth and their last surviving child abandoned him. Venturing to Oka, Quebec, he enjoyed some success and influence among the Iroquois and Algonquins as a healer. After informing a Sulpician priest that he was a pagan healer and wished to convert to Catholicism, his influence among the Iroquois declined. He was baptized on January 17, 1869 as Joseph-Antoine and died several days later.

Since the 1970s renewed interest in Copway's work has been spurred by scholars and Natives alike seeking an authentic Native voice. Copway's works are by no means unproblematic. They are in English, his second language, probably heavily edited by his wife, written with a Western audience in mind by an individual attempting to fit solely into the white world.

Karl S. Hele

References and Further Reading
Copway, George. 1847. *The Life, History and Travels of Kah-ge-ga-gah-bowh (George Copway)*. Albany: Weed & Parsons.
Copway, George. 1850. *The Ojibwa Conquest; A Tale of the Northwest.* . . . New York. Putman.
Copway, George. 1850. *The Traditional History and Characteristic Sketches of the Ojibway Nation*. New York: Charles Gilpin.
Copway, George. [1851] 1970. *Recollections of a Forest Life or the Life and Travels of Kah-ge-ga-gah-bowh or George Copway, Chief of the Ojibwa Nation*. Toronto, ON: Canadiana House.
Copway, George. 1851. *Running Sketches of Men and Places in England, France, Germany, Belgium and Scotland*. New York: Riker.
Smith, Donald B. 1976. "Kahgegagagahbowh." In *Dictionary of Canadian Biography: Volume IX, 1861–1870*. Edited by Francess G. Halpenny and Jean Hamelin, 419–421. Toronto, ON: University of Toronto Press.
Smith, Donald B. 1988. "The Life of George Copway or Kah-ge-ga-gah-bowh (1818–1869)—and a Review of His Writings." *Journal of Canadian Studies* 23, no. 3: 5–38.
Smith, Donald, and A. Lavonne Brown Rouf, eds. 1997. *Life, Letters and Speeches: George Copway (Kahgegahbowh)*. Lincoln: University of Nebraska Press.
Walker, Cheryl. 1997. "The Terms of George Copway's Surrender." In *Indian Nation: Native American Literature and Nineteeth-Century Nationalisms*, 84–110. Durham, NC: Duke University Press.

Cornplanter

Cornplanter (John O'Bail, ca. 1735–1836) was a major Seneca leader during the late eighteenth century who figured prominently in the shifting alliances that accompanied the American Revolution. He became a personal friend of George Washington through the Tammany Society, a fraternal order that adopted some Native costumes and rituals and which observed the fusion of European and Native American cultures in America.

Cornplanter's father was a white trader, John O'Bail (sometimes Abeel). Some sources contend he was Irish; others say he was Dutch. All agree, however, that he was one of the biggest sellers of liquor to the Senecas. O'Bail had been heard to boast that his trade had a profit margin of 1,000 percent. While some Englishmen detested O'Bail, they relied on his intelligence about the French, gathered from Indians with whom he did business.

Cornplanter was raised by his Seneca mother; he knew his father only slightly, having met him a few times as a child. In 1780, Cornplanter led a raiding party in the Schoharie Valley that took a large number of prisoners, his father included. Cornplanter released his father, who still made his living by bartering guns, rum, and other goods for furs. Cornplanter invited O'Bail to join his Seneca family in his old age, but the elder O'Bail chose to return to his European-American family at Fort Plain, New York.

As an ally of the French in the French and Indian War (1754–1763), Cornplanter's warriors raided several British settlements. He may have been part of the French force that defeated British General Edward Braddock and his aide George Washington at Fort Duquesne (now Pittsburgh).

During the American Revolution, the Iroquois Grand Council could not reach consensus on alliance. Cornplanter generally favored neutrality. Joseph Brant spoke eloquently about the necessity of going to war in alliance with the British, stating that neutrality would lead to disaster and that the Americans or the British might turn on the Confederacy with a vengeance. Red Jacket and Cornplanter argued against Brant. They insisted that this quarrel was among the whites; interfering in something they did not fully understand was a mistake. As the meeting broke up in a furor, Brant called Cornplanter a coward. The people gathered at Irondequoit divided into two camps and discussed the issue of going to war. In general, the Senecas were disposed to neutrality. However, the words of Brant stung the ears of the Senecas, who could not bear to be called cowards. Finally, after lengthy discussion, the Senecas were swayed along with other wavering groups to take up the British cause.

After the Revolution, Cornplanter secured for his people a tract of land along the Allegheny River. He brought in Quaker teachers and helped sustain a prosperous agricultural community that included large herds of cattle. Cornplanter signed several treaties on behalf of the Senecas, including those concluded at Fort Stanwix in 1784 and others at various locations in 1789, 1797, and 1802. Through his many associations with Euro-Americans (including a trip to England), Cornplanter sometimes wore English clothing and displayed English mannerisms. On one occasion, fellow Senecas tore off Cornplanter's English clothes, greased his body, and dressed him in traditional attire.

In April 1786, the Tammany Society welcomed Cornplanter and five other Senecas to Philadelphia. In a remarkable ceremony, the Tammany sachems escorted the Senecas from their lodgings at the Indian Queen Tavern to Tammany's wigwam on the banks of the Schuylkill River for a conference. Within a few days, Cornplanter and the Senecas proceeded to New York City to address Congress.

In Philadelphia on May 1, 1786, St. Tammany's Day was marked with the usual celebrations and feasts, after which a portrait of Cornplanter was presented. More than a dozen toasts were given,

Seneca chief Cornplanter took part in negotiating the treaties signed at Fort Stanwix in 1784 and Fort Harmar in 1789. However, he did not actually sign either document. (Getty Images)

including: "The Great Council Fire of the United States—May the 13 fires glow in one blended blaze and illumine the Eagle in his flight to the stars," "Our great grand sachem George Washington, Esq.," "Our Brother Iontonkque or the Corn Plant—May we ever remember that he visited our wigwam and spoke a good talk from our great-grandfathers," and "The Friendly Indian Nations—our warriors and young men who fought, bled and gave good council for our nation."

Later in his life, Cornplanter lost some of his prestige among the Senecas because of his easy agreement to land cessions. He retained enough influence, however, to bring the Senecas to the American side in the War of 1812. Shortly before he died in 1836, Cornplanter had a dream that indicated his friendship with all Euro-Americans had been mistaken. After the dream, he destroyed all the presents that had been given him by non-Indians.

Cornplanter's people occupied the 1,300-acre piece of land along the Allegheny River that had been given them by George Washington until the

midtwentieth century, when the Army Corps of Engineers decided that the land better suited the public convenience under water. The scope of the Army's engineering projects had grown grandiosely since Washington himself helped survey the mountains that now comprise West Virginia, long before the pursuit of electricity became a legally valid reason for the state to seize land. In 1964, the bones of Cornplanter's people were moved from their land to make way for rising waters behind the Kinzua Dam. In the valleys at the Western Door, Senecas still ask sardonically if George Washington had ever asked Cornplanter if he knew how to swim.

Bruce E. Johansen

See also American Revolution, Native American Participation; Brant, Joseph; French and Indian War; Red Jacket; Tammany Society.

References and Further Reading

Grinde, Donald A., Jr. 1977. *The Iroquois and the Founding of the American Nation.* San Francisco: Indian Historian Press.

Parker, Arthur Caswell. 1927. *Notes on the Ancestry of Cornplanter.* Rochester, NY: Lewis H. Morgan Chapter, New York State Archaeological Association.

Stone, William Leete. 1841. *Life and Times of Red-Jacket, or Sa-go-ye-wat-ha: Being the Sequel to the History of the Six Nations.* New York: Wiley and Putnam.

Wilson, Edmund. 1960. *Apologies to the Iroquois.* New York: Farrar, Straus, and Cudahy.

Costo, Rupert

From the 1930s to the 1950s, Rupert Costo (Cahuilla, 1906–1989) was active in national and tribal politics, serving both as a vocal critic of the Indian New Deal in the 1930s and as tribal chairman of the Cahuillas in the 1950s; later, Costo became an important figure in Native American publishing.

As a football player in the 1920s at Haskell Institute and Whittier College (where he played with the future President Richard M. Nixon), Rupert Costo early in life demonstrated his athletic and intellectual aptitudes to the Indian and non-Indian world.

During the 1930s, California was a major center of opposition to Collier's Indian New Deal, and Costo was one of the principal leaders of the opposition. Costo believed that the Indian New Deal was a device to assimilate the American Indian; he believed that the Indian Reorganization Act was being used to colonize Native Americans because, in his view, genocide, treaty making and treaty breaking, substandard education, disruption of Indian culture and religion, and the Dawes Allotment Act had failed. Costo knew that partial assimilation already had taken place in Native societies through the use of "certain technologies and techniques," but he knew that total assimilation, which meant fading into the general society with a complete loss of culture and identity, was another thing altogether. Costo called the IRA, "The Indian Raw Deal" (Mails, 1990, 146).

For most of his working life, Costo was employed by the state of California in the Highway Department as an engineer. Upon his retirement, Costo and his wife, Jeannette Henry Costo (Eastern Cherokee,) founded the San Francisco–based American Indian Historical Society in 1964. The organization was often in the forefront of American Indian issues such as the protection of American Indian cemeteries and American Indian human remains, as well as the correction of American Indian textbooks. The Costos sought to develop publications that accurately reflected the historical role of Indians in American society.

Initially, the American Indian Historical Society published three journals: *Wassaja*, a national Indian newspaper; *The Indian Historian*, a respected academic journal; and the *Weewish Tree*, a national magazine for young Indian people. Rupert Costo coedited all three publications with his wife. In 1970, the society founded another publication arm, the Indian Historian Press, an American Indian–controlled publishing house that published fifty-two titles. Some of the well-known titles were Rupert Costo, ed., *Textbooks and the American Indian* (1970) and Donald A. Grinde, Jr. (Yamasee), *The Iroquois and the Founding of the American Nation* (1977).

Through his editorial column in *Wassaja*, Costo advocated increased sovereignty for Native American nations in order to enhance land and water rights. He also worked tirelessly for the protection of American Indian civil, social, and religious rights.

At the end of his life, Costo endowed the Rupert Costo Chair in American Indian History at the University of California, Riverside. Costo and his wife also established the Costo Library of the American Indian at the University of California, Riverside, one of the most comprehensive collections of American Indian books in the United States. In 1994, the University of California, Riverside, renamed its Student Services Building as Costo Hall

in honor of the outstanding contributions of both Costos to the university.

Bruce E. Johansen

See also Indian Reorganization Act.
References and Further Reading
Johansen, Bruce E. 2005. *Native North America: A History.* Westport, CT: Praeger.
Mails, Thomas E. 1990. *Fools Crow.* Lincoln: University of Nebraska Press.

Council of Energy Resource Tribes

The Council of Energy Resource Tribes (CERT) was founded in 1975 by representatives from twenty-five Native American tribes and nations that own substantial reserves of energy and other natural resources. The Denver–based CERT, by 2005 a consortium of fifty-seven American and Canadian Indian polities, works to help Native Americans recognize, protect, and exploit energy-related wealth on their lands. A. David Lester has been CERT's executive director nearly since the nonprofit group's inception. CERT pursues a cooperative relationship between private industry, particularly in the energy sector, and American Indian governments. CERT also has become a notable lobbying force for Native American energy interests within the federal government, including Congress and the Interior Department.

Native lands in the CERT consortium produce 380 billion cubic feet of natural gas annually and contain 2 trillion cubic feet of proved gas reserves. Properties overseen by CERT also hold 30 percent of the United States' coal reserves, 5 percent of its oil, and significant amounts of uranium. CERT is governed by the elected tribal leaderships of fifty-three federally recognized Indian tribes in the United States and four Canadian bands. Its members have been working toward self-management of their energy resources, from negotiating agreements, to protecting the environment, to verifying revenue payments.

CERT played a role in the North American Energy Summit that was held April 14–16, 2004, in Albuquerque, New Mexico. This event included state, provincial, Native, and national leaders from three countries and involved diverse interests seeking to develop a secure, affordable, and environmentally responsible energy system. The conference included presentations by Governors Bill Richardson of New Mexico, Bill Owens of Colorado, Janet Napolitano of Arizona, Frank Murkowski of Alaska, Dave Freudenthal of Wyoming, John Hoeven of North Dakota, and Mike Rounds of South Dakota, as well as Canadian Premiers Ralph Klein (Alberta), Gary Doer (Manitoba), and Joseph L. Handley (Northwest Territories).

Summit participants considered a number of topics: capitalizing on renewable energy resources; improving energy efficiency; determining the future of nuclear energy and fossil fuels; providing a reliable and efficient electricity grid; financing infrastructure and making it more secure; and achieving needed international collaboration. The Summit also included an Energy Futures Expo, which featured cutting-edge technologies, systems, and alternative-fuel vehicles.

CERT has supported legislation that would allow Native American governmental entities to submit "tribal energy resources agreements" covering energy and right-of-way leases to the Interior Department that, when approved, may enable agreements to proceed without prior secretarial approval. This stripped-down version of the current process could accelerate energy development on Native American lands. While the proposal has widespread support from Republicans, some Democrats fear it could dilute environmental restrictions on oil and gas drilling on Indian land and weaken the Interior Department's trust responsibilities. In addition, the hydroelectric language in the energy bill would create a licensing process that favors power providers to the detriment of Native governments, their treaty rights, and the general public, according to a position paper Senate Democrats released at a 2004 Native American forum on Capitol Hill. Instead, the Democrats favor proposals to promote transmission development on Indian lands and creating tax incentives for renewable energy that are favorable to Native governments.

Tex Hall, as president of the National Congress of American Indians, has gone on record in support of CERT's assertion that incentives will be required for Native cooperation in exploitation of energy resources residing on Native lands. Hall would like to see the Congressional Budget Office analyze how much money the energy bill would allocate for development of Native American energy resources. He also wants the U.S. Department of Energy to provide a number of $1-million to $2-million grants for wind energy demonstration projects on land with significant potential, such as the Blackfeet nation in

Montana or Hall's own Mandan, Hidatsa, and Arikara nation in North Dakota. Federal utilities, military bases, and government agencies also should include preferences for energy supplied by Indian tribes and nations in their procurement contracts, Hall believes.

Through its representatives in Washington, D.C., CERT also has lobbied the U.S. government for simplification of many arcane tax laws and regulations that discourage the development of energy resources on Native lands. The organization also has been pressing Congress to pass a measure that would allow private producers of energy to receive credits on their federal tax returns for tax payments to a given state for Native energy development. In addition to making the exploration and production of new oil wells on tribal lands more attractive, such a change would encourage more production through the exploitation of existing wells, Lester has said.

CERT has encouraged Global Energy Decisions to inventory energy resources. This consulting firm has produced a wall map portraying the West's production, transmission, consumption, and land use patterns. The map contains references to coal mines, oil and natural gas wells, pipelines, railroads, power plants, and transmission lines, as well as public lands (Indian reservations, national parks, national forests, and Bureau of Land Management districts).

In addition to its energy-related activities, CERT also plays a major role in raising money for Native American education. By 2005, CERT had raised nearly $6 million through its American Spirit Award Dinner. On June 21, 2005, CERT and the Morongo Band of Mission Indians hosted the twenty-fifth annual American Spirit Award Dinner at the $250 million Morongo Casino, Resort and Spa. The dinner was part of a three-day Indian Energy Solutions 2005 conference focusing on current Indian energy policies, economic development, market trends, alternative and renewable energy, and Native utility formation. More than 500 energy industry officials, state and federal elected leaders, Native representatives, and press attended the event.

The CERT Tribal Internship Program provides students with opportunities to work alongside senior CERT staff, Native leaders, and energy companies on technical and scientific issues, policies, and projects. Past projects have focused on reservation water quality studies, cooperative planning on environmental issues with state and local govern-ments, hazardous waste operations training, and biodiversity.

CERT also operates a Tribal Institute for Sustainable Energy and publishes *Red Earth Magazine Online*.

Bruce E. Johansen

See also Economic Development; Hazardous Waste; Indian Mineral Leasing Act; MacDonald, Peter; Mining and Contemporary Environmental Problems; Reservation Economic and Social Conditions; Tribal Sovereignty; Uranium Mining.

References and Further Reading

Council of Energy Resource Tribes. 1985. Inventory of Hazardous Waste Generators and Sites on Selected Indian Reservations. Denver: Council of Energy Resource Tribes (CERT).

Council of Energy Resource Tribes. 2001. Tribal Resource Institute in Business, Engineering, and Science (TRIBES) summer program. Available at: http://www.certredearth.com/ tribesprog.shtml. Accessed April 2, 2002.

Crazy Horse

Crazy Horse (Tashunka Witco, Oglala Lakota, ca. 1842–1877), a daring military strategist, was a major Lakota leader in the last half of the nineteenth century, during the final phases of the Plains Indian wars. Alone among Native American leaders at this time, he never signed a treaty with the United States. Crazy Horse also repudiated the idea of reservation life until his violent death in a hand-to-hand struggle with Anglo-American captors at the age of about thirty-five. Crazy Horse never wore European-style clothing, and his photograph was never taken. To Oglala Lakota and to many other Native people generally, his memory has become the essence of resistance to European colonization. Alvin Josephy, Jr. wrote, "To the Sioux, he is the greatest of all their leaders" (1961, 259).

"Crazy Horse" is an old name among the Oglalas that had been handed down generation to generation for several centuries. Crazy Horse's ancestors kept historical records for the Oglalas on buckskin, a method of historical record keeping related to the winter counts of other Sioux tribes. Crazy Horse married a Cheyenne, and thus cemented the alliance that bound both during the final phases of the Plains Indian wars. He also was a son-in-law of Red Cloud.

Crazy Horse was born about 1842 on the site of what would later become the city of Rapid City, South Dakota. His father was an Oglala spiritual leader, and his mother was a Brûlé Sioux. As a youth, Crazy Horse was called the Light-Haired One or Curly, for his relatively light, wavy hair, which was unusual among the Lakota. He received the name "Crazy Horse" from his father after a battle with the Arapahos in 1858, at about sixteen years of age.

Crazy Horse was described as having been of average height, with a complexion that was lighter than most other Lakota. He was known to wander away from his village, with the detachment of a poet, after a battle. After attaining "shirt wearer" rank in 1865, he attended leadership meetings but rarely spoke. Introverted and eccentric, Crazy Horse was shot in the face and relieved of the shirt of rank in 1870 following an attempt to steal another man's wife.

From an early age, Crazy Horse was a master of the psychological aspects of Plains warfare. He often rode into war naked, except for a breechcloth around his loins, "his body painted with white hail spots, and a red lightning streak down one cheek. . . . His battle cry was 'It's a good day to die!'" (Waters, 1992, 152). Crazy Horse was never seriously injured in battle, and he made a point of never scalping anyone he killed.

In 1874, Crazy Horse and other Lakotas learned that George Armstrong Custer had led an expedition into their sacred Black Hills and found gold at French Creek. Hordes of prospectors followed, ignoring the fact that the Black Hills had been guaranteed to the Lakotas by the Fort Laramie Treaty of 1868. Crazy Horse and others rejected government edicts that sought to keep them on the Great Sioux Reservation, arguing that all the land guaranteed to them under the 1868 treaty was theirs to use.

Several allied Native peoples, including bands of Lakotas and Cheyennes, converged at the Little Bighorn in southeastern Montana in the spring of 1876. On June 17, Crazy Horse and an estimated 1,500 warriors engaged a force under General George Crook in the valley of the Rosebud in Montana. The fight was a standoff, but Crazy Horse prevented Crook from a planned rendezvous at the Little Bighorn with two other armies.

The Indian camp at the Little Bighorn, perhaps containing as many as 5,000 people and including roughly 2,000 warriors, was scattered along the river for about three miles. The elite Seventh Cal-vary under Custer had expected only 1,000. Even after his scouts told him that the camp was much larger than he expected, Custer decided to attack the Indians on their home ground. That decision resulted in his death, as well as the demise of his entire force of about 225 men. A furious, hour-long assault led by Crazy Horse and Gall dismembered Custer's force.

After the battle of the Little Bighorn, Native peoples who remained free of reservations were hounded relentlessly by reinforced U.S. Army troops, who turned Custer into a martyr. The Lakota who had defeated Custer were pushed onto the Great Sioux Reservation, band by band. As he watched his people suffer due to the destruction of their buffalo-based economy, Crazy Horse's defiant will began to soften. On May 5, 1877, Crazy Horse and his contingent of 800 Oglalas, in 145 lodges with 1,700 ponies, formed a parade two miles long as they marched into the Red Cloud Agency to surrender. They gave up their horses and guns. Red Cloud met the Oglalas en route and guided them to Fort Robinson, near the agency.

Shortly after the surrender, Crazy Horse's wife Black Shawl became sick with tuberculosis. He asked permission to take her to Spotted Tail's people at the Brûlé Agency, forty miles away, but was denied. He escaped from Fort Robinson anyway. Several dozen soldiers chased Crazy Horse to the Brûlé Agency but failed to catch him. Instead, the Brûlé Indian agent and Spotted Tail himself convinced Crazy Horse to return to Fort Robinson.

Crazy Horse agreed to surrender and return; fifteen miles from the Brûlé Agency, however, he was surrounded by forty of Spotted Tail's Army scouts. Crazy Horse was taken prisoner and escorted back to Fort Robinson. He had heard a rumor that he would be killed or taken in chains to Fort Augustine, Florida, to be imprisoned for life. At Fort Robinson on September 5, 1877, as Crazy Horse was being led toward a stockade, he rebelled at the sight of the prison and tried to escape. Little Big Man and several other Indians grabbed Crazy Horse, as Private William Gentles ran his bayonet through Crazy Horse's body.

On his deathbed, Crazy Horse recalled why he had fought:

> I was not hostile to the white man . . . We had buffalo for food, and their hides for clothing and our tipis. We preferred hunting to a life of idleness on the reservations, where we were

driven against our will. At times, we did not get enough to eat, and we were not allowed to leave the reservation to hunt. We preferred our own way of living. We were no expense to the government then. All we wanted was peace, to be left alone. . . . They tried to confine me, I tried to escape, and a soldier ran his bayonet through me. I have spoken (Johansen and Grinde, 1997, 88–89).

After Crazy Horse's assassination, about 240 Lakota lodges, occupied by people who had supported him, migrated to Canada where they joined Sitting Bull's people in exile. With the Crazy Horse band, Sitting Bull's camp grew to about 800 lodges, before their eventual return and surrender a few months later.

Bruce E. Johansen

See also Battle of the Little Bighorn; Fort Laramie Treaty; Great Sioux Uprising; Red Cloud; Spotted Tail; Worldviews and Values.

References and Further Reading

Ambrose, Stephen E. 1986. *Crazy Horse and Custer.* New York: New American Library.

Clark, Robert A. 1976. *The Killing of Crazy Horse.* Lincoln: University of Nebraska Press.

Johansen, Bruce E., and Donald A. Grinde, Jr. 1997. *The Encyclopedia of Native American Biography.* New York: Henry Holt.

Josephy, Alvin, Jr. 1961. *The Patriot Chiefs.* New York: Viking.

Kadlecek, Edward and Mabell. 1981. *To Kill an Eagle.* Boulder, CO: Johnson Publishing.

Nabokov, Peter. 1991. *Native Testimony.* New York: Viking.

Sandoz, Mari. 1942. *Crazy Horse: Strange Man of the Oglalas.* New York: Alfred A. Knopf.

Schmitt, Martin F., and Dee Brown. 1948. *Fighting Indians of the West.* New York: Charles Scribner's Sons

Utley, Robert M. 1993. *The Lance and the Shield: The Life and Times of Sitting Bull.* New York: Henry Holt.

Waters, Frank. 1992. *Brave Are My People.* Santa Fe, NM: Clear Light Publishers.

Crook, George

Major General George Crook (1828–1890) was one of the best-known officers of the post–Civil War United States Army. His career spanned the Indian wars of the Pacific Northwest in the 1850s, the Civil

George Crook spent most of his distinguished military career on the frontier and is closely associated with many significant battles, although he also defended Indian rights in the Standing Bear trial of 1879. (Library of Congress)

War, and the campaigns against the Apaches and the northern Plains peoples during the 1870s and 1880s. Crook's military record was good, but inconsistent and well supplied with controversy. His greatest military glory came in the Southwest during the early 1870s with the offensive against the western Apaches and Yavapais. At the time of his sudden death of heart failure in 1890, Crook was among the leading figures of the American military, respected as a fighter, but he was also recognized as an Indian rights advocate.

Crook was born on September 8, 1828, on a farm near Taylorsville, Ohio. He entered West Point in 1848, studied with mediocre success, and graduated thirty-eighth in a class of forty-three in 1852. The young officer saw his first action in the Pacific Northwest and made a favorable impression on his

superiors. Although Crook was "a soldier of the West," the four years spent in the Union Army shaped his character extensively, bringing him rank (major general of volunteers), experience, and vision. In 1871, as a lieutenant colonel, he received the assignment as the commander of the Department of Arizona. There Crook orchestrated an aggressive offensive by deploying several small converging detachments, which combined regulars and indigenous enlisted men. Troops struck against the parties and camps of Yavapais and western Apaches wherever they could be found and forced them onto reservations. For his exploits Crook won the star of a brigadier general, surpassing several outraged colonels in the process who proved eager to exaggerate Crook's failures in the future.

After the Arizona campaign, Crook took the field against the Sioux and Cheyennes in 1876 and 1877, suffered a defeat at Rosebud, and managed only mediocre results in other engagements. On the Plains, Crook proved militarily inefficient, uncompromising, and often frustrated. He returned to Arizona in 1882 and again took the offensive aggressively, this time against the Chiricahua Apaches, taking his troops across the international border into Mexico in 1883. Temporary peace was followed by another war. Again Crook sent his troops after the Chiricahuas, but, following a failed peace conference in March 1886, he found his policies in disfavor at Washington. Crook resigned and witnessed General Nelson A. Miles bringing an end to armed conflict in Arizona and New Mexico later that same year. Miles and Crook rushed to claim the glory for ending the Indian conflict in the Southwest and debated over Miles' decision to exile the Chiricahuan Apaches, many whom had served in the U.S. Army, as prisoners of war into Florida.

During the decades spent in the Trans-Mississippi West, Crook grew increasingly critical of the nature of American conquest and colonization. He saw the reason for armed conflicts in the greed and ruthlessness of white invaders. Anger toward white settlers and an ambivalent federal government filled Crook with a passion for understanding indigenous cultures. He believed that through paternalistic guidance Native Americans could learn to live under the new white order. Individualism, the cash economy, and hard work were the main instruments of Crook's Indian policy. Crook also appeared in the forefront enlisting indigenous men into the Army. He usually got good results, but discovered that most military officials and policy makers did not favor indigenous soldiers doing the white regulars job. Increasingly stubborn and uncompromising, Crook became an eccentric outsider in his own army, straining his relations with the Commanding General Phil Sheridan.

Crook was and remains a mystery. He certainly was ambitious, egoistic, eager for recognition, and vengeful toward those he saw as his enemies. Through his skillful aides and political connections, including President Rutherford B. Hayes, Crook was able to promote a public image of himself as a taciturn, honest, civilian-clothed man of action. Certainly, Crook was at times an innovative commander who obtained good military results through heavy dependency on indigenous soldiers, but equally often he met failure, most notably in the Sioux War of 1876–1877. His personal life is inadequately known (he was married for twenty-four years and had no children), and even his professional achievements are clouded in debate. Perhaps Crook was the greatest Indian fighter and thinker in the post–Civil War U.S. Army, or he might have been the ablest self-promoter of mediocrity.

Janne Lahti

See also Apache Wars.
References and Further Reading
Robinson, Charles M. 2001. *General Crook and the Western Frontier.* Norman: University of Oklahoma Press.
Schmitt, Martin F., ed. 1986. *General George Crook: His Autobiography.* Norman: University of Oklahoma Press.

Cruz, Joseph de la

A veteran of twenty-five years as president of the Quinault nation, Joseph Burton de la Cruz (1937–2000) gained a national reputation by serving as president of the National Tribal Chairmen's Association (1977–1981) and as head of the National Congress of American Indians (1981–1985). De la Cruz stepped down from the Quinaults' leadership in 1994 (having held the position since 1970) to make way for Pearl Capoeman Baller, the tribe's first female chief in modern times.

At home on the Quinault nation along the Pacific coast of Washington State, de la Cruz played an active role in founding many tribal enterprises, including forestry management, land restoration, housing construction, and seafood processing. Between 1985 and 1988, de la Cruz also became

influential in fisheries management on an international level, as a mediator between the United States, Canada, and Native nations in the Pacific Salmon Fisheries Treaty.

De la Cruz's niece Jennifer Scott's most vivid memory of her uncle was of the day he defiantly drove his truck onto the Chow Chow Bridge near the Washington coast to block logging trucks from entering the Quinault Indian Reservation, in protest of Bureau of Indian Affairs land use practices. "I'll never forget him sitting there on that bridge," Scott said (McGann, 2000). But that action, which helped the Quinaults win compensation for their timber, was only one of many that de la Cruz took for Native Americans. De la Cruz worked for decades to improve Native American health care, to help secure fishing rights, and to obtain other manifestations of sovereignty and economic self-sufficiency.

Randy Scott, a Quinault Indian Tribe lobbyist, called de la Cruz the father of a self-governance policy by which Native American governments exercised line item appropriations from the government instead of getting money through the federal bureaucracy. This policy placed direct, day-to-day control over services such as police, health, land use, and education in the hands of Native governments rather than the Bureau of Indian Affairs (McGann, 2000).

While he headed the Quinaults, de la Cruz was instrumental in incorporating them into the provisions of the Boldt decision, which enforced Native fishing rights in Washington State and provided a national example for such litigation. Asserting that many visitors were not respectful of the area's ecosystem, he also ordered the closure to non-Natives of twenty-six miles of ocean beach on the Quinault Reservation north of Aberdeen.

"Joe was involved in so many issues it's hard to say what his biggest accomplishment was, there's too many to choose just one," said Pearl Capoeman-Baller, current president of Quinault Indian Nation. "Everybody turned to Joe de la Cruz. He was there to protect rights for all tribes, not just Quinault. Joe was one of the greatest Indian leaders in the United States, and he worked endlessly for the Quinault people" (McGann, 2000).

On April 16, 2000, at the age of sixty-two, Joe de la Cruz suffered a heart attack and died at Seattle–Tacoma International Airport while en route to an Oklahoma conference. De la Cruz was survived by his wife, Dorothy; his daughters Gayle de la Cruz, Tina de la Cruz, and Lisa Kyle; and his sons Joe de la Cruz and Steve de la Cruz; as well as seven grandchildren and two great-grandchildren.

"His whole life was dedicated to Indian welfare and Indian concerns," said Bernie Whitebear, of United Indians of All Tribes in Seattle. "The self-governance conference that he was going to was really appropriate. He died with his boots on. A lot of the advances that the tribes are witnessing today in regard to self-governance are a result of his early involvement in that area," Whitebear said. "He was a leader in the indigenous people's efforts throughout the world, including Canada and South America" (McGann, 2000).

Bruce E. Johansen

See also National Congress of American Indians; Tribal Sovereignty.

References and Further Reading

Johansen, Bruce E., and Donald A. Grinde, Jr. 1997. *The Encyclopedia of Native American Biography.* New York: Henry Holt.

McGann, Chris. 2000. "Indian-Rights Advocate Dies on Way to Conference." *Seattle Post-Intelligencer,* April 17. Available at: http://www.cherokee.org/Messages/DeLaCruz.html. Accessed January 16, 2007.

Curtis, Charles

Charles Curtis, a man of one-eighth Native blood, served as a member of the U.S. House of Representatives, a U.S. senator, and as vice president of the United States. Born on Indian land that later was incorporated into North Topeka, Kansas, Curtis was the son of Oren A. Curtis, an abolitionist and Civil War Union cavalry officer, and Helen Pappan, who was of Kaw and Osage ancestry. Curtis's mother died when he was three; he was thereafter raised on the Kaw Reservation and in Topeka by his maternal grandmother. Following an attack on Kaw Indians at Council Grove by Cheyenne militants, Curtis departed the Indian mission school on the Kaw Reservation in 1868 and returned to Topeka, Kansas, where he attended Topeka High School. For several years as a young man, Curtis was a jockey; he also worked odd jobs until he met A. H. Case, a Topeka lawyer. Studying the law and working as a law clerk, Curtis was admitted to the Kansas bar in 1881.

Entering politics as a Republican, Curtis was elected county prosecuting attorney in 1884 and

Charles Curtis, right, with Calvin Coolidge and Mrs. Coolidge. (Library of Congress)

1886. From 1892 to 1906, he served eight terms in the U.S. House of Representatives. He authored the Curtis Act of 1898 that dissolved tribal governments and permitted the institution of civil government within the Indian Territory, in an attempt to force the assimilation on American Indian peoples. The Curtis Act brought the allotment policy to the Five Civilized Tribes of Oklahoma, who had been exempted from the Dawes Allotment Act of 1887. The Curtis Act empowered the Dawes Commission, which had been created in 1893, to extinguish tribal title to lands in Indian Territory. Once tribal title was eliminated, the Dawes Commission allotted reservation lands to individuals. Curtis's endeavors to foster detribalization, allotment, and assimilation were opposed by many of the tribal leaders of Indian Territory. In essence, the Curtis Act paved the way for

Oklahoma statehood in 1907 by destroying tribal land titles and governments there.

Curtis served in the U.S. Senate from 1907 to 1913 and from 1915 to 1929 as the first U.S. senator of American Indian ancestry. During his tenure in the Senate, Curtis was Republican party whip (1915–1924) and then majority leader (1924–1929). As chairman of the Senate Committee on Indian Affairs in 1924, Curtis sponsored the Indian Citizenship Act that made American Indians U.S. citizens but protected their indigenous property rights. After an unsuccessful campaign for the presidential nomination, Curtis ran on the ticket with Herbert Hoover in 1928, serving as vice president from 1929 to 1933. He was a deft politician who used his Indian background for personal advantage, even though his political adversaries called him "the

Injun." Although a fiscal conservative he supported veterans' benefits, farm relief, women's suffrage, and national prohibition.

The Hoover–Curtis ticket's bid for a second term in 1932 was defeated by Franklin Delano Roosevelt. Upon his retirement in 1933, Curtis had served longer in the Congress than any other active politician of his time. After leaving public office, he headed the short-lived National Republican League and practiced law in Washington, DC. Curtis was also president of a gold mining company in New Mexico. In 1936, he died of heart disease.

Bruce E. Johansen

See also Assimilation.

References and Further Reading

Schlup, Leonard. 1983. "Charles Curtis: The Vice-President from Kansas." *Manuscripts* 35 (Summer): 183–201.

Unrau, William E. 1989. *Mixed Bloods and Tribal Dissolution: Charles Curtis and the Quest for Indian Identity.* Lawrence: University Press of Kansas.

Deganawidah

The Haudenosaunee (Iroquois) Confederacy was formed by the Huron prophet Deganawidah (called the Peacemaker in oral discourse, ca. 1100–1180). Deganawidah enlisted the aid of Aiowantha (sometimes called Hiawatha) to spread his vision of a united Haudenosaunee confederacy. Deganawidah needed a spokesman because he stuttered in a culture that relied on verbal elocution. Oral history attributes the Peacemaker's stuttering to a double row of teeth. The Confederacy originally included the Mohawks, Oneidas, Onondagas, Cayugas, and Senecas. The sixth nation, the Tuscaroras, migrated into Iroquois country early in the eighteenth century.

As Hiawatha despaired at his inability to unite the contentious Iroquois, the prophet Deganawidah entered his life and changed the nature of things. Together, the two men developed a powerful message of peace. Deganawidah's vision gave Hiawatha's oratory substance. Through Deganawidah's vision, the Iroquois formulated their Constitution.

In his vision, Deganawidah saw a giant evergreen (Great White Pine), reaching to the sky and gaining strength from three counterbalancing principles of life. The first axiom was that a stable mind and healthy body should be in balance so that peace between individuals and groups can occur. Second,

Deganawidah stated that humane conduct, thought, and speech were requirements for equity and justice among peoples. Finally, he foresaw a society in which physical strength and civil authority would reinforce the power of the clan system.

Deganawidah's tree had four white roots that stretched in the four directions of the earth. From the base of the tree a snow-white carpet of thistle down covered the surrounding countryside. The white carpet protected the peoples who embraced the three double principles. On top of the giant pine perched an eagle. Deganawidah explained that the tree was humanity, living within the principles governing relations among human beings. The eagle was humanity's lookout against enemies who would disturb the peace. Deganawidah postulated that the white carpet could be spread to the four corners of the earth to provide a shelter of peace and brotherhood for all mankind. His vision was seen as a message from the Creator to bring harmony into human existence and to unite all peoples into a single family guided by his three dual principles.

With such a powerful vision, Deganawidah and Hiawatha were able to subdue the evil Tadodaho and transform his mind. Deganawidah removed evil feelings and thoughts from the head of Tadodaho and said "thou shalt strive . . . to make reason and the peaceful mind prevail." The evil wizard became reborn into a humane person charged with implementing the message of Deganawidah. After Tadodaho had submitted to the redemption, Onondaga became the central fire of the Haudenosaunee and the Onondagas became the firekeepers of the new Confederacy. To this day, the Great Council Fire of the Confederacy is kept in the land of the Onondagas.

After Tadodaho's conversion, the clan leaders of the Five Nations gathered around the Council Fire at Onondaga to hear the laws and government of the Confederacy. The fundamental laws of the Iroquois Confederacy espoused peace and brotherhood, unity, the balance of power, the natural rights of all people, and the sharing of resources. It also made provisions for the impeachment and removal of ineffective or inappropriate leaders. Moreover, the blood feud was outlawed and replaced by a Condolence Ceremony. Under this law, a grieving family could forego the option of exacting clan revenge (the taking of the life of the murderer or a member of the murderer's clan). Instead, it could accept twenty strings of wampum (freshwater shells strung together) from the slayer's family (ten for the dead

person and ten for the life of the murderer). If a woman was killed, the price was thirty wampum strings. Through this ceremony, the league reconciled conflict while reducing interpersonal violence. Deganawidah gave strict instructions governing the conduct of the league and its deliberations. Tadodaho was to maintain the fire and call the Onondaga chiefs together to determine if an issue brought to him was pressing enough to call to the attention of the Council of the Confederacy. If the proposed issue merited Council consideration, it would assemble, and Tadodaho would kindle a fire and announce the purpose of the meeting. The rising smoke penetrating the sky is a signal to the Iroquois allies that the Council is in session. The Onondaga chiefs and Tadodaho are charged with keeping the council area free from distractions.

Bruce E. Johansen

See also Haudenosaunee Confederacy, Political
    System; Hiawatha; Iroquois Great Law of
    Peace.

References and Further Reading

Parker, Arthur Caswell. 1916. *The Constitution of the
    Five Nations, or The Iroquois Book of the Great Law.*
    Albany: University of the State of New York.
Wallace, Paul A.W. 1946. *The White Roots of Peace.*
    Philadelphia: University of Pennsylvania Press.
Wallace, Paul A. W. 1948. "The Return of Hiawatha."
    *Quarterly Journal of the New York State Historical
    Association* 29, no. 4: 385–403.
Woodbury, Hanni, Reg Henry, and Harry Webster,
    comps. 1992. *Concerning the League: The Iroquois
    League Tradition as Dictated in Onondaga.*
    *(Algonquian and Iroquoian Linguistics Memoir No.
    9).* Edited by by John Arthur Gibson and Hanni
    Woodbury. Winnipeg, MB: University of
    Manitoba Press.

Deloria, Jr., Vine

In the 1960s, a thirty-one year old Hunkpapa Sioux from the Standing Rock Reservation with a long family heritage of social, political, and spiritual leadership descended on the national scene as executive director of the National Congress of American Indians (NCAI). Vine Deloria, Jr. (1933–2005) served three years as executive director of the NCAI, an experience that profoundly impacted his view of the *tipi sapa,* or sacred black lodge his great-grandfather saw in a vision a century earlier. Shocked by what he saw in Indian Country—and how American Indians were perceived—Deloria realized new tactics were

needed if tribal people were to survive the "chaotic and extreme individualism" of America (Deloria, 1985, 20). Over the next four decades, Deloria's prolific pen would profoundly impact the way Americans and the world viewed American Indians.

Little known outside national tribal leadership and scarcely known among the masses in Indian Country, Deloria "seized the nation by its lapels" with a series of provocative and insightful books in the late 1960s and 1970s. Until that time many Indians were viewed "as ciphers rather than as contemporary people facing issues such as education, jobs, healthcare and civil rights." While Indians were suitable for wall decorations, adorning the nation's coinage, and serving as foils in Western movies, they were viewed as neither modern nor political. "Indians were an unknown quantity," Deloria once observed. "There was a huge gap in how we were perceived by the average citizen and who we actually were" (Porter, 2002, 9).

Deloria poignantly outlined his intellectual and theoretical views in a 1969 book that shook the foundations of academia and religious institutions, challenging worldwide perceptions of American Indians. *Custer Died for Your Sins: An Indian Manifesto* set Deloria on the road to national prominence, calling for Indian self-determination within a political and cultural construct that was unique and separate from the larger American political and social constraints. Peoplehood was impossible, Deloria proclaimed, "without cultural independence, which in turn is impossible without land" (Deloria, 1969, 180).

The social and historical context within which Deloria came into prominence took root in the eighteenth century. "As long as any member of my family can remember," Deloria stated in 1969, "we have been involved in the affairs of the Sioux tribe." His intellectual and leadership abilities in the struggle for Indian rights came from carrying "on the leadership qualities of his father, grandfather, and great grandfather" and "stem[med] not only from his formal education and academic position but also from an extraordinary family heritage" (Hoover, 1997, 28). In reflecting on his family, Deloria once wrote that his great grandfather (Saswe), grandfather (Philip), and father (Vine, Sr.,) "created a family heritage that has been a heavy burden but that could not have been avoided once Saswe chose the red road [of leadership]" (Deloria, 2000, 84).

Vine Deloria, Jr., was born on March 26, 1933, in Martin, South Dakota, on the Pine Ridge Reservation. After attending elementary school in Martin,

Deloria graduated from St. James Academy in Faribault, Minnesota, before serving a three-year stint in the U.S. Marine Corps and attending Iowa State University, where he earned a bachelor's of science degree in 1958. He then earned a master's degree in theology from Augustana Lutheran Seminary in Rock Island, Illinois, in 1963. While he considered following his father's—and grandfather's and great-grandfather's—footsteps into the ministries of the Episcopal Church, Deloria chose a different path that centered on tribalism and traditional religious expressions.

In 1964, Deloria accepted a position with the United Scholarship Service in Denver, Colorado, to develop a scholarship program for American Indians to attend elite eastern preparatory schools. Later that year at the Sheridan, Wyoming, convention, he found himself elected executive director of the NCAI, a position he later said he was naïve enough to accept. Expected "to solve problems presented by tribes from all over the country," Deloria found the work challenging because of "unscrupulous individuals" who made tasks difficult to solve and accented the "great gap between performers and publicity" (Deloria, 1968). Financial concerns always threatened the NCAI and it was more than once on the verge of insolvency. When he left as executive director in 1967, Deloria realized "other tactics would have to be used to further the cause for Indian rights" (Deloria, 1969, 270–273).

Part of the new tactic was training Indian attorneys who could help tribes understand their rights and responsibilities. With this in mind, Deloria returned to school in 1967 and earned a law degree from the University of Colorado in 1970. While still in law school, Deloria wrote *Custer Died for Your Sins*, a book that became his best seller and one that parlayed his family heritage and legacy of leadership into national prominence. From 1970 to 1972, Deloria taught at Western Washington State College, from 1972 to 1974 at the University of California/Los Angeles, and from 1978 to 1990 at the University of Arizona, where he established an Indian policy studies program within the political science department and an American Indian studies program in 1982. Between 1990 and 2000 he was a professor at the University of Colorado, Boulder, where he retired from academia.

Putting action together with his desire to help tribes understand their rights, Deloria was one of three Indian attorneys to establish the Institute for the Development of Indian Law in 1970. This organization provided training and training materials for tribes and educational institutions around the country. He also served in organizations such as the Citizens Crusade against Poverty, the Council on Indian Affairs, the National Office for the Rights of the Indigent, the Indian Rights Association, and the Intertribal Bison Council. He was also a founding trustee on the board of the National Museum of the American Indian. As the preeminent scholar of protecting sacred lands, enforcing treaty rights, and repatriating cultural patrimony and burial remains, Deloria won numerous awards both in and outside of Indian Country.

Among the accomplishments of Vine Deloria, Jr. is a truly extraordinary event that shifted the foundation of an entire academic discipline and, in the process, created a more favorable view of American Indians and Indian tribes. The event was the publication of *Custer Died for Your Sins*, in which Deloria indicted anthropologists and put them on alert that American Indians refused to be imprisoned in their words and writings. In the process, Deloria gave voice to a whole generation of American Indians for the development of a distinct academic discipline of American Indian studies in which Indians themselves would define what was important.

In 1989, the American Anthropological Association convened a session entitled "Custer Died for Your Sins: A Twenty-Year Retrospective on Relations Between Anthropologists and American Indians." Its purpose was to explore what changes had occurred in Indian–anthropologist relations since *Custer* was first published. Out of this session came *Indians and Anthropologists: Vine Deloria Jr., and the Critique of Anthropology*, which initiated "a new period in relations between American Indian people and anthropologists in particular, between Indians and non-Indians in America generally, and between colonized peoples and the metropolis globally" (Biolsi and Zimmerman, 1997, 4).

Easily the "most influential polemicist" of the latter half of the twentieth century, Deloria "exceeded all others with similar motives" by using the social upheavals of the sixties as his forum to "represent a voice of outrage on behalf of Native Americans" (Hoover, 1997, 31). Those tutored under, and influenced by, Deloria's scholarship have built into their thinking new ethics and morality because of *Custer* and Deloria's subsequent writings. Anthropologist Murray L. Wax once credited "the shape-shifting Deloria—lawyer, priest, political scientist, prophet, educator, and satirist"—with shifting the

Vine Deloria, Jr., a Native American scholar, author, and activist, influenced two generations of leaders, Native and non-Indian. He died in 2005. (AP Photo)

orientation of the anthropologist from a "detached observer" to a "committed and engaged participant, linked to the local community" (Wax, 1997, 59).

Deloria acknowledged progress was made. "Scholars better understand their skills and the degree to which they can assist Indians," Deloria opined. "We have certainly not found paradise, but we have seen considerable light brought to bear on problems, and we can now make choices we could not make before." Nonetheless, the social sciences continue to be "a deeply colonial academic discipline." America has a "state religion," Deloria observed, "and it is called science," which controls the process of information about and interpretation of American Indians and their cultural patrimony. Scholars hiding behind the cloak of science will again "raise their voices" against American Indians in the future, Deloria predicts, because the real battle is "over control of definitions: Who is to define what an Indian *really* is?" (Deloria, 1997b, 210–212).

Long committed to the belief of getting "knowledge into the hands of ordinary people," Deloria spent a lifetime helping tribes and tribal people understand the basis of their existence, stressing the legal and moral basis of tribal political and social life. In *Tribes, Treaties, and Constitutional Tribulations* (1999), he provided an analysis of the U.S. government and how each branch relates to Indian tribes. In *Of Utmost Good Faith* (1971), Deloria provided an anthology of Indian legal papers, including Supreme Court rulings, treaties and agreements, legislative acts, and tribal speeches. In *American Indians, American Justice* (1983), *American Indian Policy in the Twentieth Century* (1985), *Behind the Trail of Broken Treaties* (1974), and *The Nations Within* (1984), Deloria provided a legal and historical framework of tribes in the United States. In *We Talk; You Listen: New Tribes, New Turf* (1970) and *God Is Red* (1973), he expounded on his theoretical framework that tribalism was the only alternative to modern life.

Deloria's recent books focused on the ideological foundations of Western science and its fallacies. *Red Earth, White Lies* (1995), *For This Land* (1999), *Spirit and Reason* (edited by his wife Barbara Deloria in 1999), and *Evolution, Creation and Other Modern Myths* (2002) all assailed Christianity and the religion of Western science while advocating a return to tribal ways. Tribal philosophies, Deloria theorized, were superior to both Western scientific interpretations and religious dogmas. Believing the real battle for survival was ideological, Deloria spent a lifetime educating Indians and non-Indians on spiritual matters that define ideology. For these efforts, *Time* magazine recognized Deloria as one of the ten most influential religious thinkers of the twentieth century.

In toto, Deloria's writings provide an insightful, scholarly and, at times, witty view of the nature of tribes and their dealings with the United States, demonstrating how and why at a philosophical level tribalism and tribal ways are superior to mainstream Western American ways. Tribal groups, Deloria once observed, "recognize the value of relations," which creates "a society of responsibility." To belong to a tribe, one had to "feed the poor," "take care of the orphans," and "provide for the elders." In short, tribalism was relational rather than institutional and hierarchal. American Indians, Deloria wrote in 1997, must "redefine their understanding of leadership to reflect traditional Indian ways." The key to returning to traditional leadership is to return to tribal ways, including the use of storytelling to help young people "feel they belong to something of their own" (Deloria, 1997a, 2, 4).

Deloria passed away November 13, 2005, at age seventy-two, in Golden, Colorado, after surgical complications. University of Colorado professor Charles Wilkinson called him "probably the most influential American Indian of the past century. He was also a wonderful human being, brilliant, bitingly funny, and profoundly warm and compassionate, always willing to lend a hand or raise a spirit" (Johansen, 2005, 7-B).

David H. DeJong

See also National Congress of American Indians; Tribal Sovereignty.

References and Further Reading

Biolsi, Thomas, and Larry J. Zimmerman. 1997. "What's Changed, What Hasn't." In *Indians and Anthropologists: Vine Deloria Jr., and the Critique of Anthropology*, 3–23. Tucson: University of Arizona Press.

Deloria, Vine, Jr. 1968. *Where Were You When We Needed You?* Washington, DC: National Congress of American Indians.

Deloria, Vine, Jr. 1969. *Custer Died for Your Sins: An Indian Manifesto*. New York: Macmillan.

Deloria, Vine, Jr. 1985. "Out of Chaos." *Parabola* 10, no. 2: 14–22.

Deloria, Vine, Jr. 1997a. *Tribal Sovereignty and American Indian Leadership*. St. Paul, MN: American Indian Policy Center.

Deloria, Vine, Jr. 1997b. "Anthros, Indians and Planetary Realities." In *Indians and Anthropologists: Vine Deloria Jr., and the Critique of Anthropology*, 209–222. Tucson: University of Arizona Press.

Deloria, Vine, Jr. 2000. *Singing for a Spirit: A Portrait of the Dakota Sioux*. Santa Fe, NM: Clear Light Publishers.

Hoover, Herbert T. 1997. "Vine Deloria Jr., in American Historiography." In *Indians and Anthropologists: Vine Deloria Jr., and the Critique of Anthropology*. Edited by Thomas Biolsi and Larry J. Zimmerman, 27–34. Tucson: University of Arizona Press.

Johansen, Bruce E. 2005. "Indian Country Hero Leaves Lasting Legacy." *Omaha World-Herald*, November 18: 7-B.

Porter, William. 2002. "Longtime Activist Vine Deloria Jr., to receive Wallace Stegner Award for His Cultural Contributions." *Denver Post*, October 24.

Wax, Murray L. 1997. "Educating an Anthro: The Influence of Vine Deloria Jr." In *Indians and Anthropologists: Vine Deloria Jr., and the Critique of Anthropology*. Edited by Thomas Biolsi and Larry J. Zimmerman, 50–60. Tucson: University of Arizona Press.

Deskaheh

Born in 1872, elevated to the position of *royaner* (hereditary chief) of the Cayuga nation under the name Deskaheh in 1917, Levi General died June 27, 1925. He is buried at the Cayuga Longhouse in Sour Springs. Deskaheh is well-known for his unsuccessful efforts between 1921 and 1925 to stop Canadian interference in Six Nations affairs by obtaining international recognition, through the League of Nations, of Haudenosaunee (Iroquois) sovereignty.

After 1918, the Canadian government, particularly the Department of Indian Affairs and its director Duncan Campbell Scott, refused to recognize the sovereignty of the traditional Six Nations' gover-

nance system at Grand River, Ontario. Adamant that the 1784 Haldiman Treaty had confirmed Haudenosaunee independence, Deskaheh traveled to England in 1921 with a petition for King George V. The petition was received by the colonial secretary, Winston Churchill, who returned the document to Canada.

Deskaheh and his American Lawyer, George Decker, then traveled to Geneva in 1923, where they convinced the Netherlands to lay Iroquois grievances before the League of Nations. Deskaheh, as a representative of the Six Nations, approached the Dutch based on a seventeenth-century mutual aid agreement.

On April 26, 1923, the Netherlands requested that the Iroquois petition be placed before the League of Nations Council. Following Britain and Canada's response, written largely at Scott's direction, the secretariat of the League presented the petition but failed to place it on the agenda for discussion. At this point the Netherlands withdrew its support. Much to the shock of Canada, Deskaheh twice requested, on August 7 and September 4, 1923, that the League grant the Six Nations formal membership as a state. Without the support of a member nation, however, Deskaheh's application was referred until September 27, when Ireland, Panama, Persia, and Estonia requested that the petition be presented to the League and the case for Iroquoian independence be brought before the International Court. Nonetheless, by 1924 Britain convinced Deskaheh's supporters to cease interference in an internal Canadian matter.

Meanwhile, in Canada, a federal order-in-council dissolved the Six Nation's Confederacy Council and created a democratically elected government subject to the Indian Act. Once elected, members of the democratic council, at the direction of their Indian Agent Colonel Morgan, proclaimed that Deskaheh was not an official representative. Also in 1924, in a dispute over land tenure between the traditional Council and Indian Affairs, an Ontario court ruled in *Garlow v. General* that Deskaheh's lands and possessions be confiscated and sold at auction. Colonel Morgan, after the Brant County sheriff refused to interfere because his authority did not extend to the Six Nations, auctioned Deskaheh's goods.

In the fall of 1924, Deskaheh returned to England to petition the king, an effort that failed. Deskaheh finally left Europe in January 1925, gave his last speech on Iroquois and Indian rights on March 10, and, after learning that his healer had not been allowed to cross the border, died on June 27. His funeral, three days later, was well attended by Haudenosaunee and the ever-watchful Royal Canadian Mounted Police. Canadian officials hoped that with the "troublemaker's" death the sovereignty issue would disappear. At the funeral, according to Iroquois customs, his brother Alexander General was elevated to *royaner* with the name of Deskaheh.

During his visits to Europe, many reporters, diplomats, and visitors were disappointed that Deskaheh failed to live up to their stereotype of a typical Indian chief. Much to Deskaheh's credit he refused to lower himself by playing Indian. Instead, he usually wore a simple brown suit and kept regular company with his lawyer, although photographs do exist of him in traditional garb.

While seeking to promote his people's sovereignty, Deskaheh's petitions and speeches form a wonderful corpus of material on indigenous rights and their trammeling by colonial powers. The most readily available materials by Deskaheh are the *Redman's Appeal for Justice* and his final speech on March 10, 1925.

Karl S. Hele

See also Democracy and Native American Images Among Europeans.
References and Further Reading
Rostowski, Joëlle. 1987. "The Redman's Appeal for Justice: Deskaheh and The League of Nations." In *Indians and Europe: An Interdisciplinary Collection of Essays.* Edited by Christian F. Feest, 435–453. Aachen, Germany: Rader Verlag.
Woo, Li Xiu (Grace Emma Slykhuis). No date. "The Truth About Deskaheh: Part II, III, IV." *Eastern Door.* Available at: www.easterndoor.com/9–10/9–10–4.htm and www.easterndoor.com. Accessed August 1, 2004.
Woo, Li Xiu (Grace Emma Slykhuis). 1999. "Canada v. the Haudenosaunee (Iroquois) Confederacy at the League of Nations: Two Quests for Independence." Ph.D. dissertation, M. en droit international—Université du Québec à Montréal.

Dodge, Henry Chee

Henry Chee Dodge (Hastiin Adiits'a'ii, "Man Who Interprets," ca. 1857–1947) was an influential leader

of the Navajo Nation for more than half a century, serving as the reservation government's chairman from 1923 to 1928 and from 1942 to 1946. Fluent in both English and Navajo when few were, Dodge played an influential role as a translator and political leader, working to expand the size of the Navajo Nation.

Dodge was born shortly before the Navajos' Long Walk to Fort Sumner, and his mother and father died when he was very young. Indian Agent W.F.M. Arn took an interest in young Dodge upon his return from the Long Walk, because he believed him to be the son of a former Indian Agent Henry Dodge. His father probably was more likely a captive Mexican, however. Upon returning from Fort Sumner, Dodge attended school for a short time in Fort Defiance. By 1882 he was serving as the official agency interpreter, and, having shown courage several times, he was put in charge of the Navajo police force and named head chief by the Indian agent. Dodge also made the first of eight trips to Washington, D.C., accompanying a delegation of Navajos to Grover Cleveland's inauguration in 1884. On his last trip in his eighties, he asked for more schools, hospitals, land, and irrigation facilities for the Navajos.

In 1890, Dodge invested in a partnership and bought the Round Rock Trading Post, which he comanaged. In 1892, when Agent David Shipley was surrounded and beaten at Round Rock while recruiting students for the Fort Defiance Boarding School, Dodge helped rescue and defend him for three days until soldiers came to the rescue. During the 1890s, Dodge also became a successful rancher at Crystal, New Mexico, and by 1907 he was a wealthy prominent Navajo headman.

In 1914, Dodge wrote the Secretary of the Interior stressing the need for more schools so that Navajo children could learn to speak English. He also stated that the allotment of the Navajo reservation would hurt most Navajos and that state governments had no interest in helping Navajos. In 1940 Dodge criticized day schools and the teaching of the Navajo language and asked for more boarding schools.

In 1922, Dodge was appointed a member of a three-man Navajo business council to sign oil leases by the U.S. government, and in 1923 a twelve-member Navajo council was elected and chose Dodge as chairman. He worked to get the money from the oil leases to benefit all Navajos, even those living off the reservation, rather than just those from the region where the oil was located.

Indian agents for the Navajo called for stock reduction because of overgrazing as early as the 1880s. The increasing Navajo population and their livestock impinged on their neighbors, including the Pueblo Indians. Dodge worked to get more land for the Navajo by cooperating with the demands of the federal government. In the 1920s, Jacob Morgan rose to prominence as Dodge's opponent, representing young assimilated Christian Navajos educated in boarding schools. Morgan questioned whether Dodge was really a Navajo and as a fundamentalist Protestant opposed Dodge's sympathy toward Catholics, the Native American Church, and traditional Navajo religion. Another strike against Dodge was his practice of the Navajo tradition of polygamy for wealthy Navajos, having over his lifetime eight wives, four of whom were sisters, and six children.

Dodge's son Thomas, an attorney, became tribal chairman in 1932, and in 1935 he was appointed assistant superintendent for the Navajo agency in an attempt to gain Navajo support for the Indian Reorganization Act, which the Navajos voted against. When John Collier became Commissioner of Indian Affairs in 1933 he pressured Thomas to implement stock reduction to protect Navajo lands from eroding away and filling up the newly built Boulder (now Hoover) Dam on the Colorado River. Increasing Navajo discontent toward stock reduction and the council's complicity led Thomas to resign the chairmanship in 1936.

Riding the antistock reduction sentiment of most Navajos, Morgan became tribal chairman in 1938 but was defeated by Dodge in 1942. Dodge's son Ben and his daughter Annie Wauneka, a respected health educator, also served on the Navajo tribal council.

Jon Reyhner

See also Economic Development.
References and Further Reading
Brugge, David M. 1985. "Henry Chee Dodge." In *Indian Lives: Essays on Nineteenth- and Twentieth-Century Native American Leaders.* Edited by L. G. Moses and Raymond Wilson, 91–112. Albuquerque: University of New Mexico Press.
Iverson, Peter. 2002. *Diné: A History of the Navajos.* Albuquerque: University of New Mexico Press.
Niethammer, Carolyn. 2001. *I'll Go and Do More: Annie Dodge Wauneka, Navajo Leader and Activist.* Lincoln: University of Nebraska Press.

Dull Knife

The harrowing march of Dull Knife and his Cheyenne compatriots from U.S. Army captivity toward their homeland in present-day Wyoming is described in Mari Sandoz's *Cheyenne Autumn* (1953). Dull Knife (ca. 1810–1883), as he was called by the Lakota, also was called Morning Star by the Cheyennes. Dull Knife, with Little Wolf, led the trek after their exile to Indian Country (Oklahoma today) late in the 1870s and 1880s.

Dull Knife and Little Wolf were among the Cheyennes who allied with the Lakota and other Native nations who defeated George Armstrong Custer at the Little Bighorn on June 25, 1876. The Army, reinforced with fresh troops, then pursued the Lakota and their allies. By 1877, U.S. Army troops chased Dull Knife into the Bighorn mountains near the head of the Powder River. The Cheyenne were then arrested and sent to Oklahoma, where, during the next several months, many of them died.

During mid-August 1878, the Cheyennes asked Indian Agent John Miles to let them leave Oklahoma for home. Miles, on superiors' orders, refused. The Cheyennes, who lacked food, took matters into their own hands, escaping homeward on foot. Early the next day 300 surviving Cheyennes started a march to their homelands in the Powder River Country, several hundred miles away. The next day, cavalry caught up with them on the Little Medicine Lodge River. The Cheyennes refused to surrender and continued their trek, repelling other attacks. They crossed the Arkansas and South Platte rivers. At White Clay Creek, Nebraska, they split into two groups. Dull Knife led 150 people to Red Cloud Agency, where they surrendered. Little Wolf and another 150 people hid in the Nebraska Sand Hills.

Little Wolf's band surrendered to Lieutenant W. P. Clark and an Army unit of Cheyenne and Lakota scouts the following March.

Back in Nebraska, Dull Knife's band arrived at the Red Cloud agency and found it abandoned, so they marched to Fort Robinson. Dull Knife's band lived at the fort two months. Officers at the fort then were ordered by superiors to force the Cheyennes back to Oklahoma. Dull Knife refused to go. Captain Wessells, the commanding officer, locked the Cheyennes in a freezing barracks with no food or water for three days. They refused to surrender.

On January 9, 1879, the Cheyennes broke out again. Fifty of them died that evening under fire by

Dull Knife and fellow chief Little Wolf led several hundred of their people in an epic march from Oklahoma toward their homelands in Montana during 1878. (National Archives and Records Administration)

troops; twenty more died of wounds and exposure. Most who survived, fewer than 100 survivors, were directed back to Fort Robinson under guard.

Dull Knife, his wife, and son then escaped once again, traveling eighteen nights on foot, resting by day, to Pine Ridge. They ate bark and their own moccasins to survive. At the Pine Ridge agency, Bill Rowland, an interpreter, housed the family. Thirty-one other warriors also escaped Fort Robinson. Troops followed them to Hat Creek Bluffs, where they called upon the warriors to surrender. The Cheyennes answered the command with their last three bullets. More shooting followed, killing twenty-eight Cheyenne. The last three survivors

stood up, using their empty rifles as clubs, and charged the 300 soldiers, who killed them.

John Ford, the well-known director of Westerns, released a film version of *Cheyenne Autumn* in 1964, his last Western film. Some reviewers believed that Ford's film was an apology for the excessive cruelty displayed toward Native peoples in his earlier films (Crowther, n.d.). Set in 1887, the film recounts the defiant migration of 300 Cheyennes from their reservation in Oklahoma territory to their original home in Wyoming. They have done this at the behest of Chiefs Little Wolf (Ricardo Montalban) and Dull Knife (Gilbert Rolands), played as "peaceful souls who have been driven to desperate measures because the U.S. government has ignored their pleas for food and shelter" (Crowther, n.d.). In the *New York Times*, reviewer Bosley Crowther described the film as a cinematic elegy—not only for the beleaguered Cheyennes, but for John Ford's fifty years in pictures" (Crowther, n.d.).

The bones of the dead Cheyennes later were turned over to the U.S. Army Medical Museum for scientific study. On October 8, 1993, the remains were returned to a delegation of sixteen Cheyennes in Washington, D.C., for reburial under the Native American Graves Protection and Repatriation Act of 1990.

Bruce E. Johansen

See also Relocation.
References and Further Reading
Crowther, Bosley. No date. "Movie Details: *Cheyenne Autumn.*" *New York Times.* Available at: http://movies2.nytimes.com/gst/movies/movie .html?v_id=9133. Accessed November 1, 2005.
Little Eagle, Avis. 1993. "Remains of Dull Knife's Band Make Final Journey Home." *Indian Country Today*, October 14.
Sandoz, Mari. 1992. *Cheyenne Autumn.* Lincoln: University of Nebraska Press. [Originally printed in 1953 Lincoln, NE: Center for Great Plains Studies.]
Wiltsey, Norman B. 1963. *Brave Warriors.* Caldwell, ID: Caxton.

Dumont, Gabriel

Born in 1837 at Red River, Rupert's Land (Manitoba), Gabriel Dumont (Métis) died May 19, 1906, at Bellevue (St.-Isidore-de-Bellevue), Saskatchewan.

Dumont is best-known for his role as a military leader in the 1885 Riel Rebellion. Prior to 1885, he was a community leader, bison hunter, ferry operator, store owner, and farmer. After 1885, Dumont worked seasonally in Buffalo Bill's Wild West Show (1886–1888), and became a symbol for Quebec nationalists (1888–1889). He returned in 1893–1894 to Batoche, Saskatchewan. Dumont married Madeline Wilkie at St. Joseph (Walhalla, North Dakota) in 1858. Madeline died in North Dakota in the spring of 1886. The couple had no children.

Dumont grew up on the Plains with his parents and extended family. He was involved in the 1851 battle between the Métis and Yankton Dakota at Grand Coteau. Dumont rose to the position of hunting leader in the Fort Carleton region (Saskatchewan) by the 1860s. In 1872, Dumont opened a ferry service and store on the Fort Carleton Trail. He was elected head of a council of eight in 1873. This council sought to govern the St. Laurent Métis community until the Northwest Territorial government established itself. In 1874, the North West Mounted Police (NWMP) investigated the council after the Fort Carleton Hudson's Bay Company factor charged the Métis government with sedition. While the NWMP cleared the council of the allegations, it ceased to function.

From 1877 to 1884, Dumont supported Métis petitions that requested land surveys and grants, representation on the Northwest Territories governing council, as well as assistance for schooling and farming. In 1878–1879, the river lot and square lot systems were surveyed in St. Laurent. Dumont and others demanded a resurvey according to the traditional river lot system. The Métis river lot system, drawn from their French heritage, consisted of narrow strips of land that fronted a river and extended in inland. The house constructed beside the river at the front of the lot, allowed for easy access to the river and gave the Métis access to farm land as well as a wood lot at the back. The square lot system, derived from the standard grid pattern township surveys, would arbitrarily cut across the river lots. The proposed solution to the issue, through the subdivision of the square lots into smaller sections that could then be pieced together to match the river lots, was complicated, confusing and appeared unnecessary to the Métis since they already had a viable system of land allotment. Instead, after delaying the decision, the Canadian government in Ottawa offered an awkward method

of legal subdivision of the square lots to mimic the river lot layout.

By 1884, survey and treaty issues in Saskatchewan created a tense atmosphere in which non-Native immigrants, Indians, and Métis were dissatisfied with the Canadian government. While discussing further petitions in March 1884, Dumont suggested that Louis Riel, based on his success in negotiating with the Canadian government during the 1869–1870 Red River Incident, be asked for assistance. Dumont and four others returned with Riel from North Dakota in July 1884. After eight months of lobbying Ottawa, Dumont and Riel concluded in February 1885 that Métis concerns would never be addressed. Dumont's unwavering support of Riel convinced many Métis to support the declaration of a provisional government and armed rebellion.

Hostilities commenced at Duck Lake when a Métis force led by Dumont defeated approximately 100 NWMP and 200 English-speaking settler volunteers who were attempting to arrest rebel leaders. Dumont forced Major-General Frederick Middleton to halt his advance toward Batoche for two weeks after a battle at Fish Creek. Following this engagement the Métis withdrew to defensive positions at Batoche, where they were defeated after a four-day battle (May 9–12). Dumont fled to the United States on May 27 upon hearing of Riel's surrender. American authorities arrested and later released Dumont after crossing the border. While in North Dakota, Dumont attempted to raise money and a force to liberate Riel from the Regina, Saskatchewan, jail.

While working in Buffalo Bill's Wild West Show, Dumont met members of New York's French community and began speaking about the 1885 rebellion. After giving a single lecture in Quebec, which shocked the nationalist French Canadian audience with its anticlerical tone, Dumont's planned speaking tour was cancelled. He remained in Quebec until the 1890s and dictated his rebellion experiences during the winter of 1889. In 1893, Dumont applied for scrip in Winnipeg, and resettled at his Batoche homestead. His death, while visiting a favorite nephew (Alexis Dumont) in 1906, passed unnoticed by Canada.

Dumont's role in the 1885 rebellion has been represented by scholars as either secondary or equal to that of Riel. Historians basing their work on Dumont's dictation of his experiences have focused on Riel's interference in military matters to explain why the Métis lost. According to Roderick C. Macleod (2004), documents and events indicate that neither Dumont nor Riel sought a far-reaching military campaign and engaged Canadian forces only when they entered Métis lands. Moreover, the Métis would have eventually been defeated regardless of Dumont's military acumen.

Karl S. Hele

See also Riel, Louis.
References and Further Reading
MacLeod, Roderick C. "Dumont, Gabriel." *Dictionary of Canadian Biography Online.* Available at: http://www.biographi.ca/EN/ShowBio.asp?BioId=40814&query=Dumont. Accessed December 30, 2004.
Stanley, George F. G. 1992. *The Birth of Western Canada: A History of the Riel Rebellions.* Toronto, ON: University of Toronto Press.
Woodcock, George W. 2003. *Gabriel Dumont.* Peterborough: Broadview Press.
Woodcock, George W. "Dumont, Gabriel." *The Canadian Encyclopedia.* Available at: http://www.thecanadianencyclopedia.com/index.cfm?PgNm=TCE&Params=A1ARTA0002444. Accessed December 30, 2004.

EchoHawk, Larry

Nationally distinguished for his work as a lawyer, legislator, and attorney general, Larry EchoHawk (Pawnee, b. 1948) started out on this path when the Shoshone-Bannock tribes of the Fort Hall Reservation hired him as their chief general counsel in the late 1970s. Over the next few years he won a seat in the Idaho Legislature, held the post of prosecuting attorney for Bannock County, and in 1991 was elected as attorney general of the state of Idaho. In 1994 he ran for governor of the state but lost. Since that time he has served as a law professor at Brigham Young University.

EchoHawk was born to a full-blooded Pawnee father and a German mother who raised him in Farmington, New Mexico. His father was an alcoholic. In elementary school he learned that Indians were dirty, savage heathens. He wasn't quite sure what to think of the fact that his legendary great-grandfather had fought on the side of the cavalry during the Indian Wars. During this time he struggled with his identity. At age fourteen he joined the Mormon Church. After reading the Book of Mormon he no longer felt inferior and found renewed pride in his heritage. He began to set goals and soon

excelled in high school athletics. As a child he had never expected to attend college, but when Brigham Young University (BYU) offered him a football scholarship in 1966 he accepted.

At BYU, EchoHawk excelled both on and off the football field. He was named to the Western Athletic Conference All-Academic football team in 1969 and prepared, upon graduation, to become a coach and educator. His older brother, John EchoHawk, persuaded him to change his career plans. John was soon to become the executive director of the Native American Rights Fund. He told Larry that attending law school would give him the power to change people's lives. Larry believed him and obtained his JD from the University of Utah in 1973.

After graduation, Larry spent a few years in Oakland working for California Indian Legal Services. In 1977 the Shoshone-Bannock tribes hired him as their attorney. He spent nine years in this position. In the 1980s he served two terms in the Idaho House of Representatives, during which he was named the best freshman legislator. In 1991 he made a bid for the position of state attorney general. Political analysts in Idaho figured he faced three disadvantages: He was a Mormon, a Democrat, and an Indian. On the national scene, however, his prospects looked quite promising. During the campaign he became the first Native American to head a state delegation at a national political convention. He prevailed and became the first American Indian in U.S. history to win a statewide election to a state constitutional office. However, not everyone viewed this as an unqualified victory for Native peoples.

Larry EchoHawk upset Idaho tribal leaders when he proposed an antigambling amendment to the state constitution. EchoHawk insisted early on that he was carrying out his obligations to uphold the state's laws. His Mormon upbringing undoubtedly was another reason for his opposition to tribal gaming. This stance cost him the support of Idaho tribes, who argued that tribal sovereignty and congressional legislation provided the necessary legal authorization for their casino operations. However, these local issues did little to stop EchoHawk's rise to national prominence. *Newsweek* named him one of twenty People to Watch in the West. In 1992 he served as a principal speaker at the Democratic national convention. EchoHawk's political fortunes began shifting two years later. Although he easily won the Democratic gubernatorial nomination, several Idaho tribes were reluctant to support him. Even though he had led his opponent in all the polls, on election day EchoHawk experienced his first loss in politics.

Since 1994, EchoHawk has served as a professor at the Brigham Young University J. Reuben Clark Law School. He has also become a stake (administrative office) president in the Mormon Church. In recent years he has called for greater tribal sovereignty and changed his stance on Indian gaming, finding it important to the economic development of tribes.

Sterling Fluharty

References and Further Reading

EchoHawk, Larry. 1995. "Achieving and Preserving the Promise of America." *Brigham Young University 1994–95 Devotional & Fireside Speeches*, 189–194. Provo, UT: Brigham Young University Publications & Graphics.
EchoHawk, Terry. 2003. *Why Do You Call Me Little Echo Hawk? The Story of My Name*. Scottsdale, AZ: Agreka Books.

Edwards, J. R.

"Junior" Edwards (Mohawk, 1958–1990) was killed during the early hours of May 1, 1990, during the culmination of firefights over commercial gaming that wracked the Akwesasne Mohawk (St. Regis) Reservation. Mathew Pyke also was killed that night, before police agencies from the United States and Canada occupied the area the next day. The body of Edwards, thirty-two, was found roughly six hundred yards from where Pyke had been killed, along the River Road in an area of Akwesasne called Snye. Edwards had been killed by a blast to the stomach.

Harold Edwards Sr., father of Edwards, said that the young man had been an innocent victim most of his life. The younger Edwards lived alone in a house owned by his father near Snye, drew welfare, and "at times, drank too much." While the younger Edwards did not overtly support gambling interests (the senior Edwards said his four other sons were gambling supporters), he was impressionable, and he sometimes associated with gaming sympathizers.

Edwards laid the blame for his son's death with the people who had brought the guns to Akwesasne. "Whoever killed my son, I don't blame them as much as the people bringing in the weapons in the first place," he said. "It's some other people who are bringing them in, and giving them to the Warriors,

and then they go crazy. I want the police to get the people who are bringing in the guns and the dope, even if they have to search every house to do it" (Johansen, 1993, 94).

Edwards' murder remains unsolved. Doug George-Kanentiio, an Akwesasne newspaper editor and antigaming activist, was charged with the murder by Quebec authorities, but was exonerated before a trial by a judge who said the charge was baseless.

Bruce E. Johansen

See also Reservation Economic and Social Conditions.
References and Further Reading
Johansen, Bruce E. 1993. *Life and Death in Mohawk Country.* Golden, CO: North American Press/Fulcrum.

Eliot, John

A Puritan missionary, translator, and writer in early colonial New England, John Eliot (1604–1690) became known as the Apostle to the Indians and is among the most famous early Anglo-American colonists. Little is known about Eliot's early life in England. Born in Widford, Hertfordshire, in August 1604, he was raised in Nazing, Essex. After enrolling at Jesus College, Cambridge, in 1618, Eliot received his baccalaureate in 1622. Eliot worked as Thomas Hooker's assistant at a Puritan academy in Essex until its closure in 1630. In 1631, Eliot arrived in Boston on the *Lyon,* a ship that also carried well-known colonists Margaret Winthrop and her stepson John Winthrop Jr. Eliot immediately took a position at the Boston church, moving in 1632 to become the teaching elder at the church in Roxbury, a position he held until 1688, two years before his death. Eliot outlived nearly every prominent first-generation Massachusetts Puritan (Cogley, 1999, 46).

Eliot is best-known for his mission work among the Algonquian-speaking peoples of Massachusetts. Around 1646, he began learning the Wôpanâak (Massachuset) language of southern New England. At this time, Eliot began the instruction of indigenous peoples in Christianity. In 1647,

A Puritan missionary, translator, and writer in early colonial New England, John Eliot became known as the Apostle to the Indians. *(Library of Congress)*

he began publishing a series of promotional tracts in England, aimed at generating financial support for proselytizing in the Massachusetts Bay colony. After some initial success with conversions among the Massachuset people, Eliot decided to establish "praying towns " where Christianized Natives could become fully assimilated to English and Christian ways of life in an atmosphere that he believed to be the key to lasting conversions.

In October 1650, Eliot and several proselytes chose the site of Natick along the Charles River as the site of the first praying town, a place where Christian Natives would live away from the influence of their unconverted friends and relatives. In total, the Puritans set up fourteen praying towns, which resembled the "reduction" type missions used in New France and Latin America, meant to remove Native people from their traditional cultures. In the praying towns, Natives adopted English dress and hairstyles, took up agriculture, and abandoned their traditional ways of life. Eliot preached to the Massachuset peoples in their Native language but stressed literacy as one of the keys to "civilizing" them. With the help of Native translators, Eliot translated and compiled what became the Indian Library, a series of pamphlets and devotional literature in the Wôpanâak language. Eliot's *A Primer or Catechism* appeared in 1654, and his translation of the entire Bible in the Native language— the first *Bible* printed in the Americas—was published in 1663. One of Eliot's famous booklets, *The Indian Dialogues* (1671), which consisted of fictional dialogues between Christian and non-Christian Natives about the benefits of conversion, illustrates the significance of literacy in the praying towns, as well as the divide in Native society that resulted from Eliot's missionary zeal.

George Tinker, an Osage religious studies scholar, suggests that Eliot's well-intentioned explicit goal—assimilating the indigenous population into English/Christian lifeways—was a significant aspect of European cultural genocide in the Americas. According to Tinker, the praying towns separated indigenous peoples from their families and community networks and were thus a major cause of social breakdown and alienation. According to Tinker, the creation of new economic, social, and government systems in the missions led to indigenous dependency on the English (Tinker, 1993, 21–41). Tinker writes: "In spite of his good intentions toward Indian peoples and his hopes for their conversion to Christianity, Eliot must be held histori-

cally accountable for the resulting cultural genocide of these peoples" (Tinker, 1993, 40).

Eliot's praying towns became weakened and were subsequently dismantled during Metacom's uprising (King Philip's War) against the English (1675). A census of the towns in 1674 reveals a population of 1,100 Christian Natives (Lepore, 1998, 370). During the bloody uprising, many indigenous peoples rejoined their communities to fight against the colonizers. John Eliot's mission work continued outside the praying towns, as he continued publishing and preaching up to his retirement in 1688.

Daniel Morley Johnson

See also Praying Villages of Massachusetts.
References and Further Reading
Cogley, Richard W. 1999. *John Eliot's Mission to the Indians Before King Philip's War.* Cambridge, MA: Harvard University Press.
Lepore, Jill. 1998. *The Name of War: King Philip's War and the Origins of American Identity.* New York: Vintage.
Tinker, George E. 1993. *Missionary Conquest: The Gospel and Native American Cultural Genocide.* Minneapolis, MN: Augsburg Fortress.
Wyss, Hilary. 2000. *Writing Indians: Literacy, Christianity, and Native Community in Early America.* Amherst: University of Massachusetts Press.

Emathla, Charley

Born a Creek in Georgia, Charley Emathla (Creek and Seminole, ca. 1790–1835) moved to Florida during the late 1820s, where he would become identified with the Seminole as an opponent of Osceola. Although many of the Georgia Creeks were forcibly relocated west of the Mississippi, Emathla settled on a small farm near Fort King (near Tampa, Florida) with a herd of cattle. He subsequently assumed a leadership role among the Seminoles. As a signatory of the Treaty of Payne's Landing in 1832, Emathla agreed to relocate to Indian Territory (later called Oklahoma). While accompanying a Seminole delegation to inspect the new lands promised in Indian Territory, he also signed the 1833 Treaty of Fort Gibson.

In June 1835, Indian Agent Wiley Thompson imprisoned Osceola, a leader of the Seminoles who opposed relocation. Having decided to resist the plans of Emathla and his supporters to leave for Oklahoma, Osceola pretended to change his posi-

Emathla, a Creek chieftain, was killed by Seminole Chief Osceola. (Library of Congress)

tion. He asked Emathla to intercede for him. Emathla, convinced of Osceola's sincerity, agreed to help. Osceola was released only after he promised to use his influence in favor of emigration.

Instead, Osceola met with other chiefs who were hostile to the move, and all agreed that death was the only appropriate penalty for any Seminole who sold his stock or otherwise prepared to leave. At this news, four hundred and fifty Indians who had agreed to emigrate fled to Fort Brooke for protection. Emathla continued to defy Osceola and openly sold his possessions. As Emathla was returning from the sale with his money, on December 18, 1835, he was ambushed and killed by Osceola's band. Some accounts say that Osceola threw the cattle money over Emathla's dead body as he awaited burial. Others say that he scattered the money to the four winds.

Osceola's faction then killed Agent Thompson on December 28, while another party massacred a military command under Major Francis Dade, after whom Dade County, Florida, is named. Their actions provoked the Second Seminole War (1835–1842).

Bruce E. Johansen

See also Osceola; Seminole Wars.

References and Further Reading
Bland, Celia. 1994. *Osceola, Seminole Rebel*. New York: Chelsea House Publishers.
Covington, James W. 1993. *The Seminoles of Florida*. Gainesville: University of Florida Press.
Mahon, John K. 1967. *History of the Second Seminole War, 1835–1842*. Gainesville: University of Florida Press.

Engels, Friedrich and the "Mother-right gens"

Karl Marx discovered the work of Lewis Henry Morgan during the late 1870s. Morgan's work contributed to American feminists' and European socialists' beliefs that one could improve society by looking back to the original state of humankind—the same sort of mirror on antiquity that Benjamin Franklin, Thomas Jefferson, and Thomas Paine had used in their analysis of American Indian societies a century earlier. In the nineteenth century as in the eighteenth, the image of the Indian served to provide antagonists to the European status quo with an alternative example of how societies ought to be organized and operated. The Iroquois Confederacy, a center of diplomatic activity in the eighteenth century, became the focus of Morgan's work in the nineteenth and so retained its pivotal position in the communication of these images between cultures.

Engels inherited Marx's copious notes on Morgan's *Ancient Society* (1877) and, after Marx's death in 1883, authored *The Origin of the Family, Private Property and the State* in 1886. Studying Morgan's account of "primitive" societies, with the Iroquois being his cornerstone, Engels provided what he believed to be an egalitarian, classless model of society that also provided justice between the sexes. In his work, Engels cited approvingly Morgan's assertion that "Democracy in government, brotherhood in society, equality in rights and privileges, and universal education, foreshadow the next higher plane of society to which experience, intelligence, and knowledge are steadily tending. It will be a revival, in a higher form, of the liberty, equality, and fraternity of the ancient gentes" (Grinde and Johansen, 1991, 230).

Engels' tone seemed to indicate that he had seen the future reflected in the past, and it worked. In this future, just as in Iroquois society, "Everything runs smoothly without soldiers, gendarmes, or police; without nobles, kings, governors, prefects, or judges;

Friedrich Engels was strongly influenced in his work on societal theory by Native American models. (Library of Congress)

prisons, without trials. All quarrels and disputes are settled by the whole body of those concerned . . . not a bit of our extensive and complicated machinery of administration is required. . . . There are no poor and needy. . . . All are free and equal—including the women" (Grinde and Johansen, 1991, 230).

Without making a specific citation, Engels evoked an image of Native American (likely Iroquois) society that was strikingly similar to Franklin's, a century before him: "All of the Indians of North America not under the dominion of the Spaniards are in that natural state, being restrained by no Laws, having no Courts, or Ministers of Justice, no Suits, no Prisons, no Governors vested with any Legal Authority. The Persuasion of Men distinguished by Reputation of Wisdom is the only Means by which others are govern'd or rather led—and the State of the Indians is probably the first State of all Nations" (Grinde and Johansen, 1991, 231).

Likewise, Jefferson wrote that American Indians had never "[s]ubmitted themselves to any laws, any coercive power or shadow of government. The only controls are their manners, and the moral sense of right and wrong. . . . There is an error into which most of the speculators on government have fallen, and which the well-known state of society of our Indians should have corrected. In their hypothesis of the origin of government, they supposed to have commenced in the patriarchal or monarchal form. Our Indians are evidently in that state of nature which has passed the association of a single family, and not yet submitted to authority of positive laws, or any acknowledged magistrate" (Grinde and Johansen, 1991, 231).

The "error" was the same one Marx and Engels had made in the first edition of *The Communist Manifesto*. Beholden to their own times and perceptions, Marx and Engels in 1848 had yet to shed their Eurocentric notions that history had begun with patriarchal, monarchial governments. Imagine how the discovery of societies that operated differently must have fascinated Marx, Engels, and the early feminists—much as it earlier had intrigued some of the United States' major architects, whose intellectual heritage we can trace back, in remarkably similar words, to Montaigne, Locke, Rousseau, among others, as well as to the American Indian confederacies (among other non-European societies), which provided the raw observational material for the philosophers and the instigators of Enlightenment-era revolutions.

Having rediscovered the "mother-right gens," Engels could scarcely contain himself: "It has the same significance for the history of primitive society as Darwin's theory of evolution has for biology, and Marx's theory of surplus value for political economy. . . . The mother-right gens has become the pivot around which this entire science turns" (Grinde and Johansen, 1991, 231).

Bruce E. Johansen

See also Democracy and Native American Images among Europeans; Marx, Karl, and Native American Societies.

References and Further Reading

Engels, Frederick. 1968. "Origin of the Family, Private Property, and the State." In *Selected Works*. Vol. 3. By Karl Marx and Frederick Engels. London: Lawrence & Wishart.

Grinde, Donald A., Jr., and Bruce E. Johansen. 1991. *Exemplar of Liberty: Native America and the Evolution of Democracy*. Los Angeles, CA: UCLA American Indian Studies Center.

Episcopal Church

The Episcopal church, a Protestant denomination, played a major role in the implementation of the Peace Policy to assimilate Indians into American society during the late nineteenth century.

The Episcopal Church of the United States of America was established in 1783 as the church for American Anglicans after the achievement of independence from Great Britain. The key features of this denomination are its governance by a General Convention selected by members and the reliance on bishops to define the work of the church in their individual geographic areas, known as dioceses.

International Anglican missionary organizations were of little consequence in the United States because the church developed its own organization for foreign and domestic missions in 1820. Episcopal mission work with Indians had the twin goals of Christianization and assimilation of Native Americans achieved through the development of Indian clergy and reservation-based schools. The emphasis on education also was a part of the church's foreign missions and its outreach to freedmen in the post–Civil War South.

Approximately two-thirds of the Episcopal church's Indian work has been and remains in South Dakota, with missions to the Navajo the most prominent of its other efforts. The focus on the Sioux of South Dakota was the result of the work of Bishops H. Benjamin Whipple of Minnesota in the 1860s and William Hobart Hare, who was named Bishop of the Niobrara District in 1873 and made responsible for all Episcopal missions to the Sioux within the Great Sioux Reservation.

The Right Reverend Mr. Whipple gained national recognition for his humane response to Indian needs following Sioux attacks on Minnesota towns in 1862. His comments helped people to distinguish between active participants and innocent Indian neighbors in the face of the general tendency to classify all Indians as hostile. Episcopal missionaries fostered by Whipple in the years before this conflict accompanied the Indian communities when they were removed to new reserves along the Missouri River. These events made it logical for the administrators of President Grant's Peace Policy to assign the Episcopal church a major role among the Sioux in the trans-Missouri West.

The church responded to the new U.S. policy by creating the Niobrara jurisdiction to administer its work with the Sioux. William Hobart Hare, who was serving as secretary for the committee overseeing foreign missions, was consecrated Bishop of the Niobrara in 1873 after Bishop Whipple rejected the extension of his ongoing responsibilities to a new region.

Bishop Hare continued the effort of Bishop Whipple to develop Indian clergy to minister to Native people. In addition, he elevated the role of the Episcopal church among the Friends of the Indians. His invitation to Herbert Welsh, an artist and social reformer, and Henry Pancoast, a lawyer, in 1882 provided a stimulus to the creation of Indian Rights Association. Hare's writings appeared in national publications and his voice was heard during meetings of the Lake Mohonk Conference. His advocacy for assimilation included support for the breakup of the Great Sioux Reservation into smaller reserves and the allotment of Indian land into individual holdings. His term of service ended with his death in 1909.

The onset of the twentieth century ended the heroic age of Episcopal missionary work among Indians. Financial support from the federal government for sectarian schools began to decline in the late nineteenth century; local and denominational sources of funds could not make up the difference. Furthermore, national attitudes toward race turned against assimilation around the start of the twentieth century. A shift toward racism occurred in the wake of American imperial ventures overseas and the onset of segregation in the South. At the same time, growing national support for cultural pluralism reduced support of assimilation by emphasizing the need to respect cultural differences. Government policies that reduced or eliminated the use of tax dollars for mission schools hit the Episcopal church's missionary work harder than the later passage of the Indian Reorganization Act of 1934, which sought to restore the traditional spiritual perspectives of Indians.

The evaluation of the missionary efforts of the Episcopal church in the early twenty-first century is mixed. Data suggest many American Indians are rejecting Christianity and turning more to traditional expressions of spirituality. Within the church are now a number of Indian clergy; in the years since the consecration of Harold Jones as the first bishop of Indian heritage, the number of Native bishops has grown. A series of face-to-face meetings connect Bishop Jones directly to the efforts of the Indian clergy created by Bishops Whipple and Hare.

The national archives of the Episcopal church are located on the campus of the Episcopal Theological

Seminary of the Southwest in Austin, Texas. Each diocese has its own archives whose locations have been determined locally.

David S. Trask

References and Further Reading
Anderson, Owanah. 1997. *400 Years: Anglican/Episcopal Mission Among American Indians.* Cincinnati, OH: Forward Movement Publications.
Cochran, Mary E. 2000. *Dakota Cross-Bearer: The Life and World of a Native American Bishop.* Lincoln: University of Nebraska Press.

Erasmus, George Henry

George Henry Erasmus, born in 1948 in Rae-Edzo, North West Territories, is widely known as a Canadian crusader for Native rights and self-government. Erasmus, who holds seven honorary doctorate degrees, came into public prominence in Canada during the early 1970s as the leader of the Indian Brotherhood of the North West Territories. He went on to become the president of the Dene Nation, the national chief of the Assembly of First Nations, and cochair of the historic Royal Commission on Aboriginal Peoples. All his life he has fought for the rights of Native peoples to control their own lives and their own lands.

A Dene raised in Yellowknife, Erasmus witnessed the impoverished plight of his people and has fought to break the cycle of alcoholism, poverty, and dependence on government handouts by advocating political sovereignty. Erasmus became a leader in the NWT Indian Brotherhood, and, at twenty-eight, he become president of the Dene Nation, a position he held for seven years. He voiced crucial environmental and land title concerns on behalf of the Dene people during the Berber pipeline inquiry in 1974, when a pipeline was being proposed to carry oil through the Mackenzie River Valley in the North West Territories. In 1975, Erasmus advocated for the historic Dene Declaration, which declared the sovereignty of the Dene Nation.

In 1985 Erasmus was elected as national chief of the Assembly of First Nations, Canada's largest Native organization. The Assembly of First Nations was born out of the National Indian Brotherhood and represents 630 First Nations communities in Canada. His goals were to unite the First Nations of Canada with the Métis and Innuits and to negotiate with the provincial and federal governments on behalf of all Native peoples in the country.

As national chief, Erasmus participated in the First Ministers Conferences on constitutional matters directly affecting aboriginal peoples of Canada. He became known there as Canada's eleventh premier. At the final conference, in 1987, the federal and provincial governments unanimously failed to recognize the inherent right of self-government for aboriginal peoples. Despite this roadblock, Erasmus and the Assembly of First Nations won support from some of the provinces and accomplished a heightened awareness of issues affecting Native peoples. Under Erasmus the public profile of the AFN rose to new heights.

Erasmus was reelected as national chief in 1988 and served until 1991. During this time he brought many aboriginal issues to the attention of the Canadian public. In one speech he expressed the frustration and anger of Native peoples toward government inaction. He warned that, if politicians did not seek peaceful solutions with his generation of leaders, the next generation may resort to violent political action. In 1990, his warning was realized in the Oka Crisis, a violent political standoff between Native peoples and the government over a proposed golf course expansion on Mohawk burial grounds.

In 1991, Erasmus was appointed as cochair to the Royal Commission on Aboriginal Peoples along with Judge René Dussault to hear from aboriginal peoples in Canada and recommend solutions to ongoing problems. After five years of hearings and studies, the Commission recommendations included that a distinct body of aboriginal government should exist within the Canadian government, that aboriginal nation governments should be given province-like power, and that the Department of Indian and Northern Affairs should be abolished and replaced with a Department of Aboriginal Relations and a Department of Indian and Inuit Services. Critics in the Canadian government rejected the recommendations as too costly and unrealistic.

Despite government inaction on issues he advocates, Erasmus is a highly respected leader. He was made an officer of the Order of Canada in 1999, after being appointed as a member in 1987. He has also been the Canadian delegate to the World Council of Indigenous Peoples.

In 1998, Erasmus became the head of a new organization, the Aboriginal Healing Foundation. The multimillion-dollar fund for the foundation was

the result of a contribution from the Canadian government as a statement acknowledging its role in inflicting damage on Native peoples through the residential school system. The purpose of the foundation is to address the legacy of physical and sexual abuse suffered by the students of the residential schools.

Aliki Marinakis

See also Assembly of First Nations; Royal Commission on Aboriginal Peoples.

References and Further Reading

CBC Archives. No date. "George Erasmus: Native Rights Crusader." Available at: http://archives.cbc.ca/300i.asp?id=1–73–516. Accessed March 13, 2005.

Indian and Northern Affairs Canada. 2004. Aboriginal People Profiles. "George Erasmus-Chief." Available at: http://www.ainac-inac.gc.ca/ks/3108_e.html. Accessed May 15, 2005.

Indian and Northern Affairs Canada. No date. "Royal Commission on Aboriginal Peoples." Available at: http://www.ainac-inac.gc.ca/ch/rcap/index_e.html. Accessed May 5, 2005.

Richardson, Boyce, ed. 1989. *Drumbeat: Anger and Renewal in Indian Country.* Toronto, ON: Summerhill Press.

McNab, David T. 2001. "Of Beads and a Crystal Vase: Michael Dorris's *The Broken Cord and Cloud Chamber.*" *West Virginia University Philological Papers* 47: 109–119.

Erdrich, Louise

Louise Erdrich is an international writer of fiction, poetry, and nonfiction, and she presently resides in Minneapolis, Minnesota. As the oldest child, she was born in Little Falls, Minnesota on June 7, 1954, and named Karen Louise by her father, with an Anglicized form of her German grandfather's name [Ludwig Erdrich (1895–1962)]. Since she was a girl, her name was Americanized to Louis and feminized to Louise. Her parents are Rita Gourneau and Ralph Louis Erdrich, who still reside in Wahpeton, North Dakota. She is an enrolled member of the Turtle Mountain Band of Chippewas residing at the Turtle Mountain Reservation in North Dakota, just south of the international border between Canada and the United States. Members of this community include Anishinabe (Ojibway or Chippeway), and Cree/Métis people. Erdrich's father is a first-generation German American, and her mother is of Anishinabe/Cree/Métis descent. This family history informs Erdrich's writings, and her stories come from these places and the families who reside there.

To date, Erdrich's life can only be described as meteoric and tragic, greatly influenced as she was by her marriage in 1981 to another German American (who was also of Irish descent), Michael Dorris (1945–1997). Dorris was raised by his mother and her two sisters, named Burkhardt, in Kentucky after his father apparently died in Germany as an American serviceman in 1945. Dorris was Erdrich's teacher and collaborator in the 1980s and 1990s, and eventually he became her literary agent. A writer as well as professor and chair of the Native studies program at Dartmouth College, Dorris was separated from Erdrich in the mid-1990s and subsequently committed suicide in April 1997. He left his three older adopted children and his three young daughters from his marriage with Louise.

Erdrich's literary works include both fiction and nonfiction, poetry, and children's books, as well as eleven collections of stories in the form of novels: *Love Medicine* (1984, republished with additional material in 1993), *The Beet Queen* (1986), *Tracks* (1988, with Michael Dorris), *The Crown of Columbus* (1991), *The Bingo Palace* (1994), *Tales of Burning Love* (1996), *The Antelope Wife* (1998), *The Last Report on the Miracles at Little No Hors* (2001), *The Master Butchers Singing Club* (2003), *Four Souls: A Novel* (2004), and *The Painted Drum, A Novel (2005).* Her poetry has been published in the following volumes: *Jacklight: Poems* (1984), *Baptism of Desire: Poems* (1989), and most recently *Original Fire: Selected and New Poems.* The last provides the images and part of the German family history, which finds its way into her *The Master Butchers Singing Club.* Her nonfiction writings include *Route 2* (1991, with Michael Dorris), *The Blue Jay's Dance: A Birth Year* (1995), and most recently *Books and Islands in Ojibwe Country* (2003). She has also published children's books: *Grandmother's Pigeon* (1996), *The Birchbark House* (1999), and *The Game of Silence* (2005). She illustrated the latter two works. Many other stories have been published in literary and other magazines and then often republished in the collections of fiction noted above. Erdrich has two clans on her mother's side of her family, both of which are significant. On her Anishinabe side, Erdrich is a Be-nays, a bird of the Great Blue Heron (Crane) Clan. In the Anishinabe clan system, the birds are spiritual leaders. On her mother's side of the family, she is also Cree/Métis of the Bear Clan. Erdrich has described her family

history in her autobiography of a birth year, *The Blue Jay's Dance.* Her great-grandmother on her mother's side was a "pure Canadian" named Virgina Grandbois (literally "Virginia of the large forest"). She reported on her family history that in 1782 "All land west of the Appalachians was still Indian territory and the people from whom I am descended on my mother's side, the Ojibwa or Anishinabe, lived lightly upon it, leaving few traces of their complicated passage other than their own teeth and bones. They levered no stones from the earth. Their houses, made of sapling frames and birchbark rolls, were not meant to last." There was no international border between Canada and the United States. In 1882 things had been altered: "The last of the Indian treaties were signed, opening up the West. Most of the Anishinabe were concentrated on small holdings of land in the territory west of the Great Lakes. The Turtle Mountain people wore trousers and calico dresses, drove wagons, spoke their own language, but also attended Holy Mass." More than one hundred years later, her maternal grandfather Patrick Gourneau, a former tribal chair, passed away. Erdrich then went home to Turtle Mountain—always border country inhabited by the Anishinabe, Cree, and Métis—for the funeral at St. Ann's Church. She described the graveyard: "The graves of Ojibwa, Cree, and Mitchif Catholics, guarded by statutes of cast concrete and plastic, march up a windy hill. Our Catholic great-great-grandparents are buried behind the church, and the pagans, the traditionals, lie yet in another graveyard, where the uneven markers are crowded by sage and wild prairie rose." In the section entitled "Three Photographs," Erdrich provides a brief glimpse into the richness of the mother's family history. "Mary Lefavor," my grandmother—Ojibwa, French, and Scots [and certainty Métis/Cree], perhaps a descendent of the Selkirkers of Rudolph's land (Canada)—stand beside a fellow first communicant."

As a youngster growing up in Wahpeton, North Dakota, Erdrich was influenced by her father, who paid her a nickel for each story she wrote. Ralph Erdrich taught at the Bureau of Indian Affairs boarding school in the town, and thus none of the family's children were allowed to attend that school. Louise and her brothers and sisters went to the local schools in Wahpeton in what has been described as a fairly diverse community of German-Americans, Norwegian-Americans, and Native Americans residing along the banks of the Red River. After completing high school, Erdrich worked at many small short-term jobs in the American West, and these experiences have found their way into her works of fiction. At the age of twenty-eight, she applied to Dartmouth College and became one of the first women admitted to the first coeducational class in the history of that college. (The same year [1972] Dorris came to Dartmouth and began the Native studies program.) After graduation, Erdrich returned home and spent some time teaching poetry in the local community. Returning to the East, she entered the graduate writing program at Johns Hopkins University in 1976, and, upon graduation, remained in the eastern United States writing poetry and working at various writing jobs. She returned to Dartmouth in 1979 to give a poetry reading and to renew her acquaintance with Dorris. For the next few years, Erdrich was a resident at New Hampshire's Macdowell Colony and then a visiting fellow and writer in residence at Dartmouth College. After her marriage, Erdrich moved from the writing of poetry to fiction, taking the images and the characters from her poetry and writing stories that were initially published in various literary magazines.

Her breakthrough came in 1981 when she won the Nelson Algren fiction contest with her story "The World's Greatest Fisherman," which is a central story in her first novel, *Love Medicine.* This work began her North Dakota series of fictional works, which have often been described as novels. In fact, her fictional works are in the form of interconnecting stories about aboriginal and nonaboriginal people that intersect for the most part with aboriginal places. Erdrich's writings can be roughly and rather arbitrarily divided into two phases, which include those published prior to 1996 and those published thereafter. The former were published in various forms of collaboration with Dorris before they were separated. The latter include those published since that time. All of her fictional collections have a dominant theme of Earth, Water, Air, or Fire.

Ute Lischke and David T. McNab

References and Further Reading
Beidler, Peter and Gay Barton. 1999. *A Reader's Guide to the Novels of Louise Erdrich.* Columbia, OH: University of Missouri Press.
Benton-Banai, Edward. 1988. *The Mishomis Book.* Minneapolis, MN: Red School House.
Chavkin, Allan, and Nancy Feyl, eds. 1994. *Conversations with Louise Erdrich & Michael Dorris.* Literary Conversations Series. Jackson: University Press of Mississippi.

Erdrich, Louise. 2002. "Fleur-de-Lis." In *Sister Nations, Native American Women Writers on Community*. Edited by Heid E. Erdrich and Laura Tohe, 114–120. St. Paul: Minnesota Historical Society Press.

Gish, Robert F. 1999. "Life into Death, Death into Life, Hunting as Metaphor and Motive in *Love Medicine*." In *The Chippewa Landscape of Louise Erdrich*. Edited by Allan Chavkin, 67–83. Tuscaloosa: University of Alabama Press.

Martin, Sandra. 2003. "Balancing Act in Art and Life." Telephone interview with Louise Erdrich. *Toronto Globe and Mail*, March 19: R3.

McNab, David T. 1999. *Circles of Time: Aboriginal Land Rights and Resistance in Ontario*. Waterloo, ON: Wilfrid Laurier University Press.

McNab, David T. 2001. "Of Beads and a Crystal Vase, Michael Dorris's *The Broken Cord and Cloud Chamber*." *West Virginia University, Philological Papers*, 47 :109–119.

McNab, David T. 2001. " 'Time Is a Fish:' The Spirit of Nanapush and the Power of Transformation in the Stories of Louise Erdrich." In *(Ad)dressing Our Words: Aboriginal Perspectives on Aboriginal Literature*. Edited by Armand Garnet Ruffo, 181–204. Penticton, BC: Theytus Books.

White Weasel, Charlie (Gourneau), Pembina, and Turtle Mountain Ojibway (Chippewa). 1994. *History from the Personal Collection and Writings of Charlie White Weasel*. Privately printed in Canada.

Erickson, Leif

Two ancient Norse sagas, *Erik's Saga* and *The Greenlanders' Saga*, describe the lives of Leif Erickson and his father, Erik the Red. Erik the Red was a notorious outlaw, who, when banished from Norway for murder, moved to Iceland where he started a family. His oldest son, Leif, was born in Iceland at the end of the eighth century. When Leif was a child, Erik was once again tried for murder and banished. Leaving his family in Iceland, Erik set out to explore the western sea. One thousand miles to the west of Iceland, he encountered a large landmass with good pasturage along its southern coast and inner fjords. He spent three years in this new land before returning to Iceland. Upon his return, he organized a group of colonists, including his family, to establish a colony in the new land, which he called Greenland.

Despite its name, Greenland has a harsh and unforgiving climate. When the settlers arrived, they found only a few wind-stunted trees and more than 80 percent of the land covered with ice year-round.

As leader of the Greenland settlement, Erik chose the best farm site for himself. He established a farm, Brattahlid, on the southern tip of the island. Erik's four children grew up at Brattahlid, where they learned the skills necessary to survive in the far north. Eventually, Leif married and had a son. After his father's death, Leif took over management of Brattahlid.

To survive in Greenland, the medieval Norse exploited all possible means of subsistence. They trapped, gathered wild plants, fished, and hunted. When wild resources were scarce, their farms helped sustain them. Considering the difficulty of life in Greenland, it is easy to understand why the Norse Greenlanders continued to search for other lands to colonize.

Around the year 1000, Leif outfitted a ship with more than thirty oarsmen and set out to explore lands to the west of Greenland. The sagas contain such a detailed description of this voyage that they have allowed modern scholars to retrace Erickson's path. His ship most likely traveled north up the western coast of Greenland, then crossed the Davis Strait to Baffin Island. Leif and his men rowed a small boat ashore on the Baffin coast, but, finding the land unsuitable, they returned to the ship and headed south to Labrador, and ultimately to a land Erickson named Vinland, which scholars believe was located on the Canadian island of Newfoundland.

Erik's Saga tells us that Erickson and his men found Vinland so appealing and hospitable that they built a large sod house there where they spent the winter. The sagas recount that Erickson named the land Vinland, meaning "land of wine," because he found grapes growing there. This element of the sagas has been hotly debated, however. Although the ruins of a Norse settlement that conforms closely to saga accounts have been discovered on Newfoundland, the ruins lie nearly 1,000 miles north of today's vines. Several theories have been offered to explain this inconsistency. The historian Helge Ingstad has suggested that the name *Vinland* is derived not from the Old Norse term for "wine," but from a similar Norse word meaning "meadow." According to this theory, the story about the grapes was a late addition to the sagas, inserted to explain the origin of Vinland.

Though they likely intended to do so, the Norse Greenlanders were not able to establish a permanent Vinland settlement. This was due at least in part to conflict between the Norse and the Native Newfoundlanders. Artifacts excavated at the L'Anse aux

Meadows Norse settlement site in Newfoundland indicate that Beothuk Indians and Dorset Eskimos occupied the area at the time of the Norse settlement. The sagas tell of conflicts between the Norse and the Natives. The Norse, who feared the Natives, were known to attack with little provocation. This resulted in vengeance attacks by the Natives, who vastly outnumbered the settlers.

Although archaeologists cannot prove that the ruins at L'Anse aux Meadows are the remains of Leif Erickson's Vinland settlement, it is clear that the Norse visited North America 500 years before Columbus. Yet Columbus and the Norse saw their discoveries in a completely different light. Unlike Columbus, the Norse did not know that they had discovered a new continent, and they received neither fame nor lasting wealth from their discovery.

Amy L. Propps

See also L'Anse aux Meadows Viking Settlement; Norse Exploration of North America.

References and Further Reading

Engstad, Helge. 2001. *The Viking Discovery of America: The Excavation of a Norse Settlement in L'Anse aux Meadows, Newfoundland*. New York: Checkmark Books.

Johnston, George, trans. 1976. *The Greenlanders' Saga*. Ottawa, ON: Oberon Press.

Jones, Gwen, trans. 1961. "Eirik the Red." *Eirik the Red and Other Icelandic Sagas*. New York: Oxford University Press.

Eskiminzin

A leader of the Arivaipa Apache band in the late nineteenth century, Eskiminzin guided his people through the turbulent first years of American colonialism in southern Arizona. Known by various names, including Es-kin-in-zin and Skimmy, "Eskiminzin' is an approximation of the Apache name, Haské Bahnzin (Anger Stands Beside Him). Haské Bahnzin lived a remarkable and difficult life, not only as a leader of a Native community threatened from every corner, but also as a farmer, warrior, husband, diplomat, rebel, father, and prisoner.

Although Haské Bahnzin was born into the Pinal band of western Apaches, he married into the closely related Arivaipa band, or *tcéjìné* (Dark Rocks People), who farmed and gathered along Arivaipa Creek and the San Pedro River in southern Arizona. Even decades after his death, Haské Bahnzin was remembered as a generous man, who welcomed relatives to gather in the San Pedro Valley. Despite the abundance of the land, Apache lifeways were not entirely tranquil. Haské Bahnzin certainly participated in the violence of war and raiding that pitted Apaches against the Mexican and American empires throughout the 1800s.

In February of 1871, after an especially harsh winter, Haské Bahnzin arrived at Camp Grant, a U.S. Army installation on the San Pedro River, asking for peace. Several months later, more than 400 Apaches had surrendered to the Army and were living peacefully at *gashdla'á cho o'aa* (Big Sycamore Stands There), five miles from Camp Grant. Nearby Chiricahua Apaches continued raiding and Tucson leaders mistakenly believed those camped at *gashdla'á cho o'aa* were responsible. In a surprise attack on *gashdla'á cho o'aa*, the Tucsonans and their Tohono O'odham allies killed more than 100 Apaches and took close to thirty children as slaves. Haské Bahnzin lost most of the Arivaipa band, as well as his own wife and children, in the Camp Grant massacre.

In the wake of the massacre, Haské Bahnzin returned to a life in the mountains. During the months that followed, people accused him of committing murders and attacks; however, none of these accusations have been convincingly proven. In 1872, he and his fellow tribesmen returned to Camp Grant, this time to have peace talks with government authorities, Tucson businessmen, and Tohono O'odham leaders. From these discussions, Eskiminzin agreed to move north and settle along the San Carlos River.

Life at San Carlos was not altogether uneventful for Haské Bahnzin. In 1874, he was arrested as a prisoner of war. Later released, he began a farm and continued to mediate among Apaches and government officials. John P. Clum, an Indian agent at San Carlos, befriended Haské Bahnzin and took him across the continent to Washington, D.C., in 1876. He made the trip east again in 1888 to meet President Grover Cleveland.

In 1877, Haské Bahnzin moved to *nadnlid cho* (Big Sunflower Hill), now the town of Dudleyville, in the San Pedro Valley. There he settled down to a successful life as a farmer and rancher. Shortly after he built a home, three or four additional Apache families joined him, also erecting houses and fences and cultivating the land. However, later that year, an Indian agent warned Haské Bahnzin that 150 armed citizens were coming to kill him. With the memory of the massacre at Camp Grant, he fled. He later said Tucsonans stole 513 sacks of grain, 523 pumpkins,

and thirty-two cattle. After his escape, Haské Bahnzin was asked if he might return to San Pedro but replied, "I would not be safe there and would feel like a man sitting on a chair with some one scratching the sand out from under the legs" (Clum 1929, 22).

Haské Bahnzin went back to San Carlos and tried to begin a new life. Several years later, he was arrested due to vague accusations of aiding Apache fugitives. Sent to Mount Vernon Barracks, Alabama, in shackles, he was eventually released with the help of his old friend, John Clum. But only a year after gaining his freedom, on December 16, 1895, Haské Bahnzin died of chronic stomach pain in obscurity and poverty. The site of his grave remains unknown today.

Chip Colwell-Chanthaphonh

See also Apache Wars; Camp Grant Massacre.
References and Further Reading
Browning, Sinclair. 2000. *Enju: The Life and Struggles of an Apache Chief from the Little Running Water.* Lincoln, NE: iUniverse.
Clum, John P. 1929. "Es-kin-in-zin." *New Mexico Historical Review* 4, no. 1: 1–27.

Franklin, Benjamin, Native American Influences

Beginning nearly two generations before the Revolutionary War, the circumstances of American diplomacy were such that opinion leaders of the English colonies and of the Iroquois Confederacy were able to meet to discuss the politics of alliance and the nature of confederation. Beginning in the early 1740s, Iroquois leaders strongly urged the colonists to form a federation similar to their own. The Iroquois' immediate practical objective was the unified management of the Indian trade and prevention of fraud. The Iroquois also stressed that the colonies should have to unify as a condition of alliance in the continuing "cold war" with France.

At a 1744 treaty council in Lancaster, Pennsylvania, Cannasatego (tadadaho, or speaker, of the Iroquois Confederacy) told colonial delegates: "Our wise forefathers established Union and Amity between the Five Nations. This has made us formidable; this has given us great Weight and Authority with our neighboring Nations. We are a powerful Confederacy; and by your observing the same methods our wise forefathers have taken, you will acquire

Benjamin Franklin achieved worldwide renown as a writer, scientist, statesman, and diplomat. (National Archives and Records Administration)

such Strength and power. Therefore whatever befalls you, never fall out with one another" (Van Doren and Boyd, 1938, 75).

Franklin probably first learned of Canassatego's advice as he set his words in type. Franklin's press issued Indian treaties in small booklets that enjoyed a lively sale throughout the colonies. Beginning in 1736, Franklin published treaty accounts on a regular basis until the early 1760s, when his defense of Indians under assault by frontier settlers cost him his seat in the Pennsylvania Assembly. Franklin subsequently served the colonial government in England.

While Franklin first read the Iroquois' urgings to unite as a printer of Indian treaties, by the early 1750s he had become directly involved in diplomacy. Early in a distinguished diplomatic career that would later make him the United States' premier envoy in Europe, Franklin attended a 1753 treaty

council at Carlisle, Pennsylvania. At this meeting with the Iroquois and Ohio Indians (Twightees, Delawares, Shawnees, and Wyandots), Franklin absorbed the rich imagery and ideas of the Six Nations at close range. On October 1, 1753, he watched the Oneida chief, Scarrooyady, and a Mohawk, Cayanguileguoa, condole the Ohio Indians for their losses against the French. Franklin listened while Scarrooyady recounted the origins of the Great Law to the Ohio Indians.

Even before the 1754 Albany Conference, Benjamin Franklin had been musing over the words of Canassatego. Using Iroquois examples of unity, Franklin sought to shame the reluctant colonists into some form of union in 1751, when he engaged in a hyperbolic racial slur (subsequent evidence shows that Franklin had a healthy respect for the Iroquois): "It would be a strange thing," he wrote in 1751, "if Six Nations of Ignorant savages should be capable of forming such an union and be able to execute it in such a manner that it has subsisted for ages and appears indissoluble, and yet that a like union should be impractical for ten or a dozen English colonies . . ." (Smyth, 1905, 3: 42).

At about the same time, Franklin became an early, forceful advocate of colonial union. All of these circumstantial strings were tied together in the summer of 1754, when colonial representatives, Franklin among them, met with Iroquois sachems at the Albany Congress to address issues of mutual concern and to develop the Albany Plan of Union, a design that echoes both English and Iroquois precedents and that would become a rough draft for the Articles of Confederation a generation later.

Bruce E. Johansen

See also Albany Congress, Native Precedents; Canassatego; Carlisle Treaty Council; Hendrick.

References and Further Reading
Bigelow, John, ed. 1868. *Autobiography of Benjamin Franklin*. Philadelphia, PA: J. B. Lippincott Co.
Boyd, Julian. [1942] 1981. "Dr. Franklin: Friend of the Indian." In *Meet Dr. Franklin*. Edited by Roy N. Lokken. Philadelphia, PA: The Franklin Institute.
Clark, Ronald W. 1983. *Benjamin Franklin: A Biography*. New York: Random House.
Grinde, Donald A., Jr., and Bruce E. Johansen. 1991. *Exemplar of Liberty: Native America and the Evolution of Democracy*. Los Angeles, CA: UCLA American Indian Studies Center.
Johansen, Bruce E. 1982. *The Forgotten Founders: Benjamin Franklin, the Iroquois and the Rationale for the American Revolution*. Ipswich, MA: Gambit.
Labaree, Leonard W., ed. 1959–Present. *The Papers of Benjamin Franklin*. New Haven, CT: Yale University Press.
Smyth, Albert H., ed. 1905–1907. *The Writings of Benjamin Franklin*. New York: Macmillan.
Van Doren, Carl, and Julian P. Boyd, eds. 1938. *Indian Treaties Printed by Benjamin Franklin 1736–1762*. Philadelphia: Historical Society of Pennsylvania.

Geronimo

The legendary war leader and medicine man Geronimo was born a Bedonkohe Apache in the 1820s at a site near the upper Gila River on the Arizona–New Mexico border (Debo, 1976, 7–9). Named Goy-ath-lay or Goyahkla, he was the chief's grandson and, although not specifically groomed to become a chief, his future activities would haunt American history. "Geronimo" is Spanish for St. Jerome, the Catholic saint of lost causes, whom Mexican troops were said to have invoked when faced with raiding parties led by him.

Young Geronimo followed established customs: He learned how to run far and fast, how to carve bows and arrows, how to hunt small game, and, importantly, how to survive. He served an apprenticeship on four hostile expeditions, becoming a horseholder for his mentor, taking care of the warriors' horses, fetching water and wood, cooking, and acting as a sentinel. Once he was accepted into the warriors' circle, Geronimo married Alope, his long-time love. Three children were born into their marriage.

Because the Bedonkohe were a small group, they frequently allied with the Mimbres Apaches under the leadership of the great Mangas Coloradas who, in 1850, led a trading venture to Janos, Mexico; Geronimo participated. While the men were away, Mexicans stole up to the encampment and killed everyone, including Geronimo's mother, Alope, and the three children (Debo, 1976, 35). His burning hatred of Mexicans never abated and motivated revenge killings for the rest of his life.

Geronimo may have participated in the Battle of Apache Pass in 1862, and certainly took part in other conflicts during those years. Other Apache leaders, such as Mangas Coloradas, Cochise, Juh, and Victorio, overshadowed Geronimo but he became more and more skilled at warfare and lived among Cochise's followers. In May 1871 he had a hand in a

fierce Arizona battle where Lieutenant Howard B. Cushing was killed (Thrapp, 1991, 548).

In 1877, Geronimo, by now notorious, joined Victorio's band on the Ojo Caliente Reservation in New Mexico. He was arrested there and put in irons by the agent, John Clum. With his followers he was moved to the San Carlos Apache Reservation, beginning a series of breakouts and surrenders that continued until the final capitulation in 1886. One year later, 1878, Geronimo was once again in Mexico and a party to raids conducted by Juh, chief of the Nednhi Apaches. The group, including Geronimo, settled for a time on the San Carlos Reservation. Breaking out in late 1881, Juh and Geronimo took their followers south into the Sierra Madre Mountains of Mexico, where they remained for one year. A sensational raid back to San Carlos, planned by Juh and Geronimo, occurred in 1882 when they extracted the Native leader Loco (at rifle point, it was said) along with several hundred of his people, and then fought with them during several skirmishes with Mexican troops. Geronimo voluntarily surrendered in early 1884 but left San Carlos about seventeen months later, by which time his reputation as a fearsome war leader had solidified. Led by Cochise's son, Naiche, and Geronimo, the group remained free until late March of 1886 when increasing military pressure caused the Apaches to yield to the Americans, instead of the Mexicans, who had promised to kill them on sight. During the arranged submission to General George Crook at Cañon de los Embudos, a site just south of the international border, Geronimo spoke twice. His poignant words have been recorded and are now summarized:

> There is one God looking down on us all. We are all children of the one God. God is listening to me. The sun, the darkness, the winds, are all listening to what we now say. I surrender myself to you . . . Once I moved about like the wind. Now I surrender to you and that is all . . . (Debo, 1976, 262).

However, a Tombstone, Arizona, liquor dealer named Tribolett entered the Apaches' encampment and supplied enough whiskey to intoxicate Geronimo and others (Debo, 1976, 264). Worried that the Apaches' absence from the Southwest would cause a drop in his profits—5,000 thirsty soldiers would be removed from the area if the Indians surrendered—Tribolett was only acting in his own self-interest. Also, he lied to Geronimo and said the

Geronimo was a legendary Apache war leader and medicine man. (National Archives and Records Administration)

soldiers would kill them at dawn unless they fled immediately.

Believing Tribolett and drinking their fill, the Naiche/Geronimo people left Embudos and remained free for the next six months, continuing to raid across the Southwest but U.S. military activity in the same region took its toll. The water holes were guarded, the wild animals killed, and the hunt for the Apaches continued relentlessly. The Indians were hungry, sick, and weary of running when, in September 1886, Geronimo sent word to Fort Bowie that he was ready to surrender. By this time General Crook had been replaced by General Nelson Miles, who agreed to meet Geronimo, Naiche, and their followers in Skeleton Canyon, Arizona. On September 4 the Apaches put down their guns for the last time. Miles quickly separated Naiche and Geronimo from their followers (Debo, 1976, 293).

The next morning, six Apaches were missing, having escaped during the night. Everyone else

remained with Naiche and Geronimo at Fort Bowie until September 8 when, along with a military guard, they rode their horses to Bowie Station and boarded a train for Florida. At Jacksonville, the men were separated from their women and children and transferred to a shuttle that took them to Pensacola. Put into boats, the seventeen warriors landed on Santa Rosa Island and were marched to Fort Pickens while their families joined other imprisoned Apaches at Fort Marion, 300 miles to the east. The promise by the American government that the Apaches would be reunited with their previously incarcerated friends and relatives was disregarded.

Fort Pickens had been abandoned for years and was in disrepair, a condition the Apaches were ordered to fix. Geronimo labored beside the warriors, weeding the parade ground, yanking grass out of the walls, cutting trees, digging latrines and cisterns, and walking on the beach under guard to collect firewood (Stockel, 1993, 105). The men cooked over fireplaces inside cavernous casemates with sandy floors, and slept on bags of old straw. Aided by their loyal friend, interpreter George Wratten, the men communicated with their families through letters including one from Geronimo to his wives and children.

> How are you at Fort Marion? How do you like it there? Have you plenty to eat, and you sleep and drink well? Send me a letter and tell me all the news. I am very satisfied here but if I only had you with me again I would be more so . . . As sure as the trees bud and bloom in the spring, so sure is my hope of seeing you again . . . Do what is right no matter how you may suffer. Write me soon a lovely letter (Skinner, 1987, 151).

In response to the many deaths at Fort Marion, on April 27, 1887, the prisoners of war were put on trains to be transferred to Mount Vernon, Alabama, about twenty-seven miles north of Mobile. Joined in May 1888 by the men from Fort Pickens, families were at long last together again. Geronimo became a justice of the peace, earning about $10 per month to enforce discipline. With proper instruction from the military, the former terror of the Southwest became mellow and sympathetic, conducting his office in a professional manner. He even cooperated with missionaries, allowing an organ to be placed in the breezeway between the two parts of his cabin.

As a consequence of public pressure regarding the continuing large number of deaths among the Alabama prisoners of war, the government relocated the surviving Apaches to Fort Sill, Oklahoma, in 1894 where they began the slow climb back to health. Under the guidance of Dutch Reformed missionaries, many Apaches adopted the Protestant religion, but Geronimo resisted until one day in the summer of 1902 when he sat in the front row of a camp meeting, listening intently and carefully considering the minister's message. In January 1903 he sat through another sermon, jumped up at its conclusion and said, "The Jesus road is good. Go right into it (Stockel, 2004, 192)." After studying catechism and participating in the requisite religious exercises, Geronimo became a Christian.

Early in February 1909, at about age eighty, he rode his horse into the nearby town of Lawton and convinced a white man to purchase a bottle of whiskey for him. Drunk, he fell on the way back to Fort Sill and lay under a tree. A heavy rain soaked him to his skin, resulting in pneumonia. Found by a military patrol early the next morning, Geronimo lived for three more days. He is buried in the Apache Prisoner of War Cemetery at Fort Sill.

H. Henrietta Stockel

See also Apache Wars; Cochise.

References and Further Reading

Debo, Angie. 1976. *Geronimo: The Man, His Time, His Place.* Norman: University of Oklahoma Press.

Skinner, Woodward B. 1987. *The Apache Rock Crumbles: The Captivity of Geronimo's People.* Pensacola, FL: Skinner Publications.

Stockel, H. Henrietta. 1993. *Survival of the Spirit: Chiricahua Apaches in Captivity.* Reno: University of Nevada Press.

Stockel, H. Henrietta. 2004. *On the Bloody Road to Jesus: Christianity and the Chiricahua Apaches.* Albuquerque: University of New Mexico Press.

Thrapp, Dan L. 1991. *Encyclopedia of Frontier Biography, Vol. II.* Lincoln: University of Nebraska Press.

Gorman, R. C.

Rudolph Carl Gorman is one of the best-known Navajo (Diné) painters, famous for his paintings, lithographs, serigraphs, painted pottery, and sculptures of graceful female figures. He is a member of the *Clauschii'* (Red Bottom People) Clan and born into the *Dibé lizhíní* (Black Sheep People) Clan. Born

R. C. Gorman was a famous Navajo painter and sculptor. (Dave G. Houser/Corbis)

on July 26, 1931, in Chinle, Arizona, he was the eldest son of Carl Nelson Gorman, a Navajo code talker, and Adella Katherine Brown. His mother and maternal grandmother, Zonnie Maria Brown, raised him at Black Mountain, Arizona, along with his five siblings. Gorman learned Navajo traditions, songs, prayers, and respect for the land from Brown. He also followed in the footsteps of his father, who was one of the first painters to break away from the 1930s studio school. Like him, R. C. Gorman developed his own unique artistic style and opened the door to a generation of painters who followed him.

Gorman began painting at age three and was later encouraged by a teacher at the Presbyterian Mission School, Jenny Lind, to pursue a career. He attended Northern Arizona University from 1950 to 1951 and from 1955 to 1956, studying literature and art, but never received an undergraduate degree. Between his periods of study, he served for four years in the U.S. Navy during the Korean War. He

later studied art in Mexico (1958), where studying the works of Diego Rivera and Rufino Tamayo changed his vision and style. In 1962 he moved to San Francisco to promote his artistic career, before moving permanently to Taos in 1968. Gorman steadily gained an international reputation over the last fifty years; his works have been widely collected and can be seen in over 100 museums in the United States, Asia, and Europe.

Gorman painted in a number of genres (watercolor, etchings, acrylics, oils, paper casts, silkscreens, stone lithographs), depicting several highly stylized subjects and producing abstracts: landscapes, nightscapes, animals, spiritual beings, and people. His distinctive themes reflect important places and beings in Dinétah, the Navajo homeland, as well as times of the day and seasons reflecting and commenting on central Navajo values. His best-known works are of the female figure, often portraits of friends and relatives who are generously

proportioned, barefoot, and draped in flowing traditional dresses, robes, and blankets common to the Navajo and Rio Grande pueblos. They are all women of strength and action. "I revere women. They are my greatest inspiration," he told an Associated Press interviewer in 1998 (Navajo Nation, 2005). This sentiment is appropriate for a member of a matrilineal society; Gorman depicts what is at the heart of Navajo society and culture: women. Gorman uses his grandmother as the focus of many of his early paintings and prints. Art lovers and many art critics say that his figures have mystique, character, strength, and lyricism and that he represents Native women in a positive manner, almost universalistic in intent. Other critics, however, dismiss Gorman's subject matter and painting style, with its warm, flowing lines and saturated colors, as unusually commercial, market driven, and stereotypical. They also dismiss Gorman himself as being interested in selling quantities of paintings rather than in pursuing innovative work. Gorman, in turn, satirically dismisses these later critics in his books and essays, poking fun at the pretentiousness of art criticism and connoisseurship.

Gorman in his later life was a prolific author and penned essays on Mexican art, petroglyphs, and cave paintings. He wrote an autobiography (Gorman, 1992) and a series of books on cooking and art, and he documented his genre in a series of books with several coauthors. He also reveled in his self-defined life style that some have called "bohemian"—complete with headbands and custom-tailored Hawaiian shirts (Obituary, 2005).

During the later half of his life, Gorman made his home in El Prado, New Mexico, near Taos and owned a gallery there, R. C. Gorman Navajo Gallery, in Taos, as well as the Nizhoni Gallery in Albuquerque, which sold his posters, lithographs, and publications. His great success as a businessperson provided him with the means to help others. In 2003 he gave his extensive library of over 1,200 books and a large collection of his art to Diné College to fulfill its guiding principle, *sa'ah naaghíí bik'eh hózhóón*, and to help preserve Diné culture, language, and history. The College of Ganado and Northern Arizona University presented him with honorary doctorates of humane letters.

Gorman passed away on November 3, 2005, at age seventy-four. In remembering him, Navajo Nation President Joe Shirley, Jr. called him the "Picasso of the Southwest" and "a child of the Navajo . . . He afforded us the opportunity to talk about ourselves to the world. When they talked about him, they talked about us" (Navajo Nation, 2005, 1).

Nancy J. Parezo

References and Further Reading
Brody, J. J. 1971. *Indian Painters and White Patrons*. Albuquerque: University of New Mexico Press.
Gorman, R. C. 1992. *The Radiance of My People*. Houston: Santa Fe Arts Gallery.
Gorman, R. C., and Virginia Dooley. 1981. *Nudes and Food: R. C. Gorman Goes Gourmet*. Flagstaff, AZ: Northland Press.
Gorman, R. C., and Virginia Dooley. 1994. *R.C. Gorman's Nudes & Foods in Good Taste*. Santa Fe, NM: Clear Light Publishers
Monthan, Doris. 1990. *R. C. Gorman—A Retrospective*. Flagstaff, AZ: Northland Press.
Navajo Nation. 2005. "Navajo Nation President Joe Shirley, Jr. Orders Flags Flown Half-staff to Honor, Remember the Late R. C. Gorman." Press release, November 6.
"Obituary: R. C. Gorman; Renowned Navajo Artist's Works Coveted by Celebrity Collectors." 2005. *New York Times*, November 13.
Parks, Stephen. 1983. *R. C. Gorman, A Portrait*. Boston: Little, Brown and Company.

Great Lakes Intertribal Council

The origins of the Great Lakes Intertribal Council (GLITC) are rooted in the collective American Indian response of the early 1960s toward the federal policies of the 1950s. In 1945 the National Congress of American Indians (NCAI) was founded to help American Indian groups make effective use of the Indian Reorganization Act of 1934. By 1960, however, the NCAI had concentrated its efforts against Congress's 1950s termination policy and the related Voluntary Relocation Program of the Bureau of Indian Affairs (BIA). In response to that policy and in collaboration with the late Sol Tax (1907–1995), then an anthropology professor at the University of Chicago, the NCAI organized a forum open to any and all American Indians in an effort to redress the intent and collective effect of these policies.

In June 1961 the American Indian Chicago Conference (AICC) was hosted on the campus of the University of Chicago, culminating with the consensual document, "The Declaration of Indian Purpose." While reflecting the moderate perspective that American Indians should work within the existing federal system, it emphatically opposed the federal policies of the 1950s, upheld sovereignty,

asserted treaty rights as interpreted by Supreme Court Justice John Marshall, and spoke up on behalf of unrecognized and underserved American Indian groups. The AICC Declaration was later presented to President John F. Kennedy in a ceremony on the lawn of the White House.

Organizations such as the NCAI and the model for intertribal cooperation afforded by the AICC motivated Indian groups throughout the United States to form cooperative, regional organizations and associations to provide administrative support and to promote social, economic, and political ties. It was in the wake of the AICC that the GLITC emerged as a community action agency under the auspices of the recently established federal Office for Economic Opportunity (OEO). Still in is formative stage, the GLITC responded to the request of the OEO to serve as a vehicle for the delivery of services and programs to its member reservations and the rural Indian communities of Wisconsin.

As part of President Lyndon B. Johnson's War on Poverty, the OEO, although a new and innovative agency committed to grassroots development, found it difficult to overcome former bureaucratic tendencies. Generally speaking, however, the OEO provided the GLITC and its membership with a useful if sometimes frustrating lesson in dealing with federal agencies besides the BIA, as well as beneficial instruction in accessing sources of nongovernmental funding.

Operating under a mission statement to support its membership "in expanding sovereignty and self-determination," the GLITC now functions as a consortium of federally recognized American Indian groups that advocates for and provides services and assistance to its membership in Wisconsin, Michigan, and Minnesota. The consortium includes the Bad River Band of Lake Superior Chippewa (Wisconsin), Lac Courte Oreilles Band of Lake Superior Chippewa (Wisconsin), Lac du Flambeau Band of Lake Superior Chippewa Indians (Wisconsin), Red Cliff Band of Lake Superior Chippewa (Wisconsin), Sokaogon Chippewa Community (Mole Lake, Wisconsin), St. Croix Band of Lake Superior Chippewa (Wisconsin), Forest County Potawatomi Community (Wisconsin), Oneida Nation (Wisconsin), Ho-Chunk Nation (Wisconsin), Stockbridge-Munsee Band of Mohican Indians (Wisconsin), Menominee Indian Tribe (Wisconsin), and the Lac Vieux Desert Tribe (Michigan).

The GLITC is administered by a board of directors composed of a respective chair for each member, along with representatives designated by each chair. The board conducts its business at regularly scheduled meetings once every other month at sites selected at previous meetings, usually held on a rotating basis at one of the membership headquarters. The day-to-day administrative and financial operations of the GLITC are conducted at the central office located in Lac du Flambeau, Wisconsin, where services are also coordinated.

As the respective local governing bodies of the GLITC membership have developed effective administrative capacities and continued the push for self-determination, they have also assumed increased responsibility for the administration and delivery of services to their own communities. The role of GLITC has therefore shifted from the direct delivery of services to its membership to supplementing and assisting local governing bodies in the administration and delivery of services, including health, aging, education, and economic development, and to political action including policy advocacy and intergovernmental relations. This is in keeping with the GLITC's mission to expand the sovereignty and self-determination of Native peoples as a collective entity comprised of independent members who are committed to gather in a self-governed forum to address, discuss, and resolve issues that require intertribal attention.

Timothy J. McCollum

See also Confederacies; National Congress of American Indians.

References and Further Reading

Loew, Patty. 2001. *Indian Nations of Wisconsin.* Madison, WI: Wisconsin Historical Society Press.

Lurie, Nancy Oestreich. 2002. *Wisconsin Indians,* rev. and exp. ed. Madison, WI: Wisconsin Historical Society Press.

Handsome Lake

Before he became a visionary, Handsome Lake (Sganyadaí:yoh, Skaniadario, 1734–August 10, 1815) led the life of a typical, well-born Seneca man with family connections to other high-status individuals. His brother (called his half brother by many non-Native scholars) was the Seneca Gaiant'waka (Chief Cornplanter), while his nephew was Sagoyewatha (Red Jacket), the famed Seneca women's speaker to the men's Grand Council. Tradition states that Sganyadaí:yoh was born into the Wolf Clan at

Conawagas, a Seneca town on the Genesee River in New York located outside modern-day Avon. A sickly child, he was unlikely to have been nominated to any lineage title due to his poor health. However, the women of the Turtle Clan took pity on him and adopted him into their clan, promising titles. Sganyadaí:yoh means "beautiful" (i.e., handsome) "lake," a reference to Lake Ontario. The term is not a personal name, but a position title of one of the Haudenosaunee Grand Council lineage (hereditary) chiefs of the Senecas.

Evolution of a Leader

As a youth, he became beloved of all, especially the women, whom he tirelessly protected, and the children, for whom he always had a story and a pouch filled with nuts bathed in maple syrup. A young woman quickly singled him out as husband material and asked her mother to arrange their marriage. As a responsible married man, he became even more popular, renowned for his good heart and strength of character. When a lineage sachem of the Wolf Clan died, the Wolf Clan Mothers quickly nominated him as successor, with the joyful permission of the Turtle Clan Mothers. To the astonishment of the Wolf and Turtle men, Handsome Lake assumed the title of the fabled sachem, Sganyadaí:yoh.

Before this stunning promotion, however, Sganyadaí:yoh was a "young man" (sometimes mistermed "warrior" in non-Native texts), also a position to which men were appointed by the women. Sganyadaí:yoh was selected to participate in the French and Indian War (1754–1763), fighting with the British–League alliance against the French. Immediately after this war, he took part in the Pontiac resistance movement that opposed the British. As more Europeans poured onto the continent, squeezing the original inhabitants, the resultant crowding made for internecine Native strife over who was to occupy the ever dwindling lands of the East. Sganyadaí:yoh fought with his Seneca brothers against the Cherokees and Choctaws of the South, as the Haudenosaunees and the Algonquins were forced by the non-Native invasion to compete for land.

When the American Revolutionary War broke out in 1776, the Continental Army, knowing that it would not be able to fight on two fronts, urgently courted all eastern Native nations, begging them to remain neutral in this "family fight" with their "bad father," King George III. In the summer of 1777 at the annual meeting of the men's Grand Council in Oswego, Sganyadaí:yoh sided with his brother, Gaiant'waka, in calling for neutrality. Eventually, however, after numerous lethal and unprovoked depredations against them by the colonial militias, the Senecas decided to go to war against the colonists. Sganyadaí:yoh submitted to the consensus, once more fighting for his people.

One morning in 1799, listening to his daughter sing a medicine song as she shelled the beans, Sganyadaí:yoh felt his consciousness slipping away. Staggering to the longhouse door, he collapsed into the arms of his relatives as his spirit wandered out of his body, floating out of the cabin and on to Sky World. Thinking her father dead, his daughter called her uncle Gaiant'waka and the rest of the village. Everyone was saddened by the news. His daughter dressed him in his burial robes, and notice went abroad that he was to be raised up (i.e., his lineage title was to be conferred upon a successor). Just then, a sachem and nephew of Sganyadaí:yoh, Taa'-wonyas (the Awl Breaker), examined the body and refused to believe that Sganyadaí:yoh's spirit had departed for good.

Handsome Lake as Visionary

Around noon the next day, Sganyadaí:yoh came out of his coma, telling his rejoicing relatives that his spirit had been visited by the Four Messengers of Sky World bringing to him the "four words" (or "matters"): *onega, gutgont, onoityeyende,* and *yondwiniyas swayas.* These four matters became the cornerstone of the Gaiwí:yo, and they consisted of prohibitions on the people. *Onega* means alcohol, the use of which was forbidden. *Gutgont* (okton) was the use of the negative spirit power, which, in the hands of the inept, did harm. (It is commonly, though inaccurately, given in English as "witchcraft.") It, too, was outlawed. *Onoityeyende* was said by some to be the practice of poisoning enemies in secret, although others more benignly rendered it "love medicine," while *yondwiniyas swayas* was "cutting the child off in the womb" or the use of birth control techniques, including abortion. These, too, were prohibited by the Gaiwí:yo.

In addition to this foundation, many more teachings came to Sganyadaí:yoh, including the condemnation of Christian missionaries. Notwithstanding this overt unfriendliness to Christian missions, Sganyadaí:yoh incorporated many Christian pre-

cepts, values, and attitudes into his Gaiwí:yo, including monotheism, sinfulness and public confession, and the submission of wives to husbands. How many of these ideas he consciously borrowed is unknown, although it is known that Sganyadaí:yoh had learned the mores and precepts of Christianity from his nephew, Henry Obail (Obeal), who had studied the Christian Bible under the Quakers in Philadelphia. However, unlike Jesus, Sganyadaí:yoh made no pretense of being a messiah or "son of God," but rather claimed to be the speaker of "the Creator."

Given the oppressive nature of his message for Haudenosaunee women—who had always controlled their own fertility, held their own councils, filled the majority of the positions as shamans, and owned all the fields and ran the clans—it is not surprising that the Clan Mothers blocked consideration of the Gaiwi:yo by the men's council for almost fifty years. Its initial reception by the people in general was quite negative. Handsome Lake was particularly opposed by Sagoyewatha (the women's speaker) and by his brother, Gaiant'waka, who heckled his teachings and put as many obstacles in his way as possible. Sagoyewatha, speaking for the Clan Mothers, denounced Sganyadaí:yoh as an imposter passing off assimilation as tradition. Stung, Sganyadaí:yoh replied that the four messengers had just revealed to him that Sagoyewatha was scheming to sell off more Iroquoian land (an attack on the Clan Mothers, who owned the land).

From that point, tensions escalated between the Clan Mothers and the followers of Sganyadaí:yoh. Around this same time, the federal government of the United States granted the Quakers the de facto power to run the New York reservations in an early program of forced assimilation. Under this program, some people gradually became so culturally desensitized to Christian proselytizing that they stopped recognizing it at the base of the Gaiwí:yo, accepting the teachings as familiar. Others regarded the Gaiwí:yo as the lesser of two evils. It was clear that the missionaries and the occupying government would forcibly prevent the older religions from being practiced, whereas the Gaiwí:yo did retain numerous traditional elements that would otherwise have been lost, such as the annual round of ceremonies, many of the older oral traditions, a masculinized version of the clan kinship, the old marriage rites, the principle (although vitiated) of reciprocity, and ecological concepts with their attendant respect for nature.

The U.S. government had reorganized the councils, installing a new system so that new elections took place. Sganyadaí:yoh was reelected to his position on the Seneca council in 1801. His election emboldening him, Sganyadaí:yoh set out to destroy his critics, actually accusing Sagoyewatha (and by implication the Clan Mothers) of witchcraft. This foolhardy accusation quickly dashed much of his growing popularity. Along with his stance against birth control, this tactic greatly outraged the women and their numerous male supporters. Sganyadaí:yoh began losing face among the people. The strength of the reaction to his attack on Sagoyewatha caused Sganyadaí:yoh to backpeddle on the issues of birth control and witchcraft, emphasizing instead popular issues related to land rights and alcohol issues.

In 1802, Sganyadaí:yoh was among a delegation of Onondaga and Seneca representatives visiting the Capitol to meet President Thomas Jefferson. He lobbied hard for an end to the sale of liquor to the Haudenosaunees, as well as for an end to fraudulent land-grabbing. He was far more successful with the administration on temperance than on land retention. Jefferson prompted his Secretary of War (the department charged with Indian affairs) to write Sganyadaí:yoh a rather patronizing letter of support on behalf of the president on the issue of his temperance work. Sganyadaí:yoh was clearly acceptable to the Euro-American overlords, if not to the Clan Mothers and their supporters.

One of the women's supporters was Gaiant'-waka, at whose town (Cornplanter's Town) Sganyadaí:yoh had been living. The people at Cornplanter's Town did not care how many letters of support he had from presidents and Quakers. By 1810, his detractors had become so numerous, and the situation so tense, that Sganyadaí:yoh was forced to move to Cold Spring, where he continued alienating people. Early in 1812, he moved to Tonawanda, taking along his chief supporters and his family, among whom was his grandson Sos'heowa, grandfather of Ely S. Parker, the first Indian Commissioner of Indian Affairs. Sos'heowa was to become Sganyadaí:yoh's successor on the Grand Council upon his death in 1815.

Handsome Lake's Final Years

During his four years at Tonawanda, he reflected on the great hostility that many had shown his teachings; being kicked out of two towns in rapid

succession preyed on his mind. Many say that he turned away from his own teachings during this time. It is certain that he had grown reluctant to tell about his visions or teach any more, distancing himself and, at times seeming to disclaim, his own revelations.

In his fourth year at Tonawanda, Sganyadaí:yoh was invited by the Onondagas to describe his "third call," a death song. He was hesitant to comply with this invitation, because his third call was his quivering song. His spirit guides returned to him, however, and advised him to go. Based on this vision, he predicted his death just as he set off for Onondaga. As word spread of his death vision, many joined his trek. Sganyadaí:yoh became increasingly depressed as he approached Onondaga; he seemed almost smitten by fear. Before the assembly he was to address, he broke down, unable to sing and denying that a spiritual meeting was in progress at all. "We are just sitting around the fire," he said (meaning that it was just a family gathering) and refused to teach. To cheer him up, the people played lacrosse, but Sganyadaí:yoh declined to watch and, again insisting that he was about to die, left the field.

His supporters took him to an Onondaga longhouse, forbidding all others to enter and swearing themselves to secrecy concerning events that took place within the longhouse. However, an Onondaga was hiding within and reported that, once inside, Sganyadaí:yoh fell into terrible distress, accusing himself of having been laggard in spreading his message and wishing that he had dared to tell *all* of the visions he had been given. (What those untold visions were, he did not reveal.) His spirit then fell quiet, leaving him once more; four days later, his body-soul followed. At eighty-two, Sganyadaí:yoh was dead.

The Longhouse Religion after Handsome Lake's Death

A half century after his death, Sganyadaí:yoh's legend outstripped his critics' complaints. Elders called a council to gather up his words, which Keepers (oral traditionalists) then committed to memory and knotted into wampum. (Sganyadaí:yoh had, himself, knotted wampum of his Gaiwí:yo.) He began to be called Sedwa'gowa'ne, meaning "our great teacher." In 1848, a recital of the the Gaiwí:yo by Sos'heowa was taken down on paper for the first time at a mourning council in Tonawanda and translated for

Lewis Henry Morgan by Donehogä'wa (Ely S. Parker). In 1851, it was published in The League of the Haudenosaunee. In 1861, the Grand Council heard (accepted) the Gaiwí:yo as legitimate. At the turn of the century, Gawaso Wanneh (Arthur Parker), himself a descendent of Sganyadaí:yoh, published another transcription. In 1994, Chief Jacob Thomas provided yet another version of the Code.

Between Sganyadaí:yoh's death in 1815 and 1900, the Longhouse Religion flowered, garnering many supporters. By the turn of the twentieth century—a nadir for all Native groups—Gawaso Wanneh observed that the teachings of Sganyadaí:yoh were on the wane and that "true believers" numbered only a few hundred (Parker, 1919, 251). By the midtwentieth century, however, the Gaiwí:yo was being recited with great frequency on the New York reservations, and, with the general Native renaissance of the 1970s, many young New York Haudenosaunees began looking into it as a way back to their roots.

Barbara Alice Mann and Bruce E. Johansen

See also Cornplanter; Longhouse Religion; Red Jacket.
References and Further Reading
Deardorff, Merle H. 1951. *The Religion of Handsome Lake: Its Origins and Development*. American Bureau of Ethnology Bulletin No. 149. Washington, DC: Bureau of American Ethnology.
Morgan, Lewis Henry. [1851] 1901. *League of the Haudenosaunee, or Iroquois*. 2 volumes. New York: Burt Franklin.
Parker, Arthur C. [Gawaso Wanneh]. 1912. *The Code of Handsome Lake, the Seneca Prophet*. New York State Museum Bulletin 163, Education Department Bulletin No. 530, November 1, 1912. Albany, NY: State University of New York Press.
Parker, Arthur C. [Gawaso Wanneh]. 1919. "Handsome Lake: The Peace Prophet [Speech, 1916]." In *The Life of Ely S. Parker, Last Grand Sachem of the Iroquois and General Grant's Military Secretary*, 244–251. Buffalo, ND: Buffalo Historical Society.
Shimony, Annemarie Anrod. [1961] 1994. *Conservatism Among the Iroquois at the Six Nations Reserve*. Syracuse, NY: Syracuse University Press.
Thomas, Chief Jacob [Cayuga], with Terry Boyle. 1994. *Teachings from the Longhouse*. Toronto, ON: Stoddart Publishing Company.
Wallace, Anthony F. C. 1970. *The Death and Rebirth of the Seneca*. New York: Alfred A. Knopf.

Harjo, Chitto

A full-blooded Muscogee (Creek) leader who valued communal land holdings and traditional ways above influences of the U.S. government, Chitto Harjo (1846–1909/1911) opposed the dissolution of Creek government allotment dictated by the Dawes Commission and the Curtis Act of 1898. He set himself and his allies against progressive mixed-blood Creeks and land speculators.

Chitto Harjo was born as Bill Harjo in 1846 near present-day Boley, Oklahoma, in what was then exclusively the Muscogee (Creek) nation after the removal of his parents with the Muscogee people from their Georgia and Alabama homelands beginning in 1832. Harjo's name derives from the Muscogee words for "snake" (pronounced "chit-toe") and a word often used as a title for Creek war leaders that translates loosely to "recklessly brave" or "brave beyond discretion" (pronounced "hah-joe"). His followers came to be called the Crazy Snakes, members of the Crazy Snake Movement (McIntosh, 1993).

Beyond his service on the federal side during the Civil War, little is known of Harjo's life until 1899 when he was selected as the speaker of the traditional ceremonial town known as Hickory Ground, a Creek ceremonial center still active in the early twenty-first century. Muscogee tradition dictates that a town's chief (or *meeko*) not speak for himself, but designate someone of status who has the oratorical skills to explain what the chief is thinking or feeling. This status as speaker both confirmed and heightened his status as a leader of, and speaker for, traditional people.

After the 1898 passage of the Curtis Act, which vastly magnified the powers of the federal government over American Indian affairs, Harjo vocalized the sentiment of many traditional Muscogee people that the U.S. government should uphold the 1832 treaty with the Creeks, which provided the terms for removal and also guaranteed the Creeks eternal sovereignty over their nation. The Curtis Act, however, enacted the process by which the tribe's government and courts would be abolished, as well as distributing the collective Creek land holdings to individual tribal members and then opening up the surplus land for sale.

After Hickory Ground's meeko became ill during a trip to Washington, D.C., Harjo assumed a leadership role and urged resistance to allotment and Muscogee national dissolution. As the Muscogee (Creek) Web site noted in 2005, Harjo's efforts "epitomized the view of all Muscogee people that they possessed an inherent right to govern themselves," and for Harjo "it was unimaginable that the Nation could be dissolved by a foreign government" (Muscogee (Creek) Nation, 2005, 38). In 1900, Harjo began traveling to ceremonial grounds throughout the Creek nation, openly advocating the formation of a new government and establishing new laws, some of which included the prohibition of commerce of any kind with European-Americans. Violators were subject to physical punishment by Snake enforcers.

Alarmed by the rebellious faction, the principal chief of the Creek nation, Pleasant Porter, alerted the federal government to the Crazy Snake movement and its anarchic implications. Subsequently, Harjo and about 100 of his followers were arrested by federal troops in January 1901 and imprisoned in Muskogee, but they were freed by a judge who cautioned the Snakes to cease their activities. Harjo continued his outward opposition to allotment, however, and was arrested again in 1902 with nine other Snake leaders. The group was promptly sent to federal prison at Fort Leavenworth, Kansas.

After finishing his two-year sentence, Harjo returned to Indian Territory where he reiterated, "We do not want our lands divided and each one given one hundred and sixty acres. This is the only land left to the Indians, and once he gives up this small strip of fertile land he will be no more" (1904). In 1905, Harjo traveled to Washington to meet with President Theodore Roosevelt but had no success in convincing Roosevelt to stop allotment. By 1906, a select U.S. Senate committee arrived in Tulsa, Oklahoma, to hear how the Creeks and Cherokees felt about allotment. Harjo made an eloquent but unheeded plea to the Senators, urging that the federal government not carve up the earth that was paid for by the relinquishment of Creek lands in Georgia and Alabama (Mann, 2001, 228).

Oklahoma statehood in 1907 ended any hope that the Crazy Snake movement would have any lasting effect on Creek politics, because its government was officially abolished upon creation of the forty-sixth state. Continuing to oppose the entire process of allotment, by 1909 Harjo and the Crazy Snakes created such fright throughout the lower Creek nation that all sorts of crimes were being attributed to them. In March of that year, Harjo was wounded in a shootout with law officers who had

1904. "Won't Take Any Part in Matter: Interior Department Not Interested in Election of Chief of the Snake Indians." *The Oklahoman,* January 3.

Chitto Harjo, or Crazy Snake, was a Muscogee (Creek) chief. (Library of Congress)

come to arrest him at his home. He escaped, however, and his disappearance led to disagreement about his final resting place. Of several reports, consensus seems to exist that he made it to the Choctaw nation, where he either died soon thereafter from his wounds or lived for about two more years before being buried in the mountains of southeastern Oklahoma.

Hugh W. Foley, Jr.

See also Curtis, Charles; General Allotment Act (Dawes Act).

Mann, Barbara Alice, ed. 2001. "'A Man of Misery': Chitto Harjo and the Senate Select Committee on Oklahoma Statehood," in Mann, ed. *Native American Speakers of the Eastern Woodlands,* 197–228. Westport, CT: Greenwood Press.

McIntosh, Kenneth Waldo. 1993. *Chitto Harjo, the Crazy Snakes and the Birth of Indian Political Activism in the Twentieth Century.* Ph.D. dissertation, Texas Christian University.

Muscogee (Creek) Nation. "History," Available at: http://www.muscogeenation-nsn.gov. Accessed May 30, 2005.

Harjo, Joy

Joy Harjo, a Muscogee Creek, poet, writer, musician, and teacher, was born in 1951 in Tulsa, Oklahoma, to a full-blooded Creek father and a Cherokee-French mother. She graduated from the University of New Mexico in 1976, having majored in creative writing, and attended the University of Iowa Writers Workshop in 1978 as part of her master of fine arts degree in creative writing. Her poetry is noted for emotional and mythic intensity in describing and connecting oral tradition to contemporary society, with a focus on identity, justice for the oppressed, and a relationship between landscape and history. Harjo's poetry challenges the contemporary Western concepts of linear time and history with the oral traditional concept of the "spiral" memory of storytelling.

In Joy Harjo's first book of poetry, *The Last Song* (1975), she explores the unwritten aspects of American Indian history. She describes the illusion of history as a past event, depicting it rather as still alive and heavily influencing the contemporary life of American Indians. She describes the past and present connections between people, animals, landscape, and language without the constraints of a linear time line. In her next book of poetry, *What Moon Drove Me to This?* (1980), Harjo continues to explore the issue of American Indian identity, with a concentration in mixed-blood ancestry. *She Had Some Horses* (1983) marks a break from an individual perspective to a more collective consciousness about injustices for oppressed people and cultures.

Secrets from the Center of the World (1989) is a chapbook focused on landscape and place, with photographs taken of Southwest landscapes by Stephen Strom. Harjo received an American Book Award and the Delmore Schwartz Memorial Award for her fourth collection of poetry, *In Mad Love and War* (1990). *The Woman Who Fell from the Sky* (1994), which received the Oklahoma Book Arts Award, focuses on the oral traditional story motif in contemporary times. *Reinventing the Enemy's Language* (1997) is a collection of nonfiction essays by Native women, coedited with Gloria Bird. *A Map to the Next World: Poetry and Tales* (2000) and *How We Became Human: New and Selected Poems* (2002) are collections of

poetry that continue to incorporate the oral tradition, with more attention to the movement into new worlds as in many traditional indigenous creation stories. Other written works by Harjo include a children's book, *The Good Luck Cat* (2000) and a screenplay for *Origin of the Apache Crown Dance* (1985).

Joy Harjo is also a saxophone musician who performs her poetry with her band, Poetic Justice. The music in *Letter from the End of the Twentieth Century* and *Native Joy for Real* (2004) is a mix of various sounds: reggae, country, rhythm and blues, jazz, and traditional American Indian song. Her many honors include the American Indian Distinguished Achievement in the Arts Award, the Josephine Miles Poetry Award, the Mountains and Plains Booksellers Award, the William Carlos Williams Award, and fellowships from the Arizona Commission on the Arts, the Witter Bynner Foundation, and the National Endowment for the Arts.

As of 2006, Harjo was an associate professor at the University of New Mexico. Harjo has also been a professor at the University of Colorado at Boulder (1985) and the University of Arizona at Tucson (1988).

DeLyssa Begay

References and Further Reading

Bruchac, Joseph. 1987. "The Story of All Our Survival: An Interview with Joy Harjo." In *Survival This Way: Interviews with American Indian Poets.* Edited by Joseph Bruchac, 87–103. Tucson: University of Arizona Press.

Carabi, Angels. 1994. "Joy Harjo." *Belles Lettres* 9, no. 4 (Summer): 46–50.

Gould, Janice. 2000. "An Interview with Joy Harjo." *Western American Literature* 35, no. 2 (Summer): 131–142.

Holmes, Kristine. 1995. "'This Woman Can Cross Any Line': Feminist Tricksters in the Works of Nora Naranjo-Morse and Joy Harjo." *Studies in American Indian Literature* 7, no. 1 (Spring): 45–63.

McAdams, Janet. 1999. "Castings for a (New) New World: The Poetry of Joy Harjo." In *Women Poets of the Americas: Toward a Pan-American Gathering.* Edited by Jacqueline V. Brogan and Cordelia C. Candelaria, 210–232. Notre Dame, IN: University of Notre Dame Press.

Harrison, William Henry

William Henry Harrison (1770–1841) initiated the pivotal expansionist pattern of treaty negotiations of nineteenth-century America. As the builder of President Thomas Jefferson's plan for Indian removal beyond the Mississippi River, Harrison negotiated six treaties between 1803 and 1810, clearing the way for American expansion into the Northwest Territories at a far faster rate than anyone expected. By the end of the War of 1812, much of this territory was prepared for statehood, which swiftly followed for Indiana and Illinois.

Harrison's efforts began in September 1802, when he formed a council at Vincennes with members of the Delaware, Eel River Miami, Kickapoo, Piankashaw, Pottawatomi, and Wea nations to ascertain who owned various lands not covered in the Treaty of Greenville (1795). In a letter to encourage the participation of the various tribes, Harrison likened the Greenville Treaty to a tree whose branches he hoped to see spread over the land under which the European-Americans and the Native Americans could live in "its shade till the end of time" (Esarey, 1922, 52). The attending tribes did not consider this council in any way indicative of a treaty or an agreement of any kind with the United States government, let alone binding. However, Harrison did. Once the council had been held, the minutes note that the purpose was to "adjust" the treaty of Greenville, and, in treaty-like language, the minutes went on to transfer land in and around Vincennes to the United States and to exchange land along the Saline River to the tribes for the exclusive right of salt making. The Delawares objected to the discussions and left. No formal treaty was drafted based on this council.

In a letter dated February 27, 1803, Jefferson sent secret advice to Harrison, wherein the president outlined his plan and vision for the settlement of the Northwest Territory, including how Harrison could help achieve those ends. In this correspondence, Jefferson made no attempt to veil his intentions when he wrote to effect that the U.S. government should promote the Indians, in particular their leaders, to do business with government trading factories (houses) and to run up debt and "be glad" to see them fall into debt. Jefferson believed that, once these important leaders found themselves steeped in debt, they would be willing to "lop them off" by selling their lands to the willing U.S. government. Thus, Americans would encroach farther toward a borderland with the Indians, and the Indians would therefore either have to join with the Americans, becoming "citizens," or be forced to move out of the area completely to some unnamed western location beyond the Mississippi River. Jefferson notes disturbingly,

William Henry Harrison, the ninth U.S. president, was elected largely on his reputation as an Indian fighter. (Library of Congress)

"The former is certainly the termination of their history . . ." He ends with a troubling refrain: "[For] their interests and their tranquility it is best they should see only the present [stat]e of their history . . ." (Esarey, 1922, 71–73). Harrison was only too eager to attend to Jefferson's ideas, making sure he obtained treaty after treaty.

The first Treaty at Fort Wayne (1803) sought to secure land ownership for the U.S. government that Harrison believed was not covered in the previous Greenville Treaty. Many leaders of the invited nations—Delawares, Miamis, Shawnees, and Weas—looked on the proceedings with suspicion. To them, the 1795 Treaty of Greenville forever secured the lands north of the Ohio. It was supposed to be a done deal. Suddenly, it appeared not to be. Some tribal leaders refused to attend at all, but others who did come walked out in disgust. Harrison was of the opinion that government Indian Agent William Wells, who was married to a Miami woman, was intriguing behind his back to make things difficult, encouraging the tribal leaders

to dissent. Following a series of setbacks and delays, by June 7 the treaty was secure and those present agreed to give up the lands in question, which were to be found on opposite sides of the territory. One section extended southwest of Fort Recovery in Ohio to just above the Ohio River on the eastern side, and the other section began just above Vincennes up to the Little Vermillion River in what would become Illinois. These two sections began a buffer zone that would cut the Indians off from the Ohio River. This treaty constituted little victory and little gain, but it was the beginning of an aggressive landgrab over the next seven years.

When a couple of Sac Indians arrived in St. Louis in 1805, Harrison wasted little time in sitting them down to negotiate a treaty to obtain a large portion of northwestern Illinois. The Sacs knew little of what they had signed, nor did they become a party to the agreement, but Harrison saw it as another gain. As these men returned to Saukenauk, the major Sac village along the Rock River, they related what had happened with Harrison. The manipulation of these men who did not even represent the tribe infuriated Black Hawk and caused the whole of the nation to be at odds with the United States into the 1830s. But it would not be until the end of the War of 1812 that Americans could take possession of this land.

The most offensive of the treaties was the second Treaty of Fort Wayne, in September 1809. Here, large portions of land filled out the remaining gaps of the buffer zone. By then, a human wall of white settlement would stand in the way of Native American access to the Ohio River. The remaining tribes would dwell in a smaller and smaller area.

Harrison's family background influenced his ends to promote himself in any way possible. Coming from one of the first families of Virginia, Harrison's father lost the family's money, forcing William Henry to end his medical education and seek a military career during the early 1790s. He became an aide to General Anthony Wayne.

It has been said that the treaty of Fort Wayne of 1809 is what tipped off the war in the west in 1812. Tecumseh met with Harrison in 1810 to protest angrily over what he knew Harrison and the U.S. government were doing by negotiating the treaties.

During the War of 1812, Harrison left office as governor to become first a militia general, then a general in the U.S. Army. His campaigns were mainly in the Old Northwest Territories and Ohio, as well as into Canada. His enemies were not just the

British, but also the Indians. The successes he made would one day become the rallying point for his presidential ambitions.

Sally Colford Bennett

See also Black Hawk's War; Northwest Ordinance.
References and Further Reading
Esarey, Logan. 1922. *Governors Messages and Letters, Volume I.* Indianapolis: Indiana Historical Commission.
Horsman, Reginald. 1961. "American Indian Policy in the Old Northwest, 1783–1812." *William and Mary Quarterly* Third Series, 18, no. 1 (January): 25–53. Billington Library, Johnson Country Community College, Overland Park, KS. Available at: http//www.jstor.org. Accessed December 9, 2002.
Kappler, Clarence J., ed. 1904. *Indian Affairs: Laws and Treaties, Volume II (Treaties).*
Washington, DC: U.S. Government Printing Office. Oklahoma State University. Library Electronic Publishing Center. Available at: http:// digital.library.okstate.edu/kappler/Vol2/ toey.htm.
Millet, Allan R. 1997. "Caesar and the Conquest of the Northwest Territory, the Second Harrison Campaign." *Timeline* 14, no. 5 (September–October): 2–21.
Owens, Robert M. 2002. "Jeffersonian Benevolence on the Ground: The Indian Land Cession Treaties of William Henry Harrison." *Journal of the Early American Republic* 22, no. 3 (Fall): 405–435.

Haudenosaunee Confederacy, Political System

At no time were Native people in America more influential in the politics of Europe than during the middle of the eighteenth century, and at that time no confederacy was more influential than that of the Haudenosaunee. The Haudenosaunee (Iroquois) Confederacy, sometimes known as the League of the Iroquois, controlled the only relatively level land route between the English colonies and French settlements ringing the Saint Lawrence Valley; the Confederacy maintained alliances with virtually every Indian nation bordering on its clusters of settlements. In this context, as France and Britain wrestled for hegemony in North America, some of the people who would do the most to shape the new United States, Benjamin Franklin the most prominent among them, cut their diplomatic teeth maintaining alliances with the Iroquois and their Native allies.

Thus, in the service of British interest, future revolutionaries such as Franklin were absorbing the Native ideas they would later use to counterpoise British tyranny in the colonies.

Peace among the formerly antagonistic Haudenosaunee nations was procured and maintained through the Great Law of Peace (*Kaianerekowa*), which was passed from generation to generation by the use of wampum, a form of written communication that outlined a complex system of checks and balances between nations and genders. A complete oral recitation of the Great Law can take several days; encapsulated versions of it have been translated into English for more than 100 years, and they provide one reason why the Iroquois are cited so often today in debates regarding the origins of United States fundamental law. While many other Native confederacies existed along the borders of the British colonies, most of the specific provisions of their governments have been lost.

To understand the provisions of the Great Law, one must understand the symbols it uses to represent the Confederacy. One was the traditional longhouse. The Confederacy itself was likened to a longhouse, with the Mohawks guarding the "eastern door," the Senecas at the "western door," and the Onondagas tending the ceremonial council fire in the middle. The primary national symbol of the Haudenosaunees was the Great White Pine, which serves throughout the Great Law as a metaphor for the Confederacy. Its branches shelter the people of the nations, and its roots spread to the four directions, inviting other peoples, regardless of race or nationality, to take shelter under the tree. The Haudenosaunees recognized no bars to dual citizenship; in fact, many influential figures in the English colonies and early United States were adopted into Iroquois nations.

Each of the five nations maintained its own council, whose leaders were nominated for qualities of "good mind" by the clan mothers of families holding hereditary rights to office titles. The Grand Council at Onondaga, drawn from the individual national councils, also could nominate sachems outside the hereditary structure, based on merit alone. These sachems, called pine tree chiefs, were said to have sprung from the body of the people as the symbolic Great White Pine springs from the earth.

Rights, duties, and qualifications of sachems were explicitly outlined, and the women could remove (or impeach) a sachem who was found guilty of any of a number of abuses of office, from

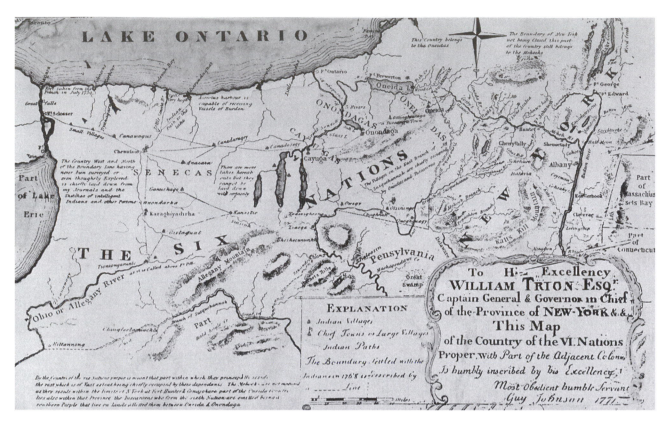

Map showing the territory of the six nations of the Iroquois Confederacy in 1771. The Iroquois were the dominant Native American diplomatic power in northeastern North America until the mideighteenth century. (North Wind Picture Archives)

missing meetings to murder. An erring chief was summoned to face charges by the war chiefs, who acted in peacetime as the peoples' eyes and ears in the council, somewhat as the role of the communication media was envisaged by Thomas Jefferson and other founders of the United States. A sachem was given three warnings, and then removed from the council if he did not mend his ways. A sachem guilty of murder lost not only his title, but also deprived his entire family of its right to representation. The women relatives holding the rights to the office were "buried" and the title transferred to a sister family.

The Great Law stipulated that leaders' skins must be seven spans thick to withstand the criticism of their constituents. The law pointed out that sachems should take pains not to become angry when people scrutinized their conduct in governmental affairs. Such a point of view pervades the writings of Jefferson and Franklin, although it was not fully codified into U.S. law until the Supreme Court decision *New York Times v. Sullivan* (1964) made it virtually impossible for public officials to

sue successfully for libel. Sachems were neither allowed to name their own successors nor carry their titles to the grave. The Great Law provided a ceremony to remove the title from a dying chief. The Great Law also provided for the removal from office of sachems who could no longer adequately function in office, a measure remarkably similar to a constitutional amendment adopted in the United States during the late twentieth century providing for the removal of an incapacitated president. The Great Law also included provisions guaranteeing freedom of religion and the right of redress before the Grand Council, and it forbade the unauthorized entry of homes—all measures that sound familiar to U.S. citizens through the Bill of Rights.

The Iroquois Confederacy is fundamentally a kinship state. The Iroquois are bound together by a clan and chieftain system that is buttressed by a similar linguistic base. However, the League of the Iroquois is much more than just a kinship state. Through the hearth, which consisted of a mother and her children, women played a profound role in

Iroquois political life. Each hearth was part of a wider group called an *otiianer*, and two or more *otiianers* constituted a clan. The word *otiianer* refers to the female heirs to the chieftainship titles of the League; the fifty authorized names for the chiefs of the Iroquois passed through the female side of the *otiianer*. The *otiianer* women selected one of the males within their group to fill a vacated seat in the League.

Such a matrilineal system was headed by a "clan mother." All the sons and daughters of a clan were related through uterine families that lived far apart. In this system, a husband went to live with his wife's family, and their children became members of the mother's clan by right of birth. Through practicing matrilineal descent, the Iroquois formed cohesive political groups that had little to do with where people lived or from what village the hearths originated.

The oldest daughter of the head of a clan sometimes succeeded her mother at her death upon the judgment of the clan. All authority sprang from the people of the various clans that made up a nation. The women who headed these clans appointed the male delegates and deputies who spoke for the clans at tribal meetings. After consultation within the clan, issues and questions were formulated and subsequently debated in council.

Iroquois political philosophy was rooted in the concept that all life is unified spiritually with the natural environment and other forces surrounding people. The Iroquois believed that the spiritual power of one person is limited, but, when combined with other individuals in a hearth, *otiianer*, or clan, spiritual power is enhanced. Whenever a person died either by natural causes or force, through murder or war, the "public" power was diminished. To maintain the strength of the group, the dead were replaced either by natural increase or by adopting captives of war. This practice of keeping clans at full strength through natural increase or adoption ensured the power and durability of the matrilineal system as well as the kinship state.

Child rearing was an important way to instill political philosophy in the youth of the Iroquois. The ideal Iroquois personality was a person who was loyal to the group but who was also independent and autonomous. Iroquois people were trained to enter a society that was egalitarian with power more equally distributed between male and female, and between young and old, than in Euro-American society. European society emphasized dominance and command structures, whereas Iroquois society was interested in collaborative behavior.

Because Iroquois society prized competence in a protector and provider more than material wealth, Iroquois children were educated to think for themselves and yet also provide for others. The Iroquois did not respect people who cowed to authority and who were submissive. Iroquois culture could be loosely called a "shame culture" because the emphasis was on honor and duty, while European culture was more guilt-oriented, since the emphasis was on an authoritarian hierarchy and advancement through the acquisition of property, status, and material possessions.

With this approach to authority, Iroquois society had none of Europe's elaborate mechanisms to control and direct the lives of the citizenry. Instead of formal instruments of authority, the Iroquois governed behavior by instilling a sense of pride and connectedness to the group through common rituals. Ostracism and shame were the punishments for transgressions until transgressors had atoned for their actions and demonstrated that they had undergone a purification process.

To sanctify and support Haudenosaunee society, the Great Law of Peace outlined the ways the that councils could function within the Iroquois nations. The origins of the League of the Iroquois arise out of the desire to resolve the problem of the blood feud. Before the founding of the League, blood revenge caused strife. Whenever clans were reduced by murder or kidnapping, relatives were bound by clan law to avenge the death or abduction of their relatives. This resulted in endless recriminations among clans. As long as justice and the control of violence resided in the clans, there was no hope of peace and goodwill.

In establishing the Conferderacy, the Iroquois built in checks and balances through the processes of consensus, removal, and public opinion. The Iroquois strictly adhered to the notion of federalism. The hereditary ("hereditary" in the Iroquois sense because the clan mothers "inherited the right" to appoint and remove peace chiefs of the Confederacy) Iroquois sachems were interested only in external matters such as war, peace, and treaty-making. The Grand Council could not interfere with the internal affairs of the tribe. Each tribe had its own sachems, but their power was limited in that they could deal only with their tribe's relations with other tribes and had no say in matters that were traditionally the concern of the clan.

The procedure for debate in the Grand Council begins with the Mohawks and Senecas (the Mohawks, Senecas, and Onondagas are called the "elder brothers"). After being debated by the Keepers of the Eastern Door (Mohawks) and the Keepers of the Western Door (Senecas), the question is then thrown across the fire to the Oneida and Cayuga statesmen (the "younger brothers") for discussion in much the same manner. Once consensus is achieved among the Oneidas and the Cayugas, the discussion is then given back to the Senecas and Mohawks for confirmation. Next the question is laid before the Onondagas for their decision.

At this stage, the Onondagas have a power similar to judicial review: They can raise objections to the proposed measure if it is believed inconsistent with the Great Law. Essentially, the legislature can rewrite the proposed law on the spot so that it can be in accord with the constitution of the Iroquois. When the Onondagas reach consensus, the *tadodaho* gives the decision to the *honowireton* (an Onondaga chief who presides over debates between the delegations) to confirm the decision if it is unanimously agreed on by all of the Onondaga sachems. Finally, the *honowireton* or *tadodaho* gives the decision of the Onondagas to the Mohawks and the Senecas so that the policy may be announced to the Grand Council as its will.

This process reflects the emphasis of the League on checks and balances, public debate, and consensus. The overall intent of such a parliamentary procedure is to encourage unity at each step. This legislative process is similar to the mechanisms of the Albany Plan of Union, the Articles of Confederation, and the U.S. Constitution.

The rights of the Iroquois citizenry are protected by portions of the Great Law, which states that, whenever an especially important matter is presented before the League Council threatening their utter ruin, the chiefs of the League must submit the matter to the decision of their people. The people of the League also can initiate impeachment proceedings and treason charges, and they can alert the Council to public opinion on a specific matter. The Iroquois people also have the power to remove sachems of the League's Council.

Upon the death or removal of a Confederacy chief, the title of the chief reverts to the women in his clan. The women protect this title and determine who will assume the position of chief. As in the power of removal, the women have the first priority in the installation of a new chief. When a position is vacant, the esteemed women of a clan gather and nominate a male member to be chief. Next, the men of the clan give their approval. After this process, the nomination is then forwarded to the Council of the League where the new chief is installed.

Public opinion is of great importance in the League of the Iroquois. Iroquois can have a direct say in the formulation of government policy even if the sachems choose to ignore the will of the people. The Great Law of Peace provides that the people can propose their own laws even when leaders fail to do so. The Great Law states that if the necessity arises to change the law, the case shall be considered and, if the new beam seems beneficial, the change, if adopted, shall be called "Added to the Rafters." This provision resembles those for popular initiative in several states of the United States, as well as the mechanism by which the federal and many state constitutions may be amended.

Through the expression of public opinion and debate, the Great Law gives the Haudenosaunee people basic rights in a distinctive and representative governmental framework. The Great Law solved disputes by giving all parties an equal hearing. The Grand Council often functioned like a think tank. Above all, political thought was the activity that went on underneath the Great Tree. For the Iroquois, the more thinkers that were beneath the tree, the better. This process is in marked contrast to European hierarchical political and educational traditions.

The League of the Iroquois a family-oriented government whose Constitution has a fixed corpus of laws that is concerned with mutual defense. Through the elimination of the clan blood feud, the state was given exclusive control over legally sanctioned violence. This process brought peace through a fundamental social contract. The Iroquois are not inclined to give much power to authorities because of the basic psychological attitudes instilled in Iroquois people. Thus, unity, peace, and brotherhood are balanced against the natural rights of all people and the necessity of sharing resources equitably. Unity for mutual defense is an abiding concept in the League. The Iroquois image of unity is a bundle of five arrows tied together to symbolize the complete union of the nations and the unbroken strength that such a unity portrays (Section 57 of the Great Law of the Iroquois). With the strength of many comes peace for future generations.

The Iroquois League accords prestige to the peace chiefs and thus seeks to reduce conflict between war and peace chiefs and the generations. The middle-aged peace chiefs are the firekeepers, encircled by warriors and providers, by women, and finally by the public at large. Although individual nations have unequal representation, this is irrelevant since each tribe votes as one. At the level of the village, the tribe, and the Grand Council, consensus devices are used to obtain unanimity and to report up and down the governmental structure. The League is not able to centralize power in matters other than mutual defense, but it is effective in diminishing friction among the Five Nations. The kinship state with its imagery of a longhouse spread afar is clearly comprehended by the Iroquois people. Iroquois power rests on the consent of the governed and is not coercive in areas of military service, taxation, and police powers. To the colonial Americans chafing under British authority, such a government and attitude toward freedom was a powerful ideal that could be used in resisting British sovereignty and tyranny.

Bruce E. Johansen

See also Albany Congress, Native Precedents; Iroquois Great Law of Peace; Wampum; Women in Native Woodlands Societies.

References and Further Reading

Fenton, William N. 1998. *The Great Law and the Longhouse: A Political History of the Iroquois Confederacy*. Norman: University of Oklahoma Press.

Gibson, John Arthur. 1992. "Concerning the League: The Iroquois League Tradition as Dictated in Onondaga." In *Algonquian and Iroquoian Linguistics Memoir No. 9*. Compiled by Hanni Woodbury, Reg Henry, and Harry Webster. Winnipeg: University of Manitoba Press.

Graymont, Barbara. 1972. *The Iroquois in the American Revolution*. Syracuse, NY: Syracuse University Press.

Grinde, Donald A., Jr., and Bruce E. Johansen. 1991. *Exemplar of Liberty: Native America and the Evolution of Democracy*. Los Angeles, CA: UCLA American Indian Studies Center.

Jacobs, Wilbur R. 1949. "Wampum, the Protocol of Indian Diplomacy." *William and Mary Quarterly* Third Series, 4, no. 3 (October): 596–604.

Mann, Barbara A., and Jerry L. Fields. 1997. "A Sign in the Sky: Dating the League of the Haudenosaunee." *American Indian Culture and Research Journal* 21, no. 2: 105–163.

Parker, Arthur C. 1916. *The Constitution of the Five Nations*. Albany: New York State Museum.

Tooker, Elisabeth. 1978. "The League of the Iroquois: Its History, Politics, and Ritual." In *Handbook of the North American Indians*. Vol. 15: *Northeast*, 418–441. Washington, DC: Smithsonian Institution.

Trigger, Bruce G., and Wilcomb E. Washburn, eds. 1996. *The Cambridge History of the Native Peoples of the Americas*. Cambridge, UK: Cambridge University Press.

Wallace, Paul A. W. 1946. *The White Roots of Peace*. Philadelphia: University of Pennsylvania Press.

Hendrick

Tiyanoga, whom the English called Hendrick (ca. 1680–1755), was a major figure in colonial affairs between 1710, when he was one of four Mohawks invited to England by Queen Anne, and 1755, when he died in battle with the French as an ally of the British. In 1754, Hendrick advised Benjamin Franklin and other colonial representatives on the principles of Iroquois government at the Albany Congress.

Hendrick, a member of the Wolf Clan, knew both Iroquois and English cultures well. He converted to Christianity and became a Mohawk preacher sometime after 1700. In England, he was painted by John Verelst and called the Emperor of the Five Nations. Hendrick was perhaps the most important individual link in a chain of alliance that saved the New York frontier and probably New England from the French in the initial stages of the Seven Year's War, which was called the French and Indian War (1754–1763) in North America.

Well-known as a man of distinction in his manners and dress, Hendrick visited England again in 1740. At that time, King George presented him with an ornate green coat of satin, fringed in gold, which Hendrick was fond of wearing in combination with his traditional Mohawk ceremonial clothing. A life-long friend of English Superintendent of Indian Affairs Sir William Johnson, Hendrick appeared often at Johnson Hall, near Albany, and had copious opportunities to rub elbows with visiting English nobles, sometimes as he arrived in war paint, fresh from battle. Thomas Pownall, a shrewd observer of colonial Indian affairs, described Hendrick as ". . . a bold artful, intriguing Fellow and has learnt no small share of European Politics, [who] obstructs and opposes all (business) where he has not been talked to first . . ." (Jacobs, 1966, 77).

Hendrick was a Mohawk who developed a relationship with the English colonies represented by William Johnson. Hendrick helped keep the Six Nations in the interests of England in its war against France. He is known for his criticism of the English for their failure to defend the Six Nations against the French, and was killed at the Battle of Lake George in 1755. (New York Public Library)

Hector Saint Jean de Crevecoeur, himself an adopted Iroquois who attended sessions of the Grand Council at Onondaga, described Hendrick in late middle age, preparing for dinner at the Johnson estate, within a few years of the Albany Congress: "[He] wished to appear at his very best . . . His head was shaved, with the exception of a little tuft of hair in the back, to which he attached a piece of silver. To the cartilage of his ears . . . he attached a little brass wire twisted into very tight spirals. A girondole (nose ring) was hung from his nose. Wearing a wide silver neckpiece, a crimson vest and a blue cloak adorned with sparkling gold, Hendrick, as was his custom, shunned European breeches for a loincloth fringed with glass beads. On his feet, Hendrick wore moccasins of tanned elk, embroidered with porcupine quills, fringed with tiny silver bells" (Grinde and Johansen, 1991, 104).

By the time Hendrick was invited to address colonial delegates at the Albany Congress in 1754, he was well known on both sides of the Atlantic, among Iroquois and Europeans alike. Hendrick played a major role in convening the Albany Congress in large part because he wished to see his friend Johnson reinstated as the English superintendent of affairs with the Six Nations. Without him, Hendrick maintained that the Covenant Chain would rust. It was Johnson himself who conducted most of the day-to-day business with the Indians at Albany.

At the Albany Congress, Hendrick repeated the advice that the Onondaga chief Canassatego had given colonial delegates at Lancaster a decade earlier, this time at a conference devoted not only to diplomacy but also to drawing up a plan for the type of colonial union the Iroquois had been requesting. The same day, at the courthouse, the colonial delegates were in the early stages of debate over the plan of union.

Hendrick was openly critical of the British at the Albany Council and hinted that the Iroquois would not ally with the English colonies unless a suitable form of unity was established among them. In talking of the proposed union of the colonies and the Six Nations on July 9, 1754, Hendrick stated, "We wish this Tree of Friendship may grow up to a great height and then we shall be a powerful people." Hendrick followed that aspiration with an analysis of Iroquois and colonial unity, when he said, "We the United Nations shall rejoice of our strength . . . and . . . we have now made so strong a Confederacy" (Grinde and Johansen, 1991, 105, 107). In reply to Hendrick's speech on Native American and colonial unity, Acting Governor James DeLancey said: "I hope that by this present Union, we shall grow up to a great height and be as powerful and famous as you were of old" (Grinde and Johansen, 1991, 107). Benjamin Franklin was commissioned to compose the final draft of the Albany Plan the same day.

Hendrick died at the Battle of Lake George in the late summer of 1755, as Sir William Johnson defeated Baron Dieskau. The elderly Mohawk was shot from his horse and bayoneted to death while on a scouting party September 8.

Bruce E. Johansen

See also Albany Congress, Native Precedents; Canassatego; Franklin, Benjamin, Native American Influences.

References and Further Reading

Grinde, Donald A., Jr., and Bruce E. Johansen. *Exemplar of Liberty: Native America and the Evolution of Democracy.* Los Angeles, CA: UCLA American Indian Studies Center, 1991.

Jacobs, Wilbur R. 1966. *Wilderness Politics and Indian Gifts.* Lincoln: University of Nebraska Press.

Wallace, Paul A. W. 1946. *The White Roots of Peace.* Philadelphia: University of Pennsylvania Press.

Hiawatha

As an historical figure, Hiawatha (ca. 1100–ca. 1180) was a Mohawk who lived at a time of great turmoil among the Iroquoian peoples. A brutal civil war had split the Five Nations (Seneca, Cayuga, Onondaga, Mohawk, and Oneida) into polarized factions. Along with the Peacemaker (Deganawida) and Jigonsaseh (the Haudenosaunee [Iroquois] Confederacy's founding clan mother), Hiawatha helped establish the *Gayansshä'gowa* (Great Law of Peace). Hiawatha is also credited with inventing wampum (freshwater shells strung together), which became vitally important to the day-to-day operations of the Iroquois League. Evolving from the strings of the Condolence Ceremony into larger and more complex belts and based on Hiawatha's original vision of wampum as a container of messages that could be passed meaningfully from person to person, wampum knotting became a form of writing essential to the administration and record keeping of the Five, and later Six, Nations. The beautiful Condolence Ceremony, which wipes the tears from the eyes of the bereaved, makes daylight for them, and covers the graves, was his creation. Hiawatha's special message was one of compassion for human suffering and, as such, was an essential complement to the Peacemaker's message of the nonviolent resolution of disputes.

At the root of the Iroquoian civil war was the blood feud, a constant series of revenge killings that seemingly could never stop. Visionaries among the Iroquois such as Hiawatha, who lived among the Onondagas, tried to call councils to eliminate the blood feud, but they were always thwarted by the evil and twisted wizard, Tadodaho, an Onondaga who used magic and spies to rule by fear and intimidation. Failing to defeat Tadadaho, Hiawatha traveled to Mohawk, Oneida, and Cayuga villages with his message of peace and brotherhood. Everywhere he went, Hiawatha's message was accepted with the proviso that he persuade the formidable Tadodaho and the Onondagas to embrace the covenant of peace.

Facing despair, Hiawatha met the prophet Deganawidah, who changed the nature of things among the Iroquois. Together, Hiawatha and Deganawidah developed a powerful message of peace. Deganawidah's vision gave Hiawatha's oratory substance. Through Deganawidah's vision, the Iroquois formulated their Constitution.

In his vision, Deganawidah saw a giant evergreen (White Pine), reaching to the sky and gaining strength from three self-counterbalancing principles of life. The first axiom was that a stable mind and healthy body should be in balance so that peace between individuals and groups could occur. Secondly, Deganawidah stated that good humane conduct, thought, and speech were requirements for equity and justice among peoples. Finally, he foresaw a society in which physical strength and civil authority would reinforce the power of the clan system.

Deganawidah's tree had four white roots that stretched to the four directions of the earth. From the base of the tree a snow-white carpet of thistledown covered the surrounding countryside. The white carpet protected the peoples that embraced the three double principles. On top of the giant pine perched an eagle. Deganawidah explained that the tree was humanity, living within the principles governing relations among human beings. The eagle was humanity's lookout against enemies who would disturb the peace. Deganawidah postulated that the white carpet could be spread to the four corners of the earth to provide a shelter of peace and brotherhood for all mankind. Deganawidah's vision was a message from the Creator to bring harmony into human existence and unite all peoples into a single family guided by his three dual principles.

With such a powerful vision, Deganawidah and Hiawatha were able to subdue the evil Tadodaho and transform his mind. In part by combing snakes from his hair, they removed evil feelings and thoughts from the head of Tadodaho and turned his mind toward reason and peace. The evil wizard became reborn into a humane person charged with implementing the message of Deganawidah. After Tadodaho had submitted to the redemption, Onondaga became the central fire of the Haudenosaunee and the Onondagas became the firekeepers of the new Confederacy. To this day, the Great Council Fire of the Confederacy is kept in the land of the Onondagas.

Hiawatha was a historical figure credited with helping to found the Iroquois Confederacy with Deganawidah (the Peacemaker). Both worked to create a confederacy between the Mohawk, Oneida, Onandagas, Cayugas, and Seneca nations. (North Wind Picture Archives)

After Tadodaho's conversion, the clan leaders of the Five Nations gathered around the Council Fire at Onondaga to hear the laws and government of the Confederacy. The fundamental laws of the Iroquois Confederacy espoused peace and brotherhood, unity, balance of power, the natural rights of all people, the impeachment and removal of the abusers of power, and the sharing of resources. Moreover, the blood feud was outlawed and replaced by a Condolence Ceremony. Under the new law, the bereaved family of a murder victim could accept twenty strings of wampum from the slayer's family (ten for the dead person and ten for the life of the murderer himself) in place of the traditional practice of exacting clan revenge. If a woman was killed, the price was thirty wampum strings. Through this ceremony, the control over legally sanctioned violence was enlarged from the clan to the League.

Hiawatha's wampum was long kept as a sacred item. One wide belt, said to have been made by Hiawatha himself, became the symbol of League unity. It contained thirty-eight rows of black wampum with a white heart in its center, flanked on either side by a white square. Everything was connected to everything else by white lines of wampum (white signifying *uki*, peace and goodness). Called the Hiawatha Belt, it was purchased by John Boyd Thatcher of Albany and deposited in the Library of Congress around the turn of the twentieth century.

The Hiawatha wampum belt symbolizes the structure of the Haudenosaunee Confederacy, with four connected squares representing the Senecas, Cayugas, Oneidas, and Mohawks. The tree of peace symbol in the center (an elongated triangle) represents the Onondagas, who tend the Central Council Fire. The belt is presently 10.5 inches wide and 21.5

inches long, but its frayed edges suggest it may have been longer in the past. The white squares and tree of peace symbol are made of purple wampum, against a background of white wampum. The Hiawatha Belt has been dated by the scholar William N. Fenton to the mideighteenth century, but this is probably not an origin date. Belts were repaired and thus replaced bead by bead over time; so they may be several centuries older than the scientific dating of existing belts indicates. A belt may have been repaired several times over the centuries, gradually changing as bead-making technology (such as the introduction of glass beads by Europeans) evolved.

In the nineteenth century, European-American ethnographers started "collecting" various Native oral traditions that, for the most part, they did not understand. Standards of scholarship were much lower at the time, and little heed was paid to the large cultural distinctions among Native American groups. Some very questionable material thus made its way into the Western chronicles, not the least of it from the fallible pen of Henry Rowe Schoolcraft. He freely made up, interpolated, and gutted traditions, mixing and matching them as he saw fit. Native sensibilities mattered little to him. One of his most fanciful and least grounded works, his *Algic Researches* (1839, 1856), contained a fractured "Myth of Hiawatha." ("Algic" was Schoolcraft's invented word for woodland cultures.)

Schoolcraft's tale about Hiawatha bore no resemblance to the historical figure cherished in Haudenosaunee tradition. Schoolcraft turned him into an Anishinabe (Ojibway, also known as Chippewa) and confused him with the Anishinabe culture hero Nanapush (also known as Manabozho). Schoolcraft knew the difference, but simply liked the sound of "Manabozho." In addition, probably out of ignorance, Schoolcraft confused Hiawatha with Tarachiawagon, one name for the Peacemaker. Finally, Schoolcraft plagiarized Joshua Clark's *Onondaga, or, Reminiscences of Earlier and Later Times* (1849), pretending that the research was his own.

The issue was only confounded further when Henry Wadsworth Longfellow used Schoolcraft's mangled version of tradition as the basis of his epic poem, "The Song of Hiawatha" (1855). Longfellow himself plagiarized the Finnish poem *Kalevala* and lifted lore from the Icelandic epic *Edda* to write his dubious "Song," creating an Iroquoian nightmare that not only cast Hiawatha as an Anishinabe-Finnish-Icelander, but also turned him into a Christian philosopher as well. Knowing nothing of the true Hiawatha and hopelessly confusing him with the Peacemaker, Longfellow presented Hiawatha as a fey imitation Jesus. Longfellow's "Song of Hiawatha" became wildly popular with nineteenth-century Euro-American readers.

Although these Western versions of the Hiawatha story are completely without foundation in Haudenosaunee oral tradition, some modern west-of-the-Mississippi Algonquins reenact Longfellow's version of "The Song of Hiawatha" at pow-wows, to the extreme discomfort of Haudenosaunee onlookers. The Iroquoian Hiawatha of history needs to be firmly disengaged from these fantastic nineteenth-century misrepresentations. Hiawatha's unflagging speakership for the Peacemaker, his message of compassion, his creation of the Condolence Ceremony, his invention of the Iroquoian writing system, and his combing the snakes from the hair of Adodaroh (Tadadaho) are what should be told about him.

Barbara Alice Mann and Bruce E. Johansen

See also Deganawidah; Haudenosaunee Confederacy, Political System; Wampum.
References and Further Reading
Howard, Helen A. 1971. "Hiawatha: Co-Founder of an Indian United Nations." *Journal of the West* 10, no. 3: 428–438.

Mann, Barbara A. Spring. 1995. "The Fire at Onondaga: Wampum as Proto-Writing." *Akwesasne Notes* New Series 1, no. 1: 40–48.

Parker, Arthur Caswell. 1916. *The Constitution of the Five Nations, or The Iroquois Book of the Great Law*. Albany: University of the State of New York.

Wallace, Paul A. W. 1948. "The Return of Hiawatha." *Quarterly Journal of the New York State Historical Association* 29, no. 4: 385–403.

Wallace, Paul A. W. 1946. *The White Roots of Peace*. Philadelphia: University of Pennsylvania Press.

Hooker Jim

In the 1850s, the Modocs traded in Yreka, California, and the traders and townspeople there gave the Indian leaders the colorful and sometimes unflattering names by which they became known. Hooker Jim (ca. 1825–1879) was a name given to a leader in the Modoc War of 1872–1873 who emerged as a rival to Kintpuash (Captain Jack). Although little is known of his early life, Hooker Jim's name became a household word throughout the United States when hostilities broke out between the Modocs and the U.S. Army. In 1864, the Modocs and Klamaths ceded

most of their land and moved onto the Klamath reservation in southern Oregon. Deeply opposed to the relocation of his people, Hooker Jim persuaded his followers to return to their aboriginal homeland in northern California. These Modocs advocated the creation of their own reservation. In 1870, about 300 Modocs under Kintpuash reestablished a community in their former homeland on the Lost River.

In November 1872, the U.S. Army visited Kintpuash's encampment on the Lost River and ordered the Modocs to the Klamath Reservation. Kintpuash opposed the order, and increasing conflict with non-Natives led to the first battle of the Modoc War. Hooker Jim and his people were living on the opposite side of the river when some ranchers fired on them, killing a woman and a baby and wounding several men. Angered by these actions, Hooker Jim and Curly Headed Doctor raided a neighboring ranch and killed twelve whites. Hooker Jim and his people then fled southward to the Lava Beds, where Kintpuash and his followers were defending themselves.

Kintpuash still believed that a peaceful settlement might be negotiated. However, the Modocs balked at the demands of the Army to hand over the men who had killed the ranchers. At a peace conference set to discuss matters, Hooker Jim and others told Kintpuash that the only way he could prove that he was not a coward would be to kill General Edward R. S. Canby. On April 11, 1873, as the conference started, Kintpuash shot Canby, wounded Indian Superintendent Alfred B. Meachum, and killed a minister.

In the weeks after the abortive conference, Hooker Jim and Kintpuash argued about the appropriate course of action. Hooker Jim deserted the fight in the Lava Beds, surrendered, and subsequently showed the Army where Kintpuash was hiding. At Kintpuash's trial in July 1873, Hooker Jim provided testimony against Kintpuash to save himself. After the trial and the execution of four leaders, Hooker Jim and about 150 other Modocs were sent to Indian Territory. Hooker Jim later died at the Quapaw Agency in Indian Territory in 1879.

Bruce E. Johansen

See also Captain Jack.
Reference and Further Reading
Johansen, Bruce E., and Donald A. Grinde, Jr. 1997. *The Encyclopedia of Native American Biography,* New York: Henry Holt.

Jackson, Andrew

Mention "Andrew Jackson" to most Americans, and the phrase "Jacksonian Democracy" may spring to mind. To the descendents of Native Americans who survived the period, however, the first comparative analogy may be to the Bataan Death March of World War II. Among Native Americans, Jackson, the seventh president of the United States, is most closely identified with the Removal Act (1830), which forced at least 100,000 Native people off their traditional homelands into involuntary exile in "Indian territory," now Oklahoma. President Andrew Jackson called Indian removal the "most arduous" of his duties as president of the United States. "I watched over it [removal] with great vigilance," Jackson recalled after he left the presidency (Rogin, 1975, 206).

Jackson was born March 15, 1767, in the Waxhaws area on the border between present-day North and South Carolina, and died June 8, 1845, at The Hermitage, Davidson County, Tennessee. Jackson's career (first as an Army general, then as president) coincided with rapid westward migration into Native lands. The explosion of westward migration after roughly 1800 generated enormous profits in land speculation. Fortunes were made in early America, not usually by working the land, but by buying early and holding large parcels for sale after demand increased dramatically because of non-Indian immigration.

As a frontier lawyer in Tennessee, Jackson acquired immense holdings with which he began a mercantile establishment and bought a plantation, including "an expensive frame house at a time when most people in the same area lived in log cabins, and spent large sums on whiskey, horses, and expensive home furnishings imported from Europe" (Rogin, 1975, 55). Jackson also quickly acquired more than a hundred slaves, making him one of frontier Tennessee's largest owners of human capital. He traded actively in slaves, and occasionally wagered them on horse races in a display of expendable wealth.

Rogin quoted a contemporary source: "Were I to characterize the United States, it would be by the appellation of the land of speculators" (Rogin, 1975, 80). Land, once ownership had been wrested from original Native owners, became the largest "futures market" available at the time, its value determined by its hoped-for future use in a newly evolving non-Indian society. As an Army general and later as president, Jackson represented the values and interests of the land-speculation industry.

Jackson did not seek the removal of the Cherokees and other Civilized Tribes—the Cherokee, Choctaw, Chickasaw, Creek, and Seminole—because they did not know how to make productive use of the land. On the contrary, four of the five (the exception being the Seminoles, who had escaped to Florida) were called "civilized" by the immigrants precisely because they were making exactly the kind of progress that the U.S. government desired of them: becoming farmers, educating their children, constituting governments modeled on the United States. Immigrants, many of them Scot and Irish, had married into Native families. Some of them owned plantations and slaves. Andrew Jackson strongly encouraged removal because his slaves and plantation placed his interests squarely among those of the races and classes whose members benefited most from Indian removal.

By the time he emerged as an advocate of Indian removal, President Jackson's name had scorched the memories of Native American peoples for decades as an Indian fighter. As a general in the U.S. Army, Jackson blazed a trail of fire throughout the South, refusing to retreat even when his superiors ordered him to relent. Between 1814 and 1824, before Jackson was elected president, he already had been the main agent for the United States in eleven treaties of cession. The land involved in these treaties included three-quarters of Alabama and Georgia, one-third of Tennessee, and one-fifth of Georgia and Mississippi (as well as smaller areas of Kentucky and North Carolina) (Rogin, 1975, 165).

In a battlefield confrontation with William Weatherford's Creeks at Horseshoe Bend, Alabama, Jackson imprisoned assistants who advised retreat. For those who retreated in battle without authorization, the penalty levied by General Jackson was harsher: "Any officer or soldier who flies before the enemy without being compelled to do so by superior force . . . shall suffer death" (Tebbel, 1966, 75).

Having subdued the Creeks, General Jackson next received orders to quell what the War Department politely called "troubles" in Georgia, principally among the Seminoles. By 1818, Jackson's troops were chasing them into Florida, which was still under Spanish jurisdiction (the area would be ceded to the United States in 1821). Having seized several Spanish forts along the way, Jackson withdrew. While he endured a debate in Congress over his cross-border expedition, Jackson also reaped popular acclaim from expansion-minded Americans that swelled his ambitions for the presidency.

Among Native Americans, President Andrew Jackson is most closely identified with the Removal Act which forced at least 100,000 Native people off their traditional homelands. (Library of Congress)

The Seminoles, most of whom were descended from Creeks, had elected to ally with the Spanish rather than the United States, an act of virtual treason to General Jackson. Furthermore, the Seminoles were giving shelter to runaway slaves. Inasmuch as the Seminoles and the escaped slaves had intermarried over generations, the pretext of Jackson's raid was the recovery of "stolen property," runaway slaves. After the United States purchased Florida from Spain, slave-hunting vigilantes invaded the area en masse, killing Seminoles as well as blacks. During the 1830s, when President Jackson proposed to remove the Seminoles from Florida to Indian Territory, they refused. Moving deep into the swamps of southern Florida (an area that, ironically, was being used as a removal *destination* for other Native peoples), the Seminoles fought 1,500 U.S. Army troops to a bloody stalemate during seven years of warfare. They were never defeated, and they never moved from their new homeland.

After Spain ceded Florida to the United States, General Jackson and other U.S. officials lost any remaining motive for treating the Indians as allies. From then on, they were defined as subjects, to be moved out as Anglo-Americans rushed into the Southeast. Jackson's policy—"move the Indians out"—became the national standard after his election as president in 1828. Alabama had already been created in 1819 from Creek and Cherokee territory; Mississippi was created in 1817 from Choctaw and Chickasaw country. These two states, along with Georgia, passed laws outlawing tribal governments and making Indians subject to state jurisdiction, after which open season was declared on remaining Native lands.

All of this activity violated treaties with the federal government. Confronted with this fact, President Jackson told the Indians that he was unable to stand by the treaties because they raised nettlesome issues of states' rights, an emerging issue in the decades before the Civil War. Instead, Jackson proposed that the Indians be moved westward.

In a message to Congress in December of 1830, in the midst of the nationwide debate over Indian removal, Jackson maintained:

> What good man would prefer a country covered with forests and ranged by a few thousand savages to our extensive republic, studded with cities, towns, and prosperous farms, embellished with all the improvements which art can devise or industry execute, occupied by more than 12 million happy people, and filled with the blessings of liberty, civilization, and religion (Satz, 1975, 44).

Jackson, who as a general told his troops to root out Indians from their "dens" and to kill Indian women and their "whelps," struck the same themes on a slightly more erudite tone as president. In his second annual message to Congress, Jackson reflected on the fact that some white Americans were growing "melancholy" over the fact that the Indians were being driven to their "tomb." These critics must understand, Jackson said, that "true philanthropy reconciles the mind to these vicissitudes as it does to the extinction of one generation to make way for another" (Stannard, 1992, 240).

During the Jackson administration, the United States concluded nearly seventy treaties with Native American nations, more than any other presidential administration. The United States acquired more

than 100 million acres of Native American land during the years Jackson was in office, in exchange for roughly $68 million (68 cents an acre) and 32 million acres west of the Mississippi River. Forty-six thousand Indians were compelled to leave their homelands and move west of the Mississippi during the same years (Satz, 1975, 97). By such means, observed de Tocqueville, "The Americans cheaply acquire whole provinces which the richest sovereigns in Europe could not afford to buy" (Satz, 1975, 98).

Their basis in U.S. law notwithstanding, Jackson thought that Indian treaties were anachronisms. "An absurdity," he called them, "not to be reconciled with the principles of our government" (McNickle, 1949, 192). He elaborated, before his election to the presidency, in a letter to President James Monroe (another advocate of Indian removal) in 1817:

> The Indians are the subjects of the United States, inhabiting its territory and acknowledging its sovereignty. Then is it not absurd for the sovereign to negotiate by treaty with the subject? I have always thought, that Congress had as much right to regulate by acts of legislation, all Indian concerns as they had of territories, are citizens of the United States and entitled to all the rights thereof, the Indians are subjects and entitled to their protection and fostering care (McNickle, 1949, 193).

The confusions of convoluted grammar aside, it is not easy to decipher what General Jackson is saying. Is he declaring the Indians to be citizens? Legally, that was not widely the case until a century later. Is he personally abrogating the treaties, which were signed by parties who had addressed each other as diplomatic peers, nation to nation, barely two generations earlier? Whatever the nature of his rhetoric, the actions of the Jackson administration made clear, especially for the Native American peoples of the South, just what Jackson meant by "protection and fostering care."

Bruce E. Johansen

See also *Cherokee Nation v. Georgia;* Forced Marches; Genocide; Indian Removal Act; Relocation; Seminole Wars; Trail of Tears; Tribal Sovereignty; *Worcester v. Georgia.*

References and Further Reading
Brandon, William. 1961. *The American Heritage Book of Indians.* New York: Dell.
Cole, Donald B. 1993. *The Presidency of Andrew Jackson.* Lawrence: University Press of Kansas.

McNickle, D'Arcy. 1949. *They Came Here First: The Epic of the American Indian.* Philadelphia, PA: J. B. Lippincott Co.

Rogin, Michael Paul. 1975. *Fathers and Children: Andrew Jackson and the Subjugation of the American Indian.* New York: Alfred A. Knopf.

Satz, Ronald N. 1975. *American Indian Policy in the Jacksonian Era.* Lincoln: University of Nebraska Press.

Stannard, David. 1992. *American Holocaust: Columbus and the Conquest of the New World.* Oxford: Oxford University Press.

Tebbel, John W. 1966. *The Compact History of the Indian Wars.* New York: Hawthorne Books.

Jackson, Helen Hunt

Helen Maria Fiske (1830–1885), who would become known later in life as Helen Hunt Jackson, was born October 15, 1830, in Amherst, Massachusetts, the daughter of Nathan Welby Fiske, a professor of languages at Amherst College. She was described as "a child of dangerous versatility and vivacity" (Mathes, 1990, 21). Variously portrayed as brilliant and something of a pest, the young Helen Fiske learned to read and write earlier than most children, drawing from collegiate surroundings, becoming a young woman "with candid beaming eyes, in which kindness contented with penetration," a "soul of fire," with the ability to "strongly love, to frankly hate" (Mathes, 1990, 22).

As a girl, Helen became close friends with the poet Emily Dickinson. Fiske, Dickinson, and Emily Fowler (who was briefly well known as an author in her later life) came to be known as the Amherst girls, a group of talented women born to Amherst faculty members. In her own time, Helen was a better-known poet than Dickinson, who spent much of her own life in obscurity.

At the age of eleven, Helen Fiske was sent to the first of several boarding schools where she spent her teenage years. By age nineteen, she had been orphaned; both of her parents died of tuberculosis. Early in her life, Helen determined to support herself as an independent woman, not an easy role in a society in which women were defined as men's property. She decided to make her living as a writer.

First known as a romantic poet, she later expanded her scope to include travel articles, short stories, novels, and books for children. Before becoming famous for her Indian reform work late in her life, she had been "an Army wife, mother, and woman of society . . . a literary person, a poet and essayist, writer of travel sketches and short stories" (Banning, 1973, xix). She was, according to her biographer Evelyn I. Banning, a woman of contradictions. While some of her writings laughed at fashion, she dressed elegantly, often beyond the station of the junior Army officer, Edward B. Hunt, whom she married at the age of twenty-two. Before the treatment of the Ponca Indians tripped her sense of indignity, Helen Hunt Jackson had been a nearly apolitical person, having taken no published position on women's suffrage or slavery, even as she "burst the bounds . . . [of] the separate sphere assigned to women during the Victorian era" (Mathes, 1990, ix).

Within the fifteen years after she married Edward Hunt, Helen gave birth to two sons and lost both of them, one at the age of one year, the other at age nine. Her husband also died, leaving her nearly alone in the world. She assuaged her loneliness by writing poetry, becoming one of the best regarded poets of nineteenth-century America. Ralph Waldo Emerson often carried her poetry in his pocket to show to friends (Banning, 1973, xx). In 1875 she married William S. Jackson of Colorado Springs, whose name she carried when her Indian reform work became well-known. At the age of forty-nine, she took up the cause of "the Indian" with a fervor that consumed her attention and energies for the last few remaining years of her short life.

Jackson's attention was turned toward the condition of Native Americans during October of 1879, shortly after Judge Elmer Dundy had ruled in *Standing Bear v. Crook.* In Boston, Jackson heard a speech describing the travail of Standing Bear and his band of Poncas who, forced off their land in northern Nebraska, had escaped reservation life in Indian Territory. They had trekked 500 miles northward during the worst of a midcontinental winter to take shelter with the U'mahas (Omahas) near the city of Omaha where, in 1879, Judge Dundy ruled that Standing Bear must be regarded as a human being under the law of habeas corpus.

After the trial, a group of Ponca Indians, including Standing Bear, visited several cities, including Chicago, New York City, Philadelphia, Baltimore, and Boston. It was in Boston, however, that support was greatest; $3,000 of the $4,000 the Poncas thought they would need to pursue their land claim was raised there (Mathes, 1989, 46). Henry Wadsworth Longfellow played a crucial role in the success of the Poncas' efforts in Boston. The Poncas stayed in Boston several weeks from late October

A successful and prolific author, Helen Hunt Jackson is best remembered for A Century of Dishonor *(1881) and* Ramona *(1884), books that helped to raise awareness of Native American rights and of their ill treatment at the hands of the U.S. government. (Library of Congress)*

into December and were presented at numerous fund-raisers. In early December, more than 1,000 Bostonians gathered at Faneuil Hall to hear Standing Bear speak. After the speeches, more than half the audience crowded the stage to shake hands with him (Mathes, 1989, 47).

After hearing their story, Jackson collected funds for the Poncas and encouraged others to take an active part in their struggles. The mayor of Boston joined a fund-raising committee for the Poncas' legal campaign to win back their homeland. Jackson herself joined Standing Bear, Thomas Henry Tibbles, and Susette "Bright Eyes" LaFlesche on a tour throughout New England. Tibbles credited Jackson's support as being one of the major factors in the Poncas' ultimate victory (Banning, 1973, 150).

Jackson's acquaintance with the Poncas started her down a new literary road. Within two years of first hearing the Poncas' heartrending story, Jackson published *A Century of Dishonor*. Three years later, with a pledge to write a novel that would become the Native American version of *Uncle Tom's Cabin*, she published the best-seller *Ramona*.

A Century of Dishonor is a factual sketch of broken treaties and corruption in the Indian Bureau; *Ramona* is a fictional account of the abuses suffered by the Mission Indians of California, based on Jackson's travels in that area shortly after *A Century of Dishonor* was published. Both books were among the best sellers of their time, one more indication of just how many non-Indians sympathized with the Native American victims of westward expansion.

Jackson's books may have been so immensely popular during the 1880s because many people in the expanding United States, finding a need to reconcile the taking of a continent with notions of their own civility, sought to deal with the "Indian Problem" in what they believed to be a civilized and humane manner. Thus, cultural genocide (a late twentieth-century phrase) was advanced in the modulated tones of civility, of doing what was believed to be best for "the Indian."

Jackson's books fueled a national debate over what would become of Native Americans who had survived subjugation by immigrant non-Natives. Most of her books combined condemnation of the government's earlier behavior with advocacy of popular solutions to the Indian Problem, such as religious instruction, boarding schools, and allotment.

After *A Century of Dishonor* was published, Jackson sent a copy of it to each member of Congress at her own expense. She then visited each representative personally to emphasize what she thought must be done to remove the stain of the dishonorable century she had described. Jackson died by the time Congress passed the General Allotment (Dawes) Act in 1887, officially adopting allotment (which she had believed would save Native Americans from extinction), at the same time turning it into a real estate vehicle for homesteaders and corporations (Indians would lose two-thirds of their remaining land base in the fifty years to follow).

Ramona, which was reprinted 300 times after Jackson's death, was adapted for stage and screen several times. "Every incident in *Ramona* . . . is true," Jackson wrote. "A Cahuilla Indian was shot two years ago exactly as Alessandro is—and his wife's name was Ramona, and I never knew this fact until Ramona was half written" (Mathes, 1986, 43).

By the middle 1880s, Jackson was suffering recurring bouts of malarial symptoms and other health problems, which gradually debilitated her. In 1885, on her deathbed, Jackson wrote of her work, "As I lie here, nothing looks to me of any value except the words I have spoken for the Indians" (Banning, 1973, 224). Her last letter, dated August 8, was written to President Grover Cleveland: "I ask you to read my *A Century of Dishonor*. I am dying happier in the belief I have that it is your hand that is destined to strike the first steady blow toward lifting the burden of infamy from our country and writing the wrongs of the Indian race . . ." (Banning, 1973, 225).

Jackson died on August 12, 1885. Upon hearing of her death, Susette LaFlesche, "shut herself into her room and wept all day long," according to her husband Thomas Henry Tibbles. "For weeks afterward she mourned the loss of this closest of her intimate friends, who had given herself wholeheartedly to save an unhappy race" (Mathes, 1986, 44).

Dickinson penned a verse in eulogy of Jackson:

Helen of Troy will die,
but Helen of Colorado, never.
"Dear friend, you can walk"
were the last words I wrote her—
"Dear friend, I can fly"—
her immortal reply (Banning, frontpiece).

Bruce E. Johansen

See also Genocide; LaFlesche, Susette Picotte;
  Standing Bear v. Crook.

References and Further Reading

Banning, Evelyn L. 1973. *Helen Hunt Jackson.* New York: Vanguard Press.
Hayes, Robert G. 1997. *A Race at Bay: New York Times Editorials on the "Indian Problem."* Carbondale: Southern Illinois University Press.
Jackson, Helen Hunt. 1972. *A Century of Dishonor: A Sketch of the United States Government's Dealings with Some of the Indian Tribes.* St. Clair Shores, MI: Scholarly Press. [Originally printed in 1888 Boston: Roberts Bros.]
Mathes, Valerie Sherer. 1986. "Helen Hunt Jackson: A Legacy of Indian Reform." *Essays and Monographs in Colorado History* 4 (1986): 25–58.
Mathes, Valerie Sherer. 1989. "Helen Hunt Jackson and the Ponca Controversy." *Montana* 39 (Winter): 42–53.
Mathes, Valerie Sherer. 1990. *Helen Hunt Jackson and Her Indian Reform Legacy.* Austin: University of Texas Press.

Jigonsaseh

"Jigonsaseh" is the position title of the Head Clan Mother of the Iroquois League. Also rendered Jikonsaseh, Gekeasawsa, and Yegonwaneh, the word is variously translated as the New Face, the Fat Face, and the Fat-Faced Lynx. Her titles in English include the Peace Queen, the Mother of Nations, the Fire Woman, the Great Woman, and the Maize Maiden. The position was created when the Great Law of Peace, also called the Constitution of the Five Nations, was established by the Iroquois League in the twelfth century.

Coming out of the Mound Builder era, the Iroquoian people experienced much scattered fighting, as the old male-dominated, hierarchical order fought the newer, more democratic orders then evolving for control of society. The old order valued hunting over agriculture, whereas the new order placed its dependency on planting, especially of corn. The fighting from New York to Ohio became quite ferocious, so that families on both sides lost valued members daily. The Iroquoian peoples north of the Saint Lawrence River and Lakes Ontario and Erie had already developed a democratic government and an economy based on agriculture. Looking south, they trembled at the thought of the fighting spreading north to them.

In the midst of this turmoil, strong spirits returned to the people to aid them in their time of need. Sapling, the Elder Twin of the First Family, reappeared among the Iroquois at the Bay of Quinte as the Peacemaker (whose name, Deganawidah, is not to be spoken). At the same time, his First Family mother, the Lynx (also known as Hanging Flowers), Sky Woman's Daughter, came as the Peace Queen. Traditionally an Attiwenderonk, she also came down from the north to bring methods of corn planting to her southern sisters. Her followers became known as the Cultivators. The Peacemaker and the Peace Queen came separately, but soon met.

Knowing that he was unable to promulgate the peace by himself, the Peacemaker sought out allies in the south, the very first of them being that Great Woman, the Head Mother of the Cultivators. He approached her with respect, urging her to add his message of Peace to her message of Corn, and, after due consideration, she agreed. However, she also insisted that he include the strong political powers of women in his Great Law. In his turn, he agreed. The two forged an alliance, coordinating their efforts thereafter.

Creating the constitutional peace required extensive lobbying over decades, but eventually the Iroquoian nations grew so disgusted with fighting that they inclined their ears ever more openly to the ways of Corn and Peace. Traditions exist of Jigonsaseh traveling tirelessly about, exhorting the people even as she evaded death squads sent by the priests to kill her. The Cultivators were often frightened for her safety on these journeys, but every time they spotted her coming home, paddling her canoe to safety.

As Jigonsaseh and Peacemaker gained followers (including Hiawatha, a formerly formidable foe), the leaders of the older culture lost theirs. Finally, with the decision of the Senecas to join the peace, only one priest obstructed their way. He was Adodaroh, the deeply feared and powerful shaman of the Onondagas, whose snake and cannibal cult had terrorized the people into submission for many years. Now, however, even Adodaroh's [a.k.a. Tadodaho or Tadadaho] once trusted lieutenant, Hiawatha, opposed him.

Representatives of all five nations—the Mohawks, Oneidas, Onondagas, Cayugas, and Senecas—gathered at Onondaga to confront Adodaroh once and for all. Deeply angry, the old priest withdrew to an island that could be approached only by canoe. Twice, the Peacemaker and Hiawatha attempted parley, but twice the old man called up the winds to blow their canoe back to shore. Finally, Jigonsaseh gave the pair a powerful medicine song to calm the waters and call the ancestors. Singing her song, the Peacemaker and Hiawatha were able to approach Adodaroh but, instead of killing or threatening him, they carried Jigonsaseh's message: If he would come over to the side of Corn and Peace, they would make him the first chairman of the Men's Grand Council of the League. Seeing his chance to retain status, the wily old man accepted their proposal.

At that point, Jigonsaseh stepped forward to announce the women's decisions regarding the people's representatives to the Men's Grand Council. She sanctioned each lineage chief, putting the horns of office on his head and announcing his election to office. Establishment of the Clan Mothers also occurred at this time, but the traditions leading to this development are obscure today. Early male anthropologists heard only the men's versions of the traditions, not realizing that there were equally important women's versions as well.

In Iroquoian culture, the names of those who attained greatness become the position titles for those who follow them in those positions. Thus the name "Adodaroh" became the position title for the Chairman of the Men's Grand Council, and the name "Jigonsaseh" became the position title for the Head Mother of the Women's Clan Council. Later Jigonsasehs continued the greatness of the first. In particular, the Jigonsaseh of the 1680s is greatly honored for defeating the Marquis de Denonville, who had been sent by Louis XIV of France along with a mighty army to destroy the Iroquois League.

After the Iroquois League was overrun by the Americans in the Revolutionary War, every attempt was made by settlers and their government to destroy Iroquoian culture. This included massive assaults on the rights and powers of women. The United States attempted to wipe out the office of the Jigonsaseh, abolishing it in 1848. The Iroquois secretly continued granting the office, however. The last recorded incumbent of the position was Gahahno (Caroline Mountpleasant), who held it until her death in 1892. The Mountpleasant family still exists, and many recognize its modern clan descendents' claim to the title.

Barbara Alice Mann

See also Haudenosaunee Confederacy, Political System.

References and Further Reading
Cusick, David. "Sketches of Ancient History of the Six Nations." [1825] 1892. In *The Iroquois Trail, or, Footprints of the Six Nations in Customs, Traditions, and History*. Edited by William Martin Beauchamp. Fayetteville, NY: H. C. Beauchamp.
Gibson, John Arthur. [1912] 1992. *Concerning the League: The Iroquois Tradition as Dictated in Onondaga by John Arthur Gibson. Memoir 9*. Edited and compiled and translated by Hanni Woodbury. Winnipeg, MB: Algonquian and Iroquoian Linguistics Memoirs.
Hewitt, John Napoleon Brinton. 1915. "Some Esoteric Aspects of the League of the Iroquois." *Proceedings of the International Congress of Americanists* 19: 322–326.
Hewitt, John Napoleon Brinton. 1920. "A Constitutional League of Peace in the Stone Age of America: The League of the Iroquois and Its Constitution." *Smithsonian Institution Series* 527–545.
Hewitt, John Napoleon Brinton. 1927. "Ethnological Studies Among the Iroquois Indians." *Smithsonian Miscellaneous Collections* 78: 237–247.

Hewitt, John Napoleon Brinton. 1931. "Field Studies Among the Iroquois Tribes." *Explorations and Field-work of the Smithsonian Institution in 1930* : 175–178.

Jemison, Pete. 1988. "Mother of Nations: The Peace Queen, a Neglected Tradition." *Akwe:kon* 5: 68–70.

Johnson, Elias. [1881] 1978. *Legends, Traditions, and Laws of the Iroquois, or Six Nations.* New York: AMS Press.

Mann, Barbara Alice. 1997. "The Lynx in Time: Haudenosaunee Women's Traditions and History." *American Indian Quarterly* 21, no. 3: 423–450.

Mann, Barbara Alice. 2000. "Jigonsaseh." In *Encyclopedia of the Haudenosaunee (Iroquois League)*. Edited by Bruce Elliott Johansen and Barbara Alice Mann, 176–180. Westport, CT: Greenwood Press.

Mann, Barbara Alice. 2004. *Iroquoian Women: The Gantowisas*, 115–116, 124–155. New York: Peter Lang, 2004.

Mann, Barbara A., and Jerry L. Fields. 1997. "A Sign in the Sky: Dating the League of the Haudenosaunee." *American Indian Culture and Research Journal* 21, no. 2: 105–163.

Parker, Arthur Caswell (Gawaso Wanneh). 1916. *The Constitution of the Five Nations, or, The Iroquois Book of the Great Law.* Albany: University of the State of New York.

Parker, Arthur Caswell (Gawaso Wanneh). 1919. *The Life of General Ely S. Parker, Last Grand Sachem of the Iroquois and General Grant's Military Secretary.* Buffalo, ND: Buffalo Historical Society.

Parker, Arthur Caswell (Gawaso Wanneh). 1928. "The Maize Maiden." In *Rumbling Wings and Other Indian Tales*, 179–191. Garden City, NY: Doubleday.

Wallace, Paul A. W. *The White Roots of Peace.* 1946. Empire State Historical Publication Series no. 56. Port Washington, NY: Ira J. Friedman.

Johnson, Emily Pauline

Born March 10, 1861, on the Six Nations reserve, upper Canada, Emily Pauline Johnson (Mohawk) died March 7, 1913, in Vancouver, British Columbia. Johnson, the first aboriginal woman to write in English about Native issues, was famous for her performances, poetry, and short stories. Since her death, Johnson's life has been claimed by a variety of political and cultural interest groups: academic, feminist, nationalist, Nativist, activist, artistic, and imperialist.

To the aboriginal community Johnson is a complex and contradictory figure. She critiqued Canada's racist policies and lamented the loss of Native culture, but she also sold Iroquoian artifacts to collectors and exploited her heritage. Her life and literary work exemplifies living with a mixed heritage in a society that reveled in the exotic while demanding assimilation.

Johnson's father, George Henry Martin Johnson, a nontraditional and proud Mohawk chief from the Wolf Clan, was a temperance advocate, a Christian, and a government interpreter. Her mother, Emily Susannah Howells, was an English-Canadian Quaker raised in the United States. Johnson was largely homeschooled, although she attended the reserve school and Brantford Collegiate Institute. After her father's death in 1884 and the family's relocation to rented accommodations in Brantford, Johnson turned to writing at age twenty-three. In 1886, as a sign of her bicultural heritage and identity, she began signing her work as E. Pauline Johnson and Tekahionwake (her great-grandfather's name). Johnson realized income from her work only after 1892. Her success began when Frank Yeigh, the president of the Young Men's Liberal Club of Toronto, invited Johnson to an evening of poetry. From this initial recital, Johnson undertook over 125 performances across southern Ontario between October 1892 and May 1893.

It was during these initial performances that Johnson began appearing in "traditional" Native costume during the first act and returned for the second in an elegant gown. Her Native costume was a buckskin dress purchased from the Hudson's Bay Company in Winnipeg. With the help of a younger sister, Johnson added a rabbit skin sleeve, bear claw necklace, hunting knife, wampum belt, Huron scalp, red wool blanket, and silver trade broaches. This costume, while reminiscent of representations of Hiawatha's Minnehaha, became Johnson's trademark. In this costume, Johnson criticized the Canadian Indian Act, offered alternative interpretations of Native life, and maintained that Canada's foundation rested on Indian and European cooperation.

From 1894 to 1909, Johnson toured Canada, the American Midwest and eastern seaboard, and she traveled three times to London, England. Although Johnson formed an important friendship with Squamish Chief Joseph Capilano and was briefly engaged to a Winnipeg insurance salesman, she

remained unmarried. In 1909, she retired to Vancouver after falling ill with breast cancer. She was buried in 1913 in Vancouver's Stanley Park.

During her lifetime, Johnson published four collections of poetry. Her first book, *The White Wampum* (London, 1895) emphasized Native topics. The second book, *Canadian Born* (Toronto, 1903), reflected Edwardian Canada's patriotic sentiments. Through the efforts of friends, Johnson's most popular volume, *Flint and Feather* (1912), as well as *Legends of Vancouver* (1912), was published shortly before her death. *Flint and Feather* remains the best-selling book of Canadian poetry. Johnson also published numerous poems, short stories, and travel narratives in a variety of magazines, such as *Mother's Magazine* (Chicago), *Boy's World* (Chicago), *Gems of Poetry* (New York), and *Week* (Toronto). Nonetheless, despite her fame and continued popularity, the English-Canadian literary canon has largely forgotten E. Pauline Johnson.

Karl S. Hele

References and Further Reading
Gray, Charlotte. 2002. *Flint and Feather: The Life and Times of E. Pauline Johnson, Tekahionwake.* New York: HarperCollins.

Johnson, E. Pauline. 1997. *Flint and Feather.* 1912. Toronto, ON: Guardian Printing.

Johnson, E. Pauline. [1912] 1997. *Legends of Vancouver.* Vancouver, BC: Douglas and MacIntyre.

Johnston, Sheila M. F. 1997. *Buckskin and Broadcloth: A Celebration of E. Pauline Johnson—Tekahionwake, 1861–1913.* Toronto, ON: Natural Heritage/Natural History.

Lyon, George W. 1990. "Pauline Johnson: A Reconsideration." *Studies in Canadian Literature* 15, no. 2: 136–159.

Rose, Marilyn J. No date. "Johnson, Emily Pauline." *Dictionary of Canadian Biography Online.* Available at: http://www.biographi.ca/EN/ShowBio.asp?BioId=41598&query=. Accessed October 16, 2004.

Rockwell, Geoffrey, and Charlotte Steward, project custodians. "Pauline Johnson Archive." McMaster University. Available at: http://www.humanities.mcmaster.ca/~pjohnson/home.html. Accessed December 18, 2004.

Rose, Marilyn J. 1997. "Pauline Johnson: New World Poet." *British Journal of Canadian Studies* 12, no. 2: 298–307.

Strong-Boag, Veronica, and Carole Gerson. 2000. *Paddling Her Own Canoe: The Times and Texts of E. Pauline Johnson Tekahionwake.* Toronto, ON: University of Toronto Press.

Johnson, William

Sir William Johnson was probably the most influential single Englishman in relations with the Iroquois and their allies during the French and Indian War. From his mansion near Albany, Johnson forayed on Indian war parties, painting himself like an Indian and taking part in ceremonial dances. He was a close friend of Hendrick (Tiyanoga), a Mahican-Mohawk leader, with whom he often traveled as a warrior. Joseph Brant fought beside Johnson at the age of thirteen. Because he successfully recruited a sizable number of Iroquois to the British interest, Johnson was made a baronet, with a £5,000 sterling award.

Johnson quickly learned the customs and language of the Mohawks. He had a number of children by Mohawk women, many of them with Mary Brant, a Mohawk clan mother and granddaughter of Hendrick. He generally was well liked among the Mohawks. Hendrick himself had a high regard for the Englishman and expressed his regard when he said, ". . . he has Large Ears and heard a great deal, and what he hears he tells us; he also has Large Eyes and sees a great way, and conceals nothing from us" (Johansen and Grinde, 1997, 185).

In June 1760, during the final thrust to defeat the French in North America, Johnson called for men to attack Montreal. About 600 warriors responded. Many Native warriors living in the Montreal area also responded to his call. Johnson reported he was sending gifts to "foreign Indians" who were switching their allegiance from the sinking French Empire. By August 5, 1760, the Native contingent had reached 1,330.

The defeat of the French and their departure from Canada at the end of the war upset the balance that the Iroquois had sought to maintain. Reluctantly, they attached themselves to the British, but they could no longer play one European power against another. The English now occupied all the forts surrounding Iroquois country. Johnson played a key role in pressing the crown to limit immigration west of the Appalachians, but land-hungry settlers ignored royal edicts, intensifying conflicts over land. In the meantime, Johnson became one of the richest men in the colonies through land transactions and trade with the Indians.

In his later years, Johnson agonized over whether to side with the British crown or the revolutionary patriots. At a meeting with the Iroquois on July 11, 1774, at his mansion near Albany, Johnson

William Johnson, British superintendent of Indian Affairs in the American colonies, 1755–1774. Johnson concluded the Treaty of Fort Stanwix with the Iroquois, persuading them to relinquish claims to territory along the frontiers of New York, Pennsylvania, and Virginia, clearing the way for European-American immigration in these areas. (National Archives of Canada)

addressed the Iroquois in the oratorical style he had learned from them, summoning them to the British cause in the coming American Revolution. Suddenly, he collapsed. He was carried to bed, where he died two hours later. The assembly of chiefs was stunned by his sudden death, but Guy Johnson, Sir William's nephew and son-in-law, stepped in to fill the breach left by his elder.

Bruce E. Johansen

See also Brant, Joseph; French and Indian War; Hendrick.

References and Further Reading

Flexner, James Thomas. 1959. *Mohawk Baronet.* New York: Harper & Row.

Graymont, Barbara. 1972. *The Iroquois in the American Revolution.* Syracuse, NY: Syracuse University Press.

Grinde, Donald A., Jr. 1977. *The Iroquois and the Founding of the American Nation.* San Francisco: Indian Historian Press.

Johansen, Bruce E., and Donald A. Grinde, Jr. 1997. *The Encyclopedia of Native American Biography.* New York: Henry Holt.

Sullivan, James, et al., eds. 1921–1965. *The Papers of Sir William Johnson.* Albany, NY: Albany: University of the State of New York.

Joseph, Younger

Hinmaton Yalatik (Thunder Traveling to Loftier Heights) was more widely known as Chief Joseph (1840–1904) of the Wallamotkin band of the Nimipu (Nez Percé). He assumed the leadership of his people in 1871 upon the death of his father, Tu-ya-kas-kas (Old Joseph). Probably most famous for his leadership during the flight of the Nez Percé from the United States Army in 1877, Chief Joseph led his people in peace, war, captivity, exile, and confinement to the reservation.

Born in 1840 near Joseph Creek in the Wallowa Valley, Joseph was the second son of Tu-ya-kas-kas, the chief of seven villages in the Wallowa region of northeast Oregon. In 1843, Tu-ya-kas-kas accepted Christianity at the Spalding Mission in Lapwai, Idaho, baptized his entire family, and took the name of Joseph. While accepting Christianity, Old Joseph continued to adhere to Nez Percé religious traditions. During the first seven years of his life, Joseph likely received some rudimentary education at the mission, including Christian training and instruction. After the killings at the Whitman Mission in 1847, Tu-ya-kas-kas and his family refused to visit the missionaries at the Spalding Mission. This distancing from white missionaries did not mean isolation from other Indian communities. While maintaining their ties to their homeland, Joseph's Wallamotkin band traveled to see Nez Percé relatives and also traded, danced, hunted, and fished with many other Columbia Plateau Indian communities.

During the 1840s and 1850s white settlers arrived in the Pacific Northwest in ever-greater numbers and placed pressure on the United States government to "solve the Indian Problem." In 1855, Tu-ya-kas-kas and many other Nez Percé and Plateau people met with Territorial Governor Isaac Stevens at Walla Walla and concluded a treaty that

Chief Joseph is probably most famous for his leadership during the flight of the Nez Percé from the U.S. Army in 1877. (Library of Congress)

set aside reservation areas for Plateau communities and opened up broad swaths of land to white settlers. The provisions of the Walla Walla Treaty of 1855 kept nearly all of the Nez Percé land holdings intact as a reservation and therefore insulated them, including Tu-ya-kas-kas's people, from the initial onslaught of white settlement. Old Joseph certainly discussed the Walla Walla council and treaty with his family and probably communicated to Joseph, Ollokot, and his other children the nature of the agreement that existed between themselves and the United States government. Shortly after the conclusion of the treaty, hostilities broke out between Plateau Indian communities and the U.S. government. The Nez Percé remained neutral, but many of their relatives in other Plateau communities suffered great hardship during the so-called Yakama War.

During the 1860s, most white settlers elected to stay out of the Wallowa region and therefore did not pose much of a threat to Joseph's people. When white miners discovered gold on the Nez Percé Reservation in 1860, the government renegotiated the 1855 Walla Walla Treaty with a small group of Nez Percé led by a lawyer. The lawyer and fifty-one Nez Percé men signed the 1863 treaty, but it did not include all Nez Percé bands and factions. The 1863 "thief" treaty provisions substantially decreased the size of the Nez Percé reservation and left Joseph's people outside the boundaries of the new reservation. From this point on, the Nez Percé were principally divided into treaty and nontreaty factions.

By 1871, the first white settlers began to arrive in the Wallowa region. Tu-ya-kas-kas died in August of 1871 and left the leadership of the Wallamotkin band to Joseph, his eldest surviving son. From the beginning of his role as leader of the Wallamotkin band, Joseph faced the great challenge of attempting to deal with increased white settlement and government efforts to remove his people to the smaller Nez Percé reservation. Despite the tumult of the times, Joseph married a young woman named Wa-win-te-piksat and started a family. Their first daughter, Kap-kap-on-mi, was born in 1865. Joseph had a total of four wives during his life while also raising nine children. All of the children except Kap-kap-on-mi died before they were two.

Joseph and his people consistently argued their case with settlers and the government, reminding all parties that Joseph's father never sold their land and was not party to any agreement that relinquished the Wallowa area to white settlement. Joseph based much of his reasoning and rhetoric on the tenets of the Washani religion, the religion of his people. For adherents of the Washani, ancestral lands were sacred, and they could not be sold or exchanged for goods. Most important, Joseph and other adherents of the Washani faith believed that their lives and the lives of their people were inextricably linked to the land. In other words, selling the land would be tantamount to selling themselves and their heritage.

Despite the vehement arguments of Joseph and his people, settlers in the Wallowa Valley failed to leave. In an attempt to resolve the problem, President Ulysses S. Grant created an executive order reservation, but the boundaries were incorrect and caused further difficulties. The executive order reservation lasted until June 1875. In 1876, the federal government sent General Oliver O. Howard to negotiate the removal of the nontreaty Nez Percé. In councils with Joseph, Ollokot, and other nontreaty leaders, Howard warned that they must move or face military action by the United States. In early

May 1877, Joseph reluctantly agreed to move to the reservation. The government placed the unrealistic deadline of June 15, 1877, on the nontreaty Nez Percé to collect their belongings and animals and move to the reservation.

After their arrival on the Camas Prairie in early June 1877, a group of younger men raided settler homes along the Salmon River. Joseph realized that this meant war and decided to move his people to more defensible positions. In this way, the flight of the Nez Percé began. After defeating the U.S. Army in three separate engagements, the nontreaty Nez Percé decided to elude pursuing forces by traveling to Montana over the LoLo Trail.

After traversing the trail, Joseph, his family, and the other nontreaty Nez Percé camped in the Big Hole Valley. On the morning of August 9, 1877, army units attacked the camp. Many Nez Percé people were killed, but warriors from the camp blunted the attack and eventually drove the Army back to entrenched positions. Joseph and the other nontreaty leaders rallied the survivors and they fled from Big Hole, turning north in an attempt to reach Canada and the camp of Sitting Bull. At the Bear Paw battlefield, the U.S. Army surrounded the remnants of the nontreaty people. Joseph, recognizing the suffering and death of his people, agreed to negotiate for an end to the fighting. He consented to a cease-fire and agreed to relinquish weapons to the Army, all with the understanding that the survivors would be returned to the Nez Percé reservation in Idaho.

The remaining 400 Nez Percé and Palouse survivors were quickly sent not to Idaho but to Fort Keogh (Montana), then to Fort Leavenworth (Kansas), and eventually to Indian Territory, where the U.S. government first placed them on the Quapaw Agency and then settled them on a piece of land on the newly created Ponca Agency. During the year and a half after their surrender, many people died from disease, malnutrition, and depression. The nontreaty Nez Percé called Indian Territory *Eekish Pah* ("hot place"). In 1885, the federal government allowed the exiled Nez Percé to return to the Pacific Northwest but divided the group into two; one group returned to the Nez Percé Reservation in Idaho and the second group, led by Joseph, was forced to settle on the Colville Indian Reservation in northern Washington State.

After 1885, Joseph and the other Nez Percé attempted to adjust to life on the Colville reservation. Joseph traveled to many places, including Washington, D.C., New York, and Seattle to speak

about his experiences and garner support for his people's return to the Wallowa Valley. On September 21, 1904, Chief Joseph died in front of his teepee in Nespelem, Washington, on the Colville Reservation. Nine months later, a large group of Nez Percé and Anglo-Americans joined to rebury Chief Joseph in a ceremony on the Colville Reservation. A large stone monument was placed on his grave and stands to this day as a memorial to Joseph's life.

Robert R. McCoy

See also Long March; Yakima.

References and Further Reading

Josephy, Alvin M., Jr. 1971. *The Nez Perce Indians and the Opening of the Northwest,* abridged ed. Lincoln: University of Nebraska Press.

Gidley, M. 1981. *Kopet: A Documentary Narrative of Chief Joseph's Last Years.* Seattle: University of Washington Press.

McWhorter, Lucullus V. 1940. *Yellow Wolf: His Own Story.* Caldwell, ID: Caxton.

Slickpoo, Allen P., Sr. 1973. *Noon Nee-Me-Poo (We, the Nez Percés): Culture and History of the Nez Percés, Volume One.* Lapwai, ID: Nez Percé Tribe.

Trafzer, Clifford E., and Richard Scheuerman. 1986. *Renegade Tribe: The Palouse Indians and the Invasion of the Inland Pacific Northwest.* Pullman: Washington State University Press.

Kicking Bird

Best-known as head of the peace faction during the Kiowa Wars of the 1870s, one of Kicking Bird's (Kiowa, 1835–1875) grandfathers was a Crow captive who had been adopted into the Kiowa nation. The Kiowas called him Watohkonk, meaning "black eagle," as well as Tene-Angpote, "eagle striking with talons" or simply "Kicking Bird." Kicking Bird's one wife was called Guadalupe. At the time of his death, Kicking Bird was a staunch proponent of education and had persuaded Thomas C. Battey, the Kiowa Indian agent, to build a school for Kiowa children.

Kicking Bird became a noted warrior as a young man. Growing older, he began to accept the counsel of Little Mountain (a principal chief of the Kiowas), who asserted that a peaceful approach to relations with the whites was better than military actions. In 1865, Kicking Bird signed the Little Arkansas Treaty, which established a Kiowa reservation that was further described in the Treaty of Medicine Lodge in 1867.

With the demise of Little Mountain in 1866, Kicking Bird became the Kiowas' major leader of the

peace party, with Satanta representing the war faction. To resolve this split in 1866, the Kiowas turned to Lone Wolf as the compromise choice for principal chief. However, Lone Wolf was unable to unite the opposing forces in his nation. During 1870, Kicking Bird was called a coward at a Sun Dance on the North Fork of the Red River. To disprove such allegations, he commanded a war party of about 100 men against a detachment of U.S. troops in Texas. During the resulting battle, Kicking Bird proved his valor by personally charging into a unit of about fifty soldiers, slaying one of them with his lance.

Kicking Bird still could not assuage his peoples' resentment regarding reservation conditions. Brian C. Hosmer wrote in a biography of him that, by late 1873, the war faction was raiding in Texas and Mexico. During these raids two young warriors, one the nephew and the other the son of paramount Chief Lone Wolf, were killed. Motivated by revenge and angered by the continued slaughter of the buffalo, Kiowa warriors attacked immigrants on the frontier. Kicking Bird kept his followers on the reservation, but some Kiowas, including Bird Bow, White Shield, White Horse, Howling Wolf, and perhaps Satanta and Lone Wolf, joined with Quanah Parker's Quahadi Comanches in the unsuccessful attack on Adobe Walls on June 27, 1874 (Hosmer, 2004).

Hosmer continued, describing the end of Satanta's career as a war chief in late 1874 and Lone Wolf's surrender early in 1975. Kicking Bird thus remained the only notable Kiowa leader.

In 1875, to influence the Kiowas, the Army gave Kicking Bird the title "principal chief." Hosmer wrote that, as chief and principal intermediary between the tribe and federal authorities, Kicking Bird was placed in charge of the hostile Indians captured during the uprising of 1874 and 1875. This position allowed Kicking Bird to protect some of his followers from danger, but it also placed him under the influence of the Army (Hosmer, 2004).

Kicking Bird's cooperation with the Army was seen as treason by some of the Kiowas. When officers from Fort Sill gave Kicking Bird a horse, Kicking Bird's reputation as a collaborator was further reinforced. Following Kicking Bird's sudden death on May 4, 1875, at Cache Creek (in Indian Territory), it was widely believed that a cup of coffee he had recently consumed had been poisoned (Hosmer, 2004). Several other Kiowas asserted that Kicking Bird was killed by witchcraft. According to Hosmer, Kiowa lore alleges that Mamanti used his medicinal powers to kill his long-time adversary. Mamanti

himself died shortly after hearing of Kicking Bird's death.

Kicking Bird was buried as a Christian at Fort Sill, Kansas, even though he had never been converted. His grave was marked by a simple wooden cross. After the cross decayed, the exact location of Kicking Bird's remains was forgotten (Hosmer, 2004).

Bruce E. Johansen

References and Further Reading

Hosmer, Brian C. 2004. "Kicking Bird." Red River Authority of Texas. Available at: http://www.rra.dst.tx.us/c_t/history/archer/people/KICKING%20BIRD.cfm. Accessed January 17, 2007.

Johansen, Bruce E., and Donald A. Grinde, Jr. 1997. *Encyclopedia of Native American Biography.* New York: Henry Holt.

Mayhall, Mildred. [1962] 1971. *The Kiowas,* 2nd ed. Norman: University of Oklahoma Press.

Nye, Wilbur Sturtevant. [1939] 1969. *Carbine and Lance: The Story of Old Fort Sill,* 3rd ed. Norman: University of Oklahoma Press.

LaDuke, Winona

Winona LaDuke (Mississippi Anishinabe, b. 1959), whose Ojibwa name, Benaysayequay, means "Thunder Woman," became one of the foremost environmental advocates in Native America during the last quarter of the twentieth century. She lectured, wrote, and pressed authorities for answers to questions on the Navajo uranium mines, on the Hydro-Quebec's construction sites at James Bay, and on the toxic waste sites on Native Alaskan and Canadian land along the Arctic Ocean. She became well-known to non-Indians as Ralph Nader's vice presidential running mate on the Green Party ticket for U.S. president in the national elections in 1996 and 2000. She also was named in 1995 by *Time* magazine as one of fifty Leaders for the Future.

LaDuke is a daughter of Vincent LaDuke, a Native rights activist in the 1950s, and Betty LaDuke, a painter. She was educated at Harvard University in the late 1970s, and in the early 1980s moved to the White Earth Ojibwa reservation in Minnesota, at Round Lake. LaDuke became involved in protests of environmental racism and in the recovery of the Native American land base. With $20,000 she received as the recipient of the first Reebok Human Rights Award, she founded the White Earth Land Recovery Program, which took action to regain the land base on her home reservation. In the early

A leading Native American activist, environmentalist, and author, Winona LaDuke works to defend the social, political, economic, and environmental rights of Native Americans. She also ran for vice president on the Green Party ticket with Ralph Nader in 1996 and 2000. (AP/Wide World Photos)

1990s, the land area of the thirty-six-mile-square reservation was 92 percent owned by non-Indians.

The White Earth Land Recovery Project maintains many other programs. One, called *Mino-Miijim*, delivers wild rice and other traditional foods, such as hominy and buffalo meat, to elderly tribal members who are afflicted with Type 2 diabetes. The program was initiated by LaDuke and Margaret Smith, an elderly former teacher (eighty-seven in 2006). The program is meant to substitute traditional foods for high-fat fast foods and government commodities that contribute to diabetes. "Oh," a tribal member exclaimed to one WELRP intern who accompanied Smith on her monthly delivery route, "[h]ere come the good commodities" (Kummer, 2004, 148).

LaDuke had refrained from electoral politics until 1996, when the Green Party asked her to run

for vice president. At the age of thirty-seven, she said the campaign allowed her a voice to propose "A new model of electoral politics. . . . I am interested in reframing the debate on issues in this society, the distribution of power, and wealth, the abuse of power, the rights of the natural world . . . and the need to consider an amendment to the U.S. Constitution in which all decisions made today would be considered in light of the impact on the seventh generation from now. . . . These are vital subjects which are all too often neglected by the rhetoric of 'major party' candidates and media" (Johansen, 1996, 3). "Until we have an environmental, economic, and social policy that is based on consideration of the impact on the seventh generation from now," said LaDuke, "we will be living in a society that is based on conquest, not one that is based on

survival. I consider myself a patriot—not to a flag, but to a land" (Johansen, 1996, 4).

During the 1996 campaign, President Bill Clinton incorporated much of her language into his own speeches. LaDuke, however, acutely criticized Clinton for talking environmentally but ignoring environmental action, by doing such things as weakening the Endangered Species Act. LaDuke supported a constitutional amendment that would define air and water as common property, to be maintained free from contamination. "The rights of the people to use and enjoy air, water, and sunlight are essential to life, liberty, and happiness," LaDuke wrote in *Indian Country Today* (October 14, 1996) (Johansen, 1996, 3).

Bruce E. Johansen

See also James Bay and Northern Quebec Agreement.

References and Further Reading
Bowermaster, Jon. 1993. "Earth of a Nation." *Harper's Bazaar*, April, n.p.
Johansen, Bruce E. 1996. "Running for Office: LaDuke and the Green Party." *Native Americas* 18, no. 4 (Winter): 3–4.
Kummer, Corby. 2004. "Going with the Grain: True Wild Rice, for the Past Twenty Years Nearly Impossible to Find, Is Slowly Being Nurtured Back to Market." *Atlantic Monthly*, May: 145–148.
LaDuke, Winona. 1999. *All Our Relations: Native Struggles for Land and Life.* Boston: South End Press.
LaDuke, Winona. 2002. *The Winona LaDuke Reader: A Collection of Essential Writings.* Stillwater, MN: Voyageur Press.
LaDuke, Winona. 2005. *Recovering the Sacred: The Power of Naming and Claiming.* Boston: South End Press.

LaFlesche, Susan Picotte

Daughter of Omaha principal Chief Joseph LaFlesche, Susan LaFlesche (Omaha, 1865–1915) became a government doctor on the Omaha Reservation during a time when cholera, influenza, tuberculosis, and other diseases were reaching epidemic proportions. She blazed a career of genius through a number of white schools, and then nearly worked herself to death serving the Omahas as a government physician.

In 1884, after two and a half years at the Elizabeth Institute for Young Ladies in Elizabeth, New Jersey, LaFlesche enrolled at the Hampton Normal and Agricultural Institute in Hampton, Virginia. This vocational school had been started by General Samuel C. Armstrong to educate freed slaves. A number of Indians also attended, and the school played a role in the designs of Lieutenant Richard Henry Pratt, who started Carlisle Indian School. LaFlesche graduated from Hampton May 20, 1886 at the top of her class. Between 1886 and 1889, she attended the Women's Medical College of Pennsylvania on a scholarship raised by her friends, many of whom were non-Indian, again graduating at the top of her class.

LaFlesche thus became one of a handful of Native American physicians in the nineteenth century, a group that includes Charles Eastman and Carlos Montezuma. She was the only Native American woman to become a medical doctor during that century. For five years, LaFlesche fought pervasive disease on the Omaha reservation, making some progress.

In December 1891, LaFlesche wrote that influenza "raged with more violence than during the two preceding years. Some families were rendered helpless by it. . . . Almost every day I was out making visits. . . . Several days the temperature was 15 to 20 degrees below zero, and I had to drive [a horse-drawn buggy] myself" (Mathes, 1985, 73). During that winter, she treated more than 600 patients.

By 1892, the intensity of her work was costing LaFlesche her health. She was beset by a number of debilitating illnesses for the rest of her life, as she ministered to the ever-present ills of the Omahas. At one point she wearily departed for Washington, D.C., to testify for the Omahas because people had threatened to convey her bodily, her mission was of such importance to them.

Back on the Omaha reservation, LaFlesche waged a tireless campaign against alcoholism, recounting stories of how Indians craving liquor used their rent money and even pawned their clothes in winter to obtain it. She wrote of one Harry Edwards, who on a winter's night in 1894, "fell from a buggy, was not missed by his drunken companions, and in the morning was found frozen to death" (Mathes, 1985, 75). From a medical point of view, LaFlesche believed that alcoholism was at the root of many of the physical, mental, and moral ills facing the Omahas and other American Indians.

In 1894, her health improving, LaFlesche married Henri Picotte, who was part French and part Sioux; she also began a new medical practice for Indians and whites at Bancroft, Nebraska. LaFlesche

practiced medicine there for the rest of her life, as her own health permitted. After LaFlesche's death on September 18, 1915, the *Walthill Times* added an extra page (in its September 24 issue) and filled it with warm eulogies to her. Friends recalled that hundreds of people in the area, Indian and Euro-American, owed their lives to her care.

The hospital that Susan LaFlesche built at Walthill has since been declared a national historic landmark. Since 1988, her memory has been celebrated at an annual festival there.

Bruce E. Johansen

See also LaFlesche, Susette Tibbles; Montezuma.
References and Further Reading

Ferris, Jeri. 1991. *Native American Doctor: The Story of Susan Laflesche Picotte*. Minneapolis, MN: Carolrhoda Books.

Mathes, Valerie Sherer. 1985. "Dr. Susan LaFlesche Picotte: The Reformed and the Reformer." In *Indian Lives: Essays on Nineteenth- and Twentieth-century Native American Leaders* Edited by L.G. Moses and Raymond Wilson. Norman: University of Oklahoma Press, 61–89.

Tong, Benson. 1999. *Susan La Flesche Picotte, M.D.: Omaha Indian Leader and Reformer*. Norman: University of Oklahoma Press.

Wilkerson, J. L. 1999. *A Doctor to Her People: Dr. Susan LaFlesche Picotte*. Kansas City, MO: Acorn Books.

LaFlesche, Susette Tibbles

Susette LaFlesche (Bright Eyes, Inshta Theamba, Omaha, 1854–1903) became a major nineteenth-century Native rights advocate through the case of the Ponca Standing Bear [*Standing Bear v. Crook*, 1879], the first legal proceeding (decided in Omaha) to establish Native Americans as human beings under U.S. law.

LaFlesche was born near Bellevue, Nebraska, the eldest daughter of Joseph "Iron Eye" LaFlesche and Mary Gale LaFlesche, daughter of an Army surgeon. Like her sister Susan, Susette LaFlesche attended the Presbyterian mission school on the Omaha reservation. Both sisters were among the most brilliant students ever to attend the school. She also studied art at the University of Nebraska.

In the late 1870s, Susette traveled with her father to Indian Territory (later Oklahoma) to render rudimentary medical attention to the Poncas with Standing Bear, whose people had been forced to move there from their former homeland along the Niobrara River in northern Nebraska. When the Poncas attempted to escape their forced exile and return to their homeland, they marched for several weeks in midwinter, finally eating their moccasins to survive, arriving at the Omaha reservation with bleeding feet. The Omahas, particularly the LaFlesche family, granted them sanctuary and sustenance.

Susette accompanied her brother Francis and Standing Bear on a lecture tour of Eastern cities in 1879 and 1880 to support the Poncas' case for a return of their homeland. Newspaper articles about the Poncas' forced exile by Omaha journalist Thomas H. Tibbles helped ignite a furor in Congress and among the public.

Tibbles, an editor at the *Omaha Herald*, was the first journalist to interview Standing Bear while the LaFlesche family sheltered the Poncas. Tibbles' accounts were telegraphed to newspapers on the East Coast. In the meantime, LaFlesche and Tibbles fell in love and married in 1882. Both also toured the East Coast with Standing Bear, "armed with news clippings on the Ponca story and endorsements from General [George] Crook, the mayor of Omaha, and leading Nebraska clergymen," raising support for the restoration of Ponca lands (Tibbles, 1880, 129).

In Boston, where support for Standing Bear's Poncas was very strong, a citizens' committee formed that included Henry Wadsworth Longfellow. While Susette LaFlesche was visiting Boston with Standing Bear, Longfellow said of her, "*This* is Minnehaha" (Tibbles, 1880, 130).

In Boston, Tibbles, LaFlesche, and Standing Bear first met Helen Hunt Jackson. The Poncas' story inflamed Jackson's conscience and changed her life. Heretofore known as a poet (and a childhood friend of Emily Dickinson), Jackson set out to write *A Century of Dishonor*, a best-selling book that described the angst of an America debating the future of the Native American peoples who had survived the last of the Indian wars. Jackson became a major figure in the Anglo-American debate over the future of Native Americans. Standing Bear and his people eventually were allowed to return home to the Niobrara River after Congress investigated the conditions under which they had been evicted. Standing Bear died there in 1908.

LaFlesche also coauthored a memoir with Standing Bear, *Ploughed Under: The Story of an Indian Chief* (1832). In ensuing years, LaFlesche and Tibbles also toured the British Isles. The couple lived in Washington, D.C., but eventually Susette returned to

Lincoln, Nebraska, where she died in 1903. She was buried in Bancroft, Nebraska. In 1994, Susette LaFlesche was inducted into the National Women's Hall of Fame.

Bruce E. Johansen

See also Jackson, Helen Hunt; LaFlesche, Susan Picotte; *Standing Bear v. Crook.*

References and Further Reading

Jackson, Helen Hunt. 1972. *A Century of Dishonor: A Sketch of the United States Government's Dealings with Some of the Indian Tribes.* St. Clair Shores, MI.: Scholarly Press. [Originally printed 1888 Boston: Roberts Bros.]

Massey, Rosemary, et al. 1979. *Footprints in Blood: Standing Bear's Struggle for Fredom and Human Dignity.* Omaha, NE: American Indian Center of Omaha.

Tibbles, Thomas Henry. [1880] 1972. *The Ponca Chiefs: An Account of the Trial of Standing Bear.* Lincoln: University of Nebraska Press.

Wilson, Dorothy Clarke. 1974. *Bright Eyes: The Story of Suzette LaFlesche.* New York: McGraw-Hill.

Francis E. Leupp was the twenty-seventh commissioner of Indian Affairs and a member of the Indian Rights Association and the U.S. Board of Indian Commissioners. Leupp was a noted Indian reform advocate who wrote prolifically on the subject. (Indian Craftsman, April 1909)

Leupp, Francis Ellington

Francis Ellington Leupp (1849–1918) is remembered in American history for his involvement in Native American issues and government policy. He served as commissioner of Indian Affairs from 1905 to 1909. Before and after his tenure in this post, Leupp was well known as an advocate of educating Indians in Anglo-American values and culture as an alternative to their anticipated extinction.

Although originally trained as a journalist who had no prior government or national political experience, Leupp's background in journalism provided an avenue into American politics. Historian Frederick E. Hoxie noted that Leupp was a "product of an old New York family, schooled in public piety by Mark Hopkins at Williams College," a prestigious institution in Williamstown, Massachusetts (Hoxie, 1997, 162). After he received an education at Williams College, Leupp worked as an editorial assistant under William Cullen Bryant for the *New York Evening Post*. In 1889, Leupp left his management position at the *Post* and moved to Washington, D.C. Fascinated with the political environment in Washington, Leupp became involved in the Civil Service Reform League and worked as the editor for the league's newspaper.

While serving as the editor for the Civil Service Reform League, Leupp developed a close relationship with one of the league's strongest supporters, Theodore Roosevelt. Leupp's friendship with Roosevelt proved critical for his future career in American government and politics. Both men shared common interests in the civil reforms of the late nineteenth century, and both closely followed numerous heated debates over Indian affairs.

When Herbert Welsh, founder of the Indian Rights Association, needed a new Washington lobbyist, Roosevelt strongly recommended Leupp for the position. At the insistence of Roosevelt, Welsh appointed Leupp to a three-year term as the association's lobbyist (Prucha, 1979, 34). Hoxie noted that Leupp "spent his three-year term hounding administrators who ignored the civil service rules, appearing at hearings on appropriations, and investigating charges of corruption and mismanagement" (Hoxie, 1997, 162). Involvement with the Indian Rights Association provided Leupp with an expertise in government policy and Indian affairs that in turn opened the door for future government appointments.

In 1896, President Grover Cleveland appointed Leupp to the Board of Indian Commissioners. When Roosevelt became president of the United States in 1901, Leupp continued to advocate Indian rights and worked closely with the Roosevelt administration on Indian policy. In 1905, Roosevelt replaced former President William McKinley's appointee, William A. Jones, with Leupp to be the new Commissioner of Indian Affairs, a position Leupp held until 1909. During his first five months as commissioner, Leupp visited Native communities across North America to look for "trouble spots" that needed his immediate attention. Leupp used this time to conduct field research for a book titled *Outlines of an Indian Policy* (1905), in which he laid out his agenda for Indian assimilation and acculturation.

During Leupp's tenure as commissioner, few issues demanded more of his time and attention than Indian education. According to Leupp, educating Indians in Anglo-American values and culture preserved Indian people from "extinction." Although Indians had always valued education, the traditional education Indian pupils received in their tribal communities did not satisfy the government's educational goals for Indian people. Unlike his predecessors, Leupp did not entirely approve of off-reservation boarding schools such as the Sherman Institute or Phoenix Indian School, but instead advocated and supported the use of reservation day schools. Leupp's philosophy of Indian education largely came from his previous experience with Indian people.

During the late nineteenth century, Leupp traveled to the Hopi Reservation in northeastern Arizona. During his visit with the Hopi, Leupp noticed how efficiently a Hopi woman and her daughters took care of their house, cooked, and washed dishes. Leupp commented that the Hopi woman "performed these housewifely duties as well as they would have been performed in most of the white settler's cabins in the Southwestern desert" (Leupp, 1910, 133). From this observation, Leupp concluded that Indian pupils who attended schools in close proximately to home influenced their parents and family to a much greater degree in comparison to those students who attended off-reservation boarding schools.

In spite of his many contributions, Leupp's tenure as commissioner is marked with controversy. A major supporter of Indian land allotment, Leupp firmly held that the government should control the sale and ownership of Indian land. Under Leupp's allotment policy, Indian people across North America lost millions of acres of land. In addition to allotment, Leupp adamantly opposed Indian isolation at the expense of Indian wishes and desires. Leupp argued that Indians who lived on reservations should not be isolated from their white neighbors. In Leupp's opinion, Indian isolation hindered Indian "progress" and slowed down the economic development of the West.

Matthew T. Sakiestewa Gilbert

See also Bureau of Indian Affairs: Establishing the Existence of an Indian Tribe; General Allotment Act (Dawes Act).

References and Further Reading
Hagen, William T. 1997. *Theodore Roosevelt and Six Friends of the Indian*. Norman: University of Oklahoma Press.
Hoxie, Frederick E. 1997. *A Final Promise: The Campaign to Assimilate the Indians, 1880–1920*. Cambridge, UK: Cambridge University Press.
Leupp, Francis E. 1910. *The Indian and His Problem*. New York: Charles Scribner's Sons.
Leupp, Francis E. 1914. *In Red Man's Land*. New York: Fleming H. Revell Company.
Prucha, Francis Paul. 1979. *The Churches and the Indian Schools*. Lincoln: University of Nebraska Press.

Little Crow

Little Crow (Cetan Wakan, Santee, or Mdewakanton Sioux), also known as Taoyateduta ("His Red Nation"), was the leader of Dakota resistance to white invasion during the U.S.–Dakota War of 1862. Born about 1810 in the Bdewakantunwan village of Kapoza (where St. Paul, Minnesota, is today), Taoyateduta came from a line of Dakota chiefs, including the first Little Crow (his great-grandfather), Cetanwakanmani (his grandfather), and Wakinyantanka (his father). Despite the fact that he was tutored well in Dakota leadership and had earned an impressive war record, when his father was suffering from a fatal accident in 1846, he indicated his support for one of Little Crow's half brothers as his successor when he passed his medals on to him. His family believed Taoyateduta had spent too many years away from Kapoza to effectively assume the chieftainship. Undaunted by this, when the waters thawed that spring, Taoyateduta returned to challenge his half brother and in the process was shot by

Mdewakanton Santee Sioux Chief Little Crow, who had previously been hospitable and accommodating toward white settlers, led a bloody Minnesota Sioux uprising in 1862 after many of his people nearly starved in U.S. captivity. The uprising was followed by the largest mass hanging in U.S. history. (Library of Congress)

a bullet that traveled through both wrists before passing into his body. Through this act of bravery, he earned the support and sympathy of the villagers, and, when he recovered from his injuries, his chieftainship was secured.

The midnineteenth century was a difficult time to assume Dakota leadership because the contest over Dakota lands and resources had reached full intensity. From the time the first treaty was signed by Cetanwakanmani in 1805, the pressure to cede Dakota lands and abandon Dakota ways only intensified. A series of land cessions in 1837, 1851, and 1858 severed large chunks for white settlement and eventually confined the Dakota to a narrow strip of reservation land bordering the Minnesota River. Taoyateduta was faced with the difficult challenge of attempting to negotiate justice in the face of repeated treaty violations by the U.S. government, continued

white incursions on Dakota land, and constant colonization efforts organized among missionaries, traders, and Indian agents that served to deeply factionalize the Dakotas and undermine Dakota leadership. He consistently sought peaceful solutions to these problems and attempted to maintain good relations with whites in southern Minnesota, tolerating the Christianizing and civilizing efforts and addressing grievances through negotiation. Given the invading settler population, however, peaceful relations were impossible to maintain as long as the Dakotas were committed to maintaining their lands and way of life.

Taoyateduta's peaceful efforts ceased when he agreed to lead the Dakotas in war at the outbreak of the U.S.–Dakota War of 1862. The Dakotas had been pushed beyond their limits in the hot summer of 1862 when they were facing starvation as a consequence of another U.S. treaty violation. When a small group of Dakota warriors killed five white settlers near Acton Township on August 17 and the Dakotas faced the likelihood of a severe backlash, they knew they could not continue to live under those circumstances. The young warriors pleaded with Taoyateduta to lead them in war, and, though he initially refused to engage in what he knew was a futile effort, he reluctantly agreed when they called him a coward. In his famous speech, he finally conceded, "Braves, you are little children—you are fools. You will die like the rabbits when the hungry wolves hunt them in the Hard Moon. Taoyateduta is not a coward: he will die with you!"

On the morning of August 18 the Dakotas began their attack on the Lower Sioux Agency, killing most of the whites they encountered and taking others, primarily women and children, as prisoners. These actions set the Minnesota frontier settlements into a panic, and terrified white settlers fled to the nearby towns and Fort Ridgely. When news of the war spread to St. Paul, Governor Alexander Ramsey commissioned Henry Sibley to lead a regiment of 1,400 men on an expedition against the Dakotas. Once the white forces were mobilized, the Dakotas moved to a defensive position and the war was quelled.

After the final battle was fought at Wood Lake on September 23, 1862, and the release of the 269 white and mixed-blood prisoners was subsequently arranged, Taoyateduta left his Minnesota homeland heartbroken. He fled the state, as did thousands of others, to either Dakota Territory or Canada. After spending time farther west attempting to rally

indigenous support for continued resistance efforts, Taoyateduta traveled to British Canada to try to build an alliance against the Americans. Without success, in the summer of 1863, he returned to Minnesota with only a small group of Dakotas.

On July 3 Taoyateduta was shot while picking raspberries with his son, Wowinape, by Nathan and Chauncey Lamson, who received bounty payments for their deed. Unfortunately, attacks on him did not end with his death. His body was dragged through the town of Hutchinson, and white boys celebrated the Fourth of July by placing firecrackers in his ears and nose. After he had been scalped, mutilated, and dismembered, his remains were displayed and kept at the Minnesota Historical Society for 108 years before they were finally returned to his family and laid to rest in Flandreau, South Dakota.

From the start of the war to the time of his death, Taoyateduta fought unceasingly for the Dakotas' right to exist in their homeland. He embodies the spirit of indigenous resistance in a struggle that persists today.

Waziyatawin Angela Wilson

See also Great Sioux Uprising.
Reference and Further Reading
Anderson, Gary C. 1986. *Little Crow: Spokesman for the Sioux.* St. Paul: Minnesota Historical Society Press.

Little Turtle

Miami leader Little Turtle was responsible for one of the biggest disasters in U.S. Army history. When he realized the futility of continuing to fight, he renounced war and became a loyal ally of the American government.

Little Turtle (Michikinikwa) was born near the Eel River in the vicinity of present-day Fort Wayne, Indiana, around 1752. His father was a chief of the Miamis, but, because his mother was a Mahican, tribal custom dictated that he could not inherit a leadership position. Nonetheless, Little Turtle displayed fine leadership and warrior qualities as a young man, and he was eventually made a Miami chief by the tribal elders. He was pro-British by nature, and in 1780 his warriors attacked and destroyed a French-Illinois expedition under Colonel Augustin de la Balme. After the American Revolution, he became a leading spokesperson for resistance to white encroachment north of the Ohio River and helped to form a loose confederation of Miami,

Shawnee, Potawatomi, and Ojibwa Indians. In 1787, Congress guaranteed the Indians that their hunting grounds would be respected. Within a few years, however, a rash of illegal settlements precipitated a fierce border war between the Indians and the frontierspeople. By 1790, when it was apparent the Indians would not accept the squatters, the American government resorted to punitive measures.

The U.S. government initially chose General Josiah Harmar, who had assembled a force of 1,100 poorly trained Pennsylvania and Kentucky militia, stiffened by 300 army regulars, to deal with the Indians. Little Turtle by this time was principal war chief of the Miamis, and he ordered his braves to

Little Turtle, chief of the Miami tribe, led militant opposition to the influx of settlers in the Ohio country in a conflict known as Little Turtle's War. However, after his defeat at the Battle of Fallen Timbers in 1794, Little Turtle became an ally of the United States. (North Wind Picture Archives)

feign retreat, luring the Americans deeper and deeper into the countryside. Harmar met no opposition until he reached Little Turtle's village, where the Indians ambushed and mauled two reconnaissance expeditions in October 1790. Having lost 262 men and accomplished nothing, the white militia withdrew to Kentucky. This victory assured Little Turtle's subsequent leadership over the Maumee Valley tribes, and they united in time to face an even greater onslaught.

In September 1791, the government dispatched General Arthur St. Clair with a force of 2,300 raw regulars and 300 Kentucky militia against the Indians. Little Turtle commanded a force of similar size, assisted by the Shawnees Blue Jacket and Tecumseh. Desertion soon reduced St. Clair's force to 1,500 men, and, encouraged by this weakness, Little Turtle abandoned his usual defensive tactics in favor of a direct assault. This tactic was something that Native Americans had never tried before. On the morning of November 4, 1791, his warriors stormed the American encampment while the soldiers were breakfasting and routed them. St. Clair, gravely ill, roused himself from bed and attempted to rally the survivors before the entire army was annihilated. A bayonet charge enabled 500 men to escape destruction but at tremendous cost, with over 600 soldiers killed and 300 wounded, and Little Turtle's losses appear to have been negligible. In November 1792 he also defeated a party of Kentuckians led by John Adair. Fearing that the dreaded "long knives" would attack again, however, Little Turtle spent the next two years shoring up tribal solidarity and soliciting help from the British.

As feared, the Americans appeared once more, this time with General Anthony Wayne at their head. Wayne spent almost two years training and equipping his force of 2,000 men and advanced carefully, building forts along the way. Little Turtle respected his professional and energetic preparations, calling him "the chief who never sleeps." The Indians harassed his line of supply with impunity, but when they rashly attacked Fort Recovery in July 1794 and were rebuffed, many grew sullen and returned home. Little Turtle took stock of "Mad Anthony" and counseled other chiefs to seek peace. "We have never been able to surprise him," he warned. "Think well of it. Something whispers to me, listen to peace." Little Turtle was ridiculed and lost command of the Indians to Blue Jacket. On August 20, 1794, Wayne crushed the confederation at the Battle of Fallen Timbers, in which Little Turtle commanded a few Miamis and

played a small role. The following year, Little Turtle was a signatory to the Treaty of Greenville, whereby the Indians gave up most of the land that comprises present-day Ohio. Containing his bitterness, he declared, "I am the last to sign the treaty; I will be the last to break it."

From that time on, Little Turtle remained a friend of the United States, and in 1797 he traveled to Washington, D.C., to meet with President George Washington and Tadeusz Kosciuszko, who presented him with a brace of pistols. He was sincere in his quest for peace and made additional land concessions with Governor William Henry Harrison, who built a house for him on the Eel River. He also took the white scout William Wells as his son-in-law and kept the Miamis out of Tecumseh's tribal coalition. Little Turtle succumbed to illness at Fort Wayne on July 14, 1812 and received a military burial.

Steve L. Danver

See also Fallen Timbers, Battle of; Tecumseh.
References and Further Reading
Carter, Harvey L. 1987. *The Life and Times of Little Turtle: First Sagamore of the Wabash.* Urbana and Chicago: University of Illinois Press
Edel, Wilbur. 1997. *Kekionga! The Worst Defeat in the History of the United States Army.* Westport, CT: Praeger.
Sword, Wiley. 1985. *President Washington's Indian War: The Struggle for the Old Northwest, 1790–1795.* Norman and London: University of Oklahoma Press.

Louis, Adrian

An enrolled member of the Lovelock Paiute, the poet and writer Adrian C. Louis was born in 1946 in northern Nevada, where he grew up the oldest of twelve children. After spending the late 1960s in San Francisco's Haight-Ashbury section, he graduated from Brown University with an MA in creative writing. Louis taught from 1984 until 1997 at Oglala Lakota College at Pine Ridge in South Dakota. Since 1999, he has been an English professor in the Minnesota State University system, in which he currently teaches and directs the creative writing program at Southwest Minnesota State University in Marshall, Minnesota.

A cofounder of the Native American Journalists Association (NAJA), Louis has produced much diverse work, including his early writing as a jour-

nalist and an editor for four tribal newspapers; a book of short stories, *Wild Indians & Other Creatures*; a novel, *Skins*; and twelve volumes of poetry: *Evil Corn; Bone & Juice; Ancient Acid Flashes Back; Skull Dance; Ceremonies of the Damned; Vortex of Indian Fevers; Blood Thirsty Savages; Days of Obsidian, Days of Grace*, with Jim Northrup, Al Hunter, and Denise Sweet; *Among the Dog Eaters; Fire Water World: Poems; Sweets for the Dancing Bears; Muted War Drums;* and *The Indian Cheap Wine Séance.*

Louis has received numerous awards and accolades. *Fire Water World* won the 1989 Poetry Center Award from San Francisco State University. Louis was named Writer of the Year for poetry in 2001 by Wordcraft Circle of Native Writers and Storytellers for *Ancient Acid Flashes Back.* He is the recipient of a Pushcart Prize and was elected to the Nevada Writers Hall of Fame in 1999. He has been granted fellowships by the Bush Foundation, the National Endowment for the Arts, the Wurlitzer Foundation, the South Dakota Arts Council, and the Lila Wallace–Reader's Digest Foundation.

Louis' most acclaimed work, *Skins*, focuses on the lives of two brothers, Rudy and Mogie Yellow Shirt, inhabitants of the Pine Ridge Reservation. Rudy is a tribal police officer surviving the death of his marriage and the dismal poverty and alcoholism among his Oglala people on the reservation. He also suffers from internalized racism, stereotyping his own people rather than truly helping them as he once sought to do. In 2002, director Chris Eyre produced *Skins* as a feature film starring Graham Greene, Eric Schweig, and Gary Farmer.

Louis' poetry is highly esteemed and focuses on much the same sort of real, hard-core, reservation-life issues found in *Skins.* He writes of his personal and the collective struggle with alcohol; the stark South Dakota landscape; government programs; poor nutrition, health, and dental care; reservation litter; and racism. His work interrogates the meaning of individual growth for Native peoples; it searches out definitions of the self in this complex and devastated world and questions what "betterment" exactly is. Louis's poetry reaches beyond the Indian world, however, showing commonality between the historical and contemporary plights of American Indians and the current situation of Iraqi people. It mourns his wife's slow loss to Alzheimer's at the same time it celebrates his love for her. Louis's poetry looks death and life in the eye squarely and challenges them both.

Kimberly Roppolo

See also Alcoholism and Substance Abuse.

References and Further Reading

"Adrian C. Louis." In *Modern American Poetry.* Available at: http://www.english.uiuc.edu/maps/poets/g_l/louis/louis.htm. Accessed March 28, 2005.

Brown Ruoff, A. LaVonne. 1990. *American Indian Literatures: An Introduction, Bibliographic Review, and Selected Bibliography.* New York: Modern Language Association of America.

Louis, Adrian. "Adrian-C-Louis.com." Available at: http://www.adrian-c-louis.com/testsite/index2.htm. Accessed March 28, 2005.

Louis, Adrian, and Karen Strom. "Adrian C. Louis." Available at: http://www.hanksville.org/storytellers/ALouis/. Accessed March 28, 2005.

Luna, James Alexander

Artist James Luna (Luiseño, from the La Jolla reservation in California, b. 1950) creates both installation art and performance art pieces that use humor and irony to question social and cultural issues, Indian identity, stereotypes of American Indians, and representations of Native Americans. Because of his unique style of art and critical subject matter, Luna has broad worldwide recognition, which is unusual for Native American artists. On the other hand, his work is not well-known by collectors who seek Native American art adhering to the stereotypes and misrepresentations of Indians, which he addresses as subject matter in his work.

His work explores issues such as socioeconomic problems that plague Native Americans, as well as the roots of those problems and their manifestations, such as substance abuse and cultural conflict. In his artwork, Luna often creates artificial environments within galleries or museums, where he reproduces an image of, or performs a representation of, a stereotype of Native Americans. His intent is to present or perform the work in such a way as to demonstrate the ridiculous nature of the stereotype or perception, showing how Native Americans are misrepresented. Further, he seeks to involve the audience in this experience so as to have them confront their beliefs and challenge their cultural perspectives and boundaries.

Luna uses a variety of media in his performances and installations, including everyday objects, audio, video, and slides. His performance art depends on interaction between the audience and artist. The performance is the artwork. Unlike

painting or sculpture, there is no actual object; this type of art must be experienced. When the performance is over, only the idea or concept of the work remains; this is the nature of performance art.

His installations utilize the same types of media to present a concept, only without his presence. In either case, the result is the same; because he uses material and/or actions that provoke a response, the viewer must choose to interact or ignore the work. Either way forces the viewer to think about the concepts to which he is drawing attention.

Installation and performance art are considered temporal, because they exist only in the moment, because one cannot collect or display conceptual works of art created through performance or temporary installation. This makes the work more provocative because it is a concept, not an object; to some this is a radical idea. However, Luna has created works that, despite the fact that they no longer exist, continue to provoke a reaction through photographic documentation.

Luna's best-known work is *The Artifact Piece,* which was both a performance and an installation. The first performance of this work took place in 1987 at the San Diego Museum of Man. In this work, he put himself on display in the museum for several days. He lay perfectly still on a bed of sand with only a sheet covering him, in a typical museum display case surrounded by exhibit labels and situated among two other cases that displayed his belongings. He was presented as though he were dead, an artifact. Visitors were not made aware that he was presenting himself as a living specimen. They were often shocked when they realized he was alive and returning their gaze all the while listening to their comments.

This work referenced and critiqued the way Native Americans have been and still are, in many cases, exhibited by museums. The point of the work was to call attention to what academics call "museumification," where Natives have been and in some cases continue to be interpreted for the public, in museums and galleries, as objects of the past and not as people of the present. This work was very successful, and it is cited and referenced by many publications, in many different fields, from art history to American Indian studies, some of which are listed in "References and Further Reading."

Luna's work is informed by both academic and personal experience as a contemporary Native American. He is formally trained as a painter, with a bachelor of fine arts in studio arts from the University of California at Irvine and a master of arts in counseling from San Diego State University. Luna currently works as an academic counselor at Palomar Community College in addition to his work as an artist

Traci L. Morris-Carlsten

See also Native American Museums.
References and Further Reading
Berlo, Janet C., and Ruth B. Phillips. 1998. *Native North American Art.* New York: Oxford University Press.
Fisher, Jean. 1992. "In Search of the 'Inauthentic.' " *Art Journal* (Fall): 44–50.
Lippard, Lucy R. 1990. *Mixed Blessings: New Art in a Multicultural America.* New York: Pantheon.
James Luna Project. Available at: http://www.jamesluna.com/. Accessed September 17, 2004.

Lyons, Oren

Oren Lyons (Onondaga, b. 1930), whose Onondaga name is Joagquisho, became known worldwide during the last half of the twentieth century as an author, publisher, and crisis negotiator, as well as a spokesperson for the Haudenosaunee in several world forums. He is also an accomplished graphic artist as well as a renowned lacrosse player and coach. In 1990, Lyons organized an Iroquois national team that played in the world Lacrosse championships in Australia. In addition, Lyons is a professor of Native American Studies at the State University of New York at Buffalo.

Lyons was educated in art at Syracuse University (1954–1958). After his graduation from college, he enjoyed a successful career as a commercial artist at Norcross Greeting Cards in New York City for more than a decade (1959–1970). Lyons began as a paste-up artist at Norcross; in a dozen years at the firm, he worked his way up to head planning director for seasonal lines.

In 1970, Lyons ended his career in the greeting card industry and returned home to the Onondaga territory, where he was condoled (installed) as a faithkeeper on the Iroquois Grand Council. Lyons also was part of a negotiating team from the Iroquois Confederacy that helped resolve the 1990 standoff between Mohawks and authorities at Kanesatake (Oka), Quebec. The Confederacy's negotiators came to occupy a crucial middle ground between the war-

riors and Canadian officials during the months of negotiations that preceded the use of armed force by the Canadian Army and police at Kanesatake and Kahnawake. The Iroquois negotiators urged both sides to concentrate on long-term solutions to problems brought to light by the summer's violence. They recommended a fair land-rights process in Canada, the creation of viable economic bases for the communities involved in the crisis, and the recognition of long-standing (but often ignored) treaty rights, including border rights.

Lyons has been involved in a number of other Iroquois rights issues, most notably the return of wampum belts to the Confederacy by the State of New York. He has spoken on behalf of the Haudenosaunee in several international forums, including the United Nations. One of Lyons's main credits as a writer is his lead authorship of *Exiled in the Land of the Free* (1992).

As a faithkeeper, Lyons has been active in bringing together religious peoples of differing traditions. On April 28, 1997, for example, he took part in an interfaith service at Saint Bartholomew's Church in New York City with leaders from Christian, Jewish, Buddhist, Sikh, Jainist, Islamic, and Hindi clergy in support of the United Nations. One aim of the service was to diminish international tensions based on religious differences.

Lyons has faced harsh attacks by independent merchants in the Iroquois Confederacy regarding his belief that some of their profits should go back to the nations in which they do business. This criticism reached a peak in the late winter of 1998, when Lyons and other supporters of the traditional council burned and bulldozed four smoke shops on Onondaga territory. Lyons and other members of the council have long maintained that sovereignty is a collective right to be exercised by a governing body, not a license to make profits because merchants on Native American territories may avoid paying New York state sales tax.

"Who represents the sovereignty of the United States?" Lyons and coauthor John C. Mohawk asked in *Cultural Survival Quarterly* (1994, 58). "Is it the New York Yankees? Bloomingdales? The *Los Angeles Times*? William F. Buckley?" Just as private enterprises do not speak for the United States, wrote Lyons and Mohawk, private Iroquois businesspeople cannot exercise national sovereignty as individuals, especially when it is used as a cover for socially debasing activities such as smuggling illegal drugs. Lyons has also been a longtime opponent

of Native American dependence on gambling for economic development: "Gaming has run its course before and each time it goes bust," Lyons has said. "Poor people are the ones who gamble. It's like chewing on your own wrist" (Slackman, 1996, A-8). When freebooting smugglers used some of their profits to establish gambling houses at Akwesasne (St. Regis) in the late 1980s, for example, Lyons and Mohawk argued that owners of the casinos and bingo halls were crippling Mohawk sovereignty rather than exercising it. "Common sense dictates," they wrote, "that the gambling operators are the greatest threat to Mohawk sovereignty" (Lyons and Mohawk, 1994, 59).

Lyons has sounded environmental warnings in a number of international forums. The venues differ, but the message is always similar: "We were told that there would come a time when we would not find clean water to wash ourselves, to cook our foods, to make our medicines, and to drink," Lyons says. Today Lyons peers into the future with great apprehension. "We were told that there would come a time when, tending our gardens, we would pull up our plants and the vines would be empty. Our precious seed would begin to disappear. . . . Can we withstand another 500 years of 'sustainable development?' I don't think so" (Lyons, 1992). "It is not too late," Lyons told the United Nations General Assembly. "We still have options. We need the courage to change our values to the regeneration of families, the life that surrounds us" (Lyons, Address, 1992).

Bruce E. Johansen

See also Haudenosaunee Confederacy, Political System.

References and Further Reading

Lyons, Oren. No date. "Address . . . to the United Nations Organization, 'The Year of Indigenous Peoples' . . . New York City, December 10, 1992." Available at: http://www.ratical.com/many_worlds/6Nations/OLatUNin92.html. Accessed January 27, 2007.

Lyons, Oren, John Mohawk, Vine Deloria, Jr., Laurence Hauptman, Howard Berman, Donald A. Grinde, Jr., Curtis Berkey, and Robert Venables. 1992. *Exiled in the Land of the Free: Democracy, Indian Nations, and the Constitution.* Santa Fe, NM: Clear Light Publishers.

Lyons, Oren, and John C. Mohawk. 1994. "Sovereignty and Common Sense." *Cultural Survival Quarterly* 17, no. 4 (Winter): 58–60.

Slackman, Michael. 1996. "A Pot of Gold: State Casinos Foreseen as Cash Cow." *Newsday*, August 31: A-8.

MacDonald, Peter

Peter MacDonald (Navajo, Hoshkaisith Begay, b. 1928) was elected chairman of the Navajo Nation four times before being removed from office by the Tribal Council in 1989 for accepting bribes and then going to a federal prison for helping incite a riot that led to the death of two of his supporters. After becoming tribal chairman in 1971, MacDonald led the Navajo government in taking advantage of the Indian self-determination movement to take over many of the governmental functions previously exercised by the U.S. government's Bureau of Indian Affairs (BIA). He also helped found the Council of Energy Resource Tribes (CERT) in 1974 and served as its chair. CERT worked to help tribes benefit more from the exploitation of their natural resources, including mining of coal and uranium.

Hoshkaisith Begay lived a traditional Navajo youth herding sheep. In his autobiography he describes attending the BIA school at Teec Nos Pos in northeastern Arizona where he received the name Peter MacDonald. He later ran away twice from the boarding school at Shiprock, New Mexico, because of the teasing, taunting, and regimentation, becoming a sixth-grade dropout. MacDonald noted that the hostile attitude toward Navajos in the BIA was emotionally devastating. Students were taught that Navajos were "superstitious savages . . . we were forced to go to church without being given an understanding of the Christian religion. We were made to feel that our parents, our grandparents, and everyone who had come before us was inferior. . . . We were constantly told that we were truly inferior to them and that we would always be inferior" (Mac-Donald, 1993, 49). At age fifteen (having lied about his age earlier to get a job), he was drafted into the Marine Corp where he was trained as a code talker. World War II ended before MacDonald could go into battle, however.

After being honorably discharged in 1946 and working for a short time, in 1948 MacDonald enrolled at Bacone, a Baptist Indian junior college in Oklahoma on the GI Bill. There he earned a general equivalency diploma (GED), then majored in sociology, and took courses in Christianity and Indian history. He went to the University of Oklahoma, working nights in the state mental hospital. The BIA encouraged MacDonald to enter a trade school when his GI Bill funds ran out. Instead, he worked two years to save enough money so that he could return to the University of Oklahoma in 1955, where he earned an electrical engineering degree in 1957.

MacDonald then went to work at Hughes Aircraft, where in a few years he became director of its Polaris missile project. He also received a taste of a corporate executive's upper-class lifestyle. Despite his success at Hughes, MacDonald took a leave in 1963 and was soon appointed director of the Navajo Division of Management, Methods and Procedures. Two years later he was placed in charge of a large War on Poverty program under the federal Office of Economic Opportunity. The Office of Navajo Economic Opportunity ran Head Start programs, community development, alcoholism rehabilitation, and many other programs that directly or indirectly affected almost every Navajo. This experience gave him the name recognition necessary to run for Navajo Nation chairman in 1970, winning by a landslide.

While he successfully negotiated better contracts for the Navajos' energy resources and worked to have Navajos run more of the programs formerly administered by the BIA, MacDonald also became enmeshed in a bitter land dispute between the Hopi and Navajo Nations. His feuding with Arizona's powerful Senator Barry Goldwater hurt the Navajos in this dispute. A strong leader, he sought to pack the tribal court with judges who would rule the way he wanted and to dictate the council's agenda.

Signs of hubris appeared in his second term when, represented by F. Lee Bailey, MacDonald was tried and acquitted of taking bribes. Some of his opponents called him "Mac Dollar." In 1982, MacDonald lost the election, partly because of his lack of success in resolving the Navajo Hopi land dispute. However, he was again elected chairman in 1986. In 1989 he was placed on administrative leave by the tribal council, and a period of political turmoil ensued that led to his going to a federal prison. He was released after being pardoned by President William Clinton in 2001.

Jon Reyhner

See also Bureau of Indian Affairs: Establishing the Existence of an Indian Tribe; Council of Energy Resource Tribes.

References and Further Reading
Bland, Celia. 1995. *Peter MacDonald: Former Chairman of the Navajo Nation.* New York: Chelsea House Publishers.
Iverson, Peter. 2002. *Diné: A History of the Navajos.* Albuquerque: University of New Mexico Press.
MacDonald, Peter. 1993. *The Last Warrior: Peter MacDonald and the Navajo.* London: Orion Books.

Major Ridge

Major Ridge (ca. 1771–1839) was one of several Cherokees who opposed John Ross and his supporters during the years leading to their removal from their homelands in the late 1820s and 1830s. As a leader of the Treaty Party, Ridge favored cooperation with the administration of Andrew Jackson, which forced the Cherokees' removal to Indian Territory, later called Oklahoma.

Nunna Hidihi (also Nungo Hattarhee, "Man on the Mountaintop Who Sees Clearly" or *"The Ridge"*) was born at Hiwassee in the Old Cherokee Nation (present-day Tennessee) about 1771. He was the son of a Cherokee man named Ogonstota and Susannah Catherine, a Scot-Cherokee woman of the Deer Clan. Shortly after his birth, Ridge's family moved to what would become northern Georgia. Having little formal education, Ridge gained most of his academic skills from his parents and neighbors. He was the uncle of Elias Boudinot and Stand Watie.

As a young man, Ridge's considerable oratorical skills facilitated his election to the Cherokee Council when he was only twenty-one. He became speaker of the Cherokee Council within a few years after that. Ridge also became a prosperous farmer and in 1792 married Princess Schoya (Susie Wickett), a full-blooded Cherokee. They had a son, John Ridge, who is sometime confused with his father.

The elder Ridge received the title "major" during the Creek War of 1813–1814 while serving under General Andrew Jackson at the Battle of Horseshoe Bend. He also joined Jackson's forces during the First Seminole War in 1818, leading a Cherokee contingent against the Seminoles.

Early in the 1830s, Major Ridge, his son John, and Elias Boudinot became leaders in the proremoval Treaty Party. On December 22, 1835, Ridge was one of the signers of the Treaty of New Echota, which exchanged the Cherokee tribal land east of the Mississippi River for lands to the west. Like a number of other leaders (Indian and white), Ridge

Major Ridge was one of several Cherokees who favored co-operation with the administration of Andrew Jackson, which forced the Cherokees' removal to Indian Territory, later called Oklahoma. (Library of Congress)

believed that the policy of removal was the best way to preserve the Cherokees in the face of rapidly expanding white encroachment. The treaty was of dubious legality, however, and was rejected by Chief John Ross and a majority of the Cherokee people. Despite its flaws, the U.S. Senate ratified the treaty.

After Major Ridge signed the Treaty of New Echota, he was reputed to have said it was his death warrant. Four years later, following the Trail of Tears, Major Ridge, John Ridge, and Boudinot were dragged from their homes and stabbed several times by a group of executioners, many of whose children and relatives had suffered fatalities during the Trail of Tears during the winter of 1838–1839. Many Cherokees believed that the treaty and Major Ridge were responsible for their losses.

Ridge's nephew Stand Watie, the future Confederate general in the Civil War, also had been targeted for assassination but escaped.

Bruce E. Johansen

See also Trail of Tears; Ross, John; *Worcester v. Georgia.*

Reference and Further Reading
John Ehle, John. 1988. *Trail of Tears: The Rise and Fall of the Cherokee Nation.* New York: Doubleday.

Mangas Coloradas

Mangas Coloradas was a Chiricahuan Apache leader during the mid-1800s. Born in approximately 1790 in southwestern New Mexico near today's Silver City, he lived through periods of Spanish and Mexican peace establishments, chronic war that followed their collapse, and the first phases of American conquest. From the 1830s to his death in 1863, Mangas Coloradas was the most prominent leader of the Chiricahuas in their struggle for regional dominance with the Mexicans and, starting in the late 1840s, with the Americans. He met a treacherous end at the hands of American soldiers, being shot as an unarmed prisoner.

Chiricahuas consisted of four major bands: the Chihennes, Chokonens, Bedonkohes, and Nednhis, which were further divided into multiple local groups. There was no single tribe in political terms, but all were related, sharing strong linguistic and cultural bonds. Mangas Coloradas probably was born as a Bedonkohe and married to the Chihenne band. For the first decades of his life he was known as Fuerte and only later received the name Kan-da-zis-tlishishen, or Mangas Coloradas ("Red/Pink Sleeves"). Born into a prominent family, he matured during the period of Spanish peace establishments, during which rations and gifts were distributed to the Apaches. Economic and political unrest provoked by the collapse of Spanish power caused this system to crumble. Struggling Mexican regimes no longer could afford to pay off the Chiricahuas. Escalating warfare became epidemic during the 1830s and continued to devastate both the Chiricahuas and the Mexicans until the 1880s. Due to the policies of extermination and treacherous acts of genocide, the Mexicans of Sonora especially gained Mangas Coloradas' hatred.

Character was the single most important factor in Mangas's rise to prominence. Mangas apparently excelled as a fierce fighter, a courageous leader, a generous statesman, a wise diplomat, and a loving family man—all traits valued in Chiricahua society. From the 1830s onward his power and prestige among the many Chiricahuan bands were exceptional. He not only controlled his own local group, which was a hybrid mix of Bedonkohes and Chihennes, but also attracted a wide following of fighting men and led many times a combined force of Chiricahuas from all bands. He gained even more influence by marrying his children wisely. For example, one daughter wedded the Chokonen leader Cochise, while others married prominent Navajo, White Mountain Apache, and Mescalero Apache men. During his life, Mangas Coloradas had at least four wives and perhaps as many as fifteen children. Overall, he was exceptionally well-connected with the many Apache divisions of the Southwest. Mexicans recognized him as the "general" of the Chiricahuas, the most prominent man of the militarily powerful people, whose cooperation and approval were vital for any significant peace initiative to succeed. He was also synonymous with Apache power and cruelty among many Mexicans, and the American invaders knew his reputation when they arrived in the late 1840s. General Stephen Kearny's army, John R. Bartlett's boundary commission, and General Edwin V. Sumner, New Mexico's military commander, all treated him as the most prominent Chiricahuan man.

At first, Mangas Coloradas advocated peaceful relations with the Americans, who shared a common enemy with him: the Mexicans. The Americans were rich in trade commodities and thus useful as partners. A lack of mutual respect, racial hatred, and economic greed, however, brought war, and, despite peace agreements, several violent incidents caused deterioration in the American–Chiricahua Apache relations throughout the 1850s and early 1860s. During the last years of the prominent chief's life, American invaders started to inundate much of his country in the roles of miners, ranchers, and farmers. Mangas himself was engaged in destructive war with the Americans during the early 1860s and was killed by them in 1863 after he had arrived for peace negotiations, was captured, and handed over to the American military. While he was a prisoner, soldiers taunted him and burned his feet, and, when Mangas Coloradas responded, he was shot down and killed, his body thrown in a ditch after being decapitated for "scientific purposes." Military reports contained a fabricated story of an escape attempt.

During his lifetime, Mangas Coloradas saw Chiricahuan power dwindle under the double pressure of Spanish/Mexican and American colonization. When he was born, the Chiricahuas were the

dominant group, but his death signaled the beginning of the end for Apache power. In a little longer than two decades, all the surviving Chiricahuas would be exiled to Florida as prisoners of war.

Janne Lahti

See also Cochise.
References and Further Reading
Sweeney, Edwin R. 1998. *Mangas Coloradas: Chief of the Chiricahua Apaches.* Norman: University of Oklahoma Press.
Worcester, Donald E. 1979. *The Apaches: Eagles of the Southwest.* Norman: University of Oklahoma Press.

Mankiller, Wilma

After a childhood in rural Oklahoma and a youthful period in the San Francisco area, Wilma Pearl Mankiller became the first woman to lead a major Indian nation in the United States.

Mankiller was born in Rocky Mountain, Oklahoma, on November 18, 1945, a daughter of a Cherokee father and a Dutch-Irish mother, one of eleven children. After spending her early years close to her people, at the age of eleven she and her family moved to San Francisco as a part of the relocation program implemented by the Bureau of Indian Affairs.

Mankiller had a difficult time adjusting to Hunter's Point, the impoverished, predominantly African American neighborhood in which her family lived. Having completed her high school education, she began to create opportunities to work for the good of Indian people. When the issue of American Indian civil rights began to gain the national spotlight in the late 1960s, Mankiller's position in the Bay Area enabled her to play a vital role in the Red Power Movement. After marrying an Ecuadorian, Hugo Olaya, and having two children, she became director of the American Indian Youth Center in East Oakland, California. Although caring for her family kept her from being present on Alcatraz Island herself when American Indian activists occupied the former federal prison in 1969, Mankiller raised money to support the protestors and visited them on Alcatraz.

Mankiller and Olaya divorced in 1977, the same year she completed her bachelor of arts at Union College. Mankiller then returned to Oklahoma, continuing her career of advocacy by addressing two of the most relevant issues to reser-

The first woman to become chief of the Cherokee Nation, Wilma Pearl Mankiller is a very well-known Native American activist nationwide. (University of Utah Women's Week Celebration)

vation communities: water and housing. At the same time, she did graduate work, earning her master's degree in community planning at the University of Arkansas in 1979. She worked for the Cherokee Nation as an economic stimulus coordinator and became the tribe's program development specialist in 1979. However, an automobile accident that year left Mankiller seriously injured and hospitalized for a lengthy period. Her health problems were compounded when she was diagnosed with systemic myasthenia gravis, a glandular autoimmune disorder requiring surgery and extending her period of recuperation. Despite her health problems, she was able to return to active political life, founding and directing the Cherokee Community Development Department in 1981.

Mankiller's activities as an advocate for treaty rights and better services earned notice. She moved

into the political structure of the Cherokee Nation during 1983 when the principal chief of the nation, Ross O. Swimmer, asked her to be his running mate. Despite receiving hate mail and death threats because of her gender, she became the first woman elected deputy principal chief. After Swimmer resigned to become head of the Bureau of Indian Affairs in December 1985, Mankiller was appointed to serve out the two years remaining in his term. Once in charge of the more than 100,000-member Cherokee Nation of Oklahoma, Mankiller concentrated on the most vital issues facing her people: unemployment, education, health care, and economic development. Her successes made her very popular with her constituents, and she became the first woman elected to lead the Cherokee Nation in 1987, when she was voted to the position of principal chief, capturing more than 80 percent of the vote. Despite continued health problems requiring a kidney transplant, she was reelected in 1991 and served as the leader of the Cherokee Nation until the end of her second term in 1995, choosing not to run for reelection due to persistent health concerns.

Even after Mankiller stepped down from her role as head of the Cherokee Nation, she continued being politically active. She continues to live in the capital of the Cherokee Nation, Tahlequah, Oklahoma, with her Cherokee second husband, Charlie Soap. Over her career, she has received numerous honors, including a special White House ceremony at the end of her term as principal chief, a Humanitarian Award from the Ford Foundation, induction into the National Women's Hall of Fame in 1993, and the nation's highest civilian honor, the Presidential Medal of Freedom, in 1998. In addition, she has published two books: her best-selling 1993 autobiography, *Mankiller: A Chief and Her People*, and *Every Day Is a Good Day: Reflections of Contemporary Indigenous Women* (2004).

Steven L. Danver

See also Occupation of Alcatraz Island; Trail of Tears; *Worcester v. Georgia*.
References and Further Reading
Champagne, Duane, ed. 1994. *Native America: Portrait of the Peoples*. Canton, MI: Visible Ink Press.
Mankiller, Wilma. 2004. *Every Day Is a Good Day: Reflections of Contemporary Indigenous Women*. Golden, CO: Fulcrum Publishing.
Mankiller, Wilma, and Michael Wallis. 1993. *Mankiller: A Chief and Her People*. New York: St. Martin's Press.

Manuelito

Manuelito, a Spanish name given him by Mexicans, is noted for his resistance to Mexican and American invasions of Navajoland, or *Dinétah*. During his lifetime, Hastiin Ch'iil Hajiin (his Native name) was committed to Navajo sovereignty and strove to maintain possession of Navajo lands.

Manuelito was born into the *Bit'ahni* Clan (Folded Arms People) near Bear Ears, Utah, around 1818. Following the teachings of the ancestors, Manuelito trained as a medicine man who followed *hózhó*, the path of harmony and balance to Old Age, the path that Navajos had been following for many generations. Manuelito's marriage to the daughter of the headman Narbona provided him with the wise leader's insight. In later years, Manuelito also found his wife Juanita to be a valuable companion.

Beginning in the late 1500s, Spaniards and then Mexicans came into the Southwest seeking their fortunes and establishing colonies. Navajos experienced cultural changes that made them herders and warriors. With the horse, Navajos ably impeded the foreigners' advances. Manuelito witnessed the shifting relationships of peace and conflict between Navajos and Mexicans. In the 1830s, Mexicans rode into Navajoland determined to break Navajo resistance and to capture women and children for the slave trade. Slavery had been known in the Southwest, but the slave trade intensified with Euro-American invasions. Slave raiders targeted Navajo women and children. In fact, raiding for Navajo slaves reached a peak during the 1830s. In a battle at Copper Pass in 1835 in the Chuska Mountains, warriors led by Narbona and Manuelito successfully defeated the Mexicans. At that time, Manuelito was a young man.

By the time the United States claimed the Southwest in 1846, Manuelito was a respected war chief, and the cycle of peace and conflict among Navajos, other tribal peoples, and the U.S. immigrants began anew. In 1851, the establishment of Fort Defiance in Navajoland preceded a war that would end in the Navajos' defeat. The conflict began over the pasturelands that lay outside the newly established fort. In 1858, General William Brooks asserted control of the pastures for U.S. Army use. In defiance, Manuelito continued to pasture his livestock on the disputed lands, whereupon Brooks ordered the livestock slaughtered. Soon afterward, a Navajo killed Brooks's black slave, and Brooks demanded that the Navajos produce the murderer for American justice. Eventually, Navajos

produced a body, most likely that of a Mexican captive. Enraged at what he considered Navajo arrogance, Brooks called for a war. In 1860 Manuelito and 1,000 warriors struck at Fort Defiance several times but were unable to take the fort.

The American Civil War turned the U.S. Army's attention away from Navajoland, and Fort Defiance was abandoned. After the war, European-American settlement again threatened the Navajos. Manuelito led the resistance and urged his people to have courage. Finding Navajos to be obstacles to white expansion, General James H. Carleton ordered their removal to a reservation near Fort Sumner, New Mexico, where the Navajos would learn the arts of civilization.

General Carleton enlisted Indian fighter Kit Carson for the campaign against the Diné. Carson and his men literally scorched Navajoland. They destroyed cornfields, peach trees, hogans, and livestock. By 1863 destitute Navajos began surrendering to the Americans. As prisoners, they endured a 300-mile journey to the internment camp. Some Navajo leaders went with their people, encouraging them to keep heart. Navajo bodies littered the trail. The old and sick were abandoned if they held up the march. Pregnant women were shot and killed if they could not keep up. Many drowned when they tried to cross the Rio Grande. At the prison, the Navajos barely survived.

Manuelito, however, vowed to remain free. The U.S. Army, fearing that he served as inspiration to others who eluded their enemy, wished to either capture or kill him. In 1865, Navajo leaders, including Herrera, met Manuelito and gave him the army's message to surrender. Manuelito refused, declaring that "his mother and his God lived in the West and he would not leave them." He would not leave his native home and the United States could kill if they pleased, but he would not leave.

Finally, in 1866, wounded and ill, Manuelito surrendered and was interned at the Bosque Rodondo prison. After four years, General Carleton reluctantly admitted that his plan was not working. There was talk of returning the Navajos to their former homes. On June 1, 1868, Manuelito and other leaders signed a treaty so that they could return to *Dinétah*. The treaty stipulated a peaceful relationship between Navajos and the United States, defined a boundary for a reservation, and required education for Navajo children. Seventeen days later, over 8,000 Navajos began the journey home. About 3,000 Navajos had died during the war.

Manuelito was one of the most accomplished Navajo war leaders and was recognized as head chief of the Navajo from 1870 to 1884. (National Archives and Records Administration)

Upon return to *Dinétah*, Manuelito remained an influential leader who articulated his concerns for the return of his people's land. He was appointed head of the first Navajo police who would keep order on the reservation. In 1874, he traveled with his wife and other Navajo leaders to Washington, D.C., to meet President Ulysses S. Grant. In 1894, Manuelito died from disease and alcoholism. His widow Juanita and his daughters carried on his messages about the importance of land for the coming generations.

Jennifer Nez Denetdale

See also Carson, Christopher "Kit"; Long Walk.
References and Further Reading

Iverson, Peter. 2002. *Diné: A History of the Navajos.* Albuquerque: University of New Mexico Press.

Kelly, Lawrence. 1970. *Navajo Roundup: Selected Correspondence of Kit Carson's Expedition Against the Navajo, 1863–1865.* Boulder, CO: Pruett Publishing Company.

Roessel, Ruth. 1973. *Navajo Stories of the Long Walk Period.* Tsaile, AZ: Navajo Community College Press.

Sundberg, Lawrence D. 1995. *Dinétah: An Early History of the Navajo People.* Santa Fe, NM: Sunstone Press.

Marx, Karl, and Native American Societies

Karl Heinrich Marx (1818–1883) was a philosopher, social scientist, historian, and revolutionary, regarded as one of the most important social thinkers of the nineteenth century, who developed Marxist theory along with Friedrich Engels (1820–1895). Their combined works constitute the basis of Marxism, a theory of philosophy (dialectical materialism), history (historical materialism), and economics that views the state as a device for the exploitation of the masses by the dominant class and that views class struggle as the catalyst for social change.

In his examination of the evolution of human society, Marx identified five basic historical developments or "regularities" in the modes of production: savagery (primitive), barbarism (nomadism), oriental despotism (slave), feudalism, and capitalism. He theorized the inevitable self-destructive end of capitalism through a proletariat revolution and rise of a superior communist society. The most extensive theoretical discussions of precapitalist societies by Marx and Engels are found in the *Grundrisse der Kritik der Politischen Ökonomie* (Outlines of the Critique of Political Economy), *Pre-Capitalist Economic Formations, The Origin of the Family, Private Property and the State,* and *Ethnological Notebooks.*

The Euro-centric presumption of an inevitable evolution of human society from primitivism to "civilization" forms the basis of the historical tension between indigenous and Marxist scholars. This critique links Marxism with other modes of Western thinking that view the "difference" of indigenous peoples and societies as deficient. Within this framework, indigenous societies are measured against Western norms of human "progress" and development. Other embedded assumptions—of human beings as superior to "nature," of religion as the opiate of the masses, and of class as the dominant unit of social organization—have contributed to a long-standing division between Marxists and Native Americans. The seminal (if not only) works among indigenous scholars are *Marxism and Native Americans* (1983)

Karl Marx, the founder of modern communism, noted the egalitarian nature of Native American cultures in notes that later were used by Friedrich Engels. (Library of Congress)

and *Culture Versus Economism: Essays on Marxism in the Multicultural Arena* (1984).

On the notion of "progress" as both inevitable and good, the indigenous critique has been virtually unanimous, viewing this understanding as inherently dismissive of the "traditional" social, political, and economic structures of indigenous societies. Bedford writes, "Aboriginals object to the Marxist vision because it sees all history unfolding after the fashion of the European model. The Marxist commitment to industrialization as the precondition of proletarian revolution means destruction of non-industrialized societies" (Bedford, 2001, 104). In other words, while "Marxism may call for more equitable distribution of the social product, more democratic control over the processes of production," capitalism is still viewed as "a necessary step toward the final solution" (Bedford, 2001, 103, 105). This notion also works to subsume indigenous peoples into the proletariat, imposing a Western class structure onto a complex and radically contingent indigenous social-political-economic-spiritual structure.

On the question of the superiority of human beings over nature and the profound anthropocentrism of Marxism, the indigenous critique is clear: The inherent trope of progress within Marxist thought pits humans against nature, wherein humans overcome their alienation from nature by consuming it (Deloria, 1983, 114–115). Or, as Grande notes, "both Marxists and capitalists view land and natural resources as commodities to be exploited; in the first instance, by capitalists for personal gain and, in the second, by Marxists for the good of all" (2004, 27).

Finally, on the issue of religion or spirituality, the tensions between the Marxist and indigenous worlds are self-evident. In several of his writings, Marx "follows the development of religion as an integral part of the repressive apparatus through its various permutations linked to the formation of caste, slavery, patriarchal monogamy and monarchy" (Rosemont, n.d.). In contrast, Vine Deloria, Jr., preeminent scholar on Native American "religious" traditions, documents the fundamental link between indigenous societies and the inherent "sacredness" of the world around them.

While the preceding critique represents the historical tenets of the Marxist–indigenous disjuncture, some scholars are beginning to revisit the presumed tension, bringing to the discourse a more nuanced reading of both Marxist and Native American thought. Bedford and Irving (2003) maintain that a close reading of Marx reveals that he is more ambivalent about the value of progress than his (indigenous) critics allow. Grande similarly notes that contemporary Marxist theorists recognize the limitations of their work and critique. She writes: "While any pedagogy with a root metaphor of 'change as progress' presents specific challenges to indigenous cultures rooted in tradition and intergeneration knowledge, revolutionary theorists do not categorically advocate change as *inherently* progressive. Rather, they are very definitive in their distinction between change that emancipates and change that merely furthers the dictates of market imperatives" (2004, 82).

This new strand of scholarship invites us to explore how Marxism may be deepened by its engagement with Native American social and political thought and how it might, in turn, deepen Native intellectualism.

Sandy Grande

See also Engels, Friedrich, and "Mother-right gens."

References and Further Reading

Bedford, David. 2001. "Marxism and the Aboriginal Question: The Tragedy of Progress." Available at: http://www.brandonu.ca/Library/CJNS/14.1/bedford.pdf. Accessed February 1, 2005.

Bedford, David, and Danielle Irving. 2003. *The Tragedy of Progress: Marxism: Modernity and the Aboriginal Question.* Halifax, CA: Fernwood Press.

Deloria, Vine, Jr. 1983. *Of Utmost Good Faith.* New York: Simon & Shuster.

Grande, Sandy. 2004. *Red Pedagogy: Native American Social and Political Thought.* Lanham, MD: Rowman & Littlefield.

Lyons, Scott L. 2005. "The Left Side of the Circle: American Indians and Progressive Politics." In *Radical Relevance: Toward a Scholarship of the Whole Left.* Edited by Laura Gray-Rosendal and Steven Rosendale. New York: State University of New York Press.

Marx, Karl. 1972. *The Ethnological Notebooks of Karl Marx.* Transcribed by Lawrence Krader. Assen, Netherlands: Van Gorcum.

Marx, Karl. [1857–1858] 1993. *Grundrisse.* Translated by Martin Niclaus. New York and Hammondsworth, UK: Penguin.

Rosemont, Franklin. No date. "Karl Marx and the Iroquois." [http://www.geocities.com/cordobakaf/marx_iroquois.html] Accessed February 1, 2007.

Massasoit

The name "Massasoit" is a title meaning "Grand Sachem" or "Great Leader" that was bestowed on Ousa Mequin (Yellow Feather), sachem of the Pokanoket and the Grand Sachem (Massasoit) of the Wampanoag Confederation.

Little is known about Massaoit (ca. 1590–1661/1662) prior to his contact with the Plymouth colony in 1621. He was born around 1590 in Montaup, a Pokanoket village near present-day Bristol, Rhode Island, and rose to leadership over eight large villages. The first documented contact of Massasoit with the English occurred in 1619. In that year, he met with Captain Thomas Dermer following the latter's voyage with Tisquantum (Squanto) to New England. William Bradford, the second governor of the Plymouth colony, described the Pokanoket sachem as "a very lust [sic] man in his best years, an able body, grave of countenance, and spare of speech. . . . His face was painted with a deep red like mulberry and he was oiled both head and face" (Josephy, 1994, 211).

Massassoit, leader of the Wampanoag, was able to maintain peaceful relations with English settlers in the area of Plymouth, Massachussetts. He and other Native Americans shared planting and fishing techniques with the colonists and fostered trade and amity between the races. (Library of Congress)

Traditionally, Massasoit is remembered for his alliance with the Pilgrims and his efforts to aid the Plymouth Colony. A calculating and skilled diplomat, he established personal relationships with the principal leaders of the Plymouth colony, including William Bradford and Edward Winslow. Concern over the possibility of conflict with the neighboring Narragansetts led Massasoit to forge an alliance with the colonists at Plymouth in March 1621. The resulting treaty was mutually beneficial, providing security for the colonists and military aid for the Wampanoags in case of hostilities with the Narragansetts. Cemented even further by Edward Winslow's resuscitation of the critically ill sachem in 1632, the alliance also served to keep the Wampanoags out of the Pequot War (1636–1637) and enabled Massasoit to resist Puritan efforts to Christianize his people.

Expanding English settlements around Massachusetts Bay brought pressures on Massasoit to cede land to the English. To this he relented, selling land in the 1650s to the colony in exchange for the maintenance of harmony. Until his death in 1661 or 1662, the Wampanoag under Massasoit and the people of the Massachusetts Bay and Plymouth colonies remained at peace.

Alan C. Downs

See also Squanto; Thanksgiving Holiday, Origins.
References and Further Reading

Axtell, James. 2001. *Natives and Newcomers: The Cultural Origins of North America.* New York: Oxford University Press.

Josephy, Alvin M., Jr. 1994. *500 Nations: An Illustrated History of North American Indians.* New York: Alfred A. Knopf.

Philbrick, Nathaniel. 2006. *Mayflower: A Story of Courage, Community, and War.* New York: Viking.

McNickle, D'Arcy

Author of *The Surrounded*, two other novels, a biography, and three book-length studies, D'Arcy McNickle was a major figure both in American Indian literature and Native studies, as well as an activist and government worker on behalf of American Indians. William D'Arcy McNickle (Métis) was born on January 18, 1904, in St. Ignatius, Montana. He was an enrolled member of the Salish and Kootenai Tribes, or Flathead. His mother, Philomena Parenteau, had fled Canada after the failed Métis revolt in 1855 and was formally adopted into the Flathead tribe. She later married local Irish rancher William McNickle. Their son D'Arcy began his education at the Catholic boarding school at St. Ignatius and then, against his mother's and his own desires, was sent to the Bureau of Indian Affairs (BIA) boarding school at Chemawa in Oregon for three years. At the age of seventeen, he began studies at the University of Montana, focusing on literature and languages such as Latin and Greek. Seeing in McNickle a talent for writing, one of his professors urged him to attend Oxford. McNickle financed his trip to England by selling his land allotment in 1925, but trouble with credit transfer prevented him from taking his degree. For a time, McNickle moved to Paris, where he wrote and played music before returning to New York in 1928.

McNickle married three times and had two daughters. In New York, he worked in various positions, among them one as an editor for *Encyclopaedia*

Brittanica and the *National Encyclopaedia of American Biography,* and intermittently took classes at the New School for Social Research and at Columbia. He continued to write, completing several short stories and his first novel, publishing *The Surrounded* in 1936. The novel focuses on the mixed-blood Archilde Leon, caught between his tribal culture and relatives on the one hand and the changes brought by colonization on the other. It is written much in the modernist tradition, at the same time highlighting cultural differences and values.

McNickle, disappointed with the lack of success of his novel and needing money, went to Washington, D.C., to work for the Federal Writers' Project and subsequently found a position with John Collier's administration at the BIA, where he work for sixteen years. Charged with the implementation of the Indian Reorganization Act of 1934, McNickle strongly advocated federal protection of tribal lands and instituting democracy in tribal governments. Gradually, he began to see the need for intertribal political organizing to advance positive change through Indian agency. In 1944, he cofounded the National Congress of American Indians for these purposes. However, with the 1950s termination and relocation policies, McNickle left the BIA to take a job with the American Indian Development Corporation. McNickle sat on the United States Civil Rights Commission and received an honorary doctorate from the University of Colorado in 1966. The same year he took a position as a professor at the University of Saskatchewan, where he developed the newly established anthropology department.

Advancing a Native perspective but writing for a non-Native audience, McNickle published a number of books, including *They Came Here First: The Epic of the American Indian* (1949), *Indians and Other Americans: A Study of Indian Affairs* (with Harold Fey, 1959, and *The Indian Tribes of the United States: Ethnic and Cultural Survival* (1962), all drawing on anthropological methods he learned in his BIA fieldwork. In 1954, working with Apache visual artist Allan Houser, McNickle published *Runner in the Sun: A Story of Indian Maize.* This young adult novel may be the first book set in precontact America written by an American Indian. He retired from the university in 1971 and published *Indian Man: The Story of Oliver La Farge,* which was nominated for a National Book Award. In 1972, he helped found the Center for the History of the American Indian at the Newberry Library in Chicago, serving as its first director. Retiring to Albuquerque to work on *Wind from an Enemy Sky,* he died of a heart attack in October 1977.

Kimberly Roppolo

See also Collier, John.
References and Further Reading

Bear Don't Walk, Scott. 1996. "McNickle, D'Arcy." In *Encyclopedia of North American Indians: Native American History, Culture, and Life from Paleo-Indians to the Present.* Edited by Frederick E. Hoxie, 369–370. Boston: Houghton-Mifflin.

Markowitz, Harvey, ed. 1995. *Ready Reference: American Indians.* Vol. 1. Pasadena, CA: Salem Press.

Malinowski, Sharon, ed. 1995. *Notable Native Americans.* Detroit, MI: Gale Research.

Means, Russell

Arguably one of the most well-known modern advocates of American Indian rights, Russell Means exhibits a spirited outspokenness that helped open a dialogue that changed the course of American Indian history in the late twentieth century. An Oglala Lakota, Means was born on November 10, 1939, on the Pine Ridge Reservation in southwestern South Dakota. Wishing to escape the limitations of reservation life, his mother, Theodora Louise Feather Means, moved the family to Vallejo, California, where his father, Walter "Hank" Means, found work as a welder at the navy shipyard on Mare Island. Hank's alcoholism contributed to an unstable family life for Russell and his teenage years were marked by school truancy, drug and alcohol abuse, and petty criminal activity.

In 1964, the twenty-six-year-old Means, recently fired from his job as a night watchman at the Cow Palace in San Francisco, accepted an invitation to accompany his father and a small assemblage of Indians living in the San Francisco Bay area on a symbolic takeover of the recently abandoned federal prison on Alcatraz Island. Russell later confided that his father's willingness to stand up for Indian treaty rights "made me proud to be his son, and to be a Lakota" (Means, 1995, 105).

Five years later, as a new cadre of urban Indians readied once again to occupy Alcatraz, Means was in Cleveland, Ohio, where he joined two Anishinabe Indians from Minnesota, Clyde Bellecourt and Dennis Banks, in their effort to develop the American Indian Movement (AIM)—arguably the principal

Russell Means, American Indian Movement (AIM) leader, speaks to a crowd of followers in South Dakota in 1974. (Bettman/Corbis)

agency for American Indian empowerment during the late 1960s and early 1970s. Means later acknowledged "here was a way to be a *real* Indian, and AIM had shown it to me. No longer would I be content to 'work within the system.' . . . Instead, like Clyde and Dennis and the others in AIM, I would get in the white man's face until he gave me and my people our just due. With that decision, my whole existence suddenly came into focus. For the first time, I knew the purpose of my life and the path I must follow to fulfill it. At the age of thirty I became a full-time Indian" (Means, 1995, 153).

On Thanksgiving Day 1970, Means, Banks, and other AIM leaders joined local Wampanoag activists in Plymouth, Massachusetts, to observe a national day of Indian mourning at the 350th anniversary celebration of the arrival of the Pilgrims. Speaking at the base of a larger-than-life statue of Chief Massasoit overlooking Plymouth Harbor, Means delivered an impassioned speech praising the ancestral Wampanoags who welcomed the Pilgrims and denouncing the white man's culture. Within twenty-four hours, Indian activists seized the *Mayflower II* (a full-scale replica of the original *Mayflower*), painted Plymouth Rock red, and brought national attention to the American Indian Movement.

Following its success at Plymouth, AIM elected Means the first national coordinator of the movement. He participated in the AIM-sponsored protest at Mount Rushmore in June 1971 and in the Trail of Broken Treaties, which led to the seizure of the Bureau of Indian Affairs building in November 1972. On the evening of February 27, 1973, Means, along with Dennis Banks, organized the occupation of Wounded Knee, South Dakota, the most renowned episode in the history of American Indian Movement. The takeover of the community, the proclamation of an Independent Oglala Nation, and the subsequent seventy-one-day siege by the federal government led to the national attention—albeit short-lived—that Means and AIM desired.

In 1974, Russell Means, beset with legal fees and court cases in the aftermath of the Wounded Knee occupation, nevertheless began his career in politics when he ran unsuccessfully for the Oglala Sioux tribal chair against the incumbent, Dick Wilson, in a contested election marked by voter fraud. In 1976, Means was tried for and acquitted of the murder of Martin Montileaux in the Longhorn Saloon in Scenic, South Dakota. Two years later he entered the South Dakota State Penitentiary, ultimately serving only twelve months of his four-year conviction for participating in a riot in a Sioux Falls courthouse in 1974. He joined Larry Flynt in 1983 in the pornographer's unsuccessful bid for the Republican presidential ticket in 1984. Hoping to force the Republican party to aid him in his struggles against the religious right in exchange for his withdrawal from the race, Flynt waged an outrageous campaign punctuated with publicity stunts. Disenchanted with the publisher's sincerity in championing First Amendment rights, Means ultimately removed his name from the ticket.

A supporter of indigenous rights worldwide, Means traveled to Nicaragua in 1986 to aid the Miskito Indians in their struggle against the Sandinistas. The move cost him the support of some of his more liberal supporters in AIM and elsewhere who saw his actions as condoning the pro-Contra deal-

ings of the Reagan administration. Likewise, his 1986 speaking tour, sponsored by Reverend Sun Myung Moon's controversial Unification Church, further isolated Means from the Left. While the so-called Moonies used his lectures on Nicaragua as a venue to distribute literature about their church, Means saw the association as a vehicle to inform the public about the plight of the Nicaraguan Indians.

In 1987, Means accepted an invitation to enter the primary race for the Libertarian party's presidential candidate in 1988. The party's principles appealed to Means and he mounted an extensive national campaign, only to lose in the end to former Republican Congressman Ron Paul at the Libertarian party convention in Seattle. With residences in both South Dakota and New Mexico, Means tried in 2001 to enter the gubernatorial race in New Mexico as a candidate from the Independent Coalition party, only to drop out after a controversy over the filing deadline. Choosing instead to run, once again, for the presidency of the Oglala Sioux tribe, Means won the primary in 2002, but lost in the general election to incumbent John Yellow Bird Steele.

In addition to his activism and political aspirations, Russell Means developed a parallel career in the arts. In 1992, Means starred as Chingachgook in *Last of the Mohicans* and provided the voice of Chief Powhatan in Disney's *Pocahontas* in 1995. He also has had roles in ten other films to date as well as numerous guest appearances on television dramas and talk shows. His autobiography, *Where White Men Fear to Tread*, was published in 1995. He also has produced two music CDs and several works of art.

Russell Means remains active in issues of Indian self-determination and injustice in North America and abroad. Most recently, he has focused his efforts on a campaign to abolish Columbus Day. No stranger to controversy, Means's exploits have reaped both supporters and critics. There is no doubt, however, that his unremitting presence on the national stage in the late twentieth century helped draw attention to issues of import to Indian peoples.

Alan C. Downs

See also American Indian Movement; Banks, Dennis; Peltier, Leonard.

References and Further Reading

Means, Russell. 1995. *Where White Men Fear to Tread.* New York: St. Martin's Griffin.

Smith, Paul Chaat, and Robert Allen Warrior. 1996. *Like a Hurricane: The Indian Movement from Alcatraz to Wounded Knee.* New York: New Press.

Metacom, and King Philip's War

Metacom (ca. 1637–1676) was the son of Massasoit, who had met the first immigrants from England in 1620 in what is now Massachusetts. The English called Metacom King Philip. He became grand sachem of the Wampanoags in 1662 and led his people and their allies in a devastating war with the English in 1675 and 1676, dying at its conclusion.

The efforts of Roger Williams, Puritan dissenter and founder of Rhode Island, helped to maintain a shaky peace along the frontiers of New England for nearly two generations after the Pequot War (1636–1637). In 1645, Williams averted another Native uprising against encroaching European-American settlements. By the 1660s, however, the aging Williams saw his lifelong pursuit of peace unravel yet again. This time, he felt more impotent than in the past: Wave after wave of colonists provided Native peoples with powerful grievances by usurping their land without permission or compensation, and yet Williams continued to believe that neither the Puritans nor any other Europeans had any right, divine or otherwise, to take Indian land. The final years of Williams's life were profoundly painful for a sensitive man who prized peace and harmony above all.

Massasoit, who had maintained peace with the newcomers since 1620, also was aging and becoming disillusioned with the colonists, as increasing numbers of European immigrants drove his people from their lands. Upon Massasoit's death in 1661, Alexander, one of Massasoit's sons, briefly served as grand sachem of the Wampanoags. However, visiting Boston in 1662, Alexander fell gravely ill and died as Wampanoag warriors rushed him into the wilderness. Upon his death, the warriors beached their canoes, buried his body in a knoll, and returned home with rumors that he had been a victim of the English. Metacom became grand sachem after Alexander's death.

Aged about twenty-five in 1662, Metacom distrusted nearly all European-Americans, Williams being one of the few exceptions. Metacom also was known as a man who did not forgive insults easily. It was once said that he chased a white man named John Gibbs from Mount Hope to Nantucket Island, about sixty miles, partially over water, after Gibbs insulted his father. Throughout his childhood, Metacom had watched his people dwindle before the English advance. By 1671, about 40,000 non-Native people lived in New England. The Native

Native American leader Metacom, also known as King Philip, led a Native alliance in King Philip's War (1676). In terms of numbers engaged and casualties sustained in proportion to population, this was one of the the bloodiest Indian wars of American history. (Library of Congress)

population, double that of the Europeans before the Pequot War, stood at about 20,000. European farms and pastures were driving away game and creating friction over land that the Indians had used without question for so many generations they had lost count of them. By 1675, the Wampanoags held only a small strip of land at Mount Hope, and settlers wanted it.

Metacom became more embittered by the day. He could see his nation being destroyed before his eyes. He and other people in his nation were interrogated by Puritan officials. Traders fleeced Indians, exchanging furs for liquor. The devastation of alco-hol and disease and the loss of land destroyed families and tradition. These were Metacom's thoughts as he prepared to go to war against the English.

As rumors of war reached Williams, he tried to keep the neighboring Narragansetts neutral, as he had done in the past. This time, he failed. Nananaw-tunu, son of Mixanno, told his close friend Williams that, while he opposed going to war, his people could not be restrained. They had decided the time had come to die fighting, rather than to expire slowly as a people. Williams' letters of this time were pervaded with sadness, as he watched the two groups he knew so well slide toward war.

Shortly after hostilities began in June 1675, Williams met with Metacom, riding with the sachem and his family in a canoe not far from Providence. Williams warned Metacom that he was leading his people to extermination. Williams compared the Wampanoags to a canoe on a stormy sea of English fury. "He answered me in a consenting, considering kind of way," Williams wrote, "[saying] My canoe is already overturned" (Giddings, 1957, 33).

When Indians, painted for war, appeared on the heights above Providence, Williams picked up his staff, climbed the bluffs, and told the war parties that, if they attacked the town, England would send thousands of armed men to crush them. "Well," one of the sachems leading the attack told Williams, "let them come. We are ready for them, but as for you, brother Williams, you are a good man. You have been kind to us for many years. Not a hair on your head shall be touched" (Straus, 1894, 220–224).

Williams was not injured, but his house was torched as he met with the Indians on the bluffs above Providence on March 29, 1676. Williams watched flames spread throughout the town. "This house of mine now burning before mine eyes hath lodged kindly some thousands of you these ten years," Williams told the attacking Indians (Swan, 1969, 14). If the colony was to survive, Williams, for the first time in his life, had to become a military commander. With a grave heart, Williams sent his neighbors out to do battle with the sons and daughters of Native people who had sheltered him during his winter trek from Massachusetts forty years earlier. As Williams and others watched from inside a hastily erected fort, nearly all of Providence burned. Fields were laid waste and cattle were slaughtered or driven into the woods.

Colonists, seething with anger, caught an Indian, and Williams was put in the agonizing position of ordering him killed, rather than watching him tortured. The war was irrefutably brutal on both sides, as the English fought with their backs literally to the sea for a year and a half before going on the offensive. At Northfield, Indians hanged two Englishmen on chains, placing hooks under their jaws. At Springfield, colonists arrested an Indian woman, then offered her body to dogs, which tore her to pieces.

In August 1676, as the Mohawks and Mohegans opted out of their alliance with the Wampanoags, the war ended. The English had exterminated most of the Narragansetts, and nearly all of Metacom's warriors, their families, and friends had been killed or driven into hiding. Metacom himself fled toward Mount Hope, then hid in a swamp. When English soldiers found him, they dragged him out of the mire, then had him drawn and quartered. His head was sent to Plymouth on a giblet, where it was displayed much as criminals' severed heads were shown off on the railings of London Bridge. Metacom's hands were sent to Boston, where a local showman charged admission for a glimpse of one of them. The remainder of Metacom's body was hung from four separate trees.

In terms of deaths in proportion to total population, King Philip's War was among the deadliest in American history. About 1,000 colonists died in the war; many more died of starvation and war-related diseases. Every Native nation bordering the Puritan settlements—those whose members, in happier days, had offered the earliest colonists their first Thanksgiving dinner—was reduced to ruin. Many of the survivors were sold into slavery in the West Indies, which served the colonists two purposes: removing them from the area and raising money to help pay their enormous war debts. Metacom's son was auctioned off with about 500 other slaves, following a brief, but intense, biblical debate over whether a son should be forced to atone for the sins of his father.

Bruce E. Johansen

See also Massasoit; Williams, Roger.
References and Further Reading
Giddings, James L. 1957. "Roger Williams and the Indians." Typescript, Rhode Island Historical Society.
Kennedy, John Hopkins. 1950. *Jesuit and Savage in New France*. New Haven, CT: Yale University Press.
Slotkin, Richard, and James K. Folsom, eds. 1978. *So Dreadful a Judgement: Puritan Responses to King Philip's War 1676–1677*. Middleton, CT: Wesleyan University Press.
Srraus, Oscar S. 1984. *Roger Williams: The Pioneer of Religious Liberty*. New York: Century Company.
Swan, Bradford F. 1969. "New Light on Roger Williams and the Indians." *Providence Sunday Journal Magazine*, November 23: 14.
Vaughan, Alden T. 1965. *New England Frontier: Puritans and Indians, 1620–1675*. Boston: Little, Brown and Company.
Wright, Ronald. 1992. *Stolen Continents*. Boston: Houghton-Mifflin.

Mills, William M.

Oglala Lakota William ("Billy") Mills distinguished himself as a distance runner, capturing the gold medal in the 10,000-meter run at the 1964 Tokyo Olympics, and later proved himself to be an inspirational speaker and caring leader.

Born in 1938 on the Pine Ridge Indian Reservation in South Dakota, he was named Makata Taka Hela, which translates as "Love Your Country" or "Respects the Earth." Mills was of mixed ancestry, a factor that caused him to feel marginalized at times as a youth. His sense of isolation was intensified when he was orphaned at the age of twelve. Athletics offered him an important release during this period.

Mills then attended Haskell Institute in Lawrence, Kansas, graduating in 1957. At the Indian boarding school, he participated in boxing and running. Eventually, he devoted himself exclusively to running, performing well enough to secure an athletic scholarship at the nearby University of Kansas. Mills blossomed under Jayhawk track coach Bill Easton. Indeed, while at the University of Kansas, he was named an all-American three times, was victorious in the Big Eight conference cross-country individual title in 1960, and contributed to two national NCAA outdoor team championships in 1959 and 1960.

After graduating in 1962 with a degree in physical education, Mills married and accepted a commission in the Marine Corps. Although he thought his athletic career had ended when he joined the service, Mills was able to continuing running. After a year and a half of training, he qualified for the U.S. Olympic team.

Despite his collegiate success, many people were dubious of Mills's prospects at the 1964 Tokyo Olympics. In fact, he had to borrow shoes because U.S. team officials felt their limited resources should be allocated to more promising competitors. His qualifying time in the 10,000-meter run was a minute slower than Australian Ron Clarke, who most observers expected would battle Tunisian Mohammad Gammoudi for the gold medal. Mills never doubted himself, however, as he set his sights on a victory in Tokyo. In what can only be described as a stunning upset, perhaps the most amazing in Olympic history, Mills surged past Clarke and Gammoudi on the last lap to become the first American to win a gold medal in the 10,000-meter run, setting an Olympic record at that

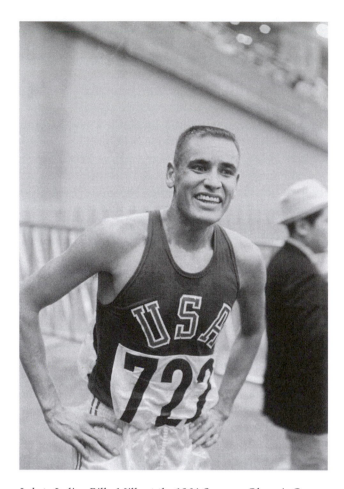

Lakota Indian Billy Mills at the 1964 Summer Olympic Games. Mills won the gold medal in the 10,000-meter race. (Bettman/Corbis)

distance. Mills also performed well in the marathon, placing fourteenth.

Mills continued running after the Olympics. Most notably, in 1965, he set U.S. records for the 10,000-meter and three miles, along with a world record in the six-mile run (27 minutes, 12 seconds), a time that has not since been surpassed.

Mills has lived a full life beyond athletics. He has been married to his wife Patricia for nearly forty years, and they have raised three daughters. After leaving the Marines, he worked as a life insurance salesperson. For much of the past thirty years, he has been an inspirational speaker, living in Sacramento. He has also taken a leading role in the empowerment of indigenous peoples. As the spokesperson for Running Strong for American Indian Youth, a division of Christian Relief Services, he has worked to help American Indian communities meet their basic needs—food, clothing, and

shelter—while implanting programs to build self-esteem and sovereignty.

Mills' life was the subject of the 1984 feature film, *Running Brave,* starring Robby Benson.

Over the past forty years, Mills has received numerous awards for his achievements as an athlete, leader, and humanitarian. In 1972, he was named one of the Ten Outstanding Young Americans by the Jaycees. Four years later, in 1976, Mills was inducted into the United States Track and Field Hall of Fame. He is also a member of the United States Olympic Hall of Fame, the National Distance Running Hall of Fame, the Kansas Hall of Fame, and the National High School Hall of Fame. In 2003 he became the first American Indian to receive the Alumni Distinguished Service Award from his alma mater.

C. Richard King

See also Thorpe, Jim.
Reference and Further Reading
Mills, Billy, and Nicholas Sparks. 2003. *Wokini: A Lakota Journey to Happiness and Understanding.* Carlsbad, CA: Hay House.

Mohawk, John C.

John C. Mohawk, regarded as "one of the foremost Iroquois scholars and activists of his generation" (Mohawk, 2006), combined the roles and talents of university professor, international negotiator, and cultural revivalist.

A long-time professor in the State University of New York at Buffalo's American Studies Department, Mohawk also directed the department's indigenous studies program. Mohawk also was known as a skilled crisis negotiator who not only helped reconcile differences between Iroquois factions, but also, during 1980, played a role in negotiating U.S.-Iranian relations. As a cultural revivalist, Mohawk initiated and led the Iroquois White Corn Project, which produced and marketed traditional Seneca white corn to restaurants, part of a larger effort by Mohawk to help maintain small-scale sustainable agriculture.

Mohawk was born to Ernie and Elsie Mohawk, into the Seneca Turtle Clan. Having graduated from Gowanda High School, Mohawk earned an undergraduate degree in history at Hartwick College during 1968 and started graduate studies at the University of Buffalo two years later. "John was the heart of the Native Studies program at the University of Buffalo," said Bruce Jackson, a longtime UB professor in American Studies. "Other people taught it, but he was the one who always provided the focus, the compassion and the guiding intelligence," said Jackson. "In addition, the students really loved him" (Mohawk, 2006).

"John had a wonderful connection with the elders [of] the Haudenosaunee (Iroquois), and they invested in him truly to hold the culture in place," said Barry White, a friend of Mohawk's for more than thirty years. "His dad, Ernie, was one of his major mentors in the thought and philosophy of the Iroquois, and people from across the Six Nations invested in him like he was a conduit for the transmission of their culture to the next generation" (Mohawk, 2006).

Mohawk was an editor of *Akwesasne Notes* between 1976 and 1983. In 1987, he helped found *Daybreak* magazine, and served as one of its editors until 1997. He also was an opinion columnist for *Indian Country Today.* Among Mohawk's best-known books are *Utopian Legacies* (2000) and *Exiled in the Land of the Free* (1992), which he co-edited with Oren Lyons.

Mohawk's ability to combine insights from the history of Europe and Native America was especially thought-provoking. In *Utopian Legacies,* Mohawk examined utopian elements in several European ideologies that became motors of oppression. "Nazism was a revitalization movement, complete with its own vision of utopia, its rationalizations for conquest and plunder, and an ability to disarm ordinary people's sense of morality and to plunge an entire nation . . . into an orgy of violence and murder," wrote Mohawk in his wide-ranging historical account of how utopian dreams often turn into searingly deadly realities. (Mohawk, 2000, 210).

To Mohawk, the legacy of utopianism is one of the defining tenets "perhaps the characterizing theme," of several Western European cultures (Mohawk, 2000, 13). Mohawk found utopian assumptions operating in some of the most powerful ideological forces shaping Christianity, Islam, and capitalism. He noted that the Christian creation story begins with the expulsion of the original human couple (Adam and Eve) from a notable Western utopia, the Garden of Eden.

In *Utopian Legacies,* Mohawk described how the abuses of capitalism spawned Marxism, its own antithesis utopia. "In pursuit of the perfectible socialist world," wrote Mohawk, "indigenous people east of the Urals were abused, dissenters were shipped to draconian gulags in Siberia, protests were

ruthlessly and brutally suppressed, [as] religious and traditional ethnic practices were outlawed" (Mohawk, 2000, 175). Following the general collapse of the Marxist utopian vision, Mohawk analyzed present-day "globalization," the pursuit of secular utopia through the accumulation of wealth. The expansion of capitalist culture to its present world-girding state has brought mass animal extinctions and steady rises in atmospheric levels of greenhouse gases. The Earth has thus become a victim of secular, industrial materialism and its appetite for fossil fuels.

Mohawk died suddenly at his home in Buffalo December 10, 2006, at age 61. Mohawk's wife, Yvonne Dion-Buffalo, who also worked in the UB American Studies Department, had died during 2005.

Bruce E. Johansen

See also Anderson, Wallace ("Mad Bear"); Lyons, Oren.

References and Further Reading

Lyons, Oren and John C. Mohawk. *Exiled in the Land of the Free: Democraacy, Indian Nations, and the U.S. Constitution.* Santa Fe, NM: Clear Light.

"Mohawk, John C., Professor; a Foremost Iroquois Scholar and Activist." *Buffalo News*, December 15, 2006. [http://www.legacy.com/buffalonews/DeathNotices.asp]

Mohawk, John C. 2000. *Utopian Legacies: A History of Conquest and Oppression in the Western World.* Santa Fe: Clear Light.

Momaday, N. Scott

Kiowa poet, novelist, artist, and educator N. Scott Momaday received critical acclaim in 1969 when he won the Pulitzer Prize for fiction for his novel, *House Made of Dawn*. The book helped to usher in a renaissance in Native American writing and placed Momaday at the forefront of the genre. In the years since *House Made of Dawn*, Momaday has published numerous books of poetry and fiction. The common theme of integrating cultural tradition into modern life unites his works. In addition to being a gifted writer, Momaday is an accomplished artist. He has exhibited his sketches, oils, acrylics, and etchings in numerous shows and used them to illustrate his books.

Momaday was born on February 27, 1934, in Lawton, Oklahoma, to Alfred and Natachee Scott Momaday. His father, a full-blooded Kiowa, and his mother, who was of French and Cherokee descent,

were both painters and teachers who instilled a strong sense of self in their son. At the age of six months, a Kiowa storyteller and tribal elder bestowed on Momaday the Kiowa name Tsoai-talee ("Rock-Tree Boy"). The name referenced a place along the Kiowa migration route known as Devil's Tower, and it forever linked Momaday to his ancestral past.

In 1936, Momaday and his family left Kiowa Country and moved to New Mexico, where they lived on the Navajo Reservation for seven years. In 1946, the family moved to the Jemez Pueblo in New Mexico after Momaday's parents accepted teaching positions at the local day school.

Growing up on the Navajo and Jemez Reservations left a lasting impression on Momaday and gave him a pan-Indian experience that has strongly influenced his writing. Living at Jemez in the mid-1940s, Momaday witnessed the changes that occurred after World War II ended. The Jemez population increased, modern conveniences became more commonplace, and returning veterans brought their off-reservation experiences home with them. Although some veterans adjusted to pueblo life, many others found the task difficult. Some left the reservation in a quest to find themselves and employment, while others remained but turned to alcohol or suicide to escape. Momaday never fell victim to the identity crises that so many Native Americans suffered after the war. He did absorb the experiences of his Navajo and Jemez neighbors, however, and he returned to those themes in his writing.

In 1958, Momaday received a BA in political science from the University of New Mexico. Unsure of his future, he accepted a teaching position on the Jicarilla Apache Reservation in New Mexico. While there, Momaday spent his free time writing, and in 1959 Stanford University awarded him the Wallace Stegner Creative Writing Scholarship for poetry. The scholarship gave Momaday an opportunity to work under respected poet Yvor Winters, who became a lifelong friend and mentor. Although he expected to return to the reservation teaching position after a year, Momaday's experiences at Stanford reshaped his career path.

In 1960, Momaday received his MA from Stanford and immediately began work on his Ph.D., which he completed in 1963. The following year, he accepted a teaching position at the University of California, Santa Barbara.

Momaday's literary breakthrough came in 1968 with the publication of *House Made of Dawn*, a classic

novel about the search for identity. The novel's main character, a Jemez man named Abel, leaves his reservation to serve in Europe during World War II. When he returns to the reservation after the war, however, Abel suffers an identity crisis. Like many returning veterans, Abel is caught between two worlds. He embarks on a journey during which a Navajo and a Kiowa help him recognize the importance of Indian culture and tradition. Only after he reconnects with his tribal heritage does Abel overcome the identity crisis that plagued him.

Since the publication of *House Made of Dawn*, Momaday has written numerous literary works that stress the importance of tradition and address the problems of Indians in modern society. Among them are *The Way to Rainy Mountain* (1969), which weaves Kiowa myths with tribal history and personal memories; *The Names* (1976), a memoir of childhood; *The Gourd Dancer* (1976), a collection of poems; and *The Ancient Child* (1989), a novel that connects Kiowa myth with Western legend. He has also held professorships at universities in the United States and Europe and continues to utilize his artistic talents.

Jennifer L. Bertolet

References and Further Reading
Momaday, N. Scott. 1968. *House Made of Dawn*. New York: Harper & Row.
Momaday, N. Scott. 1976. *The Names*. Tucson: The University of Arizona Press.
Schubnell, Matthias, ed. 1997. *Conversations with N. Scott Momaday*. Jackson: University Press of Mississippi.
Schubnell, Matthias. 1985. *N. Scott Momaday: The Cultural and Literary Background*. Norman: University of Oklahoma Press.

Montezuma

The most celebrated American Indian living in Chicago early in the twentieth century was Indian-rights advocate, writer and speaker, political organizer, and surgeon Dr. Carlos Montezuma, a graduate of the University of Illinois (1884) and the Northwestern University's Chicago Medical School (1889).

Montezuma (Mochtezuma, Wassaja, Yavapai) was born around 1866 among the Yavapai ("Almost-People to the East")—one of the thirteen bands of Pai or Pa'a (the People)—in what would become central Arizona. His birth name was Wassaja (pronounced wass-jah), a word translated from the Yuman language into English that means signaling

or beckoning. In 1871, O'odham soldiers from the Salt River area, allied with General George Crook and the U.S. Army, captured Wassaja in the Ka Vee-cum Gahk-woot (Superstition Mountains) and turned him over to photographer Carlos Gentile. Gentile took young "Carlos Montezuma" east and brought him to the Reverend G. W. Ingalls of the American Baptist Home Mission Society. Ingalls selected the pastor of the First Baptist Church in Urbana, Illinois, to raise young Carlos.

Living primarily among non-Indians for five decades following his capture, Montezuma worked for the Office of Indian Affairs (OIA) after obtaining his license to practice in Illinois. He entered government service in September 1889 at Fort Stevenson, North Dakota. In July 1890 he transferred to the Western Shoshone Agency in Nevada, where he worked until December 1892 before spending a few months in Nespelem, Colville Agency, Washington, and about three years at the United States Indian Industrial School hospital in Carlisle, Pennsylvania. He resigned in January 1896 to enter private practice in Chicago, where he remained until 1922.

Montezuma traveled with the Carlisle football team to the southwestern United States in 1901 and became reacquainted with his Yavapai relatives, who in 1903 obtained 24,680 acres of the old Fort McDowell Military Reserve (a portion of their homeland near Phoenix). During the final two decades of his life, Montezuma journeyed repeatedly to Fort McDowell, where he became increasingly familiar with his Yavapai family. With Montezuma's assistance after 1906, his Yavapai relations successfully resisted U.S. government–sponsored efforts to remove them to the Pima Salt River Reservation and build a dam on the Verde River, in the middle of the their reservation.

In Chicago after 1896, Montezuma assumed a role that purposefully was in the tradition of leadership among many American Indian peoples—that of caring for less fortunate citizens, hosting Indian visitors to his community, and advocating for the rights of Native nations. Thus, he was uniquely situated to contribute to the formation of Indian organization. During the opening decade of the twentieth century he joined efforts to politically organize Indians: In 1904 he joined with Luzena Choteau (Wyandotte from Oklahoma) to help found the National Indian Republican Association, in 1909 with Thomas L. Sloan (Omaha) and Walter Battice (Sac and Fox from Oklahoma) to form the Indian Progressive Organization, in 1911 with Laura Cornelius (Oneida from

Wisconsin) and Henry Standing Bear (Lakota from Rosebud Reservation) to organize a meeting of Indians in Columbus, Ohio, that became the Society of American Indians. In addition to his groundbreaking work creating Indian organizations, Montezuma lobbyed in Congress against OIA paternalism, fought for Yavapai land and water rights, drafted an Indian citizenship bill, gave numerous speeches—including one entitled "Let My People Go"—and published a newsletter.

Wassaja, Montezuma's newsletter, was published monthly from April 1916 to November 1922. By means of *Wassaja*, as well as numerous newspaper columns, magazine articles, and lectures, Montezuma took his one-man campaign of Indian advocacy to the public. He sometimes expressed his thoughts in verse. Countering the "vanishing Indian" thesis (commonly repeated at the time) in a piece entitled "Changing Is Not Vanishing," Montezuma wrote: "The Indian race vanishing? No, never! The race will live on and prosper forever" (Montezuma, 1987).

In 1922, suffering from the debilitating effects of diabetes and tuberculosis, Montezuma returned home to live with his relatives at Fort McDowell. He passed on January 31, 1923.

D. Anthony Tyeeme Clark (Meskwaki)

See also Boarding Schools, United States and Canada; Bureau of Indian Affairs: Establishing the Existence of an Indian Tribe; Society of American Indians.

References and Further Reading

Iverson, Peter. [1982[2001. *Carlos Montezuma and the Changing World of American Indians.* Albuquerque: University of New Mexico Press.

Montezuma, Carlos. [1916] 1987. "Changing Is Not Vanishing." In *The Papers of Carlos Montezuma, M.D.* Edited by John W. Larner, Jr. New York: Primary Source Microfilm and Scholarly Resources. [Originally appeared in *Wassaja*, June 3.]

Speroff, Leon. 2003. *Carlos Montezuma, M.D.: A Yavapai American Hero.* Portland, OR: Arnica Publishing.

Mormon Church

The interest of the Mormon Church (Church of Jesus Christ of Latter-day Saints) in Native Americans can be traced to the Book of Mormon, which was published in 1830. This book of scripture referred to Indians as Lamanites and said they were descendents of an Israelite civilization that rose and fell on the American continent. The book also contained prophecies about the Indians' receiving great blessings once they joined the Mormon Church. The church has adopted and abandoned various programs over the years to carry out its perceived responsibilities to Native Americans.

Mormon missions to the Indians began in 1830. The earliest missionaries found some tribes receptive to their message, but Indian agents prevented them from making further inroads. Non-Mormons suspected that Mormons intended to enlist Indians in their bid to establish an empire in the West. This is one reason why Mormons were persecuted and eventually driven to Utah in 1847.

When they arrived in the Great Basin, the Mormons wanted land occupied by local tribes. They made peaceful overtures to Indian chiefs, but conflict erupted as converts to the church began settling in Utah by the thousands and encroaching on lands that Native Americans used for hunting and gathering. Some of the most tragic examples of this fighting were the Mountain Meadows Massacre (1857) and the Black Hawk War (1865–1868). Despite these clashes, the Mormons made some attempts to preach the gospel and teach farming to their Native neighbors. However, the cultural gap proved largely insurmountable and the federal government relocated the Utes, Shoshones, and Paiutes to reservations in the late nineteenth century.

Relations between Native Americans and the Mormons recommenced in the 1940s. The church launched Indian missions in the Southwest and northern Plains. The Mormon missionaries on these reservations did not preach but rather promoted economic development and provided instruction in farming and ranching. In the 1950s, the church launched two educational programs for Indian students. Indian Seminary was a church program that involved constructing facilities next to federal Indian schools. Seminary teachers offered a religion class that Indian students could take during their regular school day. By the late 1960s, the annual enrollment in Indian seminary exceeded ten thousand.

The second initiative, the placement program, by contrast, required Indian students to live in the foster homes of white Mormon families during the school year. Ultimately, 70,000 Native students participated, or about 10 percent of American Indian

baby boomers. To participate in the placement program, Indian students had to obtain parental permission and become a baptized member of the church. The Mormons argued they were offering these students an education superior to that offered in reservation schools.

This program proved so appealing that, at its height in 1970, annual enrollment reached 5,000. However, evaluating the ultimate successes and failures of the program is no easy task. Critics charged the program with cultural genocide. More often than not, the students were taught that their Indian traditions were sinful and that their salvation depended on embracing Mormon beliefs and lifestyles. For most of the students, these pressures to assimilate interfered with the development of their tribal and Indian identities. Many returned home after only a year or two. A smaller percentage earned decent grades in high school, went on to obtain college degrees, and returned to their reservations with valuable skills.

Many graduates of the placement program were attracted to Brigham Young University (BYU). The enrollment of Indian students at BYU swelled to more than 500 during the early 1970s. The story of George P. Lee (Navajo) illustrates recent policy changes within the church. Lee enrolled in placement for seven years, served a mission for the church, and then earned his doctorate at BYU. In 1975 Lee became one of the highest-ranking leaders in the church. By the mid-1980s, the church was shifting its resources and programs from Native Americans and their reservations to the peoples and lands of Central and South America. Lee felt that the church had abandoned its responsibilities for Native Americans and was excommunicated in 1989 when his criticisms became public.

Sterling Fluharty

See also Missionaries, French Jesuit; Mission System, Spanish.

References and Further Reading

Jones, Sondra. 2004. "Saints or Sinners? The Evolving Perceptions of Mormon-Indian Relations in Utah Historiography." *Utah Historical Quarterly* 72, no. 1: 19–46.

Mauss, Armand L. 2003. *All Abraham's Children: Changing Mormon Conceptions of Race and Lineage.* Urbana: University of Illinois Press.

Whittaker, David J. 1985. "Mormons and Native Americans: A Historical and Bibliographical Introduction." *Dialogue* 18, no. 4: 33–64.

National Congress of American Indians

Having served in World War II, many Native Americans became increasingly active politically after the war, demanding equal voting rights and an end to discrimination. Their wartime experience intensified a renewed sense of Native American identity, reinforced religious beliefs, and exposed many Native Americans to life outside the reservations.

In several states, Native Americans were denied the right to vote, in spite of laws to the contrary. In other political activities, Native Americans resisted the construction of dams that threatened to flood reservation lands and destroy Indian fishing rights.

By the mid-1940s, Native American leaders realized that many non-Natives were not much interested in Indian affairs, that bureaucratic inertia and hostility to the Indian Reorganization Act were weakening potential benefits, and that their tribal treaty rights were in jeopardy. Originally called the Wheeler-Howard Act of 1934, the Indian Reorganization Act was an attempt to conserve and develop Indian lands and resources. This authority extended to Native Americans the legal structure that enabled them to form businesses, establish a credit system, and provide for a vocational education.

In an attempt to safeguard these and other Native American assertions, in 1944 reservation leaders and other prominent Native American professional men and women from fifty tribes met in Denver, Colorado, to form the National Congress of American Indians (NCAI), the first major intertribal organization

When the NCAI was formed, its primary concerns included the protection of Native American lands, minerals, and timber resources, as well as improving economic opportunities, education, and health care for Native Americans. Among NCAI's founding members were D'Arcy McNickle, a Flathead and employee of the Bureau of Indian Affairs who held a seat on the first national counsel, and Napoleon Johnson, a Cherokee who served as the organization's first president. They were among the early NCAI leaders who asserted that membership should be restricted to "people of Indian ancestry." As problems mounted for Native Americans, however, membership policy was changed to include non-Indians, who were offered associate memberships if they demonstrated a genuine concern for Native American issues.

One of the few postwar innovations in Native American policy was established by Congress in 1946 when the Indian Claims Commission voted to compensate Native Americans for fraud or unfair treatment by the federal government. During the next twenty-two years, the commission heard 852 claims and awarded nearly $818 million in damages to Native Americans. Otherwise, however, much of the news regarding Native American policy was bad during NCAI's early years.

Among its early platforms, the NCAI promised to "work toward the promotion of the common welfare of the aboriginal races of North America." It promised to educate non-Indians about Indian culture, preserve treaty rights, and lobby for Indian interests before the federal government. It had concern for the preservation of Indian culture and retaining the advances made under the Indian Reorganization Act, as well as pressing for the Act's fulfillment. The National Congress of American Indians became a strong lobbying force, working with other organizations, including the Indian Rights Association, to protect Native American interests before the U.S. Congress.

In 1947, part of a comprehensive study by the federal government for ways to remove waste, duplication, and inefficiency and to reduce public expenditures recommended ending the federal government's relationship with the Indian tribes. Headed by former President Herbert Hoover, this special study, which examined all phases of the national government, recommended the termination of Indian welfare by the federal government.

Anticipating this outcome and the recommendations of discontinuance of all specialized Indian activity and the Bureau of Indian Affairs, the NCAI dedicated most of its attention, for several years, to trying to correct what became known as the termination policy.

During the 1950s, the organization was a principal opponent against the termination policy, which sought to "emancipate the Indians" by terminating federal links to Indian communities and withdrawing federal support for tribal governments. The legislation called for Congress to initiate sixty separate termination bills, the last of which was to be implemented in 1962. Generally, the legislation called for the preparation of a final distribution of tribal assets to members and the removal of Indian land from federal protection.

The NCAI said that the policy of termination undermined reservation health and economic conditions and accelerated the decline of traditional cultural practices. In the wake of these negative conditions, NCAI led several tribes to campaign successfully to reverse some elements of termination. In 1953, Congress passed a resolution that called for the government to transfer federal responsibilities for tribes to the states. It also allowed states to assert legal jurisdiction over Indian reservations without tribal consent. The NCAI effectively organized opposition to these measures, with the rallying cry of "self-determination rather than termination."

Many Native Americans criticized "relocation," another postwar government program. Under the policy that began in 1948, the Bureau of Indian Affairs provided transportation, job placement, vocational training, and counseling to Native Americans who wanted to leave reservations. As a result of Native American protests, led by NCAI, federal policies began to shift away from termination and toward self-determination and the principle of autonomy.

In the 1960s, as President John F. Kennedy promised a friendlier "new frontier" in Indian affairs, the NCAI played an important role in ensuring that the federal antipoverty programs would encompass tribal communities. Additionally, this decade also witnessed the birth of several pan-Indian protest groups, with the NCAI losing its leading role to the more flamboyant, militant organizations like the National Indian Youth Council (NIYC) and the American Indian Movement (AIM), best-known for its occupation of Wounded Knee (South Dakota) in 1973.

During the 1970s even as activism accelerated, American Indians continued to be the United States' poorest minority group by many measures, including net income and mortality from several diseases. They were considered worse off than any other group, according to virtually every socioeconomic statistic. The Native American unemployment rate was ten times the U.S. national average, and 50 percent of the Native American population lived below the federal poverty line. Indian life expectancy was only forty-four years, a third less than that of the typical American at the time. Deaths caused by pneumonia, hepatitis, dysentery, strep throat, diabetes, tuberculosis, alcoholism, suicide, and homicide were two to sixty times higher than among the United States population as a whole. Half a million Native American families lived in unsanitary, dilapidated dwellings, many in shanties or abandoned automobiles. The NCAI

sought solutions to these difficulties by approaching the U.S. government.

In the 1980s and the 1990s, the NCAI promoted political causes and education through the efforts of its Washington, D.C., office, as well as programs initiated at its annual convention.

The NCAI continues to be the oldest and largest Native American organization in the United States. It was born of hostile legislation and policies that were devastating to Native American tribal nations. It continues to dedicate itself to the restoration and exercise of tribal sovereignty and the continued viability of all tribal governments.

No longer are Indians a vanishing group of Americans. The 2000 Census recorded a Native American population of more than two million, five times the number recorded in 1950. However, nearly half of all Native Americans continue to live on reservations, which cover 52 million acres in twenty-seven states, while most of the others live in urban areas. As the Indian population grows, individual Native Americans have claimed many accomplishments and are widely perceived to be productive citizens. Although Native Americans continue to face severe problems relating to employment, income, and education, they will not abandon their Indian identity and culture, nor will they be treated as dependent wards of the federal government—all aims that mirror the goals of the National Congress of American Indians.

Historically, the NCAI's political activities have followed a moderate political course, bringing together and representing a wide range of Native Americans on a variety of issues. Recently, the NCAI sent petitions to Congress to force the removal of stereotypical names, such as "Redskins," from sports team logos, license plates, and other places, as Native Americans continue to battle discrimination.

Recently, NCAI has worked to secure funding for an initiative to encourage Native Americans to pursue degrees in the field of information technology and other fields of science and technology.

Working with other Native American groups, NCAI raised relief funds for Native Americans in the Gulf states, who were victimized by Hurricane Katrina. The NCAI continues to stress the importance of preserving Native American history and cultures, as well as to protect Indian welfare. The group continues to urge Native Americans to become assimilated into non-Indian culture by stressing their common characteristics and creating the organizational forms to unite all the tribes and to retain a pluralistic relationship with the larger society by working for self-determination.

While the NCAI has had it share of criticism, it has shown, historically, that it works for the betterment of Native Americans and that it continues to fight for full inclusion. It remains a powerful voice for the collective concerns and shared identity of American Indian nations and tribes.

Fred Lindsey

See also Economic Development; Indian Reorganization Act; McNickle, D'Arcy; Relocation.

References and Further Reading

Cowger, Thomas W. 2001. *The National Congress of American Indians: The Founding Years*. Lincoln: University of Nebraska Press.

Healey, Joseph F. 2005. *Race, Ethnicity, Gender, and Class: The Sociology of Group Conflict and Change*. Thousand Oaks, CA: Pine Forge Press.

Hoxie, Frederick E. 1996. *Encyclopedia of North American Indians: Native American History, Culture, and Life from Paleo-Indians to the Present*. Boston: Houghton-Mifflin.

National Indian Youth Council

The National Indian Youth Council (NIYC) is the second-oldest national Indian organization in the United States. (The oldest is the National Congress of American Indians.) Since the termination era during the 1950s, the NIYC has fought oppressive government policies. From the mid-1960s through the early 1970s, the NIYC primarily accomplished its aims through Northwest fish-ins, Red Power protest, and Indian nationalism. While its activities since then have made headlines less often, the NIYC continues its battles through long-term projects such as political research, antidiscrimination lawsuits, and employment services benefiting various indigenous communities. Frequently at the forefront of Indian affairs, the NIYC has promoted self-determination and sovereignty and helped create a new generation of Indian leaders.

The NIYC traces its roots to Indian youth councils and college student workshops of the late 1950s. The Southwestern Regional Indian Youth Council, originated by Kiva Club students at the University of New Mexico, provided leadership training for founders of the NIYC. Herbert Blatchford (Navajo), Melvin Thom (Walker River Paiute), and Clyde Warrior (Ponca) were among the hundreds of Indian college students from nearly twenty states

who attended these youth councils and participated in debates over termination and other government policies. Each summer at the Workshop on American Indian Affairs, future founders of the NIYC stretched their minds with powerful ideas and expanded their circles of friends and influence.

The American Indian Chicago Conference in 1961 set the stage for the emergence of the NIYC. Indian college students attended this conference, along with scholars, members of the National Congress of American Indians (NCAI), and tribal leaders. However, these students wished to voice their own opinions on federal Indian policy and other concerns. They formed a youth caucus, guided the conference's outcome, and argued that Indians needed to use their combined political power in pursuit of self-determination. Ten of them gathered that fall in Gallup, New Mexico, to officially organize the NIYC. In addition to Blatchford, Thom, and Warrior, the NIYC's founders were Bernadine Eschief (Shoshone-Bannock-Pima), Rickard Karen Jacobson (Tuscarora), Howard McKinley, Jr. (Navajo), Joan Noble (Ute), Edison Real Bird (Crow), John R. Winchester (Potawatatomi), and Shirley Hill Witt (Akwesasne Mohawk). At this founding meeting, Indian women took two of the three positions within the presidency and four of the ten spots on the board of directors.

For the first few years, the NIYC founders decided to meet annually and discuss issues facing Indian students and youth across the nation. They began publishing a newsletter and by 1962 over 180 tribal councils had subscribed. In 1963 the NIYC and United Scholarship Service jointly published a new periodical, *Americans Before Columbus*. Bruce Wilkie (Makah) and Hank Adams (Assiniboine-Sioux) emerged as leaders in the NIYC. In early 1964 these two individuals played key roles in the NIYC's fish-ins in behalf of tribes in Washington State. This direct action proved so popular that by the end of 1964 membership in the NIYC reached three thousand.

The NIYC began receiving greater recognition in 1964. In May, leaders in the NIYC were invited to the Capital Conference on Indian Poverty in Washington, D.C. There they organized a youth session and stressed the need to aggressively seek funding for American Indians in the forthcoming War on Poverty. Eventually several members of the NIYC became Community Action Program directors. Before the year was over, Warrior helped Vine Deloria, Jr. become executive director of the NCAI. In

addition, the NIYC participated in the first-ever International Indian Youth Conference and received a Canadian delegation at its December meetings.

Over the next few years, the NIYC underwent several changes. Emerging in the vanguard of the Indian movement, Thom replaced Blatchford as executive director in 1965 and served until 1968. Warrior led the group from 1966 to 1968. Warrior and other orators in the NIYC denounced the colonialism of the federal government and lectured widely on the need to preserve Indian culture and identities. In 1967, the Carnegie Corporation and the Ford Foundation awarded the NIYC nearly $200,000. This allowed the NIYC to hire a small staff, set up an office in Berkeley, California, and contract with the Far West Laboratory for Educational Research and Development.

Events in 1968 and 1969 transformed the NIYC. Stan Steiner's book, *The New Indians*, appeared early in 1968, describing how the NIYC helped radicalize Indian students and other youth. Soon after this, Thom and his staff took funds earmarked for education projects and spent them on preparations for the Poor Peoples' Campaign in Washington, D.C. These actions upset the foundations and contradicted the wishes of the NIYC's board of directors. The crisis worsened when Warrior died close to the time of the campaign in Washington. These developments created a leadership vacuum in the NIYC. The students who attended the NIYC's first-ever Institute of American Indian Studies in the summer of 1968 decided to take over the NIYC's board of directors. Before long, William Pensoneau (Ponca) became president and served until 1969. In the midst of this transformation, the NIYC's headquarters moved back to New Mexico. Gerald Wilkinson (Cherokee-Catawba) agreed to become executive director around this time and began working, initially without pay, at the new office in Albuquerque.

Wilkinson realized the NIYC needed to adapt to survive. Many of the Native students who had passed through the NIYC's leadership training programs began competing with the NIYC for funding and political influence. For instance, in 1969 Wilkie became executive director of the NCAI. NIYC members obtained internships in Washington, D.C., and staffed Indian desks in major departments and agencies of the federal government. At least 250 Indian students attended the NIYC's summer Institutes in American Indian Studies and helped set up similar programs on other college campuses. Members of the NIYC also became leaders of tribes and estab-

lished Indian advocacy organizations. Wilkinson recognized the need to build membership and funds. A direct mail campaign and a resumption of the NIYC's periodical helped boost membership to 15,050 chapters by the early 1970s.

The NIYC changed during the 1970s from a direct action activist organization to one that pursued long-term projects. For example, the NIYC participated in the Trail of Broken Treaties, but its priorities lay elsewhere. Wilkinson wasted little time in obtaining the services of lawyers. With their help, the NIYC sued the BIA for its discrimination against students at schools like Intermountain and Chilocco and urged the adoption of a student bill of rights. By mid-decade Wilkinson had assembled an office with twenty people, including several staff attorneys. Some of the court cases launched and won by the NIYC during these decades dealt with issues such as affirmative action, environmental issues, religious freedom, restoration of tribal constitutions, and voting rights. One way the NIYC survived during these years was through federal funds that allowed it to provide job training and placement. Notable leaders during these years included LaVonna Weller (Caddo), who became the first female president of the NIYC in 1972, and Lawrence Roberts (Oneida), who served as president from 1974 to 1988.

Since the 1980s, the NIYC has expanded the scope of its activities and continued to provide services to Indian people and organizations. In the 1980s new projects for the NIYC included voter registration campaigns among tribes in the Southwest, voter surveys, national directories of Indian elected officials, and polling data on the views of these political leaders. During these years the NIYC also hired a young attorney named James Anaya, who helped the NIYC to become a nongovernmental organization (NGO) at the United Nations and to provide assistance to indigenous peoples facing oppression throughout Latin America. Wilkinson's death in 1989 brought additional changes to the NIYC. Norman Ration (Navajo-Laguna) became executive director and helped the NIYC to better serve the urban Indian population of New Mexico. James Nez (Navajo) has assisted with this effort as NIYC president for quite some time. The two of them brought Witt back onto the board of directors. These and other individuals have helped the NIYC to expand and open offices in Farmington and Gallup, New Mexico. In the last few years the NIYC has won the right for Navajo Indians to vote in tribal elections at polls in Albuquerque. Their most recent battles have been against low health-care funding for urban Indians across the nation.

Sterling Fluharty

See also Fishing Rights; National Congress of American Indians.

References and Further Reading

Cowger, Thomas W. 1999. *The National Congress of American Indians: The Founding Years*. Lincoln: University of Nebraska Press.

Fluharty, Sterling. 2003. "'For a Greater Indian America': The Origins of the National Indian Youth Council." Master's thesis, University of Oklahoma.

LaGrand, James B. 2002. *Indian Metropolis: Native Americans in Chicago, 1945–75*. Urbana: University of Illinois Press.

Parker, Dorothy R. 1992. *Singing an Indian Song: A Biography of D'Arcy McNickle*. Lincoln: University of Nebraska Press.

Smith, Paul Chaat, and Robert Allen Warrior. 1996. *Like a Hurricane: The Indian Movement from Alcatraz to Wounded Knee*. New York: New Press.

Steiner, Stan. 1968. *The New Indians*. New York: Harper & Row.

Warrior, Robert Allen. 1995. *Tribal Secrets: Recovering American Indian Intellectual Traditions*. Minneapolis: University of Minnesota Press.

National Museum of the American Indian

The National Museum of the American Indian (NMAI), part of the Smithsonian Institution, is the premier museum of Native American art and culture, containing the largest and most comprehensive collection of Native American art and artifacts in the world. With objects from North, South, and Central America, its holdings include approximately 800,000 objects, spanning 10,000 years of history through the present, from over a thousand Native or indigenous cultures.

The National Museum of the American Indian was created by an act of Congress (Public Law 101–185) in 1989 and signed into law by President George H. W. Bush. The acquisition of the vast holdings of the Museum of the American Indian became the foundation of the National Museum of the American Indian. The Museum of the American Indian, which was founded by George Gustav Heye

The National Museum of the American Indian opened on September 21, 2004, in Washington, D.C. The museum houses an 800,000 piece collection that honors the cultures of Native Americans from North, South, and Central America. (Jessica Sedgewick)

(1874–1957), contained the personal collections of Heye, who traveled extensively throughout the western hemisphere. With 800,000 objects and a photographic archive of 125,000 images, this collection was assembled over the period of fifty-four years, beginning at the turn of the twentieth century.

NMAI includes a smaller permanent museum, the George Gustav Heye Center located in lower Manhattan, a Cultural Resources Center that houses and cares for the collections in Suitland, Maryland, and a large permanent museum on the National Mall in Washington, D.C.

The George Gustav Heye Center, located in the Alexander Hamilton U.S. Customs House in New York City, opened in 1994. This branch of NMAI is an exhibition facility for both permanent and temporary exhibitions. It also houses a Resource Center that utilizes computer technology to teach about Native life and links the museum to current Native communities. Also, the Heye Center houses a Film and Video Center that serves the Native filmmakers and community, educators, and the general public.

Built in 1999, the Cultural Resources Center is a research and storage facility for the objects and artifacts in the NMAI collection. It is state-of-the-art in terms of the care and storage of the collection and seeks to educate new generations of museum professionals. This facility serves as the center for various museum services, including community outreach, educational outreach, and technological development. It is also a culturally sensitive facility, recognizing that some objects in the collections may have family and community connections. This facility has both public and private areas for use by

Native and non-Native researchers and visitors from tribal communities, academe, and artistic and cultural organizations.

In September 2004, NMAI opened a second, larger, permanent museum on the National Mall in Washington, D.C., in front of the U.S. Capitol. This structure was built by two construction companies, one of which is a subsidiary of the Table Mountain Rancheria of Friant, California, a federally recognized American Indian tribe. The building is 351,263 square feet, 99 feet high and has a dome that rises 120 feet in the rotunda. The creation of the new museum included consultation and collaboration with 500 Natives from 300 communities. In keeping with the consensus of consultants from Indian Country, the building includes round interior spaces, exterior water features, east-facing entrances, and many interior details that reference Native symbols from various cultures. The grand opening took place on September 21, 2004, with an elaborate morning procession of Native Americans in full regalia traditional to each of their distinctive nations. The procession stretched from the Smithsonian Institution's Castle along the Mall toward the U.S. Capitol for the dedication of the new museum.

NMAI is distinctive in that the institution works collaboratively with Native communities to sustain cultural heritage. Through extensive educational programs and community outreach between people, the museum facilitates communication and education, in addition to connections with objects, artifacts, and art. Because its exhibitions are presented from a Native perspective and in a Native voice, NMAI is dedicated not only to preserving and exhibiting cultural artifacts from the past, but also to giving a voice to contemporary indigenous peoples. According to its mission statement:

> The National Museum of the American Indian shall recognize and affirm to Native communities and the non-Native public the historical and contemporary culture and cultural achievements of the Natives of the Western Hemisphere by advancing—in consultation, collaboration, and cooperation with Natives—knowledge and understanding of Native cultures, including art, history, and language, and by recognizing the museum's special responsibility, through innovative public programming, research and collections, to protect, support, and enhance the

development, maintenance, and perpetuation of Native culture and community (NMAI, n.d., "Mission").

Traci L. Morris-Carlsten

See also Native American Museums; Native American Graves Protection and Repatriation Act.

References and Further Reading
National Museum of the American Indian (NMAI). No date. "George Gustav Heye Center." Available at: http://www.nmai.si.edu/subpage.cfm?subpage=visitor&second=ny&third=george. Accessed November 4, 2004.
National Museum of the American Indian (NMAI). No date. "Main Page." Available at: http://americanindian.si.edu/. Accessed September 15, 2004.
National Museum of the American Indian (NMAI). No date. "Press Page, Museum Mission Statement." Available at: http://americanindian.si.edu/subpage.cfm?subpage=press&second=mission. Accessed September 15, 2004.
National Museum of the American Indian (NMAI). No date. "Press Release, Grand Opening." Available at: http://americanindian.si.edu/press/releases/opening_release_July04.pdf. Accessed January 20, 2007.

Native American Church of North America

The Native American Church of North America (NAC), or Native American Church of Jesus Christ, is the largest religious organization dedicated to the use of the fruit (or "button") of the peyote cactus as the central element of its worship. However, the use of peyote in North America far predates the organization of the NAC. Peyote buttons dating to 5,000 BCE have been found in Texas, and its use in Central America appears to be more ancient still.

Opposition by European-Americans to Native use of peyote also has a very long history. When the Spanish first reached many of the isolated inland tribes of Mexico, they discovered the Indians of the Cora tribe using a previously unknown substance in their nocturnal religious rites. In 1754, Spanish historian José Ortega described "a tray filled with *peyote* which is a diabolical root [*raiz diabolica*] that is ground up and drunk by them so that they may not become weakened by the exhausting effects of so

Members of the Native American Church prepare for a prayer meeting in Mirando City, Texas, in 1996. The Church's all-night ceremonies involve the use of peyote as a sacrament. (AP/Wide World Photos)

long a function." Anthropologists have estimated that peyote has been in use among Mexican Indians for approximately 7,000 to 10,000 years. Although Ortega saw peyote as a "diabolical root," the Cora Indians saw it as a "divine cactus." The Inquisition made its use illegal in 1620, but this did not stop the spread of its use.

Anthropologist Weston La Barre estimated that the ritual and curative use of peyote was transmitted from Mexican tribes to those residing in the United States around 1870. During the next fifty years, it was diffused among various tribes throughout the Western United States. Although peyote was one of many plants used in Central American Indian ceremonies, in North American usage it became the central sacrament. Whereas prior pan-Indian movements led by people like Neolin, Tenskwatawa, and Wovoka promised a return to the pre-European state through divine and/or military means, the use of peyote became a way of accommodating and accepting the facts of modern life

while keeping a connection with traditional Indian beliefs. Further, the peyote faith became a way for Indians to deal with the crisis caused by the destruction of their traditional cultures during the nineteenth century.

By the late nineteenth century, noted anthropologist James Mooney began to research its use among Indian peoples in Oklahoma and elsewhere, even going so far as to become an advocate for its use as an expression of freedom of religion. By 1906, the use of peyote had spread to an area covering the Great Plains from Oklahoma to Nebraska. The threat of Christian missionaries' call for congressional action to ban the use of peyote caused the peyote users of the Oto, Kiowa, and Arapaho tribes to unite several diverse peyote groups and, with Mooney's support, create the Native American Church in October 1918. Although it was not and still is not representative of all Indian peyote users in the United States, the NAC was formed as a defense measure against probable government action.

Although the organization of the NAC gave peyote users a pan-Indian identity, it did little to dissuade whites and proacculturation Indians from attacking the movement. The fact that the sacrament is a mild hallucinogen caused federal, state, and local government officials to oppose the use of peyote, ignoring the purely ceremonial usage among the Indian groups. Exercising their influence on government officials were Christian leaders who claimed peyote use was, like alcohol, only used to induce euphoria. Passage of the Indian Citizenship Act and with it the official granting of constitutional rights to Indians in 1924 did not end the persecution.

The NAC has traditionally infused its rites with Christian imagery and even theology. It has no professional, paid clergy. Members are free to interpret *Bible* passages according to their own understanding. Morality is basically Christian and stresses the need to abstain from alcohol and be faithful to one's spouse. Other prominent values include truthfulness, fulfilling one's family obligations, economic self-sufficiency, praying for the sick, and praying for peace. The peyote faith stresses personal revelation and visions; individual commitment to live a life of respect, generosity, and harmony; and a heavy emphasis on the sacramental aspect of worship. Each person must come to the peyote belief of his or her own volition through an overt decision of faith. Declaring this belief makes the communicant a part of the faith community, a community that shows common concern for other members. Some communities have also included the practice of baptism. However, the amount and type of Christian influence can vary widely among and within tribal groups.

One of the most notable evangelists of the peyote religion during the last half of the nineteenth century was the Comanche Quanah Parker, who traveled from tribe to tribe spreading the new faith. Although many converted, opposition came almost immediately from many sides, both Indian and non-Indian. Many Indians who had been educated and favored assimilation saw an Indian religion as a step backward. Many were still devoted to traditional Indian cultures and could not fit the new religion into their system. Both the state and federal government banned the use of peyote, and, although some overtures were made by the Peyotists, most missionary groups condemned the new faith, blaming the use of peyote for poverty, illness, and death on the reservations. Controversy still follows the peyote faith, even in the aftermath of the 1978 passage of the American Indian Religious Freedom Act.

In his 1970 masterwork, *Custer Died for Your Sins: An Indian Manifesto*, Vine Deloria, Jr., stated that the Native American Church "appears to be the religion of the future" and that "eventually it will replace Christianity among the Indian people" (Deloria, 1970, 113). However, the fact that the theology espoused by some members of the NAC has Christian roots has caused divisions. The continual participation of Indians in traditional religions, Christianity, and peyotism has revealed Deloria's declaration to be a bit overstated, but for those who blend traditional Indian religions and Christianity, the NAC remains a vital force in the communities of which it is a part.

Steven L. Danver

See also Deloria, Vine, Jr.; Pan-Indianism; Parker, Quanah; Tenskwatawa; Wovoka.

References and Further Reading

Anderson, Edward F. 1996. *Peyote: The Divine Cactus*, 2nd ed. Tucson: University of Arizona Press.

Deloria, Vine, Jr. 1970. *Custer Died for Your Sins: An Indian Manifesto*. Norman: University of Oklahoma Press.

Fikes, Jay C. 1996. "A Brief History of the Native American Church." In *One Nation Under God: The Triumph of the Native American Church.* Edited by Huston Smith and Reuben Snake. Santa Fe, NM: Clear Light Publishers.

LaBarre, Weston. 1970. *The Peyote Cult*. North Haven, CT: Shoe String Press.

Slotkin, J. S. 1975. *The Peyote Religion: A Study in Indian-White Relations*. New York: Octagon Books.

Stewart, Omer C. 1987. *Peyote Religion: A History*. Norman: University of Oklahoma Press, 1987.

Native American Museums

Native American museums and cultural heritage centers are among the most recent of the institutions that make up the history of contemporary museums. To understand and appreciate their significance, it is important first to explore the context in which they arose. The modern museum emerged as a product of the evolution of the private collections of royal and wealthy families at the time of the Renaissance, when increased inquiry into the natural and cultural world, spurred by Western voyages of discovery, expanded the range of what was thought to be exotic, unique, and of scientific value. The first public museums began to appear by 1800, with major national museums being created by the end of the

century. National museums were developed in part not only as a reflection on ideas about what a modern, civilized country should have, but also to house the arts and crafts from colonial activities in other parts of the world. In the latter case, these "trophy" collections demonstrated the need to bring "civilization" and Christianity to those benighted and uncivilized regions, while providing exotic materials for the amusement and enjoyment of the public and scientific materials for educational and research purposes. The explosion in the numbers of museums began in the late 1800s. In the United States, for example, there were about 300 museums before 1860, approximately 700 by 1900, more than 2,000 by the start of World War II, and an estimated 14,000 today, ranging from very large natural history museums to the far more numerous local historical society museums.

By the 1950s, thousands of American and foreign museums had amassed Native American collections. In many instances, these public and private institutional collections contained important sacred and patrimonial objects, as well as tens of thousands of human remains and hundreds of thousands of funerary objects. These materials were characteristically acquired, researched, exhibited, and preserved without tribal community consultation or involvement. Museum collections had emerged from the extensive "salvage" research and collecting of Native American objects, and bodies, from the late 1800s, at a time when scholars were convinced that Native Americans and their communities would soon be extinct. There was reason for alarm, since the precontact indigenous population in North American had dropped from an estimated seven million in 1492 to only a quarter million in 1900.

Scholars at that time believed that extraordinary efforts were required to collect Native American information and objects before all trace of these cultures disappeared. The resulting massive collection of work carried out through various means resulted in a large corpus of materials being available. As a result, local, regional, and national museums were, by the 1930s, in possession of the majority of all Native American objects that had survived daily use in communities from before the reservation period. Relatively few of the older cultural heritage objects remained in their original tribal communities. During this period, tribes were not politically involved in approving or denying collecting or other research activities by outsiders (although some individuals were involved, with the knowledge of their nations),

and rarely did they have the right to interfere in such collecting. Federal and state laws did not involve tribes in archaeological project approval and regarded all archaeologically found Native American materials, including human remains, as "resources" that could be acquired and owned by institutions such as museums. Moreover, museums rarely consulted tribal representatives about any planned exhibition, educational program, or other interpretation of Native American materials. Instead, Native American history and heritage were virtually always presented to the public by museums in the absence of a Native American perspective.

Individuals, communities, and governments create museums to collect significant objects; to research, exhibit, and educationally use those objects; and to preserve them for posterity. These same goals not only motivated Native American communities to begin to establish their own museums and cultural centers during the twentieth century, but also reflected tribal communities' changing educational needs, the desire to promote pride and knowledge in their cultural heritage and history, and the need to maintain or acquire objects of heritage available to the community, including photographs and recordings. Although a few initial efforts began in the 1940s, the widespread development of Native American community museums and cultural centers began in the 1960s. New tribal efforts for self-determination, the protection of tribal sovereignty, and the pursuit of treaty rights were also occurring nationwide. This movement also mirrored renewed efforts by Native Americans to regain control over objects of heritage as well as human ancestral remains housed in nontribal museums.

Ultimately, the United States Congress passed legislation—the 1990 Native American Graves Protection and Repatriation Act (PL101–601)—which mandated that human remains and cultural objects that were culturally affiliated with federally recognized tribes be repatriated from government agencies and public museums to tribes. This complex law also has other elements, including tribal control over the disposition of human remains or cultural objects discovered on their lands or federal lands, and criminal penalties for commercial trafficking in legally restricted materials. The passage of this law spurred many tribal communities to begin work on museums and cultural centers that could house some of the cultural materials being returned to them. This change in federal law also marked the beginning of new relationships between nontribal museums and

tribal communities; specifically, some nontribal museums established new policies of consulting and collaborating with tribes prior to developing exhibits and other programs dealing with Native American materials and themes.

Some new tribal museums of the 1960s and 1970s were created because of specific cultural heritage projects. For example, the Makah Cultural and Research Center was established to house a large and very significant archaeological collection that resulted from a major excavation on their land. The Suquamish Tribal Museum was the product of a highly successful community oral-history project, and the Ak-Chin Him-Dak EcoMuseum was a part of a broader community revitalization process. These, as well as other tribal museums, were established either by tribal governments and operated through them or by tribally based organizations that usually had a relationship with their tribal governments. Today, tribal museums and cultural centers play a variety of roles and may serve both tribal and nontribal communities. Most house collections of objects and important community archival materials, develop exhibits and educational programs for their own and the broader community, and carry out research, as well as serving as points of inspiration for the work of tribal artists. Some new tribal museums are destination points for tourists, while others focus primarily on their own community and dedicate their efforts to the recovery, maintenance, and perpetuation of their heritage. Many tribal museums, for example, sponsor language programs as well as traditional arts and crafts programs, special seniors programs for the education of community youth, projects such as community oral history, and also publish educational, historical, and research materials. In some instances, tribal museums also serve as the oversight agency for the tribal government for researchers working in the community.

The National Congress of American Indians estimates that there are more than 230 tribal museums and cultural centers in the United States, while other estimates, using different definitions, place the number at less than 200. Canadian bands and tribes operate tribal heritage institutions in Canada, and entirely new museums and centers are being developed each year in both countries. A new federal grant program in the United States has been created just for tribal museum program enhancement, and a recent project led to the creation of cultural learning centers, often functioning as gallery and museum spaces, in many tribal colleges in the United States.

Many of the newest tribal museums, including the Mashantucket Pequot Museum in Connecticut, the Huhugam Heritage Center in Arizona, the Tamastlikt Cultural Institute in Oregon, and the planned Aqua Caliente Cultural Museum in California are all examples of state-of-the-art facilities with stunning architectural designs and enhanced environmental systems and approaches. These, along with other tribal museums, are also establishing new models for curating cultural materials, often involving culturally sensitive approaches for storage, access, and conservation treatments. Comparable efforts by indigenous communities in other countries have made this movement among the newest museological phenomena in the world, and an effort that is already having an impact in the broader museum community.

James D. Nason

See also National Museum of the American Indian; Native American Graves Protection and Repatriation Act.
References and Further Readings
Erikson, Patricia P. 2002. *Voices of a Thousand People: The Makah Cultural and Research Center.* Lincoln: University of Nebraska Press.
Fuller, Nancy J. 1994. "Tribal Museums." In *Native America in the Twentieth Century.* Edited by Mary Davis, 655–657. New York: Garland Publishing.
Kreps, Christina F. 2003. *Liberating Culture: Cross Cultural Perspectives on Museums, Curation, and Heritage Preservation.* New York: Routledge.
Nason, James D. 1994. "Museums and Indians." In *Native America in the Twentieth Century.* Edited by Mary Davis, 359–362. New York: Garland Publishing.

Neolin (Delaware Prophet)

Also known as the Delaware Prophet, Neolin came to prominence during the period just before and during Pontiac's Rebellion against the English in the early 1760s. His visions, preaching, and calls for Native people to return to pre-contact traditions became one of the unifying features of Pontiac's Rebellion.

Moved off their lands in eastern Pennsylvania in the wake of the fraudulent Walking Purchase, most Len-pe (also rendered Leni-Lenápe, or Delaware) were forced to move west. One of the results of this upheaval was that beginning in the

1740s, a series of "prophets," individuals conveying religious messages, began appearing among the Lenpe and other Native peoples in western Pennsylvania, eastern Ohio, and the Great Lakes region. Neolin was only the latest (and far from the last) in a long line of prophets when he came to the attention of British authorities in the early 1760s.

Neolin's religious experience began when he entered into a trance or dream in which he undertook an arduous journey to meet the Master of Life. The Master of Life showed him the path to heaven and how Europeans blocked it. He was instructed to relay a message to Native peoples that the lands the Creator made were for their use and that they should not suffer the presence of Europeans.

Neolin preached a militantly Nativistic stance toward Europeans beginning in the fall of 1761 and illustrated his message with the use of pictographs. The illustrations showed a straight path to heaven that Native people followed in pre-contact times, but sin, alcohol, and Europeans now blocked that route. The drawings also showed a grim alternative: a large fire where sinful Indians spent eternity.

Avoidance of Europeans and European goods were Neolin's overriding themes. Native people should wear animal skins instead of trade cloth, eschew European foods, use bows and arrows instead of firearms, and abstain from using alcohol. Neolin also taught his followers that fires kindled using flint and steel were not "pure." He also encouraged Native people to purify themselves by using an emetic potion known as black drink, which had long been used in the Southeast. One Shawnee community that followed Neolin engaged in the practice with such gusto that traders nicknamed their village Vomit Town. While Neolin's followers accepted his rejection of all things European in theory, doing so in practice was another matter entirely. Over the previous century and a half, Native peoples of the American Northeast had become dependent on European goods such as metal tools and cloth.

In 1763, the global conflict between France and England—called the French and Indian War in America and the Seven Year's War in Europe—came to an end. As part of the peace settlement, France surrendered all of its North American possessions, and the English garrisoned most of the former French posts in the Ohio country and the Great Lakes, including Detroit, Niagara, and Fort Pitt. Native peoples, many of whom had been allies of the French, waited to see how the British would treat them.

They did not have to wait long. Sir Jeffrey Amherst, the commander of his majesty's forces in America, ignored the advice of Sir William Johnson, the superintendent of Indian affairs, and ceased the practice of presenting Native people with diplomatic gifts. Gifts were regarded as a show of good will, and some gifts, such as gunpowder, were vital necessities to Native people, who needed it to conduct their fall and winter hunts and for warfare against their enemies. Amherst's prohibition on gifts and the high prices for British trade goods made more Native people receptive to Neolin's message, especially after it had been altered slightly by the Ottawa leader Pontiac.

The Ottawa chieftain Pontiac used Neolin's message, with its implicit and explicit hostility to Europeans, to argue for Native unity and for a war against the British. However, in his version of Neolin's teachings, Pontiac transmuted the French into friends of Native peoples who would give them trade goods for cheap prices. In many respects, this was a contravention of Neolin's (and the Master of Life's) message.

Roger M. Carpenter

See also American Revolution, Native American Participation; Johnson, William; Pontiac.

References and Further Reading

Dowd, Gregory Evans. 1992. *A Spirited Resistance: The North American Indian Struggle for Unity, 1745–1815.* Baltimore, MD: Johns Hopkins University Press.

Richter, Daniel K. 2001. *Facing East from Indian Country: A Native History of Early America.* Cambridge, MA: Belknap/Harvard University Press.

White, Richard. 1991. *The Middle Ground: Indians, Empires, and Republics in the Great Lakes Region, 1650–1815.* New York: Cambridge University Press.

Oakes, Richard

Richard Oakes (1942–1972), a Mohawk who was born on the St. Regis Reservation in New York, helped plan and implement the 1969 American Indian occupation of Alcatraz Island. His eloquence and commanding presence, his pivotal role in the takeover of Alcatraz, his development of a curriculum for the American Indian Studies Department at San Francisco State University, and his involvement in other protests in support of the Pit River and Pomo Indians make him an important figure in the

history of American Indian activism in the 1960s and 1970s.

Oakes spent time in New York City working on high steel structures before moving to California, where he married Anne Marufo. He studied under Louis Kemnitzer at San Francisco State College in the American Indian Studies Department. There, Richard was introduced to the White Roots of Peace and the Third World Liberation Strikes at Berkeley, both inspirations for his activism. While in school, Richard and other students in his program met with Belva Cottier who, through her own experiences with Alcatraz, helped lay the groundwork for the students' future takeover.

Oakes joined forces with Adam Nordwall, who was also working on plans for an occupation of Alcatraz. Their collaborative group, the Indians of All Tribes, drafted a proclamation to illustrate the grievances of American Indians in cities and on reservations and to list their demands for Alcatraz. Chief among these demands was title to the land and support to build an American Indian Museum, a Center for Native American Studies, a Spiritual Center, and a scientific center for the study of ecology and environmental protection.

November 9, 1969, saw the first attempt to take Alcatraz. Before setting sail, Richard read the Proclamation of the IAT to the gathered press, who singled him out as the leader of the movement.

As they approached Alcatraz, Oakes jumped overboard and swam to shore to claim the island by right of discovery. After being removed by the Coast Guard, Oakes and his fellow students made a second attempt to occupy Alcatraz by returning only hours later. That night, the small band of occupants on the island sang songs and danced in celebration. The next day, before the Coast Guard removed them again, Oakes once again stressed the demands of the Indians of All Tribes for title to the land. On November 20, 1969, on a third attempt, eighty-nine American Indians, including Oakes, successfully occupied Alcatraz for an extended period of time.

Oakes believed that the protest on Alcatraz had the power to prove to the federal government and to the American public that American Indians were a vibrant and powerful entity in the late twentieth century, capable of self-determination. He hoped through the media to be able to reveal the vast contributions of American Indians to society and history and to push the federal government to begin acknowledging its massive legal obligations to American Indians.

Opposition to Oakes's growing power in the media created a rift among some of the newer occupiers, who wished for a completely egalitarian society on Alcatraz and saw his influence as a threat. On January 5, 1970, Oakes's daughter Yvonne fell down a flight of stairs and was killed. In deep mourning, the Oakes family left Alcatraz and new leadership factions rose to take his place.

After leaving Alcatraz, Oakes and his family went on to support other activist movements. He took part in the protests against the occupation by the Pacific Gas and Electric Company of the Pit River lands in northern California. In Santa Rosa California, Oakes helped plan a takeover of a former Central Intelligence Agency (CIA) post, where title to the land was eventually transferred to the Pomo Indians and an American Indian Learning Center was established.

In a tragic end to a brilliant life, Richard Oakes was shot to death September 20, 1972, by a YMCA camp manager, Michael Oliver Morgan, in Santa Clara, California. Morgan asserted that Oakes had attacked him, while Oakes's defenders maintained that he had been assassinated because Morgan objected to Oakes's positions on Native-rights issues. Through his efforts on Alcatraz and elsewhere, Richard Oakes helped give an upcoming generation of American Indians a renewed sense of pride and self-respect. His accomplishments in the field of American Indian activism created a new awareness of the important place of American Indians in history and in our modern society.

Vera Parham

See also Occupation of Alcatraz Island.
References and Further Reading
Johnson, Troy R. 1996. *The Occupation of Alcatraz Island: Indian Self-Determination and the Rise of Indian Activism.* Urbana: University of Illinois Press.
Johnson, Troy R., Duane Champagne, and Joane Nagel, eds. 1997. *American Indian Activism: Alcatraz to the Longest Walk.* Urbana: University of Illinois Press.
Oakes, Richard. 1972. "Alcatraz Is Not an Island." *Ramparts* 9 (December): 35–40.

Ortiz, Simon J.

One of the most accomplished Native American poets of the twentieth century, Simon J. Ortiz (Acoma Pueblo, b. 1941) often is credited as one of

the grandfathers of Native American literature. Ortiz is a widely published poet, short story writer, and oft-cited essayist. His incorporation of Native oral traditional stories and his insistence on the creative maintenance of indigenous American philosophical traditions are among his contributions to the intellectual and literary culture of indigenous Americans, as well as to American literature as a whole.

Ortiz was born in Albuquerque, New Mexico, and raised in Deetseyamah (McCartys) on the Acoma Pueblo Reservation. He received his early education at a Bureau of Indian Affairs school. After working in the uranium mines and processing plants of New Mexico, he briefly studied chemistry at Fort Lewis College before enlisting in the U.S. Army. After his service, Ortiz studied at the University of New Mexico, where he began to publish poems in small magazines. He received his master's of fine arts as an International Writing Fellow at the University of Iowa Writers' Workshop in 1969. The same year, Ortiz was given a Discovery Award by the National Endowment for the Arts. He has since taught and spoken at numerous universities and literary festivals worldwide.

Among his best-known works is *Fight Back: For the Sake of the People, for the Sake of the Land* (1980, reissued in *Woven Stone*, 1992), a collection of poetry and prose in which Ortiz draws on the Pueblo Revolt of 1680 to illuminate similar conditions existing in modern-day America, specifically in the Southwest. Ortiz examines the 1680 revolt, in which Native Pueblo peoples, Apaches, and Navajos, along with people of mixed ethnic heritage, were successful in overthrowing the colonial Spanish power and asserting sovereignty over their indigenous homelands. The poet uses this historical occurrence to emphasize the need for solidarity among marginalized peoples in present-day America to fight oppression, particularly with regard to the land.

Ortiz again recalled American history in his 1981 collection *from Sand Creek*, this time using the war in Vietnam to explore the 1864 Sand Creek Massacre, when over 130 Cheyenne and Arapahoe people were slaughtered by U.S. troops at Sand Creek, Colorado, as part of the American westward expansion. As Ortiz writes in his introduction to the 1999 edition, *from Sand Creek* represents his attempt to "deal with history," particularly the history of America that he maintains has excluded and marginalized Native American peoples (Ortiz, 1999, Preface). According to Ortiz, the genocidal aspects of American history are a facet of the American past

that is generally unacknowledged by the dominating Euro-American culture. As such, *from Sand Creek* represents not only Ortiz's attempt to "deal with history," but serves as a reminder to the wider American public of its historical treatment of Native peoples. Ortiz examines the ties between two wartime massacres—Sand Creek and My Lai—and the reccurring themes involved in Euro-American imperialism: "splattered blood/along their mad progress; they claimed the earth" (Ortiz, 1999, 89).

Simon J. Ortiz is the author of two short story collections and has edited the acclaimed *Earth Power Coming* (1983), an anthology of indigenous short fiction from across the Americas. He has also written two books for children. One of them, *Speaking for the Generations*, which Ortiz edited in 1998, is a major collection of Native authors writing about their craft. Among his many achievements, Ortiz was an Honored Poet at the 1981 White House Salute to Poetry. Ortiz has three children, has served as lieutenant governor of Acoma Pueblo, and was the recipient of an honorary doctorate of letters degree from the University of New Mexico in 2002. Ortiz's work, including his most recent collection of poetry, *Out There Somewhere*, continues to be an integral indigenous literary response to the history of the Americas.

Daniel Morley Johnson

See also Genocide; Pueblo Revolt; Sand Creek Massacre; Uranium Mining.

References and Further Reading

Coltelli, Laura, ed. 1990. "Simon Ortiz." In *Winged Words: American Indian Writers Speak*, 103–120. Lincoln: University of Nebraska Press.

Ortiz, Simon J. 1999. *from Sand Creek: Rising in This Heart Which Is Our America*. Tucson: University of Arizona Press. [Originally printed in 1981 New York: Thunder's Mouth Press.]

Ortiz, Simon J. 2002. *Out There Somewhere*. Tucson: University of Arizona Press.

Smith, Patricia Clark. 1983. "Coyote Ortiz: 'Canis Latrans Latrans' in the Poetry of Simon Ortiz." In *Studies in American Indian Literature: Critical Essays and Course Designs*. Edited by Paula Gunn Allen, 192–210. New York: MLA.

Osceola

A charismatic warrior, Osceola (1804–January 30, 1838) led the fight against the forced removal of the Seminoles to Indian Territory in the early nineteenth century. In the Second Seminole War, Osceola emerged as the most famous defender of the Semi-

nole Indians in Florida and an outspoken opponent of U.S. expansion. Despite his prominence, most of what we know about Osceola has been colored by a combination of romanticism and racism.

Born a Creek Indian in the village of Tallassee in what is now Alabama, Osceola was originally named Billy Powell. He was the son of a British trader (William Powell) and an upper Creek woman (Polly Copinger). By virtue of the Creeks' matrilineal clan system, he grew up a full member of Creek society. He would later earn his name Osceola, which is a corruption of the Muskogee words Asin ("black drink") and Yahola ("town crier"). At other times, he went by the title Tustenuggee Tallassee or the Tallassee warrior.

In 1813, when a civil war erupted among the Creek Indians, Osceola and his mother sided with the Red Sticks, who fought against Andrew Jackson and his Creek allies. Only a child at the time, Osceola did not fight in the war, but it created disruptions in his life and in Creek society. The Treaty of Fort Jackson at the war's conclusion ceded 23 million acres to the United States, including the territory where Tallassee was located. Rather than submit to the terms of the treaty or move westward, Osceola, his mother, and many other Creeks associated with his great-uncle Peter McQueen, moved south to Florida. He, along with hundreds of other Red Sticks, joined with the Seminole Indians already living in the area.

Among the Seminoles, Osceola emerged as a prominent warrior and influential leader. He married two Seminole women, which was common under the rules of polygyny, and he had at least one and maybe two children. One wife was a Creek woman named Che-cho-ter, or "Morning Dew." His other wife, whose name remains unknown, was probably an African American woman. Hundreds of black Seminoles, many of whom were fugitive slaves, found refuge and families in Florida's Indian villages, and their presence in Florida fueled the animosity between the United States and the Seminoles.

Osceola participated in the First Seminole War (1817–1818) as a young warrior. During this war, which was initiated by Andrew Jackson's invasion of Florida, Osceola had his first experience as a Creek warrior. American troops, while seeking to return fugitive African American slaves to their masters and to destroy their ability to find refuge in Florida, captured Osceola and several other Seminoles.

Upon his return to the Seminoles, Osceola emerged as a leading warrior in his Tallassee town. His opposition to American interests increased his

A Seminole leader born around 1803, Osceola achieved his status not as a hereditary chief but rather through his clearly demonstrated skills during the Second Seminole War of 1835–1842. (Library of Congress)

stature in the community, and many Seminoles looked to the bilingual Osceola to participate in intercultural affairs. For example, in 1823, Osceola tried to put an end to the controversial Treaty of Moultrie Creek. Some accounts, probably exaggerated, have Osceola putting his knife through the yet unsigned document. Considering that in subsequent years, many Seminoles complained that they were unaware about several elements of the treaty and thus tricked into signing the agreement, Osceola's opposition may have been augmented by his literacy.

After the treaty was signed, Osceola continued to oppose U.S. interests. When the Seminoles signed the Treaty of Payne's Landing (1832) and the Treaty of Fort Gibson (1833), Osceola reemerged as a voice of opposition. In June 1835, a frustrated Wiley Thompson, who was the Indian agent to the Seminoles, arranged to have Osceola arrested. Although we do not know the exact insult that resulted in Osceola's confinement, it is clear that Thompson incarcerated the Indian leader as a means to remove

the Seminoles. Thompson put Osceola in irons until he agreed to sign a document that declared the validity of the Treaty of Payne's Landing and to bring in a band of Indians who would agree to migrate westward. When seventy-nine Seminoles arrived at Fort King to proclaim their willingness to move westward, Thompson released Osceola.

Osceola urged Seminoles to oppose the 1832 and 1833 treaties and otherwise to use armed resistance to defy any attempts to force their removal. This resistance movement resulted in the Second Seminole War. On December 18, 1835, Osceola and his followers assassinated Seminole leader Charley Emathla for his signing of the treaty and his compliance with American demands for westward migration. In November 1835, Osceola and his warriors shot Emathla as he returned home from Fort King, where he had sold his cattle, a move made necessary by his decision to move. Osceola and his warriors, in a symbolic chastisement of Emathla for selling out his Seminole neighbors for personal profit, left the money from the sale on the ground by the dead leader.

In December, Osceola led another attack, this time on Thompson, just outside of Fort King, where the Indian agent was headquartered. With the assistance of approximately sixty warriors, Osceola led a brutal attack on the man most associated with the U.S. invasion of the Seminole lands. While Osceola led the assassination of Thompson, other Seminole warriors attacked the U.S. military forces who were under the command of Major Francis Dade. In light of Osceola's attack and the general discontent among Seminole villages, the United States had sent Dade and his men to serve as reinforcements at Fort King. Before they arrived, the Seminoles attacked and routed the forces. The attack killed nearly all of the 110 men on the march.

During the resulting Second Seminole War (1935–1942), Osceola emerged as one of the more successful leaders. Although he did not benefit from hereditary ties to authority among the Seminoles, his anti-American leadership and military prowess led to his rise to Tustunuggee Tallassee and then to Tustenuggee Thlucco (head warrior) for the entire Seminole nation. His "white" heritage furthered his reputation among non-Natives, many of whom were fascinated with his upbringing. Just before his death, George Catlin further sealed Osceola's fame by painting and then distributing his portrait. In the portrait, Osceola appears in an amalgam of the finest European and Seminole clothes, armed with a rifle and adorned with gorgets around his neck and feathers in his hair.

On December 31, 1835, Osceola won a decisive victory over the United States at the Withlacoochee River. With about 250 warriors, Osceola repelled a U.S. force of nearly 800 men under General Duncan L. Clinch's command. During the fighting, Osceola was wounded but not seriously, and after he recovered, he returned to battle. Deaths were low on both sides (three Indians and four U.S. soldiers, but casualties were not. Five Indians and fifty-nine Americans were seriously wounded. Later in the war, Osceola is credited for rescuing a camp of mostly black Seminoles from the United States.

In the summer of 1837, Osceola contracted malaria. Exhausted from fighting and suffering from his illness, on October 27, 1837, Osceola sent word to General Thomas Sydney Jesup that he was desirous of a truce. Osceola and Coa Harjo traveled to Fort Peyton, where on the orders of Jesup, American soldiers captured the Indian men, who were carrying a white flag. The United States also took hostage the eighty-one Seminole men and women who accompanied Osceola to the meeting. The United States took Osceola to the Castillo San Marcos (also known as Fort Marion) in St. Augustine, where eventually 237 Seminoles were imprisoned. When it became clear that Osceola could not be convinced to support the Seminole's removal, Jesup ordered him relocated to Fort Moultrie in South Carolina.

Before his death, Osceola requested that his two wives and his children be allowed to visit him in South Carolina. With the approval of the United States, they visited the dying warrior in early 1838. Osceola died while a prisoner on January 30, 1838. Before he was buried, the medical examiner at Fort Moultrie had him decapitated. In 1843, Osceola's head, as well as some of his possessions, were put on display by Dr. Valentine Mott. After being donated to the Medical College of New York, his head disappeared during an 1865 fire.

Andrew K. Frank

See also Emathla, Charley; Jackson, Andrew; Seminole Wars.
References and Further Reading
Covington, James W. 1992. *The Seminoles of Florida.* Gainesville: University of Florida Press.
Hartley, William, and Ellen Hartley. 1973. *Osceola, the Unconquered Indian.* New York: Hawthorne Books.

Mahon, John K. 1967. *History of the Second Seminole War, 1835–1842*. Gainesville: University of Florida Press.

Miller, Susan A. 2003. *Coacoochee's Bones: A Seminole Saga*. Lawrence: University Press of Kansas.

Wickman, Patricia R. 1991. *Osceola's Legacy*. Tuscaloosa : University of Alabama Press.

Ouray

Ouray ("The Arrow," "Willy"), who was Ute and Apache, became a major presence during treaty negotiations in present-day Colorado during the late nineteenth century. He served as a spokesman for the seven Ute bands and as a peacemaker during the Ute War of 1879.

Born in Taos, New Mexico, about 1820, Ouray's father, Guera Murah, was a Jicarilla Apache who had been adopted by the Utes; his mother was a Tabeguache Ute. Throughout most of his youth, Ouray worked for Mexican sheepherders and learned Spanish. As a young man, he became a noted warrior among the Tabeguache Utes (later called the Uncompahgres) during raids against the Sioux and Kiowas. Ouray also learned English and several Indian languages, thus making him a key figure in many negotiations in the American Southwest.

Ouray's son by his first wife was taken by the Sioux in a raid on a Ute hunting camp, and he was never able to recapture him. When his first wife died in 1859, Ouray married Chipeta, a Tabeguache woman. In 1860, after his father died, Ouray was appointed chief of his band and interpreter for the U.S. government. This appointment occurred in Washington, D.C., where he was awarded medals, titles, and a $1,000 annuity.

In 1863, Ouray helped negotiate the Treaty of Conejos, in which the Utes ceded all lands east of the Continental Divide. In 1867, he helped Christopher "Kit" Carson quell a Ute uprising led by Chief Kaniatse. By 1872, however, Ouray was leading resistance to the U.S. government's seizure of lands that previously had been reserved for the Ute people. Although he was generally patient, Ouray did lose his temper during these negotiations when a U.S. government official accused the Utes of laziness. Incensed at such a characterization, Ouray replied, "We work as hard as you do. Did you ever try skinning a buffalo?" (Johansen and Grinde, 1997, 276).

Ouray served as a spokesman for the seven Ute bands, and as a peacemaker during the Ute War of 1879. (Library of Congress)

In 1873, Ouray and other Ute representatives met with a federal commission headed by Felix Brunot and were forced to compromise on the issue of land cessions. Pressured by the influx of miners and cattle owners, the Utes ceded an additional four million acres (the San Juan cession) for an annual payment of $25,000.

In 1876, when Colorado became a state, mining companies attempted to oust three White River Ute bands from their lands. "The Utes must go" became a political slogan among non-Native immigrants, in spite of the Utes' service as scouts for the U.S. Army and in state militias fighting other Native peoples.

These tensions were compounded by the policies of a new Indian agent, Nathan Meeker, who arrived in 1878. In September 1879, Meeker directed the Utes to use parts of their land for farming. Canalla, brother-in-law of Ouray and a Ute shaman, protested the conversion of grazing lands to agriculture. Canalla challenged Meeker's decision and told him to leave the agency. Meeker proceeded to request a detachment of 150 troops under Major Thomas T. Thornburgh to "pacify" the rebellious Utes. Shortly afterward, the Utes killed Meeker and seven other whites. Following subsequent bloody altercations, Ouray was able to secure a peaceful settlement because both sides respected him.

On August 27, 1880, soon after his return from Washington, D.C., Ouray died of Bright's Disease, an affliction of the kidneys, near Ignacio, Colorado. In 1925, he was reburied at Montrose, Colorado.

Bruce E. Johansen

See also Carson, Christopher "Kit"
Reference and Further Reading
Johansen, Bruce E., and Donald A. Grinde, Jr. 1997. *The Encyclopedia of Native American Biography.* New York: Henry Holt.

Owens, Louis

Of Cherokee, Choctaw, and Irish descent, Louis Owens was an extremely prolific writer, having produced five novels, two books of personal and literary essays, five books of literary criticism (two on John Steinbeck's work, a major critical interest of Owens), and three on American Indian literature, over seventy-five critical essays and chapters, and over thirty essays.

Owens was born in Lompoc, California, in 1948 and grew up in rural Mississippi and California. He was one of nine children, the second member of his family to finish high school, and the only one to attend university. With an understanding of the working class and a love of the outdoors that permeate much of his written work, Owens worked as a field laborer as well as a firefighter and forest ranger before attending graduate school. He took his Ph.D. at the University of California Davis as a University of California Regents Fellow in 1981, becoming a full professor in that system eight years later. Owens was a Fulbright lecturer in American literature at the University of Pisa and taught for a time at the University of New Mexico. Owens also was awarded

Outstanding Teacher of the Year for 1985–1986 by the International Steinbeck Society and the Distinguished Teaching Award by the University of California Santa Cruz in 1992. He was awarded a New Mexico Humanities Grant in 1987 and a National Endowment for the Arts Creative Writing Fellowship in 1989, and he was named Wordcraft Circle Writer of the Year (Prose–Personal and Critical Essays) in 1998 for *Mixblood Messages. The Sharpest Sight* was the recipient of France's 1995 Roman Noir Award, and this novel, along with *Other Destinies,* was the cowinner of the Josephine Miles/PEN Oakland Award in 1993. *Bone Game* won the Julian J. Rothbaum Prize in 1994. *Nightland* won an American Book Award in 1997. Tragically, Owens committed suicide in July 2002 in Albuquerque, New Mexico.

Owens's novels are mysteries. *The Sharpest Sight,* the first book in Oklahoma's American Indian Literature and Critical Studies Series, is not merely a whodunnit in regard to the murder of Attis McCurtain, but also a study in mixed-blood identity and continuance in the characters of Mundo Morales, a Chicano deputy sheriff seeking the killer, and Cole and Hoey McCurtain, Attis's brother and father. In this novel, Owens introduces the characters of Uncle Luther and Old Lady (Onatima) Blue Wood, whose Mississippi Choctaw approach to the world provides grounding for the other characters as well as the resolution to the mystery.

Bone Game continues Cole's saga, at the same time confronting the results of colonialism from the cruelty of the early Spanish missionaries to the present. *Wolfsong,* the novel Owens wrote first during his years as a forest ranger but published third, is an interrogation of environmentalist ethics from a Native perspective. *Nightland* delves into the world of Billy Keene and Will Striker, half-blood Cherokees caught in a New Mexico mystery, and shows the effects of capitalism and greed on American Indian cultures as well as the effects of the Vietnam War on individual American lives. *Nightland* is the only one of Owens's novels to utilize Cherokee materials, with Will and Billy paralleling the twins born to Kana'ti and Selu, the first man and first woman in Cherokee oral tradition. *Dark River,* Owens's final novel, follows Mississippi Choctaw Jacob Nashoba, displaced and working as a tribal ranger on the fictional Black Mountain Apache Reservation in eastern Arizona, the home of his estranged wife.

The comic genius and humor that appear throughout his earlier work despite their overall serious tone is perhaps most fully expressed in this

work, though it is at the same time still a mystery and, as the title suggests, "dark." It is also perhaps the most postmodern of Owens's novels, with characters such as the more-Indian-than-the-Indians Jewish anthropologist Avrum Goldberg and Jessie, the young Apache man who at first sells fake "vision quests" to unsuspecting New Agers and then, being mistaken for a wolf and shot while impersonating one in his trade, becomes ironically a real spirit helper. The autobiographical *I Hear the Train: Inventions, Reflections, Refractions* was his last work.

Kimberly Roppolo

See also Mission System, Spanish.
References and Further Reading

Kilpatrick, Jacquelyn, ed. 2004. *Louis Owens: Literary Reflections on His Life and Work.* Norman: University of Oklahoma Press.
"Louis Owens." Available at: http://www .hanksville.org/storytellers/Owens/. Accessed March 28, 2005.

Parker, Arthur C.

Arthur Caswell Parker (Gawasowaneh, 1881–1955) was an Indian intellectual who devoted over forty years of his life to New York museums. Most commentators tend to stress that he was only one-quarter Indian by blood, but he thought of himself as simply a modern assimilated Seneca Iroquois Indian of noble descent. He chose wholehearted assimilation into Euro-American culture as his life path and remained heartily resistant to the imposition of any Indian stereotype. Instead, he worked almost ceaselessly to claim, for himself and for the Iroquois, his version of an Indian ethos. At the heart of this quest lay his writing. A workaholic, he wrote 440 separate books, articles and addresses, thirty-two published newspaper articles, 114 radio scripts, and forty-five unpublished articles, speeches and plays, in addition to editing five periodicals.

Arthur C. Parker married Beulah Tahamont (Dark Cloud, Abenaki) on April 23, 1904, then married Anna Theresa Cooke on September 17, 1914, and is survived by his daughter Martha Anne Parker.

Parker began his professional life as an archaeologist in the Science Division of the New York State Museum. He was dedicated to the reconstruction of the American ethnographic past and showed few qualms about desecrating the graves of ancestors in and around his own childhood reservation to signifi-

cantly enhance the museum's collections. At the State Museum he also developed his sensory, psychological, and entertainment-orientated approach to display and created the life-sized Indian dioramas that stayed there from 1908 to 1976. As he moved into his thirties, Parker produced a number of important anthropological texts, notably *Iroquois Uses of Maize and Other Food Plants* (1910), *The Code of Handsome Lake, the Seneca Prophet* (1913), and *The Constitution of the Five Nations* (1916). However, finding his anthropological approach criticized as too "Indian" and as focused on advancing Indian culture rather than on scientific objectivity, he increasingly turned his attention to pan-Indian concerns. He gave a huge chunk of his life and energy to the challenge of making the first twentieth-century Indian reform organization, the Society of American Indians (SAI, 1911–1920s) a force to be reckoned with. He ended his involvement with the SAI, sadly disillusioned about the cohesive power of the Indian "race" but convinced that he had helped lay the foundations for vital future reform.

Parker was able to maintain his commitment to social evolution in his best-known role, as Director of the Rochester Museum, New York, from 1924 to 1946. He transformed the institution from relative obscurity to national significance, largely by presenting versions of Indian history that affirmed the triumphant nationalism of the day. He published the influential *A Manual for History Museums* in 1935. In 1939, after attracting an enormous benefaction from the industrialist Dr. Edward Bausch, he was able to add a spectacular modern building to the museum. During the New Deal years, he promoted two relief programs on the reservations of his childhood, the Tonawanda Community House and the Seneca Arts & Crafts Project. Again, his approach attracted criticism, but his efforts were a practical success. For such practical achievements, as well as his personal kindness, Parker is still remembered today on New York reservations with warmth and appreciation.

Although most of Parker's life was public indeed, he had a secret life in a host of fraternities. The group he gave his heart to was American Freemasonry, in which in 1924 he achieved the highest rank, the thirty-third degree and the title Sovereign Grand Inspector General. As a Mason, he used his Indian heritage and his writing ability to subvert the processes of exclusion that kept middle-class Indians and white Anglo-Saxon Protestants apart. A heart condition forced Parker into retirement at the age of sixty-five, whereupon he returned to writing

juvenile and children's books with Iroquois and Indian themes, part of his lifelong effort to connect the oral culture of his childhood with a positive vision of American nationalism. His children's books, especially *Skunny Wundy and Other Indian Tales* (1926), were successes, and all, in different ways, owed something to his first book-length study of tribal lore, *Seneca Myths and Folktales* (1923).

Parker was a fascinating and complex man, always deeply frustrated at, as he put it, having "to play Indian in order to be Indian" and determined to live beyond any imposed definition of what an Indian should be. Certainly, with his staunch Republican values, his eugenicist and racist views, his commitment to social evolution and to salvage ethnography, as well as his love of Freemasonry, he defies many of the usual Indian stereotypes. In sum, his illustrious family history, his remarkable life story, and the great wealth of written material he left to posterity all combine to make him one of the most fascinating Indian leaders of the postfrontier era.

Joy Porter

See also Parker, Ely; Society of American Indians.
Reference and Further Reading
Porter, Joy. 2001. *To Be Indian: The Life of Iroquois-Seneca Arthur Caswell Parker*. Norman: University of Oklahoma Press.

Ely S. Parker (1828–1905), also known as Hasanoanda, was the United States' first Native American Commissioner of Indian Affairs. (National Archives and Records Administration)

Parker, Ely

Colonel Ely Parker (Donehogawa, Seneca, 1828–1905) was secretary to General Ulysses S. Grant; he wrote the surrender ending the Civil War that General Robert E. Lee signed at Appomattox. After the Civil War, Parker became the United States' first Native American Commissioner of Indian Affairs after Grant was elected president.

Parker had planned on a legal career, passed the necessary examinations, but was denied certification because he was Indian and therefore not a U.S. citizen. Parker then switched to civil engineering, but he also had a considerable background in ethnology. He helped to inspire Lewis Henry Morgan's pioneering studies of the Iroquois that founded academic anthropology in the United States. Parker became an early member of the Grand Order of the Iroquois, a fraternal society established by Morgan.

Parker's tenure in the Indian Bureau coincided with investigations by Congress under Senator James B. Doolittle regarding corruption on the frontier. The Doolittle report received considerable publicity, finding that, in a large number of cases, Indian wars could be traced to the provocations of European-Americans who had seized Native lands illegally. Parker came into office under the aegis of a Peace Policy initiated by Congress after the publicity attending the Doolittle report, in an attempt to deal honestly with remaining Native American nations.

However, the Indian Rings, whose members had done so much to corrupt the system and profited so handsomely from government contracts for services paid but rarely delivered, made Parker's life miserable and his job impossible. During Parker's tenure as Indian Commissioner, however, he helped orchestrate considerable public outrage over the treatment of Indians nationwide, particularly those on the Plains who were being ruthlessly pursued as he served in the office. After Parker was hounded out of office, he expressed his disgust: "They made their onslaught on my poor, innocent head and made the air foul with their malicious and poisonous accusations. They were defeated, but it was no

longer a pleasure to discharge patriotic duties in the face of foul slander and abuse. I gave up a thankless position to enjoy my declining years in peace and quiet" (Johansen and Grinde, 1997, 281).

Parker had overseen a brief interlude in the destructive Indian policies of the nineteenth century, a time during which Red Cloud and his allies had forced the U.S. Army to dissemble its forts in the Powder River country and sign the Treaty of 1868, guaranteeing the Black Hills to the Lakota. In June 1870, Parker had hosted Red Cloud and a companion chief, Red Dog, as they visited Washington, D.C., and spoke at the Cooper Union.

This was Parker's evaluation of U.S. Indian policies:

> The white man has been the chief obstacle in the way of Indian civilization. The benevolent measures attempted by the government for their advancement has been almost uniformly thwarted by the agencies employed to carry them out. The soldiers, sent for their protection, too often carried demoralization and disease into their midst. The agent appointed to be their friend and counselor, business manager, and the [manager] of government bounties, frequently went among them only to enrich himself in the shortest possible time, at the cost of the Indians, and spend the largest available sum of the government money with the least ostensible beneficial result (Johansen and Grinde, 1997, 281).

Long before the subject came to the attention of scholars, Parker noted the debt of the U.S. political system to the Iroquois. In an "Address to the New York Historical Society, May 28, 1847," Parker noted the fascination of the U.S. founders with the Iroquois League: "Glad were your forefathers to sit upon the thresholds of the Longhouse[;] rich did they hold themselves in getting the mere sweepings from its door" (Johansen 1999, 147).

During his later years, Parker made a large amount of money playing the stock market but was ruined when he was forced to pay the bond of another man who had defaulted. After retiring from service with the U.S. government, Parker was appointed New York City building superintendent in 1876. He held the post until he died in 1905. Parker is buried in Buffalo, New York, in a common plot with his grandfather, Red Jacket.

Bruce E. Johansen

See also Grant Peace Policy; Parker, Arthur C.; Red Cloud.

References and Further Reading
Armstrong, William N. 1978. *Warrior in Two Camps: Ely S. Parker.* Syracuse, NY: Syracuse University Press.
Armstrong, Virginia Irving. 1971. *I Have Spoken: American History Through the Voices of the Indians.* Chicago: Swallow Press.
Johansen, Bruce E. 1999. *Native Americans and the Evolution of Democracy: A Supplementary Bibliography.* Westport, CT: Greenwood Press.
Johansen, Bruce E., and Donald A. Grinde, Jr. 1997. *The Encyclopedia of Native American Biography,* 280–282. New York: Henry Holt.
Nabokov, Peter. 1991. *Native Testimony.* New York: Viking.
Parker, Arthur C. 1919. *The Life of General Ely S. Parker, Last Grand Sachem of the Iroquois and General Grant's Military Secretary.* Buffalo, NY: Buffalo Historical Society Publications 23.

Parker, Quanah

Although Quanah ("Sweet Fragrance") Parker played a role of great historical significance to the Comanche people and in his role in spreading peyote religion in Oklahoma, controversy surrounds his life. He was born sometime between 1845 and 1863, to a mother, Cynthia Ann Parker, who had been captured from her white family as a nine-year-old and raised as Comanche. Though most of her family was killed during the raid, Cynthia began a new life as a Comanche girl and was given the name of Preloch. She married Pete Nocona in her teens and gave birth to Quanah near Cedar Lake, Texas. The couple also had a daughter who lived to adulthood and a son who died in childhood. Cynthia, along with the daughter, Topsannah, were recaptured by the Texas Rangers in 1861. Both suffered greatly from their removal; Topsannah died in the mid 1860s, and Cynthia in 1870. Pete Nocona passed away in 1866 or 1867.

Quanah was ridiculed by other Comanches for his mixed ancestry; although he was Comanche culturally, he stood out because of his height and thinness, as well as his relatively light skin and gray eyes. Depending on one's opinion on the year of his birth, his role in the tribe during the mid and late-nineteenth century is debatable. It is certain that he fought as a warrior in the Battle of Adobe Walls in 1875 in the Comanches' last great effort to protect the

Quanah Parker was a Comanche leader. (Library of Congress)

buffalo on their Texas lands from eradication by white opportunists. He is noted by a white man who counciled with the Comanches regarding their surrender as being "a young man of much influence with his people" (Hagan, 1996, 468). Whether he was too young, as some say, to be a war chief who led his people in resisting the reservation for two years following the battle is unknown.

After the onset of reservation life, however, Quanah's role becomes more clear. Although he resisted cutting his hair and giving up any of his eight wives (five of whom he married simultaneously and several of whom were young widows in need of financial support), Quanah was named a band chief by the Indian agent early on and was eventually named a judge in 1886 and principal chief in 1890. When Anglo-American cattle owners encroached on reservation land, Quanah became one of the earliest advocates of leasing and took a position monitoring the land boundaries, for which the cattlepeople paid him. He was also given cattle from time to time and set up his own herd with these and a bull given to him by Charles Goodnight (b. 1836), one of the most prosperous Anglo-American cattle raisers of the time. With the money he earned, Quanah built his famed home, the ten-roomed, double-porched Star House.

During the early reservation era, Quanah traveled throughout Texas and Oklahoma as a popular celebrity who led many parades on horseback in full regalia. He was one of five chiefs who rode in Theodore Roosevelt's inaugural parade in 1900. Over the years, Quanah made twenty trips to Washington, D.C., working to improve allotment conditions for his people, though he was unable to delay it as long as he wished. Quanah and other Comanches suffered from the loss of lease lands and the use of communally held property, and his finances would continue to trouble him until the end of his life. Two of his wives also left him during this time. Late in his life, Quanah traveled actively as a roadman, leading and attending peyote meetings throughout Oklahoma and testifying on behalf of his religion before state committees. He died on February 23, 1911, and was buried next to his mother and his sister, whom he had moved from Texas and reburied in Cache County, Oklahoma. He was survived by two remaining wives, Tonarcy and Topay, as well as sixteen of the twenty-four children he is known to have fathered. Quanah, Preloch, and Topsannah were all removed to Fort Sill Military Cemetery outside Lawton, Oklahoma, in 1957.

Kimberly Roppolo

See also General Allotment Act (Dawes Act).
References and Further Reading
Hagan, William. 1996. "Parker, Quanah." In *Encyclopedia of North American Indians: Native American History, Culture, and Life from Paleo-Indians to the Present.* Edited by Frederick E. Hoxie, 468–69. Boston: Houghton-Mifflin.
Malinowski, Sharon, ed. 1995. *Notable Native Americans.* Detroit, MI: Gale Research.
Malinowski, Sharon, and Simon Glickman, eds. 1996. *Native North American Biography.* Vol. 2. New York: UXL.
Markowitz, Harvey, ed. 1995. *Ready Reference: American Indians.* Vol. 1. Pasadena, CA: Salem Press.

Peltier, Leonard

Leonard Peltier (Lakota and Anishinabe, b. 1944) is an American Indian Movement (AIM) activist who has served three decades of two consecutive life sentences in the federal prison system following his conviction for killing Federal Bureau of Investigation Agents Jack Coler and Ronald Williams on the Pine Ridge Reservation during a shoot-out in June 1975. Many people believe that Peltier was wrongly convicted on falsified evidence, and he is widely considered a symbol of aboriginal peoples' political struggles worldwide, especially in the United States and Canada. Peltier also has become an artist and author while in prison.

Peltier is considered a political prisoner by Amnesty International and other human-rights advocates around the world. The United Nations High Commissioner on Human Rights, the Dalai Lama, and the European Parliament, among others, have all called for his release ("The Case of Leonard Pelitier . . . ," n.d.).

His struggles began early, growing up in poverty on the Turtle Mountain Reservation in North Dakota. He witnessed U.S. government policies that forced Native families off their reservations and into cities and that caused the withdrawal of essential services from those who chose to remain. In this climate, Peltier became active in organizing and protesting for the rights of his people. By the early 1970s, he was strongly involved with the American Indian Movement.

In 1972, Peltier took part in the Trail of Broken Treaties, a demonstration requesting the U.S. government to investigate treaty violations over the last 100 years. When met with a negative response from the Bureau of Indian Affairs, the demonstrators occupied the Bureau of Indian Affairs Washington, D.C., headquarters for a week. The result was the promise of a hearing on AIM-initiated grievances. Another result was intense FBI scrutiny of the occupation's leaders, including Russell Means, Dennis Banks, and Peltier.

Through AIM's activites, Peltier came to the Pine Ridge Indian Reservation in South Dakota, where the 1975 shoot-out occurred. By the time AIM activists arrived, circumstances on the Pine Ridge Reservation included extreme poverty, violence, and fear.

Richard Wilson had been elected tribal chairman on the Pine Ridge Reservation in 1972 and had since been in conflict with the traditional Oglala people. Wilson represented big business, and he ignored demands and rights of traditional people on the reservation. Wilson's policies reduced the people to extreme poverty and fear. He enforced his regime and economic policies by misusing federal money to employ a personal police force, which he trained, armed, and deployed to control the residents of the Pine Ridge Reservation. This force called itself Guardians of the Oglala Nation, or the GOON squad. This squad committed violent acts of intimidation, violence, and outright murder against the traditional Indian people on the reservation. Despite the presence of FBI agents on the reservation at that time, the murders went largely uninvestigated. Appeals to the Bureau of Indian Affairs also were ignored. In fact, the U.S. federal government provided funding for the GOON squad.

In 1973, traditional people at Pine Ridge asked AIM for help, and approximately 300 traditionals, AIM members, and supporters occupied the village of Wounded Knee, South Dakota, in protest of Wilson and his GOON squad. The background to this occupation included the historical relevance of the site, where in 1890 the U.S. Cavalry massacred 300 people, including many women and children. Under siege by the FBI and BIA, the occupiers of Wounded Knee in 1973 lasted seventy-one days, until U.S. government officials agreed to investigate conditions on the Pine Ridge Reservation. The investigation never occurred, but many AIM members were charged with various legal offenses related to the occupation.

Between 1973 and 1976, at least sixty-six people died violently at Pine Ridge (other deaths may not have been documented). The FBI is charged with investigating major crimes on U.S. Indian reservations, but these deaths were only lightly investigated, if at all. The majority of victims were members or supporters of AIM and the traditional Oglala people. During this time, the murder rate on the Pine Ridge Reservation was the highest in the country (Johansen and Maestas, 1979, 97–120; Messerschmidt, 1983, 6).

In 1974, Means ran for tribal chairman against Wilson. In a climate of stress and fear, with allegations of rampant fraud, Wilson narrowly won the election. The BIA refused to oversee the election or to investigate it for irregularities and fraud.

In this context, the traditional council of chiefs asked AIM to provide protection, alleging a lack of legal protection from Wilson and the GOON squad.

Leonard Peltier, American Indian Movement leader, being extradited to the United States in 1976 to face trial for the murder of two FBI agents a year earlier. (Bettman/Corbis)

A small group of AIM members responded, including Peltier, who arrived in March 1975. The AIM activists and local traditionalists set up a spiritual camp on the property of Cecilia and Harry Jumping Bull, who had been constantly under threat from the GOONs (Clark, 1999, xvi).

A month before the shoot-out occurred at Jumping Bull's, the FBI, aware of AIM's presence, increased its own presence in and around the reservation. On June 26, 1975, FBI Agents Williams and Coler entered the Jumping Bull compound following a red pick-up truck, and gunfire erupted. During the firefight, the agents were killed. A Native American man, Joe Stuntz, also died that day; his murder was never investigated. By the end of the day, FBI and other law enforcement agencies had occupied the reservation and the AIM members involved, including Peltier, had fled the area.

Two months later, a car carrying Michael Anderson, Rob Robideau, Norman Charles, and others exploded. The FBI found a gun in the wreckage that it claimed was the murder weapon used against Coler and Williams. In November 1975, Dino Butler, Rob Robideau, Peltier, and a youth, Jimmy Eagle,

were indicted for the murders of Williams and Coler. At this time Peltier was in Canada fighting extradition. Butler and Robideau were tried together and acquitted. The jury concluded Butler and Robideau acted in self-defense against the paramilitary assault on Pine Ridge by the FBI. Charges against Jimmy Eagle were dropped, and the full force of governmental prosecution was then directed at Peltier, who was later extradited from Canada, to stand trial before an all-white jury in U.S. District Court, Fargo, North Dakota, in April of 1977.

Preparing its case against Peltier, the FBI coerced Myrtle Poor Bear into signing three false affidavits that directly implicated him in the killing of the two agents. Later, the FBI admitted that Poor Bear was not even on the scene the day of the killings (Clark, 1999, xviii).

Peltier was found guilty of two counts of murder and sentenced to two consecutive life sentences. The trial, presided over by Judge Paul Benson, was based on false evidence in the Poor Bear affidavits, on a bullet that was incorrectly connected to the alleged murder weapon, and on testimony given by other witnesses under coercion from the FBI.

At the trial, the prosecution presented fifteen days of evidence, and the defense was limited to six days. Peltier's defense team had the same evidence as was presented in the Bulter and Robideau trial indicating FBI misconduct but was not permitted to present most of it to the jury. Peltier also was not allowed to assert self-defense. Peltier's appeals to the Eighth Circuit Court and the U.S. Supreme Court were both denied. In 1993, even in the face of evidence of FBI misconduct and the admission of one of the prosecutors that the government does not know who killed the agents, the Eighth Circuit Court denied Peltier's appeal a second time.

With the assistance of Bobby Garcia, Dallas Thundershield, and Roque Dueñas, Peltier escaped from Lompoc federal prison in July of 1979. Thundershield was killed during the escape, and Garcia and Peltier were captured six days later. At his escape trial, Judge Lawrence Lydick prohibited Peltier from presenting evidence of his reasons for fleeing prison, and Peltier was sentenced for the maximum of seven years for escape and possession of a weapon. Garcia was sentenced to five years. Garcia was found dead in his cell a year later, and Roque Dueñas disappeared in a fishing accident (Messerschmidt, 1983, 139).

Many who have studied the Peltier case claim to this day that Peltier was wrongly convicted and is

thus a political prisoner. He is considered an important American Indian leader who fought to protect the rights of his people, as well as a symbol of the ongoing oppression of American Indian people at the hands of the U.S. federal government.

Aliki Marinakis

See also American Indian Movement; Means, Russell; Pine Ridge, Political Murders; Trail of Broken Treaties; Wilson, Richard.

References and Further Readings

Apted, Micheal. 1992. *Incident at Oglala: The Leonard Peltier Story.* Film produced by Robert Redford. "Case of Leonard Peltier: Native American Prisoner." No date. Available at: www.freepeltier.org. Accessed March 30, 2005.

Clark, Ramsey. 1999. "Preface." In *Prison Writings: My Life Is My Sundance.* By Leonard Peltier, xiii–xxii. New York: St. Martin's Press.

Johansen, Bruce, and Roberto Maestas. 1979. *Wasi'chu: The Continuing Indian Wars.* New York: Monthly Review Press.

Messerschmidt, Jim. 1983. *The Trial of Leonard Peltier.* Boston: South End Press.

Matthiessen, Peter. 1992. *In the Spirit of Crazy Horse: The Story of Leonard Peltier and the FBI's War on the American Indian Movement.* New York: Penguin.

Peltier, Leonard. 1999. *Prison Writings: My Life Is My Sundance.* New York: St. Martin's Press.

Penn, William, Quakers, and Native Americans

William Penn (1644–1718) was an important English Quaker and a voice for religious tolerance in Europe and North America. He founded the Pennsylvania colony (the state's name is Anglicized Latin for "Penn's forest"). The colony's original principles included scrupulous attention to nonviolence (which remains a central tenet of the Quaker creed) as well as fairness in relations with Native Americans, most notably the Leni Lenápes, whom Europeans called the Delawares.

Penn's memory has been a presence throughout Native American history, especially in the Northeast. Quaker influence is particularly notable in the religion of Handsome Lake (known today as the Longhouse Religion) among the Iroquois. Quakers often were invited as trustworthy observers at treaty councils and other crucial events by Native Americans in the Northeast who suspected the motives of other European-Americans. As recently as 1990, Quakers were invited to act as observers in clashes between factions on the Akwesasne Mohawk reservation. The Society of Friends, which still maintains its headquarters in Philadelphia, devotes substantial resources to Native American history and relations.

Penn's "holy experiment" was designed to grant asylum to the persecuted under conditions of equality and freedom, at a time when a person could be punished severely in Puritan Boston merely for professing Quakerism and when Protestants persecuted Catholics, Catholics persecuted Protestants, and both persecuted Quakers and Jews. The French philosopher Voltaire, a champion of religious toleration, offered lavish praise: "William Penn might, with reason, boast of having brought down upon earth the Golden Age, which in all probability, never had any real existence but in his dominions" (Powell, n.d.).

Penn's vision for his colony could be compared in many ways to that of Roger Williams, who had founded Providence Plantations (later Rhode Island) a few decades earlier. Like Penn, Williams was a dissenter from theocracy who welcomed many faiths at a time of deadly religious conflict in England. Williams also practiced very cordial relations with neighboring Native Americans. Like Penn, Williams carried on his campaign for religious tolerance on both sides of the Atlantic.

The most specific description of Penn's mother, Margaret, comes from a neighbor, the acid-tongued diarist Samuel Pepys, who described her as a "fat, short, old Dutch woman, but one who hath been heretofore pretty handsome" (Powell, n.d.). She did the child rearing because her husband was seldom at home. His father, William Penn, Sr., was a much sought-after naval commander because he knew the waters around England and could handle a ship in bad weather and get the most from his crew.

William Penn, Jr. was born on October 14, 1644, in London. He developed an early interest in religion, having heard a speech by Thomas Loe, a missionary for the Society of Friends, known by the then-derisive name Quakers. Founded in 1647 by the English preacher George Fox, Quakers formed a mystical Protestant sect emphasizing a direct relationship with God. An individual's conscience, not the *Bible,* was believed by the Quakers to be the ultimate authority; their doctrine resembled that of the modern Unitarians. Quakers had no clergy and no churches. Rather, they held meetings at which participants meditated silently and spoke when moved to

William Penn makes a treaty with Native Americans in Pennsylvania in 1737. Penn, a Quaker, campaigned for peace and religious tolerance. (Library of Congress)

do so. They favored plain dress and a simple life (Powell, n.d.).

Penn studied Greek and Roman classics and became a religious rebel at Oxford University, where he defied Anglican church officials by visiting John Owen, a professor who had been dismissed for advocating tolerant humanism. Penn also protested compulsory chapel attendance, a position for which he was expelled from Oxford at age seventeen. Penn's parents then sent him to France, where he enrolled at l'Academie Protestante.

Returning to England by 1664, Penn studied at Lincoln's Inn, a prestigious London law school in London. Penn attended Quaker meetings (a criminal act) and was arrested several times. As an aristocrat, he was released, but he insisted that all Quakers be treated equally. Penn was imprisoned six times in England for speaking his mind on matters of religion. While incarcerated, he wrote several pamphlets that provided a theoretical basis for Quakerism, meanwhile attacking intolerance. Penn also devoted considerable time to challenging oppressive government policies in court; one of his cases helped protect the right to trial by jury. Penn used his diplomatic skills and family connections to get large numbers of Quakers out of jail. He also saved many from the gallows (Powell, n.d.).

As a result of these activities, the junior Penn's father disowned him. After his release from jail, Penn lived in several Quaker households. When Penn attacked the Catholic and Anglican doctrine of the trinity, the Anglican bishop had him imprisoned in the infamous Tower of London. Ordered to recant, Penn declared from his cold isolation cell: "My prison shall be my grave before I will budge a jot; for I owe my conscience to no mortal man" (Powell, n.d.). In the Tower, Penn wrote several pamphlets defining the principal elements of Quakerism, the best-known being *No Cross, No Crown*, which presented a pioneering historical case for religious toleration. During this time, the British Parliament passed the Conventicle Act, which aimed to suppress religious dissent as sedition. Having won his release from prison on legal grounds, Penn challenged the Act by preaching Quakerism at public meetings. Penn later used his legal training to prepare an historic defense of religious toleration in court. The jury acquitted all defendants, but the Lord Mayor of London refused to accept this verdict. He hit the jury members with fines and ordered them held in brutal Newgate prison (Powell, n.d.). They sued the mayor for false arrest and won, establishing a major precedent protecting their right of trial by jury.

Convinced that religious toleration was not possible in England, Penn requested a charter for an American colony. On March 4, 1681, realizing that he could rid England of the nettlesome Quakers, Charles II signed a charter for territory west of the Delaware River and north of Maryland. In 1681, from England, Penn sent William Markham as his deputy to establish a government at Uppland (later renamed Chester, now a suburb of Philadelphia) and instructed commissioners to plot Philadelphia (a name derived from ancient Greek meaning "city of brotherly love"), which was laid out a few miles north of the point where the Delaware and the Schuylkill rivers converge.

The First Frame of Government, which Penn and the initial land purchasers adopted on April 25, 1682, expressed ideals anticipating the Declaration of

Independence: "Men being born with a title to perfect freedom and uncontrolled enjoyment of all the rights and privileges of the law of nature . . . . No one can be put out of his estate and subjected to the political view of another, without his consent" (Powell, n.d.). This document provided for secure private property, nearly unlimited free enterprise, a free press, and trial by jury, as well as religious toleration. In contrast to the English penal code, which commended the death penalty for roughly 200 offenses, Penn reserved it for two: murder and treason. Penn also encouraged women's education and participation in public debate (Powell, n.d.).

Pennsylvania's legal structure included a humane penal code that (in 1701) extended civil rights to criminals and encouraged the emancipation of slaves, although Penn himself owned human capital. Emancipation did not become official Quaker doctrine until 1758. Even under such a system, however, the representative assembly was left in an inferior position to the executive, which was controlled by the proprietors of the colony.

Penn realized that much of the land his supporters occupied was held by Native Americans, most notably the Delawares (Leni Lenápes), who had never been defeated militarily by the Swedes or the Dutch, who had earlier claimed the area. True to his nonviolent doctrines, Penn refused to fortify Philadelphia, making friendly relations with Native neighbors a practical necessity. Penn also inspired confidence among Native peoples by traveling among them unarmed and without bodyguards.

In 1682, Penn met with the chiefs of the Delaware nation and signed a Great Treaty at the village of Shackamaxon, near the present-day Kensington district of Philadelphia, that pledged long-lasting goodwill between the Native Americans and the immigrating Europeans. Philadelphia quickly grew into an urban area of almost 20,000 people, for a time the largest city in the British colonies. The city retained its reputation as a beacon of freedom for many decades, during which time Benjamin Franklin, for one, moved there from Puritan Boston.

The negotiation of a treaty with the Leni Lenápes also affirmed Penn's claim to the land for his investors, who would have been much less interested in a venture lacking clear title. The treaty also implied diplomatic relations with the powerful Haudenosaunee (Iroquois) Confederacy, with whom the Lenápe were subsidiary allies. Therefore, a chain of friendship (later called the Covenant Chain in frontier diplomacy) was engaged by Penn, although his less scrupulous successors disregarded its provisions in their rush to acquire land. The treaty invoked the rights of both parties to share some areas that European-Americans subsequently took for themselves.

Throughout his tenure as chief executive of Pennsylvania, Penn maintained peaceful relations with the area's indigenous peoples, including the Susquehannocks and Shawnees, as well as the Leni Lenápe. His abilities as a sprinter—he could outrun many Natives—won him respect. He also learned local Native languages well enough to conduct negotiations without interpreters. From the very beginning, Penn acquired Native land through peaceful, voluntary exchange.

Penn was a shrewd businessman who competed with Lord Baltimore, founder of Maryland, for territorial rights. Using his friendly relations with Native peoples, Penn outmaneuvered Maryland agents, a fact that is evident today to anyone who compares the relative sizes of Pennsylvania and Maryland. Most notably, Penn bested Baltimore at acquiring trading rights with the Haudenosaunee Confederacy. Thus, when Benjamin Franklin began his diplomatic career in the early 1750s as Pennsylvania envoy to the Iroquois, he was filling a role first explored by Penn.

By 1701 Penn had returned to England for the rest of his life. He tried from a distance to administer his declining estate, until he experienced a debilitating stroke in 1712. Four months later, he suffered a second stroke. After that, Penn experienced difficulty speaking and writing until he died on July 30, 1718.

Bruce E. Johansen

See also Democracy and Native American Images among Europeans; Handsome Lake.

References and Further Reading

Dunn, Richard S., and Mary M., eds. 1981–1987. *The Papers of William Penn*. Philadelphia: University of Pennsylvania Press.

Dunn, Richard S., and Mary M., eds. 1986. *The World of William Penn*. Philadelphia: University of Pennsylvania Press.

Lutz, Norma Jean. 2000. *William Penn: Founder of Democracy*. New York: Chelsea House Publishers.

Powell, Jim. No date. "The Freeman: Ideas on Liberty. William Penn, America's First Great Champion for Liberty and Peace. Available at: http://www.quaker.org/wmpenn.html. Accessed January 20, 2007.

Watson, John F. 1857. *Annals of Philadelphia and Pennsylvania in the Olden Time*. Philadelphia: E. Thomas.

Plenty Coups

Plenty Coups (1848–1932), whose Crow name (Aleek-chea-ahoosh) meant "Many Achievements," was the principal chief of the Crows during the late stages of the Plains wars. He spearheaded the Crow strategy to cooperate with the U.S. Army in its pursuit of the Cheyennes, Sioux, Arapahoes, and other "hostiles" following the Battle of the Little Bighorn (1876). Plenty Coups' Crows provided scouts for George Armstrong Custer before his loss at the Little Bighorn and mourned his death.

Plenty Coups was groomed for chieftainship from an early age, and he was paid uncommon attention as a child by the Crows. When he was nine years of age, one of his brothers was killed by the Sioux, provoking a lifelong enmity. The Sioux had earlier pushed the Crows westward into the Little Bighorn country from the Black Hills area. Their new homeland was located in the midst of one of the last surviving large buffalo runs on the Plains, and it became a site of competition between the Crows and their traditional enemies.

At a young age, Plenty Coups was beset by harrowing dreams in which the buffalo disappeared from the Plains and white men's cattle replaced them. He told the dreams to the Crows' spiritual leaders, who concluded that the Crows would suffer less if they cooperated with the invaders. Plenty Coups had a healthy appetite for battle and joined the warriors of the Crow by taking his first scalp (and capturing two horses) at age fifteen. Nevertheless, he hearkened to the spiritual advisors' words and determined to cooperate with the invaders.

Following Plenty Coups' vision, 135 Crow warriors volunteered to serve as scouts for General George Crook during the 1876 campaign that resulted in the deaths of Custer and 225 of his troopers at the Little Bighorn. Plenty Coups worried that Crook was not prepared for Crazy Horse's Lakotas when they met in battle June 16, 1876. He was correct; Crazy Horse routed Crook and his Indian allies in a battle that presaged Custer's Last Stand nine days later.

After the Custer battle, the Crows under Plenty Coups continued to support the U.S. Army as it drove the Cheyennes and Sioux into subjugation. Crow warriors aided in the pursuit of Sitting Bull into Canada, the defeat of the northern Cheyennes, and the surrender of Crazy Horse. Plenty Coups urged his people to become farmers and ranchers, abandoning his own teepee for a log farmhouse.

Plenty Coups was an important Crow leader during the late nineteenth and early twentieth centuries. (Library of Congress)

Plenty Coups also opened a general store so that the Crows could buy trade goods at fair prices. Plenty Coups traveled to Washington, D.C., several times after 1880 to assure trade and aid for the Crows. He was noted for his sagacity in business dealings.

Not all of the Crows supported him, however; like other Native American tribes and nations, they suffered great losses due to disease and warfare. Many young warriors also resented being confined to a reservation. Nearly 300 Crow opponents of Plenty Coups joined forces in the fall of 1887 with the young firebrand Sword Bearer, who sought to prove his acumen as a warrior by leading a horse raid on the neighboring Blackfeet. Upon his return, Sword Bearer and his companions paraded through the Crow village with their captured horses and confronted the local Indian agent, H. E. Williamson, who sent to Fort Custer for troops. Sword Bearer's group then galloped into the mountains and

spurred a rash of rumors of an alliance with the Cheyennes and Sioux that would destroy white settlements and Plenty Coups' "good Indians." Plenty Coups later persuaded Sword Bearer to lay down his arms.

While Plenty Coups was a longtime ally of the non-Natives, he was often critical of their character. He said that, while the Crows agreed to be friendly with them, they found that the non-Natives too often promised to do one thing and then, when they acted at all, did another: "They spoke very loudly when they said their laws were made for everybody; but we soon learned that although they expected the Crows to keep them, they thought nothing of breaking them themselves" (Johansen and Grinde, 1997, 293). During World War I, Plenty Coups encouraged young Crow men to leave the enforced idleness and alcoholism of the reservation and join the U.S. Army. After the war, in 1921, he was chosen to represent all American Indians at the dedication of the Tomb of the Unknown Soldier, in Arlington, Virginia. In 1928, his health failing, Plenty Coups willed his personal real estate, including about 200 acres of land, to the U.S. government for the future use of the Crow people. Plenty Coups died on March 3, 1932. The Crow council so revered him that its members refused to name another principal chief in his place.

Bruce E. Johansen

See also Crow; Battle of the Little Bighorn; Reservation Economic and Social Conditions.

References and Further Reading

Hamilton, Charles. 1972. *Cry of the Thunderbird.* Norman: University of Oklahoma Press.

Johansen, Bruce E., and Donald A. Grinde, Jr. 1997. *The Encyclopedia of Native American Biography.* New York: Henry Holt.

Linderman, Frank B. 1962. *Plenty-Coups: Chief of the Crows.* Lincoln: University of Nebraska Press.

Wagner, Glendolin Damon. [1933] 1987. *Blankets and Moccasins: Plenty Coups and his People, the Crows.* Lincoln: University of Nebraska Press.

Pocahontas

Pocahontas (Powhatan, ca. 1595–1617) was the favorite daughter of Powhatan (ca. 1547–1618), the paramount chief of the Powhatan Confederacy when the first English colonists arrived at Jamestown in 1607. In actuality, Pocahontas (also Pokahantes or Pokahantesu, meaning "the playful one" or "the spoiled child") was the nickname of a girl named Matoaka. Later, she was baptized with the name of Rebecca.

Powhatan's name among his own people was Wahunsonacock. He was a remarkable figure who probably had assembled most of the Powhatan Confederacy during his tenure as leader of one of its bands. The tidewater confederacy included about 200 villages organized into several small nation-states when the English encountered it for the first time. Wahunsonacock was about sixty years of age when Jamestown was founded in 1607. He and other Native people in the area may have met with other Europeans before the Jamestown colonists. The Spanish had established a mission on the York River in 1570 that was destroyed by indigenous warriors. Gangs of pirates also occasionally sought shelter along the Carolina outer banks as they waited for the passage of Spanish galleons flush with booty from Mexico, Mesoamerica, and Peru.

In the beginning, as Wahunsonacock sought peace with the English, the colonists were in no demographic position to compete with the Natives. Within the first few years after Jamestown was founded, the peoples of the Powhatan Confederacy could have eradicated the English settlement with ease. Jamestown, in fact, would not have survived in its early years without their help. Of 900 colonists who landed during the first three years (1607–1610), only 150 were alive in 1610. Most of the colonists were not ready for the rugged life of founding a colony; many died of disease, exposure to unanticipated cold weather, and starvation. At one point within a year of their landfall in America, the Jamestown colonists became so hungry that some of them engaged in cannibalism. According to John Smith's journals, one colonist killed his wife, "powdered" (salted) her, "and had eaten part of her before it was known; for which he was executed, as he well deserved" (Page, 2003, 159).

As her prominent father's daughter, Pocahontas enjoyed considerable power, even as a young woman. For instance, although the incident is shrouded in ambiguity, Pocahontas allegedly saved the life of Jamestown's Captain John Smith in 1608, when she was thirteen years old. As the leader of the Jamestown settlement, Smith had been taken captive by Pocahontas's uncle, Opechancanough. Just before Chief Powhatan was to behead Smith (so the story goes), Pocahontas intervened on Smith's behalf. Smith, in an account of the incident published later, never mentioned Pocahontas's intervention, however, so the whole story may have been invented.

Young Pocahontas was said to have saved the life of Captain John Smith in the mythical version of an event that has many historical interpretations. (Library of Congress)

When Smith departed for England the next year, Indian–white relations deteriorated. Pocahontas was coaxed onto an English ship on the Potomac in 1612 and then taken as a hostage to Jamestown to bargain for the release of Virginia captives held by the Powhatans. During her detention at Jamestown, she became a convert to Christianity. At this time, John Rolfe also courted Pocahantas. With her father's consent, she married Rolfe in April of 1613. The union facilitated a period of peaceful relations between the Powhatans and the English immigrants.

In 1616, Pocahontas and Rolfe journeyed to Great Britain with Sir Thomas Dale and several Indians. In England, she was received as the daughter of an emperor. King James I and Queen Anne met Pocahontas at court, and her portrait was painted. While at Gravesend, England, en route for return to Virginia in 1617, Pocahontas died of a European disease (perhaps smallpox) while waiting to board a ship. She was buried in the yard of St. George's Parish Church at Gravesend; memorials were built to her there, as well as in Jamestown. Powhatan, her father, passed away the next year. In 1622, Opechancanough, her uncle, made war with the colonists, and Rolfe was killed in that conflict.

Pocahontas's son, Thomas Rolfe, Jr., was educated in London and then returned to North America in 1641, where he became a successful entrepreneur. As a result of tensions between the European immigrants and American Indians, the younger Rolfe had to plead with Virginia authorities to allow him to visit his Indian relatives. To this day, several Virginia families proudly trace their ancestry to the Rolfe family and thus to Pocahontas.

Bruce E. Johansen

See also Powhatan.
References and Further Reading
Page, Jake. 2003. *In the Hands of the Great Spirit: The 20,000 Year History of the American Indian.* New York: Free Press.
Tilton, Robert S. 1994. *Pocahontas: The Evolution of an American Narrative.* Cambridge, UK: Cambridge University Press.

Pontiac

Frank Waters characterized Pontiac (Ponteach, Ottawa, ca. 1720–1769) as "a man of steel pounded between a British hammer and a French anvil" (Waters, 1992, 35). Pontiac, after whom General Motors named an automobile model, tried to erect a Native confederacy to block Euro-American immigration into the Old Northwest.

Pontiac was a man of medium build and dark complexion who highly valued personal fidelity. If Pontiac owed a debt, he would scratch a promissory note on birch bark with his sign, the otter. The notes were always redeemed. He was an early ally of the French in 1755 at Fort Duquesne, now the site of Pittsburgh, along with an alliance of Ottawas, Ojibwas, Hurons, and Delawares. Pontiac played a major role in the French defeat of English General Edward Braddock in 1755, during the opening battles of what came to be known as the French and Indian War in America.

Pontiac was probably born along the Maumee River in present-day northern Ohio of an Ottawa father and a Chippewa mother. He married Kantuckeegan and had two sons, Otussa and Shegenaba. Pontiac held no hereditary chieftainship among the Ottawas, but by about 1760 his oratorical skills and

Ottawa chief Pontiac passes a pipe to Major Robert Rogers in 1760. Pontiac let Rogers and his forces pass through Indian territory unmolested during the French and Indian War. (Library of Congress)

reputed courage as a warrior had raised him to leadership. By 1763, Pontiac also had formed military alliances with eighteen other Native peoples from the Mississippi River to Lake Ontario.

After the British defeat of the French in 1763, Pontiac found himself faced on the southern shore of Lake Erie with an English force that included Robert Rogers' legendary Rangers, who were self-trained as forest warriors. Rogers told Pontiac that the land he occupied was now British, having been ceded by France, and that his force was talking possession of French forts. Pontiac said that, while the French might have surrendered, his people had not. After four days of negotiations, Rogers agreed with Pontiac's point of view. Rogers was allowed to continue to the former French fort on the present-day site of Detroit, and power was transferred as hundreds of Indians watched. Rogers and Pontiac became friends.

Pontiac now looked forward to peaceful trading with the British, but, when Rogers left the area, fur traders began swindling the Indians, getting them addicted to cheap liquor. Pontiac sent a belt of red wampum, signifying the taking up of arms, as far east as the Iroquois Confederacy, then southward along the Mississippi. He appealed for allies, telling the assembled chiefs of each nation he visited that if they did not unify and resist colonization, the English would flood them, like waves of an endless sea.

By the spring of 1763, a general uprising was being planned by combined forces of the Ottawas, Hurons, Delawares, Senecas, and Shawnees. On May 9, each group was to attack the nearest English fort. Pontiac's plan was betrayed to the commander of the British fort at Detroit by an Ojibwa woman, known as Catherine among the English, with whom he had made love. Pontiac laid siege to the fort at Detroit, and other members of the alliance carried out their respective roles, but an appeal for the support of the French fell on deaf ears. After a siege that lasted through the winter and into the spring of 1764, the fort received outside reinforcements, tipping the balance against Pontiac after fifteen months.

After the rebellion, European-American immigrants moved into the Ohio Valley in increasing numbers, and the prestige of the aging Pontiac leader began to decline among his former allies. Pontiac now counseled peace. The younger warriors were said to have "shamed" him and possibly beat him in their frustration. With a small band of family and friends, Pontiac was forced to leave his home village and move to Illinois.

On April 20, 1769, Pontiac was murdered in Cahokia, Illinois. According to one account, he was stabbed by a Peoria Indian who may have been bribed with a barrel of whiskey by an English trader named Williamson.

Bruce E. Johansen

See also Cahokia; Fur Trade; Wampum.

References and Further Reading

Blackbird, Andrew J. 1897. *History of the Ottawa and the Chippewa Indians of Michigan.* Ypsilanti, MI. Harbor Springs, MI: Babcock and Darling.

Hays, Wilma P. 1965. *Pontiac: Lion in the Forest.* Boston: Houghton-Mifflin.

Parkman, Francis. 1868. *History of the Conspiracy of Pontiac.* Boston: Little, Brown & Company..

Peckham, Howard H. 1947. *Pontiac and the Indian Uprising.* Chicago: University of Chicago Press.

Rogers, Robert. 1765. *A Concise Account of North America.* London.

Waters, Frank. 1992. *Brave Are My People.* Santa Fe, NM: Clear Light Publishers.

Powhatan

Wahunsonacock, better known to the early Virginia colonists as Powhatan (ca. 1547–1618), was the principal chief of a federation usually called the Powhatan Confederacy. He also was the father of Pocahontas.

The name "Powhatan" (meaning "falling waters") was taken from one of his favorite dwelling places, the falls of the James River near present-day Richmond. Powhatan was probably born during the 1540s. He inherited control over six small tribes in Virginia (most likely from his mother) and systematically added other tribes to his dominion through warfare and intimidation until he was the chief of an estimated thirty tribal groups united in what has become known as the Powhatan Confederacy. In total, he was the leader of more than 14,000 people and oversaw an estimated 8,500 square miles of land.

In spite of Powhatan's control over the Tidewater Virginia region, other hostile Native American tribes frequently came into conflict with his people. A series of Indian wars in the sixteenth century compelled Powhatan to maintain a strong warrior class, composed of an estimated 3,000 men. The Native Americans in Virginia were therefore a warring soci-

Powhatan, also known as Wahunsonacock, was the principal chief of the Powhatan Confederacy in Virginia during the late sixteenth and early seventeenth centuries. (Library of Congress)

ety and constantly fighting to either defend or expand their hunting grounds against other tribes in the area.

By the late sixteenth century, Powhatan had heard about white men who occasionally appeared in North America. In fact, it is possible that a contingent of his warriors killed the last of the Roanoke settlers sometime in the early seventeenth century. Powhatan was wary of Europeans but viewed them as possible allies in his struggles against other Native American tribes in the region.

About sixty years of age when Jamestown was founded, Powhatan initially greeted the English colonists with a degree of cordiality. Captain John Smith described him as a man of dignified bearing. As relations between the two peoples deteriorated, Powhatan developed a harsher attitude toward the newcomers. Nevertheless, for the first few years of the Jamestown settlement, colonists relied heavily on Powhatan and his people for food.

There were periodic outbreaks of violence between the two groups, but in general Powhatan managed to maintain peace, and no major wars between the Indians and the settlers erupted during his lifetime. Most devastating to the Powhatans, however, were the diseases that the immigrants brought with them from Europe, particularly smallpox, which nearly obliterated the Indian population. After Powhatan's death from smallpox in 1618, he was succeeded as chief of the Powhatan Confederacy by his half brother, Opechancanough, who was more aggressive when dealing with the Jamestown colonists.

Bruce E. Johansen

See also Pocahontas.
References and Further Reading
Hodge, Frederick Webb, ed. 1910. *Handbook of American Indians.* Bureau of American Ethnology Bulletin 30. Washington, DC: Smithsonian Institution.
Rountree, Helen C. 1990. *Pocahontas's People: The Powhatan Indians of Virginia Through Four Centuries.* Norman: University of Oklahoma Press.

Red Cloud

Red Cloud, whose Oglala name Makhpiya-luta literally means "Scarlet Cloud," was a major leader of the Oglala Lakota during the late phases of the Plains Indian wars. His name refers to an unusual formation of crimson clouds that hovered over the western horizon as he was born. At one point, during the 1860s, Red Cloud and his allies forced the United States to concede considerable territory in and around the Black Hills. The Sioux reservation at that time was defined in the Fort Laramie Treaty of 1868.

When he was born, about 1820, the world of Red Cloud's people was largely independent of non-Native immigrants. When he died, in 1909, his people had been pushed onto a tiny fraction of their former land and imprisoned in a concentration camp. Born into the heyday of the Plains horse culture, Red Cloud died in the era of the "vanishing race."

As a young man, Red Cloud learned like most other Sioux boys to fight and hunt. Very quickly, he proved himself adept at both. Red Cloud was especially known as a fierce warrior who was always

Red Cloud, an Oglala Lakota leader, with William Blackmore.
(National Archives and Records Administration)

ready to take an enemy's scalp. He had five children and possibly as many as six wives.

In 1865, Red Cloud and his allies refused to sign a treaty permitting the passage of immigrants across their lands from Fort Laramie, along the Powder River, to the gold fields of Montana. Red Cloud was angered by the rapid and ruthless encroachment of non-Natives on the lands of his people. In the first Fort Laramie Treaty (1851), the United States had promised to "protect the aforesaid Indian nations against the commission of all depredations by the people of the said United States." However, while non-Natives were swarming onto the northern Plains and committing depredations and treaty violations, the energies of the U.S. Army were being directed not toward protecting the Indians but toward fighting the Civil War.

Following the war, the Army turned its attention to protecting not the Indians, according to the treaty obligation, but the invading non-Natives. In

December 1866, Captain William J. Fetterman bragged that he could ride with eighty men across the whole of Sioux country. He set out with eighty-one men and high ambitions, only to be led into a deadly ambush by Crazy Horse and a dozen warriors, who killed all of them. Still, at this time the Sioux dominated the northern Plains. When U.S. Army troops built forts without the Indians' permission, war parties cut off food supplies to Fort Phil Kearney in northern Wyoming and laid siege to the outpost for two years. In 1868, with the wagon road still closed, the government signed a treaty at Fort Laramie that caused the forts to be dismantled. According to the 1868 Fort Laramie Treaty, the Powder River country and the Black Hills were reserved for the Lakotas forever.

Red Cloud advised trading with whites but otherwise avoiding them. His valor as a warrior was legendary. He had counted more than eighty coups (strikes against an enemy), and once returned from battle against a contingent of Crows with an arrow through his body. In the late 1860s, Red Cloud was about forty-five years old. Once a trader at Wolf Point asked him why he continued to pursue the diminishing herds of buffalo rather than settle on a reservation. "Because I am a red man," he said. "If the Great Spirit had desired me to be a white man, he would have made me so in the first place. He put in your heart certain wishes and plans, in my heart he put other and different desires. Each man is good in his sight. It is not necessary for eagles to be crows. Now we are poor but we are free. No white man controls our footsteps. If we must die, we die defending our rights" (Johansen and Grinde, 1997, 313).

Despite the best efforts of Red Cloud and other patriots, however, by the mid-1870s, most Plains Indians knew they could not persevere against the invaders. As the Plains wars ended, Red Cloud settled at Red Cloud Agency, Nebraska. He counseled peace and was even accused of "selling out" by some younger Oglalas. He later was moved to the Great Sioux Reservation where, in 1881, Indian Agent V. T. McGillycuddy stripped Red Cloud of his chieftainship.

During the 1870s and 1880s, Red Cloud fought the Army's regulations and opposed the reservation system, but at the same time he provided aid to Yale Professor Othniel C. March, who was searching the area for dinosaur bones. In exchange, March said he would take Sioux allegations of mistreatment "to the highest levels" of government (Milner, 1990, 387).

March investigated Red Cloud's complaints of rotten food and unmet promises. The Yale professor uncovered massive profiteering by Indian Rings in the Grant administration, sparking a congressional investigation and several newspaper exposés. At one point, March confronted Grant personally. March and Red Cloud became friends for the rest of their lives. Red Cloud said that he appreciated the fact that March did not forget his promise after he got what he wanted.

Red Cloud's biographer George E. Hyde characterized him in old age as "wrinkled, stooped, and almost blind" (Hyde, 1967, 336). Red Cloud was sometimes given to ironic bitterness over what had become of him and his people: "I, who used to control 5,000 warriors, must tell Washington when I am hungry. I must beg for that which I own" (Hyde, 1967, 336). Red Cloud spent his final years in retirement, having little to do with his people's affairs. He died on December 10, 1909.

Bruce E. Johansen

See also Treaty of Fort Laramie (1851); Fort Laramie Treaty (1868).

References and Further Reading
Armstrong, Virginia Irving. 1971. *I Have Spoken: American History Through the Voices of the Indians*. Chicago: Swallow Press.
Brininstool, E. A. 1953. *Fighting Indian Warriors*. New York: Bonanza Books.
Hyde, George E. 1967. *Red Cloud's Folk: A History of the Oglala Sioux Indians*. Norman: University of Oklahoma Press.
Johansen, Bruce E., and Donald A. Grinde, Jr. 1997. *The Encyclopedia of Native American Biography*. New York: Henry Holt.
Milner, Richard. 1990. "Red Cloud." In *The Encyclopedia of Evolution*, 387–388. New York: Henry Holt.
Olson, James C. 1965. *Red Cloud and the Sioux Problem*. Lincoln: University of Nebraska Press.
Powers, William K. 1969. *Indians of the Northern Plains*. New York: Putnam.

Red Jacket

Red Jacket (ca. 1758–1830) considered himself, first and foremost, an orator. An avowed traditionalist, he is most famous for his speeches denouncing the presence of Christian missionaries on the reservations and for opposing the sale of Indian lands. Never actually appointed a sachem, he nonetheless became a very influential Seneca chief. Although he was sometimes accused of cowardice, demagoguery, and alcoholism, Red Jacket's speeches are among the most compelling explanations of aboriginal sovereignty in U.S. history. In addition to his significance as a political figure in the early national period, Red Jacket became popular because he was an extraordinarily dynamic speaker. His speeches, of which dozens are extant, are notable for their sarcasm and disarming humor.

Red Jacket's birth name was Otetiani ("Always Ready"). According to Arthur C. Parker, he was born to a Seneca mother of the Wolf Clan named Ahweyneyonh ("Drooping Flower" or "Blue Flower"). His father was Thadahwahnyeh, a Cayuga of the Turtle Clan. There are a number of rival stories about the date and location of his birth, but Christopher Densmore argues that he was probably born in 1758 on the west side of Lake Cayuga, near either Geneva or Canoga. He was drawn to public speaking at a young age and was rumored to practice the art by himself in the woods, although this story seems fanciful.

Red Jacket served as a message runner for the British during the Revolutionary War. For this work, he was awarded a red jacket, from which his English name derived. Later in life, he was as well-known as Red Jacket as by his Seneca name, with his Christian children taking the last name of Jacket. Shortly after the war, Red Jacket was recognized by the Senecas for his verbal skills, appointed as a minor chief, and renamed Sagoywatha (roughly pronounced, Shay-go-ye-watha), which has been variously translated as "disturber of dreams," "keeper awake," or "he keeps them awake." In the early years of his political work among the Seneca, he served to convene councils with condolence speeches. He also served as speaker for the clan mothers, charged with conveying their deliberations to the councils of sachems and warriors.

Although distinguished for his verbal abilities during the Revolution, he also earned a reputation for cowardice that followed him for many years afterward. Cornplanter, an influential Seneca warrior, claimed that Red Jacket fled from the Battle of Newtown. Joseph Brant was fond of retelling a story that Red Jacket and a friend smeared themselves with the blood of a slaughtered cow to claim that they had been in battle. As a result, Brant called him Cowkiller, an unflattering name by which he was designated in most British council records of the 1790s and early 1800s. Fighting on the American side during the War of 1812, however, Red Jacket

Although Red Jacket fought against the United States during the American Revolution, he became a steadfast ally in the War of 1812. (Library of Congress)

redeemed his martial reputation by fighting with distinction at the Battle of Chippewa.

Several diplomatic triumphs in the 1790s significantly raised Red Jacket's stature. He was an active participant at the U.S.–Haudenosaunee (Six Nations, or Iroquois) councils of Tioga Point and Newtown in 1790 and 1791. He served as a leading spokesman for a Seneca deputation that met George Washington in Philadelphia in 1792. While in Philadelphia, Red Jacket (among other chiefs) was given a large chest medal by the president, which he wore proudly for the rest of his life. Most importantly, he was a principal negotiator at the 1794 Treaty of Canandaigua, where the Seneca secured nearly four million acres of land in perpetuity. The terms of this treaty have served as the basis for a series of successful Haudenosaunee land claims in New York State since the 1970s.

In 1797, Red Jacket attended the Treaty of Big Tree, where the Senecas sold much of the land guaranteed to them by the Treaty of Canandaigua. At this famous council, Red Jacket spoke on behalf of the sachems to oppose the sale, but, once the warriors and clan mothers overruled the sachems, Red Jacket successfully argued to double the proposed size of the Buffalo Creek Reservation. Because of this apparent change in position, the historian William Leete Stone charged him with duplicitous conduct. The allegation was supported by his Indian political rivals, such as Joseph Brant, but it has little substance to it.

Red Jacket's most famous speech, a reply to the Reverend Jacob Cram in 1805, was one of several speeches he gave in the early 1800s that explained why the Indians did not want Christian missionaries in their midst. The speech is noteworthy for his condensed history of white–Native relations and his objection to Cram's attempt to "force your religion upon us." Although the level of sarcasm is difficult to gauge, Red Jacket told Cram that the Senecas might ask him back only if they saw that Christianity could soften the habits of the white frontiersman living on their borders. The speech's authenticity has been a topic of debate, but Red Jacket gave many such speeches on the topic over the decade (Densmore, 1999; Robie, 1986). Furthermore, Red Jacket had become a minor celebrity on this issue. He often took pride in the publication of his speeches, and he saw to it that they were properly translated.

In addition to his reply to Cram, other famous performances include his May 1811 replies to the Ogden Land Company agent, John Richardson, and the missionary, John Alexander. These speeches contain very clear examples of Red Jacket's acerbic wit. After rejecting Alexander's overtures, Red Jacket concluded with the gentle request that the missionary forbear his generous offers, "lest our heads should be too much loaded, and by and by burst" (Stone, 1841, 204).

By the end of the War of 1812, the Senecas lived on ten reservations totaling about 200,000 acres. They were beset by land companies externally and Christianity internally.

By 1819, two leading Seneca chiefs, Young King and Captain Pollard, had become Christian. After the conversion of his grandson, Red Jacket allied with the so-called Pagan party, and he began to stridently condemn the encroachment of missionaries and land companies. Every year, he and other traditionalist chiefs lobbied the governor and legislature

to support Seneca self-determination. He succeeded in obliging the state to pass a law that prohibited missionaries living on Native lands from 1821 to 1824.

Red Jacket spent the 1820s denouncing the corrupt practices of the Ogden Land Company agents who succeeded in buying large portions of Seneca lands in August 1826. Red Jacket traveled to Washington to overturn the sale but he was unable to do so. At the same time, Secretary of Indian Affairs Thomas McKenney convinced the Christian chiefs to depose Red Jacket as a troublemaker, which they did in 1827. A year later, having proved corruption during the federal inquiry into the sale, Red Jacket was reinstated as a chief in July of 1828. Even though Red Jacket's protests were successful in preventing federal ratification of the Ogden sale of 1826, the lands were not returned. (Shortly afterward, the land sale of 1838 rendered it a moot issue.) Exhausted by his political efforts, pinched for money, and trying to make peace with his Christian wife, Red Jacket went on a commercial speaking tour the following year, traveling in museum shows from Boston to New York. He died of cholera on January 20, 1830.

There are four principal biographies of Red Jacket. The first, by William Leete Stone, was published in 1841. It contains a wealth of primary and anecdotal information because Stone was able to interview and correspond with many people who knew Red Jacket personally. More importantly, Stone reprinted as many of Red Jacket's speeches as he could obtain, thinking that future generations of historians would benefit more from the original documents than from historians' glosses of them. Stone's transcripts compare very accurately with extant manuscripts. Stone occasionally changes a preposition or inserts a period for clarity, but he did not dress up the vocabulary. The translations Stone used were principally those of Jasper Parrish, a federal Indian agent who was captured as a child by the Senecas and who spoke both Mohawk and Seneca fluently. The only major weakness of Stone's biography is that he accepted the opinions of Red Jacket's lifelong opponents, namely Thomas Morris, Joseph Brant, and Thomas McKenney, all of whom were invested in protecting their own reputations.

Niles Hubbard's 1886 biography largely reprints Stone's material without Stone's biases. Arthur C. Parker's 1952 biography is important for its sources in Seneca oral tradition, but it seems to have been intended as a children's book, not an academic history. The best recent biography is Christo-

pher Densmore's, which avoids the demonization and hagiography of the earlier works and which puts dates and places to many of the events Stone did not document.

Granville Ganter

See also Canandaigua (Pickering) Treaty; Cornplanter; Haudenosaunee Confederacy, Political System; Parker, Arthur C.

References and Further Reading

Blacksnake, Governor. "Narrative." "Notes of Border History." Lyman C. Draper Collection of Indian Artifacts. Microfilm. Reel 47, vol. 4: 13–82.

Densmore, Christopher. 1987. "More on Red Jacket's Reply." *New York Folklore* 13, no. 3–4: 121–122.

Densmore, Christopher. 1999. *Red Jacket: Iroquois Diplomat and Orator.* Syracuse, NY: Syracuse University Press.

Ganter, Granville. 2000. " 'You Are a Cunning People Without Sincerity': Sagoyewatha and the Trials of Community Representation." In *Speakers of the Northeastern Woodlands.* Edited by Barbara Mann, 165–195. Westport, CT: Greenwood Press.

Hubbard, Niles J. 1886. *An Account of Sa-Go-Ye-Wat-Ha, or Red Jacket and His People.* Albany: Joel Munsell's Sons.

Parker, Arthur C. 1943. "The Unknown Mother of Red Jacket." *New York History* 24, no. 4 (October): 525–533.

Parker, Arthur C. [1952] 1998. *Red Jacket: Last of the Seneca.* Lincoln: University of Nebraska Press.

Robie, Harry. 1986. "Red Jacket's Reply: Problems in the Verification of a Native American Speech Text." *New York Folklore* 12, no. 3–4: 99–117.

Stone, William Leete. 1841. *The Life and Times of Sa-Go-Ye-Wat-Ha, or Red-Jacket.* New York: Wiley and Putnam.

Riel, Louis

More than a century after his execution, Louis Riel (Métis) remains perhaps the most controversial figure in Canadian history. Considered a traitor by some and a hero by others, Riel twice attempted to establish independent provinces in an effort to secure the rights of Native and Métis peoples in the Canadian west. Something of a mystic, Riel led two rebellions against the Canadian government, fifteen years apart, in 1869–1870 and again in 1885.

The son of a Fort Garry (present-day Winnipeg) miller, Riel's father, also named Louis, led the successful Courthouse Rebellion in 1849. The younger Riel attended college in Montreal and returned west

Louis Riel, Métis chieftain and leader of the Northwest Rebellion. (Corbis)

in 1869. Canada had become a confederation in 1867, and the newly established federal government wished to establish its control over the western territories as quickly as possible, beginning with present-day Manitoba. In 1869, the government began surveying lands along the Red River and dividing them into 800-acre square townships, ignoring Métis land-use patterns that were based on the older French system of dividing land into narrow strips, beginning at the waterfront, stretching back through individual fields, and terminating in a common pasture known as the "hay privilege."

Many of the first government allotments were given to the Canada Firsters, Protestant Orangemen from Ontario who detested Catholicism, the French language, and Native peoples. Expecting resistance from the Métis, a party of Canada Firsters seized a small post near Fort Garry but surrendered when Riel arrived with a larger and better armed force. Riel formed a governing body for Manitoba, the Comite National des Métis and became its president.

Unwilling to launch an invasion of the western territories, the Canadian government chose to negotiate with the Métis. At this point Riel made his first miscalculation.

The Métis released most of their Canadian prisoners, but one of them, Thomas Scott, became embroiled in a confrontation with Riel. Tried by Riel and the Comite National des Métis for bearing arms against the state, Scott was executed in 1870, a move that turned public opinion against the Métis. In response, the Canadian government sent a force to Manitoba to arrest Riel, who fled for his life. Over the next few years, other members of the jury that had convicted Scott were murdered, while Louis Riel disappeared. However, the Métis elected him to three terms in the Canadian Parliament in absentia.

As Protestant Canadians began moving into Manitoba, Métis peoples moved farther west, settling along the Saskatchewan River. By the 1880s, the Métis, Cree, and other Native peoples recognized that the northern plains were undergoing a dramatic transformation. Violence increased as American whisky traders sold their goods. Bison herds shrank drastically due to overhunting by American and Canadian hide hunters. Canadian government surveyors appeared in Saskatchewan, and, just as they had done fifteen years earlier in Manitoba, they began laying out new square townships.

The most dramatic change, however, was the building of the Canadian Pacific Railroad (CPR), which increased the white presence on the Canadian plains. Worried about retaining their lands and way of life, the Métis decided to organize an opposition to the government under Louis Riel. There was just one problem: No one knew where Riel was. A small party of Métis were assigned the task of finding Louis Riel, and they found him quietly teaching Native children in Montana, where he had married and was raising a family. He agreed to return to Canada to organize a Métis government.

Riel quickly organized the Provisional Government of Saskatchewan, authored a Métis bill of rights, and put together a 400-man strong army. Riel's initial campaigns against the government attempted to avoid bloodshed. The Métis seized government stores, cut communications, and interfered with the building of the CPR. However, the Métis got into a shooting battle with a force of Mounties at Duck Lake, Saskatchewan. This encounter had two immediate results. First, it persuaded some Crees (but not most) to join Riel. It also prompted the Canadian government to organize a

large military expedition to crush the Métis. The troops were shipped west, traveling part of the way on the not yet completed CPR. The Métis were defeated at Batoche, and, after hiding in the woods for a few days, Riel surrendered to government troops.

Riel was tried in Reigna, charged with the murder of Thomas Scott some fifteen years before. Despite questions concerning his fitness to stand trial and calls for mercy from French Catholics, he was hanged in November 1885.

Roger M. Carpenter

See also Métis Nation Accord.

References and Further Reading

Beal, Bob, and Rod MacLeod. 1984. *Prairie Fire: The Northwest Rebellion of 1885*. Edmonton: Hurtig Publishers.

Ens, Gerhard J. 1996. *Homeland to Hinterland: The Changing Worlds of the Red River Métis in the Nineteenth Century*. Toronto, ON: University of Toronto Press.

Flanagan, Thomas. 2000. *Riel and the Rebellion: 1885 Reconsidered*. Toronto, ON: University of Toronto Press

Rogers, Will

Born in 1879 to a Cherokee ranching family in Oologah, Indian Territory (now Oklahoma), Will Rogers, an enrolled member of the Cherokee Nation, became an internationally known vaudevillian, actor, writer, orator, and humanitarian before his death in an airplane crash in 1935. He was extraordinarily well-known during the 1920s and 1930s—some suggest the most well-known celebrity of his day—because of his multifaceted career and keen wit.

During his youth, Rogers became an adept trick roper, a line of work that would affect his life's work. He left the Territory in 1897 to work as a cowboy but came across a better opportunity, especially considering the declining role of cowboys at the turn of the century: He joined Texas Jack's Wild West Show and later the Wirth Brothers Circus as a livestock handler and trick roper, taking the stage name the Cherokee Kid. Rogers moved to vaudeville in 1904, where he added humorous, usually political, commentary to his stage performances. Rogers' act eventually offered as much (if not more) personal commentary

Will Rogers on horseback with his children, ca. 1941. (Library of Congress)

as trick roping. In 1918, Rogers joined the Ziegfeld Follies, where he was one of its few male performers. He became such a popular performer that President Woodrow Wilson attended his performances. Other presidents maintained close ties to Rogers. Calvin Coolidge invited him to stay at 1600 Pennsylvania Avenue, and Franklin Roosevelt communicated with Rogers often.

In 1922, Rogers began writing a weekly column for McNaught Syndicate. These were the most widely read columns in the country in the late 1920s and early 1930s. Rogers' column, which discussed current politics in a palatable way, was published in 600 newspapers across the country, from the *New York Times* to the *Tulsa Daily World*, and read by 40 million people. Rogers consistently defined himself as an American Indian in his writings and occasionally offered biting commentary about the sordid ties between his tribe and the U.S. government. His fans became so enthusiastic that he was considered a possible Democratic candidate for president of the United States in 1924, 1928, and 1932.

In addition to his stage and journalistic careers, Rogers spent the late 1920s mastering two new technologies that ignited a technological revolution: radio and film. His film celebrity—he starred or appeared in seventy-one films—exceeded that of Clark Gable, Shirley Temple, and Mae West by 1934. And his radio shows were listened to by millions.

Rogers traveled extensively from the latter part of the 1920s until the end of his life. In 1926, he traveled Europe on an assignment to write a series of articles entitled "Letters of a Self-Made Diplomat to His President" for the *Saturday Evening Post*. In 1927 he visited Russia and Mexico; in 1931 he toured Central America for the benefit of Managua's earthquake victims (he donated $5,000 of his own money to the relief effort); and in 1932 he explored Asia, dining with the emperor of Manchuria and sipping tea with Japan's minister of war. Finally, in 1934 Rogers and his family—comprised of his wife Betty and his three children, Bill, Mary, and Jim—toured the world.

These trips were all made with the assistance of emerging air technology, which Rogers supported wholeheartedly. Rogers befriended many early aviators, including Charles Lindbergh and Wiley Post. During 1935, Post and Rogers died in an airplane crash in Alaska. A tremendous outpouring of grief followed Rogers' death, and many memorials were erected in his honor, including the Shrine of the Sun in Colorado. A statue of Rogers stands in National Statuary Hall in Washington, D.C., a testament to his influence on American politics, as well as on U.S. popular culture and humor.

Amy M. Ware

See also Humor, as Value.
References and Further Reading
Justice, Daniel Heath. 2002. "Our Fires Survive the Storm: Removal and Defiance in the Cherokee Literary Tradition." Ph.D. dissertation, University of Nebraska.
Rogers, Will. 1973–1983. *The Writings of Will Rogers.* 21 volumes. Stillwater, OK: Oklahoma State University Press.
Yagoda, Ben. 1993. *Will Rogers: A Biography.* Norman: University of Oklahoma Press.

Rose, Wendy

A noted poet and anthropologist with over twelve books to her credit, Wendy Rose, of Hopi, Miwok, and European ancestry, is also a visual artist. Rose was born Bronwen Elizabeth Edwards on May 7, 1948, in Oakland, California. She grew up with her mother, brother, and stepfather in the San Francisco Bay Area. A high school dropout, she became involved in San Francisco's bohemian culture in her teens and began writing.

Rose attended Cabrillo and Contra Costa Junior Colleges and the University of California at Berkeley from 1966 to 1980, taking a master's degree in cultural anthropology at Berkeley in 1978 and completing coursework for a Ph.D. in anthropology. From 1978 to 1983, Rose taught in the Native American studies and ethnic studies programs at Berkeley, then at Fresno State University in 1983–1984. Since that time, she has served as head of the American Indian studies program at Fresno City College. She was nominated for a Pulitzer Prize in poetry in 1980.

Ranging in themes from personal and cultural identity to activism to indictments of genocidal acts, her writing has been anthologized widely. Her first volume of poetry, *Hopi Roadrunner Dancing*, was published in 1973 and contains several poems that refer to the occupation of Alcatraz Island by an intertribal group of Indians in an attempt to raise public awareness of Native issues. *Long Division: A Tribal History* (1976) and *Academic Squaw: Reports to the World from the Ivory Tower* (1977) both include poems that chronicle Rose's ongoing issues with the conflict between anthropological methods and respect for the people and cultures studied. "Academic Squaw"

is written from the perspective of a Lakota woman murdered and dismembered along with her infant in the Wounded Knee Massacre of 1890. It is preceded by an epigraph from the *Plains Indian Art Auction Catalog*, chronicling prices for the items stolen from the men, women, and children slain there. This is a common technique of Rose, and this particular poem has been often reprinted. *Lost Copper* (1980), which contains the shorter "Builder Kachina: A Home-Going Cycle" and was originally printed as a twelve-page chapbook in 1979, further explores Rose's quest for a sense of connectedness to her people and asserts an association with the earth from a personal and cultural perspective.

What Happened When the Hopi Hit New York, published in 1982, focuses on landscapes and investigates the graffiti of contemporary culture using an anthropological method. *Going to War with All My Relations* (1993) and *The Halfbreed Chronicles & Other Poems* (1985) contain many strong poems protesting injustice on the behalf of oppressed people, who include such diverse figures as Truganinny, the last full-blooded Tasmanian, a woman whose body was put on display in museums for over eighty years despite her protest at seeing her husband's remains defiled in this way prior to her death, and Julia Pastrana, a Mexican woman who was put on tour as a curiosity because of her facial deformities and a medical condition that caused excessive hair growth.

Rose's subsequent books of poetry include *Now Poof She Is Gone* (1994), *Bone Dance: New and Selected Poems, 1965–1992* (1994), and *Itch Like Crazy* (2002). Her poetry continues to explore her earlier themes as well as feminism from a Native perspective. Rose also authored a monograph entitled *Aboriginal Tattooing in California* in 1979. "Neon Scars," an autobiographical essay published in 1987 in Brian Swann and Arnold Krupat's collection, *I Tell You Now: Autobiographical Essays by Native American Writers*, recounts her personal experiences as a survivor of abuse and its impetus for her poetry. Rose has served as an editor for *American Indian Quarterly*, one of the most noted scholarly journals in the field of Native studies, and remains involved in community and academic projects.

Kimberly Roppolo

See also Katsinas; Ortiz, Simon J.
References and Further Reading
Champagne, Duane, ed. 1994. *The Native North American Almanac*. Detroit, MI: Gale Research.
Johansen, Bruce E., and Donald A. Grinde, Jr., eds. 1997. *The Encyclopedia of Native American Biography: Six Hundred Life Stories of Important People, from Powhatan to Wilma Mankiller*. New York: Henry Holt.
Malinowski, Sharon, ed. 1995. *Notable Native Americans*. Detroit, MI: Gale Research.
"Wendy Rose." *Voices from the Gaps: Women Writers of Color*. Available at: http://voices.cla.umn.edu/newsite/authors/ROSEwendy.htm. Accessed March 29, 2005.

Ross, John

John Ross (1790–1866) acted as principal chief of the Cherokee Nation from 1828 to 1866. While only one-eighth Cherokee according to blood quantum, he served his people as a dedicated and passionate public servant during a tumultuous time in Cherokee history. He led his nation through a remarkable revitalization after the majority of Cherokees were forced to move from their southeastern homeland to the Indian Territory along the devastating Trail of Tears (1838).

Ross was born in Turkey Town, Cherokee Nation, now located in Alabama. His father and grandfather were traders who married into the Cherokee Nation. He received private tutoring during his early years and became a successful young merchant and plantation owner. Like other well-off Cherokees of his day, Ross owned African slaves. By the 1830s, he was one of the Cherokee Nation's wealthiest men.

As evidenced by his early life, Ross advocated, as Cherokee leader, a particular form of assimilation—one that maintained Cherokee sovereignty and independence—as a means of preservation in the face of encroaching white pressure and influence, but he did so in the context of mainstream U.S. values, including those of Christianity. Despite the fact that he spoke little, if any, Cherokee, Ross was adamantly supported by Cherokee traditionalists because of his intense dedication to the preservation of a unified nation located in their southeastern homeland. These followers called him Tsan Usdi, or Little John, and later Cooweescoowee.

Beginning in 1816, Ross became increasingly involved and dedicated to Cherokee politics. In 1827, Ross was chosen to head the Cherokee's constitutional convention. Once ratified, this constitution became the first such written document among

Native North American tribes. The following year, Ross was elected chief of a government that challenged what remained of the Cherokees' traditional governing system.

Pressures on the Cherokees from the state of Georgia to relocate west of the Mississippi River mounted in the 1830s. Georgians began settling on Cherokee lands, and with Andrew Jackson, a well-known Indian fighter, elected to the U.S. presidency in 1828, the state had a strong sympathizer in Washington, D.C. Despite Supreme Court decisions that supported the Cherokees' right to their land, Jackson and later President Martin Van Buren would force the tribe to relocate.

Still, Ross had the support of the majority of Cherokee citizens and was fighting to keep his nation's homeland intact. However, a small group of dissenters, who considered removal to Indian Territory a promising solution to white encroachment, signed the Treaty of New Echota in 1835, ceding Cherokee land for new land to the west. Ross fought the sham treaty as best he could and then led his people along the Trail of Tears in 1838, a disastrous trip that would take the lives of at least one-quarter of the traveling population. Once these Cherokees reached those already settled in the West, they faced division and near civil war trying to create a unified government. It was not until 1846, after the revengeful executions of several treaty signers (not with Ross's direct knowledge), that the Cherokee Nation became unified once again.

From 1846 until the outbreak of the American Civil War in 1861, the Cherokees prospered under Ross's leadership. A newspaper, the *Cherokee Advocate,* was established, Cherokee education became a top priority, and the new settlers experienced general prosperity. With the outbreak of war, however, the Cherokees were once again divided, this time between Union and Confederate sympathies. This split, however, echoed that which occurred in the tribe thirty years before: New Echota Treaty signers sided with the Confederate cause. Ross and his supporters hoped the Cherokee people would remain neutral, but challengers such as Stand Watie, who raised a Cherokee regiment for service in the Confederate Army, dashed Ross's hopes of continued peace within the nation. After a victory at Wilson's Creek, Missouri, increased the Confederacy's strength in the region, Ross resigned himself and his people to an alliance with the South. Ross continued to serve as head of the Cherokee Nation and as emissary to the United States. Ross returned to the Cherokee Nation before his death in 1866.

Amy M. Ware

See also Cherokee Nation v. Georgia; Trail of Tears; Worcester v. Georgia.
References and Further Reading
Moulton, Gary E. 1978. *John Ross: Cherokee Chief.* Athens: University of Georgia Press.
Ross, John. 1984. *The Papers of Chief John Ross.* 2 volumes. Edited by Gary E. Moulton. Norman: University of Oklahoma Press.

Sacagawea or Sakakawea

Sacagawea (also Sakakawea) was the American Indian woman who served as interpreter, guide, emissary, and counselor for the Lewis and Clark expedition of 1804–1806. She assisted the group as they surveyed the continent between Fort Mandan near Bismarck, North Dakota, and Fort Clatsop near Astoria, Oregon. She and her husband, Toussaint Charbonneau, joined the exploring party on April 7, 1805, and left it on August 17, 1806, spending a period of seventeen months with the American explorers. Sacagawea, was nicknamed Janey by William Clark, has become an historic icon symbolizing the ingenuity and endurance of Native American women. Among the most engaging figures in U.S. history, her own genealogical history is claimed by at least two major Indian communities, and there is some disagreement over the spelling, pronunciation, and meaning of her name. As a historical personage her young adult life was documented, but her ensuing years remain a mystery: She died either in South Dakota in her middle twenties or in Wyoming when nearly 100 years old. The contention over her history, coupled with the unique legacy of being the only woman to participate in the Corps of Discovery, has made her larger in death than she was in life. More than a century after her death, she is one of the most well-known, studied, revered, and celebrated American women.

Sacagawea, it is asserted, was born in the late 1780s in a northern Shoshone village located near present-day Tendoy, Idaho. The people to which she would have belonged were known as the Agaidikas, or the Salmoneaters, and were the ancestors of today's Lemhi Shoshone living at Fort Hall and near Salmon, Idaho. Around 1800, when Sacagawea was about twelve or fourteen years old, she and her band

were in winter camp near the Three Forks area of the Upper Missouri River in Montana, when a hunting or warring party of the Hidatsa tribe captured and took her to the Knife River village of Metaharta near Washburn, North Dakota. In that region, she met French Canadian fur trader Toussaint Charbonneau whom the Americans later hired as an interpreter. When Lewis and Clark arrived in late 1804 to stay among the Hidatsa and to build Fort Mandan, Sacagawea was one of Charbonneau's two wives. She was fluent in Hidatsa and Shoshone, and Charbonneau spoke Hidatsa, French, and Gros Ventre. Her knowledge of topography and her familiarity with Native custom inspired Lewis and Clark to ask that she, with her infant son Jean Baptiste, join the exploring party. The baby had been born only weeks earlier, on February 11, 1805, and was affectionately nicknamed Pomp or Pompy by Clark.

Sacagawea's contributions to the success of the Lewis and Clark expedition were substantial, if not undisputed. As a mother with baby in arms, she lent credibility to the peaceful intentions of the Corps of Discovery. She augmented the health and diet of the explorers, bringing to the attention of the captains a variety of berries as well as edible plants such as wild artichokes, onions, camas, and nuts, where they could be found, and how they could be prepared. She identified roots for medicinal purposes, provided information that Lewis used in writing scientific descriptions, translated languages, recognized geographical landmarks, and recommended the best routes to travel. On one occasion she rescued journals and instruments after a boat capsized, and in November 1805 she cast her vote in favor of the group's remaining on the Pacific Coast. At Fort Clatsop she traded the beads off her buckskin dress to help procure needed supplies.

In a fortuitous reunion with her estranged brother, the Shoshone Chief Cameahwait, she indirectly lent much needed assistance when he allowed the explorers to trade with his band for horses and he provided the Americans with a knowledgeable escort (Old Toby) for the journey west across the Bitterroot Mountains and on to the Columbia River. Modern historians have largely dismissed Sacagawea's services as a pilot and guide, but her assistance was truly remarkable when considered in the broader context of what her role encompassed.

Following the return of the expedition to the Hidatsa-Mandan villages in August 1806, Sacagawea faded into the mists of temporal obscurity. There are

Statue of Sacagawea, a Native American woman who accompanied the Lewis and Clark Expedition during its journey to the Pacific Ocean during 1804–1806. Sacagawea's presence made the expedition seem less threatening to the various tribes that the group encountered. The explorers also probably would have become lost without her knowledge of local peoples and the terrain. (Library of Congress)

two predominant theories concerning her origins and ultimate fate. The first one asserts that around 1810 William Clark invited Sacagawea (Hidatsa for "Bird Woman"), Charbonneau, and their son to St. Louis, so that Jean Baptiste could begin his education. The Charbonneaus would assume possession of 320 acres of land given by the U.S. government as partial compensation for Toussaint's services to the expedition. The Charbonneaus left Jean Baptiste in the care of Clark and by 1812 were reported to be at Fort Manuel, a fur trading post on the Missouri River. There, on December 20, Sacagawea died of what was called putrid fever.

The alternate version alleges that Sacajawea (Shoshone "Boat Pusher" or "Launcher") lived for many years and died on April 9, 1884, on the Wind

River Indian Reservation in west central Wyoming. According to this version, she traveled through a large part of the West, remarried perhaps several times, and eventually reunited with her tribe, becoming a respected and influential elder.

Today Sacagawea is one of the most venerated women in American history. She has been memorialized in movies, documentaries, and books and in countless magazine and newspaper stories. Her hypothetical likeness has been the subject of numerous artworks, paintings, and statues, and her face adorns both a postage stamp and a one dollar coin. In 2003, the state of North Dakota installed a bronze of her in National Statuary Hall, U.S. Capitol Building, Washington, D.C.

SuAnn M. Reddick and Cary C. Collins

See also Clark, George Rogers; Oregon Trail.
References and Further Reading
Sally McBeth. 1998. *Essie's Story: The Life and Legacy of a Shoshone Teacher.* Lincoln: University of Nebraska Press.
Mann, John W. W. 2004. *Sacajawea's People: The Lemhi Shoshones and the Salmon River Country.* Lincoln: University of Nebraska Press.
McBeth, Sally. 2003. "Memory, History, and Contested Pasts: Reimagining Sacajawea/ Sacagawea." *American Indian Culture and Research Journal* 27: 1–32.
Thomasma, Kenneth. 1997. *The Truth About Sacajawea.* Jackson, WY: Grandview Publishing.

Scholder, Fritz

Born in Breckenridge, Minnesota, Fritz Scholder (1937–2005) was, along with Oscar Howe, Allan Houser, R. C. Gorman, Maria Martinez, and T. C. Cannon, among the first Native American artists to receive international acclaim. Although he maintained an ambivalent relationship to his indigenous identity throughout his lifetime, Scholder is best-known for his vivid, unconventional images of Native Americans. Juxtaposing figures in traditional dress with contemporary elements, Scholder's work reevaluated and reinterpreted stereotypical, romantic, and conventional representations of Native Americans. The series of Native American paintings Scholder produced are simultaneously brutal and beautiful, magical and humorous, reflecting the lived, quotidian experiences of late twentieth-century indigenous people.

For example, one of his most famous images, *Super Indian #2 (with ice-cream cone)*, features a buf-

falo dancer in traditional regalia taking a break to eat strawberry ice cream. As with most of his Native-themed paintings, the dancer appears in disembodied space with no familiar background to give the figure context. In the painting, the dancer seems to be sitting against a wall in a gymnasium or some other indoor public space. The ambiguity of the figure's location leads the viewer to question the ways in which Native Americans are often distilled in timeless space, outside the context of the various communities to which they belong.

Scholder's images of Native Americans aren't comfortable or comforting. His Indians smoke and drink alcohol, and they are often draped in the U.S. flag. They critique Euro-American colonization in paintings such as *Portrait of a Massacred Indian*, which portrays a Plains warrior whose head has been shattered, and illustrate the Indian Everyman in works such as *Indian with Beer Can*, a study of a grim, sunglass-wearing man seated next to a Coors can who flashes his sharp, skeletal teeth at the viewer. As a result, his work has been controversial with non-Natives who prefer romantic visions of Indians, as well as with Native Americans who find his representations of the paradoxical and darker aspects of living as an indigenous person in the United States to be disrespectful.

Scholder's father, who was of Luiseño and German ancestry, worked for the Bureau of Indian Affairs. At various times during his career, Scholder alternately embraced and maintained a distance from his identity as a tribal person, an attitude that created distrust in the larger Native American community. In an interview, Scholder claimed that "I was mislabeled an Indian artist . . . I grew up in public schools and I'm not Indian" (Academy of Achievement, 1996, 3). Similarly, he wrote, "I am a non-Indian Indian" (Scholder, 1979).

Although he didn't grow up near his tribal relatives in San Diego County, California, Scholder did spend much of his childhood on or near reservations. As a high school student in Pierre, South Dakota, he took classes with Oscar Howe, the acclaimed Lakota artist. In addition to indigenous influences, Scholder's work was shaped by the San Francisco Bay area figurative style of Wayne Thiebaud, with whom he shared gallery space in the 1950s, as well as work by artists as far ranging as Picasso, Matisse, Bacon, and Rauschenberg. In addition to painting Native American images, Scholder has produced sculpture, photography, poetry, and multimedia work, touching on themes from his trav-

els to places as far-reaching as Romania and Egypt. Scholder's work has substantially influenced the American art scene and was the subject of two major retrospectives and a PBS documentary.

Scholder taught art history at the Institute of American Indian Arts in Santa Fe in 1964 but left to pursue his own artistic ambitions full-time. In 1967 he began his Indian series, possibly because of his experience working with Native American students at IAIA and becoming excited by the fresh, innovative, and contemporary works the young people were generating there. In 1972, the Smithsonian Institution and the U.S. Information Service organized an exhibition of Scholder's work and invited him to tour Europe with T. C. Cannon, a Caddo/Kiowa artist and former student, a trip that launched both of the artists' international careers. Scholder's work in the 1980s grew out of the Indian series but returned to broader and more abstract themes. In the 1990s, he painted a new Indian series, Rot/Red, and in 2002 his last major show, Orchids and Other Flowers, dealt with the artist's reaction to 9/11.

Michelle H. Raheja

See also Gorman, R. C.

References and Further Reading

Academy of Achievement. No date. "Fritz Scholder." Available at: http://www.achievement.org. Accessed February 6, 2006.

Scholder, Fritz. 1979. *Indian Kitsch.* Flagstaff, AZ: Northland Press.

Taylor, Joshua C., et al. 1982. *Fritz Scholder.* New York: Rizzoli International Publications.

Seattle

Seattle (ca. 1786–1866) was a Duwamish Indian village leader, born on Blake Island in Elliott Bay, near the site where a town was founded in 1853 and today, as a great city, still honors his memory. Seattle's people were the Coast Salish, who spoke a form of Lushootseed. As the correct pronunciation of his name (Seath'tl, Duwamish-Suquamish Lushootseed) would be impossible to render exactly in English, its spelling has taken a number of forms, among them See-yat, Sealth, Seath'tl, and S'ia. He was descended from nobility through both maternal ancestors of the Duwamish and his father's Suquamish tribes, and he is still held in high esteem by the Coast Salish and other Native people.

Long before non-Native settlers began to arrive in the Puget Sound region, Seattle had established

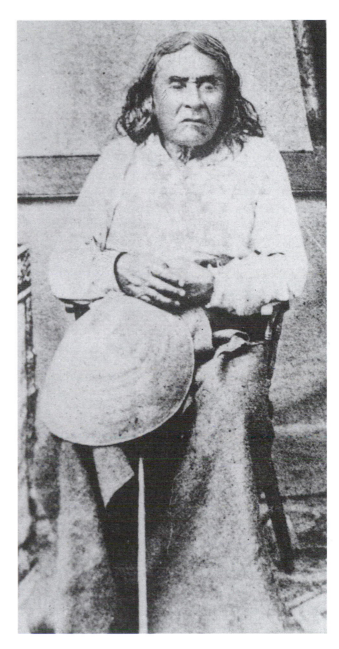

Chief Seath'tl (anglicized as "Seattle") was a Duwamish and Suquamish leader whose people moved from the present-day site of the city that bears his name. (Library of Congress)

an impressive reputation as a warrior among local groups. With the arrival of the Americans and their lust for Indian land, Seattle refocused his energies on peacemaking, and, having proven his leadership capabilities in both war and peace, he was the logical choice for the American officials to appoint as chief prior to treaty negotiations with Washington Governor Isaac I. Stevens. Seattle and Patkanim,

representing the Duwamish and Snoqualmie bands, met in March 1854, when the newly appointed governor was called to mediate a dispute between whites and Indians near Whidbey Island.

Although Seattle was an exceptional orator in his own language, he rarely spoke the trade language, Chinook Jargon, and used little or no English. An American settler, Henry A. Smith, later claimed that he had been present when Seattle spoke to Governor Stevens and, supposedly hearing the chief speak through an interpreter, kept notes on the chief's oration. In 1887, the *Seattle Sunday Star* published an article in which Smith reconstructed and published a version of Chief Seattle's statement. Through translation, appropriation, modification, and embellishment by a series of non-Native writers over the ensuing century, the speech is still embraced and marketed as an eloquent prophecy and environmental plea from a wise Native American elder and leader. However, as the historian Clarence B. Bagley has observed, "Doubtless Chief Seattle and the other chiefs present expressed its thoughts and sentiments in their own language forming the thread of the speech, but to Doctor Smith belongs the credit for its beautiful wording and delightful imagery" (Bagley, 1931, 255).

The earliest documentation of Seattle's name and activities in Puget Sound were contained in the records of the Hudson's Bay Company at Fort Nisqually. The company built a trading post in 1833 and established the Puget Sound Agricultural Company on a large land claim located between the Nisqually River and Commencement Bay. Seattle was on several occasions mentioned in the fort's *Journal of Daily Occurrences*, sometimes as "Le Gros" in reference to his physical appearance. His early relationship with the British, known by the Indians as King George men, was not always positive. One of the chief traders, knowing that Seattle was a frequent visitor at the fort and that he often engaged in violent raids and vengeful attacks on other local Indians, asked him to sign a peace treaty.

In 1847, Seattle led a Suquamish war party against the Chemakums near Port Townsend, losing a son during the battle. According to some sources, that event affected him deeply and prompted his conversion to Christianity. Other historians have suggested that his motives were more pragmatic and that he reinforced his political and social status through expanded allegiances. In either circumstance, records indicate that Catholic priests baptized him sometime before 1850, christening him Noah.

Seattle's family name, Si'a, derived from the Duwamish matrilineal line through his mother, Sholitza, but Seattle predominantly represented the Suquamish tribe of his father, Shweabe. He also made his home among the Suquamish at Agate Pass where, under his jurisdiction, the plank longhouse known as Oleman House was extended to 1,000 feet in length to accommodate his followers. Two of his wives bore him several children and some of his sons and grandsons became tribal leaders. His daughter, Angeline, was a famous citizen of Seattle and together they were the subjects of Clarence Bagley's article "Chief Seattle and Angeline."

Around 1904, the American Benjamin F. Shaw wrote about an encounter with Seattle in 1850 when the Native chief supposedly expressed a desire for white settlement. Shaw was affiliated with Colonel M. T. Simmons, and both of them were assigned in 1853 to appoint leaders of the Puget Sound tribes for the purpose of negotiating treaties with Governor Stevens. Seattle was officially designated as the chief of the Duwamish and Suquamish by Simmons and Shaw, and on January 22, 1855, he signed the Treaty of Point Elliott. The two tribes had been traditional enemies for generations and a separate reservation was established at Port Madison for the Suquamish, but the Duwamish never received land of their own.

Chief Seattle died on June 7, 1866, when he was approximately eighty years old. He was buried at Suquamish, Washington.

SuAnn M. Reddick and Cary C. Collins

See also Fishing Rights; Potlatch.
References and Further Reading
Anderson, Eva Greenslit. 1943. *Chief Seattle.* Caldwell, ID: Caxton.
Bagley, Clarence. 1931. "Chief Seattle and Angeline." *Washington Historical Quarterly* 22: 243–275.
Clark, Jerry L. 1985. "Thus Spoke Chief Seattle: The Story of an Undocumented Speech." *Prologue* 18: 58–65.
Furtwangler, Albert. 1997. *Answering Chief Seattle.* Seattle: University of Washington Press.
Kaiser, Rudolf. 1984. "Chief Seattle's Speech(es): American Origin and European Reception." .
Special Collections. Seattle: University of Washington

Sequoyah

Sequoyah (ca. 1770–1843), the inventor of the Cherokee syllabary (a set of written symbols that represent spoken syllables), became the only individual

in world history to invent a written language by himself.

Sequoyah was born in Taskigi, now within the state of Tennessee. His father was an American trader and his mother a Cherokee. He spent his early life as a hunter and fur trader but was crippled in a hunting accident (he subsequently worked as a silversmith). In the Creek War of 1813 and 1814, Sequoyah served under General Andrew Jackson.

In 1809, Sequoyah initiated work on a Cherokee alphabet. He hoped to aid his tribe in becoming literate in their own tongue, a tool that not only would help the tribe communicate in new ways and over many miles, but also would ensure, he hoped, the survival of the Cherokee language and cultural identity. After much frustration—and after his workshop was burned down by skeptical tribespeople—Sequoyah realized that an alphabet based on the Cherokee language would be exceedingly difficult to master. A syllabary based on phonetics would be easier to learn, Sequoyah concluded, and worked to perfect his system. His syllabary consists of eighty-six characters.

Although Sequoyah's project was met with skepticism by some Cherokees, his project was embraced within a few years after the official recognition of the project by tribal leaders. Nearly twelve years after the commencement of his project, Sequoyah presented his syllabary to the Cherokee Council in 1821. In a short time—some suggest only a few months—children and adults were able to read and write using Sequoyah's system. Soon after, parts of the *Bible* were translated into Cherokee, showing how missionaries hoped to incorporate the language into their work. In addition, the Cherokee constitution (1828) and the *Cherokee Phoenix and Indian Advocate*, a weekly newspaper first published in 1828, were printed in both English and Cherokee. Today, the syllabary is still used by many Cherokees, both in Oklahoma and North Carolina, and it represents a strong tie to a heritage distinct from other American cultural groups.

The syllabary's completion and dissemination throughout the Cherokee Nation in 1821 occurred at an important time of change for the Cherokees and other tribes. Unlike the tribes that used a lack of literacy as a powerful form of resistance, the Cherokee used their syllabary as a form of defiance in the face of growing pressures from the United States, pressures that would eventually force the relocation of most of the Cherokees. The syllabary continues to

Born half-Cherokee Sequoyah originated the Cherokee alphabet in 1821, thereby helping thousands of Native Americans to become literate. He is probably the only person to have invented a written language single-handedly. (Library of Congress)

symbolize cultural independence among many Cherokees.

Sequoyah accompanied the Cherokees forcibly removed by the U.S. government on the Trail of Tears in 1838 to Indian Territory, which would later become Oklahoma. Once there, he became president of the western Cherokees and presented the Cherokee Act of Union, which united the eastern and western Cherokee peoples. Sequoyah's death is something of a mystery. In 1842 he joined an expedition to locate a lost band of Cherokees who migrated west during the American Revolution. He never returned and his remains were never found. Many believe that Sequoyah died in Mexico and is buried somewhere near San Fernando, Tamaulipas. Still, Sequoyah, who never learned English fluently, is honored in a variety of ways by his tribe, by the state of Oklahoma, and by the giant redwood trees along the northern California coast that bear his name.

Amy M. Ware

See also *Cherokee Phoenix and Indian Advocate;* Ross, John; Trail of Tears.

References and Further Reading
Bender, Margaret. 2002. *Signs of Cherokee Culture: Sequoyah's Syllabary in Eastern Cherokee Life.* Chapel Hill: University of North Carolina Press.
Foreman, Grant. 1938. *Sequoyah.* Norman: University of Oklahoma Press.
Mooney, James. 1996. *Myths of the Cherokee.* New York: Dover Publications.

Sitting Bull

The Siouan words *"Tatanka-Iyotanka"* describe a stubborn buffalo seated on his haunches. The name was given to a Hunkpapa Sioux who emerged as a resistance leader against U.S. colonialism in the northern Plains. He was called Sitting Bull.

Around 1831, Sitting Bull was born along the Grand River at a place known as Many Caches in present-day South Dakota. Originally, he received the name Jumping Badger from his father, who bore the name Sitting Bull. His mother, Her-Holy-Door, created a close bond with him during his formative years. His childhood behavior earned him the alias Slow. He entered combat at age fourteen, counting his first coup on the Crow and earning the honor of his father's name. With distinction, he entered the Strong Heart, the Kit Fox, and the Silent Eaters societies. He married his first wife in 1851, but she died during childbirth. After his father died in 1859, he married two additional wives. They gave birth to two daughters and a son. In addition, he adopted his nephew, One Bull, as a son.

Sitting Bull became known as a *blotaunka*, or war chief, in the Strong Hearts, a warrior society. Standing five feet ten inches in height, he possessed a muscular frame and dark braided hair. As he matured, Sitting Bull earned acclaim as a singer, an artist, and a dancer. The scars on his chest, back, and arms testified to his repeated sacrifices in Sun Dances. He embodied the cardinal virtues of his people, that is, bravery, fortitude, generosity, and wisdom. He traded furs with the Chouteau company at Fort Pierre and encountered U.S. soldiers at Fort Berthold. In 1864, he fought against blue-clad regulars at the Battle of Killdeer Mountain. Thereafter, he laid siege to the newly established Fort Rice as well as Fort Buford.

By the 1870s, Sitting Bull's reputation as a *wichasha wakan*, or holy man, elevated his power among the Lakota Sioux. He was anointed *wakiconza*, a supreme chief, seeking to unite the diverse bands and contentious factions into a spirited resistance movement. In a ceremony, he was borne into a large circle on a buffalo robe and crowned with a magnificent headdress. He denounced the *wasichu*, or white people, who were invading Sioux country along the Powder and Yellowstone Rivers.

Sitting Bull tried to stop their invasion into the *Paha Sapa* (Black Hills), where gold was found by prospectors. Even though the Fort Laramie Treaty guaranteed the "unceded" territory near the Great Sioux reservation as a traditional hunting ground, officials in Washington, D.C., broke their promises. They announced that tribes not settled on the reservation by January 31, 1876, would be considered "hostile." In fact, three columns of soldiers were deployed to drive them into confinement under the surveillance of government agents. One column, led by Brigadier General George Crook, moved north from Fort Fetterman. Under Colonel John Gibbon, another column headed east from western Montana. The third column, commanded by General Alfred Terry, marched westward from Fort Abraham Lincoln. Surrounded on all sides, the off-reservation Sioux had nowhere to escape.

Thus began the Great Sioux War. In the Spring of 1876, Sitting Bull communicated with Wakantanka, or the Great Mystery, at the top of a butte. He received a dream about a dust storm propelled by high winds from the east. He saw uniformed troops advancing, their weapons and horse trimmings glistening in the sunlight. When the approaching fury crashed into a rolling cloud, thunder pealed, lightning cracked, and rains poured. The tempest passed, leaving an open sky.

On June 6, 1876, roughly 3,000 Lakotas and Cheyennes joined Sitting Bull for a Sun Dance along the Rosebud Creek in Montana. Following purification in a sweat lodge, he entered the dance circle. After staring into the blazing orb overhead, he offered his flesh and slashed his arms 100 times. As blood flowed from his body, Sitting Bull received another vision. He foresaw the mounted bluecoats attacking—"as many as grasshoppers." However, they descended upside down toward the ground as they rode. They possessed no ears and therefore could not heed the warnings to turn back.

Inspired by his visions, the Oglala war chief Crazy Horse organized a band of 500 warriors for action. On June 17, he surprised Crook's troops at the Battle of the Rosebud. Then the Sioux and their allies moved their camps to the valley of the Little Bighorn River at a place the Sioux called Greasy

A Hunkpapa Lakota Sioux, Sitting Bull is one of the most celebrated Indian leaders in American history. Sitting Bull participated in many famous battles, most notably the Battle of the Little Bighorn in 1876, and joined Buffalo Bill's Wild West Show in 1885. (Library of Congress)

Grass. In search of an elusive enemy, Colonel George Armstrong Custer of the Seventh Cavalry located their camps on June 25 with the help of Crow scouts. Outnumbered more than four to one, he ignored the warnings of his scouts and led the troops toward the camps. Along the Little Bighorn, 261 men of the Seventh Cavalry died that day.

After the stunning loss at the Little Bighorn, Lieutenant General Phil Sheridan deployed 2,500 additional troops to avenge the death of Custer. Congress took away the Black Hills in violation of the Fort Laramie Treaty and seized another 40 million acres of promised land. Sitting Bull, however, refused to accept defeat. He and his loyalists fled beyond the reach of the armed forces by crossing the border into Canada. General Terry traveled north to offer Sitting Bull a pardon in exchange for settling on the reservation, but he defiantly rejected the offer.

With the buffalo herds dwindling, Sitting Bull finally decided to end his exile. On July 19, 1881, he told his young son, Crow Foot, to hand his rifle to the commanding officer of Fort Buford in Montana. After the gesture, he spoke: "I wish to be remembered as the last man of my tribe to surrender my rifle." He donned a pair of sunglasses to protect his sensitive eyes and boarded a steamer for Bismarck. Dispatched to Fort Randall, he and his followers were prisoners of war for nearly two years.

Assigned to the Standing Rock Agency after 1883, Sitting Bull lived in a cabin. Devoted to his family, he retained his two wives. His two adult daughters were married and presented him with grandchildren. He continued to raise five children in his immediate household, including two pairs of twins and a daughter named Standing Holy. His mother, Her-Holy-Door, lived with the family until her death in 1884. He fathered two more children thereafter. Although he eschewed Christianity, he sent his children to a nearby Christian school to learn to read and to write.

The government agent, James McLaughlin, permitted Sitting Bull to participate in a traveling exhibition in 1884. In 1885, the legendary figure was allowed to join Buffalo Bill's Wild West show, earning $50 a week for appearing on horseback in an arena. On tour, he profited from the sale of his autograph and pictures. He stayed with the show only four months, having the opportunity to shake hands with President Grover Cleveland while in Washington, D.C.

After returning home, Sitting Bull spoke against the unjust policies of the agency. He openly defied the land agreements of 1888 and 1889, which threw half the Great Sioux Reservation open to non-Indian settlement and divided the rest into six separate reservations. "I would rather die an Indian," he prophetically stated, "than live a white man." Indeed, he received a vision of a meadowlark telling him that he would die at the hands of the Sioux.

In the fall of 1890, a Miniconjou Sioux named Kicking Bear came to Sitting Bull with news of the Ghost Dance religion, which promised to restore the traditional way of life. Though skeptical of the religion at first, he planted a prayer tree at Standing Rock. He began dancing while wearing a shirt with a painted red cross. When attempting to arrest him at his cabin on December 15, 1890, a Lakota Sioux policeman shot him in the head, and his final vision came to pass. His killing led to the tragic events at Wounded Knee two weeks later.

Sitting Bull died a martyr in the last days of Sioux resistance to U.S. colonialism. He was originally buried at Fort Yates, North Dakota, but in 1953 according to some sources, his remains were relocated to Mobridge, South Dakota. Researchers continue to disagree about the actual location of his bones, and grave sites are maintained in both locations. On March 6, 1996, the Standing Rock Sioux Tribal Council voted to change the name of the tribal community college to Sitting Bull College (SBC). As a tribute to his spirit, the institution adopted its motto from his words: "Let us put our minds together to see what we can build for our children."

Brad D. Lookingbill

See also Battle of the Little Bighorn; Black Hills
(*Paha Sapa*); Cody, William Frederick; Crazy
Horse; Wounded Knee, South Dakota,
Massacre at.

References and Further Reading

Anderson, Gary C. 1996. *Sitting Bull and the Paradox of Lakota Nationhood.* New York: HarperCollins.

Ostler, Jeffrey. 2004. *The Plains Sioux and U.S. Colonialism from Lewis and Clark to Wounded Knee.* Cambridge, UK: Cambridge University Press.

Sitting Bull College. No date. Available at: http://www.sittingbull.edu. Accessed February 14, 2005.

Utley, Robert. 1993. *The Lance and the Shield: The Life and Times of Sitting Bull.* New York: Ballantine Books.

White, Richard. 1978. "The Winning of the West: The Expansion of the Western Sioux in the Eighteenth and Nineteenth Centuries." *Journal of American History* 65 (September): 321–323.

Smith, John

One of the best-known figures from the period of early American history, John Smith was briefly the leader of the first successful English colony at Jamestown and a lifelong promoter of English colonization efforts in North America. Born in England in 1580, Smith fought as a solider against the Turks in Hungary. Upon returning to England, he joined the Virginia Company's colonization venture to the Chesapeake in 1607. As a soldier with worldly experience, and not a respecter of class, Smith made himself unpopular with some of the gentry during the trip, who, upon arriving in Virginia, opened the company's instructions for the colony and were

appalled to learn that Smith had been appointed their leader.

Fearful that the Spanish were attempting to find and destroy the colony, the English established Jamestown at a defensible site a few miles inland along the James River. However, the Jamestown colony was situated next to a swamp teeming with disease-carrying mosquitoes, and, taking their water from the sluggish, brackish, and salty James, many colonists soon became ill. Smith managed to alleviate the effects of disease somewhat by having the colony disperse to smaller settlements during the summer months.

Most of the colonists lacked useful skills and were unused to the hard labor needed for the colony to succeed. When a number of the colonists refused to work, Smith issued an order proclaiming that "He that doth not work shall not eat." Nevertheless, the colony ran short on food. Lacking the hunting skills to take advantage of the local game and fearful of the local Powhatan Indians, the colonists remained inside Jamestown's palisades and starved.

While much of Europe was aghast at tales of Spanish atrocities in the Americas, Smith admired the actions of Cortes, Pizzaro, and other conquistadores, and he thought it best for the English to emulate Spanish policies (or what he believed were Spanish policies) toward Native peoples. However, Smith found that he lacked the military wherewithal to coerce the local Powhatan Confederacy, and he may have also realized that the Powhatans were very different from the Natives of Central and South America. Smith managed to obtain food from the Powhatans through a combination of barter, bullying, and theft. At one point, he seized the half brother of Powhatan, Opechancanough, as a hostage in exchange for maize. This act earned the colonists Opechancanough's undying hostility, and he later led two destructive wars against Virginia.

Captured by the Powhatans during one of his explorations, Smith was apparently marked to die. Smith later described a scene in which he was restrained while an executioner prepared to cudgel him to death. At the last moment, Powhatan's favorite child, Pocahontas, threw herself between Smith and the executioner's club and persuaded her father to spare his life. Smith seemed to think that Pocahontas acted on her own initiative. However, it has been argued that Smith misunderstood what happened. Pocahontas's act of rescuing him and her father's granting him his life may have been part of a ritual that, in the eyes of Native peoples, made Smith

References and Further Reading
Barbour, Philip L. 1964. *The Three Worlds of Captain John Smith.* London: Macmillan.
Kupperman, Karen Ordahl, ed. 1988. *Captain John Smith: A Select Edition of His Writings.* Chapel Hill: University of North Carolina Press.

The English soldier and adventurer Captain John Smith helped found the Jamestown colony in 1607 and provided leadership during its crucial early years. (Library of Congress)

a tributary of Powhatan. There is also the possibility that the incident may have never occurred. Smith's narrative of his adventures in Virginia went through several editions, but not until 1625, long after the other principals in the drama (Pocahontas and Powhatan) were dead, did he mention this incident.

Smith's considerable leadership skills and his imposition of a military style of discipline helped the Jamestown colony to survive. However, his wariness of the Powhatans set the tone for an uneasy relationship for the next half century.

Smith remained a proponent of English colonization until his death in 1630. To his credit, Smith's writings about North America were realistic descriptions of the land and its commodities. But for the most part, Smith viewed Native peoples as savages and valuable only as trade partners. He believed that they must either become "civilized" or be pushed aside by the English.

Roger M. Carpenter

See also Pocahontas; Powhatan.

Smohalla

Like Wovoka, the Paiute progenitor of the Ghost Dance, the Wanapam prophet *šmúxala* (generally rendered as Smohalla, meaning "dreamer") rose to prominence during the late nineteenth century as the symbolic head of a major religious revitalization movement. Like the Ghost Dance, Smohalla's creed, called *waasaní* (Washani, "dancers" or "worship") in the Sahaptin language, mingled indigenous beliefs with Christian concepts but explicitly renounced Euro-American culture. By urging the Indians of the Columbia Plateau to reject white ways and refuse land cessions, the so-called Dreamer Cult inspired strong resistance to federal policies designed to isolate and assimilate Native Americans.

Smohalla lived during a period of wrenching change for the indigenous peoples of the Plateau. Born around 1815 in present-day eastern Washington State, he may have witnessed the arrival of the first British and American fur traders to enter Wanapam territory along the Columbia River. The newcomers brought useful goods, but they also introduced alcohol and diseases that ravaged Native communities and undermined the status of traditional shamans. With the traders came Catholic Iroquois and Jesuit priests, from whom Smohalla probably learned the Christian theology and rituals that influenced Washani. Missionary activity intensified in the 1830s with the arrival of Protestant ministers, but Indian enthusiasm quickly waned as anger mounted over the growing stream of Euro-American emigrants arriving on the Oregon Trail. By 1850, Smohalla and other "dreamer prophets" had begun preaching that their people should shun white "civilization" and never sell any piece of their Earth Mother. Despite such spiritual objections, four treaties signed in 1855 ceded millions of acres to the United States and established reservations where Plateau Indians would presumably settle down as yeomen farmers. Many refused to obey, however, and among the "renegades" Washani became a powerful source of hope.

Smohalla built his reputation and his religion on a series of prophetic visions. Already deemed a potent *iyánca* ("one who trains or disciplines") by his own people, he attracted numerous followers from across the Plateau by promising them deliverance from the American onslaught. His methods and message closely resembled those of Indian prophets of earlier eras. Besides predicting eclipses and other natural phenomena, he periodically entered deep, death-like trances during which he claimed to visit the afterworld and receive instructions from the Creator. Above all, Smohalla declared, Indians must stop tilling the earth or face divine retribution. When a military officer attempted to convince him otherwise, he retorted:

> You ask me to plow the ground! Shall I take a knife and tear my mother's bosom? Then when I die she will not take me to her bosom to rest.
>
> You ask me to dig for stone! Shall I dig under her skin for her bones? Then when I die I can not enter her body to be born again.
>
> You ask me to cut grass and make hay and sell it, and be rich like the white men, but how dare I cut off my mother's hair?

The Creator would reward obedience to his creed with world renewal. If Indians faithfully performed the *wáashat* (Washat, or Prophet Dance), the whites would die off or disappear, deceased relatives would return to life, and the land would revert to its pristine state. Until then, Indians must cast off white ways, seek wisdom in dreams, and reject the reservation system and allotment. Smohalla also preached pacifism, as did most of his disciples, but their teachings gave spiritual sanction to the defiance of federal authority.

By the late 1860s, Smohalla's growing influence had earned him the enmity of government officials and some tribal leaders. He clashed repeatedly with Chief Moses of the Columbia-Sinkiuse, who considered him a rival, and a bitter quarrel with the Walla Walla dreamer Homily prompted Smohalla to move his base from Wallula to the winter village of P'na near Priest Rapids. His greatest enemies, however, were the Indian agents who accused him and his disciples of corrupting their reservation kin. Agency officials clamored continually for the removal and confinement of all renegade Dreamers, but Smohalla maintained amicable relations with the military authorities at Fort Walla Walla. Because the Wanapams remained peaceful and their lands were unde-

sirable to white settlers, the Army saw little reason to force the issue. Smohalla stayed off the reservation until his death in 1895, and his creed survived continuing efforts to suppress it. Although Washani's millenarian and Nativistic aspects soon faded, its forms of worship continue to influence tribal life through the Seven Drums Religion practiced across the interior Northwest.

Andrew H. Fisher

See also Dreamer Cult; Handsome Lake; Seven Drums Religion; Wovoka.

References and Further Reading

Du Bois, Cora. 1938. "The Feather Cult of the Middle Columbia." *General Series in Anthropology No. 7.* Menasha, WI: George Banta Printing Company.

Relander, Click. 1956. *Drummers and Dreamers.* Caldwell, ID: Caxton.

Ruby, Robert, and John A. Brown. 1989. *Dreamer Prophets of the Columbia Plateau: Smohalla and Skolaskin.* Norman: University of Oklahoma Press.

Spier, Leslie. 1935. "The Prophet Dance of the Northwest and Its Derivatives: The Source of the Ghost Dance." *General Series in Anthropology No. 1.* Menasha, WI: George Banta Printing Company.

Society of American Indians

The Society of American Indians (SAI, 1911–1920s) was a cross-tribal group created on the tide of progressive feeling that swept through American politics during the early decades of the twentieth century. It developed alongside the religious intertribalism of the peyote faith and the Native American Church and eventually was completely eclipsed by the city-based fraternal intertribalism that crystallized during the 1920s. It pushed for national Indian reform, sought to initiate and direct change in government policy, and presented itself as the modern, united Indian representative body of the era. Made up primarily of educated, middle-class Indians, it can be seen positively as an important fraternity that laid the foundations for the more effective Indian reform of the rest of the century. It built on a long tradition of intertribal unity and action, invoking the legacy of Joseph Brant (Thayendanega) and Tecumseh. Less positively, its disintegration can also be seen as indicative of the illusory nature of the inclusive dream at the core of American rhetoric at the beginning of the twentieth century. The SAI hoped to serve as a modern, proud, and unified Indian elite

and to spearhead the full integration of Indian people in American culture, but found instead that the general reevaluation of Indian capabilities they desired was not about to happen. The "race leadership" the SAI offered was neither wanted nor understood by the most Indians, nor was it desired by the dominant society.

The SAI's agenda was comparable to that of the National Association for the Advancement of Colored People (NAACP), formed just a few years previously; both organizations campaigned for the legal and political recognition of their people and spread the word through their own journals. A specifically Indian identity made the SAI unique among the other bodies, such as the Indian Rights Association and the Lake Mohonk Conference of the Friends of the Indian, with a voice in Indian reform debates. Yet although it was "of Indians, by Indians, and for Indians," the SAI shared the same basic agenda as other non-Indian reform organizations: final detribalization and the individual absorption of Indians into American society as patriotic citizens.

SAI core leadership was always small but it included men like Dr. Charles A. Eastman, the prominent physician, lecturer, and author; Dr. Carlos Montezuma, at the time one of the most recognized Indians in the country; the writer, museum man, and anthropologist Arthur C. Parker; the then most powerful Indian executive within the Bureau of Indian Affairs, Supervisor of Employment Charles E. Daganett; the community activist Gertrude Bonnin; the Reverends Sherman Coolidge and Henry Roe Cloud; and the Indian lawyers Thomas L. Sloan and Hiram Chase. SAI successes included its *Quarterly Journal* (renamed in 1916 *The American Indian Magazine*), a number of well-received conferences, a meeting with President Woodrow Wilson in 1914, the inauguration of an Indian Day and various other efforts designed to move perceptions of Indians away from the Wild West show stereotype and to foster Indian citizenship and self-help. Almost from the outset, however, the organization was plagued by internal conflict, by apathy on the part of the membership, and by a lack of funding. Especially bitter disputes arose over the appropriate role of the Bureau of Indian Affairs, both in Indian life and in the organization, over the role of peyote in Indian life, and over Indian citizenship.

What Indian people wanted most at this time was recognition of their claims and a resolution of their complaints, rather than rhetoric about self-help as a panacea for all social ills. The SAI was run by

Charles Eastman, a Sioux, championed Native American causes from the Wounded Knee Massacre in 1890 until he died in 1939. His writings interpreted Native American ways of life for white Americans during a time of considerable misunderstanding. (Library of Congress)

and for the emerging educated Indian middle class, and it failed to bring about any practical legislative change. It also failed to garner either the funds or the broad-based support needed to renegotiate the Indian position in American society. However, when the Committee of One Hundred met in 1923, it included much of the core membership of the SAI and its resolutions were generally similar to the SAI's early overall agenda. In turn, that consensus fed into the Meriam Report of 1928, the document that revealed in a politically significant fashion the failures of previous government policy and that fueled the ensuing movement to revive tribalism and to use social science to ease Indian integration into American society.

Joy Porter

See also Brant, Joseph; Meriam Report; Montezuma; Parker, Arthur C.; Tecumseh.

Reference and Further Reading
Porter, Joy. 2001. *To Be Indian: The Life of Iroquois-Seneca Arthur Caswell Parker.* Norman: University of Oklahoma Press.

Sohappy, Sr., David

The name David Sohappy, Sr. (Wanapam), has come to symbolize the struggle of Indian peoples of the Columbia River and its tributaries to preserve the salmon runs that have nourished and sustained their societies for thousands of years.

Sohappy's ancestors traded fish with the 1805 Lewis and Clark expedition. Kettle Falls in Washington and Celilo Falls near The Dalles in Oregon were two of the largest Indian fisheries in North America and gathering places for the Indian nations of the Plateau and beyond. The biggest part of the Native diet has always been fish. Catching salmon is a way of life, and religious beliefs and ceremonies are closely tied to preserving the fish runs. In 1855, treaties were signed with Northwest Indian nations pledging that "for as long as the sun shines, as long as the mountains stand, and as long as the river flows," the River People would be able to fish at their accustomed places. Yet by the end of the nineteenth century, environmental degradation caused by fish wheels (mechanized fish harvesters), canneries, logging, and agriculture had seriously endangered the fish and impacted the lives of the "River People."

Seventeen dams constructed on the Columbia and Snake River spawning grounds also had a deleterious effect. Nevertheless, since the late 1950s, the Indians of the Northwest have found themselves the official scapegoat for the salmon decline, accused of overfishing. "Can an Indian save a salmon" was one of the racist slogans gracing bumper stickers on non-Indian cars in the 1980s.

David Sohappy, Sr. was born in 1925. His name is derived from *souiehappie,* meaning "shoving something under a ledge" in the Wanapam Indian language. (*Wana* means "river," and *pam* means "people of.") The original Wanapam villages ranged from the mouth of the Little White Salmon River upstream to Priest Rapids. Sohappy's family was evicted from their ancestral home at Priest Rapids and White Bluff in the 1940s to make room for the Hanford nuclear facility. Eventually, David and his family moved to Cook's Landing at the mouth of the Little White Salmon River in Washington.

David Sohappy followed the old Wanapam religion his entire life, a religion that spurns violence and alcohol consumption. He is a lineal descendent of the Indian prophet Smohalla, who founded the Waashat (or dreamer) religion. He told his followers that "God commanded that the lands and fisheries should be common to all who lived upon them; that they were never to be marked off or divided, but that the people should enjoy the fruits that God planted in the land, and the animals that lived upon it, and the fishes in the water . . . This is the old law." The Wanapam refused to participate in the 1855 treaty negotiations with the United States and resisted government efforts to remove them to the Yakama Indian Reservation. Smohalla's teachings inspired resistance to federal assimilationist policies.

Sohappy grew up on his grandmother's allotted land on the Yakama Indian Reservation. He was taught to follow the seasonal food cycles of traditional Wanapam culture that consisted of wild game, fish, roots, and huckleberries. He fished for salmon without regard to season or limit, and he followed the traditional practices of salmon conservation handed down by his ancestors. He was taught that to fish is to give thanks to the Creator and to show respect for the Creator's gift of life, salmon. He believed that only the Creator—not the state, federal, or even Native governments—could control his traditional fishing practices.

Sohappy believed that he could live where he fished, at Cook's Landing on the Columbia River, especially since the government never kept its promise to provide new houses and fishing sites for those displaced by dam construction. Cook's Landing is one of five small fishing sites approved by the federal government "in lieu" of the thirty-seven Indian communities flooded out by the construction of Bonneville Dam in 1933. No matter what the need, he never accepted welfare, unemployment compensation, or surplus commodities. Instead, he and his family ate salmon at almost every meal, traded or sold fish for other food staples and their modest cash needs, gathered roots and berries, and hunted. Sohappy also provided salmon for tribal ceremonies and conducted religious ceremonies in the family longhouse.

In 1981, fish runs were at an all-time low, and federal enforcement agencies proclaimed the disappearance of 40,000 Chinook salmon between Boneville and McNary dams on the Columbia River. This was District Six, an area designated by the courts exclusively for Indian fishing. Federal officials

then charged that the fish were taken by Indian poachers, chief among whom were David Sohappy and members of his extended family.

On June 17, 1982, David Sohappy, his wife, son, and seventy-five other Indian fishermen were arrested for fishing out of season. The Sohappys' front door was kicked down and the house ransacked by local, state, and federal agents. A sting operation, code-named Salmonscam, had been under way for fourteen months to entrap the Indian fisherfolk who openly took salmon in defiance of state regulations, asserting their treaty right to fish. David Sohappy and his son were convicted under the Lacey Amendment to the Black Bass Act, and each was sentenced to five years in federal prison. Other Indian fishers received lesser sentences. In contrast, two non-Indian poachers received only thirty days in prison and a suspended sentence, respectively.

During the trial, testimony about Sohappy's religion and traditional fish conservation practices was not allowed. It was later found that most of the "missing fish" Sohappy and his fellow River Indians were accused of poaching were not missing after all. Finding the dams difficult to navigate, the fish had simply spawned in tributaries along the Columbia before reaching McNary Dam. In addition, an aluminum plant located upriver from The Dalles Dam had spilled fluorides into the river, confusing the fish that were not killed by the effluent.

David, an elder and spiritual leader in the Feather Cult of the Waashat or Seven Drums Religion, spent twenty months in a federal prison before an international protest and the intervention by Senator Daniel Inouye, chairman of the Senate Select Committee on Indian Affairs, led to his release in June of 1988. A ruling by the Yakama tribal court had already found Sohappy and the other defendants not guilty of the poaching charges. Meanwhile, at Sohappy's home at Cook's Landing, federal officials issued an eviction notice. He took the eviction notice to court and won in what turned out to be his last battle before his untimely death three years later. Having suffered diabetic strokes in prison, Sohappy's health broke and he died in a nursing home on May 6, 1991.

This was not the first time that David Sohappy had tested the white man's unjust laws that violated Indian treaty rights. During the 1960s and 1970s the Northwest fishing struggle centered on the much publicized fish-ins in western Washington at Frank's Landing. Meanwhile, on the Columbia, Sohappy fished according to his traditional religious beliefs, using fish traps he had built from driftwood until state game and fishing officials raided his camp and beat family members. In 1968 he and his cousin, Richard Sohappy, and a dozen others were jailed on the charge of illegal fishing.

The two Sohappys then became plaintiffs in the landmark federal case of *Sohappy v. Smith*. On July 8, 1969, U.S. District Court Judge Robert C. Belloni ruled that Indian fishers are allowed to harvest their fair share of the Columbia River salmon runs. A few years later in 1974, Judge George Boldt ruled that the "fair and equitable" in the earlier decision meant 50 percent of harvestable fish and that authority to regulate tribal fishing on and off the reservations was reserved for the Indian treaty nations. Yet despite these favorable legal decisions, the states of Washington and Oregon continued to interfere with Indian fishing, and federal authorities stepped up their harassment of the Sohappys.

When he died, David Sohappy was buried according to the old religion of his ancestors, with traditional songs and wrapped in a Pendleton blanket. His attorney, Tom Keefe, Jr. recalled that solemn occasion:

> And while the sun chased a crescent moon across the Yakima Valley, I thanked David Sohappy for the time we had spent together, and I wondered how the salmon he had fought to protect would fare in his absence. Now he is gone, and natural runs of Chinook that fed his family since time immemorial are headed for the Endangered Species Act list. "Be glad for my dad," David Sohappy, Jr., told the mourners. "He is free now, he doesn't need any tears" (Grinde and Johansen, 1995, 166).

Steve Talbot

See also Fishing Rights; Salmon, Economic and Spiritual Significance of; Seven Drums Religion.

References and Further Reading

Grinde, Donald A., and Bruce E. Johansen. 1995. *Ecocide of Native America: Environmental Destruction of Indian Lands and Peoples*, 145–169. Santa Fe, NM: Clear Light Publishers.

Hunn, Eugene S. 1996. "Columbia River Indians." *Native America in the Twentieth Century: An Encyclopedia*. Edited by Mary B. Davis, 127–128. New York: Garland Publishing.

Ulrich, Roberta. 1999. "Conviction and Eviction." In *Empty Nets: Indians, Dams, and the Columbia River*. Corvallis: Oregon State University Press.

Spotted Tail

Spotted Tail (*Sinte Gleska*) was a *Sicangu* (upper Brûlé Lakota), born in 1823 in the Ring band (*tiyospe*), a community of bilaterally related extended families on the White River in south central South Dakota. He learned to hunt bison, to conduct raiding expeditions against the Pawnee, to protect his community's southern lands that lay beyond the Platte River in western Nebraska, and to take the proper path toward leadership under the guidance of Little Thunder, leader of the Ring band. By midcentury, he became a Shirt Wearer (*Wicasa*), the official band executive for the council (*Wiscas Itacans*), locating good hunting and campgrounds, deciding family disputes, and negotiating with foreign officials.

Traders were part of Spotted Tail's early life, but increased non-Native immigration to Oregon in 1843, to Utah in 1847, and to California in 1849 brought overland travelers through the Brûlés' Platte River territories, and soon the American military followed to protect the immigrants. These events forever changed Spotted Tail's life.

In 1854, a Mormon emigrant abandoned a lame cow and a Minniconju Lakota killed the animal. This "Mormon cow affair" convinced the brash recent West Point graduate Lieutenant John Lawrence Grattan to take a detachment and demand that Little Thunder's Brûlé band pay compensation and release the guilty Lakota to military control. After an unfruitful negotiation, Grattan's men fired their heavy artillery and the Lakota retaliated, killing the entire unit. After learning of Grattan's fate, Secretary of War Jefferson Davis ordered General William S. Harney to prepare a punitive campaign against the guilty tribespeople. The following year at Ash Hollow in western Nebraska, Harney's expedition attacked Little Thunder's band, killing eighty-six people and taking prisoners. Harney then demanded the surrender and imprisonment of the leading men. Spotted Tail (among others) surrendered at Fort Laramie in the fall of 1855. He was incarcerated at Fort Leavenworth and later Fort Kearny before returning to his people the following fall. Upon his return, he decided to stand with Little Thunder and avoid war with the whites but to continue to fight the traditional Pawnee foes.

In 1866, Spotted Tail succeeded Little Thunder as headman of the Ring Band and joined with Swift Bear of the Corn band for protection. Together they stood for peace, signing the Fort Laramie Treaty of 1868 and moving to the Whetstone Agency on the Missouri River. There Spotted Tail killed Big Mouth

Spotted Tail was a leader of the Brûlé Lakota who sought compromise with the invading whites. Spotted Tail disagreed with Red Cloud, wanting to negotiate to allow whites to pass through Indian lands on their way to the gold mines in Montana. Spotted Tail became a leader of the Oglala Sioux after Red Cloud was deposed in 1881, but he was assassinated shortly thereafter. (Mercaldo Archives)

during a leadership dispute in 1869. The agency was moved to northwest Nebraska shortly afterward, and then war began in the north when Sitting Bull and Crazy Horse's followers refused to stay inside the boundaries of the Great Sioux Reservation. At the same time, miners violated Lakota boundaries and invaded the Black Hills. The escalating frustration culminated on the banks of the Greasy Grass Creek when Lakota soldiers and their allies destroyed Brevet General George A. Custer's entire command.

While Crazy Horse and Sitting Bull fought, Spotted Tail's agency was known as a peace camp. As General Nelson Miles pursued the warring chiefs, General George Crook sought Spotted Tail's help and in the fall of 1876 unilaterally and illegally declared that the United States "recognized Spotted Tail as chief of all the Sioux." Spotted Tail, with U.S.

backing, maintained his status by signing the Black Hills Treaty (Agreement) in 1876 that enabled the United States to take control of that region. In early 1877, with Crook's urging, Spotted Tail went north on a peace mission seeking Crazy Horse's surrender. The two men met and Crazy Horse accepted the terms Spotted Tail presented. The war was nearly over when Crazy Horse surrendered in late spring and Sitting Bull and his people went to Canada in an effort to retain their independence.

After briefly moving their people to the old Ponca Agency on the Missouri River, Spotted Tail and other upper Brûlé leaders moved in the summer of 1878 to the Rosebud Agency in south central South Dakota. At Rosebud, old tribal conflicts merged into new battles. Spotted Tail tried to follow Lakota tradition but lacked credibility because he owed his position to U.S. intervention. As he attempted to maintain control over all the Brûlé bands, Spotted Tail encountered increasing tension between himself and Two Strike, White Thunder, Crow Dog, and Hollow Horn Bear. Rosebud leaders sent some children to the Carlisle boarding school in 1879, and Spotted Tail removed the children without Brûlé authority, violating tribal political protocol. These ill feelings erupted following a meeting in early August 1881, when Crow Dog shot Spotted Tail, killing him instantly.

Richmond Clow

See also Black Hills (*Paha Sapa*); Crazy Horse; Sitting Bull.

References and Further Reading

Bray, Kingsley M. 2002. "Spotted Tail and the Treaty of 1868." *Nebraska History* 83, no. 1: 19–35.

Clow, Richmond L. 1998. "The Anatomy of a Lakota Shooting: Crow Dog and Spotted Tail." *South Dakota History* 28, no. 4: 209–227.

Hyde, George E. 1961. *Spotted Tail's Folk: A History of the Brule Sioux* Norman: University of Oklahoma Press.

Seagle, William. 1970. "The Murder of Spotted Tail." *Indian Historian* 3, no. 4: 10–22.

Worcester, Donald F. 1964. "Spotted Tail: Warrior, Diplomat." *American West* 1, no. 4: 38–46, 87.

Squanto

Best-known for serving as an interpreter for the Pilgrims and for showing them how to survive in New England, Squanto (died 1622) was a Patuxet Indian who, in a few short years, traveled (sometimes unwillingly) from North America, to Spain and England, and back to New England.

Squanto (rendered as Tisquantum by William Bradford) stepped into history in 1614, when English sea captain Thomas Hunt abducted roughly twenty Native men from Cape Cod. Hoping to sell the Indians as slaves, Hunt took his human cargo to Spain, where he sold a few of the Indians before Spanish authorities seized the rest and sent them to live with Catholic friars so that they could be instructed in Christianity. Little is known about Squanto's time in Spain or how he left the country, but by 1617 he was living in the London home of the Newfoundland Company's treasurer, John Slany. Hoping to use Squanto as an interpreter and go-between, the English took him to Newfoundland in 1618. He returned to his native Patuxet while serving as a guide and interpreter for Thomas Dermer's 1619 expeditions to Cape Cod and Martha's Vineyard. As Dermer prepared to sail around Cape Cod, Squanto left to seek out his own people. In the few years since Squanto had been abducted, New England's Native populations had been devastated by European diseases, often carried by English fishermen who came ashore to dry their catch and to trade. Squanto returned to Patuxet and discovered that nearly all of his people had perished in an epidemic.

Without Squanto to act as an interpreter, Dermer had difficulty dealing with the Native peoples of the area, who had good reason to be suspicious of English intentions. The Indians rightly viewed the English as kidnappers, and they also rightly believed that the English had something to do with the diseases that ravaged their communities in coastal New England. When Dermer returned to the southern New England coast a year later, he was captured by a group of Native people and held until Squanto interceded. Squanto joined Dermer, but the expedition was attacked by Native people at Martha's Vineyard. The Pokanokets seized Squanto as a captive, while Dermer, wounded several times, made his way back to Virginia, where he died shortly thereafter.

In November 1620, the Pilgrims landed on Cape Cod. The Pokanokets were undoubtedly aware of the English presence, but, like other Native peoples, they maintained a cautious distance from the Plymouth settlement and its inhabitants. In the spring of 1621, Samoset, an Abenaki, made the initial contact with the English. A few days after this meeting, Samoset and Squanto translated the terms of the first treaty between the English and the Pokanoket

leader, Massasoit. For his part, Massasoit probably looked upon the English as potential allies against the more numerous and powerful Narragansetts, who had been relatively untouched by the recent epidemics of European disease.

Due to his extensive contact with the English, Squanto had far better command of their language than did Samoset, and the Pokanokets permitted him to remain in the Plymouth settlement. Squanto helped the Pilgrims obtain a quantity of maize, trained them in the planting and harvesting of the crop, and guided them on their excursions out of the Plymouth settlement. He also attempted to rebuild the Patuxets, scouring the region for survivors of the smallpox epidemic. This angered the Pokanokets, who saw this as a challenge, but the Plymouth colony protected Squanto. Squanto attempted to gain a measure of influence among other Native people in the area, claiming that, if they did not heed him, he could persuade his English friends to send a plague among them. While the Plymouth settlers did not approve of Squanto's actions, they realized that he was critical to their success, due to his abilities as a translator. At one point, the Pilgrims nearly went to war with nearby Native groups over the mere rumor that they had killed Squanto. When Squanto died in 1622, he asked the English to pray for him so that he could go to their heaven.

Roger M. Carpenter

See also Canonicus; Massasoit.

References and Further Reading
Salisbury, Neal. 1982. *Manitou and Providence: Indians, Europeans, and the Making of New England.* Oxford: Oxford University Press.
Salisbury, Neal. 1999. "Squanto: Last of the Patuxet." In *The Human Tradition in Colonial America.* Edited by Ian K. Steele and Nancy L. Rhoden, 21–36. Wilmington, DE. Scholarly Resources.

St. Clair, Arthur

Arthur St. Clair was born in England in 1737. In his youth, he entered the British Army with the rank of ensign. He came to America during the French and Indian War as an officer in the Sixtieth of Foot. At the end of hostilities, St. Clair retired from his commission, settling first in Boston and then moving to the Pennsylvania frontier, where he purchased some 4,000 acres in the Ligonier Valley, the title to which was disputed because it was west of the 1763 Royal Proclamation Line and controversial because only

the Haudenosaunees gave up claims to that area in the 1768 Treaty of Fort Stanwix. Other Native nations, such as the Delawares and the Shawnees, still considered the area to be Indian Country. Later, in the Ohio country, St. Clair continued his willingness to participate in the extension of disputed white settlements.

As the political situation between Great Britain and her North American colonies deteriorated in the early 1770s, St. Clair sided with the opposition to British rule. In July 1775 he was commissioned as a colonel in a regiment of Pennsylvania militia. Within a year, he joined the Continental Army and participated in the battles of Trenton (1776) and Princeton (1777).

In the course of his campaigning with the Continental Army, St. Clair earned the trust of George Washington. This trust led to St. Clair's appointment and brief service as an adjutant general of the Continental Army in 1777. Then Washington sent St. Clair to the northern department to help shore up the defenses. There he committed his most well-known act of the war when he abandoned Fort Ticonderoga between July 2 and 5, 1777, during General John Burgoyne's invasion of New York. While some assert that his military reasoning was sound, many contemporaries suspected St. Clair of disloyalty for abandoning the post. Many Patriots, including important figures in Congress feared that the campaign was lost and worried that they were henceforth risking their lives uselessly on other fronts in New York.

St. Clair's poor military planning at Ticonderoga would be evident again on the Ohio frontier. St. Clair could have delayed Burgoyne either by fortifying the heights across the lake from the fort (by failing to do this, he was careless at best and incompetent at worst) or by sustaining what would have been a long and admittedly bloody siege, which at least would have thrown Burgoyne even further off schedule. St. Clair held no important field commands for the remainder of the war. His last command was at West Point in October 1780. On November 3, 1783, Arthur St. Clair retired from the Continental Army, having attained the rank of Major General.

The retired officer next involved himself in national politics, serving in the Continental Congress from November 2, 1785, until November 28, 1787, eventually securing election to the post of president of the body. Next he was made first governor of the Northwest Territory, a post he held from 1789 until

1802. It was in his role as territorial governor that St. Clair had his most profound effects with respect to Native American history.

As governor, St. Clair speculated in Ohio land and ignored Indian rights as he oversaw the rapid, often tumultuous, and often illegal settlement of the Northwest Territory under the Ordnance of 1787. In January of 1789, as one his first acts in the new office, Arthur St. Clair presided over the Fort Harmar Conference, to speed European-American immigration to the area.

Shortly after the conference ended in a series of agreements known as the Fort Harmar Treaty, a force under Colonel Josiah Harmar was defeated in a concerted attack by a Native American alliance under Little Turtle. Harmer's defeat stunned the Army, whose commanders knew that the Old Northwest would remain closed to immigrants as long as Little Turtle's alliance held. Harmar's defeat pulled St. Clair back into military service.

St. Clair resumed his rank of major general, and gathered an army of 2,000 men during the summer of 1791, then marched into the Ohio country. About a quarter of the men deserted en route. To keep the others happy, St. Clair permitted about 200 soldiers' wives to travel with the army. Despite Harmar's defeat, they seemed to have little inkling of what lay in wait for them.

On November 4, 1791, the Miami/Mohican Little Turtle was one of the principal chiefs among a coalition of Shawnees, Miamis, Delawares, Potawatomis, Ottawas, Chippewas, and Wyandots in the Old Northwest (Ohio country), which defeated St. Clair's army of 1,400 soldiers. About 1,200 warriors, rallied by Little Turtle and aided by an element of surprise, lured St. Clair's forces into the same sort of trap as Colonel Harmar's force had fallen into, this time near St. Mary's Creek, a tributary of the Wabash River. Thirty-eight officers and 598 enlisted men died in the battle; 242 others were wounded, many of whom later died. Fifty-six wives also lost their lives, bringing the total death toll to about 950, a death toll higher than any inflicted on the United States by the British in any single battle of the American Revolution. The death toll was four times the number sustained by General George Armstrong Custer's unit at the Little Bighorn in 1876. After the battle, St. Clair resigned his commission in disgrace.

A Congressional Court of Inquiry later found St. Clair blameless in the defeat, instead placing the blame on Congress for not authorizing the campaign until late in the season, thus forcing it to rely heavily on militia. The work of subjugating the Indian nations in the Northwest Territory next fell to Anthony Wayne. His campaign led eventually to the Battle of Fallen Timbers in 1794 and to the subsequent Treaty of Greeneville (also known as Greenville) in 1795. Arthur St. Clair died in poverty in 1818.

James R. McIntyre, Robert W. Venables, and Bruce E. Johansen

See also Fallen Timbers, Battle of; Northwest Ordinance.

References and Further Reading
Millet, Allan R., and Peter Maslowski. 1994. *For the Common Defense: A Military History of the United States of America.* New York: Free Press.
Prucha, Francis P. 1977. *The Sword of the Republic: The United States Army on the Frontier, 1783–1846.* Bloomington: Indiana University Press.
Sword, Wiley. 1985. *President Washington's Indian War: The Struggle for the Old Northwest, 1790–1795.* Norman: University of Oklahoma Press.
Weigley, Russell F. 1967. *History of the United States Army.* New York: Macmillan.

Standing Bear (Ponca); *Standing Bear v. Crook* (1879)

The *Standing Bear vs. Crook* court case began with the last request of a dying son and ended with a groundbreaking legal decision. For the first time, Native Americans were considered human beings under the law.

In 1877, the U.S. government told Chief Standing Bear ("Machunazha") and his Poncas that they must move from their Nebraska reservation to the Indian Territory (Oklahoma). The government sent several tribal leaders to examine their new land, promising the Ponca that they could return to Nebraska if they were dissatisfied. The chiefs rejected the land as being barren, full of rocks and unsuitable for farming. However, they were told they had no choice; the tribe was moving.

Many Poncas died en route. By the end of 1878, only 430 of the 710 Poncas who had been sent to the Indian Territory were still alive; the rest had been lost to starvation and disease. One of the last to die was Standing Bear's 16-year-old son. He asked that his body be buried with those of his ancestors. Standing Bear promised, and in January 1879, he

headed north with a small burial party. They traveled by hidden trails and reached the Omaha Indian reservation before soldiers caught up with them.

General George Crook was ordered to arrest and return the Poncas. When he saw them, Crook was saddened by their pitiable condition and impressed with their stoicism. He contacted the *Omaha Daily Herald*'s assistant editor Thomas Henry Tibbles, and enlisted his help. Crook believed his removal order was cruel, but felt powerless to do anything about it himself. He encouraged Tibbles to use his newspaper to "... fight against those who are robbing these helpless people" (Brown, 1970, 340–341).

Tibbles was able to enlist the help of two prominent attorneys, A. J. Poppleton and J. L. Webster. Using the Fourteenth Amendment as the basis of their case, they persuaded Judge Elmer S. Dundy to grant an application for a writ of *habeas corpus*. Webster quoted from the amendment, which states that all *persons* born or naturalized in the United States are citizens of the United States and cannot be deprived of life, liberty, or property without due process of law. Webster inferred that the Indians must then be citizens since they were born "on our soil. "If they are not citizens," he said, "what are they? Are they wild animals, deer to be chased by every hound?" (*Omaha Herald,* May 3, 1879, 8).

The second day of the trial climaxed with Standing Bear's testimony: "... You see me standing here. Where do you think I come from? From the water, the woods or where? God made me and he put me on my land. But, I was ordered to stand up and leave my land. When I got down there it seemed as if I was in a big fire. One-hundred and fifty-eight of my people were burned up; now I stand before you. I came away to save my wife and children and friends. I never want to go back there again. I want to go back to my old reservation to live there and be buried in the land of my fathers . . ." (*Omaha Herald,* May 3, 1879, 8).

The trial ended with Judge Dundy declaring Standing Bear "a person under the law," and thus entitled to basic human rights. (*Omaha Republican,* May 12, 1879, 1). When the news reached the Ponca still in Oklahoma, Standing Bear's brother, Big Snake, decided to test the law and headed north with thirty of his followers. However, Dundy had written the law to apply only in the case of Standing Bear, so orders were sent to arrest Big Snake. He was bayoneted and killed while resisting arrest.

The first attempt by Indians to fulfill the high hopes created by Judge Dundy's decision had ended in the tragic death of an innocent man. Standing Bear, who had started the entire process by his simple desire to return his dead son to the land of his birth, now had a brother to bury as well. It had only been a few months since newspapers across the country had called for citizenship rights for peaceful Indians, but it was not until 1924, forty-five years later, that those citizenship rights, which had seemed so attainable in the spring of 1879, would finally be given to the First Americans.

Hugh J. Reilly

See also Jackson, Helern Hunt; LaFlesche, Susette.
References and Further Reading
Berkhofer, Robert F. 1978. *The White Man's Indian.* New York: Alfred A. Knopf.
Brown, Dee. 1970. *Bury My Heart at Wounded Knee: An Indian History of the American West.* New York: Bantam Books.
Coward, John M. "Creating the Ideal Indian: The Case of the Poncas." *Journalism History* 21 (Autumn, 1995) 112–121.
Knight, Oliver. 1960. *Following the Indian Wars.* Norman: University of Oklahoma Press.
Martin, John L., and Nelson, Harold L., "The Historical Standard in Press Analysis." *Journalism Quarterly* 33 (1956): 456–466.
Omaha Bee, 20, June, 1877–21, May, 1879.
Omaha Herald, 1, April, 1879–22, May, 1879.
Omaha Republican, 2, June, 1877–12, May, 1879.
Tibbles, Thomas Henry. 1957. *Buckskin and Blanket Days: Memoirs of a Friend of the Indians.* New York: Doubleday and Company.

Standing Bear, Luther

Remembered for his work as an author, schoolteacher, rancher, store clerk, post office assistant, minister's aide, actor, lecturer, and chief of his *tiospaye* (extended family), Luther Standing Bear was one of the most widely known Lakota advocates for Indians in the early twentieth century.

Standing Bear was born between 1863 and 1868 at Ota Kte ("Breaking Up of Camp") at Fort Robinson, Nebraska. He was among the first class enrolled in 1879 at the U.S. Indian Industrial School in Carlisle, Pennsylvania, located in an abandoned U.S. Army military facility. He completed his final term in 1884 and returned to the Rosebud and Pine Ridge Reservations in South Dakota, where he lived off and on again for the next twenty-one years.

Standing Bear's experience at Carlisle taught him lessons that the non-Indian architects of government Indian education never intended. He became an advocate for using education as an instrument to defend Indian nations. In his third book, *Land of the Spotted Eagle* (1933), Standing Bear recognized that the subjects taught with the well-being of Indian peoples in mind would be different from those that non-Indians taught: "The Indian, by the very sense of duty, should become his own historian, giving his account of the race—fairer and fewer accounts of the wars and more of statecraft, legends, language, oratory, and philosophical conceptions" (Standing Bear, 1933, 254).

In 1891, Standing Bear was among the founders of the Oglala Society of the Pine Ridge Reservation, where gatherings in the Allen Issue Station District offered opportunities, in his words, "where we could discuss matters of importance to the tribe, and suggest ways and means to better our conditions" (Standing Bear, 1928, 235). In 1912 he joined the Society of American Indians, a critical forum at the headwaters of a century-long process among Indians to reclaim the authority to represent themselves in culture, policies, and politics. After 1916, in California, he was a member of the American Indian Progressive Association and the National League for Justice to the American Indian.

For one season, until the serious injuries he suffered in a train wreck almost ended his life in 1904, Standing Bear was an actor in the Wild West shows produced by William F. Cody. In 1905 he was chosen to replace his deceased father as chief of his *tiospaye*. After the government reclassified him as a U.S. citizen, Standing Bear worked in Iowa at a dry goods firm and at the 101 Ranch in Oklahoma. He moved to Los Angeles in 1916, where he became an actor in Hollywood Westerns. Standing Bear's early silent films included *White Oak* (1921). His later sound movies included *The Santa Fe Trail* (1930), *The Conquering Horde* (1931), *Circle of Death* (1935), and *Fighting Pioneers* (1935).

In addition to essays and articles, Standing Bear published four books between 1928 and 1934 with the help of his niece: *My People the Sioux* (1928), *My Indian Boyhood* (1931), *Land of the Spotted Eagle* (1933), and *Stories of the Sioux* (1934). Negotiating the problem of representing Indians in a second language was his most enduring accomplishment. Standing Bear wrote to correct injustices—to represent, in his words, "explanations [of things done by the Indian] that are more often than not

Luther Standing Bear was one of the most widely known Lakota advocates for Indians in the early twentieth century. (Library of Congress)

erroneous" (Standing Bear, 1933, 42). In the language of the destroyers of indigenous worlds, he fought back against predictions of Indian demise, destructive government policies, and the contagious diseases that slaughtered his and other extended families. He located the cause of these problems outside of Indian cultures. "The Lakotas were blessed with good health . . . [a]nd as far as I can remember there was no such thing as a contagious disease" (Standing Bear, 1933, 60). He located the cure inside Indian cultures: "It is the unquenchable spirit that has saved him—his clinging to Indian ways, Indian thought, and tradition, that has kept him and is keeping him today" (Standing Bear, 1933, 190).

Standing Bear died in Huntington, California, on February 19, 1939, during the filming of *Union Pacific*.

D. Anthony Tyeeme Clark (Meskwaki)

See also Boarding Schools, United States and Canada; Crook, George; Society of American Indians.

References and Further Reading

Ellis, Richard N. 1985. "Luther Standing Bear: 'I Would Raise Him to Be an Indian.'" In *Indian Lives: Essays on Nineteenth-and Twentieth-Century Native Americans*. Edited by L. G. Moses and Raymond Wilson, 138–157. Albuquerque: University of New Mexico Press.

Standing Bear, Luther. [1928] 1975. *My People the Sioux*. Lincoln: University of Nebraska Press.

Standing Bear, Luther. [1933] 1978. *Land of the Spotted Eagle*. Lincoln: University of Nebraska Press.

Sullivan, General John and the Haudenosaunee Holocaust of 1779

The term "holocaust" is wedded in the public mind to the experience of the Jews of Europe from 1933 to 1945. However, the Iroquois experienced a holocaust during the eighteenth century in upstate New York, western Pennsylvania, and Ohio during the American Revolution (Parker, 1926, 126). Ever since the 1779 scorched-earth attacks by General John Sullivan, General James Clinton, Colonel Goose Van Schaick, and Colonel Daniel Brodhead, the immigrants have been known to eastern Natives as the Town Destroyers (ASP, 1998, 1: 140).

Typically, American histories slim the coordinated assaults by these military operatives down to the Sullivan campaign, ignoring the full intent and extent of the orders of George Washington, their commander in chief. Washington ordered his lead general, Sullivan, to destroy the Iroquois utterly, not because of their alliance with the British, but very specifically because he considered "the Six Nations of Indians, with their associates and adherents" the enemy. He consequently announced his "immediate objects" to be "the total destruction and devastation of their settlements" (Sparks, 1855, 6: 264). The Revolutionary Army was "to lay waste all the settlements around, with instructions to do it in the most effectual manner, that the country may not be merely overrun, but destroyed" (Sparks, 1855, 6: 265). Washington even specified that terrorism was part of his order, for the Army was to make it a point " to rush on with the war-whoop and fixed bayonet" because "[n]othing w[ould] disconcert and terrify the Indians more than this" (Sparks, 1855, 6: 265).

Washington thus ordered total war, for the people being rushed upon with fixed bayonet were women, children, and old folks. The American battle cry of danger to settlers on the "frontiers"—i.e., Native lands as yet unseized—was a pretext and a rationale for whipping up armies to commit genocide, the preferred method for "clearing" the land of its original people in favor of European settlers (Mann, 2005, 51–54). Furthermore, Washington had what today would be viewed as a serious conflict of interest in ordering the attacks, for the ultimate prize was Ohio, and the Washington family basically owned the Ohio Company, which speculated heavily in real estate that was then in the fiercely protected possession of Native nations (Kutler, 2003, 6: 175). He had personally surveyed Ohio Company land for speculation during the French and Indian War (Clark, 1995, 22, 27–28; Fitzpatrick, 1925, 1: 43–46, 77, 416, 449).

Moreover, the Continental Congress paid its army recruits in land warrants, issued on property to be seized in Ohio. The only way to pay its debts was actually to break the Haudenosaune (Iroquois) League and appropriate Ohio, a move that would enrich Washington. Should the new United States fail to take Ohio, to pay its debts, and to establish its financial and political credit, European nations would reclaim the states as their colonies. These complex interactions explain the absolute and driving need of Washington to break the League and seize Ohio, a feat that he finally managed in 1795 (Mann, 2004, 135–201).

Washington's plan called for a two-pronged attack by the major forces under Sullivan at Easton, New Jersey, and under Clinton at Canajoharie, New York, converging on upstate and western New York. Van Schaick was specifically to target the Onondagas (as the perceived seat of Iroquoian government). Meantime, Brodhead was to rush north from Fort Pitt to meet up with the combined forces of Sullivan, Clinton, and Van Schaick in western New York, thus cutting the New York Iroquois off from Pennsylvania and Ohio aid. If possible, the combined armies were, after devastating the Iroquois, to march on Niagara, the British headquarters, but that was always more of a desire than an actual goal.

In fact, due to Sullivan's petulant dawdling, Van Schaick's attack occurred in April 1779, well before the main force left (Egly, 1992, 60–65). Also ready in April, Brodhead was told to stand down, given the laggardly pace of the main army, but he went ahead with his original orders, setting up forts along the

Allegheny Mountains in the spring and summer and setting off on August 6, 1779, to meet Sullivan's main force (Cook, 1972, 307–308; Hammond, 1939, 3: 88; Sparks, 6: 206, 224–225). Finally, on August 9, 1779, Sullivan and Clinton simultaneously lumbered out of their separate headquarters, meeting up at Tioga (Cook, 1972, 84, 93, 201). Whereas Van Schaick marched with the main body, Brodhead never quite hooked up with it, attaining only Olean Point, forty miles distant from the main force (Edson, 1879, 663; Mann, 2005, 46; Stone, 1924, 95).

It is important to understand that the Iroquois did not want the war, avoided participating in it as long as they could, and, once coerced into it, chose removing women, children, and elders from harm's way over standing to fight the Revolutionary Army. At the outset of British–American hostilities, League speakers explicitly told both sides that they were neutral. This did not stop the Americans from attacking any and all "Indians," including those allied with them, or the British from deliberately engineering an attack by the Americans on the neutral Senecas at the Battle of Oriskany to drag the League into the war on the crown's side. The resultant disagreement among League nations as to their stances led to the incident in which the fire at Onondaga was put out in 1777, but this simply meant that the issue was tabled, with each of the League's constituent nations free to form its own policy. The League itself was not dissolved, as many Western historians still erroneously assert (Mann, 2005, 10–15).

To ensure that the Iroquois would be wiped off the face of the earth, Congress authorized Washington to raise a total army of 5,163, to be shared among Van Schaick (558), Clinton (1,500), and Sullivan (2,500), with Brodhead to join the fray, bringing his 605 men from Fort Pitt (Egly, 1992, 61; Hammond, 1939, 3: 147; NYSHA 1933, 4: 202). By contrast, the Iroquois League, at its peak in 1777, had but a thousand soldiers (Cruikshank, 1893, 35). By 1779, those numbers had dwindled. By the time of the one "battle" of the Sullivan campaign, fought at Newtown (Elmira, New York) on August 29, 1779, the Confederate forces under Thayendenegea (Joseph Brant), the Mohawk war chief, and Colonel John Butler, the British commander, had seriously thinned.

According to Butler, the *combined* strength of the British and Native Confederates amounted to fewer than six hundred men the day of the Newtown battle (Flick, 1929, 282). In his formal report, Sullivan greatly exaggerated this number to 1,500, but even his own commanders falsified that count at the time,

John Sullivan became a brigadier general in the Continental Army. In 1779 he led a brutal, "scorched earth" expedition against elements of the Six Nations whom he defined as enemies. (Library of Congress)

and historians since then have pegged the Native numbers at those reported by Thayendanegea and Butler (Cook, Journals: 298, officers. Graymont, 1972, 208; Mann, 2005, 80, 82–84). Furthermore, whereas Sullivan's men had been feasting their way across Iroquois on crops they were destroying, the British and Native troops were literally starving, living on rations of seven ears of green corn per day each, with many suffering greatly from the "Ague" (Cruikshank, 1893, 71; Flick, 1929, 284, 293). The Battle of Newtown was therefore a complete rout of the Confederacy, but the Native purpose had never been to defeat the Sullivan army. The Iroquois were buying time to evacuate their people.

The American attacks of 1779 had the intended genocidal effect, destroying a total of at least sixty towns, a number that would, even today, knock out any state of the Union. Van Schaick racked up three towns (Cook, 1972, 17, 193; Egly, 1992, 62; Mann, 2005, 28–36); Brodhead, sixteen (Edson, 1879, 663; Flick, 1929, 285, 291; Mann, 2005, 39–48; Stone, 1924, 94, 95, 96); and Sullivan-Clinton, forty-one (Cook, 1972, 380–82). The destruction was complete, with all

housing within the sweep of the combined armies completely burned, all crops looted (to support the Americans) and/or burned, all household and farm implements destroyed or looted, and all of the once magnificent peach and apple orchards of the League cut down. In addition, all animals of the fields and forests were consumed by the Americans, along with the fishes of the waters. The American soldiers took numerous scalps for the lucrative bounties that the states and Congress offered on Native dead, with one soldier, Timothy Murphy, racking up thirty-three scalps by himself (Cook, 1972, 162). American soldiers also skinned Natives, making shoes and other items from their tanned "hides" (for skinning, see Cook, 1972, 8, 240, 244, 279; for a detailed description of the destruction, see Mann, 2005, 58–106).

Because the American attacks of 1778 had already induced famine in Iroquoia (Mann, 2005, 20–22), there was no buffer for the effects of the Sullivan campaign. In addition, the winter of 1779–1780 was the severest on record, with New York harbor freezing solid and snows drifting several feet high from New York through Ohio, precluding hunting (Edson, 1879, 667; Seaver, 1990, 60). As the Seneca adoptee Mary Jemison so wrenchingly documented the effect on Natives at the time, "but what were our feelings when we found that there was not a mouthful of any kind of sustenance left, not even enough to keep a child one day from perishing with hunger" (Seaver, 1990, 59). Thousands of Natives died as an immediate result of the dire starvation caused by the attacks. Many more died as refugees, 5,036 at Niagara (Graymont, 1972, 220; Mann, 2005, 106–108), and another 5,000 at British Detroit (Haldiman Papers, 10: 444–445, Mann, 2005, 111).

The Americans lost no time in seizing the land that had recently hosted Iroquoian farms; the settlers ploughed up corn charred in the Sullivan despoliation (Wright, 1943, 4: 3). In 1879, a massive centennial was mounted in New York to celebrate the Sullivan campaign as a great moment in U.S. history (Cook, 1972, 331–579), and it is still celebrated to this day by Euro-Americans who, hopefully, do not realize that they are exalting an act of genocide.

Barbara Alice Mann

See also American Revolution Native American Participation; Brant, Joseph; Genocide; Haudenosaunee Confederacy, Political System.

References and Further Reading

American State Papers (ASP). [1832] 1998. Class II. 2 volumes. Buffalo, NY: William S. Hein & Co.

Clark, Harrison. 1995. *All Cloudless Glory: The Life of George Washington, from Youth to Yorktown.* Washington, DC: Regnery Publishing, 1995.

Cook, Frederick. 1972. *Journals of the Military Expedition of Major General John Sullivan Against the Six Nations of Indians in 1779.* 1887. Freeport, NY: Books for Libraries Press.

Cruikshank, Ernest. 1893. *The Story of Butler's Rangers and the Settlement of Niagara.* Welland, ON: Tribune Printing House.

Edson, Obed. 1879. "Brodhead's Expedition Against the Indians of the Upper Allegheny, 1779." *Magazine of American History* 3, no. 11 (November): 649–675.

Egly, T. W., Jr. 1992. *Goose Van Schaick of Albany, 1736–1789, The Continental Army's Senior Colonel.* Hampton, NH: T. W. Egly, Jr.

Fitzpatrick, John C. ed. 1925. *The Diaries of George Washington, 1748–1799.* 4 volumes. Boston: Houghton-Mifflin.

Flick, Alexander C. 1929. "New Sources on the Sullivan–Clinton Campaign in 1779." *Quarterly Journal of the New York State Historical Society* 10, no. 3 (July): 185–224.

Flick, Alexander C. 1929. "New Sources on the Sullivan–Clinton Campaign in 1779." *Quarterly Journal of the New York State Historical Society* 10, no. 4 (October): 265–317.

Graymont, Barbara. 1972. *The Iroquois in the American Revolution.* Syracuse, NY: Syracuse University Press.

Hammond, Otis G. 1939. *Letters and Papers of Major-General John Sullivan, Continental Army.* Vol. 3: *1779–1795.* Concord, NH: New Hampshire Historical Society.

"Haldiman Papers, The." 1908. *Collections and Researches Made by the Pioneer Society of the State of Michigan,* 2nd ed. Vol. 10, 210–672. Lansing: Wynkoop Hallenbeck Crawford Company, State Printers.

Kutler, Stanley I., ed.-in-chief. 2003. *Dictionary of American History.* 10 volumes. New York: Charles Scribner's Sons.

Mann, Barbara Alice. 2005. *George Washington's War on Native America, 1779–1782.* Westport, CT: Praeger.

Mann, Barbara Alice. 2004. "The Greenville Treaty of 1795: Pen-and-Ink Witchcraft in the Struggle for the Old Northwest." In *Enduring Legacies: Native American Treaties and Contemporary Controversies.* Edited by Bruce E. Johansen, 135–201. Westport, CT: Praeger.

New York State Historical Association (NYSHA). 1933. *History of the State of New York.* 6 volumes. New York: Columbia University Press.

Parker, Arthur Caswell (Gawaso Waneh). [1926] 1970. *An Analytical History of the Seneca Indians, Researches and Transactions of the New*

York State Archaeological Association, Lewis H. Morgan Chapter. Millwood, NY: Kraus Reprint.

Seaver, James E. [1823] 1990. *A Narrative of the Life of Mrs. Mary Jemison.* Syracuse, NY: Syracuse University Press.

Sparks, Jared, ed. 1855. *The Writings of George Washington; Being His Correspondence, Addresses, Messages, and Other Papers, Official and Private, Selected and Published from the Original Manuscripts.* 12 volumes. Boston: Little, Brown and Company.

Stone, William L. [1838] 1969. *Life of Joseph Brant— Thayendanegea: Including the Border Wars of the American Revolution, and Sketches of the Indian Campaign of Generals Harmar, St. Clair, and Wayne, and Other Matters Connected with the Indian Relations of the United States and Great Britain, from the Peace of 1783 to the Indian Peace of 1795.* 2 volumes. Milwood, NY: Kraus Reprint.

Stone, Rufus B. 1924. "Brodhead's Raid on the Senecas." *Western Pennsylvania Historical Magazine* 7, no. 2 (April): 88–101.

Wright, Albert Hazen. 1943. *The Sullivan Expedition of 1779: Contemporary Newspaper Comment.* Studies in History, nos. 5, 6, 7, and 8. 4 parts. Ithaca, NY: A. H. Wright.

Tammany Society

Many colonial Americans viewed American society as a synthesis of Native American and European cultures. The Tammany Society, a classic example of the blending of the two cultures, was a broad-based popular movement that reinforced the founders' usage of symbols and ideological concepts indigenous to North America. The celebration of Tammany Day may have been an attempt to adapt May Day and other Old World holidays to the new American environment.

Subsequently, when it inherited the patriotic mantle of the Sons of Liberty in Philadelphia, the Tammany Society espoused a philosophy that America was a unique synthesis of the best and noblest aspects of Europe and America. Building on their own experiences with American Indians, founding fathers like James Madison and Thomas Jefferson used the Tammany Society and its membership to forge a new democratic party after the formation of the U.S. Constitution. Other founding fathers like Benjamin Franklin, John Dickinson, and Benjamin Rush became influential members of the Society.

To the Tammany Society, American Indians were more than a symbol of freedom. To members of the Revolutionary generation, American Indians represented a wellspring of new ideas that freed Europeans from the antiquated ideas of class and autocratic government that had so long existed in Europe. In the late eighteenth century, Tammany Society members from Georgia to Rhode Island to the Ohio River frequently consulted with American Indian leaders and sought to study American Indian languages and ideas. The Society's members emphasized concepts and values that founders such as Franklin and Jefferson found in Native societies, including a weak executive (except in war), popular participation in government, and charity for the poor. Even James Madison was compelled to seek out the Iroquois and their council when he became disillusioned with the Articles of Confederation in 1784.

Although the early history of the Tammany Society is ambiguous, it appears that King Tammany, a Delaware chief friendly to William Penn, became a popular figure in the folklore of early Pennsylvania. The Tammany Society became an avenue for the expression of a regional American identity by the mideighteenth century. The Society's ability to synthesize American and European values and to forge a new identity made it a potent force in creating a national identity as well. Its use of an amalgam of American Indian symbols and the figure of Christopher Columbus denotes that the American colonists were willing and able to change both American Indian and European values in their quest for a viable American identity before, during, and after the American Revolution.

The Tammany Society believed that Penn's friendship with the Delaware chief, Tammany, was a product of Penn's sincerity in dealing with the Delawares. Perhaps Penn's initial successes with the Delawares and also with the Iroquois were based on the common understanding of the amicable feelings of peace among all human beings that leads to an equitable and just society.

Initially, Penn dealt with the Unami (Turtle Totem) Leni Lenápe (Delaware) tribe when he came to Pennsylvania, and Delaware Chief Tammany played a prominent role in the early treaties negotiated with Penn. Although the real Tammany's mark appeared on only two treaties (June 23, 1683 and June 15, 1692), he was destined to become a legendary figure in U.S. and Pennsylvania history and folklore. Tradition has it that Tammany's name

meant "the affable" and that he was one of the Delaware Indians who welcomed William Penn on his arrival in America on October 27, 1682. By July 6, 1694, in a meeting between the Provincial Council of Pennsylvania and a delegation of Indians, Tammany had become a strong supporter of the whites and their policies. From these facts and folklore, a legendary Tammany was constructed in the early eighteenth century that was the white man's friend and counselor.

Chief Tammany's mythic importance among the people of Philadelphia crystallized when a group of Quakers established the Schuylkill Fishing Company in 1732. Claiming that their fishing rights in the Schuylkill River had been given to them by the Delaware chief and friend to William Penn, Tammany, the company adopted him as its patron saint. The saint's day was designated as May 1, the traditional beginning of the fishing season. At this time, Chief Tammany was viewed by many Philadelphians as a nature spirit whose ritual day was celebrated to ensure a bountiful fishing season, but he seems also to have been associated with a resolve to protect the fishing rights (and, by proxy, the political rights) of its members.

Within a decade, the Schuylkill Fishing Company began to fictionalize Tammany by creating mottoes attributed to him. In 1747, the company gave a cannon to the Association Battery of Philadelphia, stamped *Kwanio Che Keeteru* ["This is my right, and I will defend it"], a phrase attributed to Tammany. The phrase was ripe with implications for the increasingly restless colonists. By the time of the Stamp Act crisis eighteen years later, images of the American Indian, often as Tammany, were being used widely as a symbol of resistance to British authority. The colonists were beginning to forge a new identity, calling themselves "Americans," a word used in place of their former European nationalities. The colonists were surprisingly conscious of the composite European-American identity they were creating.

The influence of the Tammany Society extended to the end of the nineteenth century; its members often brought prominent Iroquois leaders, such as Cornplanter, to Philadelphia to meet with important political figures, including George Washington.

Bruce E. Johansen

See also Cornplanter; Penn, William, Quakers, and Native Americans.

References and Further Reading

Dunn, Richard S., and Mary M. Dunn, eds. 1982. *The Papers of William Penn.* Philadelphia: University of Pennsylvania Press.

Kilroe, Edwin P. 1913. *St. Tammany and the Origin of the Tammany Society.* New York: Private Printing.

Myers, Albert C., ed. 1983. *William Penn's Own Account of the Lenni Lenape or Delaware Indians.* Wilmington, DE: Middle Atlantic Press.

Tecumseh

The Shawnee Tecumseh (ca. 1768–1813), was a major military leader and alliance builder who sought to stop European-American expansion into the Ohio Valley area early in the nineteenth century, after alliances led by Pontiac and Little Turtle had failed. For a time, Tecumseh assembled an alliance that posed the last major obstacle to Anglo-American expansion across the Ohio Valley westward to the Mississippi River.

Tecumseh was born about 1768 near present-day Oldtown, Ohio. He fought as a young warrior at the Battle of Fallen Timbers. Tecumseh's influence grew rapidly as he came of age, not only because of his acumen as a statesman and a warrior, but also because he forbade the torture of prisoners. Immigrants and Tecumseh's Native American allies trusted Tecumseh implicitly.

Tecumseh was raised from birth to make war on the encroaching European-Americans by his mother, Methoataske, whose husband, the Shawnee Puckeshinwa, had been killed in cold blood by immigrants when Tecumseh was a boy. Tecumseh and his mother found him dying. As he watched his father die, Tecumseh vowed to become like "a fire spreading over the hill and valley, consuming the race of dark souls" (Johansen and Grinde, 1997, 383). A few years later, Tecumseh's hatred for the immigrants was compounded by the murder of Cornstalk, a Shawnee chief who had been his mentor.

By the turn of the century, as the number of non-Indian immigrants grew, Tecumseh began to assemble the Shawnees, Delawares, Ottawas, Ojibwas, Kickapoos, and Wyandots into a confederation with the aim of establishing a permanent Native American confederation that would act as a buffer zone between the United States to the east and English Canada to the north. One observer recalled Tecumseh as a commanding speaker. His voice was

said to have "resounded over the multitude, his words like a succession of thunderbolts" (Johansen and Grinde, 1997, 384).

Rallying Native allies with an appeal for alliance about 1805, Tecumseh urged all Indians in the area to unite as brothers, as sons of one Mother Earth. He scoffed at the idea of selling the land. Why not sell the air? He asked. The sale of land, to Tecumseh, was contrary to the ways of nature. He tried to unite the southern tribes by appealing to history:

Where today are the Pequot? Where are the Narragansett, the Mohican, the Pocanet, and other powerful tribes of our people? They have vanished before the avarice and oppression of the white man, as snow before the summer sun. Will we let ourselves be destroyed in our turn, without an effort worthy of our race? Shall we, without a struggle, give up our homes, our lands, bequeathed to us by the Great Spirit? The graves of our dead and everything that is dear and sacred to us? I know you will say with me: never! Never!" (Armstrong, 1984, 45).

Tecumseh told representatives of southern Native nations that they faced extinction: Our broad domains are fast escaping from our grasp. Every year our white intruders become more greedy, exacting, oppressive, and overbearing. Before the palefaces came among us, we enjoyed the happiness of unbounded freedom, and were acquainted with neither riches, wants, nor oppression. How is it now? Wants and oppression are our lot. Dare we move without asking, by your leave. Are we not being stripped, day by day, of the little that remains of our ancient liberty? Do they not even kick and strike us as they do their blackfaces? How long will it be before they will tie us to a post and whip us, and make us work for them? Shall we wait for that moment or shall we die fighting before submitting to such ignominy? (Johansen and Grinde, 1997, 384).

Territorial governor (and U.S. Army general) William Henry Harrison tried to undermine the growing strength of Tecumseh's Native alliance by negotiating treaties with individual Native nations. Because only a portion of each nation's warriors elected to follow Tecumseh, Harrison found it easy enough to find "treaty Indians" among those who did not elect to fight. By 1811, Harrison had negotiated at least fifteen treaties, all of which Tecumseh repudiated.

Harrison's wariness of Tecumseh's power sprung from a deep respect for him. "The implicit obedience and respect which the followers of Tecumseh pay to him is really astonishing and more than any other circumstance bespeaks him [as] one of those uncommon geniuses, which spring up occasionally to produce revolutions and to overturn the established order of things," said Harrison. He continued: "If it were not for the vicinity of the United States, he would, perhaps, be the founder of an Empire that would rival in glory Mexico or Peru. No difficulties deter him" (Hamilton, 1972, 159).

Tecumseh was particularly galled by Harrison's choice as his territorial capital the village of Chillicothe, the same site (with the same name) as the Shawnees' former principal settlement. The name itself is anglicized Shawnee for "principal town." At one treaty council, Tecumseh found himself seated next to Harrison on a bench. Tecumseh slowly but aggressively pushed Harrison off the edge of the bench, then told him that this was what the immigrants were doing to his people. They were being slowly squeezed off their lands. During his last conference with Tecumseh, Harrison bid the chief to take a chair. "Your father requests you take a chair," an interpreter told Tecumseh, to which he replied, defiantly: "My father! The sun is my father and the Earth is my mother. I will repose upon her bosom" (Gill, 1987, 14). Tecumseh then sat, cross-legged, on the ground.

Tecumseh also was angry over Harrison's treaty of September 30, 1809, with the Delawares, Potawatomies, Miamis, Kickapoos, Wea, and Eel River peoples. For $8,200 in cash and $2,350 in annuities, Harrison had laid claim on behalf of the United States to roughly 3 million acres of rich hunting land along the Wabash River in the heart of the area in which Tecumseh wished to build his Native confederacy. When Tecumseh and his brother, also a Shawnee war chief, complained to Harrison that the treaty terms were unfair, Harrison at first rebuked Tecumseh by saying that the Shawnees had not even been part of the treaty. The implicit refusal to recognize Tecumseh's alliance angered the Indians even more. Realizing that Tecumseh's influence made it politic for him to do so, Harrison agreed to meet with him. At a meeting on August 12, 1810, each side drew up several hundred battle-ready warriors and

soldiers. Harrison agreed to relay Tecumseh's complaints to the president, and Tecumseh said that his warriors would join the Americans against the British if Harrison would annul the treaty.

Nothing came of Harrison's promises, and, the following year, bands of warriors allied with Tecumseh began ranging out of the settlement of Tippecanoe to terrorize nearby farmsteads and small backwoods settlements. Harrison said he would wipe out Tippecanoe if the raids did not stop; Tecumseh said they would stop when the land signed away under the 1810 treaty was returned. Tecumseh then journeyed southward to bring the Creeks, Chickasaws, and Choctaws into his alliance. Tecumseh carried the message that he had used to recruit other allies:

> Brothers—When the white men first set foot on our grounds, they were hungry. They had no place on which to spread their blankets, or to kindle their fires. They were feeble; they could do nothing for themselves. Our fathers commiserated with their distress, and shared freely with them whatever the Great Spirit had given his red children. They gave them food when hungry, medicine when sick, spread skins for them to sleep on, and gave them ground so that they might hunt and raise corn. Brothers—the white people are like poisonous serpents: when chilled, they are feeble, and harmless, but invigorate them with warmth, and they sting their benefactors to death (Johansen and Grinde, 1997, 385–386).

Tecumseh failed, for the most part, to bring new allies into his alliance. While he was traveling, the command of the existing alliance fell to Tecumseh's brother, Tenskwatawa, who was called The Prophet. On September 26, 1811, Harrison decamped at Vincennes with more than 900 men, two-thirds of them Indian allies. He built a fort and named it after himself on the present-day site of Terre Haute, Indiana. Harrison then sent two Miamis to The Prophet to demand the return of property Harrison alleged had been stolen in the raids, along with the surrender of Indians he accused of murder. The Miamis did not return to Harrison's camp. The governor's army marched to within sight of Tippecanoe and met with Tenskwatawa, who invited them to make camp, relax, and negotiate. Harrison's forces did stop, but set up in battle configurations, as The Prophet's warriors readied an attack.

Within two hours of pitched battle, Harrison's forces routed the Indians, then burned the village of Tippecanoe as Tenskwatawa's forces scattered into the woods. Returning to the devastation from his travels, Tecumseh fled to British Canada, where, in the War of 1812, he was put in command of a force of whites and Indians as a British brigadier general. Harrison's forces met Tecumseh at the Battle of the Thames, in what is now Ontario, east of today's Windsor. Tecumseh was killed during that battle on October 5, 1813. After it, some of the Kentucky militia who had taken part in it found a body they thought was Tecumseh's and cut strips from it for souvenirs. His warriors, who had dispersed in panic when Tecumseh died, said later that they had taken his body with them. Having committed twenty thousand men and $5 million to the cause, the United States had effectively terminated armed Indian resistance in the Ohio Valley and the surrounding areas.

Bruce E. Johansen

See also Fallen Timbers, Battle of; Harrison, William Henry; Tenskwatawa.

References and Further Reading

Armstrong, Virginia Irving. 1984. *I Have Spoken: American History Through the Voices of the Indians.* Athens, OH: Swallow Press.

Eckert, Allan W. 1992. *A Sorrow in Our Heart: The Life of Tecumseh.* New York: Bantam.

Edmunds, R. David. 1983. *The Shawnee Prophet.* Lincoln: University of Nebraska Press.

Edmunds, R. David. 1984. *Tecumseh and the Quest for Indian Leadership.* Boston: Little, Brown and Company.

Gill, Sam. 1987. *Mother Earth: An American Story.* Chicago: University of Chicago Press.

Hamilton, Charles, ed. 1972. *Cry of the Thunderbird.* Norman: University of Oklahoma Press.

Johansen, Bruce E., and Donald A. Grinde, Jr. 1997. *The Encyclopedia of Native American Biography.* New York: Henry Holt.

Tekakwitha, Kateri

Kateri (Catherine) Tekakwitha, a seventeenth-century Mohawk, is the only Native American to have been beatified (acclaimed at one step from sainthood) by the Roman Catholic Church. Her life also reflects the tensions between Christians and the Mohawks who refused to be converted.

Tekakwitha, who became known as the Lily of the Mohawks, was born in 1656 in Ossernenon (also known as Auriesville), New York, to a Mohawk father and an Algonquian mother who had been Christianized, then taken captive by the Mohawks a few years before Kateri's birth. She was born into a world of deadly tension between Native peoples and immigrant Jesuit priests. During the 1640s, eight Jesuits were tortured and killed in Ossernenon, after which, in 1667, the French sent troops to avenge the murders. Kateri thus spent much of her youth in a village under French military and religious occupation; the Mohawks had been compelled to accept Jesuits in their midst under duress.

Some of the priests had done their best to convince Mohawks in Ossernenon and the vicinity that their God would punish Natives who did not adopt their faith. After a deadly smallpox epidemic swept the area during Tekakwitha's youth (killing her younger brother, mother, and father), the priests were marked men. Catherine contracted smallpox and her face was disfigured by it, but she didn't die. Orphaned at the age of four, an uncle took responsibility for her.

Despite the fact that the uncle detested the Jesuits, he was ordered to lodge three of them in his home following the occupation of the village in 1667. Kateri became their hostess at the age of eleven. In subsequent years, she continued to bond with the missionaries to the point of refusing to marry in order to maintain her virginity. In retaliation, some of Kateri's relatives withheld food and threatened her life. Resisting these pressures, however, Tekakwitha continued to befriend the priests as several of her neighbors were converted gradually to Catholicism. She was baptized with the name Catherine in 1676. After that, she was harassed as she walked to the village chapel; on one occasion, a warrior taunted Kateri with a wax axe. Others accused Tekakwitha of inviting her uncle into bed to compromise her purported Christian virginity.

Shortly after the sexual rumors, Kateri moved to the Saint Francis Xavier mission in Kahnawake, near Montreal. Her uncle is said to have followed her, threatening to kill Kateri and family members who had accompanied her to Kahnawake; He was not successful. At the mission, she studied Christian theology intensively. Kateri continued to resist pressure to marry, eventually becoming associated with the nuns at the Hotel Dieu hospital in Ville Marie (Montreal). In 1679, Tekakwitha took a formal vow of chastity under Catholic auspices, the first Iroquois to do so.

Controversy attended her vow, however. Kateri stopped participating in hunting expeditions after her half-sister alleged that her husband had been seduced by the purported virgin. Instead, Kateri remained at the mission, practicing penance to the point of self-punishment, saying the Rosary for long periods of time barefoot at the foot of a cross planted in snow, eating food laced with ashes, and sometimes sleeping on a bed of thorns. The mission's priests did not dissuade her. Instead, they acclaimed her reverence and dedication to God.

On April 17, 1680, at the end of a long winter of self-inflicted suffering, Kateri fell ill and died during Holy Week. Since that time, a body of myth has grown up around her life and premature death. It is said, for example, that as Kateri died her face radiated light and lost all the scars inflicted on her by smallpox. Some people who pray in her memory are said to have experienced miracle cures.

In 1884, the Jesuits petitioned the Vatican for her canonization as a saint. In 1943, she was venerated by the Vatican, and, in 1980, she was declared beatified, another step toward sainthood. At least 300 full or partial biographies of Kateri's life have been published, in twenty languages, the most recent in 2005 (Greer, 2005, xi). She also has been the subject of several plays, operas, and films; places where she was known to have lived have become pilgrimage sites for devout Catholics.

Despite all of her postmortem acclaim, at least one ethnohistorian, K. I. Koppedrayer, asserts, based on his examination of historical records, that the Jesuits invented Kateri Tekakwitha to provide an exemplary model for conversions of Native Americans to Catholicism. He points to a lack of independent oral history as an indication that she was an entirely fabricated figure.

Bruce E. Johansen

See also Haudenosaunee Confederacy, Political System; Missionaries, French Jesuit.
References and Further Reading
Greer, Allan. 2005. *Mohawk Saint: Catherine Tekakwitha and the Jesuits.* New York: Oxford University Press.
Koppedrayer, K. I. 1993. "The Making of the First Iroquois Virgin: Early Jesuit Biographies of the Blessed Kateri Tekakwitha." *Ethnohistory* 40 (Spring): 277–306.

Tenskwatawa

Tenskwatawa probably was born in 1775 at Old Piqua, Ohio; he died November 1836 at present-day Kansas City, Kansas. Tenskwatawa, also known as the Shawnee Prophet or simply The Prophet, was an important religious political leader in the early nineteenth century Great Lakes–Ohio Valley region.

Tenskwatawa was born as part of a set of triplets into a family of at least six older brothers and sisters. Prior to his birth, their Shawnee war chief father, Puckeshinwa, died in the 1775 Battle of Point Pleasant, Ohio. Their Creek mother, Methoataske, left the Ohio in 1779 and entrusted her children— Tenskwatawa, Tecumseh (who would grow up to be one of the most famous orators and military leaders of all time), and another child—to an older sister, Tecumapease. His childhood name was Lalawethika ("rattle" or "noisemaker").

In 1804 Lalawethika assumed the role of community shaman when the renowned shaman Penagashea died. Lalawethika had been studying with him since 1795. After a series of visions in 1805, Lalawethika changed his name to Tenskwatawa, meaning "The Open Door." In the visions Tenskwatawa met the Master of Life who showed him heaven and hell, as well as giving him instructions on how to avoid one while gaining admission to the other. Tenskwatawa preached that Indians must give up alcohol, reject Christianity, destroy their medicine bags, and respect all life. If the Master of Life's teachings were followed, Tenskwatawa claimed that the dead and animals would be restored. Adherents were given "prayer sticks" inscribed with prayers for the Master of Life (Edmunds, 2004). He also claimed that Americans were products of the evil Great Serpent who, assisted by witches, spread death and destruction. Tenskwatawa nonetheless proposed that trade continue with the Anglo-Americans, but only on terms set by the Indians until it was no longer needed. Finally, the Nativist vision of Tenskwatawa and Tecumseh included a call for pan-Indian unity to resist encroachments on Indian lands by Europeans (Dowd, 1992, 382–383). Of the brothers, Tenkswatawa's approach was more spiritual, while Tecumseh's was more pragmatic, but both were very persuasive.

Immediately following his vision and explanations, Tenskwatawa and Tecumseh established a village near Greenville, Ohio, and called for all Indian people to settle there. This settlement was a direct challenge to the 1795 Treaty of Greenville. Tenskwatawa participated in witchcraft trials among the

A Shawnee mystic and the brother of Tecumseh, Tenskwatawa appointed himself prophet in 1805. Laulewasika was his given name, but he adopted the name Elkswatawa, and later Tenskwatawa, The Prophet. (Hulton Archive/Getty Images)

Delawares and Wyandots in 1806. Those accused of witchcraft were individuals who appeared to be acculturated to the immigrants' ways. As his prestige and popularity grew, the settlement of Greenville proved to be inadequate. This resulted in the establishment of Prophetstown in 1808 at the mouth of the Tippecanoe River.

Here the brothers' influence was interpreted as a threat by governor of Indiana William Henry Harrison. In 1811, when Tecumseh was in the South building a pan-Indian coalition, Harrison and about 1,000 men attacked Prophetstown, defeating Tenskwatawa and his followers. This event was the nadir of Tenskwatawa's power among the Great Lakes nations. Prophetstown was rebuilt shortly after Harrison left the area, and Tenskwatawa continued to participate in the major events of the War of 1812, although he did not participate in any of the

actual fighting. In 1813, at the Battle of the Thames, Tenskwatawa fled with the British, leaving Tecumseh and dozens of other warriors to die while protecting their retreat. The American victory in this battle effectively ended British and Indian power in the Old Northwest.

Denied admission to the United States in 1815, Tenskwatawa and a few Shawnee followers remained in Upper Canada until 1824. In 1826, two years after his return, Tenskwatawa and the Shawnees were removed from the Ohio Valley. They traveled to Kaskaskia and western Missouri, eventually reaching the Shawnee reservation in Kansas in 1828. Tenskwatawa sat for a portrait by American artist George Catlin in 1832 and died in 1836.

Karl S. Hele

See also Catlin, George; Harrison, William Henry; Tecumseh.

References and Further Reading

Allan, Robert S. No date. "Tecumseh." *The Canadian Encyclopedia.* Available at: http://www .thecanadianencyclopedia.com/ index.cfm?PgNm=TCE&Params =A1ARTA0007898. Accessed December 20, 2004.

Dowd, Gregory Evans. 1992a. *A Spirited Resistance: The North American Indian Struggle for Unity, 1745–1815.* Baltimore, MD: Johns Hopkins University Press.

Dowd, Gregory Evans. 1992b. "Thinking and Believing: Nativism and Unity in the Ages of Pontiac and Tecumseh." *American Indian Quarterly* 16: 309–335.

Edmunds, R. David. No date. "Tenskwatawa." *Dictionary of Canadian Biography Online.* Available at: http://www.biographi.ca/ EN/ShowBio.asp?BioId=37811&query =tenskwatawa. Accessed December 19, 2004.

Edmunds, R. David. 1984. *Tecumseh and the Quest for Indian Leadership.* Boston: Little, Brown and Company.

Gilbert, Bil. 1990. *God Gave Us This Country: Tekamthi and the First American Civil War.* New York: Anchor Book.

Thorpe, Jim

Hailed as the greatest athlete during the first half of the twentieth century, Jim Thorpe excelled in football, baseball, and track. Born James Francis Thorpe on May 28, 1888, in Indian Territory (now Oklahoma), Thorpe and his twin brother Charles were the second and third children of six. His father, Hiram Thorpe, was of Irish and Sac-Fox Indian descent. His mother was one-quarter French and three-quarters Chippewa, being the granddaughter of the famous Sac-Fox leader, Black Hawk. Thorpe's Indian name was Wa-tho-huck, meaning Bright Path.

One year after Jim and Charles were born, the Thorpe family acquired a 160-acre farm in Oklahoma during the Oklahoma land rush of 1889. Thorpe was an extremely active child and learned how to ride, swim, and hunt at a young age. He was educated at the Sac-Fox reservation school, the Haskell Institute in Lawrence, Kansas, and finally the Carlisle Indian School in Pennsylvania beginning in 1904.

Thorpe wanted to study to become an electrician at Carlisle, but ended up learning to be a tailor. While at Carlisle, he became more active in organized sports, particularly football. His athletic ability brought him to the attention of Carlisle's athletic coach, "Pop" Warner, who decided to groom Thorpe for track, as well as football. Warner elevated Thorpe from the junior varsity to the varsity football team, where he spent most of the 1908 season on the bench.

During the summer of 1909, Thorpe traveled southward to work on a farm as part of his work commitment to the Carlisle School. He joined the Carolina League and played professional baseball for Winston-Salem, Fayetteville, and Rocky Mount, remaining for the 1910 season as well. In 1911, he returned to Carlisle for two years to complete his education and, at Warner's urging, set his sights on competing in the 1912 Olympics in track and field.

The Olympic Games of 1912 at Stockholm, Sweden, represented the pinnacle of Thorpe's athletic career. He competed in both the five-event pentathlon (running broad jump, javelin throw, 200-meter race, discus, and 1,500-meter race) and the ten-event decathlon (100-meter dash, running broad jump, shotput, running high jump, 400-meter race, discus throw, 110-meter high hurdles, pole vault, javelin throw, and 1,500-meter race). In the pentathlon, Thorpe placed first in four out of the five events. In the decathlon, he set a record that would not be broken for another fifteen years. His achievements earned him the gold medal in both events. King Gustav V of Sweden proclaimed him to be "the greatest athlete in the world," to which Thorpe famously replied, "Thanks, King."

Hailed as the greatest athlete of the first half of the twentieth century, Jim Thorpe excelled in football, baseball, track, and other sports. (National Archives and Records Administration)

In January 1913, however, a scandal erupted when Olympic officials realized that Thorpe had played professional baseball, thus making him ineligible for the Olympics because he had compromised his amateur standing. The Amateur Athletic Union stripped him of his Olympic medals and removed his accomplishments from the Olympic record.

When Thorpe returned to the United States, in 1913, he married Iva Miller in the first of his three marriages. The couple had four children, three daughters, and a son. Thorpe continued to play college football and was named to the all-American team. Upon his graduation from Carlisle in 1913, Thorpe returned to professional baseball and joined the New York Giants as a right fielder. Thorpe continued playing baseball until 1919, at various times for the Giants, the Cincinnati Reds, and the Boston Braves. In 1920, Thorpe helped organize the American Professional Football Association (which became the National Football League in 1922) and served as the organization's first president. He also played for teams in Canton (Ohio), New York, and St. Petersburg (Florida).

Following his divorce from Iva in 1924, Thorpe married Freeda Kirkpatrick. The couple had four sons. He retired from football in 1929 and moved to Hollywood, where he tried to sell his life story. Although Metro-Goldwyn-Mayer (MGM) bought the rights, the picture was never made, and Thorpe turned instead to writing, publishing a book for the 1932 Olympics held in Los Angeles entitled *Jim Thorpe's History of the Olympics*. Ultimately, he ended up working construction and appearing in bit parts in films. His one significant role was as a supporting character in the 1937 Errol Flynn film, *The Green Light*.

He returned to Oklahoma in 1937 and became active in Native American affairs. In 1940, he embarked on a public lecture tour across the United States, speaking on current sports, his own career, the importance of sports in American life, and Native American culture. Too old for active military service during World War II, Thorpe briefly joined the merchant marines in June 1945. Divorced from Freeda in 1949, in June of the same year, he married for the third time, to Patricia Gladys Askew. After the war ended, he returned to California, where in late 1949 Warner Brothers acquired the rights to his life story and began production on *Jim Thorpe, All-American* (1951), with Burt Lancaster playing the title role. Thorpe was given a generous payment for his story and was retained as a technical advisor.

In 1950, a poll among nearly 400 Associated Press sports writers selected Thorpe as the greatest athlete and greatest football player of the first half of the twentieth century, choosing him over Babe Ruth, Ty Cobb, Red Grange, and Jack Dempsey, among others. At the same time, he was inducted into the college and pro football halls of fame. He died in 1953.

Efforts to have Thorpe's Olympic medals and records reinstated had begun in the late 1930s. Finally, in 1982, these efforts by his supporters paid off when the International Olympic Committee

returned Thorpe's name to their record books and restored his medals to his family.

See also Boarding Schools, United States and Canada; Mills, William M.
References and Further Reading
Foner, Eric, and John A. Garraty, eds. 1991. *The Reader's Companion to American History.* Boston: Houghton-Mifflin.
Wheeler, Robert W. 1981. *Jim Thorpe: The World's Greatest Athlete.* Norman: University of Oklahoma Press.

Tribal Colleges

Tribal colleges are unique institutions of higher education that cater specifically to the needs of Native American students to facilitate their educational achievement. Tribal colleges haves existed for more than thirty years and have grown in number to more than thirty individual institutions. They are governed by Native American nations and tribes, but they remain separate from the reservation governments. They stress Native values and service to Native communities, while providing the essentials of a typical educational experience beyond secondary level. A traditional liberal arts curriculum is taught from a Native perspective, with an emphasis on preparing students for success in either their tribal community or beyond.

Community

Since first contact with Europeans, American Indians have been stripped of large parts of their homelands, their means of subsistence, and, in some cases, almost every facet of their cultures, including language, religion, and even family ties. Wherever Native American peoples have managed to hold together the remaining fragments of their culture it has been a community effort. When these communities have had disagreements, they have generally resolved them by consensus, procedures still used today. Now, many of these communities have been able to reconstruct their fragmented cultures, as best they can, in a new venue: tribally controlled community colleges (TCCCs).

During the second half of the twentieth century, American Indians began to assert their entitlement to national sovereignty, legally, economically, and culturally. This assertiveness led to empowerment,

which in turn led to the acts signed into U.S. law allowing for Indian self-determination. One of these acts is the Tribally Controlled Community College Assistance Act of 1978.

Governance

During the 1960s, the civil rights movement was affecting change across the nation. Newly active minority groups were embroidering their specific ideas for justice into the social fabric of the United States, often by force. The Nixon administration responded to this outcry by acting on the ideals set in place during the Kennedy administration. The Indian Empowerment Assistance Program was manifested in signing into law several acts to encourage and assist Native American nations and tribes to create a new future for themselves (Boxberger, 1989, 130–132). A series of new federal laws resulted from this program, including the Indian Financing Act of 1974, the Indian Education Acts of 1972 and 1974, the Indian Self-Determination and Education Assistance Act of 1975, the Indian Child Welfare Act of 1978, and the American Indian Religious Freedom Act of 1978 (Boyer, 1989, 24).

Possibly the most important and most empowering act to have come out of this era is the Tribally Controlled Community College Assistance Act of 1978 (Boyer, 1989, 24). This act provides the basis for a system of institutions of higher education that would operate in accordance with a unique set of principles and guidelines based on Native values and traditions. The Act makes it possible to acquire an education that shares, rather than stifles, the worldview of its Native American students.

Each TCCC is chartered by a specific tribe or tribes. Most are governed by boards made up of tribal community members, which operate with autonomy from the tribal government (Boyer, 1989, 32).

Generally, the presidents of these colleges and their administrative staffs are Native Americans, and often the positions are held by women; roughly one-third of the presidents were women at the time of Boyer's study (Boyer, 1989, 32).

Curriculum

These centers of Native American education offer an opportunity to reconstruct the missing elements of tribal cultures and to reverse the economic decay that

afflicts Native peoples. These schools can provide a way of regaining self-esteem and a sense of autonomy, viable options for the control of common resources and local prosperity, without compromising traditional tribal values.

Tribal colleges seek not to transport students to a life in the past, but to understand the past as the origin of traditional Native values that can offer a sound coping mechanism for contemporary life and the basis for a future in which Native peoples can find self-realization and continued self-determination. At the same time, tribal colleges can prepare students to manage their own affairs and those of their communities, thus breaking the cycle of dependency (Boyer, 1989, 51–52).

Both individual students and communities in which they live can profit from the reconstruction and revitalization of tribal culture that occurs in the reservation community colleges. In an effort to reestablish the knowledge and pride in tribal heritage, the tribally controlled institutions create what can be described as a cultural renaissance in the communities they serve (Boyer, 1989, 52–53).

The important distinction to be made about the Native American experience in a tribal college, compared to that of a non-Indian institution, is that value is placed on tribal knowledge, beliefs, and lifeways; in other words, the tribal college builds self-esteem and pride in the Native heritage. In addition, students in Native community colleges are also provided a viable education in mainstream areas of study, so that they are prepared for careers in the world inside or outside the tribal realm (Boyer, 1989, 54).

When a core group of tribal college graduates achieves academic success and becomes educational and community leaders, their accomplishments serve entire communities. For example, a growing number of Indian graduates are entering the ranks of tribal teaching staffs. Graduates who remain on their reservations after graduation offer the seeds of social stability, economic growth, and future leadership (Boyer, 1989, 60).

An important aspect of Indians teaching Indians is the creation of an environment that emphasizes traditional cultures. An ability to transcend the shortcomings of European language, for example, is necessary to comprehend such ideas as the "numinous" aspects of Native American culture, such as the infusion of divinity into the natural world (Boxberger, 1989, 133).

Faculty

Many faculty positions at tribal colleges are filled by non-Indians. However, Native Americans fill most administrative positions and account for most of the student body. Tribal colleges are working to produce more Native American teachers. Due to failed policies of the past, however, Indian instructors are scarce. Fortunately, many of the available non-Indian instructors understand the individual and common needs and are aware of community values. Often they come to Native communities planning to stay for a short time. Still other non-Indian instructors make their homes in Native communities and are accepted by the members of tribes with whom they work (Boyer, 1989, 32–33).

Short-time faculty often keep programs going, only to be replaced. Such turnover changes the character of programs and upsets their continuity, affecting the perceptions of students. A high turnover rate of faculty and staff can be attributed to a combination of factors such as isolation, low pay, and heavy teaching loads compared to their colleagues' at non-Indian community colleges (Boyer, 1989, 33).

However, many institutions forge strong, lasting administrations, and manage the frequent changes well. This relative lack of turmoil is one of the goals of the American Indian Higher Education Consortium: to promote the kind of professional relationships in the administration that will reduce pressure and create a stable environment and working relations for tribal and college administrators (Boyer, 1989, 33).

Students

At the heart of any discussion about education are the students. Without them, all other facets of education are irrelevant. No matter what their ethnicity or cultural background, all students enter education with some learned behaviors, outlooks on life, and patterns of learning and understanding, or lifeways, already in place. Many students share attributes of the dominant or mainstream society, and their lifeways are similar. Learning within the mainstream methodology is relatively easy for them. However, many members of minorities—American Indians among them—have their own unique lifeways. These lifeways may be fragmented, but they are still ingrained and still different from those of mainstream students. Thus, learning and understanding

in a mainstream environment may prove to be extremely difficult for them. This, coupled with many forms of ethnic bias, can cause an individual of any minority group—in this case, an American Indian—to have a negative self-image and low self-esteem. When one of the fundamental differences in lifeways is the method of learning or understanding, then persons in a minority may believe that they are intellectually incapable of academic success.

Jim Cummins has written that most Western indigenous groups "have been conquered, subjugated, segregated, and regarded as inherently inferior by the dominant group. Educational failure is regarded by the dominant group as the natural consequence of the minority group's inherent inferiority" (Cummins, 1988, 3). This idea not only becomes a self-fulfilling prophecy, but part of the generational, stereotypical baggage that the members of this group have to bear.

Students at Native-controlled colleges are typically older than most college students (about twenty-nine to thirty-three years of age). Most are women, and most (as high as 68 percent in some colleges) have children. In the Native-controlled colleges that Boyer cited, more than half of the students were unemployed the year before attending school; up to 98 percent below Census Bureau poverty guidelines. Most students attending tribal colleges are residents of the reservation. Many Indian students see the tribal college as a place to transition from high school to a non-Indian college (Boyer, 1989, 31).

Daniel R. Gibbs

See also American Indian Higher Education Consortium; Education.

References and Further Readings

Boyer, P. 1989. *Tribal Colleges: Shaping the Future of Native America.* Princeton, NJ: Carnegie Foundation for the Advancement of Teaching. Web site of the Foundation http://www.carnegiefoundation.org/

Cummins, Jim. 1988. "The Empowerment of Indian Students." In *Teaching American Indian Students.* Edited by Jon Reyhner. Norman: University of Oklahoma Press.

Reyhner Jon. 1988. *Teaching American Indian Students.* Norman: University of Oklahoma Press.

Szasz, Margaret Connell. 1977. *Education and the American Indian: The Road to Self-Determination Since 1928.* Albuquerque: University of New Mexico Press.

"Tribal Colleges: An Introduction." No date. Prepared by the American Indian Higher Education Consortium, The Institute for Higher Education Policy. Available at: http://www.aihec.org/. Accessed January 20, 2007.

Uncas

For most Americans, the name "Uncas" conjures up the fictional character of James Fenimore Cooper's *The Last of the Mohicans.* The historical Uncas (1588?–1683), however, was a Mohegan (not a Mohican) and far from being the last of his tribe. Uncas recognized, earlier than other Native leaders, that the arrival of English colonists permanently altered the balance of power in southern New England. He closely allied himself with the newcomers, and for more than four decades he presided over the rise of the Mohegans. Under his leadership, the Mohegans rendered valuable military assistance to both the Plymouth and Massachusetts Bay colonies during the Pequot War and King Philip's War. Because of Uncas's willingness to enter into alliances with the New England colonies against other Native peoples, as well as his part in slaying the Narragansett sachem Miantonomo, some scholars of Native America have cast him as a historical villain. However, his actions also strengthened the Mohegans, enabling them to retain a measure of independence in colonial New England, long after other Native peoples had been displaced or coerced into moving into one of the Praying Towns.

At the time of English and Dutch settlement, the Mohegans were a small southern New England tribe that occupied the lands between the Connecticut and Thames Rivers. Dominated by the more numerous and powerful Pequots, the Mohegans paid them tribute in the form of goods and wampum. On at least five occasions, Uncas attempted to undermine the authority—whether by a coup or other means is not documented—of the Pequot sachem, Sassacus. He always failed, and Sassacus forced him into exile among the Narragansetts. Each time, however, Sassacus permitted Uncas to return and retain leadership of the Mohegans, but only after ritually humiliating himself. Sassacus further punished Uncas each time by reducing the amount of Mohegan territory under his control. Uncas and the Mohegans were finally

able to throw off Pequot domination by siding with Massachusetts Bay and Plymouth Bay Colonies when the Pequot War erupted in 1637. The colonial military leaders were distrustful of Uncas and the Mohegans at first, but he demonstrated his loyalty by delivering to them four Pequot heads and a captive. He also participated in planning and leading the attack on the Pequot's stronghold at Mystic. As a reward for his services, Uncas received a large share of the Pequot prisoners. While the colonists sold most of their Pequot prisoners as slaves and shipped them to British sugar colonies in the Caribbean, the Mohegans adopted most of their prisoners and incorporated them into the tribe.

Seeking even closer ties to the English, Uncas enhanced his standing with them by occasionally feeding them rumors of Indian plots against their colonies. By presenting himself as an ally, Uncas and his people avoided displacement and received comparably favorable treatment from the English. The Mohegans were able to retain a good deal of autonomy.

Uncas proved useful yet again to the New England colonies when the Narragansett sachem Miantonomo, who had been an English ally during the Pequot War, began to speak out against them. Miantnomo approached other Native groups and argued that, just as the English thought of themselves as "English," Native people should unite in the face of the European invasion and stop thinking of themselves as Narragansetts, Nipmucks, or Pokonokets. At about this time, Miantonomo signed a treaty with Massachusetts that required him to notify the colony if he went to war against another Native American tribe. Miantonomo sought, and was granted, permission to attack the Mohegans, who had been waylaying Narragansett hunters. Captured by the Mohegans during the ensuing war, Miantonomo reportedly attempted to purchase his freedom. Despite receiving a ransom from the Narragansetts for Miantonomo's safe return, Uncas turned him over to the colony of Connecticut. Wanting to be rid of a troublesome Native leader but not wanting Miantonomo's blood on their hands, the Connecticut authorities gave him back to Uncas, with the implicit understanding he would have Miantonomo executed.

Uncas lent further assistance to the New England colonies during King Philip's War in 1675–1676. While he could no longer lead warriors in the field himself, his son, Oweneco, assisted the English. After the war, Uncas reaffirmed his alliance to the colony and began selling Mohegan lands to them until his death in 1683.

Roger M. Carpenter

See also Cooper, James Fenimore; Metacom and King Philip's War; Pequot War; Praying Villages of Massachusetts.

References and Further Reading
Jennings, Francis. 1975. *The Invasion of America: Indians, Colonialism, and the Cant of Conquest.* Chapel Hill: University of North Carolina Press.
Oberg, Michael Leroy. 2003. *Uncas: First of the Mohegans.* Ithaca, NY: Cornell University Press.

Victorio

Considered by historians to be one of the greatest guerilla fighters and military strategists (Keenan, 1998, 16), Mimbres Apache Chief Victorio was born about 1825 in southwestern New Mexico (Thrapp, 1988, 1483–1485). Legends about his origins persist, most stating that he was a captured Mexican boy raised among the Apaches, but proof is lacking. Biduyé, as he was called by tribal members, was renamed by his enemies when he became a respected war leader, even though he tried very hard to find a course other than war. Victorio kept on the path of peace until the American government, in the form of the Indian Bureau and the military, demanded too much and war ensued. Through it all, he had an unyielding desire to live at Ojo Caliente, New Mexico, Victorio's ancestral home.

Mimbres Apaches actually lived near what is today known as Monticello, New Mexico. They called themselves the *Chihenne*, the Red Paint people. Their early leader was Mangas Coloradas, a notable chief. Following their customs, the boy Victorio undoubtedly participated in long established ceremonies beginning when he received his first moccasins and his first haircut. Later, he competed with other boys in footraces, took baths in ice-cold water all year to "harden" his body, imitated in play the elders' decision-making process, and learned the names and characteristics of animals, birds, plants, and the elements.

At about age sixteen, as an apprentice, Victorio rode along on the first of four raids, on which the older warriors acted as his teachers and tested his skills in the many aspects of warfare, a necessary exercise before a young man made the transition to a fighter for his people. By 1850 Victorio started to be

noticed by the American military as a skilled warrior; in 1853 he affixed an "X" as his signature to a formal agreement with the American government. Although the document was never ratified by the U.S. Senate and thus became invalid, Victorio's signature was a sign of his growing leadership status.

Victorio conducted a successful raid in 1855, taking his accomplices into the Mexican states of Sonora and Chihuahua to bring back large numbers of captives and livestock. In July 1862, he took part in the significant Apache Pass battle and continued to participate in numerous skirmishes and depredations with white settlers and the American military. In 1863, after the death of Mangas Coloradas, Victorio assumed leadership of the group. In September 1879 he and sixty warriors raided a cavalry unit camped near a small Hispanic settlement in southwestern New Mexico. The Apaches killed five soldiers and three civilians, galloping off with sixty-eight horses and mules. The attack signaled the start of the Victorio War.

By January of 1880, Victorio had led his people in battles across three states, leaving the pursuing U.S. Army baffled at every turn. He fought Mexicans, settlers, Texas Rangers, and the Ninth Cavalry in New Mexico, Texas, and Mexico, winning engagements at almost every contact. The Ninth Cavalry, known as Buffalo Soldiers, was one of six black regiments formed after the Civil War to help keep peace on the Western frontier. On April 6, 1880, seventy-one members of the Ninth Cavalry, led by Captain Henry Carroll, cautiously approached Victorio's camp in the Hembrillo Basin, a natural stronghold, in south central New Mexico. They were immediately surrounded by a larger force of about 150 Apaches under Victorio's leadership, firing volley after volley from behind stacked breastworks erected on the surrounding ridgetops. Despite all efforts, Victorio's warriors were ultimately driven from their positions (Laumbach, 2000, 248).

Victorio's son Washington was killed in a battle on June 5, 1880 (Thrapp, 1974, 282), after which the weary chief divided his forces and moved with about 200 followers toward Mexico. Victorio took his people to an unmistakable site on the plains, three rocky peaks called *Tres Castillos*, where they were eventually attacked by an irregular group of Mexicans and Tarahumara Indians. Fighting continued for hours until the dawn of October 15, 1880, when Victorio was dead, either by his own hand or from a bullet fired by one of the Indians, as were sixty warriors and eighteen women and children. Sixty-eight

women and children were taken captive, along with 180 animals. Prisoners were gathered, the adolescent boys were taken to a nearby arroyo and shot, while the remaining women and children were enslaved.

H. Henrietta Stockel

See also Mangas Coloradas.

References and Further Reading
Ball, Eve. 1970. *In the Days of Victorio.* Tucson: University of Arizona Press.
Keenan, Jerry. 1988. "Mimbres Apache War Chief Victorio May Have Been America's Greatest Guerilla Fighter." *Wild West Magazine,* June: 16–18, 75.
Laumbach, Karl W. 2000. *Hembrillo: An Apache Battlefield of the Victorio War.* White Sands Missile Range, New Mexico. Archaeological Research Report No. 00-06, Human Systems Research, Inc.
Thrapp, Dan L. 1974. *Victorio and the Mimbres Apaches.* Norman: University of Oklahoma Press.
Thrapp, Dan L. 1988. *Encyclopedia of Frontier Biography.* Vol. 3. Lincoln: University of Nebraska Press.
Utley, Robert M. March. 1984. "The Buffalo Soldiers and Victorio." *New Mexico Magazine,* 47–50, 53–54.

Warrior, Clyde

Indian nationalist, social critic, student activist, renowned fancy dancer, and youth leader, Clyde Warrior (Ponca, 1939–1968) was a major figure in the Native American student–youth movement of the 1960s. He helped found the National Indian Youth Council (NIYC). His ideas changed how Indian people thought about activism and nationalism. Thousands were inspired by his charisma, commitment, and clamor for change.

Warrior was born during the Great Depression near Ponca City, Oklahoma. His grandparents raised him traditionally. As a young man, he became instrumental in the revival of Ponca songs and dances. By 1957 the newspapers were already calling him a world champion dancer. In 1958 Warrior won an award in the design category at a state-level high school art competition. By early 1961 he was attending Cameron Junior College in Lawton, Oklahoma.

Early in the spring of 1961, Warrior traveled to the University of Oklahoma to attend a regional planning conference for the American Indian Chicago Conference. Before the semester was over,

he returned to the University of Oklahoma to join 300 Indian youth and students for the annual meeting of the Southwestern Regional Indian Youth Council. Although he was a newcomer to the youth council movement, which had emerged in the Southwest, Warrior became its president. The young people who elected him were amazed at his confidence and Indian pride.

In June 1961, Clyde Warrior attended the American Indian Chicago Conference with nearly thirty students from the Workshop on American Indian Affairs. They were frustrated that older Indian leaders expected them to run errands. The students did this, but they also took matters into their own hands. Several won election to leadership positions at the conference. For instance, Warrior served on the Drafting Committee and helped revise the Declaration of Indian Purpose. The students also formed a youth caucus. During the conference Warrior performed a ceremonial song and announced that he had prayed in behalf of the confused delegates. He also helped the youth caucus to seize the microphone and told the conference delegates to stop being so deferential toward white people.

When the conference concluded, Warrior and several of the students returned to Colorado for the remainder of their summer workshop. Many of the students had been radicalized by their experience in Chicago and grew impatient with the slow and steady approach to change advocated by their instructors. Some of the students stayed, others left early, and the most committed among them, including Warrior, assembled in August at Gallup, New Mexico. At this meeting the students discussed their goals, elected officers, and decided to call their organization the National Indian Youth Council. Warrior was elected to its board of directors.

Between late 1961 and 1964 Warrior cemented his reputation as a national Indian leader. He was nominated for a spot on his tribal council. He presided over a National Indian Youth Conference and was in demand on college campuses as a speaker. He returned to the Workshop on American Indian Affairs, served as coeditor of its student newsletter, and soon became coeditor of the University of Chicago periodical *Indian Voices*. He worked with Marlon Brando and publicists in New York City to help tribes in Washington State secure their fishing rights. At the March on Washington and Freedom Summer, he increased his knowledge of civil rights strategies. He was invited to speak in Washington, D.C., on how the War on Poverty could bene-fit American Indians. In late 1964 he published his influential essay, "Which One Are You? Five Types of Indians."

During the last four years of his life, Warrior maintained a demanding schedule. He married and became a father. The NIYC elected him its president. Colleges called him for speaking engagements. His testimony before the president's National Advisory Commission on Rural Poverty was reprinted as "We Are Not Free." He represented the NIYC at Martin Luther King Jr.'s anti-Vietnam peace march in New York City. The John Hay Whitney Foundation awarded him an Opportunity Fellowship for graduate work in American Studies. These activities took a toll on Warrior. He put on weight and the excessive drinking harmed his liver. He died suddenly while working on an Oklahoma summer school project in July 1968. In his honor, the NIYC organized the Clyde Warrior Institute in American Indian Studies.

Sterling Fluharty

See also Fishing Rights; National Indian Youth Council.
References and Further Reading
Smith, Paul Chaat, and Robert Allen Warrior. 1996. *Like a Hurricane: The Indian Movement from Alcatraz to Wounded Knee.* New York: New Press.
Steiner, Stan. 1968. *The New Indians.* New York: Harper & Row.

Washakie

Washakie's Shoshonis allied with Plenty Coups' Crows to assist the U.S. Army against the Cheyennes, Sioux, and others who were defined by the United States as "hostile" during the final phases of the Plains Wars, beginning in the 1870s. Washakie's accommodation helped him bargain for a sizable, fertile reservation in the Shoshonis' homeland, while "hostile" Cheyennes, Sioux, and their allies were assigned to arid reservations and treated miserably after their surrenders.

Various accounts place Washakie's birth at between 1798 and 1804. His father, Pasego, was of mixed blood; his mother was Shoshoni. Pasego was killed by Flatheads when Washakie was a child. As a young man, Washakie developed his skills as a warrior by riding for several years with a band of Bannocks. He stood six feet tall, married several women, and had twelve children. His reputation was mainly as a warrior (although he was rarely aggressive after

his youth), but he also was known among the Shoshoni as an excellent singer.

By the 1840s, large numbers of gold seekers on their way to California were passing through the Shoshonis' homeland in present-day Wyoming, but few settled in the area. A few years later, a large party of Mormons under Brigham Young settled on the southern edge of the Shoshone homeland at the Great Salt Lake. In 1851, Washakie rejected the terms of a proposed treaty that would have diminished Shoshoni lands, and allied for a time with the Mormons, before the federal government asserted authority over them as part of Utah's bid for statehood. In 1869, Washakie negotiated the Treaty of Fort Bridger, which set apart 3 million acres for the Shoshonis in their traditional homeland.

By the mid-1870s, the Plains Wars were drawing to a close. Washakie allied with the Crows and the U.S. Army at the Little Bighorn. Plenty Coups worried that General George Crook was not prepared for Crazy Horse's Lakotas when they met in battle, along with Washakie's Shoshones, June 16, 1876. He was correct; Crazy Horse routed Crook and his Indian allies in a battle that presaged Custer's Last Stand nine days later.

O. O. Howard, who is best-known as the commander who pursued Chief Joseph and other non-treaty Nez Percés on their Long March in 1877, recalled Washakie as "a tall, big man with fine eyes and a great deal of hair. He spoke broken English, but could make himself understood. He was a great eater. . . . He ate very politely, but was like a giant taking his food" (Johansen and Grinde, 1997, 410).

Howard said that Washakie was famous for his skill as a buffalo hunter. Despite his support for the immigrants, Washakie and his people had their share of troubles with broken treaties. In 1870, land that had been set aside for the Shoshonis and Bannocks by a treaty signed in 1864 was demanded for white settlement. Many young Shoshoni warriors called for war, but Washakie forbade it.

Washakie allied with the whites out of necessity, not choice. He chafed at being confined on a reservation. In 1878, at a meeting called by the governor of Wyoming, Washakie said:

> The white man, who possesses this whole vast country from sea to sea, who roams over it at pleasure and lives where he likes, cannot know the cramp we feel in this little spot, with the undying remembrance of the fact, which you know as well as we, that every foot of what

Washakie was a Shoshoni chief and representative for both the Shoshoni and Bannock peoples. He negotiated the surrender of the Green River Valley in eastern Utah and southern Wyoming, which provided for the construction of the Union Pacific Railway. (National Archives and Records Administration)

you proudly call America, not very long ago belonged to the Red Man. The Great Spirit gave it to us, [and] there was room enough for all his tribes; all were happy in their freedom (Johansen and Grinde, 1997, 410).

The whites had superior tools and weapons, said Washakie, and "hordes of men" to use against the Indians. He continued: "We . . . sorry remnants of tribes once mighty, are cornered on little spots of the earth, all ours by right—cornered like guilty prisoners, and watched by men with guns who are more than anxious to kill us off" (Johansen and Grinde, 1997, 410).

When Washakie was an elderly man, his eldest son (also named Washakie) was killed in a drunken

brawl with a white man. The elder Washakie was grieved by the fact that his son had passed onto the Spirit World in disgrace, "like an Arapaho," he said. (The Shoshonis and Arapahoe were bitter enemies, even in the face of overwhelming white encroachment.) Washakie also opposed the Ghost Dance, but he urged his people to continue the Sun Dance, which they had borrowed from the Sioux.

Despite such doubts, Washakie was such a source of support for the U.S. Army that in 1878 it named a frontier fort after him in the Wind River Valley. Washakie died in his sleep on February 20, 1900. He was buried with the honors accorded a captain in the post cemetery at Fort Washakie.

Two statues of Washakie memorialize him in the Salt Lake City area. The most notable is downtown, where he is part of the Brigham Young Monumental Group, along with other people (all American non-Natives) who gave great aid to initial Mormon settlement in the Salt Lake Valley.

Bruce E. Johansen

See also Mormon Church; Plenty Coups.
References and Further Reading
Armstrong, Virginia Irving. 1971. *I Have Spoken: American History Through the Voices of the Indians.* Chicago: Swallow Press.
Hebard, Grace Raymond. 1995. *Washakie: Chief of the Shoshones.* Lincoln: University of Nebraska Press.
Howard, O. O. 1908–1989. *Famous Indian Chiefs I Have Known.* Lincoln: University of Nebraska Press.

Watie, Stand

Stand Watie (1806–1871) was the only American Indian to hold the Confederate rank of brigadier general during the U.S. Civil War. He was also the last Confederate general to surrender, laying down his arms in June of 1865, more than two months after the surrender of the South at Appomattox. In addition, Watie served as principal chief of the Confederate Cherokee Nation, part of a governmental fissure that occurred within the larger Cherokee Nation due not only to the Civil War, but also to past disagreements over Cherokee removal.

Born into the Cherokee Nation in 1806 in what is now Georgia, Stand Watie was raised by a full-blood Cherokee father and a mixed-blood mother.

His family is full of well-known Cherokee leaders. Elias Boudinot, Watie's brother, was the founder of the *Cherokee Phoenix* and a signer of the 1835 Treaty of New Echota, which ignited the removal of the Cherokee from their lands in the southeastern United States. Similarly, Major Ridge, Watie's uncle, was a factional chief in the Cherokee Nation. John Rollin Ridge, Watie's cousin, became a well-known Cherokee poet and author in California during the second half of the nineteenth century. While Watie may not be as well-known as his kin, his role in nineteenth-century Cherokee politics is crucial to understanding the tribe's rocky transition from their eastern homeland to their new land in the Territory.

Watie was among a small group of dissenters who considered removal to Indian Territory a promising solution to white encroachment on Cherokee land. He was thus one of the signers of the Treaty of New Echota in 1835, which ceded Cherokee land for new land out west. This treaty was considered fraudulent by the majority of the Cherokees living in the East and solidified a divide between pro- and antiremoval parties in the tribe.

Watie and his cosigners moved to the Territory (today Oklahoma) in 1837, before the devastating forced removal of most remaining tribal members along the Trail of Tears in 1838. At least one-quarter (approximately 4,000) of the traveling population died along the way. Once the remainder of the tribe, led by John Ross, arrived and settled in the Territory, the pro- and antiremoval parties clashed. In 1839, Watie's relatives—Boudinot, Major Ridge, and his son John Ridge—were executed by the antiremoval party for betraying their tribe. As a member of this influential family, Watie was now considered the leader of the proremoval Cherokees.

Strife among the tribe's factions continued until 1846, when peace was made by way of a new treaty with the U.S. government. Between 1846 and the outbreak of the Civil War, Watie had a family and began a legal practice. He also became a member of the Knights of the Golden Circle, a mainly white proslavery organization.

In 1861, with the secession of the South from the Union, Watie raised the Cherokee Regiment of Mounted Rifles. He used this regiment's influence to pressure John Ross, the Cherokee's principal chief (and longtime foe of Watie and the Confederate States), to side with the Confederacy. Watie's tactics worked and, soon after the war's beginning,

Stand Watie was a Cherokee leader and served as a Confederate general. (National Archives and Records Administration)

Ross briefly sided with the South. In 1862, however, as Ross fled the Territory for Philadelphia, Watie was elected principal chief of the Confederate Cherokees.

Watie participated in battles at Pea Ridge (1861), Wilson's Creek (1861), and the first Battle of Cabin Creek (1863), among others, and was promoted to brigadier general in 1864. The general was known for his guerilla war tactics.

After the Civil War, Watie left politics behind in large part and returned home, where he died a few years later in 1871.

Amy M. Ware

See also Major Ridge; Ross, John; Trail of Tears.
References and Further Reading
Cunningham, Frank. [1959] 1998. *General Stand Watie's Confederate Indians.* Norman: University of Oklahoma Press.
Franks, Kenny A. 1979. *Stand Watie and the Agony of the Cherokee Nation.* Memphis, TN: Memphis State University Press.

Welch, James

James Welch (1940–2003), a novelist associated with the modern Native American literary renaissance, was born in Browning, Montana, of Blackfeet, Gros Ventre, and European heritage and spent his early childhood on the Blackfeet Reservation of Montana. His family lived in a number of western cities before turning to farming on the Fort Belknap Reservation following Welch's graduation from high school in Minneapolis, Minnesota. As a child he always wanted to be a writer. His literary career began in earnest as an undergraduate at the University of Montana (BA, 1965), where he was nurtured by the notable collection of writers who gathered around Richard Hugo and William Kittredge in Missoula, a city that remained the geographical center of Welch's life as a writer.

The five novels written by Welch present distinct episodes of American Indian experience that are unified by their portrayal of Indian culture's richness and the heartache of its dislocation. The reader can examine the novels in the order they were written or note that they can be reorganized into a historical chronology of Indian experience. *Fools Crow* (1986) is the story of the Blackfeet from the era of the American Civil War through the Marias River massacre of January 1870, which marked the end of independent life for the tribe.

Next in historical sequence is *The Heart Song of Charging Elk* (2000), the story of an Oglala Sioux who becomes separated from William F. "Buffalo Bill" Cody's Wild West Show while on tour in Europe and lives out his life in France. After a number of years he rejects the opportunity to rejoin the Cody show and return to South Dakota.

Two other works, *Winter in the Blood* (1974) and *The Death of Jim Loney* (1979), address isolated men negotiating indefinite time frames in the midst of twentieth-century reservation life. Their personal problems rise out of tenuous ties to their families and cultural traditions on the Fort Belknap reservation. *Winter in the Blood* suggests a recovery of cultural and family connections. Jim Loney pursues suicide at the hands of a law enforcement officer when he allows himself to be shot by his pursuers. The most recent historical setting occurs in *The Indian Lawyer* (1990), the story of a "successfully assimilated" Blackfeet Indian who used athletic prowess to advance his intellectual interests with college and legal degrees and a position in an

important Helena law firm. At the end of the book Sylvester Yellow Calf abandons his Helena legal practice and a campaign for Congress to return to the reservation and an unspecified future.

In addition to his novels, Welch began his writing career with a collection of poetry, *Riding the Earthboy 40* (published in 1971, revised and expanded in 1976). He also has ventured into memoir and history with *Killing Custer* (1994), occasioned by his work as an advisor to a television program, "Last Stand at Little Big Horn."

Welch's work appears frequently in general literary anthologies and those devoted to Indian writers. Literary analysts have approached his work from a variety of angles, including his understanding of the importance of place and his status as an Indian writer. Welch's landscapes are not photographic images of the world of the Fort Belknap reservation and neighboring towns. Readers feel the importance of place even though it is not possible to locate the exact physical settings for the action in his books. His landscape details seep into his narratives in ways that present lives embedded in the land. Welch's mixed-blood ancestry includes ties to a white trader killed by Blackfeet warriors on the eve of the Marias River Massacre, the event that concludes *Fools Crow*. Critics concerned with blood quanta of Indian writers do not include Welch among those whose perspectives, visions, or ancestries are questionable.

Honors for Welch's work include the Native Writer's Circle's lifetime achievement award in 1997 and the French government's 1995 medal designating him a *Chevalier of the l'Ordre des Artes et des Lettres* (Knight of the Order of Arts and Letters) for *Fools Crow*. While speaking of the Blackfeet in *Fools Crow*, Welch revealed something of his overall goals as a writer: "They weren't particularly noble Indians. They weren't particularly bad Indians. They were human beings. That's really what I wanted to get across, the idea that historical Indians were human beings. They weren't cliches."

David S. Trask

See also Cody, William Frederick; Battle of the Little Bighorn.

References and Further Reading

Lincoln, Kenneth. 1983. *Native American Renaissance.* Berkeley: University of California Press.

McFarland, Ron. 2000. *Understanding James Welch.* Columbia: University of South Carolina Press.

Nelson, Robert M. 1993. *Place and Vision: The Function of Landscape in Native American Fiction.* American Indian Studies. Edited by Rodney Simard. New York: Peter Lang.

Schorcht, Blanca. 2003. *Storied Voices in Native American Texts: Harry Robinson, Thomas King, James Welch and Leslie Marmon Silko.* Indigenous Peoples and Politics. Edited by Franke Wilmer. New York: Routledge.

Whitman, Marcus and Narcissa

On November 29, 1847, a small group of Cayuse Indians entered the Waiilatpu mission in the eastern reaches of the Oregon Country and killed fourteen white men, women, and children. Among the dead were Marcus and Narcissa Whitman, the Presbyterian evangelists who had established the station eleven years earlier in a blush of religious zeal and optimism. The killings, forever since memorialized as the Whitman Massacre, have been the subject of extensive historical study and widely differing interpretations. To early commentators, the Whitmans represented martyrs for the national cause of Manifest Destiny, fallen Christian soldiers in the battle between civilization and savagery that gave Americans title to the West. More recently, scholars have applied ethnohistorical methods in an effort to better understand the motives of the Cayuse perpetrators and the context in which they acted. What emerges from such analysis is not a simple story of victims and villains but a complex drama involving frustrated ambitions, clashing expectations, and cultural misunderstandings.

The Whitman Massacre ended the first phase of missionary activity on the Columbia Plateau. Initially, the Indians of the region had expressed substantial interest in learning more about Christianity. In the late eighteenth century, a Native oracle called the Spokane Prophet had reputedly foretold the coming of the whites, who would "bring with them a book and will teach you everything, and after that the world will fall to pieces." The idea that whites were spiritually potent but potentially dangerous people gained credence in the early 1800s, when fur traders introduced both miraculous new goods and terrible new diseases such as smallpox. While traditional shamans struggled to cope with the recurring epidemics and their concomitant loss of status, the survivors sought explanations and solutions for

American missionary Marcus Whitman was murdered by a Cayuse in his home on November 29, 1847, near present-day Walla Walla, Washington. His wife, Narcissa and twelve associates were also killed in what became known as the Whitman Massacre. (Hulton Archive/Getty Images)

their misfortunes. Many concluded that the whites' immense "spirit powers" stemmed from their religion, and in 1832 a delegation of four Nez Percé and Flathead men journeyed to St. Louis seeking the Book of Heaven. Their visit stirred tremendous excitement in the Protestant evangelical community, which perceived the delegation as a heathen plea for salvation and a chance to counteract Catholic influence in the region. The American Board of Commissioners for Foreign Missions (ABCFM) quickly dispatched the Whitmans, among others, and in 1836 the Whitmans established their station at Waiilatpu to proselytize the Cayuses, Umatillas, and Walla Wallas.

After a promising start, the enthusiasm and idealism that had inspired the mission quickly dissolved into mutual disappointment and distrust. Profound cultural differences and communication problems hindered conversion efforts, while Christianity failed to deliver the tangible benefits many Indians had hoped to obtain. The Whitmans' deep ethnocentrism strained relations further, breeding resentment and suspicion on both sides. By the early 1840s, the Whitmans had begun limiting their con-

tact with Indians and catering primarily to the growing stream of immigrants on the nearby Oregon Trail. The ABCFM moved to close the station in 1842 after hearing critical reports from another missionary, but Marcus traveled back to Boston and convinced the board to rescind its order. The Indians were less favorably disposed when he returned a year later leading a train of a thousand new settlers. More arrived every year thereafter, and with them came fresh outbreaks of scarlet fever, whooping cough, and measles. A devastating measles epidemic in 1847 convinced some Cayuses of Whitman's evil intentions. A physician by training, Marcus had often treated their sick, but in the Plateau society a shaman with too much power could become a sorcerer who inflicted harm on others. The traditional sanction for sorcery was death.

On November 29, two Cayuse men named Tomahas and Tiloukaikt entered the Whitman house to request medicine. As Marcus argued with Tiloukaikt, Tomahas slipped behind the doctor and delivered the first of several tomahawk blows to his head. A party of Indians then killed Narcissa, ten other men, and two children before leaving with about fifty captives. As the news spread, most of the other Christian missions on the Plateau were abandoned. Although the Hudson's Bay Company ransomed the hostages a month later, war raged for two years until the Cayuses agreed to surrender five men to face American justice. They were hanged in Oregon City following a summary trial presided over by the mountain man Joe Meek. On the scaffold, Tiloukaikt declared, "Did not your missionaries tell us that Christ died to save his people? So die we, to save our people." The massacre and the war actually hastened the creation of the Oregon Territory, however, and in 1855 the remaining Cayuses signed a treaty ceding the bulk of their land to the United States.

Andrew H. Fisher

See also Oregon Trail; Hudson's Bay Company.
References and Further Reading
Cebula, Larry. 2003. *Plateau Indians and the Quest for Spiritual Power, 1700–1850.* Lincoln: University of Nebraska Press.
Jeffrey, Julie Roy. 1991. *Converting the West: A Biography of Narcissa Whitman.* Norman: University of Oklahoma Press.
Miller, Christopher L. 1985. *Prophetic Worlds: Indians and Whites on the Columbia Plateau.* Piscataway, NJ: Rutgers University Press.

Williams, Roger

One of America's earliest cultural pluralists and advocates of the separation of church and state, Roger Williams founded Providence, Rhode Island, as a safe haven for early European settlers who had suffered religious persecution. He also believed in forging good relations with the Native peoples of New England. Rather than fight for title to the land, Williams argued that colonists should negotiate and pay a fair price for it. His policy proved effective, as Rhode Island had the most peaceful Indian relations in all the colonies.

Williams was born in London, England, about 1603. His father was a hardworking shopkeeper who hoped to carve out a better life for his children. Young Roger eventually went off to college at Cambridge University, where he studied to become a minister. He later landed a job as the private chaplain of nobleman, Sir William Masham. While work-

ing for Masham, Williams became increasingly interested in the Massachusetts Bay Colony, of which he had heard rousing stories. In 1631, Williams decided to give up his life in England and set off for America, where he hoped to establish himself in what was already being viewed in some quarters as a land of opportunity.

Once in Massachusetts Bay, Williams found himself at odds with the colony's leadership. He criticized the king and believed that the colony should completely separate itself from the Church of England, rather than try to reform or purify it. Williams believed in religious freedom, arguing that governments were not divinely sanctioned and therefore they had no right to establish state religions. He also claimed that the colony's royal charter was null and void because the settlers had not purchased the land from the Native people. The colony's leaders considered such talk as tantamount to blasphemy, and Williams was eventually banished from Massachu-

Narragansett protect British colonist Roger Williams. Williams developed a good relationship with the Narragansetts, a situation that enabled him to negotiate an end to the Pequot War in 1637, thereby helping the Puritans who had exiled him. (Library of Congress)

setts Bay in 1636. Rather than head back to England, he decided to move south and establish the colony of Providence near Narragansett Bay. Williams invited all religious refugees to the new colony and set up a trading post at Cocumscussoc, where he met and befriended the local indigenous people.

Unlike his belligerent neighbors to the north at Massachusetts Bay, Williams made peace and forged positive relations with the Natives. He insisted on adequately compensating the Narragansett Indians for their lands. Only after he fairly purchased the territory around Providence did he apply to London for a colonial charter. But Williams did not stop there. He went on to further the Narragansetts' trust by learning their language and familiarizing himself with their culture. He saw in Indian society a degree of harmony, humanity, and hospitality that was decidedly lacking among his own people. Williams documented his observations and the Narragansett language in his book, *A Key into the Language of America: Or, An help to the Language of the Natives in that part of America, called New-England* [sic]. Considered the first ethnoanthropological study of American Indians, Williams' account records Narragansett culture, analyzing everything from their religious beliefs to their sleeping habits.

Though Williams was a staunch advocate of Indian land rights, he was also a pragmatist and a realist. Hence, when the Pequots went to war with Massachusetts Bay over that colony's encroachment on Native land, Williams convinced the Narragansetts to remain neutral. He believed that only death and destruction would come to the Indians if they fought the colonists. Williams' peace policy and dealings with the Native peoples were effective; relations between whites and the Narragansetts remained cordial for nearly forty years. But the burgeoning white population's continual expansion onto Indian lands inevitably led to further conflict.

In 1675, Wampanoag Chief Metacom took on Massachusetts Bay, resulting in what came to be known as King Philip's War—the bloodiest conflict to that time. Though the Narragansetts had not taken sides in the war, colonists preemptively attacked them, resulting in the Great Swamp Massacre. With 500 to 600 dead—most of which were women and children—the Narragansett leadership ignored Williams' pleas and decided to side with Metacom in his fight against the colonists. They launched an assault on Providence, burning the town to the ground. Williams, in turn, accepted a commission as captain in the local militia and fought his former friends. In the end, the Narragansetts and Wampanoags could not match the firepower of the colonists, and they suffered a devastating loss in the war.

After King Philip's War, Williams' vision of a peaceful land where Indians and whites lived side by side, each learning from the other, came crashing down. With all of his former Narragansett friends gone, he lived out his last days a broken man among the rubble and ashes of Providence. Roger Williams died in the winter of 1683.

Bradley Shreve

See also Canonicus; Land Cessions, Colonial, Early National

References and Further Reading

Miller, Perry. 1953. *Roger Williams: His Contribution to the American Tradition*. Indianapolis, IN: Bobbs-Merrill Company.

Rubertone, Patricia E. 2001. *Grave Undertakings: An Archaeology of Roger Williams and the Narragansett Indians*. Washington, DC: Smithsonian Institution.

Williams, Roger. [1643] 1973. *A Key into the Language of America*. Detroit, MI: Wayne State University Press.

Wilson, Richard

Richard Wilson (Oglala Lakota, 1936–1990) was chairman of the Pine Ridge Indian Reservation tribal council during the 1973 Wounded Knee occupation, as well as during its violent aftermath. From the early 1970s until his defeat for the chairman's office by Al Trimble in 1976, Wilson outfitted a tribal police force that was often called the goon squad. This police force, which took "GOON" to mean Guardians of the Oglala Nation, was financed with tribal money from the federal government and cooperated closely with the Federal Bureau of Investigation (FBI).

One result of the escalating conflict between Oglala Lakota traditionalists allied with the American Indian Movement (AIM) and Wilson was the seventy-one-day occupation of Wounded Knee in 1973. The conflict between Wilson and AIM likely sprang from political differences: Wilson, a supporter of the Viet Nam war, saw dissent by AIM and by students as acts of ungrateful citizens who were dupes of the Communists. The local context of the occupation included an effort to publicly confront Wilson's policies, which often favored non-Indian ranchers, farmers, and corporations.

Richard Wilson, president of the Oglala Sioux Tribal Council, held a previously unreleased list in 1973 given to him and later authenticated by a U.S. Justice Department official, showing names of American Indian Movement (AIM) militants occupying Wounded Knee, South Dakota, and the counts the Justice Department has against them. (Bettmann/Corbis)

The struggle between AIM and Wilson also took place in the realm of tribal electoral politics. When Wilson sought reelection in 1974, Russell Means, an Oglala who had helped found AIM, challenged him. In the primary Wilson trailed Means, 667 votes to 511 votes. Wilson won the final election over Means by fewer than 200 votes in balloting that the U.S. Commission on Civil Rights later found to be permeated with fraud. The Civil Rights Commission recommended a new election, which was not held; Wilson answered his detractors by stepping up the terror, examples of which were described in a chronology kept by the Wounded Knee Legal Defense-Offense Committee. One of the GOON's favorite weapons was the automobile; officially, such deaths could be reported as "traffic accidents."

Wilson had a formidable array of supporters on the reservation, many of whom criticized AIM for being urban-based and insensitive to reservation res-

idents' needs. Mona Wilson, one of Wilson's daughters, who was seventeen years old in 1973, recalled him crying in his mother's arms at the time. Speaking about the events two decades later, Wilson's wife, Yvonne, and two daughters recalled him as a kind and compassionate father who had the interests of his people at heart. They said that Wilson supported AIM when it protested the 1972 murder of Raymond Yellow Thunder in the reservation border town of Gordon, Nebraska. Only later, as events culminated in the weeks-long siege of Wounded Knee, did Wilson and AIM leaders become deadly enemies.

Wilson was the first Oglala Lakota tribal chairperson to serve two consecutive terms. He worked as a self-employed plumber, owner of a gas station, and on other short-term projects after his defeat by Trimble for the tribal chairmanship in 1976. Wilson also held the traditional role of pipe carrier. He was

known for feeding anyone who came to his door, and he had a major role in beginning a Lakota community college on the reservation, as well as a number of other tribal enterprises.

Wilson died of a heart attack in 1990, as he was preparing to run for a third term as tribal chairman.

Bruce E. Johansen

See also American Indian Movement; Banks, Dennis; Means, Russell; Peltier, Leonard; Pine Ridge Political Murders.

References and Further Reading

Johansen, Bruce E., and Roberto F. Maestas. 1979. *Wasi'chu: The Continuing Indian Wars*. New York: Monthly Review Press.

LaMay, Konnie. 1993. "20 Years of Anguish." *Indian Country Today*, February 25. n.p.

Matthiessen, Peter. 1991. *In the Spirit of Crazy Horse*. New York: Viking.

U.S. Commission on Civil Rights. 1974. "Report of Investigation: Oglala Sioux Tribe, General Election, 1974." October, mimeographed. Washington, DC: Civil Rights Commission.

Winnemucca

A diplomatic, influential leader during a fraught time in northern Paiute (Numa) history, Winnemucca (died 1880) worked hard, yet ultimately unsuccessfully to ensure peaceful relations with non-Natives, and he earned the distinction (especially among non-Natives) of being first overall chief of the northern Paiute. The northern Paiute traditionally ranged in present-day central and eastern California, western Nevada, and eastern Oregon. Prior to assuming responsibility as chief, Winnemucca (also known as Po-i-to or Old Winnemucca) is remembered as a father, medicine man, and an antelope charmer (Hopkins, 1994, 55). Public knowledge of Winnemucca's life begins with his acquisition of political power. When Captain Truckee, Winnemucca's father-in-law, left on an expedition to California, probably when accompanying Captain John Fremont in the mid-1840s, he appointed Winnemucca the band leader. Winnemucca's status as "chief" was recognized internally among the northern Paiute, distinguishing him from leaders who were appointed and acknowledged only by non-Natives (Hopkins, 1994, 10, 194).

Winnemucca assumed leadership of the northern Paiute at a critical moment in Paiute history. Regular contact with non-Natives had begun only a few years earlier, under Truckee's leadership, and changes to everyday life were imminent. Truckee had welcomed non-Natives with joy, because their arrival signaled the fulfillment of a Paiute prophecy (Hopkins, 1994, 6–7). In a dream, however, Winnemucca saw non-Natives bringing bloodshed and destruction among the northern Paiutes, and he did not celebrate the growing non-Native presence. He sought peaceful relations with non-Natives whenever possible but did not stand by to see his people abused.

In 1855 Winnemucca negotiated the Honey Lake Valley agreement with non-Native citizens of Honey Lake, California, to minimize conflict between the communities. According to the agreement, when a member of one party committed a crime against a member of the other, the communities would negotiate and turn over the perpetrator, thereby eliminating the need for continued conflict. By 1860, Winnemucca was accused of not abiding by the terms of his own agreement when he was unhelpful in the investigation of the murder of D. E. Demming, believed to be murdered by Paiutes. The agreement had collapsed on both

Winnemucca (The Giver), was a Paviotso or Paiute chief of western Nevada. (National Archives and Records Administration)

sides: Winnemucca would not turn over members of his community each time an Anglo accused a Paiute, and the Honey Lake community was rapidly filling with new citizens who had no regard for the 1855 agreement. At the same time, Winnemucca was outraged by the non-Natives' exploitation of another agreement in which non-Native cattle herders leased land from northern Paiutes. He traveled to Virginia City in hopes of gaining legal support but came away unsuccessful (Knack and Stewart, 1984, 65).

In the spring of 1860, tensions between Paiutes and non-Natives grew until they culminated in the Pyramid Lake War. Winnemucca participated in the conflict at Pyramid Lake, although by 1862 he was exchanging gifts with Governor James Nye on neutral ground in an effort to maintain peace. In 1865, thirty Paiutes were massacred at Pyramid Lake, including Winnemucca's wives, several daughters, and other family members (Knack and Stewart, 1984, 79). Nevertheless, in 1867 Winnemucca sent a letter to Carson City in hopes of negotiating peace for his people once again.

By this time, Winnemucca was widely recognized by the Mormons and other non-Natives, and some of his own people, as the first overall chief of the northern Paiutes. In 1870, the 5,000 northern Paiutes still operated in small, semiautonomous bands of fifty to 200 that acknowledged linguistic and cultural ties. Each had its own chief, yet many acknowledged Winnemucca as a form of chief over all (Stewart, 1939, 129). Notably, Winnemucca never organized all of his subchiefs but was known as the "traveling chief" (Stewart, 1939, 130). He negotiated with Indian agents and the military on behalf of his people as they lost land and freedom and became increasingly dependent on government rations for survival.

Following the Bannock Wars, Winnemucca and his daughter Sarah (who would become famous as an educator and writer) traveled to Washington, D.C., and met with Secretary of the Interior Carl Schurz and President Rutherford B. Hayes to inform them of the northern Paiutes' primary concerns: their lack of essential supplies, exploitation by Indian agents, and the government's unfulfilled promises to help them settle in a permanent, peaceful home. Winnemucca and his daughter worked to ensure peace for the northern Paiutes, but, as bearers of promises that the federal government never upheld, their favor fluctuated in the eyes of some

Paiutes. Nevertheless, Winnemucca continued caring for his people until his death in 1880.

Amy S. Fatzinger

See also Mormon Church; Winnemucca, Sarah.
References and Further Reading

Hopkins, Sarah Winnemucca. [1883] 1994. *Life Among the Piutes: Their Wrongs and Claims.* Reno: University of Nevada Press.

Knack, Martha C., and Omer C. Stewart. 1984. *As Long as the River Shall Run: An Ethnohistory of Pyramid Lake Indian Reservation.* Berkeley: University of California Press.

Stewart, Omer C. 1939. "The Northern Paiute Bands." In *University of California Publications in Anthropological Records.* Edited by A. L. Kroeber, et al., 127–150. Berkeley: University of California Press.

Winnemucca, Sarah

Also known as Thocmetony ("Shell Flower"), Sonometa ("White Shell"), and the Princess, Sarah Winnemucca (or Hopkins, her married name) was one of the earliest Native American women writers to capture the flavor and characteristics of her Paiute culture. She also traveled extensively to give lectures describing the wrongs done to her fellow Native Americans.

Winnemucca was born about 1844 among the Paiute people (then spelled Piute) at Humboldt Sink in what is now Nevada. Her father, Winnemucca II, was chief of the tribe and was the son of Captain Truckee, a wise and knowing Paiute chief. Although she lived for a portion of her childhood in the San Joaquin Valley area of California, she returned to Nevada, where she moved into the home of a white family and was named Sarah Winnemucca. She had attended a convent school in California, and that seems to have been her only formal education.

Starting in 1868, Winnemucca served as an interpreter between her people on the Paiute reservation and the whites who surrounded it. In 1876, she taught at the Indian school on the Malheur Reservation in Oregon. She also served as the guide and interpreter to General Oliver O. Howard during the Bannock War in Oregon in 1878.

When the Paiute were forcibly removed to the Yakima Indian Reservation in what is now Washington State in 1879, Winnemucca and her father traveled to Washington, D.C., to try to reverse the decision, but to no avail. She then began lecturing in San

and Mary Tyler Peabody Mann. In 1883, as a result of the lectures on behalf of her people, she published *Life Among the Piutes: Their Wrongs and Claims,* which Mann edited for her. A personal and tribal history, the work documented her people's moral character and achievements and examined Indian–white relations, a theme previously unexplored in earlier Native American writings.

Winnemucca lived only eight years after the publication of her famed work, and, in that time, she fought continuously to return the Paiute lands to her people. She died of tuberculosis on her sister's ranch near Monida, Montana, on October 16, 1891. The Paiute people remembered her as "Mother."

References and Further Reading
Canfield, Gae Whitney. 1983. *Sarah Winnemucca of the Northern Paiutes.* Norman: University of Oklahoma Press.
Hopkins, Sarah Winnemucca. 1994. *Life Among the Piutes: Their Wrongs and Claims.* Reno: University of Nevada Press.
Zanjani, Sally Springmeyer. 2001. *Sarah Winnemucca.* Lincoln: University of Nebraska Press.

Women of All Red Nations

Women of All Red Nations (WARN) was formed in the middle 1970s "to address issues directly facing Indian women and their families" (Wittstock and Salinas, 2006). WARN has some notable alumnae. For example, Winona LaDuke, who ran for vice president of the United States on the Green party ticket with Ralph Nader in 1996 and 2000, was a WARN founding member.

When the American Indian Movement (AIM) began in the 1960s, women members found themselves playing supporting (and, some asserted, subservient) roles. In 1974, at Rapid City, South Dakota, Native women from more than thirty nations met and decided, among other things, that "truth and communication are among our most valuable tools in the liberation of our lands, people, and four-legged and winged creations" (Johansen, 1998, 44). The formation of WARN enabled politically active Native American women to speak with a collective voice on issues that affected them intensely. At the same time, WARN members, with chapters throughout the United States, worked to support a large number of Native American men in prisons.

Sarah Winnemucca, one of the earliest Native American woman writers to capture the flavor and characteristics of her Paiute culture, traveled extensively during the late-nineteenth century to give lectures describing the wrongs done to her fellow Native Americans. (Library of Congress)

Francisco about the wrongs perpetrated against her people, and she became a leading spokesperson for those who saw the government's policy toward Native Americans as cruel and unjust. Although she met in 1880 with President Rutherford B. Hayes and Interior Secretary Carl Schurz, who promised to help return her people to their reservation, nothing was done for the Paiute.

In 1881, Winnemucca married Lieutenant L. H. Hopkins, a white army officer who sympathized with her plight. She then conducted an extensive lecture tour of the East Coast, and she was sponsored by woman suffrage advocates Elizabeth Peabody

Members of WARN also form liaisons with non-Native feminist groups, such as the National Organization of Women, to advocate policies of concern to minority women. The group's main priorities include the improvement of educational opportunities, health and medical care (including reproductive rights), resistance to violence against women, an end to stereotyping, support for treaties, and protection of the environment, including campaigns against uranium mining and milling, a long-time threat to Lakota and Navajo women as well as men.

One critical issue raised by WARN is the widespread sterilization of Native American women in government-run hospitals, an extension of a eugenics movement aimed at impeding the population increase of groups believed by some in government to be poor and/or mentally defective. These programs had ended for most of non-Indian groups after World War II (Germany's Nazis having given eugenics an extremely bad reputation), but they continued on Indian reservations through the 1970s. Wherever Indian activists gathered during the Red Power years of the 1970s, conversation inevitably turned to the number of women who had had their tubes tied or their ovaries removed by the Indian Health Service. Communication spurred by activism provoked a growing number of Native American women to piece together and name what amounted to a national eugenics policy carried out with copious federal funding.

WARN and other women's organizations publicized the sterilizations, which were performed after pro forma "consent" of the women being sterilized. The "consent" sometimes was not offered in the women's language, and often followed threats that they would die or lose their welfare benefits if they had more children. At least two fifteen-year-old girls were told they were having their tonsils out before their ovaries were removed. The enormity of government-funded sterilization, as well as its eugenics context, has been documented by Sally Torpy (1998) in her thesis, "Endangered Species: Native American Women's Struggle for Their Reproductive Rights and Racial Identity, 1970s–1990s," written at the University of Nebraska at Omaha.

No one even today knows exactly how many Native American women were sterilized during the 1970s. One basis for calculation is provided by the General Accounting Office, whose study covered only four of twelve IHS regions over four years (1973–1976). Within those limits, the study documented the sterilization of 3,406 Indian women. Another estimate was provided by Lehman Brightman (Lakota), who devoted much of his life to the issue. His educated guess (without exact calculations to back it up) is that 40 percent of Native women and 10 percent of Native men were sterilized during the decade. Brightman estimates that the total number of Indian women sterilized during the decade was between 60,000 and 70,000. The women of WARN played a central role in bringing involuntary sterilization of Native American women to an end.

Bruce E. Johansen

See also American Indian Movement; LaDuke, Winona; Reservations Economic and Social Conditions.

References and Further Reading
Johansen, Bruce E. 1998. "Reprise/Forced Sterilizations." *Native Americas* 15 (Winter): 4, 44–47.
Torpy, Sally J. 1998. "Endangered Species: Native American Women's Struggle for Their Reproductive Rights and Racial Identity: 1970's–1990's." Masters thesis, University of Nebraska.
Wittstock, Laura Waterman, and Elaine J. Salinas. 2006. "A Brief History of the American Indian Movement." Available at: http://www.aimovement.org/ggc/history.html. Accessed May 16, 2006.

Wovoka

Numu (northern Paiute) seer, holy man, and prophet of the 1890 Ghost Dance movement. After experiencing a vision, Wovoka (Jack Wilson, ca. 1858–1932) began preaching to the local Numu on the Walker River Reservation. Word of his teachings spread rapidly to reservations as far east as Oklahoma, and the Ghost Dance of 1890 became one of the most widespread and famous pan-Indian religious movements of the nineteenth century.

Wovoka (the [wood] cutter) was born sometime between 1856 and 1863 in either the Smith or Mason Valleys of western Nevada. His father was named Numu-tibo'o ("Northern Paiute White Man"), and Wovoka had at least two younger brothers. As a child of about eight, he began working on the Mason Valley ranch of David and Abigail Wilson. There he acquired the name by which he was more commonly known by local whites and Indians alike: Jack Wil-

son. The Wilsons were devout United Presbyterians, and it is reasonable to suspect that this early exposure to Christianity influenced the development of the Ghost Dance doctrine. Wovoka and his wife Mary (who by various accounts was Numu or Bannock) had a number of children but only three daughters survived to adulthood.

Wovoka grew up in a spiritual tradition based in shamanism and prophecy. Two decades before his vision, a previous version of the Ghost Dance had emerged from Walker River. James Mooney, the first to study the religion, believed that Wovoka's father was the 1870 Ghost Dance prophet, but subsequent scholarship has determined that the prophet was a Fish Lake Valley Paiute named Wodziwob. Wovoka's father may have had some involvement with the earlier Ghost Dance but the details remain obscure. Wovoka demonstrated his power to followers in ways common for Numu shamans—weather control and invulnerability. Although he was not practicing as a shaman when he experienced his visions, he later became a noted healer.

Wovoka experienced his first vision on New Year's Day 1889. He reported traveling to heaven and meeting God. He was instructed to return to Earth and tell the people to lead good and loving lives and to follow a ritual that, if faithfully observed, would reunite them with their deceased loved ones and friends in a world without "death or sickness or old age." The basic ceremony in 1890 was identical to that of 1870—the Great Basin Round Dance. Within the circle, men, women, and children alternated sexes, interlocked fingers, and shuffled slowly to the left, all the while singing the numerous songs revealed to individual dancers in visions. The first dances probably took place early in 1889, and by the time of the second dances later that spring Indians from across the Great Basin were already in attendance.

Wovoka's doctrine was similar to the 1870 movement but exhibited some very important differences. The only written version of Wovoka's doctrine recorded by a Native person was the Messiah Letter, written by the Caspar Edson (Arapaho) in August 1891. On one level the intent of the 1890 Ghost Dance was to bring a radical transformation of the existing order—a renewal of the earth and reunification of all people—but on another its effect was redemptive. Wovoka preached a gospel of peace, love, and accommodation that, by eliminating many of the causes of internal discord, served to strengthen Indian communities. Wovoka's message was flexible and allowed room for individual and cultural interpretation. He told his followers to live at peace with the whites: "Do not fight. Do always right." On the other hand his words could also be interpreted to suggest that whites would not survive the coming cataclysm. His doctrine also exhibited far greater Christian influence than the earlier movement. Wovoka reportedly claimed he was Jesus and allegedly showed the stigmata of crucifixion to a number of Native seekers, including the Cheyenne holy man Porcupine.

The massacre of Lakota Ghost Dancers at Wounded Knee in December of 1890 did not end the practice of the religion, as is popularly believed. Wovoka continued to be a renowned healer and spiritual leader into the twentieth century. Individual Indians and delegations corresponded with and visited him until his death in September 1932. He was buried beside his wife Mary in the Walker River Reservation cemetery.

Gregory E. Smoak

See also Ghost Dance Religion; Wounded Knee, South Dakota, Massacre at.
References and Further Reading
Hittman, Michael. 1997. *Wovoka and the Ghost Dance.* Expanded ed. Lincoln: University of Nebraska Press.
Mooney, James. *The Ghost Dance Religion and the Sioux Outbreak of 1890.* Reprint ed. Lincoln: University of Nebraska Press.

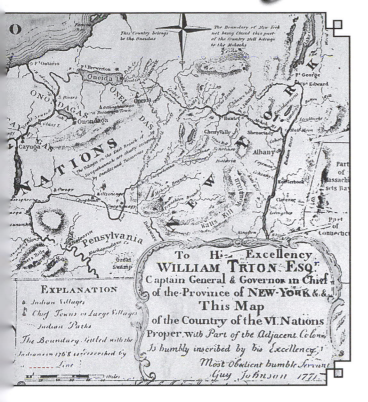

Iroquois Great Law of Peace

Probably dating back to the mid-twelfth century, the Iroquois Great Law of Peace is accredited to legendary Huron leader Deganawidah, who lived in what is now upstate New York. Deganawidah formed a Native American confederation of five Haudenosaunee (Iroquois) in the region. Sometimes referred to as the Five Nations, the Iroquois Confederacy had many allies over a large area. The confederacy emerged as the strongest Native American confederacy in North America when European immigration began and remained so until the American Revolution. The Confederacy split during that conflict, mostly siding with the British (the Oneidas siding with the Patriots and the Senecas split). Afterward, the Confederacy was forced to cede much of its land to the Americans.

The Iroquois Great Law is a remarkable statement of human rights, and some of its principles have influenced the evolution of democracy worldwide, including the U.S. Constitution of 1787. What follows are a few brief excerpts of a condensation of the oral history that was first written during the 1880s. A complete version of the Great Law takes about four eight-hour days to recite; the last person who could recite it from memory was Jake Thomas, a Cayuga (1922–1998). The oral history has been recited in several versions. One that has been published, in Onondaga and English, is Hanni Woodbury, comp. Concerning the League: The Iroquois League Tradition as Dictated in Onondaga by John Arthur Gibson *(Winnipeg: University of Manitoba Press, 1992).*

I am Dekanawidah and with the Five Nations' Confederate Lords I plant the Tree of Great Peace. I plant it in your territory, Adodarhoh, and the Onondaga Nation, in the territory of you who are Firekeepers.

I name the tree the Tree of the Great Long Leaves. Under the shade of this Tree of the Great Peace we spread the soft white feathery down of the globe thistle as seats for you, Adodarhoh, and your cousin Lords.

We place at the top of the Tree of the Long Leaves an Eagle who is able to see afar. If he sees in the distance any evil approaching or any danger

threatening he will at once warn the people of the Confederacy.

Whenever the Confederate Lords shall assemble for the purpose of holding a council, the Onondaga Lords shall open it by expressing their gratitude to their cousin Lords and greeting them, and they shall make an address and offer thanks to the earth where men dwell, to the streams of water, the pools, the springs and the lakes, to the maize and the fruits, to the medicinal herbs and trees, to the forest trees for their usefulness, to the animals that serve as food and give their pelts for clothing, to the great winds and the lesser winds, to the Thunderers, to the Sun, the mighty warrior, to the moon, to the messengers of the Creator who reveal his wishes and to the Great Creator who dwells in the heavens above, who gives all the things useful to men, and who is the source and the ruler of health and life.

Every Onondaga Lord (or his deputy) must be present at every Confederate Council and must agree with the majority without unwarrantable dissent, so that a unanimous decision may be rendered.

All the business of the Five Nations Confederate Council shall be conducted by the two combined bodies of Confederate Lords. First the question shall be passed upon by the Mohawk and Seneca Lords, then it shall be discussed and passed by the Oneida and Cayuga Lords. Their decisions shall then be referred to the Onondaga Lords, [Fire Keepers] for final judgment.

In all cases the procedure must be as follows: when the Mohawk and Seneca Lords have unanimously agreed upon a question, they shall report their decision to the Cayuga and Oneida Lords who shall deliberate upon the question and report a unanimous decision to the Mohawk Lords. The Mohawk Lords will then report the standing of the case to the Firekeepers, who shall render a decision as they see fit in case of a disagreement by the two bodies, or confirm the decisions of the two bodies if they are identical. The Fire Keepers shall then report their decision to the Mohawk Lords who shall announce it to the open council.

Rights, Duties and Qualifications of Lords

If at any time it shall be manifest that a Confederate Lord has not in mind the welfare of the people or disobeys the rules of this Great Law, the men or women of the Confederacy, or both jointly, shall come to the Council and upbraid the erring Lord through his War Chief. If the complaint of the people through the War Chief is not heeded the first time it shall be uttered again and then if no attention is given a third complaint and warning shall be given. If the Lord is contemptuous the matter shall go to the council of War Chiefs. The War Chiefs shall then divest the erring Lord of his title by order of the women in whom the titleship is vested. When the Lord is deposed the women shall notify the Confederate Lords through their War Chief, and the Confederate Lords shall sanction the act. The women will then select another of their sons as a candidate and the Lords shall elect him. Then shall the chosen one be installed by the Installation Ceremony.

If a Lord of the Confederacy of the Five Nations should commit murder the other Lords of the Nation shall assemble at the place where the corpse lies and prepare to depose the criminal Lord. If it is impossible to meet at the scene of the crime the Lords shall discuss the matter at the next Council of their Nation and request their War Chief to depose the Lord guilty of crime, to "bury" his women relatives and to transfer the Lordship title to a sister family.

Certain physical defects in a Confederate Lord make him ineligible to sit in the Confederate Council. Such defects are infancy, idiocy, blindness, deafness, dumbness, and impotency. When a Confederate Lord is restricted by any of these conditions, a deputy shall be appointed by his sponsors to act for him, but in case of extreme necessity the restricted Lord may exercise his rights.

The Lords of the Confederacy of the Five Nations shall be mentors of the people for all time. The thickness of their skin shall be seven spans—which is to say that they shall be proof against anger, offensive actions, and criticism. Their hearts shall be full of peace and good will and their minds filled with a yearning for the welfare of the people of the Confederacy. With endless patience they shall carry out their duty and their firmness shall be tempered with a tenderness for their people. Neither anger nor fury shall find lodgment in their minds and all their words and actions shall be marked by calm deliberation.

All Lords of the Five Nations Confederacy must be honest in all things. They must not idle or gossip, but be men possessing those honorable qualities that make true Royaneh. It shall be a serious wrong for anyone to lead a Lord into trivial affairs, for the people must ever hold their Lords high in estimation out of respect to their honorable positions.

Should any man of the Nation assist with special ability or show great interest in the affairs of the Nation, if he proves himself wise, honest, and worthy of confidence, the Confederate Lords may elect him to a seat with them and he may sit in the Confederate Council. He shall be proclaimed a "Pine Tree sprung up for the Nation" and shall be installed as such at the next assembly for the installation of Lords. Should he ever do anything contrary to the rules of the Great Peace, he may not be deposed from office—"no one shall cut him down"—but thereafter everyone shall be deaf to his voice and his advice. Should he resign his seat and title no one shall prevent him. A Pine Tree chief has no authority to name a successor nor is his title hereditary.

People of the Five Nations members of a certain clan shall recognize every other member of that clan, irrespective of the Nation, as relatives. Men and women, therefore, members of the same clan are forbidden to marry.

The lineal descent of the people of the Five Nations shall run in the female line. Women shall be considered the progenitors of the Nation. They shall own the land and the soil. Men and women shall follow the status of the mother. The women heirs of the Confederated Lordship titles shall be called Royaneh [Noble] for all time to come. The women of the Forty Nine [Fifty, with an empty seat for the Peacemaker]. Royaneh families shall be the heirs of the Authorized Names for all time to come.

If the female heirs of a Confederate Lord's title become extinct, the title right shall be given by the Lords of the Confederacy to the sister family whom they shall elect and that family shall hold the name and transmit it to their (female) heirs, but they shall not appoint any of their sons as a candidate for a title until all the eligible men of the former family shall have died or otherwise have become ineligible.

Five arrows shall be bound together very strong and each arrow shall represent one nation. As the five arrows are strongly bound this shall symbolize the complete union of the nations. Thus are the Five Nations united completely and enfolded together, united into one head, one body, and one mind. Therefore they shall labor, legislate, and council together for the interest of future generations.

The Lords of the Confederacy shall eat together from one bowl the feast of cooked beaver's tail. While they are eating they are to use no sharp utensils for if they should they might accidentally cut one another and bloodshed would follow. All measures must be taken to prevent the spilling of blood in any way.

The people [are vested] with the right to correct their erring Lords. In case a part or all the Lords pursue a course not vouched for by the people and heed not the third warning of their women relatives, then the matter shall be taken to the General Council of the women of the Five Nations. If the Lords notified and warned three times fail to heed, then the case falls into the hands of the men of the Five Nations. The War Chiefs shall then, by right of such power and authority, enter the open council to warn the Lord or Lords to return from the wrong course. If the Lords heed the warning they shall say, "we will reply tomorrow." If then an answer is returned in favor of justice and in accord with this Great Law, then the Lords shall individually pledge themselves again by again furnishing the necessary shells for the pledge. Then shall the War Chief or Chiefs exhort the Lords urging them to be just and true.

When a member of an alien nation comes to the territory of the Five Nations and seeks refuge and permanent residence, the Lords of the Nation to which he comes shall extend hospitality and make him a member of the nation. Then shall he be accorded equal rights and privileges in all matters except as after mentioned.

No body of alien people [which have been] adopted temporarily shall have a vote in the council of the Lords of the Confederacy, for only they who have been invested with Lordship titles may vote in the Council. Aliens have nothing by blood to make claim to a vote and should they have it, not knowing all the traditions of the Confederacy, might go against its Great Peace. In this manner the Great Peace would be endangered and perhaps be destroyed.

When the men of the Five Nations, now called forth to become warriors, are ready for battle with an obstinate opposing nation that has refused to accept the Great Peace, then one of the five War Chiefs shall be chosen by the warriors of the Five Nations to lead the army into battle. It shall be the duty of the War Chief so chosen to come before his warriors and address them. His aim shall be to impress upon them the necessity of good behavior and strict obedience to all the commands of the War Chiefs. He shall deliver an oration exhorting them with great zeal to be brave and courageous and never to be guilty of cowardice. At the conclusion of his oration he shall march forward and commence the War Song . . .

The rites and festivals of each nation shall remain undisturbed and shall continue as before

because they were given by the people of old times as useful and necessary for the good of men.

A certain sign shall be known to all the people of the Five Nations which shall denote that the owner or occupant of a house is absent. A stick or pole in a slanting or leaning position shall indicate this and be the sign. Every person not entitled to enter the house by right of living within it upon seeing such a sign shall not approach the house either by day or by night but shall keep as far away as his business will permit.

Christopher Columbus: Journal

Christopher Columbus kept a detailed journal of his travels in America that is not only a rich source for descriptions of the peoples he met, but also reveals his assumptions about them.

IN THE NAME OF OUR LORD JESUS CHRIST

Whereas, Most Christian, High, Excellent, and Powerful Princes, King and Queen of Spain and of the Islands of the Sea, our Sovereigns, this present year 1492, after your Highnesses had terminated the war with the Moors reigning in Europe . . .

Friday, 3 August, 1492. Set sail from the bar of Saltes at 8 o'clock, and proceeded with a strong breeze till sunset, sixty miles or fifteen leagues south, afterwards southwest and south by west, which is the direction of the Canaries.

Tuesday, 25 September. . . . At sunset Martin Alonzo called out with great joy from his vessel that he saw land, and demanded of the Admiral a reward for his intelligence. The Admiral says, when he heard him declare this, he fell on his knees and returned thanks to God, and Martin Alonzo with his crew repeated Gloria in excelsis Deo, as did the crew of the Admiral. Those on board the Nina ascended the rigging, and all declared they saw land. The Admiral also thought it was land, and about twenty-five leagues distant.

Wednesday, 26 September. Continued their course west till the afternoon, then southwest and discovered that what they had taken for land was nothing but clouds.

Thursday, 11 October. Steered west-southwest; and encountered a heavier sea than they had met with before in the whole voyage. Saw pardelas and a green rush near the vessel. The crew of the *Pinta* saw a cane and a log; they also picked up a stick which appeared to have been carved with an iron tool, a piece of cane, a plant which grows on land, and a board. The crew of the Nina saw other signs of land, and a stalk loaded with rose berries. These signs encouraged them, and they all grew cheerful. Sailed this day till sunset, twenty-seven leagues.

After sunset steered their original course west and sailed twelve miles an hour till two hours after midnight, going ninety miles, which are twenty-two leagues and a half; and as the *Pinta* was the swiftest sailer, and kept ahead of the Admiral, she discovered land and made the signals which had been ordered. The land was first seen by a sailor called Rodrigo de Triana, although the Admiral at ten o'clock that evening standing on the quarter-deck saw a light . . . near a small island, one of the Lucayos, called in the Indian language Guanahani. Presently they descried people, naked, and the Admiral landed in the boat, which was armed, along with Martin Alonzo Pinzon, and Vincent Yanez his brother, captain of the Nina. The Admiral bore the royal standard, and the two captains each a banner of the Green Cross. . . .

Numbers of the people of the island straightway collected together. Here follow the precise words of the Admiral: "As I saw that they were very friendly to us, and perceived that they could be much more easily converted to our holy faith by gentle means than by force, I presented them with some red caps, and strings of beads to wear upon the neck, and many other trifles of small value, wherewith they were much delighted, and became wonderfully attached to us. Afterwards they came swimming to the boats, bringing parrots, balls of cotton thread, javelins, and many other things which they exchanged for articles we gave them, such as glass beads, and hawk's bells; which trade was carried on with the utmost good will. But they seemed on the whole to me, to be a very poor people. They all go completely naked, even the women, though I saw but one girl. All whom I saw were young, not above thirty years of age, well made, with fine shapes and faces; their hair short, and coarse like that of a horse's tail, combed toward the forehead, except a small portion which they suffer to hang down behind, and never cut.

Some paint themselves with black, which makes them appear like those of the Canaries, neither black nor white; others with white, others with red, and others with such colors as they can find. Some paint the face, and some the whole body; others only the eyes, and others the nose. Weapons they have none, nor are acquainted with them, for I showed them swords which they grasped by the blades, and cut

themselves through ignorance. They have no iron, their javelins being without it, and nothing more than sticks, though some have fish-bones or other things at the ends. They are all of a good size and stature, and handsomely formed.

Saturday, 13 October. At daybreak great multitudes of men came to the shore, all young and of fine shapes, very handsome; their hair not curled but straight and coarse like horse-hair, and all with foreheads and heads much broader than any people I had hitherto seen; their eyes were large and very beautiful; they were not black, but the color of the inhabitants of the Canaries, which is a very natural circumstance, they being in the same latitude with the island of Ferro in the Canaries. They were straight-limbed without exception, and not with prominent bellies but handsomely shaped. They came to the ship in canoes, made of a single trunk of a tree, wrought in a wonderful manner considering the country; some of them large enough to contain forty or forty-five men, others of different sizes down to those fitted to hold but a single person.

Powhatan: Remarks to Captain John Smith

One of the most powerful Indian leaders in North America during the early seventeenth century, Powhatan ruled over a large confederacy from his base in Virginia. He had an erratic relationship with the Jamestown colonists, as the two sides maintained a tenuous peace. Nevertheless, despite their mutual suspicion, Powhatan supplied the colonists with food during several crucial periods and thus saved the fledgling colony from total disaster. Powhatan was succeeded at his death in 1618, by his brother Opechancanough, who was far less tolerant of the colonists and organized the devastating Massacre of 1622, in which one-third of the white population died at Indian hands.

Captain Smith, some doubt I have of your coming hither . . . for many do inform me, your coming is not for trade, but to invade my people and possess my Country. . . . I am now grown old, and must soon die; and the succession must descend, in order, to my brothers, Opitchapan, Opekankanough, and Catataugh, and then to my two sisters, and their two daughters. I wish their experience was equal to mine; and that your love to us might not be less than ours to you. Why should you take by force that from us which you can have by love? Why should you destroy us, who have provided you with food? What can you get by war? We can hide our provisions, and fly into the woods; and then you must consequently famish by wronging your friends. What is the cause of your jealousy? You see us unarmed, and willing to supply your wants, if you will come in a friendly manner, and not with swords and guns, as to invade an enemy. I am not so simple, as not to know it is better to eat good meat, lie well, and sleep quietly with my women and children; to laugh and be merry with the English; and, being their friend, to have copper, hatchets, and whatever else I want, than to fly from all, to lie cold in the woods, feed upon acorns, roots, and such trash, and to be so hunted, that I cannot rest, eat, or sleep. In such circumstances, my men must watch, and if a twig should break, all would cry out, "Here comes Capt. Smith": and so, in this miserable manner, to end my miserable life; and, Capt. Smith, this might be soon your fate too, through your rashness and unadvisedness. I, therefore, exhort you to peaceable councils; and, above all, I insist that the guns and swords, the cause of all our jealousy and uneasiness, be removed and sent away.

Massasoit Peace Treaty

The Wampanoag chief Massasoit was the first Indian leader to deal with the New England colonists shortly after the Pilgrims' arrival in Plymouth, Massachusetts, in late 1620. At the Pilgrims' request, Massasoit agreed to this treaty in March 1621. Both sides worked hard to maintain peace as long as Massasoit lived, despite bitter conflicts between Indians and colonists in other parts of New England. The chief died in 1662 and was succeeded by his son, Metacom, who led the Wampanoags in King Philip's War against the colonists from 1676 to 1677.

1. That neither he nor any of his should injure or do hurt to any of our people.
2. And if any of his did hurt to any of ours, he should send the offender, that we might punish him.
3. That if any of our tools were taken away when our people were at work, he should cause them to be restored; and if ours did any harm to any of his, we would do the like to them.

4. If any did unjustly war against him, we would aid him; if any did war against us, he should aid us.

5. He should send to his neighbor confederates, to certify them of this, that they might not wrong us, but might be likewise comprised in the conditions of peace.

6. That when their men came to us, they should leave their bows and arrows behind them, as we should do our pieces when we came to them.

Lastly, that doing thus, King James would esteem of him as his friend and ally.

John Mason: A Brief History of the Pequot War

The Pequot War of 1636 was the first and one of the most brutal of the American Indian wars. The result of fighting among the tribes and their shifting alliances with the American colonists, the war ended with the complete annihilation of the Pequot tribe, particularly after the gruesome Indian massacre at Fort Mystic. When the war ended in 1637, the few surviving Pequots were sold off into slavery. The Pequot War cleared the path for white expansion in southern New England and was generally regarded as a great triumph by the colonists.

Major John Mason served as commander of the Connecticut forces. He wrote this history of the war around 1670, although it did not appear in print until 1736, when Boston minister and historian Thomas Prince published it with his own introduction and explanatory notes.

In the Beginning of May 1637 there were sent out by Connecticut Colony Ninety Men under the Command of Capt. John Mason against the Pequots, with Onkos an Indian Sachem living at Mohegan [Note: Onkos, usually called Uncas, the Great Sachem of the Moheags] who was newly revolted from the Pequots; being Shipped in one Pink, one Pinnace, and one Shallop; who sailing down the River of Connecticut fell several times a ground, the Water being very low: The Indians not being wonted to such Things with their small Canoes, and also being impatient of Delays, desired they might be set on Shoar, promising that they would meet us at Saybrook; which we granted: They hastening to their Quarters, fell upon Thirty or forty of the Enemy near Saybrook Fort, and killed seven of them outright; having only one of theirs wounded, who was sent back to Connecticut in a Skiff; Capt. John Underhill also coming with him, who informed us what was performed by Onkos and his Men; which we looked at as a special Providence; for before we were somewhat doubtful of his Fidelity: Capt. Underhill then offered his Service with nineteen Men to go with us, if Lieutenant Gardner would allow of it, who was Chief Commander at Saybrook Fort; which was readily approved of by Lieutenant Gardner and accepted by us; In lieu of them we sent back twenty of our Soldiers to Connecticut.

. . . Their Numbers far exceeded ours: having sixteen Guns with Powder and Shot, as we were informed by the two Captives forementioned (where we declared the Grounds of this War) who were taken by the Dutch and restored to us at Saybrook; which indeed was a very friendly Office and not to be forgotten. . . . They were on Land, and being swift on Foot, might much impede our Landing, and possibly dishearten our Men; we being expected only by Land, there being no other Place to go on Shoar but in that River, nearer than Narragansett.

. . . We Marched thence towards Pequot, with about five hundred Indians: But through the Heat of the Weather and want of Provisions some of our Men fainted: And having Marched about twelve Miles, we came to Pawcatuck River, at a Ford where our Indians told us the Pequots did usually Fish; there making an Alta, we stayed some small time: The Narragansett Indians manifesting great Fear, in so much that many of them returned, although they had frequently despised us, saying, That we durst not look upon a Pequot, but themselves would perform great Things; though we had often told them that we came on purpose and were resolved, God assisting, to see the Pequots, and to fight with them, before we returned, though we perished. I then enquired of Onkos, what he thought the Indians would do? Who said, The Narragansetts would all leave us, but as for Himself He would never leave us: and so it proved: For which Expressions and some other Speeches of his, I shall never forget him. Indeed he was a great Friend, and did great Service.

And after we had refreshed our selves with our mean Commons, we Marched about three Miles, and came to a Field which had lately been planted with Indian Corn: There we made another Alt, and called our Council, supposing we drew near to the Enemy: and being informed by the Indians that the Enemy had two Forts almost impregnable; but we were not

at all Discouraged, but rather Animated, in so much that we were resolved to Assault both their Forts at once. But understanding that one of them was so remote that we could not come up with it before Midnight, though we Marched hard; whereat we were much grieved, chiefly because the greatest and bloodiest Sachem there resided, whose name was Sassacous: We were then constrained, being exceedingly spent in our March with [extreme] Heat and want of Necessaries, to accept of the nearest.

We then Marching on in a silent Manner, the Indians that remained fell all into the Rear, who formerly kept the Van; (being possessed with great Fear) we continued our March till about one Hour in the Night: and coming to a little Swamp between two Hills, there we pitched our little Camp; much wearied with hard Travel, keeping great Silence, supposing we were very near the Fort; as our Indians informed us; which proved otherwise: The Rocks were our Pillows; yet Rest was pleasant: The Night proved Comfortable, being clear and Moon Light: We appointed our Guards and placed our Sentinels at some distance; who heard the Enemy Singing at the Fort, who continued that Strain until Midnight, with great Insulting and Rejoycing, as we were afterwards informed: They seeing our Pinnaces sail by them some Days before, concluded we were afraid of them and durst not come near them, the Burthen of their Song tending to that purpose.

In the Morning, we awaking and seeing it very light, supposing it had been day, and so we might have lost our Opportunity, having purposed to make our Assault before Day; rowsed the Men with all expedition, and briefly commended ourselves and Design to God, thinking immediately to go to the Assault; the Indians shewing us a Path, told us that it led directly to the Fort. We held on our March about two Miles, wondering that we came not to the Fort, and fearing we might be deluded: But seeing Corn newly planted at the Foot of a great Hill, supposing the Fort was not far off, a Champion Country being round about us; then making a stand, gave the Word for some of the Indians to come up: At length Onkos and one Wequash appeared; We demanded of them, Where was the Fort? They answered On the Top of that Hill: Then we demanded, Where were the Rest of the Indians? They answered, Behind, exceedingly afraid: We wished them to tell the rest of their Fellows, That they should by no means Fly, but stand at what distance they pleased, and see whether English Men would now Fight or not. Then Capt. Underhill came up, who Marched in the Rear; and commend-

ing ourselves to God, divided our Men: There being two Entrances into the Fort, intending to enter both at once: Captain Mason leading up to that on the North East Side; who approaching within one Rod, heard a Dog bark and an Indian crying Owanux! Owanux! which is Englishmen! Englishmen! We called up our Forces with all expedition, gave Fire upon them through the Pallizado; the Indians being in a dead indeed their last Sleep: Then we wheeling off fell upon the main Entrance, which was blocked up with Bushes about Breast high, over which the Captain passed, intending to make good the Entrance, encouraging the rest to follow. Lieutenant Seeley endeavoured to enter; but being somewhat cumbred, stepped back and pulled out the Bushes and so entred, and with him about sixteen Men: We had formerly concluded to destroy them by the Sword and save the Plunder.

Whereupon Captain Mason seeing no Indians, entred a Wigwam; where he was beset with many Indians, waiting all opportunities to lay Hands on him, but could not prevail. At length William Heydon. . . . Notwithstanding the statement by Trumbull and others, that Davis cut the bowstring and saved the life of Mason, there is reason, well supported by tradition, for believing that this service was performed by Heydon, and that the incident occurred at this very moment. It will be seen that Mason entered the fort on one side, that Davis entered on the opposite with Captain Underhill, and that he could therefore not have been near. The sword of Heydon that is said to have cut the bowstring is in the possession of the Connecticut Historical Society.] espying the Breach in the Wigwam, supposing some English might be there, entred; but in his Entrance fell over a dead Indian; but speedily recovering himself, the Indians some fled, others crept under their Beds: The Captain going out of the Wigwam saw many Indians in the Lane or Street; he making towards them, they fled, were pursued to the End of the Lane, where they were met by Edward Pattison, Thomas Barber, with some others; where seven of them were Slain, as they said. The Captain facing about, Marched a slow Pace up the Lane he came down, perceiving himself very much out of Breath; and coming to the other End near the Place where he first entred, saw two Soldiers standing close to the Pallizado with their Swords pointed to the Ground: the Captain told them that We should never kill them after that manner: The Captain also said, We must Burn them; and immediately stepping into the Wigwam where he had been before, brought

out a Firebrand, and putting it into the Matts with which they were covered, set the Wigwams on Fire. Lieutenant Thomas Bull and Nicholas Omsted beholding, came up; and when it was thoroughly kindled, the Indians ran as Men most dreadfully Amazed.

And indeed such a dreadful Terror did the Almighty let fall upon their Spirits, that they would fly from us and run into the very Flames, where many of them perished. And when the Fort was thoroughly Fired, Command was given, that all should fall off and surround the Fort; which was readily attended by all; only one Arthur Smith being so wounded that he could not move out of the Place, who was happily espied by Lieutenant Bull, and by him rescued.

The Fire was kindled on the North East Side to windward; which did swiftly over-run the Fort, to the extream Amazement of the Enemy, and great Rejoycing of our selves. Some of them climbing to the Top of the Pallizado; others of them running into the very Flames; many of them gathering to windward, lay pelting at us with their Arrows; and we repayed them with our small Shot: Others of the Stoutest issued forth, as we did guess, to the Number of Forty, who perished by the Sword.

What I have formerly said, is according to my own Knowledge, there being sufficient living Testimony to every Particular.

But in reference to Captain Underhill and his Parties acting in this Assault, I can only intimate as we were informed by some of themselves immediately after the Fight, Thus They Marching up to the Entrance on the South West Side, there made some Pause; a valiant, resolute Gentleman, one Mr. Hodge, stepping towards the Gate, saying; If we may not Enter, wherefore came we here; and immediately endeavoured to Enter; but was opposed by a sturdy Indian which did impede his Entrance; but the Indian being slain by himself and Sergeant Davis, Mr. Hedge Entred the Fort with some others; but the Fort being on Fire, the Smoak and Flames were so violent that they were constrained to desert the Fort.

Thus were they now at their Wits End, who not many Hours before exalted themselves in their great Pride, threatning and resolving the utter Ruin and Destruction of all the English, Exulting and Rejoycing with Songs and Dances: But God was above them, who laughed his Enemies and the Enemies of his People to Scorn, making them as a fiery Oven: Thus were the Stout Hearted spoiled, having slept their last Sleep, and none of their Men could find their Hands: Thus did the Lord judge among the Heathen, filling the Place with dead Bodies!

And here we may see the just Judgment of God, in sending even the very Night before this Assault, One hundred and fifty Men from their other Fort, to join with them of that Place, who were designed as some of themselves reported to go forth against the English, at that very Instant when this heavy Stroak came upon them where they perished with their Fellows. So that the Mischief they intended to us, came upon their own Pate: They were taken in their own snare, and we through Mercy escaped. And thus in little more than one Hour's space was their impregnable Fort with themselves utterly Destroyed, to the Number of six or seven Hundred, as some of themselves confessed. There were only seven taken captive, and about seven escaped. (The place of the Fort being called Mistick), this Fight was called Mistick Fight: And Mr. Increase Mather, from a Manuscript he met with, tells us; It was on Friday, May 26. 1637, a memorable Day!

Of the English, there were two Slain outright, and about twenty Wounded: Some Fainted by reason of the sharpness of the Weather, it being a cool Morning, and the want of such Comforts and Necessaries as were needful in such a Case; especially our [Surgeon] [Note: This surgeon, whose name was Pell, had been attached to Saybrook Fort and was sent on the expedition by Gardener.] was much wanting, whom we left with our Barks in Narragansett Bay, who had Order there to remain until the Night before our intended Assault.

And thereupon grew many Difficulties: Our Provision and Munition near spent; we in the enemies Country, who did far exceed us in Number, being much enraged: all our Indians, except Onkos, deserting us; our Pinnaces at a great distance from us, and when they would come we were uncertain.

But as we were consulting what Course to take, it pleased God to discover our Vessels to us before a fair Gale of Wind, sailing into Pequot Harbour, to our great Rejoycing.

We had no sooner discovered our Vessels, but immediately came up the Enemy from the other Fort; Three Hundred or more as we conceived. The Captain lead out a file or two of Men to Skirmish with them, chiefly to try what temper they were of, who put them to a stand: we being much encouraged thereat, presently prepared to March towards our Vessels: Four or Five of our Men were so wounded that they must be carried with the Arms

of twenty more. We also being faint, were constrained to put four to one Man, with the Arms of the rest that were wounded to others; so that we had not above forty Men free: at length we hired several Indians, who eased us of that Burthen, in carrying of our wounded Men. And Marching about one quarter of a Mile; the Enemy coming up to the Place where the Fort was, and beholding what was done, stamped and tore the Hair from their Heads: And after a little space, came mounting down the Hill upon us, in a full career, as if they would over run us; But when they came within Shot, the Rear faced about, giving Fire upon them: Some of them being Shot, made the rest more wary: Yet they held on running to and fro, and shooting their Arrows at Random. There was at the Foot of the Hill a small Brook, where we rested and refreshed our selves, having by that time taught them a little more Manners than to disturb us.

We then Marched on towards Pequot Harbour; and falling upon several Wigwams, burnt them: The Enemy still following us in the Rear, which was to windward, though to little purpose; yet some of them lay in Ambush behind Rocks and Trees, often shooting at us, yet through Mercy touched not one of us; And as we came to any Swamp or Thicket, we made some Shot to clear the Passage. Some of them fell with our Shot; and probably more might, but for want of Munition; But when any of them fell, our Indians would give a great Shout, and then would they take so much Courage as to fetch their Heads. And thus we continued, until we came within two Miles of Pequot Harbour; where the Enemy gathered together and left us; we Marching on to the Top of an Hill adjoining to the Harbour, with our Colours flying; having left our Drum at the Place of our Rendezvous the Night before: We seeing our Vessels there Riding at Anchor, to our great Rejoycing, and came to the Water-Side, we there sat down in Quiet.

Captain Patrick being Arrived there with our Vessels, who as we were informed was sent with Forty Men by the Massachusetts Colony, upon some Service against the Block Islanders; Who coming to the Shore in our Shallop with all his Company, as he said to Rescue us, supposing we were pursued, though there did not appear any the least sign of Such a Thing.

Thus did the Lord scatter his Enemies with his strong Arm! The Pequots now became a Prey to all Indians. Happy were they that could bring in their Heads to the English: Of which there came almost daily to Winsor, or Hartford. But the Pequots grow-

ing weary hereof, sent some of the Chief that survived to mediate with the English; offering that If they might but enjoy their Lives, they would become the English Vassals, to dispose of them as they pleased. Which was granted them. Whereupon Onkos and Myantonimo were sent for; who with the Pequots met at Hartford. The Pequots being demanded, how many of them were then living? Answered, about One Hundred and Eighty, or two Hundred. There were then given to Onkos, Sachem of Monheag, Eighty; to Myantonimo, Sachem of Narragansett, Eighty; and to Nynigrett, (He was usually called Ninnicraft.) Twenty, when he should satisfy for a Mare of Edward Pomroye's killed by his Men. The Pequots were then bound by Covenant, That none should inhabit their native Country, nor should any of them be called Pequots any more, but Moheags and Narragansetts forever. Shortly after, about Forty of them went to Moheag; others went to Long Island; the rest settled at Pawcatuck, a Place in Pequot Country, contrary to their late Covenant and Agreement with the English.

William Johnson: Report Regarding the Iroquois Confederacy

Superintendent of Indian Affairs in British North America Sir William Johnson possessed a keen awareness of the importance of Native Americans to British policy in fighting the French for control of North America. He sent this report to the Board of Trade in London in the fall of 1763, stressing the strength of the Iroquois Confederacy, which influenced alliances across wide areas in the present-day middle Atlantic, Northeast, and adjacent Ohio Valley. Johnson believed that, if the British would befriend the Iroquois and supply them with weapons, the Iroquois would stymie French aggression in North America.

As Original proprietors, this Confederacy claim the Country of their residence, South of Lake Ontario to the great Ridge of the Blew Mountains, with all the Western part of the province of New York towards Hudsons River, west of the Caats Kill, thence to Lake Champlain, and from Regioghne a Rock at the East side of said lake to Osswegatche on La Gattell on the River St. Lawrence (having long ceded their claim North of said line in favour of the Canada Indians as Hunting ground) thence up the River St. Lawrence and along the South side of Lake Ontario to Niagara.

In right of conquest, they claim all the Country (comprehending the Ohio) along the great Ridge of Blew Mountains at the back of Virginia, thence to the head of the Kentucke River, and down the same to the Ohio above the Rifts, thence Northerly to the South end of Lake Michigan, then along the eastern shore of said lake to Missillimackinac, thence easterly across the North end of Lake Huron to the great Ottwawa River (including the Chippawea or Mississagey Country) and down the said River to the Island of Montreal.—However, these more distant claims being possessed by many powerful Nations, the Inhabitants have long began to render themselves independent by the assistance of the French, and the great decrease of the Six Nations; but their claim to the Ohio, and thence to the Lakes is not in the least disputed by the Shawanese Delawares etc., who never transacted any Sales of Land or other matters without their consent, and who sent Deputys to the grand Council at Onondaga on all important occasions.

Pontiac: Reasons for Making War on the English Speech

An outgrowth of the French and Indian War, Pontiac's Rebellion of 1763 illustrated the complicated nature of Euro-Indian alliances in the seventeenth and eighteenth centuries. The uprising was a brief attempt of French-allied Native Americans to win back Canada for the French after the French had been utterly defeated in the French and Indian War. Pontiac, a Delaware, delivered this speech at a meeting of French and Native Americans on May 5, 1763.

My brothers, we have never had in view to do you any evil. We have never intended that any should be done you. But amongst my young men there are, as amongst you, some who, in spite of all precautions which we take, always do evil. Besides, it is not only for my revenge that I make war upon the English, it is for you, my brothers, as for us. When the English, in their councils, which we have held with them, have insulted us, they have also insulted you, without your knowing anything about it, and as I know, and all our brothers know, the English have taken from you all means of avenging yourselves, by disarming you and making you write on a paper, which they have sent to their country, which they could not make us do; therefore, I will avenge you

equally with us, and I swear annihilation as long as any of them shall remain on our land. Besides, you do not know all the reasons which oblige me to act as I do. I have told you only that which regards you. You will know the rest in time. I know well that I pass amongst many of my brothers for a fool, but you will see in the future if I am such as is said, and if I am wrong. I also know well that there are amongst you, my brothers, some who take the part of the English, to make war against us, and that only pains me on their account. I know them well, and when our father shall have come, I will name them and point them out to him, and they will see whether they or we shall be the most content in the future.

I doubt not, my brothers, that this war tries you, on account of the movements of our brothers, who all the time go and come to your houses. I am sorry for it but do not believe, my brothers, that I instigate the wrong which is done to you, and for proof that I do not wish it, remember the war of the Foxes, and the manner in which I have behaved in your interest. It is now seventeen years that the Sauteux and Ottawas of Michelimakinak and all the nations of the north have come with the Sacs and Foxes to annihilate you. Who has defended you? Was it not I and my people? When Mekinak, great chief of all the nations, said in his council that he would carry to his village the head of your commander, and eat his heart and drink his blood, have I not taken up your interest by going to his camp and telling him, if he wanted to kill the French, he must commence with me and my people? Have I not helped you to defeat them and drive them away? When or how came that? Would you, my brothers, believe that I to-day would turn my arms against you? No, my brothers, I am the same French Pondiak who lent you his hand seventeen years ago. I am a Frenchman, and I want to die a Frenchman! And I repeat to you they are both your interests and mine which I revenge. Let me go on. I don't ask your assistance, because I know you cannot give it. I only ask of you provisions for me and all my people. If, however, you would like to aid me, I would not refuse you. You would cause me pleasure, and you would sooner be out of trouble. For I warrant you, when the English shall be driven from here or killed, we shall all retire to our villages according to our custom, and await the arrival of our father, the Frenchman. These, you see, my brothers, are my sentiments. Rest assured, my brothers, I will watch that no more wrong shall be done to you by my people, nor by other Indians.

What I ask of you is that our women be allowed to plant our corn on the fallows of your lands. We shall obliged to you for that.

The Royal Proclamation of 7 October 1763

This Proclamation was an attempt that did not succeed to satisfy Native Americans for a dividing line that would halt encroachment on their lands.

1763, OCTOBER 7.
BY THE KING.
A Proclamation
George r.

Whereas We have taken into Our Royal Consideration the extensive and valuable Acquisitions in America, secured to Our Crown by the late Definitive Treaty of Peace, concluded at Paris the Tenth Day of February last, and being desirous, that all Our loving Subjects, as well of Our Kingdoms as of Our Colonies in America, may avail themselves, with all convenient Speed, of the great Benefits and Advantages which must accrue therefrom to their Commerce, Manufactures, and Navigation; We have thought fit, with the Advice of Our Privy Council, to issue this Our Royal Proclamation, hereby to publish and declare to all Our loving Subjects, that We have, with the Advice of Our said Privy Council, granted Our Letters Patent under Our Great Seal of Great Britain, to erect within the Countries and Islands ceded and confirmed to Us by the said Treaty, Four distinct and separate Governments, stiled and called by the Names of Quebec, East Florida, West Florida, and Grenada, and limited and bounded as follows; viz.

First. The Government of Quebec, bounded on the Labrador Coast by the River St. John, and from thence by a Line drawn from the Head of that River through the Lake St. John to the South End of the Lake nigh Pissin; from whence the said Line crossing the River St. Lawrence and the Lake Champlain in Forty five Degrees of North Latitude, passes along the High Lands which divide the Rivers that empty themselves into the said River St. Lawrence, from those which fall into the Sea; and also along the North Coast of the Baye des Chaleurs, and the Coast of the Gulph of St. Lawrence to Cape Rosieres, and from thence crossing the Mouth of the River St. Lawrence by the West End of the Island

of Antiocosti, terminates at the aforesaid River of St. John.

Secondly. The Government of East Florida, bounded to the Westward by the Gulph of Mexico, and the Apalachicola River; to the Northward, by a Line drawn from that Part of the said River where the Chatahouchee and Flint Rivers meet, to the Source of St. Mary's River, and by the Course of the said River to the Atlantick Ocean; and to the Eastward and Southward, by the Atlantick Ocean, and the Gulph of Florida, including all Islands within Six Leagues of the Sea Coast.

Thirdly. The Government of West Florida, bounded to the Southward by the Gulph of Mexico, including all Islands within Six Leagues of the Coast from the River Apalachicola to Lake Pentchartain; to the Westward, by the said Lake, the Lake Mauripas, and the River Mississippi; to the Northward, by a Line drawn due East from that Part of the River Mississippi which lies in Thirty one Degrees North Latitude, to the River Apalachicola or Chatahouchee; and to the Eastward by the said River.

. . . And whereas We are desirous, upon all Occasions, to testify Our Royal Sense and Approbation of the Conduct and Bravery of the Officers and Soldiers of Our Armies, and to reward the same, We do hereby command and impower Our Governors of Our said Three New Colonies, and all other Our Governors of Our several Provinces on the Continent of North America, to grant, without Fee or Reward, to such Reduced Officers as have served in North America during the late War, and to such Private Soldiers as have been or shall be disbanded in America, and are actually residing there, and shall personally apply for the same, the following Quantities of Lands, subject at the Expiration of Ten Years to the same Quit-Rents as other Lands are subject to in the Province within which they are granted, as also subject to the same Conditions of Cultivation and Improvement; viz.

To every Person having the Rank of a Field Officer, Five thousand Acres.—To every Captain, Three thousand Acres.—To every Subaltern or Staff Officer, Two thousand Acres.—To every Non-Commission Officer, Two hundred Acres.—To every Private Man, Fifty Acres.

We do likewise authorize and require the Governors and Commanders in Chief of all Our said Colonies upon the Continent of North America, to grant the like Quantities of Land, and upon the same Conditions, to such Reduced Officers of Our Navy, of like Rank, as served on Board Our Ships of War in

North America at the Times of the Reduction of Louisbourg and Quebec in the late War, and who shall personally apply to Our respective Governors for such Grants.

And whereas it is just and reasonable, and essential to Our Interest and the Security of Our Colonies, that the several Nations or Tribes of Indians, with whom We are connected, and who live under Our Protection, should not be molested or disturbed in the Possession of such Parts of Our Dominions and Territories as, not having been ceded to, or purchased by Us, are reserved to them, or any of them, as their Hunting Grounds; We do therefore, with the Advice of Our Privy Council, declare it to be Our Royal Will and Pleasure, that no Governor or Commander in Chief in any of Our Colonies of Quebec, East Florida, or West Florida, do presume, upon any Pretence whatever, to grant Warrants of Survey, or pass any Patents for Lands beyond the Bounds of their respective Governments, as described in their Commissions; as also, that no Governor or Commander in Chief in any of Our other Colonies or Plantations in America, do presume, for the present, and until Our further Pleasure be known, to grant Warrants of Survey, or pass Patents for any Lands beyond the Heads or Sources of any of the Rivers which fall into the Atlantick Ocean from the West and North-West, or upon any Lands whatever, which, not having been ceded to, or purchased by Us as aforesaid, are reserved to the said Indians, or any of them.

And We do further declare it to be Our Royal Will and Pleasure, for the present as aforesaid, to reserve under Our Sovereignty, Protection, and Dominion, for the Use of the said Indians, all the Lands and Territories not included within the Limits of Our said Three New Governments, or within the Limits of the Territory granted to the Hudson's Bay Company, as also all the Lands and Territories lying to the Westward of the Sources of the Rivers which fall into the Sea from the West and North West, as aforesaid; and We do hereby strictly forbid, on Pain of Our Displeasure, all Our loving Subjects from making any Purchases or Settlements whatever, or taking Possession of any of the Lands above reserved, without Our especial Leave and Licence for that Purpose first obtained.

And We do further strictly enjoin and require all Persons whatever, who have either wilfully or inadvertently seated themselves upon any Lands within the Countries above described, or upon any other Lands, which, not having been ceded to, or purchased by Us, are still reserved to the said Indians as aforesaid, forthwith to remove themselves from such Settlements.

And whereas great Frauds and Abuses have been committed in the purchasing Lands of the Indians, to the great Prejudice of Our Interests, and to the great Dissatisfaction of the said Indians; in order therefore to prevent such Irregularities for the future, and to the End that the Indians may be convinced of Our Justice, and determined Resolution to remove all reasonable Cause of Discontent, We do, with the Advice of Our Privy Council, strictly enjoin and require, that no private Person do presume to make any Purchase from the said Indians of any Lands reserved to the said Indians, within those Parts of Our Colonies where We have thought proper to allow Settlement; but that if, at any Time, any of the said Indians should be inclined to dispose of the said Lands, that same shall be purchased only for Us, in Our Name, at some publick Meeting or Assembly of the said Indians to be held for that Purpose by the Governor or Commander in Chief of Our Colonies respectively, within which they shall lie . . .

Resource

Royal Proclamation of 7 October 1763. Available at: http://www.ainc-inac.gc.ca/ch/rcap/sg/sga4_e.html. Accessed January 27, 2007.

Fort Stanwix Treaty

The Fort Stanwix Treaty, signed on October 22, 1784, near Rome, New York, brought fighting between the United States and the Iroquois Confederacy to an end following the American Revolution, in which the Iroquois had served as allies of the British.

Articles concluded at Fort Stanwix, on the twenty-second day of October one thousand seven hundred and eighty-four, between Oliver Wolcott, Richard Butler, and Arthur Zee, Commissioners Plenipotentiary from the United States, in Congress assembled, on the one Part, and the Sachems and Warriors of the Six Nations, on the other.

The United States of America give peace to the Senecas, Mohawks, Onondagas and Cayugas, and receive them into their protection upon the following conditions:

ARTICLE 1

Six hostages shall be immediately delivered to the commissioners by the said nations, to remain in possession of the United States, till all prisoners, white and black, which were taken by the said Senecas, Mohawks, Onondagas and Cayugas, or by any of them, in the late war, from among the people of the United States, shall be delivered up.

ARTICLE 2

The Oneida and Tuscarora nations shall be secured in the possession of the lands on which there are settled.

ARTICLE 3

A line shall be drawn, beginning at the mouth of a creek about four miles east of Niagara, called Oyonwayea, or Johnston's Landing-Place, upon the lake named by the Indians Oswego, and by us Ontario; from thence southerly in a direction always four miles east of the carrying-path, between Lake Erie and Ontario, to the mouth of Tehoseroron or Buffaloe Creek on Lake Erie; then south to the north boundary of the state of Pennsylvania; thence west to the end of the said north boundary; then south along the west boundary of the said state, to the river Ohio; the said land from the mouth of the Oyonwayea to the Ohio, shall be the western boundary of the lands of the Six Nations, so that the Six Nations shall and do yield to the United States, all claims to the country west of the said boundary, and then they shall be secured in the peaceful possession of the lands they inhabit east and north of the same, reserving only six miles square round the fort of Oswego, to the United States, for the support of the same.

ARTICLE 4

The Commissioners of the United States, in consideration of the present circumstances of the Six Nations, and in executing of the humane and liberal views of the United States upon the signing of the above articles, will order goods to be delivered to the said Six Nations for their use and comfort.

Oliver Wolcott
Richard Butler
Arthur Lee
Mohawks:
    Onogwendahonji, his x mark
    Touighnatogon, his x mark
Onondagas:
    Oheadarighton, his x mark
    Kendarindgon, his x mark

Senekas:
    Tayagonendagighti, his x mark
    Tehonwaeaghrigagi, his x mark
Oneidas:
    Otyadonenghti, his x mark
    Dagaheari, his x mark
Cayuga:
    Oraghgoanendagen, his x mark
Tuscaroras:
    Ononghsawenghti, his x mark,
    Tharondawagon, his x mark
Seneka Abeal:
    Kayenthoghke, his x mark
Witness:
    Sam. Jo. Atlee
    James Dean
    Wm. Maclay
    Saml. Montgomery
    Fras. Johnston
    Derick Lane, captain
    Pennsylvaina Commissioners
    John Mercer, lieutenant
    Aaron Hill
    William Pennington, lieutenant
    Alexander Campbell
    Mahlon Hord, ensign
    Saml. Kirkland, missionary
    Haugh Peeles

Northwest Ordinance

Chiefly written by Rufus King and Nathan Dane of Massachusetts and adopted by the Confederation Congress on July 13, 1787, the Northwest Ordinance provided for the governance of the territories, but it also made a provision for the eventual admission of between three and five states from those territories. Since the new states would have the same rights as the original thirteen, the law ensured that the United States would not become a colonial power on the North American continent. A number of provisions within the Northwest Ordinance would later be emulated in the U.S. Constitution and the Bill of Rights. The states eventually carved from the Northwest Ordinance are Ohio, Indiana, Illinois, Michigan, and Wisconsin.

An Ordinance for the government of the Territory of the United States northwest of the River Ohio.

So soon as there shall be five thousand free male inhabitants of full age in the district, upon giving proof thereof to the governor, they shall receive

authority, with time and place, to elect a representative from their counties or townships to represent them in the general assembly: Provided, That, for every five hundred free male inhabitants, there shall be one representative, and so on progressively with the number of free male inhabitants shall the right of representation increase, until the number of representatives shall amount to twenty five; after which, the number and proportion of representatives shall be regulated by the legislature: Provided, That no person be eligible or qualified to act as a representative unless he shall have been a citizen of one of the United States three years, and be a resident in the district, or unless he shall have resided in the district three years; and, in either case, shall likewise hold in his own right, in fee simple, two hundred acres of land within the same; Provided, also, That a freehold in fifty acres of land in the district, having been a citizen of one of the states, and being resident in the district, or the like freehold and two years residence in the district, shall be necessary to qualify a man as an elector of a representative.

The representatives thus elected, shall serve for the term of two years; and, in case of the death of a representative, or removal from office, the governor shall issue a writ to the county or township for which he was a member, to elect another in his stead, to serve for the residue of the term.

The general assembly or legislature shall consist of the governor, legislative council, and a house of representatives. The Legislative Council shall consist of five members, to continue in office five years, unless sooner removed by Congress; any three of whom to be a quorum . . .

The governor, judges, legislative council, secretary, and such other officers as Congress shall appoint in the district, shall take an oath or affirmation of fidelity and of office; the governor before the president of congress, and all other officers before the Governor. As soon as a legislature shall be formed in the district, the council and house assembled in one room, shall have authority, by joint ballot, to elect a delegate to Congress, who shall have a seat in Congress, with a right of debating but not voting during this temporary government.

And, for extending the fundamental principles of civil and religious liberty, which form the basis whereon these republics, their laws and constitutions are erected; to fix and establish those principles as the basis of all laws, constitutions, and governments, which forever hereafter shall be formed in the

said territory: to provide also for the establishment of States, and permanent government therein, and for their admission to a share in the federal councils on an equal footing with the original States, at as early periods as may be consistent with the general interest:

. . . Inhabitants of the said territory shall always be entitled to the benefits of the writ of habeas corpus, and of the trial by jury; of a proportionate representation of the people in the legislature; and of judicial proceedings according to the course of the common law. All persons shall be bailable, unless for capital offenses, where the proof shall be evident or the presumption great. All fines shall be moderate; and no cruel or unusual punishments shall be inflicted. No man shall be deprived of his liberty or property, but by the judgment of his peers or the law of the land; and, should the public exigencies make it necessary, for the common preservation, to take any person's property, or to demand his particular services, full compensation shall be made for the same. And, in the just preservation of rights and property, it is understood and declared, that no law ought ever to be made, or have force in the said territory, that shall, in any manner whatever, interfere with or affect private contracts or engagements, bona fide, and without fraud, previously formed.

Religion, morality, and knowledge, being necessary to good government and the happiness of mankind, schools and the means of education shall forever be encouraged. The utmost good faith shall always be observed towards the Indians; their lands and property shall never be taken from them without their consent; and, in their property, rights, and liberty, they shall never be invaded or disturbed, unless in just and lawful wars authorized by Congress; but laws founded in justice and humanity, shall from time to time be made for preventing wrongs being done to them, and for preserving peace and friendship with them.

The said territory, and the States which may be formed therein, shall forever remain a part of this Confederacy of the United States of America, subject to the Articles of Confederation, and to such alterations therein as shall be constitutionally made; and to all the acts and ordinances of the United States in Congress assembled, conformable thereto.

. . . There shall be neither slavery nor involuntary servitude in the said territory, otherwise than in

the punishment of crimes whereof the party shall have been duly convicted: Provided, always, That any person escaping into the same, from whom labor or service is lawfully claimed in any one of the original States, such fugitive may be lawfully reclaimed and conveyed to the person claiming his or her labor or service as aforesaid.

Lewis and Clark Expedition: Journals

In 1804, Meriwether Lewis and William Clark set out from St. Louis, Missouri, with fifty men to explore the vast new lands the United States had acquired from France with the Louisiana Purchase of 1803. President Thomas Jefferson had commissioned the two former soldiers to investigate the new U.S. territory with an eye toward expansion and eventual settlement. Aided by a Native American woman named Sacajawea, the Lewis and Clark Expedition traveled all the way to the coast of Oregon before returning to Washington, D.C., with their maps and notes in 1806. Below is an excerpt of their journals from the expedition.

April 07, 1805
[Meriwether Lewis]
Fort Mandan

Our vessels consisted of six small canoes, and two large perogues. This little fleet altho' not quite so rispectable as those of Columbus or Capt. Cook, were still viewed by us with as much pleasure as those deservedly famed adventurers ever beheld theirs; and I dare say with quite as much anxiety for their safety and preservation. [W]e were now about to penetrate a country at least two thousand miles in width, on which the foot of civilized man had never trodden; the good or evil it had in store for us was for experiment yet to determine, and these little vessels contained every article by which we were to expect to subsist or defend ourselves . . . enterta[in]ing as I do, the most confident hope of succeeding in a voyage which had formed a da[r]ling project of mine for the last ten years, I could but esteem this moment of my departure as among the most happy of my life. The party are in excellent health and sperits, zealously attached to the enterprise, and anxious to proceed; not a whisper of murmur or discontent to be heard among them, but all act in unison, and with the most perfict harmony.

April 07, 1805
[Patrick Gass]

About 5 o'clock in the afternoon we left fort Mandan in good spirits. Thirty one men and a woman [Sacagawea] went up the river and thirteen returned down it in the boat. We had two periogues and six canoes, and proceeded about four miles, and encamped opposite the first Mandan village, on the North side.

April 07, 1805
[John Ordway]

. . . our Intrepter and them that went with him returned brought with them 4 of the RickaRee Savages. . . . they Informed us that only 10 of their nation had come up to the Mandanes villages to treat & Smoak a peace pipe with them . . . they brought a letter from Mr Tabbo who lives with [the] R.Ree . . . with news that 3 of the Souix [sic] chiefs was going down on the Big barge to see their Great father and that Some of the Rick a Ree chiefs was going also.

About 5 oClock we all went on board fired the Swivel and Set off on our journey. [A]t the Same time the barge Set off for St Louis 2 frenchmen in a perogue in company with them. they took down the letters and all the writings which was necessary to go back to the States also Some curious animals such as Goat Skins & horns, a barking Squerrell Some Mountain Rams horns a prarie hen & badgers Some birds cauled magpies & a number of other curious things too tedious to mention &.C.

The returning party, in charge of Corporal Warfington, consisted, in addition to the leader, of six private soldiers, Gravelines, who had been engaged as pilot, and two other Frenchmen. Temporarily accompanying it, also, were the two engages, Rivet and Degie, and a lame Arikara who had been granted the privilege of transportation in the boat to his tribal home. The party was to be joined at the Arikara village by Tableau, the trader, and four hands, making a party of fifteen to descend the river. None of them had originally intended to become permanent members of the exploring expedition with the exception of Newman and Reed, the two men who had been discharged for misconduct.]

April 08, 1805
[Patrick Gass]

The woman that is with us is a squaw of the Snake nation of Indians, and wife to our interpreter.

We expect she will be of service to us, when passing through that nation.

Tenskwataya (The Prophet): System of Religion Speech (1808)

Tenkswataya, a Shawnee popularly known as The Prophet, forged a Native American alliance in the Midwest with the help of his brother Tecumseh in the early 1800s. The Prophet was the spiritual leader behind the movement and preached a gospel of a pan-Indian religion intended to unite all the tribes into a single, powerful unit, capable of bargaining with the Americans. The Prophet delivered this speech to the governor of Indiana Territory, William Henry Harrison, in August 1808.

Father, It is three years since I first began with that system of religion which I now practice. The white people and some of the Indians were against me; but I had no other intention but to introduce among the Indians, those good principles of religion which the white people profess. I was spoken badly of by the white people, who reproached me with misleading the Indians; but I defy them to say that I did anything amiss.

Father, I was told that you intended to hang me. When I heard this, I intended to remember it, and tell my father, when I went to see him, and relate to him the truth.

I heard, when I settled on the Wabash, that my father, the governor, had declared that all the land between Vincennes and fort Wayne, was the property of the Seventeen Fires. I also heard that you wanted to know, my father, whether I was God or man; and that you said if I was the former, I should not steal horses. I heard this from Mr. Wells, but I believed it originated with himself.

The Great Spirit told me to tell the Indians that he had made them, and made the world [and] that he had placed them on it to do good, not evil.

I told all the red skins, that the way they were in was not good, and that they ought to abandon it.

That we ought to consider ourselves as one man; but we ought to live agreeably to our several customs, the red people after their mode, and the white people after theirs; particularly, that they should not drink whiskey; that it was not made for them, but the white people, who alone knew how to use it; and that it is the cause of all the mischief which the Indians suffer; and that they must always follow the directions of the Great Spirit, and we must listen to him, as it was he that made us: determine to listen to nothing that is bad: do not take up the tomahawk, should it be offered by the British, or by the long knives: do not meddle with any thing that does not belong to you, but mind your own business, and cultivate the ground, that your women and your children may have enough to live on.

I now inform you, that it is our intention to live in peace with our father and his people forever.

My father, I have informed you what we mean to do, and I call the Great Spirit to witness the truth of my declaration. The religion which I have established for the last three years, has been attended to by the different tribes of Indians in this part of the world. Those Indians were once different people; they are now but one: they are all determined to practice what I have communicated to them, that has come immediately from the Great Spirit through me.

Brother, I speak to you as a warrior. You are one. But let us lay aside this character, and attend to the care of our children, that they may live in comfort and peace. We desire that you will join us for the preservation of both red and white people. Formerly, when we lived in ignorance, we were foolish; but now, since we listen to the voice of the Great Spirit, we are happy.

I have listened to what you have said to us. You have promised to assist us: I now request you, in behalf of all the red people, to use your exertions to prevent the sale of liquor to us. We are all well pleased to hear you say that you will endeavor to promote our happiness. We give you every assurance that we will follow the dictates of the Great Spirit.

We are all well pleased with the attention that you have showed us; also with the good intentions of our father, the President. If you give us a few articles, such as needles, flints, hoes, powder, &c., we will take the animals that afford us meat, with powder and ball.

Tecumseh: Speech to Governor William Henry Harrison

In the early 1800s, the most powerful Native American of his day, Tecumseh forged a pan-Indian alliance

among Midwestern tribes with the help of his brother, Tenskwataya (The Prophet). They hoped to prevent American expansion by claiming that Native Americans held collective rights to land that could not be sold or bartered without the consent of all. On August 12, 1810, Tecumseh delivered this speech to Governor William Henry Harrison of the Indiana Territory. Harrison would later be his chief adversary during the War of 1812.*

It is true I am a Shawanee [sic]. My forefathers were warriors. Their son is a warrior. From them I only take my existence; from my tribe I take nothing. I am the maker of my own fortune; and oh! that I could make that of my red people, and of my country, as great as the conceptions of my mind, when I think of the Spirit that rules the universe. I would not then come to Governor Harrison, to ask him to tear the treaty, and to obliterate the landmark; but I would say to him, Sir, you have liberty to return to your own country.

The being within, communing with past ages, tells me, that once, nor until lately, there was no white man on this continent. That it then all belonged to red men, children of the same parents, placed on it by the Great Spirit that made them, to keep it, to traverse it, to enjoy its productions, and to fill it with the same race. Once a happy race.

Since made miserable by the white people, who are never contented, but always encroaching. The way, and the only way to check and stop this evil, is, for all the red men to unite in claiming a common and equal right in the land, as it was at first, and should be yet; for it never was divided, but belongs to all, for the use of each. That no part has a right to sell, even to each other, much less to strangers; those who want all, and will not do with less. The white people have no right to take the land from the Indians, because they had it first; it is theirs. They may sell, but all must join. Any sale not made by all is not valid. The late sale is bad. It was made by a part only. Part do not know how to sell. It requires all to make a bargain for all.

All red men have equal rights to the unoccupied land. The right of occupancy is as good in one place as in another. There cannot be two occupations in the same place. The first excludes all others. It is not so in hunting or travelling; for there the same ground will serve many, as they may follow each other all day; but the camp is stationary, and that is occupancy. It belongs to the first who sits down on his blanket or skins, which he has thrown upon the ground, and till he leaves it no other has a right.

Johnson v. M'Intosh

This decision was one of several adjudicated by U.S. Supreme Court Justice John Marshall during the 1820s and 1830s that define the relationship of Native Americans with the U.S. government to this day. It was sthe first of the "Marshall Trilogy," with Cherokee Nation v. Georgia *(1831) and* Worcester v. Georgia *(1832) that underlie most of the government's presumptive powers vis à vis American Indians.*

21 U.S. 543, 5 L.Ed. 681, 8 Wheat. 543 (1823)
March 10, 1823

"ERROR to the District Court of Illinois. This was an action of ejectment for lands in the State and District of Illinois, claimed by the plaintiffs under a purchase and conveyance from the Piankeshaw Indians, and by the defendant, under a grant from the United States. It came up on a case stated, upon which there was a judgment below for the defendant.

. . . Mr. Chief Justice MARSHALL delivered the opinion of the Court.

The plaintiffs in this cause claim the land, in their declaration mentioned, under two grants, purporting to be made, the first in 1773, and the last in 1775, by the chiefs of certain Indian tribes, constituting the Illinois and the Piankeshaw nations; and the question is, whether this title can be recognised in the Courts of the United States?

The facts, as stated in the case agreed, show the authority of the chiefs who executed this conveyance, so far as it could be given by their own people; and likewise show, that the particular tribes for whom these chiefs acted were in rightful possession of the land they sold. The inquiry, therefore, is, in a great measure, confined to the power of Indians to give, and of private individuals to receive, a title which can be sustained in the Courts of this country. . . .

. . . The United States, then, have unequivocally acceded to that great and broad rule by which its civilized inhabitants now hold this country. They hold, and assert in themselves, the title by which it was acquired. They maintain, as all others have maintained, that discovery gave an exclusive

right to extinguish the Indian title of occupancy, either by purchase or by conquest; and gave also a right to such a degree of sovereignty, as the circumstances of the people would allow them to exercise.

The power now possessed by the government of the United States to grant lands, resided, while we were colonies, in the crown, or its grantees. The validity of the titles given by either has never been questioned in our Courts. It has been exercised uniformly over territory in possession of the Indians. The existence of this power must negative the existence of any right which may conflict with, and control it. An absolute title to lands cannot exist, at the same time, in different persons, or in different governments. An absolute, must be an exclusive title, or at least a title which excludes all others not compatible with it. All our institutions recognise the absolute title of the crown, subject only to the Indian right of occupancy, and recognise the absolute title of the crown to extinguish that right. This is incompatible with an absolute and complete title in the Indians.

We will not enter into the controversy, whether agriculturists, merchants, and manufacturers, have a right, on abstract principles, to expel hunters from the territory they possess, or to contract their limits. Conquest gives a title which the Courts of the conqueror cannot deny, whatever the private and speculative opinions of individuals may be, respecting the original justice of the claim which has been successfully asserted. The British government, which was then our government, and whose rights have passed to the United States, asserted title to all the lands occupied by Indians, within the chartered limits of the British colonies. It asserted also a limited sovereignty over them, and the exclusive right of extinguishing the title which occupancy gave to them. These claims have been maintained and established as far west as the river Mississippi, by the sword. The title to a vast portion of the lands we now hold, originates in them. It is not for the Courts of this country to question the validity of this title, or to sustain one which is incompatible with it.

Although we do not mean to engage in the defence of those principles which Europeans have applied to Indian title, they may, we think, find some excuse, if not justification, in the character and habits of the people whose rights have been wrested from them.

The title by conquest is acquired and maintained by force. The conqueror prescribes its limits. Humanity, however, acting on public opinion, has established, as a general rule, that the conquered shall not be wantonly oppressed, and that their condition shall remain as eligible as is compatible with the objects of the conquest. Most usually, they are incorporated with the victorious nation, and become subjects or citizens of the government with which they are connected. The new and old members of the society mingle with each other; the distinction between them is grandually [sic] lost, and they make one people. Where this incorporation is practicable, humanity demands, and a wise policy requires, that the rights of the conquered to property should remain unimpaired; that the new subjects should be governed as equitably as the old, and that confidence in their security should gradually banish the painful sense of being separated from their ancient connexions, and united by force to strangers.

When the conquest is complete, and the conquered inhabitants can be blended with the conquerors, or safely governed as a distinct people, public opinion, which not even the conqueror can disregard, imposes these restraints upon him; and he cannot neglect them without injury to his fame, and hazard to his power.

But the tribes of Indians inhabiting this country were fierce savages, whose occupation was war, and whose subsistence was drawn chiefly from the forest. To leave them in possession of their country, was to leave the country a wilderness; to govern them as a distinct people, was impossible, because they were as brave and as high spirited as they were fierce, and were ready to repel by arms every attempt on their independence.

What was the inevitable consequence of this state of things? The Europeans were under the necessity either of abandoning the country, and relinquishing their pompous claims to it, or of enforcing those claims by the sword, and by the adoption of principles adapted to the condition of a people with whom it was impossible to mix, and who could not be governed as a distinct society, or of remaining in their neighbourhood, and exposing themselves and their families to the perpetual hazard of being massacred.

Frequent and bloody wars, in which the whites were not always the aggressors, unavoidably ensued. European policy, numbers, and skill, prevailed. As the white population advanced, that of the Indians necessarily receded. The country in the immediate neighbourhood of agriculturists became unfit for them. The game fled into thicker and more unbroken forests, and the Indians followed. The soil,

to which the crown originally claimed title, being no longer occupied by its ancient inhabitants, was parcelled out according to the will of the sovereign power, and taken possession of by persons who claimed immediately from the crown, or mediately, through its grantees or deputies.

That law which regulates, and ought to regulate in general, the relations between the conqueror and conquered, was incapable of application to a people under such circumstances. The resort to some new and different rule, better adapted to the actual state of things, was unavoidable. Every rule which can be suggested will be found to be attended with great difficulty.

However extravagant the pretension of converting the discovery of an inhabited country into conquest may appear; if the principle has been asserted in the first instance, and afterwards sustained; if a country has been acquired and held under it; if the property of the great mass of the community originates in it, it becomes the law of the land, and cannot be questioned. So, too, with respect to the concomitant principle, that the Indian inhabitants are to be considered merely as occupants, to be protected, indeed, while in peace, in the possession of their lands, but to be deemed incapable of transferring the absolute title to others. However this restriction may be opposed to natural right, and to the usages of civilized nations, yet, if it be indispensable to that system under which the country has been settled, and be adapted to the actual condition of the two people, it may, perhaps, be supported by reason, and certainly cannot be rejected by Courts of justice. . . .

. . . It has never been contended, that the Indian title amounted to nothing. Their right of possession has never been questioned. The claim of government extends to the complete ultimate title, charged with this right of possession, and to the exclusive power of acquiring that right. The object of the crown was to settle the seacoast of America; and when a portion of it was settled, without violating the rights of others, by persons professing their loyalty, and soliciting the royal sanction of an act, the consequences of which were ascertained to be beneficial, it would have been as unwise as ungracious to expel them from their habitations, because they had obtained the Indian title otherwise than through the agency of government. The very grant of a charter is an assertion of the title of the crown, and its words convey the same idea. The country granted, is said to be 'our island called Rhode-Island;' and the charter contains an actual grant of the soil, as well as of the powers of government.

. . . The letter was written a few months before the charter was issued, apparently at the request of the agents of the intended colony, for the sole purpose of preventing the trespasses of neighbours, who were disposed to claim some authority over them. The king, being willing himself to ratify and confirm their title, was, of course, inclined to quiet them in their possession.

This charter, and this letter, certainly sanction a previous unauthorized purchase from Indians, under the circumstances attending that particular purchase, but are far from supporting the general proposition, that a title acquired from the Indians would be valid against a title acquired from the crown, or without the confirmation of the crown.

The acts of the several colonial assemblies, prohibiting purchases from the Indians, have also been relied on, as proving, that, independent of such prohibitions, Indian deeds would be valid. But, we think this fact, at most, equivocal. While the existence of such purchases would justify their prohibition, even by colonies which considered Indian deeds as previously invalid, the fact that such acts have been generally passed, is strong evidence of the general opinion, that such purchases are opposed by the soundest principles of wisdom and national policy.

After bestowing on this subject a degree of attention which was more required by the magnitude of the interest in litigation, and the able and elaborate arguments of the bar, than by its intrinsic difficulty, the Court is decidedly of opinion, that the plaintiffs do not exhibit a title which can be sustained in the Courts of the United States; and that there is no error in the judgment which was rendered against them in the District Court of Illinois.

Resource

Johnson v. M'Intosh. Available at:
http://www.law.nyu.edu/kingsburyb/spring03/
    indigenousPeoples/classmaterials/class10/
    A.%20Johnson%20v_%20McIntosh.htm.
    Accessed January 20, 2007.

Cherokee Nation v. Georgia

Resisting removal, the Cherokees sued in federal court under a clause in the Constitution (Article III, Section 2) that allows foreign citizens or states to seek legal redress against states in the union. In this case, the Cherokees were

suing as an independent nation seeking redress because the state of Georgia had extended its power over Cherokee territory, extinguished the authority of the Cherokee government, and executed one of its citizens. U.S. Supreme Court Chief Justice John Marshall skirted the issue by deciding that the Cherokees were not an independent country, but instead a "domestic dependent nation." Marshall thus threw the case out of court, deciding that the Cherokees had no grounds on which to sue under the Constitution.

Writing for the majority in Cherokee Nation v. Georgia, *Marshall said that the Cherokees possessed a limited sovereignty: "They may, more correctly, perhaps be denominated domestic dependent nations. . . . Their relation to the United States resembles that of a ward to his guardian." These phrases, interpreted by the Bureau of Indian Affairs, became the legal justification for the colonial system that was being imposed on Indians as Anglo-American settlement exploded across North America in the nineteenth century.*

Cherokee Nation v. Georgia (1831)
30 U.S. 1

Mr Chief Justice MARSHALL delivered the opinion of the Court.

This bill is brought by the Cherokee Nation, praying an injunction to restrain the State of Georgia from the execution of certain laws of that State which, as is alleged, go directly to annihilate the Cherokees as a political society and to seize, for the use of Georgia, the lands of the Nation which have been assured to them by the United States in solemn treaties repeatedly made and still in force.

If Courts were permitted to indulge their sympathies, a case better calculated to excite them can scarcely be imagined. A people once numerous, powerful, and truly independent, found by our ancestors in the quiet and uncontrolled possession of an ample domain, gradually sinking beneath our superior policy, our arts and our arms, have yielded their lands by successive treaties, each of which contains a solemn guarantee of the residue, until they retain no more of their formerly extensive territory than is deemed necessary to their comfortable subsistence. To preserve this remnant, the present application is made.

Before we can look into the merits of the case, a preliminary inquiry presents itself. Has this Court jurisdiction of the cause?

The third article of the Constitution describes the extent of the judicial power. The second section closes an enumeration of the cases to which it is extended, with "controversies" "between a State or the citizens thereof, and foreign states, citizens, or subjects." A subsequent clause of the same section gives the supreme Court original jurisdiction in all cases in which a State shall be a party. The party defendant may then unquestionably be sued in this Court. May the plaintiff sue in it? Is the Cherokee Nation a foreign state in the sense in which that term is used in the Constitution?

The counsel for the plaintiffs have maintained the affirmative of this proposition with great earnestness and ability. So much of the argument as was intended to prove the character of the Cherokees as a State as a distinct political society, separated from others, capable of managing its own affairs and governing itself, has, in the opinion of a majority of the judges, been completely successful. They have been uniformly treated as a State from the settlement of our country. The numerous treaties made with them by the United States recognize them as a people capable of maintaining the relations of peace and war, of being responsible in their political character for any violation of their engagements, or for any aggression committed on the citizens of the United States by any individual of their community. Laws have been enacted in the spirit of these treaties. The acts of our Government plainly recognize the Cherokee Nation as a State, and the Courts are bound by those acts.

A question of much more difficulty remains. Do the Cherokees constitute a foreign state in the sense of the Constitution?

The counsel have shown conclusively that they are not a State of the union, and have insisted that, individually, they are aliens, not owing allegiance to the United States. An aggregate of aliens composing a State must, they say, be a foreign state. Each individual being foreign, the whole must be foreign.

This argument is imposing, but we must examine it more closely before we yield to it. The condition of the Indians in relation to the United States is perhaps unlike that of any other two people in existence. In the general, nations not owing a common allegiance are foreign to each other. The term foreign nation is, with strict propriety, applicable by either to the other. But the relation of the Indians to the United States is marked by peculiar and cardinal distinctions which exist nowhere else.

The Indian Territory is admitted to compose a part of the United States. In all our maps, geographical treatises, histories, and laws, it is so considered.

In all our intercourse with foreign nations, in our commercial regulations, in any attempt at intercourse between Indians and foreign nations, they are considered as within the jurisdictional limits of the United States, subject to many of those restraints which are imposed upon our own citizens. They acknowledge themselves in their treaties to be under the protection of the United States; they admit that the United States shall have the sole and exclusive right of regulating the trade with them, and managing all their affairs as they think proper; and the Cherokees, in particular, were allowed by the treaty of Hopewell, which preceded the Constitution, "to send a deputy of their choice, whenever they think fit, to Congress." Treaties were made with some tribes by the State of New York, under a then unsettled construction of the confederation by which they ceded all their lands to that State, taking back a limited grant to themselves in which they admit their dependence.

Though the Indians are acknowledged to have an unquestionable, and heretofore unquestioned right to the lands they occupy, until that right shall be extinguished by a voluntary cession to our government, yet it may well be doubted whether those tribes which reside within the acknowledged boundaries of the United States can, with strict accuracy, be denominated foreign nations. They may, more correctly, perhaps, be denominated domestic dependent nations. They occupy a territory to which we assert a title independent of their will, which must take effect in point of possession when their right of possession ceases. Meanwhile they are in a state of pupilage. Their relation to the United States resembles that of a ward to his guardian.

They look to our government for protection; rely upon its kindness and its power; appeal to it for relief to their wants; and address the President as their Great Father. They and their country are considered by foreign nations, as well as by ourselves, as being so completely under the sovereignty and dominion of the United States that any attempt to acquire their lands, or to form a political connexion with them, would be considered by all as an invasion of our territory and an act of hostility.

These considerations go far to support the opinion that the framers of our Constitution had not the Indian tribes in view when they opened the courts of the union to controversies between a State or the citizens thereof, and foreign states.

In considering this subject, the habits and usages of the Indians in their intercourse with their white neighbours ought not to be entirely disregarded. At the time the Constitution was framed, the idea of appealing to an American court of justice for an assertion of right or a redress of wrong had perhaps never entered the mind of an Indian or of his tribe. Their appeal was to the tomahawk, or to the Government. This was well understood by the Statesmen who framed the Constitution of the United States, and might furnish some reason for omitting to enumerate them among the parties who might sue in the courts of the union. Be this as it may, the peculiar relations between the United States and the Indians occupying our territory are such that we should feel much difficulty in considering them as designated by the term foreign state were there no other part of the Constitution which might shed light on the meaning of these words. But we think that, in construing them, considerable aid is furnished by that clause in the eighth section of the third article which empowers Congress to "regulate commerce with foreign nations, and among the several States, and with the Indian tribes."

In this clause, they are as clearly contradistinguished by a name appropriate to themselves from foreign nations as from the several States composing the union. They are designated by a distinct appellation, and as this appellation can be applied to neither of the others, neither can the appellation distinguishing either of the others be in fair construction applied to them. The objects to which the power of regulating commerce might be directed are divided into three distinct classes—foreign nations, the several States, and Indian tribes. When forming this article, the convention considered them as entirely distinct. We cannot assume that the distinction was lost in framing a subsequent article unless there be something in its language to authorize the assumption.

The counsel for the plaintiffs contend that the words "Indian tribes" were introduced into the article empowering Congress to regulate commerce for the purpose of removing those doubts in which the management of Indian affairs was involved by the language of the ninth article of the confederation. Intending to give the whole power of managing those affairs to the government about to be instituted, the convention conferred it explicitly, and omitted those qualifications which embarrassed the exercise of it as granted in the confederation. This may be admitted without weakening the construction which has been intimated. Had the Indian tribes been foreign nations in the view of the convention,

this exclusive power of regulating intercourse with them might have been, and most probably would have been, specifically given in language indicating that idea, not in language contradistinguishing them from foreign nations. Congress might have been empowered "to regulate commerce with foreign nations, including the Indian tribes, and among the several States." This language would have suggested itself to statesmen who considered the Indian tribes as foreign nations, and were yet desirous of mentioning them particularly.

It has been also said that the same words have not necessarily the same meaning attached to them when found in different parts of the same instrument—their meaning is controlled by the context. This is undoubtedly true. In common language, the same word has various meanings, and the peculiar sense in which it is used in any sentence is to be determined by the context. This may not be equally true with respect to proper names. "Foreign nations" is a general term, the application of which to Indian tribes, when used in the American Constitution, is at best extremely questionable. In one article in which a power is given to be exercised in regard to foreign nations generally, and to the Indian tribes particularly, they are mentioned as separate in terms clearly contradistinguishing them from each other. We perceive plainly that the Constitution in this article does not comprehend Indian tribes in the general term "foreign nations," not, we presume, because a tribe may not be a nation, but because it is not foreign to the United States. When, afterwards, the term "foreign state" is introduced, we cannot impute to the convention the intention to desert its former meaning and to comprehend Indian tribes within it unless the context force that construction on us. We find nothing in the context, and nothing in the subject of the article, which leads to it.

The Court has bestowed its best attention on this question, and, after mature deliberation, the majority is of opinion that an Indian tribe or Nation within the United States is not a foreign state in the sense of the Constitution, and cannot maintain an action in the Courts of the United States.

A serious additional objection exists to the jurisdiction of the Court. Is the matter of the bill the proper subject for judicial inquiry and decision? It seeks to restrain a State from the forcible exercise of legislative power over a neighbouring people, asserting their independence, their right to which the State denies. On several of the matters alleged in the bill, for example, on the laws making it criminal to exercise the usual powers of self-government in their own country by the Cherokee Nation, this Court cannot interpose, at least in the form in which those matters are presented.

That part of the bill which respects the land occupied by the Indians, and prays the aid of the Court to protect their possession may be more doubtful. The mere question of right might perhaps be decided by this Court in a proper case with proper parties. But the Court is asked to do more than decide on the title. The bill requires us to control the Legislature of Georgia, and to restrain the exertion of its physical force. The propriety of such an interposition by the Court may be well questioned. It savours too much of the exercise of political power to be within the proper province of the judicial department. But the opinion on the point respecting parties makes it unnecessary to decide this question.

If it be true that the Cherokee Nation have rights, this is not the tribunal in which those rights are to be asserted. If it be true that wrongs have been inflicted, and that still greater are to be apprehended, this is not the tribunal which can redress the past or prevent the future.

The motion for an injunction is denied.

Resource

Cherokee Nation v. Georgia. Available at: http://supct.law.cornell.edu/supct/html/historics/USSC_CR_0030_0001_ZO.html. Accessed January 20, 2007.

Worcester v. Georgia

This decision was one of several adjudicated by U.S. Supreme Court Justice John Marshall during the 1820s and 1830s that define the relationship of Native Americans with the U.S. government to this day. It was the third of the "Marshal Trilogy," with Johnson v. M'Intosh *(1823) and* Cherokee Nation v. Georgia *(1831) that underlie most of the government's presumptive powers vis à vis American Indians.*

Worcester v. Georgia upheld limited sovereignty for the Cherokee Nation in 1832 against President Andrew Jackson's demands for removal. Jackson's actions ultimately comprised contempt of the Supreme Court (an impeachable offense under the Constitution). In the incendiary years before the Civil War, however, the political cost

of following the Supreme Court's rulings upholding Cherokee sovereignty proved too great for Jackson's sense of political expediency or for Congress.

The specific issue that spurred the lawsuit was the refusal by Samuel Worcester, a missionary among the Cherokees, to sign an oath acknowledging Georgia's sovereignty while on Cherokee land. The case thus became a test of the Cherokees' right to a homeland within the bounds of Georgia. The state's officials argued that the Constitution prohibited the establishment of one state within the boundaries of another.

Justice Marshall wrote that Native nations had always been considered distinct, independent political communities, retaining original natural rights. Georgia's law, according to Marshall, interfered forcibly with the relations between the United States and the Cherokee Nation, the regulation of which, according to the settled principles of the U.S. Constitution, is committed exclusively to the federal government.

31 U.S. 515 . . .

A writ of error was issued to "The Judges of the Superior Court for the County of Gwinett in the State of Georgia" commanding them to send to the Supreme Court of the United States the record and proceedings in the said Superior Court of the County of Gwinett, between the State of Georgia, plaintiff, and Samuel A. Worcester, defendant, on an indictment in that Court. The record of the Court of Gwinnett was returned, certified by the clerk of the Court, and was also authenticated by the seal of the Court. It was returned with, and annexed to, a writ of error issued in regular form, the citation being signed by one of the Associate Justices of the Supreme Court and served on the Governor and Attorney General of the State more than thirty days before the commencement of the term to which the writ of error was returnable.

By the Court: The Judicial Act, so far as it prescribes the mode of proceeding, appears to have been literally pursued. In February, 1979, a rule was made on this subject in the following words:

> It is ordered by the Court that the clerk of the Court to which any writ of error shall be directed may make return of the same by transmitting a true copy of the record, and of all proceedings in the same, under his hand and the seal of the Court.
>
> This has been done. But the signature of the judge has not been added to that of the

clerk. The law does not require it. The rule does not require it.

The plaintiff in error was indicted in the Supreme Court for the County of Gwinnett in the State of Georgia, . . . The indictment and plea in this case draw in question the validity of the treaties made by the United States with the Cherokee Indians; if not so, their construction is certainly drawn in question, and the decision has been, if not against their validity, "against the right, privilege, or exemption specifically set up and claimed under them." They also draw into question the validity of a statute of the State of Georgia

> On the ground of its being repugnant to the Constitution, treaties, and laws of the United States, and the decision is in favour of its validity. . . . The relation between the Europeans and the natives was determined in each case by the particular government which asserted and could maintain this preemptive privilege in the particular place. The United States succeeded to all the claims of Great Britain, both territorial and political, but no attempt, so far as it is known, has been made to enlarge them. So far as they existed merely in theory, or were in their nature only exclusive of the claims of other European nations, they still retain their original character, and remain dormant. So far as they have been practically exerted, they exist in fact, are understood by both parties, are asserted by the one, and admitted by the other.

. . . Certain it is that our history furnishes no example, from the first settlement of our country, of any attempt, on the part of the Crown, to interfere with the internal affairs of the Indians farther than to keep out the agents of foreign powers who, as traders or otherwise, might seduct them into foreign alliances. The King purchased their lands when they were willing to sell, at a price they were willing to take, but never coerced a surrender of them. He also purchased their alliance and dependence by subsidies, but never intruded into the interior of their affairs or interfered with their self-government so far as respected themselves only.

The third article of the treaty of Hopewell acknowledges the Cherokees to be under the protection of the United States of America, and of no other power.

This stipulation is found in Indian treaties generally. It was introduced into their treaties with Great Britain, and may probably be found in those with other European powers. Its origin may be traced to the nature of their connexion with those powers, and its true meaning is discerned in their relative situation.

The general law of European sovereigns respecting their claims in America limited the intercourse of Indians, in a great degree, to the particular potentate whose ultimate right of domain was acknowledged by the others. This was the general state of things in time of peace. It was sometimes changed in war. The consequence was that their supplies were derived chiefly from that nation, and their trade confined to it. Goods, indispensable to their comfort, in the shape of presents, were received from the same hand. What was of still more importance, the strong hand of government was interposed to restrain the disorderly and licentious from intrusion into their country, from encroachments on their lands, and from the acts of violence which were often attended by reciprocal murder. The Indians perceived in this protection only what was beneficial to themselves—an engagement to punish aggressions on them. It involved practically no claim to their lands, no dominion over their persons. It merely bound the Nation to the British Crown as a dependent ally, claiming the protection of a powerful friend and neighbour and receiving the advantages of that protection without involving a surrender of their national character.

This is the true meaning of the stipulation, and is undoubtedly the sense in which it was made. Neither the British Government nor the Cherokees ever understood it otherwise.

The same stipulation entered [into] with the United States is undoubtedly to be construed in the same manner they receive the Cherokee Nation into their favour and protection. The Cherokees acknowledge themselves to be under the protection of the United States, and of no other power. Protection does not imply the destruction of the protected. The manner in which this stipulation was understood by the American Government is explained by the language and acts of our first President.

So with respect to the words "hunting grounds." Hunting was, at that time, the principal occupation of the Indians, and their land was more used for that purpose than for any other. It could not, however, be supposed that any intention existed of restricting the full use of the lands they reserved.

To the United States, it could be a matter of no concern whether their whole territory was devoted to hunting grounds or whether an occasional village and an occasional cornfield interrupted, and gave some variety, to the scene.

These terms had been used in their treaties with Great Britain, and had never been misunderstood. They had never been supposed to imply a right in the British Government to take their lands or to interfere with their internal government.

The sixth and seventh articles stipulate for the punishment of the citizens of either country who may commit offences on or against the citizens of the other. The only inference to be drawn from them is that the United States considered the Cherokees as a nation.

The ninth article is in these words:

> For the benefit and comfort of the Indians, and for the prevention of injuries or oppressions on the part of the citizens or Indians, the United States, in Congress assembled, shall have the sole and exclusive right of regulating the trade with the Indians and managing all their affairs as they think proper.

To construe the expression "managing all their affairs" into a surrender of self-government would be a perversion of their necessary meaning, and a departure from the construction which has been uniformly put on them. The great subject of the article is the Indian trade. The influence it gave made it desirable that Congress should possess it. The commissioners brought forward the claim with the profession that their motive was "the benefit and comfort of the Indians and the prevention of injuries or oppressions." This may be true as respects the regulation of their trade and as respects the regulation of all affairs connected with their trade, but cannot be true as respects the management of their affairs. The most important of these is the cession of their lands and security against intruders on them. Is it credible that they could have considered themselves as surrendering to the United States the right to dictate their future cessions and the terms on which they should be made, or to compel their submission to the violence of disorderly and licentious intruders? It is equally inconceivable that they could have supposed themselves, by a phrase thus slipped into an article on another and more interesting subject, to have divested themselves of the right of self-government

on subjects not connected with trade. Such a measure could not be "for their benefit and comfort," or for "the prevention of injuries and oppression." Such a construction would be inconsistent with the spirit of this and of all subsequent treaties, especially of those articles which recognise the right of the Cherokees to declare hostilities and to make war. It would convert a treaty of peace covertly into an act annihilating the political existence of one of the parties. Had such a result been intended, it would have been openly avowed.

The Treaty of Holston, negotiated with the Cherokees in July, 1791, explicitly recognising the national character of the Cherokees and their right of self-government, thus guarantying their lands, assuming the duty of protection, and of course pledging the faith of the United States for that protection, has been frequently renewed, and is now in full force.

. . . The Indian nations had always been considered as distinct, independent political communities retaining their original natural rights as undisputed possessors of the soil, from time immemorial, with the single exception of that imposed by irresistible power, which excluded them from intercourse with any other European potentate than the first discoverer of the coast of the particular region claimed, and this was a restriction which those European potentates imposed on themselves, as well as on the Indians. The very term "nation," so generally applied to them, means "a people distinct from others." The Constitution, by declaring treaties already made, as well as those to be made, to be the supreme law of the land, has adopted and sanctioned the previous treaties with the Indian nations, and consequently admits their rank among the powers who are capable of making treaties. The words "treaty" and "nation" are words of our own language, selected in our diplomatic and legislative proceedings by ourselves, having each a definite and well understood meaning. We have applied them to Indians as we have applied them to the other nations of the earth. They are applied to all in the same sense.

. . . The act of the State of Georgia under which the plaintiff in error was prosecuted is consequently void, and the judgment a nullity.

The acts of the Legislature of Georgia interfere forcibly with the relations established between the United States and the Cherokee Nation, the regulation of which, according to the settled principles of our Constitution, is committed exclusively to the Government of the Union.

They are in direct hostility with treaties, repeated in a succession of years, which mark out the boundary that separates the Cherokee country from Georgia; guaranty to them all the land within their boundary; solemnly pledge the faith of the United States to restrain their citizens from trespassing on it; and recognise the preexisting power of the Nation to govern itself.

They are in equal hostility with the acts of Congress for regulating this intercourse and giving effect to the treaties.

The forcible seizure and abduction of the plaintiff in error, who was residing in the Nation with its permission and by authority of the President of the United States, is also a violation of the acts which authorize the Chief Magistrate to exercise his authority. . . .

Resource

Worcester v. Georgia. Available at: http://supct.law .cornell.edu/supct/html/historics/USSC_CR_ 0031_0515_ZS.html. Accessed January 20, 2007.

Andrew Jackson: Indian Removal Message to Congress

President Andrew Jackson's message on the removal of Southern Indians, part of his first annual message to the U.S. Congress in December 1829, advocated policies that called for the expulsion of Native Americans from their lands in the eastern United States and exiled them to reservations in the West. Despite some public sympathy for the Native Americans, especially the Cherokee in Georgia, Jackson argued that, if the Indians remained in existing states, they would constitute a foreign people, contradicting the prohibition of states within other states found in Article IV, Section 3 of the Constitution. Congress subsequently adopted the Indian Removal Act of 1830, approving Jackson's proposed policy. The Supreme Court decisions in Cherokee Nation v. Georgia *(1831) and* Worcester v. Georgia *(1832) proved inadequate to protect Native American interests in the face of state, presidential, and congressional momentum, and they were ultimately forced off their land, culminating in the devastating and dramatic removal of the Cherokees in 1838 on the Trail of Tears.*

It gives me pleasure to announce to Congress that the benevolent policy of the government, steadily pursued for nearly thirty years, in relation to the

removal of the Indians beyond the white settlements is approaching to a happy consummation. Two important tribes have accepted the provision made for their removal at the last session of Congress, and it is believed that their example will induce the remaining tribes also to seek the same obvious advantages.

The consequences of a speedy removal will be important to the United States, to individual states, and to the Indians themselves. The pecuniary advantages which it promises to the government are the least of its recommendations. It puts an end to all possible danger of collision between the authorities of the general and state governments on account of the Indians. It will place a dense and civilized population in large tracts of country now occupied by a few savage hunters. By opening the whole territory between Tennessee on the north and Louisiana on the south to the settlement of the whites it will incalculably strengthen the southwestern frontier and render the adjacent states strong enough to repel future invasions without remote aid. It will relieve the whole state of Mississippi and the western part of Alabama of Indian occupancy, and enable those states to advance rapidly in population, wealth, and power.

It will separate the Indians from immediate contact with settlements of whites; free them from the power of the states; enable them to pursue happiness in their own way and under their own rude institutions; will retard the progress of decay, which is lessening their numbers, and perhaps cause them gradually, under the protection of the government and through the influence of good counsels, to cast off their savage habits and become an interesting, civilized, and Christian community. These consequences, some of them so certain and the rest so probable, make the complete execution of the plan sanctioned by Congress at their last session an object of much solicitude.

Toward the aborigines of the country no one can indulge a more friendly feeling than myself, or would go further in attempting to reclaim them from their wandering habits and make them a happy, prosperous people. I have endeavored to impress upon them my own solemn convictions of the duties and powers of the general government in relation to the state authorities. For the justice of the laws passed by the states within the scope of their reserved powers they are not responsible to this government. As individuals we may entertain and express our opinions of their acts, but as a government we have as little right to control them as we have to prescribe laws for other nations.

With a full understanding of the subject, the Choctaw and the Chickasaw tribes have with great unanimity determined to avail themselves of the liberal offers presented by the act of Congress, and have agreed to remove beyond the Mississippi River. Treaties have been made with them, which in due season will be submitted for consideration. In negotiating these treaties, they were made to understand their true condition, and they have preferred maintaining their independence in the Western forests to submitting to the laws of the states in which they now reside. These treaties, being probably the last which will ever be made with them, are characterized by great liberality on the part of the government. They give the Indians a liberal sum in consideration of their removal, and comfortable subsistence on their arrival at their new homes. If it be their real interest to maintain a separate existence, they will there be at liberty to do so without the inconveniences and vexations to which they would unavoidably have been subject in Alabama and Mississippi.

Humanity has often wept over the fate of the aborigines of this country, and philanthropy has been long busily employed in devising means to avert it, but its progress has never for a moment been arrested, and one by one have many powerful tribes disappeared from the earth. To follow to the tomb the last of his race and to tread on the graves of extinct nations excite melancholy reflections. But true philanthropy reconciles the mind to these vicissitudes as it does to the extinction of one generation to make room for another. In the monuments and fortresses of an unknown people, spread over the extensive regions of the West, we behold the memorials of a once powerful race, which was exterminated or has disappeared to make room for the existing savage tribes. Nor is there anything in this which, upon a comprehensive view of the general interests of the human race, is to be regretted. Philanthropy could not wish to see this continent restored to the condition in which it was found by our forefathers. What good man would prefer a country covered with forests and ranged by a few thousand savages to our extensive republic, studded with cities, towns, and prosperous farms, embellished with all the improvements which art can devise or industry execute, occupied by more than 12 million happy people, and filled with all the blessings of liberty, civilization, and religion?

The present policy of the government is but a continuation of the same progressive change by a milder process. The tribes which occupied the countries now constituting the Eastern states were annihilated or have melted away to make room for the whites. The waves of population and civilization are rolling to the westward, and we now propose to acquire the countries occupied by the red men of the South and West by a fair exchange, and, at the expense of the United States, to send them to a land where their existence may be prolonged and perhaps made perpetual.

Doubtless it will be painful to leave the graves of their fathers; but what do they more than our ancestors did or than our children are now doing? To better their condition in an unknown land our forefathers left all that was dear in earthly objects. Our children by thousands yearly leave the land of their birth to seek new homes in distant regions. Does humanity weep at these painful separations from everything, animate and inanimate, with which the young heart has become entwined? Far from it. It is rather a source of joy that our country affords scope where our young population may range unconstrained in body or in mind, developing the power and faculties of man in their highest perfection. These remove hundreds and almost thousands of miles at their own expense, purchase the lands they occupy, and support themselves at their new homes from the moment of their arrival. Can it be cruel in this government when, by events which it cannot control, the Indian is made discontented in his ancient home to purchase his lands, to give him a new and extensive territory, to pay the expense of his removal, and support him a year in his new abode? How many thousands of our own people would gladly embrace the opportunity of removing to the West on such conditions? If the offers made to the Indians were extended to them, they would be hailed with gratitude and joy.

And is it supposed that the wandering savage has a stronger attachment to his home than the settled, civilized Christian? Is it more afflicting to him to leave the graves of his fathers than it is to our brothers and children? Rightly considered, the policy of the general government toward the red man is not only liberal but generous. He is unwilling to submit to the laws of the states and mingle with their population. To save him from this alternative, or perhaps utter annihilation, the general government kindly offers him a new home, and proposes to pay the whole expense of his removal and settlement.

In the consummation of a policy originating at an early period, and steadily pursued by every administration within the present century—so just to the states and so generous to the Indians—the executive feels it has a right to expect the cooperation of Congress and of all good and disinterested men. The states, moreover, have a right to demand it. It was substantially a part of the compact which made them members of our Confederacy. With Georgia there is an express contract; with the new states an implied one of equal obligation. Why, in authorizing Ohio, Indiana, Illinois, Missouri, Mississippi, and Alabama to form constitutions and become separate states, did Congress include within their limits extensive tracts of Indian lands, and, in some instances, powerful Indian tribes? Was it not understood by both parties that the power of the states was to be coextensive with their limits, and that, with all convenient dispatch, the general government should extinguish the Indian title and remove every obstruction to the complete jurisdiction of the state governments over the soil? Probably not one of those states would have accepted a separate existence—certainly it would never have been granted by Congress—had it been understood that they were to be confined forever to those small portions of their nominal territory the Indian title to which had at the time been extinguished.

It is, therefore, a duty which this government owes to the new states to extinguish as soon as possible the Indian title to all lands which Congress themselves have included within their limits. When this is done the duties of the general government in relation to the states and the Indians within their limits are at an end. The Indians may leave the state or not, as they choose. The purchase of their lands does not alter in the least their personal relations with the state government. No act of the general government has ever been deemed necessary to give the states jurisdiction over the persons of the Indians. That they possess by virtue of their sovereign power within their own limits in as full a manner before as after the purchase of the Indian lands; nor can this government add to or diminish it.

May we not hope, therefore, that all good citizens, and none more zealously than those who think the Indians oppressed by subjection to the laws of the states, will unite in attempting to open the eyes of those children of the forest to their true condition, and by a speedy removal to relieve them from all the

evils, real or imaginary, present or prospective, with which they may be supposed to be threatened.

Cherokee Nation Memorial

In this excerpt of the Cherokee Nation Memorial, the Cherokees present a plea to the American people not to force them from their ancestral lands in the face of the Indian Removal Act of 1830. Their plea went unheard, and President Andrew Jackson ordered them off their lands in Georgia in 1833. Although the Cherokees contested the order in the U.S. courts, they were compelled to leave Georgia in 1838 and make an arduous journey to the newly established Indian Country in present-day Oklahoma on a trip so fraught with disease, disaster, and death that it came to be known as the Trail of Tears.

We are aware that some persons suppose it will be for our advantage to remove beyond the Mississippi. We think otherwise. Our people universally think otherwise. Thinking that it would be fatal to their interests, they have almost to a man sent their memorial to Congress, deprecating the necessity of a removal. . . . It is incredible that Georgia should ever have enacted the oppressive laws to which reference is here made, unless she had supposed that something extremely terrific in its character was necessary in order to make the Cherokees willing to remove. We are not willing to remove; and if we could be brought to this extremity, it would be not by argument, nor because our judgment was satisfied, not because our condition will be improved; but only because we cannot endure to be deprived of our national and individual rights and subjected to a process of intolerable oppression.

We wish to remain on the land of our fathers. We have a perfect and original right to remain without interruption or molestation. The treaties with us, and laws of the United States made in pursuance of treaties, guaranty our residence and our privileges, and secure us against intruders. Our only request is, that these treaties may be fulfilled, and these laws executed.

But if we are compelled to leave our country, we see nothing but ruin before us. The country west of the Arkansas territory is unknown to us. From what we can learn of it, we have no prepossessions in its favor. All the inviting parts of it, as we believe, are preoccupied by various Indian nations, to which it has been assigned. They would regard us as intruders. . . . The far greater part of that region is, beyond all controversy, badly supplied with wood and water; and no Indian tribe can live as agriculturists without these articles. All our neighbors . . . would speak a language totally different from ours, and practice different customs. The original possessors of that region are now wandering savages lurking for prey in the neighborhood. . . . Were the country to which we are urged much better than it is represented to be, . . . still it is not the land of our birth, nor of our affections. It contains neither the scenes of our childhood, nor the graves of our fathers.

. . . We have been called a poor, ignorant, and degraded people. We certainly are not rich; nor have we ever boasted of our knowledge, or our moral or intellectual elevation. But there is not a man within our limits so ignorant as not to know that he has a right to live on the land of his fathers, in the possession of his immemorial privileges, and that this right has been acknowledged by the United States; nor is there a man so degraded as not to feel a keen sense of injury, on being deprived of his right and driven into exile. . . .

Indian Removal Act

President Andrew Jackson was a strong supporter of legislation to remove American Indians from across the United States to "Indian Territory," now Oklahoma, a measure bitterly opposed by most Native Americans. The measure was politically popular with immigrants seeking the rich lands occupied for thousands of years by the Cherokees and others.

May 28, 1830
Chapter CXLVIII

An Act to provide for an exchange of lands with the Indians residing in any of the states or territories, and for their removal west of the river Mississippi. Be it enacted by the Senate and House of Representatives of the United States of America, in Congress assembled, That it shall and may be lawful for the President of the United States to cause so much of any territory belonging to the United States, west of the river Mississippi, not included in any state or organized territory, and to which the Indian title has been extinguished, as he may judge necessary, to be divided into a suitable number of districts, for the reception of such tribes or nations of Indians as may choose to exchange the lands where they now reside, and remove there; and to cause each of said districts to be so described by natural or artificial marks, as to be easily distinguished from every other.

Sec. 2 *And be it further enacted*, That it shall and may be lawful for the President to exchange any or all of such districts, so to be laid off and described, with any tribe or nation of Indians now residing within the limits of any of the states or territories, and with which the United States have existing treaties, for the whole or any part or portion of the territory claimed and occupied by such tribe or nation, within the bounds of any one or more of the states or territories, where the land claimed and occupied by the Indians, is owned by the United States, or the United States are bound to the state within which it lies to extinguish the Indian claim thereto.

Sec. 3 *And be it further enacted*, That in the making of any such exchange or exchanges, it shall and may be lawful for the President solemnly to assure the tribe or nation with which the exchange is made, that the United States will forever secure and guarantee to them, and their heirs or successors, the country so exchanged with them; and if they prefer it, that the United States will cause a patent or grant to be made and executed to them for the same: *Provided always*, That such lands shall revert to the United States, if the Indians become extinct, or abandon the same.

Sec. 4 *And be it further enacted*, That if, upon any of the lands now occupied by the Indians, and to be exchanged for, there should be such improvements as add value to the land claimed by any individual or individuals of such tribes or nations, it shall and may be lawful for the President to cause such value to be ascertained by appraisement or otherwise, and to cause such ascertained value to be paid to the person or persons rightfully claiming such improvements. And upon the payment of such valuation, the improvements so valued and paid for, shall pass to the United States, and possession shall not afterwards be permitted to any of the same tribe.

Sec. 5 *And be it further enacted*, That upon the making of any such exchange as is contemplated by this act, it shall and may be lawful for the President to cause such aid and assistance to be furnished to the emigrants as may be necessary and proper to enable them to remove to, and settle in, the country for which they may have exchanged; and also, to give them such aid and assistance as may be necessary for their support and subsistence for the first year after their removal.

Sec. 6 *And be it further enacted*, That it shall and may be lawful for the President to cause such tribe or nation to be protected, at their new residence, against all interruption or disturbance from any other tribe or nation of Indians, or from any other person or persons whatever.

Sec. 7 *And be it further enacted*, That it shall and may be lawful for the President to have the same superintendence and care over any tribe or nation in the country to which they may remove, as contemplated by this act, that he is now authorized to have over them at their present places of residence: *Provided*, That nothing in this act contained shall be construed as authorizing or directing the violation of any existing treaty between the United States and any of the Indian tribes.

Sec. 8 *And be it further enacted*, That for the purpose of giving effect to the provisions of this act, the sum of five hundred thousand dollars is hereby appropriated, to be paid out of any money in the treasury, not otherwise appropriated.

Resource

Indian Removal Act. Available at: http://academic .udayton.edu/race/02rights/native10.htm. Accessed January 20, 2007.

Black Hawk: Surrender Speech

The Black Hawk War of 1832 lasted only fifteen weeks but marked the demise of both the Sauk and Fox tribes as political and military forces in the Midwest. The leader and guiding spirit behind the conflict, Chief Black Hawk, delivered this address at the time of his surrender to U.S. Army troops in August 1832. Spending a year in prison after his capture, upon his release Black Hawk traveled around the country as something of a public attraction, subsequently publishing his autobiography.

Black-hawk is an Indian. He has done nothing for which an Indian ought to be ashamed. He has fought for his countrymen, the squaws and papooses, against white men, who came, year after year, to cheat them and take away their lands. You know the cause of our making war. It is known to all white men. They ought to be ashamed of it. The white men despise the Indians, and drive them from their homes. But the Indians are not deceitful. The white men speak bad of the Indian, and look at him spitefully. But the Indian does not tell lies; Indians do not steal.

An Indian, who is as bad as the white men, could not live in our nation; he would be put to

death, and eaten up by the wolves. The white men are bad schoolmasters; they carry false looks, and deal in false actions; they smile in the face of the poor Indian to cheat him; they shake them by the hand to gain their confidence, to make them drunk, to deceive them, and ruin our wives. We told them to let us alone, and keep away from us; but they followed on, and beset our paths, and they coiled themselves among us, like the snake. They poisoned us by their touch. We were not safe. We lived in danger. We were becoming like them, hypocrites and liars, adulterers, lazy drones, all talkers, and no workers.

We looked up to the Great Spirit. We went to our great father. We were encouraged. His great council gave us fair words and big promises; but we got no satisfaction. Things were growing worse. There were no deer in the forest. The opossum and beaver were fled; the springs were drying up, and our squaws and papooses without victuals to keep them from starving; we called a great council, and built a large fire. The spirit of our fathers arose and spoke to us to avenge our wrongs or die. We all spoke before the council fire. It was warm and pleasant. We set up the war-whoop, and dug up the tomahawk; our knives were ready, and the heart of Blackhawk swelled high in his bosom, when he led his warriors to battle. He is satisfied. He will go to the world of spirits contented. He has done his duty. His father will meet him there, and commend him.

Treaty of Guadalupe Hidalgo

This treaty was negotiated at the conclusion of the Mexican-American War (1846–1848), and provided for the transfer of land from Mexico to the United States that now comprises Arizona, New Mexico, Utah, Colorado, Nevada, and California. The following clause was meant to protect the liberty and property of the Mexican citizens who were absorbed into the United States. Their lands often were seized by immigrants in violation of the treaty.

ARTICLE IX. Mexicans who, in the territories aforesaid, shall not preserve the character of citizens of the Mexican Republic, conformably with what is stipulated in the preceding article, shall be incorporated into the Union of the United States, and be admitted at the proper time (to be judged of by the Congress of the United States) to the enjoyment of all the rights of citizens of the United States, according to the principles of the Constitution; and in the

meantime shall be maintained and protected in the free enjoyment of their liberty and property, and secured in the free exercise of their religion without restriction.

Treaty of Fort Laramie

This treaty, as signed, was ratified by the Senate with an amendment changing the annuity in Article 7 from fifty to ten years, subject to acceptance by the tribes. Assent of all the tribes except the Crows was procured and in subsequent agreements this treaty has been recognized as in force.

Articles of a treaty made and concluded at Fort Laramie, in the Indian Territory, between D. D. Mitchell, superintendent of Indian affairs, and Thomas Fitzpatrick, Indian agent, commissioners specially appointed and authorized by the President of the United States, of the first part, and the chiefs, headmen, and braves of the following Indian nations, residing south of the Missouri River, east of the Rocky Mountains, and north of the lines of Texas and New Mexico, viz, the Sioux or Dahcotahs, Cheyennes, Arrapahoes, Crows. Assinaboines, Gros-Ventre Mandans, and Arrickaras, parties of the second part, on the seventeenth day of September, A. D. one thousand eight hundred and fifty-one.

ARTICLE 1.
The aforesaid nations, parties to this treaty, having assembled for the purpose of establishing and confirming peaceful relations amongst themselves, do hereby covenant and agree to abstain in future from all hostilities whatever against each other, to maintain good faith and friendship in all their mutual intercourse, and to make an effective and lasting peace.
ARTICLE 2.
The aforesaid nations do hereby recognize the right of the United States Government to establish roads, military and other posts, within their respective territories.
ARTICLE 3.
In consideration of the rights and privileges acknowledged in the preceding article, the United States bind themselves to protect the aforesaid Indian nations against the commission of all depredations by the people of the said United States, after the ratification of this treaty.

ARTICLE 4.

The aforesaid Indian nations do hereby agree and bind themselves to make restitution or satisfaction for any wrongs committed, after the ratification of this treaty, by any band or individual of their people, on the people of the United States, whilst lawfully residing in or passing through their respective territories.

ARTICLE 5.

The aforesaid Indian nations do hereby recognize and acknowledge the following tracts of country, included within the metes and boundaries hereinafter designated, as their respective territories, viz:

The territory of the Sioux or Dahcotah Nation, commencing the mouth of the White Earth River, on the Missouri River: thence in a southwesterly direction to the forks of the Platte River: thence up the north fork of the Platte River to a point known as the Red Bute, or where the road leaves the river; thence along the range of mountains known as the Black Hills, to the head-waters of Heart River; thence down Heart River to its mouth; and thence down the Missouri River to the place of beginning.

The territory of the Gros Ventre, Mandans, and Arrickaras Nations, commencing at the mouth of Heart River; thence up the Missouri River to the mouth of the Yellowstone River; thence up the Yellowstone River to the mouth of Powder River in a southeasterly direction, to the head-waters of the Little Missouri River; thence along the Black Hills to the head of Heart River, and thence down Heart River to the place of beginning.

The territory of the Assinaboin Nation, commencing at the mouth of Yellowstone River; thence up the Missouri River to the mouth of the Muscle-shell River; thence from the mouth of the Muscle-shell River in a southeasterly direction until it strikes the head-waters of Big Dry Creek; thence down that creek to where it empties into the Yellowstone River, nearly opposite the mouth of Powder River, and thence down the Yellowstone River to the place of beginning.

The territory of the Blackfoot Nation, commencing at the mouth of Muscle-shell River; thence up the Missouri River to its source; thence along the main range of the Rocky Mountains, in a southerly direction, to the head-waters of the northern source of the Yellowstone River; thence down the Yellowstone River to the mouth of Twenty-five Yard Creek; thence across to the head-waters of the Muscle-shell River, and thence down the Muscle-shell River to the place of beginning.

The territory of the Crow Nation, commencing at the mouth of Powder River on the Yellowstone; thence up Powder River to its source; thence along the main range of the Black Hills and Wind River Mountains to the head-waters of the Yellowstone River; thence down the Yellowstone River to the mouth of Twenty-five Yard Creek; thence to the head waters of the Muscle-shell River; thence down the Muscle-shell River to its mouth; thence to the head-waters of Big Dry Creek, and thence to its mouth.

The territory of the Cheyennes and Arrapahoes, commencing at the Red Bute, or the place where the road leaves the north fork of the Platte River; thence up the north fork of the Platte River to its source; thence along the main range of the Rocky Mountains to the head-waters of the Arkansas River; thence down the Arkansas River to the crossing of the Santa Fé road; thence in a northwesterly direction to the forks of the Platte River, and thence up the Platte River to the place of beginning.

It is, however, understood that, in making this recognition and acknowledgement, the aforesaid Indian nations do not hereby abandon or prejudice any rights or claims they may have to other lands; and further, that they do not surrender the privilege of hunting, fishing, or passing over any of the tracts of country heretofore described.

ARTICLE 6.

The parties to the second part of this treaty having selected principals or head-chiefs for their respective nations, through whom all national business will hereafter be conducted, do hereby bind themselves to sustain said chiefs and their successors during good behavior.

ARTICLE 7.

In consideration of the treaty stipulations, and for the damages which have or may occur by reason thereof to the Indian nations, parties hereto, and for their maintenance and the improvement of their moral and social customs, the United States bind themselves to deliver to the said Indian nations the sum of fifty thousand dollars per annum for the term of ten years, with the right to continue the same at the discretion of the President of the United States for a period not exceeding five years thereafter, in provisions, merchandise, domestic animals, and agricultural implements, in such proportions as may be deemed best adapted to their condition by the Presi-

dent of the United States, to be distributed in proportion to the population of the aforesaid Indian nations.
ARTICLE 8.

It is understood and agreed that should any of the Indian nations, parties to this treaty, violate any of the provisions thereof, the United States may withhold the whole or a portion of the annuities mentioned in the preceding article from the nation so offending, until, in the opinion of the President of the United States, proper satisfaction shall have been made.

In testimony whereof the said D. D. Mitchell and Thomas Fitzpatrick commissioners as aforesaid, and the chiefs, headmen, and braves, parties hereto, have set their hands and affixed their marks, on the day and at the place first above written.

D. D. Mitchell
Thomas Fitzpatrick
Commissioners.

Sioux:
　　Mah-toe-wha-you-whey, his x mark.
　　Mah-kah-toe-zah-zah, his x mark.
　　Bel-o-ton-kah-tan-ga, his x mark.
　　Nah-ka-pah-gi-gi, his x mark.
　　Mak-toe-sah-bi-chis, his x mark.
　　Meh-wha-tah-ni-hans-kah, his x mark.

Cheyennes:
　　Wah-ha-nis-satta, his x mark.
　　Voist-ti-toe-vetz, his x mark.
　　Nahk-ko-me-ien, his x mark.
　　Koh-kah-y-wh-cum-est, his x mark.

Arrapahoes:
　　Bè-ah-té-a-qui-sah, his x mark.
　　Neb-ni-bah-seh-it, his x mark.
　　Beh-kah-jay-beth-sah-es, his x mark.

Crows:
　　Arra-tu-ri-sash, his x mark.
　　Doh-chepit-seh-chi-es, his x mark.

Assinaboines:
　　Mah-toe-wit-ko, his x mark.
　　Toe-tah-ki-eh-nan, his x mark.
　　Mandans and Gros Ventres:
　　Nochk-pit-shi-toe-pish, his x mark.
　　She-oh-mant-ho, his x mark.

Arickarees:
　　Koun-hei-ti-shan, his x mark.
　　Bi-atch-tah-wetch, his x mark.

In the presence of—
　　A. B. Chambers, secretary.
　　S. Cooper, colonel, U.S. Army.
　　R. H. Chilton, captain, First Drags.

Thomas Duncan, captain, Mounted Riflemen.
Thos. G. Rhett, brevet captain R. M. R.
W. L. Elliott, first lieutenant R. M. R.
C. Campbell, interpreter for Sioux.
John S. Smith, interpreter for Cheyennes.
Robert Meldrum, interpreter for the Crows.
H. Culbertson, interpreter for Assiniboines
　　and Gros Ventres.
Francois L'Etalie, interpreter for Arick arees.
John Pizelle, interpreter for the Arrapahoes.
B. Gratz Brown.
Robert Campbell.
Edmond F. Chouteau.

Chief Sea'th'l's Farewell Speech

An important leader of the Coast Salish in the Puget Sound region of Washington State, the Duwamish-Suquamish Chief Sea'th'l' delivered the following speech in 1854 at a reception for Washington's Territorial Governor Isaac Stevens, who was attempting to buy significant tracts of land from the local Indians. The elderly chief spoke no English, so his speech was translated into Chinook, a trade jargon, and then into English. Henry Smith, a prominent citizen of the new city of Seattle, the name anglicized from the chief's, took notes but did not publish the following version until 1887. Many years after that, the speech was frequently edited and paraphrased in an attempt to make it more amenable to assertions that Sea'th'l' spoke in environmental metaphors. These versions have been quoted so often that many people do not know them from a translation that itself was removed from the original speech by more than thirty years and by an intervening conversion to a trade jargon. In whatever version they appear, however, Sea'th'l's words have become symbolic of a love for the earth as well as the struggles Native Americans faced in opposing European-American expansion settlement.

Yonder sky that has wept tears of compassion upon my people for centuries untold, and which to us appears changeless and eternal, may change. Today is fair. Tomorrow it may be overcast with clouds. My words are like the stars that never change. Whatever Seattle says, the great chief at Washington can rely upon with as much certainty as he can upon the return of the sun or the seasons. The white chief says that Big Chief at Washington sends us

greetings of friendship and goodwill. This is kind of him for we know he has little need of our friendship in return. His people are many. They are like the grass that covers vast prairies. My people are few. They resemble the scattering trees of a storm-swept plain. The great, and I presume good, White Chief sends us word that he wishes to buy our land but is willing to allow us enough to live comfortably. This indeed appears just, even generous, for the Red Man no longer has rights that he need respect, and the offer may be wise, also, as we are no longer in need of an extensive country.

There was a time when our people covered the land as the waves of a wind-ruffled sea cover its shell-paved floor, but that time long since passed away with the greatness of tribes that are now but a mournful memory. I will not dwell on, nor mourn over, our untimely decay, nor reproach my paleface brothers with hastening it, as we too may have been somewhat to blame.

Youth is impulsive. When our young men grow angry at some real or imaginary wrong, and disfigure their faces with black paint, it denotes that their hearts are black, and that they are often cruel and relentless, and our old men and old women are unable to restrain them. Thus it has ever been. Thus it was when the white man began to push our forefathers ever westward. But let us hope that the hostilities between us may never return. We would have everything to lose and nothing to gain. Revenge by young men is considered gain, even at the cost of their own lives, but old men who stay at home in times of war, and mothers who have sons to lose, know better.

Our good father in Washington. . . . I presume he is now our father as well as yours, since King George has moved his boundaries . . . our great and good father, I say, sends us word that if we do as he desires he will protect us. His brave warriors will be to us a bristling wall of strength, and his wonderful ships of war will fill our harbors, so that our ancient enemies far to the northward, the Haidas and Tsimshians will cease to frighten our women, children, and old men. Then in reality he will be our father and we his children. But can that ever be? Your God is not our God! Your God loves your people and hates mine! He folds his strong protecting arms lovingly about the paleface and leads him by the hand as a father leads an infant son. But, He has forsaken His Red children, if they really are His. Our God, the Great Spirit, seems also to have forsaken us. Your God makes your people wax

stronger every day. Soon they will fill all the land. Our people are ebbing away like a rapidly receding tide that will never return. The white man's God cannot love our people or He would protect them. They seem to be orphans who can look nowhere for help. How then can we be brothers? How can your God become our God and renew our prosperity and awaken in us dreams of returning greatness? If we have a common Heavenly Father He must be partial, for He came to His paleface children. We never saw Him. He gave you laws but had no word for His red children whose teeming multitudes once filled this vast continent as stars fill the firmament. No; we are two distinct races with separate origins and separate destinies. There is little in common between us.

To us the ashes of our ancestors are sacred and their resting place is hallowed ground. You wander far from the graves of your ancestors and seemingly without regret. Your religion was written upon tablets of stone by the iron finger of your God so that you could not forget. The Red Man could never comprehend nor remember it. Our religion is the traditions of our ancestors, the dreams of our old men, given them in solemn hours of the night by the Great Spirit; and the visions of our sachems, and is written in the hearts of our people.

Your dead cease to love you and the land of their nativity as soon as they pass the portals of the tomb and wander away beyond the stars. They are soon forgotten and never return. Our dead never forget this beautiful world that gave them being. They still love its verdant valleys, its murmuring rivers, its magnificent mountains, sequestered vales and verdant lined lakes and bays, and ever yearn in tender fond affection over the lonely hearted living, and often return from the happy hunting ground to visit, guide, console, and comfort them.

Day and night cannot dwell together. The Red Man has ever fled the approach of the White Man, as the morning mist flees before the morning sun. However, your proposition seems fair and I think that my people will accept it and will retire to the reservation you offer them. Then we will dwell apart in peace, for the words of the Great White Chief seem to be the words of nature speaking to my people out of dense darkness.

It matters little where we pass the remnant of our days. They will not be many. The Indian's night promises to be dark. Not a single star of hope hovers above his horizon. Sad-voiced winds moan in the distance. Grim fate seems to be on the Red Man's

trail, and wherever he will hear the approaching footsteps of his fell destroyer and prepare stolidly to meet his doom, as does the wounded doe that hears the approaching footsteps of the hunter.

A few more moons, a few more winters, and not one of the descendants of the mighty hosts that once moved over this broad land or lived in happy homes, protected by the Great Spirit, will remain to mourn over the graves of a people once more powerful and hopeful than yours. But why should I mourn at the untimely fate of my people? Tribe follows tribe, and nation follows nation, like the waves of the sea. It is the order of nature, and regret is useless. Your time of decay may be distant, but it will surely come, for even the White Man whose God walked and talked with him as friend to friend, cannot be exempt from the common destiny. We may be brothers after all. We will see.

We will ponder your proposition and when we decide we will let you know. But should we accept it, I here and now make this condition that we will not be denied the privilege without molestation of visiting at any time the tombs of our ancestors, friends, and children. Every part of this soil is sacred in the estimation of my people. Every hillside, every valley, every plain and grove, has been hallowed by some sad or happy event in days long vanished. Even the rocks, which seem to be dumb and dead as the swelter in the sun along the silent shore, thrill with memories of stirring events connected with the lives of my people, and the very dust upon which you now stand responds more lovingly to their footsteps than yours, because it is rich with the blood of our ancestors, and our bare feet are conscious of the sympathetic touch. Our departed braves, fond mothers, glad, happy hearted maidens, and even the little children who lived here and rejoiced here for a brief season, will love these somber solitudes and at eventide they greet shadowy returning spirits. And when the last Red Man shall have perished, and the memory of my tribe shall have become a myth among the White Men, these shores will swarm with the invisible dead of my tribe, and when your children's children think themselves alone in the field, the store, the shop, upon the highway, or in the silence of the pathless woods, they will not be alone. In all the earth there is no place dedicated to solitude. At night when the streets of your cities and villages are silent and you think them deserted, they will throng with the returning hosts that once filled them and still love this beautiful land. The White Man will never be alone.

Let him be just and deal kindly with my people, for the dead are not powerless. Dead, did I say? There is no death, only a change of worlds.

Sand Creek Massacre: Report of the Joint Committee on the Conduct of the War

The brutal Sand Creek massacre of November 29, 1865, resulted in the murder of more than two hundred Cheyennes, many of them women and children. The attack was led by U.S. Army Colonel John M. Chivington, whose sanity many historians now question. Chivington ordered his troops to slaughter every Indian in the Sand Creek village and to take no prisoners. Chivington's order was even more diabolical because the Indians had previously surrendered to the U.S. government and were ostensibly under U.S. protection at the time. The massacre compelled the Cheyenne to break off peace talks with the Americans and led to a vicious war during 1867–1869.

In the summer of 1864, Governor [John] Evans, of Colorado Territory, as acting superintendent of Indian Affairs, sent notice to the various bands and tribes of Indians within his jurisdiction that such as desired to be considered friendly to the whites should at once repair to the nearest military post in order to be protected from the soldiers who were to take the field against the hostile Indians.

About the close of the summer, some Cheyenne Indians, in the neighborhood of the Smoke Hills, sent word to Major [Edward W.] Wynkoop, the commandant of the post of Fort Lyon, that they had in their possession, and were willing to deliver up, some white captives they had purchased of other Indians. Major Wynkoop, with a force of over 100 men, visited these Indians and received the white captives. On his return he was accompanied by a number of the chiefs and leading men of the Indians, whom he had invited to visit Denver for the purpose of conferring with the authorities there in regard to keeping peace. Among them were Black Kettle and White Antelope of the Cheyennes, and some chiefs of the Arapahoes. The council was held and these chiefs stated that they were very friendly to the whites, and always had been, and that they desired peace. Governor Evans and Colonel Chivington, the commander of that military district, advised them to

repair to Fort Lyon and submit to whatever terms the military commander there should impose. This was done by the Indians, who were treated somewhat as prisoners of war, receiving rations, and being obliged to remain within certain bounds.

A northern band of the Cheyennes, known as the Dog Soldiers, had been guilty of acts of hostility; but all the testimony goes to prove that they had no connexion with Black Kettle's band, but acted in spite of his authority and influence. Black Kettle and his band denied all connexion with or responsibility for the Dog Soldiers, and Left Hand and his band of Arapahoes were equally friendly.

These Indians, at the suggestion of Governor Evans and Colonel Chivington, repaired to Fort Lyon and placed themselves under the protection of Major Wynkoop. They were led to believe that they were regarded in the light of friendly Indians, and would be treated as such so long as they conducted themselves quietly.

The treatment extended to those Indians by Major Wynkoop does not seem to have satisfied those in authority there, and for some cause, which does not appear, he was removed, and Major Scott J. Anthony was assigned to the command of Fort Lyon; but even Major Anthony seems to have found it difficult at first to pursue any different course toward the Indians he found there. They were entirely within the power of the military. Major Anthony, having demanded their arms, which they surrendered to him, they conducted themselves quietly, and in every way manifested a disposition to remain at peace with the whites. For a time even he continued issuing rations to them as Major Wynkoop had done; but it was determined by Major Anthony, (whether upon his own motion or as the suggestion of others does not appear) to pursue a different course towards these friendly Indians. They were called together and told that rations could no longer be issued to them, and they had better go where they could obtain subsistence by hunting. At the suggestion of Major Anthony (and from one in his position a suggestion was the equivalent to a command) these Indians went to place on Sand Creek, about thirty-five miles from Fort Lyon, and there established their camp, their arms being restored to them. He told them that he then had no authority to make peace with them; but in case he received such authority he would inform them of it. In his testimony he says:

"I told them they might go back on Sand Creek, or between there and the headwaters of the Smoky Hill, and remain there until I received instructions from the department headquarters, from General [Samuel R.] Curtis; and that in case I did receive any authority to make peace with them I would go right over and let them know it. I did not state to them that I would give them notice in case we intended to attack them. They went away with that understanding, and in case I received instructions from department headquarters I was to let them know it."

To render the Indians less apprehensive of any danger, One Eye, a Cheyenne chief, was allowed to remain with them to obtain information for the use of the military authorities. He was employed at $125 a month, and several times brought to Major Anthony, at Fort Lyon, information of proposed movements of other, hostile bands. Jack Smith, a half-breed son of John S. Smith, an Indian interpreter, employed by the government, was also there for the same purpose. A U.S. soldier was allowed to remain there, and two days before the massacre Mr. Smith, the interpreter, was permitted to go there with goods to trade with the Indians. Everything practicable seems to have been done to remove from the minds of the Indians any fear of approaching danger; and when Colonel Chivington commenced his movement he took all of the precautions in his power to prevent these Indians learning of his approach. For some days all travel on that route was forcibly stopped by him, not even the mail being allowed to pass. On the morning of 28 November he appeared at Fort Lyon with over 700 mounted men and two pieces of artillery. One of his first acts was throw a guard around the post to prevent any one from leaving it. At this place Major Anthony joined him with 125 men and two pieces of artillery.

That night, the entire party started from Fort Lyon, and, by a forced march, arrived at the Indian camp, on Sand creek, shortly after daybreak. The Indian camp consisted of about 100 lodges of Cheyennes, under Black Kettle, and from 8 to 10 lodges of Arapahoes under Left Hand. It is estimated that each lodge contained five or more persons, and that more than one-half were women and children.

Upon observing the approach of the soldiers, Black Kettle, the head chief, ran up to the top of his lodge an American flag, which had been presented to him some years before by Commissioner [of Indian Affairs Alfred B.] Greenwood, with a small white flag under it, as he had been advised to do in case he met with any troops on the prairies. Mr. Smith, the interpreter, supposing that they might be strange troops, unaware of the character of the Indi-

ans encamped there, advanced from his lodge to meet them, but was fired upon, and returned to his lodge.

And then the scene of murder and barbarity began. Men, women, and children were indiscriminately slaughtered. In a few minutes all the Indians were flying over the plain in terror and confusion. A few who endeavored to hide themselves under the bank of the creek were surrounded and shot down in cold blood, offering but feeble resistance. From the sucking babe to the old warrior, all who were overtaken were deliberately murdered. Not content with killing women and children, who were incapable of offering any resistance, the soldiers indulged in acts of barbarity of the most revolting character; such, it is to be hoped, as never before disgraced the acts of men claiming to be civilized. No attempt was made by the officers to restrain the savage cruelty of the men under their command, but they stood by and witnessed these acts without one word of reproof, if they did not incite their commission. For more than two hours the work of murder and barbarity was continued, until more than one hundred dead bodies, three fourths of them women and children, lay on the plain as evidences of the fiendish malignity and cruelty of the officers who had sedulously and carefully plotted the massacre, and of the soldiers who had so faithfully acted out the spirit of their officers.

It is difficult to believe that beings in the form of men, and disgracing the uniform of United States soldiers and officers, could commit or countenance the commission of such acts of cruelty and barbarity as are detailed in the testimony, but which your committee will not specify in the report. It is true that there seems to have existed among the people inhabiting the region of country a hostile feeling towards the Indians. Some of the Indians had committed acts of hostility towards the whites; but no effort seems to have been made by the authorities there to prevent these hostilities, other than by the commission of even worse acts. The hatred of the whites to the Indians would seem to have been inflamed and excited to the utmost; the bodies of persons killed at a great distance, whether by Indians or not, . . . were brought to the capital of the Territory and exposed to the public gaze for the purpose of inflaming still more the already excited feeling of the people. Their cupidity was appealed to, for the governor in a proclamation calls upon all, "either individually or in such parties as they may organize," "to kill and destroy as enemies of the country, whatever they may be found, all such hostile Indians," authorizing them to "hold to their own private use and benefit all the property of said hostile Indians that they may capture." What Indians he would ever term friendly it is impossible to tell. His testimony before your committee was characterized by such prevarication and shuffling as has been shown by no witness they have examined during the four years they have been engaged in their investigations; and for the evident purpose of avoiding admission that he was fully aware that the Indians massacred so brutally at Sand Creek, were then, and had been, actuated by the most friendly feelings towards the whites, and had done all in their power to restrain those less friendly disposed.

The testimony of Major Anthony, who succeeded an officer disposed to treat these Indians with justice and humanity, is sufficient of itself to show how unprovoked and unwarranted was this massacre. He testifies that he found these Indians in the neighborhood of Fort Lyon when he assumed command of that post; that they professed their friendliness to the whites, and their willingness to do whatever he demanded of them; that they delivered their arms up to him; and they went to and encamped upon the place designated by him; that they gave him information from time to time of acts of hostility which were meditated by other and hostile bands, and in every way conducted themselves properly and peaceably, and yet he says it was fear and not principle which prevented his killing them while they were completely in his power. And when Colonel Chivington appeared at Fort Lyon, on his mission of murder and barbarity, Major Anthony made haste to accompany him with men and artillery, although Colonel Chivington had no authority whatever over him.

As to Colonel Chivington, your committee can hardly find fitting terms to describe his conduct. Wearing the uniform of the United States, which should be the emblem of justice and humanity; holding the important position of commander of a military district, and therefore having the honor of the government to that extent in his keeping, he deliberately executed a foul and dastardly massacre which would have disgraced the veriest savage among those who were the victims of his cruelty. Having full knowledge of their friendly character, having himself been instrumental to some extent in placing them in their position of fancied security, he took advantage of their inapprehension and defenceless condition to gratify the worst passions

that ever cursed the heart of man. It is thought by some that desire for political preferment prompted him to this cowardly act; that he supposed that by pandering to the inflamed passions of an excited population he could recommend himself to their regard and consideration. Others think it was to avoid being sent where there was more of danger and hard service to be performed; that he was willing to get up a show of hostility on the part of the Indians by committing himself acts which savages themselves would never premeditate. Whatever may have been his motive, it is to be hoped that the authority of this government will never again be disgraced by acts such as he and those acting with him have been guilty of committing.

There were hostile Indians not far distant, against which Colonel Chivington could have led the force under his command. Major Anthony testifies that but three of four days' march from his post were several hundreds of Indians, generally believed to be engaged in acts of hostility towards the whites. And he deliberately testifies that only the fear of them prevented him from killing those who were friendly and entirely within his reach and control. It is true that to reach them required some days of hard marching. It was not to be expected that they could be surprised as easily as those on Sand creek; and the warriors among them were almost, if not quite, as numerous as the soldiers under the control of Colonel Chivington. Whatever influence this may have had upon Colonel Chivington, the truth is that he surprised and murdered in cold blood, the unsuspecting men, women, and children on Sand Creek, who had every reason to believe they were under the protection of the United States authorities, and then returned to Denver and boasted of the brave deeds he and the men under his command had performed.

The Congress of the United States, at its last session, authorized the appointment of a commission to investigate all matters relating to the administration of Indian Affairs within the limits of the United States. Your committee most sincerely trust that the result of their inquiry will be the adoption of measures which will render impossible the employment of officers, civil and military, such as have heretofore made the administration of Indian Affairs in this country a byword and [of] reproach.

In conclusion, your committee are of the opinion that for the purpose of vindicating the cause of justice and upholding the honor of the nation, prompt and energetic measures should be at once taken to remove from office those who have thus disgraced the government by whom they are employed, and to punish, as their crimes deserve, those who have been guilty of these brutal and cowardly acts.

Treaty with the Kiowa, Comanche, and Apache

Oct. 21, 1867. | 15 Stats., 589. | Ratified, July 25, 1868. | Proclaimed Aug. 25 1868.

Articles of a treaty concluded at the Council Camp on Medicine Lodge Creek, seventy miles south of Fort Larned, in the State of Kansas, on the twenty-first day of October, eighteen hundred and sixty-seven, by and between the United States of America, represented by its commissioners duly appointed thereto to-wit: Nathaniel G. Taylor, William S. Harney, C. C. Augur, Alfred S. [H.] Terry, John B. Sanborn, Samuel F. Tappan, and J. B. Henderson, of the one part, and the Kiowa, Comanche, and Apache Indians, represented by their chiefs and headmen duly authorized and empowered to act for the body of the people of said tribes (the names of said chiefs and headmen being hereto subscribed) of the other part, witness:

Whereas, on the twenty-first day of October, eighteen hundred and sixty-seven, a treaty of peace was made and entered into at the Council Camp, on Medicine Lodge Creek, seventy miles south of Fort Larned, in the State of Kansas, by and between the United States of America, by its commissioners Nathaniel G. Taylor, William S. Harney, C. C. Augur, Alfred H. Terry, John B. Sanborn, Samuel F. Tappan, and J. B. Henderson, of the one part, and the Kiowa and Comanche tribes of Indians, of the Upper Arkansas, by and through their chiefs and headmen whose names are subscribed thereto, of the other part, reference being had to said treaty; and whereas, since the making and signing of said treaty, at a council held at said camp on this day, the chiefs and headmen of the Apache nation or tribe of Indians express to the commissioners on the part of the United States, as aforesaid, a wish to be confederated with the said Kiowa and Comanche tribes, and to be placed, in every respect, upon an equal footing with said tribes; and whereas, at a council held at the same place and on the same day, with the chiefs and headmen of the said Kiowa and Comanche Tribes,

they consent to the confederation of the said Apache tribe, as desired by it, upon the terms and conditions hereinafter set forth in this supplementary treaty: Now, therefore, it is hereby stipulated and agreed by and between the aforesaid commissioners, on the part of the United States, and the chiefs and headmen of the Kiowa and Comanche tribes, and, also, the chiefs and headmen of the said Apache tribe, as follows, to-wit:

ARTICLE 1.

The said Apache tribe of Indians agree to confederate and become incorporated with the said Kiowa and Comanche Indians, and to accept as their permanent home the reservation described in the aforesaid treaty with said Kiowa and Comanche tribes, concluded as aforesaid at this place, and they pledge themselves to make no permanent settlement at any place, nor on any lands, outside of said reservation.

ARTICLE 2.

The Kiowa and Comanche tribes, on their part, agree that all the benefits and advantages arising from the employment of physicians, teachers, carpenters, millers, engineers, farmers, and blacksmiths, agreed to be furnished under the provisions of their said treaty, together with all the advantages to be derived from the construction of agency buildings, warehouses, mills, and other structures, and also from the establishment of schools upon their said reservation, shall be jointly and equally shared and enjoyed by the said Apache Indians, as though they had been originally a part of said tribes; and they further agree that all other benefits arising from said treaty shall be jointly and equally shared as aforesaid.

ARTICLE 3.

The United States, on its part, agrees that clothing and other articles named in Article X. of said original treaty, together with all money or other annuities agreed to be furnished under any of the provisions of said treaty, to the Kiowa and Comanches, shall be shared equally by the Apaches. In all cases where specific articles of clothing are agreed to be furnished to the Kiowas and Comanches, similar articles shall be furnished to the Apaches, and a separate census of the Apaches shall be annually taken and returned by the agent, as provided for the other tribes. And the United States further agrees, in consideration of the incorporation of said Apaches, to increase the annual appropriation of money, as provided for in Article X. of said treaty, from twenty-five thousand to thirty thousand dollars; and the latter amount shall be annually appropriated, for the period therein named, for the use and benefit of said three tribes, confederated as herein declared; and the clothing and other annuities, which may from time to time be furnished to the Apaches, shall be based upon the census of the three tribes, annually to be taken by the agent, and shall be separately marked, forwarded, and delivered to them at the agency house, to be built under the provisions of said original treaty.

ARTICLE 4.

In consideration of the advantages conferred by this supplementary treaty upon the Apache tribe of Indians, they agree to observe and faithfully comply with all the stipulations and agreements entered into by the Kiowas and Comanches in said original treaty. They agree, in the same manner, to keep the peace toward the whites and all other persons under the jurisdiction of the United States, and to do and perform all other things enjoined upon said tribes by the provisions of said treaty; and they hereby give up and forever relinquish to the United States all rights, privileges, and grants now vested in them, or intended to be transferred to them, by the treaty between the United States and the Cheyenne and Arapahoe tribes of Indians, concluded at the camp on the Little Arkansas River, in the State of Kansas, on the fourteenth day of October, one thousand eight hundred and sixty-five, and also by the supplementary treaty, concluded at the same place on the seventeenth day of the same month, between the United States, of the one part, and the Cheyenne, Arapahoe, and Apache tribes, of the other part. In testimony of all which, the said parties have hereunto set their hands and seals at the place and on the day hereinbefore stated.

N. G. Taylor, [SEAL.]
President of Indian Commission.
Wm. S. Harney, [SEAL.]
Brevet Major-General, Commissioner, &c.
C. C. Augur, [SEAL.]
Brevet Major-General.
Alfred H. Terry, [SEAL.]
Brevet Major-General and Brigadier-General.
John B. Sanborn. [SEAL.]
Samuel F. Tappan. [SEAL.]
J. B. Henderson. [SEAL.]

On the part of the Kiowas:

Satanka, or Sitting bear, his x mark, [SEAL.]
Sa-tan-ta, or White Bear, his x mark, [SEAL.]
Wah-toh-konk, or Black Eagle, his x mark, [SEAL.]

Ton-a-en-ko, or Kicking Eagle, his x mark, [SEAL.]
Fish-e-more, or Stinking Saddle, his x mark, [SEAL.]
Ma-ye-tin, or Woman's Heart, his x mark, [SEAL.]
Sa-tim-gear, or Stumbling Bear, his x mark, [SEAL.]
Sa-pa-ga, or One Bear, his x mark, [SEAL.]
Cor-beau, or The Crow, his x mark, [SEAL.]
Sa-ta-more, or Bear Lying Down, his x mark,
    [SEAL.]

On the part of the Comanches:

Parry-wah-say-men, or Ten Bears, his x mark,
    [SEAL.]
Tep-pe-navon, or Painted Lips, his x mark, [SEAL.]
To-she-wi, or Silver Brooch, his x mark, [SEAL.]
Cear-chi-neka, or Standing Feather, his x mark,
    [SEAL.]
Ho-we-ar, or Gap in the Woods, his x mark, [SEAL.]
Tir-ha-yah-gua-hip, or Horse's Back, his x mark,
    [SEAL.]
Es-a-man-a-ca, or Wolf's Name, his x mark, [SEAL.]
Ah-te-es-ta, or Little Horn, his x mark, [SEAL.]
Pooh-yah-to-yeh-be, or Iron Mountain, his x mark,
    [SEAL.]
Sad-dy-yo, or Dog Fat, his x mark, [SEAL.]

On the part of the Apaches:

Mah-vip-pah, Wolf's Sleeve, his x mark, [SEAL.]
Kon-zhon-ta-co, Poor Bear, his x mark, [SEAL.]
Cho-se-ta, or Bad Back, his x mark, [SEAL.]
Nah-tan, or Brave Man, his x mark, [SEAL.]
Ba-zhe-ech, Iron Shirt, his x mark, [SEAL.]
Til-la-ka, or White Horn, his x mark, [SEAL.]

Attest:

Ashton S. H. White, secretary.
Geo. B. Willis, reporter.
Philip McCusker, interpreter.
John D. Howland, clerk Indian Commission.
Sam'l S. Smoot, United States surveyor.
A. A. Taylor.
J. H. Leavenworth, United States Indian agent.
Thos. Murphy, superintendent Indian affairs.
Joel H. Elliott, major, Seventh U.S. Cavalry.

Treaty with the Navajo

This treaty with the Navajo outlined their land holdings after the United States had attempted to remove the entire nation and break up the same lands less than a decade earlier. The removal caused so much suffering that public opinion demanded the Navajos be allowed to return home on lands guaranteed by law. The Navajos continue to live on these lands today, which comprise the largest and most populous reservation within the United States.

June 1, 1868. | 15 Stats., p. 667. | Ratified July 25, 1868. | Proclaimed Aug. 12, 1868.

Articles of a treaty and agreement made and entered into at Fort Sumner, New Mexico, on the first day of June, one thousand eight hundred and sixty-eight, by and between the United States, represented by its commissioners, Lieutenant-General W. T. Sherman and Colonel Samuel F. Tappan, of the one part, and the Navajo Nation or tribe of Indians, represented by their chiefs and head-men, duly authorized and empowered to act for the whole people of said nation or tribe, (the names of said chiefs and head-men being hereto subscribed,) of the other part, witness:

ARTICLE 1.

From this day forward all war between the parties to this agreement shall forever cease. The Government of the United States desires peace, and its honor is hereby pledged to keep it. The Indians desire peace, and they now pledge their honor to keep it.

. . .

ARTICLE 2.

The United States agrees that the following district of country, to wit: bounded on the north by the 37th degree of north latitude, south by an east and west line passing through the site of old Fort Defiance, in Cañon Bonito, east by the parallel of longitude which, if prolonged south, would pass through old Fort Lyon, or the Ojo-de-oso, Bear Spring, and west by a parallel of longitude about 109λ 30φ west of Greenwich, provided it embraces the outlet of the Cañon-de-Chilly, which cañon is to be all included in this reservation, shall be, and the same is hereby, set apart for the use and occupation of the Navajo tribe of Indians, and for such other friendly tribes or individual Indians as from time to time they may be willing, with the consent of the United States, to admit among them; and the United States agrees that no persons except those herein so authorized to do, and except such officers, soldiers, agents, and employees of the Government, or of the Indians, as may be authorized to enter upon Indian reservations in discharge of duties imposed by law, or the orders of the President, shall ever be permitted to pass over, settle upon, or reside in, the territory described in this article. . . .

ARTICLE 9.

In consideration of the advantages and benefits conferred by this treaty, and the many pledges of friendship by the United States, the tribes who are parties to this agreement hereby stipulate that they

will relinquish all right to occupy any territory outside their reservation, as herein defined, but retain the right to hunt on any unoccupied lands contiguous to their reservation, so long as the large game may range thereon in such numbers as to justify the chase; and they, the said Indians, further expressly agree:

1st. That they will make no opposition to the construction of railroads now being built or hereafter to be built across the continent.

2d. That they will not interfere with the peaceful construction of any railroad not passing over their reservation as herein defined.

3d. That they will not attack any persons at home or travelling, nor molest or disturb any wagon-trains, coaches, mules, or cattle belonging to the people of the United States, or to persons friendly therewith.

4th. That they will never capture or carry off from the settlements women or children.

5th. They will never kill or scalp white men, nor attempt to do them harm.

6th. They will not in future oppose the construction of railroads, wagon-roads, mail stations, or other works of utility or necessity which may be ordered or permitted by the laws of the United States; but should such roads or other works be constructed on the lands of their reservation, the Government will pay the tribe whatever amount of damage may be assessed by three disinterested commissioners to be appointed by the President for that purpose, one of said commissioners to be a chief or head-men of the tribe.

7th. They will make no opposition to the military posts or roads now established, or that may be established, not in violation of treaties heretofore made or hereafter to be made with any of the Indian tribes.

ARTICLE 10.

No future treaty for the cession of any portion or part of the reservation herein described, which may be held in common, shall be of any validity or force against said Indians unless agreed to and executed by at least three-fourths of all the adult male Indians occupying or interested in the same; and no cession by the tribe shall be understood or construed in such manner as to deprive, without his consent, any individual member of the tribe of his rights to any tract of land selected by him as provided in article [5] of this treaty.

ARTICLE 11.

The Navajos also hereby agree that at any time after the signing of these presents [legal instruments] they will proceed in such manner as may be required of them by the agent, or by the officer charged with their removal, to the reservation herein provided for, the United States paying for their subsistence en route, and providing a reasonable amount of transportation for the sick and feeble.

ARTICLE 12.

It is further agreed by and between the parties to this agreement that the sum of one hundred and fifty thousand dollars appropriated or to be appropriated shall be disbursed as follows, subject to any condition provided in the law, to wit:

1st. The actual cost of the removal of the tribe from the Bosque Redondo reservation to the reservation, say fifty thousand dollars.

2d. The purchase of fifteen thousand sheep and goats, at a cost not to exceed thirty thousand dollars.

3d. The purchase of five hundred beef cattle and a million pounds of corn, to be collected and held at the military post nearest the reservation, subject to the orders of the agent, for the relief of the needy during the coming winter.

4th. The balance, if any, of the appropriation to be invested for the maintenance of the Indians pending their removal, in such manner as the agent who is with them may determine.

5th. The removal of this tribe to be made under the supreme control and direction of the military commander of the Territory of New Mexico, and when completed, the management of the tribe to revert to the proper agent.

ARTICLE 13.

The tribe herein named, by their representatives, parties to this treaty, agree to make the reservation herein described their permanent home, and they will not as a tribe make any permanent settlement elsewhere, reserving the right to hunt on the lands adjoining the said reservation formerly called theirs, subject to the modifications named in this treaty and the orders of the commander of the department in which said reservation may be for the

time being; and it is further agreed and understood by the parties to this treaty, that if any Navajo Indian or Indians shall leave the reservation herein described to settle elsewhere, he or they shall forfeit all the rights, privileges, and annuities conferred by the terms of this treaty; and it is further agreed by the parties to this treaty, that they will do all they can to induce Indians now away from reservations set apart for the exclusive use and occupation of the Indians, leading a nomadic life, or engaged in war against the people of the United States, to abandon such a life and settle permanently in one of the territorial reservations set apart for the exclusive use and occupation of the Indians. . . .

Resource

Treaty with the Navajo. Available at: http://digital.library.okstate.edu/kappler/ Vol2/treaties/nav1015.htm. Accessed January 20, 2007.Fort Laramie Treaty

Fort Laramie Treaty (1868)

Signed in the Wyoming Territory on November 6, 1868, the Fort Laramie Treaty was perhaps the most significant treaty between the United States and the Sioux. The two sides failed to maintain the terms of the treaty, however, resulting in the outbreak of the Sioux War just eight years later.

ARTICLES OF A TREATY MADE AND CONCLUDED BY AND BETWEEN Lieutenant General William T. Sherman, General William S. Harney, General Alfred H. Terry, General O. O. Augur, J. B. Henderson, Nathaniel G. Taylor, John G. Sanborn, and Samuel F. Tappan, duly appointed commissioners on the part of the United States, and the different bands of the Sioux Nation of Indians, by their chiefs and headmen, whose names are hereto subscribed, they being duly authorized to act in the premises.

ARTICLE I

From this day forward all war between the parties to this agreement shall forever cease. The government of the United States desires peace, and its honor is hereby pledged to keep it. The Indians desire peace, and they now pledge their honor to maintain it.

If bad men among the whites, or among other people subject to the authority of the United States, shall commit any wrong upon the person or property of the Indians, the United States will, upon proof made to the agent, and forwarded to the Commissioner of Indian Affairs at Washington city, proceed at once to cause the offender to be arrested and punished according to the laws of the United States, and also reimburse the injured person for the loss sustained.

If bad men among the Indians shall commit a wrong or depredation upon the person or property of any one, white, black, or Indian, subject to the authority of the United States, and at peace therewith, the Indians herein named solemnly agree that they will, upon proof made to their agent, and notice by him, deliver up the wrongdoer to the United States, to be tried and punished according to its laws, and, in case they willfully refuse so to do, the person injured shall be reimbursed for his loss from the annuities, or other moneys due or to become due to them under this or other treaties made with the United States; and the President, on advising with the Commissioner of Indian Affairs, shall prescribe such rules and regulations for ascertaining damages under the provisions of this article as in his judgment may be proper, but no one sustaining loss while violating the provisions of this treaty, or the laws of the United States, shall be reimbursed therefor.

ARTICLE II

The United States agrees that the following district of country, to wit, viz: commencing on the east bank of the Missouri river where the 46th parallel of north latitude crosses the same, thence along low-water mark down said east bank to a point opposite where the northern line of the State of Nebraska strikes the river, thence west across said river, and along the northern line of Nebraska to the 104th degree of longitude west from Greenwich, thence north on said meridian to a point where the 46th parallel of north latitude intercepts the same, thence due east along said parallel to the place of beginning; and in addition thereto, all existing reservations of the east back of said river, shall be and the same is, set apart for the absolute and undisturbed use and occupation of the Indians herein named, and for such other friendly tribes or individual Indians as from time to time they may be willing, with the consent of the United States, to admit amongst them; and the United States now solemnly agrees that no persons, except those herein designated and authorized so to do, and except such officers, agents, and employees of the government as may be authorized to enter upon Indian reservations in discharge of duties enjoined by law, shall ever be permitted to pass over,

settle upon, or reside in the territory described in this article, or in such territory as may be added to this reservation for the use of said Indians, and henceforth they will and do hereby relinquish all claims or right in and to any portion of the United States or Territories, except such as is embraced within the limits aforesaid, and except as hereinafter provided.

. . .

ARTICLE XII

No treaty for the cession of any portion or part of the reservation herein described which may be held in common, shall be of any validity or force as against the said Indians unless executed and signed by at least three-fourths of all the adult male Indians occupying or interested in the same, and no cession by the tribe shall be understood or construed in such manner as to deprive, without his consent, any individual member of the tribe of his rights to any tract of land selected by him . . .

. . .

ARTICLE XVI

The United States hereby agrees and stipulates that the country north of the North Platte river and east of the summits of the Big Horn mountains shall be held and considered to be unceded Indian territory, and also stipulates and agrees that no white person or persons shall be permitted to settle upon or occupy any portion of the same; or without the consent of the Indians, first had and obtained, to pass through the same; and it is further agreed by the United States, that within ninety days after the conclusion of peace with all the bands of the Sioux nation, the military posts now established in the territory in this article named shall be abandoned, and that the road leading to them and by them to the settlements in the Territory of Montana shall be closed.

Canadian Treaties Numbers 1 through 11

Canada negotiated eleven treaties with Native peoples between 1871 and 1921, in sequential numbers, all specifying which lands were to be ceded, the locations and sizes of reserves (often with individual or family allotted land specified), and small annuities, guarantees of schools, farm equipment, and other equipment, as well as the prohibition of liquor sales and presents. Some of the treaties also reserved hunting and fishing rights. The treaties were rather similar except for the specific areas ceded and reserved. The first of the following treaties lists all the common elements, while the next ten list only the Native peoples involved and the lands ceded. Note that not all of the treaties are cited here, but those not cited were similar except for the groups of people and territories affected. The treaties seem to have been printed on a common form.

TREATIES 1 AND 2 BETWEEN HER MAJESTY THE QUEEN AND THE CHIPPEWA AND CREE INDIANS OF MANITOBA AND COUNTRY ADJACENT WITH ADHESIONS

Treaty No. 1

ARTICLES OF A TREATY made and concluded this third day of August in the year of Our Lord one thousand eight hundred and seventy-one, between Her Most Gracious Majesty the Queen of Great Britain and Ireland by Her Commissioner, Wemyss M. Simpson, Esquire, of the one part, and the Chippewa and Swampy Cree Tribes of Indians, inhabitants of the country within the limits hereinafter defined and described, by their Chiefs chosen and named as hereinafter mentioned, of the other part.

Whereas all the Indians inhabiting the said country have pursuant to an appointment made by the said Commissioner, been convened at a meeting at the Stone Fort, otherwise called Lower Fort Garry, to deliberate upon certain matters of interest to Her Most Gracious Majesty, of the one part, and to the said Indians of the other, and whereas the said Indians have been notified and informed by Her Majesty's said Commissioner that it is the desire of Her Majesty to open up to settlement and immigration a tract of country bounded and described as hereinafter mentioned, and to obtain the consent thereto of her Indian subjects inhabiting the said tract, and to make a treaty and arrangements with them so that there may be peace and good will between them and Her Majesty, and that they may know and be assured of what allowance they are to count upon and receive year by year from Her Majesty's bounty and benevolence.

The Chippewa and Swampy Cree Tribes of Indians and all other the Indians inhabiting the district hereinafter described and defined do hereby cede, release, surrender and yield up to Her Majesty the Queen and successors forever all the lands included within the following limits, that is to say: Beginning at the international boundary line near its junction with the Lake of the Woods, at a point due north from the centre of Roseau Lake; thence to run due north to the centre of Roseau Lake; thence northward to the centre of

White Mouth Lake, otherwise called White Mud Lake; thence by the middle of the lake and the middle of the river issuing therefrom to the mouth thereof in Winnipeg River; thence by the Winnipeg River to its mouth; thence westwardly, including all the islands near the south end of the lake, across the lake to the mouth of Drunken River; thence westwardly to a point on Lake Manitoba half way between Oak Point and the mouth of Swan Creek; thence across Lake Manitoba in a line due west to its western shore; thence in a straight line to the crossing of the rapids on the Assiniboine; thence due south to the international boundary line; and thence eastwardly by the said line to the place of beginning. To have and to hold the same to Her said Majesty the Queen and Her successors for ever; and Her Majesty the Queen hereby agrees and undertakes to lay aside and reserve for the sole and exclusive use of the Indians the following tracts of land, that is to say: For the use of the Indians belonging to the band of which Henry Prince, otherwise called Mis-koo-ke-new is the Chief, so much of land on both sides of the Red River, beginning at the south line of St. Peter's Parish, as will furnish one hundred and sixty acres for each family of five, or in that proportion for larger or smaller families; and for the use of the Indians of whom Na-sha-ke-penais, Na-na-wa-nanaw, Ke-we-tayash and Wa-ko-wush are the Chiefs, so much land on the Roseau River as will furnish one hundred and sixty acres for each family of five, or in that proportion for larger or smaller families, beginning from the mouth of the river; and for the use of the Indians of which Ka-ke-ka-penais is the Chief, so much land on the Winnipeg River above Fort Alexander as will furnish one hundred and sixty acres for each family of five, or in that proportion for larger or smaller families, beginning at a distance of a mile or thereabout above the Fort; and for the use of the Indians of whom Oo-za-we-kwun is Chief, so much land on the south and east side of the Assiniboine, about twenty miles above the Portage, as will furnish one hundred and sixty acres for each family of five, or in that proportion for larger or smaller families, reserving also a further tract enclosing said reserve to comprise an equivalent to twenty-five square miles of equal breadth, to be laid out round the reserve, it being understood, however, that if, at the date of the execution of this treaty, there are any settlers within the bounds of any lands reserved by any band, Her Majesty reserves the right to deal with such settlers as She shall deem just, so as not to diminish the extent of land allotted to the Indians.

And with a view to show the satisfaction of Her Majesty with the behaviour and good conduct of Her Indians parties to this treaty, She hereby, through Her Commissioner, makes them a present of three dollars for each Indian man, woman and child belonging to the bands here represented.

And further, Her Majesty agrees to maintain a school on each reserve hereby made whenever the Indians of the reserve should desire it.

Within the boundary of Indian reserves, until otherwise enacted by the proper legislative authority, no intoxicating liquor shall be allowed to be introduced or sold, and all laws now in force or hereafter to be enacted to preserve Her Majesty's Indian subjects inhabiting the reserves or living elsewhere from the evil influence of the use of intoxicating liquors shall be strictly enforced.

Memorandum of things outside of the Treaty which were promised at the Treaty at the Lower Fort, signed the third day of August, A.D. 1871.

- *For each Chief who signed the treaty, a dress distinguishing him as Chief.*
- *For braves and for councillors of each Chief a dress; it being supposed that the braves and councillors will be two for each Chief.*
- *For each Chief, except Yellow Quill, a buggy.*
- *For the braves and councillors of each Chief, except Yellow Quill, a buggy.*
- *In lieu of a yoke of oxen for each reserve, a bull for each, and a cow for each Chief; a boar for each reserve and a sow for each Chief, and a male and female of each kind of animal raised by farmers, these when the Indians are prepared to receive them.*
- *A plough and a harrow for each settler cultivating the ground.*
- *These animals and their issue to be Government property, but to be allowed for the use of the Indians, under the superintendence and control of the Indian Commissioner.*
- *The buggies to be the property of the Indians to whom they are given.*
- *The above contains an inventory of the terms concluded with the Indians.*

Treaty No. 2
ARTICLES OF TREATY made and concluded this twenty-first day of August, in the year of Our

Lord one thousand eight hundred and seventy-one, between Her Most Gracious Majesty the Queen of Great Britain and Ireland, by Her Commissioner Wemyss M. Simpson, Esquire, of the one part, and the Chippewa Tribe of Indians, inhabitants of the country within the limits hereinafter defined and described, by their Chiefs chosen and named as hereinafter mentioned, of the other part.

The Chippewa Tribe of Indians and all other Indians inhabiting the district hereinafter described and defined do hereby cede, release, surrender and yield up to Her Majesty the Queen, and Her successors forever, all the lands included within the following limits, that is to say:

All that tract of country lying partly to the north and partly to the west of a tract of land ceded to Her Majesty the Queen by the Indians inhabiting the Province of Manitoba, and certain adjacent localities, under the terms of a treaty made at Lower Fort Garry on the third day of August last past, the land now intended to be ceded and surrendered being particularly described as follows, that is to say: Beginning at the mouth of Winnipeg River, on the north line of the lands ceded by said treaty; thence running along the eastern shore of Lake Winnipeg northwardly as far as the mouth of Beren's River; thence across said lake to its western shore, at the north bank of the mouth of the Little Saskatchewan or Dauphin River; thence up said stream and along the northern and western shores thereof, and of St. Martin's Lake, and along the north bank of the stream flowing into St. Martin's Lake from Lake Manitoba by the general course of such stream to such last-mentioned lake; thence by the eastern and northern shores of Lake Manitoba to the mouth of the Waterhen River; thence by the eastern and northern shores of said river up stream to the northernmost extremity of a small lake known as Waterhen Lake; thence in a line due west to and across lake Winnepegosis; thence in a straight line to the most northerly waters forming the source of the Shell River; thence to a point west of the same two miles distant from the river, measuring at right angles thereto; thence by a line parallel with the Shell River to its mouth, and thence crossing the Assiniboine River and running parallel thereto and two miles distant therefrom, and to the westward thereof, to a point opposite Fort Ellice; thence in a south-westwardly course to the north-western point of the Moose Mountains; thence by a line due south to the United States frontier; thence by the frontier eastwardly to the westward line of said tract ceded by treaty as aforesaid; thence bounded thereby by the west, northwest and north lines of said tract, to the place of beginning, at the mouth of Winnipeg River.

Resource

Treaties 1 and 2. Available at: http://www .ainc-inac.gc.ca/pr/trts/trty1–2_e.html. Accessed January 20, 2007.

Treaty No. 3

BETWEEN HER MAJESTY THE QUEEN AND THE SAULTEAUX TRIBE OF THE OJIBBEWAY INDIANS AT THE NORTHWEST ANGLE ON THE LAKE OF THE WOODS WITH ADHESIONS

ARTICLES OF A TREATY made and concluded this third day of October, in the year of Our Lord one thousand eight hundred and seventy-three, between Her Most Gracious Majesty the Queen of Great Britain and Ireland, by Her Commissioners, the Honourable Alexander Morris, Lieutenant-Governor of the Province of Manitoba and the North-west Territories; Joseph Alfred Norbert Provencher and Simon James Dawson, of the one part, and the Saulteaux Tribe of the Ojibway Indians, inhabitants of the country within the limits hereinafter defined and described, by their Chiefs chosen and named as hereinafter mentioned, of the other part.

The Saulteaux Tribe of the Ojibbeway Indians and all other the Indians inhabiting the district hereinafter described and defined, do hereby cede, release, surrender and yield up to the Government of the Dominion of Canada for Her Majesty the Queen and Her successors forever, all their rights, titles and privileges whatsoever, to the lands included within the following limits, that is to say:-

Commencing at a point on the Pigeon River route where the international boundary line between the Territories of Great Britain and the United States intersects the height of land separating the waters running to Lake Superior from those flowing to Lake Winnipeg; thence northerly, westerly and easterly along the height of land aforesaid, following its sinuosities, whatever their course may be, to the point at which the said height of land meets the summit of the watershed from which the streams flow to Lake Nepigon; thence northerly and westerly, or whatever may be its course, along the ridge separating the waters of the Nepigon and the Winnipeg to the height of land dividing the waters of the Albany and the

Winnipeg; thence westerly and north-westerly along the height of land dividing the waters flowing to Hudson's Bay by the Albany or other rivers from those running to English River and the Winnipeg to a point on the said height of land bearing north forty-five degrees east from Fort Alexander, at the mouth of the Winnipeg; thence south forty-five degrees west to Fort Alexander, at the mouth of the Winnipeg; thence southerly along the eastern bank of the Winnipeg to the mouth of White Mouth River; thence southerly by the line described as in that part forming the eastern boundary of the tract surrendered by the Chippewa and Swampy Cree tribes of Indians to Her Majesty on the third of August, one thousand eight hundred and seventy-one, namely, by White Mouth River to White Mouth Lake, and thence on a line having the general bearing of White Mouth River to the forty-ninth parallel of north latitude; thence by the forty-ninth parallel of north latitude to the Lake of the Woods, and from thence by the international boundary line to the place beginning.

The tract comprised within the lines above described, embracing an area of fifty-five thousand square miles, be the same more or less. To have and to hold the same to Her Majesty the Queen, and Her successors forever.

Resource
Treaty 3. Available at: http://www.ainc-inac.gc
.ca/pr/trts/trty3_e.html. Accessed January 20, 2007.

Treaty No. 4
BETWEEN HER MAJESTY THE QUEEN AND THE CREE AND SAULTEAUX TRIBES OF INDIANS AT THE QU'APPELLE AND FORT ELLICE

ARTICLES OF A TREATY made and concluded this fifteenth day of September, in the year of Our Lord one thousand eight hundred and seventy-four, between Her Most Gracious Majesty the Queen of Great Britain and Ireland, by Her Commissioners, the Honourable Alexander Morris, Lieutenant Governor of the Province of Manitoba and the North-West Territories; the Honourable David Laird, Minister of the Interior, and William Joseph Christie, Esquire, of Brockville, Ontario, of the one part; and the Cree, Saulteaux and other Indians, inhabitants of the territory within the limits hereinafter defined and described by their Chiefs and Headmen, chosen and named as hereinafter mentioned, of the other part.

The Cree and Saulteaux Tribes of Indians, and all other the Indians inhabiting the district hereinafter described and defined, do hereby cede, release, surrender and yield up to the Government of the Dominion of Canada, for Her Majesty the Queen, and Her successors forever, all their rights, titles and privileges whatsoever, to the lands included within the following limits, that is to say:—

Commencing at a point on the United States frontier due south of the northwestern point of the Moose Mountains; thence due north to said point of said mountains: thence in a north-easterly course to a point two miles due west of Fort Ellice; thence in a line parallel with and two miles westward from the Assiniboine River to the mouth of the Shell River; thence parallel to the said river and two miles distant therefrom to its source; thence in a straight line to a point on the western shore of Lake Winnipegosis, due west from the most northern extremity of Waterhen Lake; thence east to the centre of Lake Winnipegosis; thence northwardly, through the middle of the said lake (including Birch Island), to the mouth of Red Deer River; thence westwardly and southwestwardly along and including the said Red Deer River and its lakes, Red Deer and Etoimaini, to the source of its western branch; thence in a straight line to the source of the northern branch of the Qu'Appelle; thence along and including said stream to the forks near Long Lake; thence along and including the valley of the west branch of the Qu'Appelle to the South Saskatchewan; thence along and including said river to the mouth of Maple Creek; thence southwardly along said creek to a point opposite the western extremity of the Cypress Hills; thence due south to the international boundary; thence east along the said boundary to the place of commencement. Also all their rights, titles and privileges whatsoever to all other lands wheresoever situated within Her Majesty's North-West Territories, or any of them. To have and to hold the same to Her Majesty the Queen and Her successors for ever.

Resource
Treaty 4. Available at: http://www.ainc-inac.gc
.ca/pr/trts/trty4_e.html. Accessed January 20, 2007.

Treaty No. 5

BETWEEN HER MAJESTY THE QUEEN AND THE SAULTEAUX AND SWAMPY CREE TRIBES OF INDIANS AT BEREN'S RIVER AND NORWAY HOUSE WITH ADHESIONS

ARTICLES OF A TREATY made and concluded at Beren's River the 20th day of September, and at Norway House the 24th day of September, in the year of Our Lord one thousand eight hundred and seventy-five, between "Her Most Gracious Majesty the Queen" of Great Britain and Ireland, by Her Commissioners the Honourable Alexander Morris, Lieutenant-Governor of the Province of Manitoba and the North-west Territories, and the Honourable James McKay, of the one part, and the Saulteaux and Swampy Cree tribes of Indians, inhabitants of the country within the limits hereinafter defined and described, by their Chiefs, chosen and named as hereinafter mentioned, of the other part.

The Saulteaux and Swampy Cree Tribes of Indians and all other the Indians inhabiting the district hereinafter described and defined, do hereby cede, release, surrender and yield up to the Government of the Dominion of Canada, for Her Majesty the Queen and Her successors for ever, all their rights, titles and privileges whatsoever to the lands included within the following limits, that is to say:

Commencing at the north corner or junction of Treaties Nos. 1 and 3; then easterly along the boundary of Treaty No. 3 to the "Height of Land," at the northeast corner of the said treaty limits, a point dividing the waters of the Albany and Winnipeg Rivers; thence due north along the said "Height of Land " to a point intersected by the 53° of north latitude; and thence north-westerly to "Favourable Lake"; thence following the east shore of said lake to its northern limit; thence north-westerly to the north end of Lake Winnipegoosis; then westerly to the "Height of Land" called "Robinson's Portage"; thence north-westerly to the east end of "Cross Lake"; thence north-westerly crossing "Foxes Lake"; thence north-westerly to the north end of "Split Lake"; thence south-westerly to "Pipestone Lake," on "Burntwood River "; thence south-westerly to the western point of "John Scott's Lake"; thence south-westerly to the north shore of "Beaver Lake"; thence south-westerly to the west end of "Cumberland Lake"; thence due south to the "Saskatchewan River"; thence due south to the north-west corner of the northern limits of Treaty No. 4, including all territory within the said limits,

and all islands on all lakes within the said limits, as above described; and it being also understood that in all cases where lakes form the treaty limits, ten miles from the shore of the lake should be included in the treaty.

And also all their rights, titles and privileges whatsoever to all other lands wherever situated in the North-west Territories or in any other Province or portion of Her Majesty's dominions situated and being within the Dominion of Canada;

The tract comprised within the lines above described, embracing an area of one hundred thousand square miles, be the same more or less.

To have and to hold the same to Her Majesty the Queen, and Her successors forever.

Resource

Treaty 5. Available at: http://www.ainc-inac.gc.ca/ pr/trts/trty5_e.html. Accessed January 20, 2007.

Treaty No. 8

MADE JUNE 21, 1899 AND ADHESIONS, REPORTS, ETC.

ARTICLES OF A TREATY made and concluded at the several dates mentioned therein, in the year of Our Lord one thousand eight hundred and ninety-nine, between Her most Gracious Majesty the Queen of Great Britain and Ireland, by Her Commissioners the Honourable David Laird, of Winnipeg, Manitoba, Indian Commissioner for the said Province and the Northwest Territories; James Andrew Joseph McKenna, of Ottawa, Ontario, Esquire, and the Honourable James Hamilton Ross, of Regina, in the Northwest Territories, of the one part; and the Cree, Beaver, Chipewyan and other Indians, inhabitants of the territory within the limits hereinafter defined and described, by their Chiefs and Headmen, hereunto subscribed, of the other part:

. . . The said Commissioners have proceeded to negotiate a treaty with the Cree, Beaver, Chipewyan and other Indians, inhabiting the district hereinafter defined and described, and the same has been agreed upon and concluded by the respective bands at the dates mentioned hereunder, the said Indians DO HEREBY CEDE, RELEASE, SURRENDER AND YIELD UP to the Government of the Dominion of Canada, for Her Majesty the Queen and Her successors for ever, all their rights, titles and privileges whatsoever, to the lands included within the following limits, that is to say:

Commencing at the source of the main branch of the Red Deer River in Alberta, thence due west to the central range of the Rocky Mountains, thence northwesterly along the said range to the point where it intersects the 60th parallel of north latitude, thence east along said parallel to the point where it intersects Hay River, thence northeasterly down said river to the south shore of Great Slave Lake, thence along the said shore northeasterly (and including such rights to the islands in said lakes as the Indians mentioned in the treaty may possess), and thence easterly and northeasterly along the south shores of Christie's Bay and McLeod's Bay to old Fort Reliance near the mouth of Lockhart's River, thence southeasterly in a straight line to and including Black Lake, thence southwesterly up the stream from Cree Lake, thence including said lake southwesterly along the height of land between the Athabasca and Churchill Rivers to where it intersects the northern boundary of Treaty Six, and along the said boundary easterly, northerly and southwesterly, to the place of commencement.

AND ALSO the said Indian rights, titles and privileges whatsoever to all other lands wherever situated in the Northwest Territories, British Columbia, or in any other portion of the Dominion of Canada.

TO HAVE AND TO HOLD the same to Her Majesty the Queen and Her successors for ever.

Resource

Treaty 8. Available at: *http://www.ainc-inac.gc .ca/pr/trts/trty8_e.html*. Accessed January 20, 2007.

Treaty No. 9

THE JAMES BAY TREATY (TREATY No. 9) (MADE IN 1905 AND 1906) AND ADHESIONS MADE IN 1929 AND 1930

ARTICLES OF A TREATY made and concluded at the several dates mentioned therein, in the year of Our Lord one thousand and nine hundred and five, between His Most Gracious Majesty the King of Great Britain and Ireland, by His Commissioners, Duncan Campbell Scott, of Ottawa, Ontario, Esquire, and Samuel Stewart, of Ottawa, Ontario, Esquire; and Daniel George MacMartin, of Perth, Ontario, Esquire, representing the province of Ontario, of the one part; and the Ojibeway, Cree and other Indians, inhabitants of the territory within the limits hereinafter defined and described, by their chiefs, and headmen hereunto subscribed, of the other part:—

Whereas, the Indians inhabiting the territory hereinafter defined have been convened to meet a commission representing His Majesty's government of the Dominion of Canada at certain places in the said territory in this present year of 1905, to deliberate upon certain matters of interest to His Most Gracious Majesty, of the one part, and the said Indians of the other.

And whereas, the said commissioners have proceeded to negotiate a treaty with the Ojibeway, Cree and other Indians, inhabiting the district hereinafter defined and described, and the same has been agreed upon, and concluded by the respective bands at the dates mentioned hereunder, the said Indians do hereby cede, release, surrender and yield up to the government of the Dominion of Canada, for His Majesty the King and His successors for ever, all their rights titles and privileges whatsoever, to the lands included within the following limits, that is to say: That portion or tract of land lying and being in the province of Ontario, bounded on the south by the height of land and the northern boundaries of the territory ceded by the Robinson-Superior Treaty of 1850, and the Robinson-Huron Treaty of 1850, and bounded on the east and north by the boundaries of the said province of Ontario as defined by law, and on the west by a part of the eastern boundary of the territory ceded by the Northwest Angle Treaty No. 3; the said land containing an area of ninety thousand square miles, more or less.

And also, the said Indian rights, titles and privileges whatsoever to all other lands wherever situated in Ontario, Quebec, Manitoba, the District of Keewatin, or in any other portion of the Dominion of Canada.

To have and to hold the same to His Majesty the King and His successors for ever.

And His Majesty the King hereby agrees with the said Indians that they shall have the right to pursue their usual vocations of hunting, trapping and fishing throughout the tract surrendered as heretofore described, subject to such regulations as may from time to time be made by the government of the country, acting under the authority of His Majesty, and saving and excepting such tracts as may be required or taken up from time to time for settlement, mining, lumbering, trading or other purposes.

Resource

Treaty 9. Available at: http://www.ainc-inac.gc .ca/pr/trts/trty9_e.html. Accessed January 20, 2007.

Treaty No. 11
TREATY No. 11 (JUNE 27, 1921) AND ADHESION (JULY 17, 1922) WITH REPORTS, ETC.

ARTICLES OF A TREATY made and concluded on the several dates mentioned therein in the year of Our Lord One thousand Nine hundred and Twenty-One, between His Most Gracious Majesty George V, King of Great Britain and Ireland and of the British Dominions beyond the Seas, by His Commissioner, Henry Anthony Conroy, Esquire, of the City of Ottawa, of the One Part, and the Slave, Dogrib, Loucheux, Hare and other Indians, inhabitants of the territory within the limits hereinafter defined and described, by their Chiefs and Headmen, hereunto subscribed, of the other part:—

WHEREAS, the Indians inhabiting the territory hereinafter defined have been convened to meet a commissioner representing His Majesty's Government of the Dominion of Canada at certain places in the said territory in this present year of 1921, to deliberate upon certain matters of interest to His Most Gracious Majesty, of the one part, and the said Indians of the other.

AND WHEREAS the said Commissioner has proceeded to negotiate a treaty with the Slave, Dogrib, Loucheux, Hare and other Indians inhabiting the district hereinafter defined and described, which has been agreed upon and concluded by the respective bands at the dates mentioned hereunder, the said Indians do hereby cede, release, surrender and yield up to the Government of the Dominion of Canada, for His Majesty the King and His Successors forever, all their rights, titles, and privileges whatsoever to the lands included within the following limits, that is to say:

Commencing at the northwesterly corner of the territory ceded under the provisions of Treaty Number Eight; thence northeasterly along the height-of-land to the point where it intersects the boundary between the Yukon Territory and the Northwest Territories; thence northwesterly along the said boundary to the shore of the Arctic ocean; thence easterly along the said shore to the mouth of the Coppermine river; thence southerly and southeasterly along the left bank of said river to Lake Gras by way of Point lake; thence along the southern shore of Lake Gras to a point situated northwest of the most western extremity of Aylmer lake; thence along the southern shore of Aylmer lake and following the right bank of the Lockhart river to Artillery lake; thence along the western shore of Artillery lake and following the right bank of the Lockhart river to the site of Old Fort Reliance where the said river enters Great Slave lake, this being the northeastern corner of the territory ceded under the provisions of Treaty Number Eight; thence westerly along the northern boundary of the said territory so ceded to the point of commencement; comprising an area of approximately three hundred and seventy-two thousand square miles.

AND ALSO, the said Indian rights, titles and privileges whatsoever to all other lands wherever situated in the Yukon Territory, the Northwest Territories or in any other portion of the Dominion of Canada.

To have and to hold the same to His Majesty the King and His Successors forever.

AND His Majesty the King hereby agrees with the said Indians that they shall have the right to pursue their usual vocations of hunting, trapping and fishing throughout the tract surrendered as heretofore described, subject to such regulations as may from time to time be made by the Government of the Country acting under the authority of His Majesty, and saving and excepting such tracts as may be required or taken up from time to time for settlement, mining, lumbering, trading or other purposes.

Resource
Treaty 11. Available at: http://www .ainc-inac.gc.ca/pr/trts/trty11_e.html. Accessed January 20, 2007.

Two Moon: Account of the Battle of the Little Bighorn

The United States was gearing up to celebrate its hundredth birthday as a nation when General George Armstrong Custer disobeyed orders and attacked a large settlement of Sioux and Cheyenne on the Little Bighorn River in what is now southeastern Montana. The resulting battle is described here by a Native American witness.

That spring I was camped on Powder River with fifty lodges of my people—Cheyennes. The place is near what is now Fort McKenney. One morning soldiers charged my camp. They were in command of Three Fingers [Colonel R. S. McKenzie]. We were surprised and scattered, leaving our ponies. The soldiers ran all our horses off. That night the soldiers

slept, leaving the horses [to] one side; so we crept up and stole them back again, and then we went away.

We traveled far, and one day we met a big camp of Sioux at Charcoal Butte. We camped with the Sioux, and had a good time, plenty grass, plenty game, good water. Crazy Horse was head chief of the camp. Sitting Bull was camped a little ways below, on the Little Missouri River.

Crazy Horse said to me, "I'm glad you are come. We are going to fight the white man again."

The camp was already full of wounded men, women, and children.

I said to Crazy Horse, "All right. I am ready to fight. I have fought already. My people have been killed, my horses stolen; I am satisfied to fight."

I believed at that time the Great Spirits had made Sioux, put them there [he drew a circle to the right], and the white men and Cheyennes here [indicating two places to the left], expecting them to fight. The Great Spirits I thought liked to see the fight; it was to them all the same like playing. So I thought then about fighting.

About May, when the grass was tall and the horses strong, we broke camp and started across the country to the mouth of the Tongue River. Then Sitting Bull and Crazy Horse and all went up the Rosebud. There we had a big fight with General [George] Crook, and whipped him. Many soldiers were killed—few Indians. It was a great fight, much smoke and dust.

From there we all went over the divide, and camped in the valley of Little Horn. Everybody thought, "Now we are out of the white man's country. He can live there, we will live here." After a few days, one morning when I was in camp north of Sitting Bull, a Sioux messenger rode up and said, "Let everybody paint up, cook, and get ready for a big dance."

Cheyennes then went to work to cook, cut up tobacco, and get ready. We all thought to dance all day. We were very glad to think we were far away from the white man.

I went to water my horses at the creek, and washed them off with cool water, then took a swim myself. I came back to the camp afoot. When I got near my lodge, I looked up the Little Horn towards Sitting Bull's camp. I saw a great dust rising. It looked like a whirlwind. Soon Sioux horsemen came rushing into camp shouting: "Soldiers come! Plenty white soldiers."

I ran into my lodge, and said to my brother-in-law, "Get your horses; the white man is coming. Everybody run for horses."

Outside, far up the valley, I heard a battle cry, Hay-ay, hay-ay! I heard shouting, too, this way [clapping his hands very fast]. I couldn't see any Indians. Everybody was getting horses and saddles. After I had caught my horse, a Sioux warrior came again and said, "Many soldiers are coming."

Then he said to the women, "Get out of the way, we are going to have hard fight."

I said, "All right, I am ready."

I got on my horse, and rode out into my camp. I called out to the people all running about: "I am Two Moon, your chief. Don't run away. Stay here and fight. You must stay and fight the white soldiers. I shall stay even if I am to be killed."

I rode swiftly toward Sitting Bull's camp. There I saw the white soldiers fighting in a line. Indians covered the flat. They began to drive the soldiers all mixed up—Sioux, then soldiers, then more Sioux, and all shooting. The air was full of smoke and dust. I saw the soldiers fall back and drop into the river-bed like buffalo fleeing. They had not time to look for a crossing. The Sioux chased them up the hill, where they met more soldiers in wagons, and then messengers came saying more soldiers were going to kill the women, and the Sioux turned back. Chief Gall was there fighting. Crazy Horse also.

I then rode toward my camp, and stopped squaws from carrying off lodges. While I was sitting on my horse I saw flags come up over the hill to the east like that [he raised his finger-tips]. Then the soldiers rose all at once, all on horses, like this [he put his fingers behind each other to indicate that Custer appeared marching in columns of fours]. They formed into three bunches [squadrons] with a little ways between. Then a bugle sounded, and they all got off horses, and some soldiers led the horses back over the hill.

Then the Sioux rode up the ridge on all sides, riding very fast. The Cheyennes went up the left way. Then the shooting was quick, quick. Pop—pop—pop very fast. Some of the soldiers were down on their knees, some standing. Officers all in front. The smoke was like a great cloud, and everywhere the Sioux went the dust rose like smoke. We circled all round him—swirling like water round a stone. We shoot, we ride fast, we shoot again. Soldiers drop, and horses fall on them. Soldiers in line drop, but one man rides up and down the line—all the time shouting. He rode a sorrel horse with white face and white fore-legs. I don't know who he was. He was a brave man.

Indians keep swirling round and round, and the soldiers killed only a few. Many soldiers fell. At last all horses killed but five. Once in a while some man would break out and run toward the river, but he would fall. At last about a hundred men and five horsemen stood on the hill all bunched together. All along the bugler kept blowing his commands. He was very brave too. Then a chief was killed. I hear it was Long Hair [Custer], I don't know; and then the five horsemen and the bunch of men, may be [about] forty, started toward the river. The man on the sorrel horse led them, shouting all the time. He wore a buckskin shirt, and had long black hair and mustache. He fought hard with a big knife. His men were all covered with white dust. I couldn't tell whether they were officers or not. One man all alone ran far down toward the river, then round up over the hill. I thought he was going to escape, but a Sioux fired and hit him in the head. He was [a sergeant] the last man. He wore braid on his arms.

All the soldiers were now killed, and the bodies were stripped. After that no one could tell which were officers. The bodies were left where they fell. We had no dance that night. We were sorrowful.

Next day four Sioux chiefs and two Cheyennes and I, Two Moon, went upon the battlefield to count the dead. One man carried [a] Little bundle of sticks. When we came to dead men, we took a little stick and gave it to another man, so we counted the dead. There were 388. There were thirty-nine Sioux and seven Cheyennes killed and about a hundred wounded.

Some white soldiers were cut with knives, to make sure they were dead; and the war women had mangled some. Most of them were left just where they fell. We came to the man with the big mustache; he lay down the hills towards the river. The Indians did not take his buckskin shirt. The Sioux said, "That is a big chief. That is Long Hair." I don't know. I had never seen him. The man on the white-faced horse was the bravest man.

That day as the sun was getting low our young men came up the Little Horn riding hard. Many white soldiers were coming in a big boat, and when we looked we could see the smoke rising. I called my people together, and we hurried up the Little Horn, into Rotten Grass Valley. We camped there three days, and then rode swiftly back over our old trail to the east. Sitting Bull went back into the Rosebud and down the Yellowstone, and away to the north. I did not see him again.

Chief Joseph: I Will Fight No More Forever Speech

Following their refusal to surrender, the Nez Percé were forced out of their homeland in Idaho and chased north and eastward about 1,700 miles through rough country during 1877. After they were slowly starved and reduced in numbers in several battles with U.S. Army troops, Chief Joseph the Younger, their leader, decided finally to surrender. The following is extracted from his speech on that occasion.

Tell General [Howard O.] Howard that I know his heart. What he told me before I have in my heart. I am tired of fighting. Our chiefs are killed. Looking Glass is dead, Tu-hul-hil-sote is dead. The old men are all dead. It is the young men who now say yes or no. He who led the young men is dead. It is cold and we have no blankets. The little children are freezing to death. My people—some of them have run away to the hills and have no blankets and no food. No one knows where they are—perhaps freezing to death. I want to have time to look for my children and see how many of them I can find. Maybe I shall find them among the dead. Hear me, my chiefs, my heart is sick and sad. From where the sun now stands I will fight no more against the white man.

Helen Hunt Jackson: *A Century of Dishonor*

Helen Hunt Jackson, who was best known in her time as a poet, turned to writing exposes of government misconduct in Indian affairs late in her life. Her major book on this subject, A Century of Dishonor, *was a best-seller.*

There are within the limits of the United States between 250 and 300,000 Indians, exclusive of those in Alaska. The names of the different tribes and bands, as entered in the statistical table the Indian Office Reports, number nearly 300. One of the most careful estimates which have been made of their numbers and localities gives them as follows: "In Minnesota and States east of the Mississippi, about 32,500; in Nebraska, Kansas, and the Indian Territory, 70,650; in the Territories of Dakota, Montana, Wyoming, and Idaho, 65,000; in Nevada and the Territories of Colorado, New Mexico, Utah, and Arizona, 84,000; and on the Pacific slope, 48,000."

Of these, 130,000 are self-supporting on their own reservations, "receiving nothing from the Government except interest on their own moneys, or annuities granted them in consideration of the cession of their lands to the United States."

. . . Of the remainder, 84,000 are partially supported by the Government—the interest money due them and their annuities, as provided by treaty, being inadequate to their subsistence on the reservations where they are confined. . . .

There are about 55,000 who never visit an agency, over whom the Government does not pretend to have either control or care. These 55,000 "subsist by hunting, fishing, on roots, nuts, berries, etc., and by begging and stealing"; and this also seems to dispose of the accusation that the Indian will not "work for a living." There remains a small portion, about 31,000, that are entirely subsisted by the Government.

There is not among these 300 bands of Indians one which has not suffered cruelly at the hands either of the Government or of white settlers. The poorer, the more insignificant, the more helpless the band, the more certain the cruelty and outrage to which they have been subjected. This is especially true of the bands on the Pacific slope. These Indians found themselves all of a sudden surrounded by and caught up in the great influx of gold-seeking settlers, as helpless creatures on a shore are caught up in a tidal wave. There was not time for the Government to make treaties; not even time for communities to make laws. The tale of the wrongs, the oppressions, the murders of the Pacific-slope Indians in the last thirty years would be a volume by itself, and is too monstrous to be believed.

It makes little difference, however, where one opens the record of the history of the Indians; every page and every year has its dark stain. The story of one tribe is the story of all, varied only differences of time and place; but neither time nor place makes any difference in the main facts. Colorado is as greedy and unjust in 1880 as was Georgia in 1830, and Ohio in 1795; and the United States Government breaks promises now as deftly as then, and with an added ingenuity from long practice.

One of its strongest supports in so doing is the wide-spread sentiment among the people of dislike to the Indian, of impatience with his presence as a "barrier to civilization" and distrust of it as a possible danger. The old tales of the frontier life, with its horrors of Indian warfare, have gradually, by two or three generations' telling, produced in the average mind something like an hereditary instinct of questioning and unreasoning aversion which it is almost impossible to dislodge or soften. . . .

President after president has appointed commission after commission to inquire into and report upon Indian affairs, and to make suggestions as to the best methods of managing them. The reports are filled with eloquent statements of wrongs done to the Indians, of perfidies on the part of the Government; they counsel, as earnestly as words can, a trial of the simple and unperplexing expedients of telling truth, keeping promises, making fair bargains, dealing justly in all ways and all things. These reports are bound up with the Government's Annual Reports, and that is the end of them. . . .

The history of the Government connections with the Indians is a shameful record of broken treaties and unfulfilled promises. The history of the border white man's connection with the Indians is a sickening record of murder, outrage, robbery, and wrongs committed by the former, as the rule, and occasional savage outbreaks and unspeakably barbarous deeds of retaliation by the latter, as the exception.

Taught by the Government that they had rights entitled to respect, when those rights have been assailed by the rapacity of the white man, the arm which should have been raised to protect them has ever been ready to sustain the aggressor.

The testimony of some of the highest military officers of the United States is on record to the effect that, in our Indian wars, almost without exception, the first aggressions have been made by the white man. . . . Every crime committed by a white man against an Indian is concealed and palliated. Every offense committed by an Indian against a white man is borne on the wings of the post or the telegraph to the remotest corner of the land, clothed with all the horrors which the reality or imagination can throw around it. Against such influences as these are the people of the United States need to be warned.

To assume that it would be easy, or by any one sudden stroke of legislative policy possible, to undo the mischief and hurt of the long past, set the Indian policy of the country right for the future, and make the Indians at once safe and happy, is the blunder of a hasty and uninformed judgment. The notion which seems to be growing more prevalent, that simply to make all Indians at once citizens of the United States would be a sovereign and instantaneous panacea for all their ills and all the Government's perplexities, is a very inconsiderate one.

To administer complete citizenship of a sudden, all round, to all Indians, barbarous and civilized alike, would be as grotesque a blunder as to dose them all round with any one medicine, irrespective of the symptoms and needs of their diseases. It would kill more than it would cure. Nevertheless, it is true, as was well stated by one of the superintendents of Indian Affairs in 1857, that, "so long as they are not citizens of the United States, their rights of property must remain insecure against invasion. The doors of the federal tribunals being barred against them while wards and dependents, they can only partially exercise the rights of free government, or give to those who make, execute, and construe the few laws they are allowed to enact, dignity sufficient to make them respectable. While they continue individually to gather the crumbs that fall from the table of the United States, idleness, improvidence, and indebtedness will be the rule, and industry, thrift, and freedom from debt the exception. The utter absence of individual title to particular lands deprives every one among them of the chief incentive to labor and exertion— the very mainspring on which the prosperity of a people depends."

All judicious plans and measures for their safety and salvation must embody provisions for their becoming citizens as fast as they are fit, and must protect them till then in every right and particular in which our laws protect other "persons" who are not citizens. . . .

However great perplexity and difficulty there may be in the details of any and every plan possible for doing at this late day anything like justice to the Indian, however, hard it may be for good statesmen and good men to agree upon the things that ought to be done, there certainly is, or ought to be, no perplexity whatever, or difficulty whatever, in agreeing upon certain things that ought not to be done, and which must cease to be done before the first steps can be taken toward righting the wrongs, curing the ills, and wiping out the disgrace to us of the present conditions of our Indians.

Cheating, robbing, breaking promises—these three are clearly things which must cease to be done. One more thing, also, and that is the refusal of the protection of the law to the Indian's rights of property, "of life, liberty, and the pursuit of happiness."

When these four things have ceased to be done, time, statesmanship, philanthropy, and Christianity can slowly and surely do the rest. Till these four things have ceased to be done, statesmanship and philanthropy alike must work in vain, and even Christianity can reap but small harvest.

Ex Parte Crow Dog

In this case, the U.S. Supreme Court denied federal jurisdiction over the murder of an Indian by another Indian in Indian country, citing relevant treaties. The court reasoned that federal jurisdiction would deny Indians trial by their peers. The U.S. Congress reacted to this ruling by passing the Major Crimes Act of 1885, which subjected reservation Indians to federal jurisdiction for murder and other major crimes. Today this law and others still restrict the scope of operation for reservation courts.

The petitioner is in the custody of the marshal of the United States for the territory of Dakota, imprisoned in the jail of Lawrence county, in the first judicial district of that territory, under sentence of death, adjudged against him by the district court for that district, to be carried into execution January 14, 1884. That judgment was rendered upon a conviction for the murder of an Indian of the Brule Sioux band of the Sioux nation of Indians, by the name of Sin-ta-ge-le-Scka, or in English, Spotted Tail, the prisoner also being an Indian of the same band and nation, and the homicide having occurred, as alleged in the indictment, in the Indian country, within a place and district of country under the exclusive jurisdiction of the United States and within the said judicial district. The judgment was affirmed on a writ of error, by the supreme court of the territory. It is claimed on behalf of the prisoner that the crime charged against him, and of which he stands convicted, is not an offense under the laws of the United States; that the district court had no jurisdiction to try him, and that its judgment and sentence are void. It therefore prays for a writ of habeas corpus, that he may be delivered from an imprisonment which he asserts to be illegal. . . .

The district courts of the territory of Dakota are invested with the same jurisdiction in all cases arising under the laws of the United States as is vested in the circuit and district courts of the United States. Rev. St. §§ 1907–1910. The reservation of the Sioux Indians, lying within the exterior boundaries of the territory of Dakota, was defined by article 2 of the treaty concluded April 29, 1868, (15 St. 635,) and by section 1839 Rev. St., it is excepted out of and constitutes no part of that territory. The object of this exception is stated to be to exclude the jurisdiction of

any state or territorial government over Indians within its exterior lines, without their consent, where their rights have been reserved and remain unextinguished by treaty. But the district courts of the territory having, by law, the jurisdiction of district and circuit courts of the United States, may, in that character, take cognizance of offenses against the laws of the United States, although committed within an Indian reservation, when the latter is situate within the space which is constituted by the authority of the territorial government the judicial district of such court. . . .

Nevertheless, although the section of the act of 1834 containing the definition of that date has been repealed, it is not to be regarded as if it had never been adopted, but may be referred to in connection with the provisions of its original context which remain in force, and may be considered in connection with the changes which have taken place in our situation, with a view of determining from time to time what must be regarded as Indian country, where it is spoken of in the statutes. It is an admitted rule in the interpretation of statutes that clauses which have been repealed may still be considered in construing the provisions that remain in force. BRAMWELL, L. J. in *Atty. Gen. v. Lamplough*, 3 Exch. Div. 223–227; Hardc. St. 217; *Savings Bank v. Collector*, 3 Wall. 495–513; *Com. v. Bailey*, 13 Allen, 541. This rule was applied in reference to the very question now under consideration in *Bates v. Clark*, 95 U.S. 204, decided at the October term, 1877. It was said in that case by Mr. Justice MILLER, delivering the opinion of the court, that 'it follows from this that all the country described by the act of 1834 as Indian country remains Indian country so long as the Indians retain their original title to the soil, and ceases to be Indian country whenever they lose that title, in the absence of any different provision by treaty or by act of congress.' In our opinion that definition now applies to all the country to which the Indian title has not been extinguished within the limits of the United States, even when not within a reservation expressly set apart for the exclusive occupancy of Indians, although much of it has been acquired since the passage of the act of 1834, and notwithstanding the formal definition in that act has been dropped from the statutes, excluding, however, any territory embraced within the exterior geographical limits of a state, not excepted from its jurisdiction by treaty or by statute at the time of its admission into the Union, but saving, even in respect to territory not thus excepted and actually in the exclusive occupancy of

Indians, the authority of congress over it, under the constitutional power to regulate commerce with the Indian tribes, and under any treaty made in pursuance of it. *U.S. v. McBratney*, 104 U.S. 621. . . .

By the Indian appropriation act of August 15, 1876, congress appropriated $1,000,000 for the subsistence of the Sioux Indians, in accordance with the treaty of 1868, and 'for purposes of their civilization,' (19 St. 192) but coupled it with certain conditions relative to a cession of a portion of the reservation, and with the proviso 'that no further appropriation for said Sioux Indians for subsistence shall hereafter be made until some stipulation, agreement, or arrangement shall have been entered into by said Indians with the president of the United States, which is calculated and designed to enable said Indians to become self-supporting.' In pursuance of that provision the agreement was made, which was ratified in part by the act of congress of February 28, 1877. The enactment of this agreement by statute, instead of its ratification as a treaty, was in pursuance of the policy which had been declared for the first time in a proviso to the Indian appropriation act of March 3, 1871, (16 St. 566 c. 120) and permanently adopted in section 2079 of the Revised Statutes, that thereafter 'no Indian nation or tribe within the territory of the United States shall be acknowledged or recognized as an independent nation, tribe, or power with whom the United States may contract by treaty,' but without invalidating or impairing the obligation of subsisting treaties. . . . It must be remembered that the question before us is whether the express letter of section 2146 of the Revised Statutes, which excludes from the jurisdiction of the United States the case of a crime committed in the Indian country by one Indian against the person or property of another Indian, has been repealed. If not, it is in force and applies to the present case. The treaty of 1868 and the agreement and act of congress of 1877, it is admitted, do not repeal it by any express words. What we have said is sufficient at least to show that they do not work a repeal by necessary implication. A meaning can be given to the legislation in question, which the words will bear, which is not unreasonable, which is not inconsistent with its scope and apparent purposes, whereby the whole may be made to stand. Implied repeals are not favored. The implication must be necessary. There must be a positive repugnancy between the provisions of the new laws and those of the old. *Wood v. U.S.* 16 Pet. 342; *Daviess v. Fairbairn*, 3 How. 636; *U.S. v. Tynen*, 11 Wall. 88; *State v. Stoll*, 17 Wall. 425.

The language of the exception is special and express; the words relied on as a repeal are general and inconclusive. The rule is, generalia specialibus non derogant. 'The general principle to be applied,' said BOVILL, C. J., in *Thorpe v. Adams,* L. R. 6 C. P. 135, 'to the construction of acts of parliament is that a general act is not to be construed to repeal a previous particular act, unless there is some express reference to the previous legislation on the subject, or unless there is a necessary inconsistency in the two acts standing together.' 'And the reason is,' said Wood, V. C., in *Fitzgerald v. Champneys,* 30 Law J. Ch. 782; 2 Johns. & H. 31–54, 'that the legislature having had its attention directed to a special subject, and having observed all the circumstances of the case and provided for them, does not intend, by a general enactment afterwards, to derogate from its own act when it makes no special mention of its intention so to do.'

The nature and circumstances of this case strongly reinforce this rule of interpretation in its present application. It is a case involving the judgment of a court of special and limited jurisdiction, not to be assumed without clear warrant of law. It is a case of life and death. It is a case where, against an express exception in the law itself, that law, by argument and inference only, is sought to be extended over aliens and strangers; over the members of a community, separated by race, by tradition, by the instincts of a free though savage life, from the authority and power which seeks to impose upon them the restraints of an external and unknown code, and to subject them to the responsibilities of civil conduct, according to rules and penalties of which they could have no previous warning; which judges them by a standard made by others, and not for them, which takes no account of the conditions which should except them from its exactions, and makes no allowance for their inability to understand it. It tries them not by their peers, nor by the customs of their people, nor the law of their land, but by superiors of a different race, according to the law of a social state of which they have an imperfect conception, and which is opposed to the traditions of their history, to the habits of their lives, to the strongest prejudices of their savage nature; one which measures the red man's revenge by the maxims of the white man's morality. It is a case, too, of first impression, so far as we are advised; for, if the question has been mooted heretofore in any courts of the United States, the jurisdiction has never before been practically asserted as in the present instance.

The provisions now contained in sections 2145 and 2146 of the Revised Statutes were first enacted in section 25 of the Indian intercourse act of 1834. 4 St. 733. Prior to that, by the act of 1796, (1 St. 469,) and the act of 1802, (2 St. 139,) offenses committed by Indians against white persons, and by white persons against Indians, were specifically enumerated and defined, and those by Indians against each other were left to be dealt with by each tribe for itself, according to its local customs. The policy of the government in that respect has been uniform. As was said by Mr. Justice MILLER, delivering the opinion of the court in *U. S. v. Joseph,* 94 U.S. 614, 617:

'The tribes for whom the act of 1854 was made were those semi-independent tribes whom our government has always recognized as exempt from our laws, whether within or without the limits of an organized state or territory, and, in regard to their domestic government, left to their own rules and traditions, in whom we have recognized the capacity to make treaties, and with whom the governments, state and national, deal, with a few exceptions only, in their national or tribal character, and not as individuals.'

To give to the clauses in the treaty of 1868 and the agreement of 1877 effect, so as to uphold the jurisdiction exercised in this case, would be to reverse in this instance the general policy of the government towards the Indians, as declared in many statutes and treaties, and recognized in many decisions of this court, from the beginning to the present time. To justify such a departure, in such a case, requires a clear expression of the intention of congress, and that we have not been able to find. It results that the first district court of Dakota was without jurisdiction to find or try the indictment against the prisoner; that the conviction and sentence are void, and that his imprisonment is illegal.

The writs of habeas corpus and certiorari prayed for will accordingly be issued.

William T. Sherman: Report on the End of the Indian Problem

. . . I now regard the Indians as substantially eliminated from the problem of the Army. There may be spasmodic and temporary alarms, but such Indian wars as have hitherto disturbed the public peace and tranquillity are not probable. The Army has been a large factor in producing this result, but it is not the

only one. Immigration and the occupation by industrious farmers and miners of land vacated by the aboriginies [sic] have been largely instrumental to that end, but the railroad which used to follow in the rear now goes forward with the picket-line in the great battle of civilization with barbarism, and has become the greater cause. I have in former reports, for the past fifteen years, treated of this matter, and now, on the eve of withdrawing from active participation in public affairs, I beg to emphasize much which I have spoken and written heretofore. The recent completion of the last of the four great transcontinental lines of railway has settled forever the Indian question, the Army question, and many others which have hitherto troubled the country. . . .

General Allotment Act (Dawes Act)

The Dawes Act, named after its principal sponsor, Senator Henry Dawes, was advanced as a mechanism to assimilate Native Americans by giving them individual landholdings and, in some cases, citizenship rights. Allotment also broke up collective Indian landholdings and threw open as much as 90 percent of them to non-Indian immigrants.

An Act to Provide for the Allotment of Lands in Severalty to Indians on the Various Reservations, and to Extend the Protection of the Laws of the United States and the Territories over the Indians, and for Other Purposes.

Be it enacted by the Senate and House of Representatives of the United States of America in Congress assembled, That in all cases where any tribe or band of Indians has been, or shall hereafter be, located upon any reservation created for their use, either by treaty stipulation or by virtue of an act of Congress or executive order setting apart the same for their use, the President of the United States be, and he hereby is, authorized, whenever in his opinion any reservation or any part thereof of such Indians is advantageous for agricultural and grazing purposes, to cause said reservation, or any part thereof, to be surveyed, or resurveyed if necessary, and to allot the lands in said reservation in severalty to any Indian located thereon in quantities as follows:

To each head of a family, one-quarter of a section; To each single person over eighteen years of age, one-eighth of a section; To each orphan child under eighteen years of age, one-eighth of a section;

and To each other single person under eighteen years now living, or who may be born prior to the date of the order of the President directing an allotment of the lands embraced in any reservation, one-sixteenth of a section:

Provided, That in case there is not sufficient land in any of said reservations to allot lands to each individual of the classes above named in quantities as above provided, the lands embraced in such reservation or reservations shall be allotted to each individual of each of said classes pro rata in accordance with the provisions of this act: And provided further, That where the treaty or act of Congress setting apart such reservation provides the allotment of lands in severalty in quantities in excess of those herein provided, the President, in making allotments upon such reservation, shall allot the lands to each individual Indian belonging thereon in quantity as specified in such treaty or act: And provided further, That when the lands allotted are only valuable for grazing purposes, an additional allotment of such grazing lands, in quantities as above provided, shall be made to each individual.

SEC. 2. That all allotments set apart under the provisions of this act shall be selected by the Indians, heads of families selecting for their minor children, and the agents shall select for each orphan child, and in such manner as to embrace the improvements of the Indians making the selection . . .

SEC. 3. That the allotments provided for in this act shall be made by special agents appointed by the President for such purpose . . .

SEC. 4. That where any Indian not residing upon a reservation, or for whose tribe no reservation has been provided by treaty, act of Congress, or executive order, shall make settlement upon any surveyed or unsurveyed lands of the United States not otherwise appropriated, he or she shall be entitled, upon application to the local land-office for the district in which the lands are located, to have the same allotted to him or her, and to his or her children, in quantities and manner as provided in this act for Indians residing upon reservations . . .

SEC. 5. That upon the approval of the allotments provided for in this act by the Secretary of the Interior, he shall cause patents to issue therefor in the name of the allottees, which patents shall be of the legal effect, and declare that the United States does and will hold the land thus allotted, for the period of twenty-five years, in trust for the sole use and benefit of the Indian to whom such allotment shall have been made, or, in case of his decease, of his heirs

according to the laws of the State or Territory where such land is located, and that at the expiration of said period the United States will convey the same by patent to said Indian, or his heirs as aforesaid, in fee, discharged of said trust and free of all charge or incumbrance whatsoever: Provided, That the President of the United States may in any case in his discretion extend the period . . . That at any time after lands have been allotted to all the Indians of any tribe as herein provided, or sooner if in the opinion of the President it shall be for the best interests of said tribe, it shall be lawful for the Secretary of the Interior to negotiate with such Indian tribe for the purchase and release by said tribe, in conformity with the treaty or statute under which such reservation is held, of such portions of its reservation not allotted as such tribe shall, from time to time, consent to sell, on such terms and conditions as shall be considered just and equitable between the United States and said tribe of Indians, which purchase shall not be complete until ratified by Congress, and the form and manner of executing such release prescribed by Congress: Provided however, That all lands adapted to agriculture, with or without irrigation so sold or released to the United States by any Indian tribe shall be held by the United States for the sole purpose of securing homes to actual settlers and shall be disposed of by the United States to actual and bona fide settlers only tracts not exceeding one hundred and sixty acres to any one person, on such terms as Congress shall prescribe, subject to grants which Congress may make in aid of education: And provided further, That no patents shall issue therefor except to the person so taking the same as and homestead, or his heirs, and after the expiration of five years occupancy thereof as such homestead; and any conveyance of said lands taken as a homestead, or any contract touching the same, or lieu thereon, created prior to the date of such patent, shall be null and void. And the sums agreed to be paid by the United States as purchase money for any portion of any such reservation shall be held in the Treasury of the United States for the sole use of the tribe or tribes Indians . . .

SEC. 6. That upon the completion of said allotments and the patenting of the lands to said allottees, each and every number of the respective bands or tribes of Indians to whom allotments have been made shall have the benefit of and be subject to the laws, both civil and criminal, of the State or Territory in which they may reside; and no Territory shall pass or enforce any law denying any such

Indian within its jurisdiction the equal protection of the law. And every Indian born within the territorial limits of the United States to whom allotments shall have been made under the provisions of this act, or under any law or treaty, and every Indian born within the territorial limits of the United States who has voluntarily taken up, within said limits, his residence separate and apart from any tribe of Indians therein, and has adopted the habits of civilized life, is hereby declared to be a citizen of the United States, and is entitled to all the rights, privileges, and immunities of such citizens, whether said Indian has been or not, by birth or otherwise, a member of any tribe of Indians within the territorial limits of the United States without in any manner affecting the right of any such Indian to tribal or other property.

SEC. 7. That in cases where the use of water for irrigation is necessary to render the lands within any Indian reservation available for agricultural purposes, the Secretary of the Interior be, and he is hereby, authorized to prescribe such rules and regulations as he may deem necessary to secure a just and equal distribution thereof among the Indians residing upon any such reservation. . . .

SEC. 8. That the provisions of this act shall not extend to the territory occupied by the Cherokees, Creeks, Choctaws, Chickasaws, Seminoles, and Osage, Miamies and Peorias, and Sacs and Foxes, in the Indian Territory, nor to any of the reservations of the Seneca Nation of New York Indians in the State of New York, nor to that strip of territory in the State of Nebraska adjoining the Sioux Nation on the south added by executive order.

SEC. 9. That for the purpose of making the surveys and resurveys mentioned in section two of this act, there be, and hereby is, appropriated, out of any moneys in the Treasury not otherwise appropriated, the sum of one hundred thousand dollars, to be repaid proportionately out of the proceeds of the sales of such land as may be acquired from the Indians under the provisions of this act.

SEC. 10. That nothing in this act contained shall be so construed to affect the right and power of Congress to grant the right of way through any lands granted to an Indian, or a tribe of Indians, for railroads or other highways, or telegraph lines, for the public use, or condemn such lands to public uses, upon making just compensation.

SEC. 11. That nothing in this act shall be so construed as to prevent the removal of the Southern Ute Indians from their present reservation in Southwest-

ern Colorado to a new reservation by and with consent of a majority of the adult male members of said tribe.

Approved, February, 8, 1887.

Sitting Bull: Speech on Keeping Treaties (1890)

What treaty that the whites have kept has the red man broken? Not one. What treaty that the whites ever made with us red men have they kept? Not one. When I was a boy the Sioux owned the world. The sun rose and set in their lands. They sent 10,000 horsemen to battle. Where are the warriors to-day? Who slew them? Where are our lands? Who owns them? What white man can say I ever stole his lands or a penny of his money? Yet they say I am thief. What white woman, however lonely, was ever when a captive insulted by me? Yet they say I am a bad Indian. What white man has ever seen me drunk? Who has ever come to me hungry and gone unfed? Who has ever seen me beat my wives or abuse my children? What law have I broken? Is it wrong for me to love my own? Is it wicked in me because my skin is red; because I am a Sioux; because I was born where my fathers lived; because I would die for my people and my country?

Wounded Knee Massacre: Testimony of the Sioux (1890)

Turning Hawk [speaking through an interpreter]: Mr. Commissioner, my purpose today is to tell you what I know of the condition of affairs at the agency where I live. A certain falsehood [the Ghost Dance] came to our agency from the west which had the effect of a fire upon the Indians, and when this certain fire came upon our people those who had far-sightedness and could see into the matter made up their minds to stand up against it and fight it. The reason we took this hostile attitude to this fire was because we believed that you yourself would not be in favor of this particular mischief-making thing; but just as we expected, the people in authority did not like this thing and we were quietly told that we must give up or have nothing to do with this certain movement. Though this is the advice from our good friends in the East, there were, of course, many silly young men who were longing to become identified with the movement, although they knew that there was nothing absolutely bad, nor did they know there was anything absolutely good, in connection with the movement.

In the course of time we heard that the soldiers were moving toward the scene of the trouble. After awhile some of the soldiers finally reached our place and we heard that a number of them also reached our friends at Rosebud. Of course, when a large body of soldiers is moving toward a certain direction they inspire a more or less amount of awe, and it is natural that the woman and children who see this large moving mass are made afraid of it and be put in a condition to make them run away. At first we thought that Pine Ridge and Rosebud were the only two agencies where soldiers were sent, but finally we heard that the other agencies fared likewise. We heard and saw that half our friends at Rosebud agency, from fear at seeing the soldiers, began the move of running away from their agency toward ours [Pine Ridge], and when they had gotten inside of our reservation they there learned that right ahead of them at our agency was another large crowd of soldiers, and while the soldiers were there, there was constantly a great deal of false rumor flying back and forth. The special rumor I have in mind is the threat that the soldiers had come there to disarm the Indians entirely and to take away all their horses from them. That was the oft-repeated story.

So constantly repeated was this story that our friends from Rosebud, instead of going to Pine Ridge, the place of their destination, veered off and went to some other direction toward the "Bad Lands." We did not know definitely how many, but understood there were 300 lodges of them, about 1,700 people. Eagle Pipe, Turning Bear, High Hawk, Short Bull, Lance, No Flesh, Pine Bird, Crow Dog, Two Strike, and White Horse were the leaders.

The people after veering off in this way, many of them who believe in peace and order at our agency, were very anxious that some influence should be brought upon these people. In addition to our love of peace we remembered that many of these people were related to us by blood. So we sent out peace commissioners to the people who were thus running away from their agency.

I understood at the time that they were simply going away from fear because of so many soldiers. So constant was the word of these good men from Pine Ridge agency that finally they succeeded in getting away half of the party from Rosebud, from the

place where they took refuge, and finally were brought to the agency at Pine Ridge. Young-Man-Afraid-of-His-Horses, Little Wound, Fast Thunder, Louis Shangreau, John Grass, Jack Red Cloud, and myself were some of these peacemakers.

The remnant of the party from Rosebud not taken to the agency finally reached the wilds of the Bad Lands. Seeing that we had succeeded so well, once more we went to the same party in the Bad Lands and succeeded in bringing these very Indians out of the depths of the Bad Lands and were being brought toward the agency. When we were about a day's journey from our agency we heard that a certain band of Indians from the Cheyenne River agency was coming toward Pine Ridge in flight [those are considered to be from Big Foot's band].

Captain Sword: Those who actually went off of the Cheyenne River agency probably number 303, and there were [some] from the Standing Rock reserve with them, but as to their number I do not know. There were a number of Oglallas, old men and several school boys, coming back with that very same party, and one of the very seriously wounded boys was a member of the Oglalla boarding school at Pine Ridge agency. He was not on the warpath, but was simply returning to his agency and to his school after a summer visit to his relatives on the Cheyenne River.

Turning Hawk: When we heard that these people were coming toward our agency we also heard this. These people were coming toward Pine Ridge agency, and when they were almost on the agency they were met by the soldiers and surrounded and finally taken to the Wounded Knee creek, and there at a given time their guns were demanded. When they had delivered them up, the men were separated from their families, from their tipis, and taken to a certain spot. When the guns were thus taken and the men thus separated, there was a crazy man, a young man of very bad influence and in fact a nobody, among that bunch of Indians [who] fired his gun, and of course the firing of a gun must have been the breaking of a military rule of some sort, because immediately the soldiers returned fire and indiscriminate killing followed.

Spotted Horse: This man shot an officer in the army; the first killed this officer. I was a voluntary scout at that encounter and I saw exactly what was done, and that was what I noticed; that the first shot killed an officer. As soon as this shot was fired the Indians immediately began drawing their knives, and they were exhorted from all sides to desist, but this was not obeyed. Consequently the firing began immediately on the part of the soldiers.

Turning Hawk: All the men who were in a bunch were killed right there, and those who escaped that first fire got into the ravine, and as they went along up the ravine for a long distance they were pursued on both sides by the soldiers and shot down, as the dead bodies showed afterwards. The women were standing off at a different place from where the men were stationed, and when the firing began, those of the men who escaped the first onslaught went in one direction up the ravine, and then the women, who were bunched together at another place, went entirely in a different direction through an open field, and the women fared the same fate as the men who went up the deep ravine.

American Horse: The men were separated, as has already been said, from the women, and they were surrounded by the soldiers also. When the firing began, of course the people who were standing immediately around the young man who fired the first shot were killed right together, and then they turned their guns, Hotchkiss guns, etc., upon the women who were in the lodges standing there under a flag of truce, and of course as soon as they were fired upon they fled, the men fleeing in one direction and the women running in two different directions. So that there were three general directions in which they took flight.

There was a woman with an infant in her arms who was killed as she almost touched the flag of truce, and the women and children of course were strewn all along the circular village until they were dispatched. Right near the flag of truce a mother was shot down with her infant; the child not knowing that its mother was dead was still nursing, and that especially was a very sad sight. The women as they were fleeing with their babies were killed together, shot right through, and the women who were very heavy with child were also killed. All the Indians fled in these three directions, and after most all of them had been killed a cry was made that all those who were not killed or wounded should come out of their places of refuge, and as soon as they came in sight a number of soldiers surrounded them and butchered them there.

Of course we all feel very sad about this affair. I stood very loyal to the government all through those troublesome days, and believing so much in the government and being so loyal to it, my disappointment was very strong, and I have come to Washington with a very great blame on my heart. Of course it

would have been all right if only the men were killed; we would almost feel grateful for it. But the fact of the killing of the women, and more especially the killing of the young boys and girls who are to go to make up the future strength of the Indian people, is the saddest part of the whole affair and we feel it very sorely.

I was not there at the time before the burial of the bodies, but I did go there with some of the police and the Indian doctor and a great many people, men from the agency, and we went through the battlefield and saw where the bodies were from the track of the blood.

Turning Hawk: I had just reached the point where I said that the women were killed. We heard, besides the killing of the men, of the onslaught also made upon the women and children, and they were treated as roughly and indiscriminately as the men and boys were.

Of course this affair brought a great deal of distress upon all the people, but especially upon the minds of those who stood loyal to the government and who did all that they were able to do in the matter of bringing about peace. They especially have suffered much distress and are very much hurt at heart. These peacemakers continued on in their good work, but there were a great many fickle young men who were ready to be moved by the change in the events there, and consequently, in spite of the great fire that was brought upon all, they were ready to assume any hostile attitude. These young men got themselves in readiness and went in the direction of the scene of battle so they might be of service there. They got there and finally exchanged shots with the soldiers. This party of young men was made up from Rosebud, Oglalla [Pine Ridge], and members of any other agencies that happened to be there at the time. While this was going on in the neighborhood of Wounded Knee [the Indians and soldiers exchanging shots] the agency, our home, was also fired into by the Indians. Matters went on in this strain until the evening came on, and then the Indians went off down by White Clay creek. When the agency was fired upon by the Indians from the hillside, of course the shots were returned by the Indian police who were guarding the agency buildings.

Although fighting seemed to have been in the air, yet those who believed in peace were still constant in their work. Young-Man-Afraid-of-His-Horses, who had been on a visit to some other agency in the north or northwest, returned, and immediately went out to the people living about White Clay creek, on the border of the Bad Lands, and brought his people out. He succeeded in obtaining the consent of the people to come out of their place of refuge and return to the agency. Thus the remaining portion of the Indians who started from Rosebud were brought back into the agency. Mr. Commissioner, during the days of the great whirlwind out there, these good men tried to hold up a counteracting power, and that was "Peace." We have now come to realize that peace has prevailed and won the day. While we were engaged in bringing about peace our property was left behind, of course, and most of us lost everything, even down to the matter of guns with which to kill ducks, rabbits, etc., shotguns, and guns of that order. When Young-Man-Afraid brought the people in and their guns were asked for, both men who were called hostile and men who stood loyal to the government delivered up their guns.

Lone Wolf v. Hitchcock (1902)

On January 6, 1901, a rule to show cause why a temporary injunction should not be granted was issued. In response to this rule an affidavit of the Secretary of the Interior was filed, in which, in substance, it was averred that the complainant (Lone Wolf) and his wife and daughter had selected allotments under the act of June 6, 1900, and the same had been approved by the Secretary of the Interior, and that all other members of the tribes, excepting twelve, had also accepted and retained allotments in severalty, and that the greater part thereof had been approved before the bringing of this suit. . . . The appellants base their right to relief on the proposition that by the effect of the article just quoted the confederated tribes of Kiowa, Comanche, and Apache were vested with an interest in the lands held in common within the reservation, which interest could not be divested by Congress in any other mode than that specified in the said twelfth article, and that as a result of the said stipulation the interest of the Indians in the common lands fell within the protection of the fifth amendment to the Constitution of the United States, and such interest—indirectly at least—came under the control of the judicial branch of the Government. We are unable to yield our assent to this view.

The contention, in effect, ignores the status of the contracting Indians and the relation of dependency they bore and continue to bear toward the Government of the United States. To uphold the

claim would be to adjudge that the indirect operation of the treaty was to materially limit and qualify the controlling authority of Congress in respect to the care and protection of the Indians, and to deprive Congress, in a possible emergency, when the necessity might be urgent for a partition and disposal of the tribal lands, of all power to act if the assent of the Indians could not be obtained.

Now, it is true that in decisions of this court the Indian right of occupancy of tribal lands, whether declared in a treaty or otherwise created, has been stated to be sacred, or, as sometimes expressed, as sacred as the fee of the United States in the same lands . . . —But in none of these cases was there involved a controversy between Indians and the Government respecting the power of Congress to administer the property of the Indians. The questions considered in the cases referred to, which either directly or indirectly had relation to the nature of the property rights of the Indians, concerned the character and extent of such rights as respected States or individuals. In one of the cited cases it was clearly pointed out that Congress possessed a paramount power over the property of the Indians by reason of its exercise of guardianship over their interests, and that such authority might be implied, even though opposed to the strict letter of a treaty with the Indians. Thus, in *Beecher v. Wetherby* (95 U. S., 525), discussing the claim that there had been a prior reservation of land by treaty to the use of a certain tribe of Indians, the court said (p. 525):

> But the right which the Indians held was only that of occupancy. The fee was in the United States, subject to that right, and could be transferred by them whenever they chose. The grantee, it is true, would take only the naked fee, and could not disturb the occupancy of the Indians; that occupancy could only be interfered with or determined by the United States. It is to be presumed that in this matter the United States would be governed by such considerations of justice as would control a Christian people in their treatment of an ignorant and dependent race. Be that as it may, the propriety or justice of their action toward the Indians with respect to their lands is a question of governmental policy, and is not a matter open to discussion in a controversy between third parties, neither of whom derives title from the Indians.

Plenary authority over the tribal relations of the Indians has been exercised by Congress from the beginning, and the power has always been deemed a political one, not subject to be controlled by the judicial department of the Government. Until the year 1871 the policy was pursued of dealing with the Indian tribes by means of treaties, and of course a moral obligation rested upon Congress to act in good faith in performing the stipulations entered into on its behalf. But, as with treaties made with foreign nations (*Chinese Exclusion Cases*, 130 U. S., 581, 600), the legislative power might pass laws in conflict with treaties made with the Indians . . .

The power exists to abrogate the provisions of an Indian treaty, though presumably such power will be exercised only when circumstances arise which will not only justify the Government in disregarding the stipulations of the treaty, but may demand, in the interest of the country and the Indians themselves, that it should do so. When, therefore, treaties were entered into between the United States and a tribe of Indians it was never doubted that the power to abrogate existed in Congress, and that in a contingency such power might be availed of from considerations of governmental policy, particularly if consistent with perfect good faith toward the Indians . . .

The power of the General Government over these remnants of a race once powerful, now weak and diminished in numbers, is necessary to their protection, as well as to the safety of those among whom they dwell. It must exist in that Government, because it never has existed anywhere else; because the theater of its exercise is within the geographical limits of the United States; because it has never been denied, and because it alone can enforce its laws on all the tribes . . .

In view of the legislative power possessed by Congress over treaties with the Indians and Indian tribal property we may not specially consider the contentions pressed upon our notice that the signing by the Indians of the agreement of October 6, 1892, was obtained by fraudulent misrepresentations and concealment; that the requisite three-fourths of adult male Indians had not signed, as required by the twelfth article of the treaty of 1867, and that the treaty as signed had been amended by Congress without submitting such amendments to the action of the Indians, since all these matters, in any event, were solely within the domain of the legislative authority, and its action is conclusive upon the courts.

The act of June 6, 1900, which is complained of in the bill, was enacted at a time when the tribal relations between the confederated tribes of Kiowas, Comanches, and Apaches still existed, and that statute and the statutes supplementary thereto dealt with the disposition of tribal property and purported to give an adequate consideration for the surplus lands not allotted among the Indians or reserved for their benefit. Indeed, the controversy which this case presents is concluded by the decision in *Cherokee Nation v. Hitchcock* (187 U. S., 294), decided at this term, where it was held that full administrative power was possessed by Congress over Indian tribal property. In effect, the action of Congress now complained of was but an exercise of such power, a mere change in the form of investment of Indian tribal property, the property of those who, as we have held, were in substantial effect the words of the Government. We must presume that Congress acted in perfect good faith in the dealings with the Indians of which complaint is made, and that the legislative branch of the Government exercised its best judgment in the premises. In any event, as Congress possessed full power in the matter, the judiciary can not question or inquire into the motives which prompted the enactment of this legislation. If injury was occasioned, which we do not wish to be understood as implying, by the use made by Congress of its power, relief must be sought by an appeal to that body for redress and not to be courts. The legislation in question was constitutional, and the demurrer to the bill was therefore rightly sustained. . . .

Geronimo: His Own Story (1906)

COMING OF THE WHITE MEN

About the time of the massacre of "Kaskiyeh" [1858] we heard that some white men were measuring land to the south of us. In company with a number of other warriors I went to visit them. We could not understand them very well, for we had no interpreter, but we made a treaty with them by shaking hands and promising to be brothers. Then we made our camp near their camp, and they came to trade with us. We gave them buckskin, blankets, and ponies in exchange for shirts and provisions. We also brought them game, for which they gave us some money. We did not know the value of this money, but we kept it and later learned from the Navajo Indians that it was very valuable.

Every day they measured land with curious instruments and put down marks which we could not understand. They were good men, and we were sorry when they had gone on into the west. They were not soldiers. These were the first white men I ever saw. . . .

Not long after this some of the officers of the United States troops invited our leaders to hold a conference at Apache Pass [Fort Bowie]. Just before noon the Indians were shown into a tent and told that they would be given something to eat. When in the tent they were attacked by soldiers. Our chief, Mangus-Colorado, and several other warriors, by cutting through the tent, escaped; but most of the warriors were killed or captured. Among the Bedonkohe Apaches killed at this time were Sanza, Kladetahe, Niyokahe, and Gopi. After this treachery the Indians went back to the mountains and left the fort entirely alone. I do not think that the agent had anything to do with planning this, for he had always treated us well. I believe it was entirely planned by the soldiers . . .

After this trouble all of the Indians agreed not to be friendly with the white men any more. There was no general engagement, but a long struggle followed. Sometimes we attacked the white men, sometimes they attacked us. First a few Indians would be killed and then a few soldiers. I think the killing was about equal on each side. The number killed in these troubles did not amount to much, but this treachery on the part of the soldiers had angered the Indians and revived memories of other wrongs, so that we never again trusted the United States troops.

GREATEST OF WRONGS

Perhaps the greatest wrong ever done to the Indians was the treatment received by our tribe from the United States troops about 1863. The chief of our tribe, Mangus-Colorado, went to make a treaty of peace for our people with the white settlement at Apache Tejo, New Mexico. It had been reported to us that the white men in this settlement were more friendly and more reliable than those in Arizona, that they would live up to their treaties and would not wrong the Indians.

Mangas-Colorado, with three other warriors, went to Apache Tejo and held a council with these citizens and soldiers. They told him that if he would come with his tribe and live near them, they would issue to him, from the Government, blankets, flour,

provisions, beef, and all manner of supplies. Our chief promised to return to Apache Tejo within two weeks. When he came back to our settlement he assembled the whole tribe in council. I did not believe that the people at Apache Tejo would do as they said and therefore I opposed the plan, but it was decided that with part of the tribe Mangus-Colorado should return to Apache Tejo and receive an issue of rations and supplies. If they were as represented, and if these white men would keep the treaty faithfully, the remainder of the tribe would join him and we would make our permanent home at Apache Tejo . . . No word ever came to us from them. From other sources, however, we heard that they had been treacherously captured and slain. In this dilemma we did not know just exactly what to do, but fearing that the troops who had captured them would attack us, we retreated into the mountains near Apache Pass . . . After we had disbanded our tribe the Bedonkohe Apaches reassembled near their old camp vainly waiting for the return of Mangas-Colorado and our kinsmen. No tidings came save that they had all been treacherously slain. Then a council was held, and as it was believed that Mangus-Colorado was dead, I was elected Tribal Chief. . . .

REMOVALS

While returning from trailing the Government troops we saw two men, a Mexican and a white man, and shot them off their horses. With these two horses we returned and moved our camp. My people were suffering much and it was deemed advisable to go where we could get more provisions. Game was scarce in our range then, and since I had been Tribal Chief I had not asked for rations from the Government, nor did I care to do so, but we did not wish to starve.

We had heard that Chief Victoria of the Chihenne [Oje Caliente] Apaches was holding a council with the white men near Hot Springs in New Mexico, and that he had plenty of provisions. We had always been on friendly terms with this tribe, and Victoria was especially kind to my people. With the help of the two horses we had captured, to carry our sick with us, we went to Hot Springs. We easily found Victoria and his band, and they gave us supplies for the winter. We stayed with them for about a year, and during this stay we had perfect peace. We had not the least trouble with Mexicans, white men, or Indians. When we had stayed as long as we should, and had again accumulated some supplies, we decided to leave Victoria's band. When I told him that we were going to

leave he said that we should have a feast and dance before we separated.

The festivities were held about two miles above Hot Springs, and lasted for four days. There were about four hundred Indians at this celebration. I do not think we ever spent a more pleasant time than upon this occasion. No one ever treated our tribe more kindly than Victoria and his band. We are still proud to say that he and his people were our friends.

When I went to Apache Pass (Fort Bowie) I found General Howard in command, and made a treaty with him. This treaty lasted until long after General Howard had left our country. He always kept his word with us and treated us as brothers. We never had so good a friend among the United States officers as General Howard. We could have lived forever at peace with him. If there is any pure, honest white man in the United States army, that man is General Howard. . . .

IN PRISON AND ON THE WAR PATH

Soon after we arrived in New Mexico two companies of scouts were sent from San Carlos. When they came to Hot Springs they sent word for me and Victoria to come to town. The messengers did not say what they wanted with us, but as they seemed friendly we thought they wanted a council, and rode in to meet the officers. As soon as we arrived in town soldiers met us, disarmed us, and took us both to headquarters, where we were tried by court-martial. They asked us only a few questions and then Victoria was released and I was sentenced to the guardhouse. Scouts conducted me to the guardhouse and put me in chains. When I asked them why they did this they said it was because I had left Apache Pass.

I do not think that I ever belonged to those soldiers at Apache Pass, or that I should have asked them where I might go. Our bands could no longer live in peace together, and so we had quietly withdrawn, expecting to live with Victoria's band, where we thought we would not be molested. They also sentenced seven other Apaches to chains in the guardhouse.

I do not know why this was done, for these Indians had simply followed me from Apache Pass to Hot Springs. If it was wrong (and I do not think it was wrong) for us to go to Hot Springs, I alone was to blame. They asked the soldiers in charge why they were imprisoned and chained, but received no answer.

I was kept a prisoner for four months, during which time I was transferred to San Carlos. Then I think I had another trial, although I was not present.

In fact I do not know that I had another trial, but I was told that I had, and at any rate I was released. . . .

In the summer of 1883 a rumor was current that the officers were again planning to imprison our leaders. This rumor served to revive the memory of all our past wrongs—the massacre in the tent at Apache Pass, the fate of Mangus Colorado, and my own unjust imprisonment, which might easily have been death to me. Just at this time we were told that the officers wanted us to come up the river above Geronimo to a fort [Fort Thomas] to hold a council with them. We did not believe that any good could come of this conference, or that there was any need of it; so we held a council ourselves, and fearing treachery, decided to leave the reservation. We thought it more manly to die on the war path than to be killed in prison. . . .

THE FINAL STRUGGLE

We started with all our tribe to go with General [George] Crook back to the United States, but I feared treachery and decided to remain in Mexico. . . . I have suffered much from such unjust orders as those of General Crook. Such acts have caused much distress to my people. I think that General Crook's death was sent by the Almighty as a punishment for the many evil deeds he committed.

Soon General Miles was made commander of all the western posts, and troops trailed us continually. They were led by Captain Lawton, who had good scouts. The Mexican soldiers also became more active and more numerous. We had skirmishes almost every day, and so we finally decided to break up into small bands. With six men and four women I made for the range of mountains near Hot Springs, New Mexico. We passed many cattle ranches, but had no trouble with the cowboys. We killed cattle to eat whenever we were in need of food, but we frequently suffered greatly for water. At one time we had no water for two days and nights and our horses almost died from thirst. We ranged in the mountains of New Mexico for some time, then thinking that perhaps the troops had left Mexico, we returned. On our return through Old Mexico we attacked every Mexican found, even if for no other reason than to kill. We believed they had asked the United States troops to come down to Mexico to fight us. . . .

I sent my brother Porico [White Horse] with Mr. George Wratton on to Fort Bowie to see General Nelson Miles, and to tell him that we wished to return to Arizona; but before these messengers returned I met two Indian scouts—Kayitah, a Chokonen Apache, and Marteen, a Nedni Apache. They were serving as scouts for Captain Lawton's troops. They told me that General Miles had come and had sent them to ask me to meet him. So I went to the camp of the United States troops to meet General Miles.

When I arrived at their camp I went directly to General Miles and told him how I had been wronged, and that I wanted to return to the United States with my people, as we wished to see our families, who had been captured and taken away from us.

General Miles said to me:

"The President of the United States has sent me to speak to you. He has heard of your trouble with the white men, and says that if you will agree to a few words of treaty we need have no more trouble. Geronimo, if you will agree to a few words of treaty all will be satisfactorily arranged."

So General Miles told me how we could be brothers to each other. We raised our hands to heaven and said that the treaty was not to be broken. We took an oath not to do any wrong to each other or to scheme against each other.

Then he talked with me for a long time and told me what he would do for me in the future if I would agree to the treaty. I did not greatly believe General Miles, but because the President of the United States had sent me word I agreed to make the treaty, and to keep it. Then I asked General Miles what the treaty would be. General Miles said to me:

"I will take you under Government protection; I will build you a house; I will fence you much land; I will give you cattle, horses, mules, and farming implements. You will be furnished with men to work the farm, for you yourself will not have to work. In the fall I will send you blankets and clothing so that you will not suffer from cold in the winter time. There is plenty of timber, water, and grass in the land to which I will send you. You will live with your tribe and with your family. If you agree to this treaty you shall see your family within five days."

I said to General Miles:

"All the officers that have been in charge of the Indians have talked that way, and it sounds like a story to me; I hardly believe you."

He said:

"This time it is the truth."

I said:

"General Miles, I do not know the laws of the white man, nor of this new country where you are to send me, and I might break the laws."

He said:

"While I live you will not be arrested."

Then I agreed to make the treaty. (Since then I have been a prisoner of war, I have been arrested and placed in the guardhouse twice for drinking whisky.)

We stood between his troopers and my warriors. We placed a large stone on the blanket before us. Our treaty was made by this stone, as it was to last until the stone should crumble to dust; so we made the treaty, and bound each other with an oath.

I do not believe that I have ever violated that treaty; but General Miles never fulfilled his promises. . . .

A PRISONER OF WAR

When I had given up to the Government they put me on the Southern Pacific Railroad and took me to San Antonio, Texas, and held me to be tried by their laws.

In forty days they took me from there to Fort Pickens [Pensacola], Florida. Here they put me to sawing up large logs. There were several other Apache warriors with me, and all of us had to work every day. For nearly two years we were kept at hard labor in this place and we did not see our families until May, 1887. This treatment was in direct violation of our treaty made at Skeleton Canyon.

After this we were sent with our families to Vermont, Alabama, where we stayed five years and worked for the Government. We had no property, and I looked in vain for General Miles to send me to that land of which he had spoken; I longed in vain for the implements, house, and stock that General Miles had promised me. . . . We were not healthy in this place, for the climate disagreed with us. . . .

When General Miles last visited Fort Sill I asked to be relieved from labor on account of my age. I also remembered what General Miles had promised me in the treaty and told him of it. He said I need not work any more except when I wished to, and since that time I have not been detailed to do any work. I have worked a great deal, however, since then, for, although I am old, I like to work and help my people as much as I am able.

Winters v. United States (1908)

Winters v. United States has become the most influential case in defining Native American water rights.

APPEAL from the United States Circuit Court of Appeals for the Ninth Circuit to review a decree which affirmed a decree of the Circuit Court for the District of Montana, enjoining a diversion of the waters of Milk river. Affirmed. . . .

Statement by Mr. Justice McKenna:

This suit was brought by the United States to restrain appellants and others from constructing or maintaining dams or reservoirs on the Milk river in the state of Montana, or in any manner preventing the water of the river or its tributaries from flowing to the Fort Belknap Indian Reservation.

An interlocutory order was granted, enjoining the defendants in the suit from interfering in any manner with the use by the reservation of 5,000 inches of the water of the river. The order was affirmed by the circuit court of appeals. 74 C. C. A. 666, 143, Fed. 740. Upon the return of the case to the circuit court, an order was taken pro confesso against five of the defendants. The appellants filed a joint and several answer, upon which and [a]. . . decree was entered making the preliminary injunction permanent. The decree was affirmed by the circuit court of appeals. 78 C. C. A. 546, 148 Fed. 684.

The allegations of the bill, so far as necessary to state them, are as follows: On the 1st day of May 1888, a tract of land, the property of the United States, was reserved and set apart 'as an Indian reservation as and for a permanent home and abiding place of the Gros Ventre and Assiniboin bands or tribes of Indians in the state (then territory) of Montana, designated and known as the Fort Belknap Indian Reservation.' The tract has ever since been used as an Indian reservation and as the home and abiding place of the Indians. Its boundaries were fixed and defined as follows . . .

Milk river, designated as the northern boundary of the reservation, is a nonnavigable stream. Large portions of the lands embraced within the reservation are well fitted and adapted for pasturage and the feeding and grazing of stock, and since the establishment of the reservation the United States and the Indians have had and have large herds of cattle and large numbers of horses grazing upon the land within the reservation, 'being and situate along and bordering upon said Milk river.' Other portions of the reservation are 'adapted for and susceptible of farming and cultivation and the pursuit of agriculture, and productive in the raising thereon of grass, grain, and vegetables,' but such portions are of dry and arid character, and, in order to make them productive, require large quantities of water for the purpose of irrigating them. In 1889 the

United States constructed houses and buildings upon the reservation for the occupancy and residence of the officers in charge of it, and such officers depend entirely for their domestic, culinary, and irrigation purposes upon the water of the river. In the year 1889, and long prior to the acts of the defendants complained of, the United States, through its officers and agents at the reservation, appropriated and took from the river a flow of 1,000 miners' inches, and conducted it to the buildings and premises, used the same for domestic purposes and also for the irrigation of land adjacent to the buildings and premises, and by the use thereof raised crops of grain, grass, and vegetables. Afterwards, but long prior to the acts of the defendants complained of, to wit, on the 5th of July, 1898, the Indians residing on the reservation diverted from the river for the purpose of irrigation a flow of 10,000 miners' inches of water to and upon divers and extensive tracts of land, aggregating in amount about 30,000 acres, and raised upon said lands crops of grain, grass, and vegetables. And ever since 1889 and July, 1898, the United States and the Indians have diverted and used the waters of the river in the manner and for the purposes mentioned, and the United States 'has been enabled by means thereof to train, encourage, and accustom large numbers of Indians residing upon the said reservation to habits of industry and to promote their civilization and improvement.' It is alleged with detail that all of the waters of the river are necessary for all those purposes and the purposes for which the reservation was created, and that in furthering and advancing the civilization and improvement of the Indians, and to encourage habits of industry and thrift among them, it is essential and necessary that all of the waters of the river flow down the channel uninterruptedly and undiminished in quantity and undeteriorated in quality.

It is alleged that, 'notwithstanding the riparian and other rights' of the United States and the Indians to the uninterrupted flow of the waters of the river, the defendants, in the year 1900, wrongfully entered upon the river and its tributaries above the points of the diversion of the waters of the river by the United States and the Indians, built large and substantial dams and reservoirs, and, by means of canals and ditches and water ways, have diverted the waters of the river from its channel, and have deprived the United States and the Indians of the use thereof. And this diversion of the water, it is alleged, has continued until the present time, to the irreparable injury

of the United States, for which there is no adequate remedy at law. . . .

And it is again alleged that the waters of the river are indispensable to defendants, are of the value of more than $100,000 to them, and that if they are deprived of the waters 'their lands will be ruined, it will be necessary to abandon their homes, and they will be greatly and irreparably damaged, the extent and amount of which damage cannot now be estimated, but will greatly exceed $100,000,' and that they will be wholly without remedy if the claim of the United States and the Indians be sustained.

Messrs. Edward C. Day and James A. Walsh for appellants.

Mr. Justice McKenna delivered the opinion of the court . . .

The case, as we view it, turns on the agreement of May, 1888, resulting in the creation of Fort Belknap Reservation. In the construction of this agreement there are certain elements to be considered that are prominent and significant. The reservation was a part of a very much larger tract which the Indians had the right to occupy and use, and which was adequate for the habits and wants of a nomadic and uncivilized people. It was the policy of the government, it was the desire of the Indians, to change those habits and to become a pastoral and civilized people. If they should become such, the original tract was too extensive; but a smaller tract would be inadequate without a change of conditions. The lands were arid, and, without irrigation, were practically valueless. And yet, it is contended, the means of irrigation were deliberately given up by the Indians and deliberately accepted by the government. The lands ceded were, it is true, also arid; and some argument may be urged, and is urged, that with their cession there was the cession of the waters, without which they would be valueless, and 'civilized communities could not be established thereon.' And this, it is further contended, the Indians knew, and yet made no reservation of the waters. We realize that there is a conflict of implications, but that which makes for the retention of the waters is of greater force than that which makes for their cession. The Indians had command of the lands and the waters,—command of all their beneficial use, whether kept for hunting, 'and grazing roving herds of stock,' or turned to agriculture and the arts of civilization. Did they give up all this? Did they reduce the area of their occupation and give up the waters which made it valuable or adequate? And, even regarding the allegation of the answer as true, that there are springs and streams on

the reservation flowing about 2,900 inches of water, the inquiries are pertinent. If it were possible to believe affirmative answers, we might also believe that the Indians were awed by the power of the government or deceived by its negotiators. Neither view is possible. The government is asserting the rights of the Indians. But extremes need not be taken into account. By a rule of interpretation of agreements and treaties with the Indians, ambiguities occurring will be resolved from the standpoint of the Indians. And the rule should certainly be applied to determine between two inferences, one of which would support the purpose of the agreement and the other impair or defeat it. On account of their relations to the government, it cannot be supposed that the Indians were alert to exclude by formal words every inference which might militate against or defeat the declared purpose of themselves and the government, even if it could be supposed that they had the intelligence to foresee the 'double sense' which might some time be urged against them.

Another contention of appellants is that if it be conceded that there was a reservation of the waters of Milk river by the agreement of 1888, yet the reservation was repealed by the admission of Montana into the Union, February 22, 1889, 'upon an equal footing with the original states.' The language of counsel is that 'any reservation in the agreement with the Indians, expressed or implied, whereby the waters of Milk river were not to be subject of appropriation by the citizens and inhabitants of said state, was repealed by the act of admission.' But to establish the repeal counsel rely substantially upon the same argument that they advance against the intention of the agreement to reserve the waters. The power of the government to reserve the waters and exempt them from appropriation under the state laws is not denied, and could not be. *United States v. Rio Grande Dam & Irrig. Co.* 174 U. S. 702, 43 L. ed. 1141, 19 Sup. Ct. Rep. 770; *United States v. Winans,* 198 U. S. 371, 49 L. ed. 1089, 25 Sup. Ct. Rep. 662. That the government did reserve them we have decided, and for a use which would be necessarily continued through years. This was done May 1, 1888, and it would be extreme to believe that within a year Congress destroyed the reservation and took from the Indians the consideration of their grant, leaving them a barren waste,—took from them the means of continuing their old habits, yet did not leave them the power to change to new ones.

Appellants' argument upon the incidental repeal of the agreement by the admission of Montana into the Union, and the power over the waters of Milk river which the state thereby acquired to dispose of them under its laws, is elaborate and able, but our construction of the agreement and its effect make it unnecessary to answer the argument in detail. For the same reason we have not discussed the doctrine of riparian rights urged by the government.

Decree affirmed.

Indian Citizenship Act (1924)

An Act To Authorize the Secretary of the Interior to issue certificates of citizenship to Indians.

Be it enacted . . . That all non-citizen Indians born within the territorial limits of the United States be, and they are hereby, declared to be citizens of the United States: Provided, That the granting of such citizenship shall not in any manner impair or otherwise affect the right of any Indian to tribal or other property.

Meriam Report (1928)

CHAPTER I
GENERAL SUMMARY OF FINDINGS AND RECOMMENDATIONS

The Conditions Among the Indians. An overwhelming majority of the Indians are poor, even extremely poor, and they are not adjusted to the economic and social system of the dominant white civilization. . . .

In justice to the Indians, it should be said that many of them are living on lands from which a trained and experienced white man could scarcely wrest a reasonable living. In some instances the land originally set apart for the Indians was of little value for agricultural operations other than grazing. In other instances part of the land was excellent but the Indians did not appreciate its value. Often when individual allotments were made, they chose for themselves the poorer parts, because those parts were near a domestic water supply or a source of firewood, or because they furnished some native product important to the Indians in their primitive life. Frequently the better sections of the land originally set apart for the Indians have fallen into the hands of the whites, and the Indians have retreated to the poorer lands remote from markets. . . .

Suffering and Discontent.

Some people assert that the Indians prefer to live as they do; that they are happier in their idleness and irresponsibility. The question may be raised whether these persons do not mistake for happiness and content an almost oriental fatalism and resignation. The survey staff found altogether too much evidence of real suffering and discontent to subscribe to the belief that the Indians are reasonably satisfied with their condition. The amount of serious illness and poverty is too great to permit of real contentment. The Indian is like the white man in his affection for his children, and he feels keenly the sickness and the loss of his offspring. . . .

The Work of the Government in Behalf of the Indians.

The work of the government directed toward the education and advancement of the Indian himself, as distinguished from the control and conservation of his property, is largely ineffective. The chief explanation of the deficiency in this work lies in the fact that the government has not appropriated enough funds to permit the Indian Service to employ an adequate personnel properly qualified for the task before it.

Absence of Well-Considered, Broad Educational Program.

The outstanding evidence of the lack of adequate, well-trained personnel is the absence of any well considered, broad educational program for the Service as a whole. Here the word education is used in its widest sense and includes not only school training for children but also activities for the training of adults to aid them in adjusting themselves to the dominant social and economic life which confronts them. It embraces education in economic production and in living standards necessary for the maintenance of health and decency.

Work for the Promotion of Health.

The inadequacy of appropriations has prevented the development of an adequate system of public health administration and medical relief work for the Indians . . . .

The hospitals, sanatoria, and sanatorium schools maintained by the Service, despite a few exceptions, must be generally characterized as lacking in personnel, equipment, management, and design. The statement is sometimes made that, since the Indians live according to a low scale, it is not necessary for the government to furnish hospital facilities for them which are comparable with those supplied for poor white people in a progressive community. The survey staff regards this basis of judging facilities as unsound. The question is whether the hospitals and sanatoria are efficient institutions for the care and treatment of patients, and this question must generally be answered in the negative. . . .

Formal Education of Indian Children.

For several years the general policy of the Indian Service has been directed away from the boarding school for Indian children and toward the public schools and Indian day schools. More Indian children are now in public schools maintained by the state or local governments than in special Indian schools maintained by the nation. It is, however, still the fact that the boarding school, either reservation or non-reservation, is the dominant characteristic of the school system maintained by the national government for its Indian wards.

The survey staff finds itself obliged to say frankly and unequivocally that the provisions for the care of the Indian children in boarding schools are grossly inadequate. . . .

The medical attention given Indian children in the day schools maintained by the government is also below a reasonable standard. . . .

Economic Education and Development on the Reservations.

At a few reservations energetic and resourceful superintendents with a real faculty for leadership have demonstrated that the economic education of the Indian is entirely possible. These superintendents have been handicapped in part by their own lack of training in several of the fields which are involved in a well-rounded, effective program of economic and social education, but even more by the general absence of trained and experienced assistants in these different fields.

Even under the best conditions, it is doubtful whether a well-rounded program of economic advancement framed with due consideration of the natural resources of the reservation has anywhere been thoroughly tried out. The Indians often say that programs change with superintendents. Under the poorest administration there is little evidence of anything which could be termed an economic program.

Everywhere the lack of trained subordinate personnel in immediate contact with the Indians is striking. For years the Indian Service has had field

positions with the title "Farmer." The duties of this position would more properly be described by the title "Field Clerk," or in some instances " General Laborer." The duties have rarely been those of an agricultural teacher and demonstrator, and the qualifications required have not been such as are necessary for teachers or leaders in agriculture. The salaries have been so low that, as a rule, the Service is fortunate if it gets a really good agricultural laborer with sufficient education to perform his clerical duties. Some exceptions must be noted. One or two well-trained agricultural teachers employed as farmers have shown what is possible, but in general the economic and industrial education of adult reservation Indians has been neglected.

Even less has been done toward finding profitable employment for Indians. As has been said, the schools do little for their graduates. Little is done on the reservations. In a few jurisdictions labor services are maintained chiefly in recruiting Indians for temporary unskilled labor. This employment service is largely mass work, not individualized, and it does not often seek to find the Indian an opportunity for a permanent position that offers him a chance to work up or one that will arouse his interest.

Family and Community Development.

The Indian Service has not appreciated the fundamental importance of family life and community activities in the social and economic development of a people. The tendency has been rather toward weakening Indian family life and community activities than toward strengthening them. The long continued policy of removing Indian children from the home and placing them for years in boarding school largely disintegrates the family and interferes with developing normal family life. The belief has apparently been that the shortest road to civilization is to take children away from their parents and insofar as possible to stamp out the old Indian life. The Indian community activities particularly have often been opposed if not suppressed. The fact has been appreciated that both the family life and the community activities have many objectionable features, but the action taken has often been the radical one of attempting to destroy rather than the educational process of gradual modification and development. . . .

Legal Protection and Advancement.

Much of the best work done by the Indian Service has been in the protection and conservation of Indian property, yet this program has emphasized the property rather than the Indian. Several legal situations exist which are serious impediments to the social and economic development of the race. . . .

Many Indian tribes still have outstanding against the government claims arising out of the old treaties and laws. The existence of these claims is a serious impediment to progress. The Indians look forward to getting vast sums from these claims; thus the facts regarding their economic future are uncertain. They will hardly knuckle down to work while they still hope the government will pay what they believe is due them. Some Indians, mostly mixed bloods, are maintaining their tribal connections and agitating because they have rights under these claims. Attorneys are naturally interested, and a few are perhaps inclined to urge the Indians to press claims which have comparatively little real merit. . . .

Failure to Develop Cooperative Relationships.

The Indian Service has not gone far enough in developing cooperative relationships with other organizations, public and private, which can be of material aid to it in educational developmental work for the Indians. . . .

Recommendations.

The fundamental requirement is that the task of the Indian Service be recognized as primarily educational, in the broadest sense of that word, and that it be made an efficient educational agency, devoting its main energies to the social and economic advancement of the Indians, so that they may be absorbed into the prevailing civilization or be fitted to live in the presence of that civilization at least in accordance with a minimum standard of health and decency.

To achieve this end, the Service must have a comprehensive, well-rounded educational program, adequately supported, which will place it at the forefront of organizations devoted to the advancement of a people. This program must provide for the promotion of health, the advancement of productive efficiency, the acquisition of reasonable ability in the utilization of income and property, guarding against exploitation, and the maintenance of reasonably high standards of family and community life. It must extend to adults as well as to children and must place special emphasis on the family and the community. Since the great majority of the Indians are ultimately to merge into the general population, it should cover the transitional period and should endeavor to instruct Indians in

the utilization of the services provided by public and quasi-public agencies for the people at large in exercising the privileges of citizenship and in making their contribution in service and in taxes for the maintenance of the government. It should also be directed toward preparing the white communities to receive the Indian. By improving the health of the Indian, increasing his productive efficiency, raising his standard of living, and teaching him the necessity for paying taxes, it will remove the main objections now advanced against permitting Indians to receive the full benefit of services rendered by progressive states and local governments for their populations. By actively seeking cooperation with state and local governments and by making a fair contribution in payment for services rendered by them to untaxed Indians, the national government can expedite the transition and hasten the day when there will no longer be a distinctive Indian problem and when the necessary governmental services are rendered alike to whites and Indians by the same organization without discrimination.

In the execution of this program, scrupulous care must be exercised to respect the rights of the Indian. This phrase "rights of the Indian" is often used solely to apply to his property rights. Here it is used in a much broader sense to cover his rights as a human being living in a free country. Indians are entitled to unfailing courtesy and consideration from all government employees. They should not be subjected to arbitrary action. Recognition of the educational nature of the whole task of dealing with them will result in taking the time to discuss with them in detail their own affairs and to lead rather than to force them to sound conclusions. The effort to substitute educational leadership for the more dictatorial methods now used in some places will necessitate more understanding of and sympathy for the Indian point of view. Leadership will recognize the good in the economic and social life of the Indians in their religion and ethics and will seek to develop it and build on it rather than to crush out all that is Indian. The Indians have much to contribute to the dominant civilization, and the effort should be made to secure this contribution, in part because of the good it will do the Indians in stimulating a proper race pride and self respect. . . .

Medical Service.

Adequate appropriations should be made markedly to accelerate the progress of the present administration in developing a real system of preventive medicine and public health service for the Indians. . . .

The medical examination of the Indian children must therefore be of the highest standard. . . .

School System.

The first and foremost need in Indian education is a change in point of view. Whatever may have been the official governmental attitude, education for the Indian in the past has proceeded largely on the theory that it is necessary to remove the Indian child as far as possible from his home environment; whereas the modern point of view in education and social work lays stress on upbringing in the natural setting of home and family life. The Indian educational enterprise is peculiarly in need of the kind of approach that recognizes this principle; that is less concerned with a conventional school system and more with the understanding of human beings. . . .

Routinization must be eliminated. The whole machinery of routinized boarding school and agency life works against that development of initiative and independence which should be the chief concern of Indian education in and out of school. The routinization characteristic of the boarding schools, with everything scheduled, no time left to be used at the child's own initiative, every moment determined by a signal or an order, leads just the other way. . . .

The boarding schools demand special consideration. Under the section on health the recommendations have been summarized that relate to the health of the child: better diet, less over-crowding, less heavy productive work, more thorough physical examinations, and better correlation of remediable defects. These factors have an important bearing on education itself that need not be discussed in this brief summary. . . .

The industrial training must be subjected to the tests of practical use. The Indian Service must attempt to place the Indians who leave the school and help them to become established in productive enterprise either on the reservations or in white communities. It must be prepared to enter into cooperative arrangements with employers so that boys and girls shall have opportunity to gain experience in commercial employment while still having some official connection with the school. In this way the school can place its emphasis on helping the pupil to acquire the necessary fundamental skill and then getting him a job where he can apply this skill in an occupation for which there is a local demand. . . .

The present policy of placing Indian children in public schools near their homes instead of in boarding schools or even in Indian Service day schools is, on the whole, to be commended. It is a movement in the direction of the normal transition; it results as a rule in good race contacts, and the Indians like it. The fact must be recognized, however, that often Indian children and Indian families need more service than is ordinarily rendered by public schools, as has just been elaborated in the discussion of boarding schools. The Indian Service must, therefore, supplement the public school work by giving special attention to health, industrial and social training, and the relationship between home and school. . . .

The Indian day schools should be increased in number and improved in quality and should carry children at least through the sixth grade. The Hopi day schools are perhaps the most encouraging feature of the Indian school system. More can perhaps be done in providing transportation to day schools. Where Indians come in to camp near the day schools, special activities should be undertaken for them. In general the day schools should be made community centers for reaching adult Indians in the vicinity as well as children, and they should be tied into the whole program adopted for the jurisdiction.

Improving General Economic Conditions.

The primary object of the Indian Service in the field of general economic conditions should be to increase the amount and the productivity of Indian labor so that the Indians can support themselves adequately through earned income. . . .

At some jurisdictions the economic resources are apparently insufficient, even if efficiently used, to support the Indian population according to reasonable standards. In some cases the Indians were given poor lands; in others during the course of years the whites have gained possession of the desirable lands. Nothing permanent is to be achieved by trying to make the Indians wrest a living from lands which will not yield a decent return for the labor expended. Some Indians on more promising land are personally interested in pursuits which cannot be followed on the reservations. The "let down your bucket where you are" policy, wise as it is for certain conditions, cannot therefore be exclusively followed. The Indian Service must seek to find suitable employment off the reservation for Indians who have no real chance there or

who desire to seek other employment. In some instances, as in the Navajo country, the situation can be met in part by securing them more land, but, in general, the solution lies in an intelligent employment service. . . .

This shift into industry cannot be made hurriedly or as a wholesale movement if it is to be successful. Employment finding should be individualized and should seek to place the Indians, usually the younger rather than the older Indians, in lines of work in which they are interested and which offer opportunity for advancement and for establishing a permanent home for themselves and, if they are married, for their families. The mass placing of large numbers of Indians in unskilled temporary jobs which offer no permanent opportunity and involve either separation from their families, or the makeshift of group camping, is at best a temporary expedient. Where it involves keeping children out of school and a low type of camp life, it probably does more harm than good. In placing Indians in temporary jobs of this character, the government should see that their wages are fair and their living conditions are up to a reasonable standard. The Indians should not be exploited as a source of cheap labor. . . .

The problem of inherited land should be given thorough detailed study by the Division of Planning and Development. . . . The policy of individual allotment should be followed with extreme conservatism. Not accompanied by adequate instruction in the use of property, it has largely failed in the accomplishment of what was expected of it. It has resulted in much loss of land and an enormous increase in the details of administration without a compensating advance in the economic ability of the Indians. The difficult problem of inheritance is one of its results. Before more allotments are made, the Service should be certain that it has the staff to do the educational work essential to the success of the policy. . . .

In some jurisdictions the tribe is possessed of great natural resources which are not susceptible of individual allotment and which, from the standpoint of sound national economy, should be preserved in large working units so that they may be conserved and used effectively. The two outstanding illustrations are the timber lands on the Klamath Reservation in Oregon and the timber lands and the power sites on the Menominee Reservation in Wisconsin. Only to a limited extent is it possible for these Indians to work with these great resources.

The more progressive Klamath Indians are anxious to get possession of their share of the tribal wealth so that they may use it as capital in individual enterprise . . .

The survey staff suggests that an experiment be tried in these jurisdictions with the modern business device of the corporation. The corporation would own the property, keep it intact, and conserve and operate it as a great national asset. . . .

Taxation of Property of Indians.

The question of subjecting the property of Indians to state and county taxes should be approached from the educational standpoint. It is essential that the Indians be educated to utilize the services furnished by local and state governments and that they learn the obligation to contribute to the support of these activities. On the other hand, the educational process should be gradual and the relationship between benefits received and tax payments therefore should be obvious. It is a serious mistake suddenly to change the status of an Indian from that of a tax-exempt person to a person subject to the full burden of state and county taxes, especially where the general property tax is in force, the brunt of which falls on land. The Indian has land value out of all proportion to his income from the use of that land, and thus the general property tax, when applied to him, violates the fundamental canon that taxation should be related to capacity to pay. An income tax would be a far better form of taxation for first lessons for the Indians. The imposition of the full weight of the general property tax tends to the loss of the Indians' land. . . .

Improving Family and Community Life.

The program developed for each jurisdiction should place special emphasis on family life and community activities. Experience has abundantly demonstrated that the family as a whole is the social unit of major importance in the development of a people. The importance of community activities has also been generally recognized. Among the Indians, community activities are probably even more important than among white people because the Indians' social and economic system was and is communistic. Individualism is almost entirely lacking in their native culture. Thus, work with communities as a whole will follow a natural line and will result in accelerated group progress.

The program should embrace health, home making with special emphasis on diet, the use of money, the supplementing of income by home activities, and organized recreation and other community activities.

In all these activities the Indian point of view and the Indian interests should be given major consideration. In home design and construction the effort should be made to adapt characteristically Indian things to modern uses. . . . In supplementing the Indian incomes and in home decoration, encouragement should be given to native Indian arts and industries. They appeal to the Indians' interest, afford an opportunity for self-expression, and, properly managed, will yield considerable revenue, much more than can be secured by encouraging them to duplicate the handiwork of the whites. Their designs can be readily adapted to articles for which the commercial demand is reasonably good. Persons who have interested themselves in this field uniformly report that the demand for Indian art work of high quality materially exceeds the supply, and that insofar as there is an over supply, it consists of work of poor quality. A little intelligent cooperation and aid in marketing would doubtless tend rapidly to correct this difficulty.

In recreation and in other community activities the existing activities of the Indians should be utilized as the starting point. That some of their dances and other activities have objectionable features is, of course, true. The same thing is true of the recreation and the community activities of almost any people. The object should be not to stamp out all the native things because a few of them have undesirable accompaniments but to seek to modify them gradually so that the objectionable features will ultimately disappear. The native activities can be supplemented by those activities borrowed from the whites that make a distinct appeal to the Indians, notably athletics, music, and sewing, and other close work demanding manual skill. The Indians themselves should have a large hand in the preparation of the program. . . .

Maintenance of Order and Administration of Justice.

The differences existing among the several jurisdictions with respect to such vital matters as the degree of economic and social advancement of the Indians, the homogeneity of the population, and their proximity to white civilization are so great that no specific act of Congress either conferring jurisdiction over the restricted Indians on state courts or providing a legal code and placing jurisdiction in the

United States courts appears practicable. The law and the system of judicial administration to be effective must be specially adapted to the particular jurisdiction where they are to be applied, and they must be susceptible of change to meet changing conditions until the Indians are ready to merge into the general population and be subjected, like other inhabitants, to the ordinary national and state laws administered by United States and state courts exercising their normal jurisdictions. . . .

Protection of the Property Rights of Indians.

No evidence warrants a conclusion that the government of the United States can, at any time in the near future, relinquish its guardianship over the property of restricted Indians, secured to the Indians by government action. The legal staff of the Indian Service charged with the duty of protecting Indian rights should be materially strengthened and should be authorized to act more directly. . . .

The Settlement of Claims.

The unsettled legal claims against the government should be settled at the earliest possible date. A special commission should be created to study those claims which have not yet been approved by Congress for submission to the Court of Claims. . . .

Citizenship.

All Indians born in the United States are now citizens. The Supreme Court of the United States has held that citizenship is not incompatible with continued guardianship or special protective legislation for Indians. The soundness of this decision is not open to question. It is good law and sound economic and social policy. In handling property, most of the restricted Indians are still children. True friends of the Indians should urge retention of restrictions until the Indian is economically on his feet and able to support himself by his own efforts according to a minimum standard of health and decency in the presence of white civilization.

Missionary Activities.

The outstanding need in the field of missionary activities among the Indians is cooperation. . . . The missionaries should consider carefully a material broadening of their program and an increase in the number and kinds of contacts with the Indians. Their best work has usually been in the field of education. For adult Indians their main offering has been church activities similar to those conducted in white communities, and those activities apparently make little appeal to the Indians. The missionaries need to have a better understanding of the Indian point of view of the Indian's religion and ethics, in order to start from what is good in them as a foundation. Too frequently, they have made the mistake of attempting to destroy the existing structure and to substitute something else without apparently realizing that much in the old has its place in the new. . . .

The belief is that it is a sound policy of national economy to make generous expenditures in the next few decades with the object of winding up the national administration of Indian affairs. The people of the United States have the opportunity, if they will, to write the closing chapters of the history of the relationship of the national government and the Indians. The early chapters contain little of which the country may be proud. It would be something of a national atonement to the Indians if the closing chapters should disclose the national government supplying the Indians with an Indian Service which would be a model for all governments concerned with the development and advancement of a retarded race.

Wheeler Howard (Indian Reorganization) Act (1934)

An Act To conserve and develop Indian lands and resources; to extend to Indians the right to form business and other organizations; to establish a credit system for Indians; to grant certain rights of home rule to Indians; to provide for vocational education for Indians; and for other purposes. . . .
SEC. 2.

The existing periods of trust placed upon any Indian lands and any restriction on alienation thereof are hereby extended and continued until otherwise directed by Congress.
SEC. 3.

The Secretary of the Interior, if he shall find it to be in the public interest, is hereby authorized to restore to tribal ownership the remaining surplus lands of any Indian reservation heretofore opened, or authorized to be opened, to sale, or any other form of disposal by Presidential proclamation, or by any of the public-land laws of the United States: *Provided, however,* That valid rights or claims of any persons to any lands so withdrawn existing on the date of the withdrawal shall not be affected by this Act. . . .

SEC. 4.

Except as herein provided, no sale, devise, gift, exchange or other transfer of restricted Indian lands or of shares in the assets of any Indian tribe or corporation organized hereunder, shall be made or approved: *Provided, however,* That such lands or interests may, with the approval of the Secretary of the Interior, be sold, devised, or otherwise transferred to the Indian tribe in which the lands or shares are located or from which the shares were derived or to a successor corporation; and in all instances such lands or interests shall descend or be devised, in accordance with the then existing laws of the State, or Federal laws where applicable, in which said lands are located or in which the subject matter of the corporation is located, to any member of such tribe or of such corporation or any heirs of such member: *Provided further,* That the Secretary of the Interior may authorize voluntary exchanges of lands of equal value, and the voluntary exchange of shares of equal value whenever such exchange, in his judgment, is expedient and beneficial for or compatible with the proper consolidation of Indian lands and for the benefit of cooperative organizations.

SEC. 5.

The Secretary of the Interior is hereby authorized, in his discretion, to acquire through purchase, relinquishment, gift, exchange, or assignment, any interest in lands, water rights or surface rights to lands, within or without existing reservations, including trust or otherwise restricted allotments whether the allottee be living or deceased, for the purpose of providing land for Indians. . . . Title to any lands or rights acquired pursuant to this Act shall be taken in the name of the United States in trust for the Indian tribe or individual Indian for which the land is acquired, and such lands or rights shall be exempt from State and local taxation.

SEC. 6.

The Secretary of the Interior is directed to make rules and regulations for the operation and management of Indian forestry units on the principle of sustained-yield management, to restrict the number of livestock grazed on Indian range units to the estimated carrying capacity of such ranges, and to promulgate such other rules and regulations as may be necessary to protect the range from deterioration, to prevent soil erosion, to assure full utilization of the range, and like purposes.

SEC. 7.

The Secretary of the Interior is hereby authorized to proclaim new Indian reservations on lands acquired pursuant to any authority conferred by this Act, or to add such lands to existing reservations: *Provided,* That lands added to existing reservations shall be designated for the exclusive use of Indians entitled by enrollment or by tribal membership to residence at such reservations.

SEC. 8.

Nothing contained in this Act shall be construed to relate to Indian holdings of allotments or homesteads upon the public domain outside, of the geographic boundaries of any Indian reservation now existing or established hereafter. . . .

SEC. 10.

There is hereby authorized to be appropriated, out of any funds in the Treasury not otherwise appropriated, the sum of $10,000,000 to be established as a revolving fund from which the Secretary of the Interior, under such rules and regulations as he may prescribe, may make loans to Indian chartered corporations for the purpose of promoting the economic development of such tribes and of their members, and may defray the expenses of administering such loans. Repayment of amounts loaned under this authorization shall be credited to the revolving fund and shall be available for the purposes for which the fund is established. A report shall be made annually to Congress of transactions under this authorization.

SEC. 11.

There is hereby authorized to be appropriated, out of any funds in the United States Treasury not otherwise appropriated, a sum not to exceed $250,000 annually, together with any unexpended balances of previous appropriations made pursuant to this section, for loans to Indians for the payment of tuition and other expenses in recognized vocational and trade schools: *Provided,* That not more than $50,000 of such sum shall be available for loans to Indian students in high schools and colleges. Such loans shall be reimbursable under rules established by the Commissioner of Indian Affairs.

SEC. 12.

The Secretary of the Interior is directed to establish standards of health, age, character, experience, knowledge, and ability for Indians who may be appointed, without regard to civil-service laws, to the various positions maintained, now or hereafter, by the Indian Office, in the administration of functions or services affecting any Indian tribe. Such qualified Indians shall hereafter have the preference to appointment to vacancies in any such positions. . . .

SEC. 15.

Nothing in this Act shall be construed to impair or prejudice any claim or suit of any Indian tribe against the United States. It is hereby declared to be the intent of Congress that no expenditures for the benefit of Indians made out of appropriations authorized by this Act shall be considered as offsets in any suit brought to recover upon any claim of such Indians against the United States.

SEC. 16.

Any Indian tribe, or tribes, residing on the same reservation, shall have the right to organize for its common welfare, and may adopt an appropriate constitution and bylaws, which shall become effective when ratified by a majority vote of the adult members of the tribe, or of the adult Indians residing on such reservation, as the case may be, at a special election authorized and called by the Secretary of the Interior under such rules and regulations as he may prescribe. Such constitution and bylaws when ratified as aforesaid and approved by the Secretary of the Interior shall be revocable by an election open to the same voters and conducted in the same manner as hereinabove provided. Amendments to the constitution and bylaws may be ratified and approved by the Secretary in the same manner as the original constitution and bylaws.

In addition to all powers vested in any Indian tribe or tribal council by existing law, the constitution adopted by said tribe shall also vest in such tribe or its tribal council the following rights and powers: To employ legal counsel, the choice of counsel and fixing of fees to be subject to the approval of the Secretary of the Interior; to prevent the sale, disposition, lease, or encumbrance of tribal lands, interests in lands, or other tribal assets without the consent of the tribe; and to negotiate with the Federal, State, and local Governments. The Secretary of the Interior shall advise such tribe or its tribal counsel of all appropriation estimates or Federal projects for the benefit of the tribe prior to the submission of such estimates to the Bureau of the Budget and the Congress.

SEC. 17.

The Secretary of the Interior may, upon petition by at least one-third of the adult Indians, issue a charter of incorporation to such tribe: . . .

SEC. 18.

This Act shall not apply to any reservation wherein a majority of the adult Indians, voting at a special election duly called by the Secretary of the Interior, shall vote against its application. It shall be the duty of the Secretary of the Interior, within one year after the passage and approval of this Act, to call such an election, which election shall be held by secret ballot upon thirty days' notice.

SEC. 19.

The term "Indian" as used in this Act shall include all persons of Indian descent who are members of any recognized Indian tribe now under Federal jurisdiction, and all persons who are descendants of such members who were, on June 1, 1934, residing within the present boundaries of any Indian reservation, and shall further include all other persons of one-half or more Indian blood. For the purposes of this Act Eskimos and other aboriginal peoples of Alaska shall be considered Indians. The term "tribe" wherever used in this Act shall be construed to refer to any Indian tribe, organized band, pueblo, or the Indians residing on one reservation. The words "adult Indians" wherever used in this Act shall be construed to refer to Indians who have attained the age of twenty-one years.

House Concurrent Resolution 108 (1953)

Whereas it is the policy of Congress, as rapidly as possible, to make the Indians within the territorial limits of the United States subject to the same laws and entitled to the same privileges and responsibilities as are applicable to other citizens of the United States, to end their status as wards of the United States, and to grant them all of the rights and prerogatives pertaining to American citizenship; and

Whereas the Indians within the territorial limits of the United States should assume their full responsibilities as American citizens: Now, therefore, be it

Resolved by the House of Representatives (the Senate concurring), That it is declared to be the sense of Congress that, at the earliest possible time, all of the Indian tribes and the individual members thereof located within the States of California, Florida, New York, and Texas, and all of the following named Indian tribes and individual members thereof, should be freed from Federal supervision and control and from all disabilities and limitations specially applicable to Indians: The Flathead Tribe of Montana, the Klamath Tribe of Oregon, the Menominee Tribe of Wisconsin, the Potowatamie Tribe of Kansas and Nebraska, and those members of the Chippewa Tribe who are on the Turtle Mountain Reservation,

North Dakota. It is further declared to be the sense of Congress that, upon the release of such tribes and individual members thereof from such disabilities and limitations, all offices of the Bureau of Indian Affairs in the States of California, Florida, New York, and Texas and all other offices of the Bureau of Indian Affairs whose primary purpose was to serve any Indian tribe or individual Indian freed from Federal supervision should be abolished. It is further declared to be the sense of Congress that the Secretary of the Interior should examine all existing legislation dealing with such Indians, and treaties between the Government of the United States and each such tribe, and report to Congress at the earliest practicable date, but not later than January 1, 1954, his recommendations for such legislation as, in his judgment, may be necessary to accomplish the purposes of this resolution.

Public Law 280 (1953)

AN ACT To confer jurisdiction on the State of California, Minnesota, Nebraska, Oregon, and Wisconsin, with respect to criminal offenses and civil causes of action committed or arising on Indian reservations within such States, and for other purposes.

Be it enacted by the Senate and House of Representatives of the United States of America in Congress assembled, That chapter 53 of title 18, United States Code, is hereby amended by inserting at the end of the chapter analysis preceding section 1151 of such title the following new item:

1162. State jurisdiction over offenses committed by or against Indians in the Indian country.
SEC. 2.

Title 18, United States Code, is hereby amended by inserting in chapter 53 thereof immediately after section 1161 a new section, to be designated as section 1162, as follows:

1162. STATE JURISDICTION OVER OFFENSES COMMITTED BY OR AGAINST INDIANS IN THE INDIAN COUNTRY

(a) Each of the States listed in the following table shall have jurisdiction over offenses committed by or against Indians in the areas of Indian country listed opposite the name of the State to the same extent that such State has jurisdiction over offenses committed elsewhere within the State, and the criminal laws of such State shall have the same force and effect within such Indian country as they have elsewhere within the State:

State of	Indian country affected
California	*All Indian country within the State*
Minnesota	*All Indian country within the State, except the Red Lake Reservation*
Nebraska	*All Indian country within the State*
Oregon	*All Indian country within the State, except the Warm Springs Reservation*
Wisconsin	*All Indian country within the State, except the Menominee Reservation*

(b) Nothing in this section shall authorize the alienation, encumbrance, or taxation of any real or personal property, including water rights, belonging to any Indian or any Indian tribe, band, or community that is held in trust by the United States or is subject to a restriction against alienation imposed by the United States; or shall authorize regulation of the use of such property in a manner inconsistent with any Federal treaty, agreement, or statute or with any regulation made pursuant thereto; or shall deprive any Indian or any Indian tribe, band, or community of any right, privilege, or immunity afforded under Federal treaty, agreement, or statute with respect to hunting, trapping, or fishing or the control, licensing, or regulation thereof.

(c) The provisions of sections 1152 and 1153 of this chapter shall not be applicable within the areas of Indian country listed in subsection (a) of this section.
SEC. 3.

Chapter 85 of title 28, United States Code, is hereby amended by inserting at the end of the chapter analysis preceding section 1331 of such title the following new item:

1360. State civil jurisdiction in actions to which Indians are parties.
SEC. 4.

Title 28, United States Code, is hereby amended by inserting in chapter 85 thereof immediately after section 1359 a new section, to be designated as section 1360, as follows:

§ 1360. STATE CIVIL JURISDICTION IN ACTIONS TO WHICH INDIANS ARE PARTIES

(a) Each of the States listed in the following table shall have jurisdiction over civil causes of action between Indians or to which Indians are parties which arise in the areas of Indian country listed opposite the name of the State to the same extent that such State has jurisdiction over other civil

causes of action, and those civil laws of such State that are of general application to private persons or private property shall have the same force and effect within such Indian country as they have elsewhere within the State:

State of	Indian country affected
California	All Indian country within the State
Minnesota	All Indian country within the State, except the Red Lake Reservation
Nebraska	All Indian country within the State
Oregon	All Indian country within the State, except the Warm Springs Reservation
Wisconsin	All Indian country within the State, except the Menominee Reservation

(b) Nothing in this section shall authorize the alienation, encumbrance, or taxation of any real or personal property, including water rights, belonging to any Indian or any Indian tribe, band, or community that is held in trust by the United States or is subject to a restriction against alienation imposed by the United States; or shall authorize regulation of the use of such property in a manner inconsistent with any Federal treaty, agreement, or statute or with any regulation made pursuant thereto; or shall confer jurisdiction upon the State to adjudicate, in probate proceedings or otherwise, the ownership or right to possession of such property or any interest therein.

(c) Any tribal ordinance or custom heretofore or hereafter adopted by an Indian tribe, band, or community in the exercise of any authority which it may possess shall, if not inconsistent with any applicable civil law of the State, be given full force and effect in the determination of civil causes of action pursuant to this section.
SEC. 5.

Section 1 of the Act of October 5, 1949 (63 Stat. 705, ch. 604), is hereby repealed, but such repeal shall not affect any proceedings heretofore instituted under that section.
SEC. 6.

Notwithstanding the provisions of any Enabling Act for the admission of a State, the consent of the United States is hereby given to the people of any State to amend, where necessary, their State constitution or existing statutes, as the case may be, to remove any legal impediment to the assumption of civil and criminal jurisdiction in accordance with the provisions of this Act: *Provided,* That the provisions of this Act shall not become effective with respect to

such assumption of jurisdiction by any such State until the people thereof have appropriately amended their State constitution or statutes as the case may be.
SEC. 7.

The consent of the United States is hereby given to any other State not having jurisdiction with respect to criminal offenses or civil causes of action, or with respect to both, as provided for in this Act, to assume jurisdiction at such time and in such manner as the people of the State shall, by affirmative legislative action, obligate and bind the State to assumption thereof.

Approved, August 15, 1953.

Indian Civil Rights Act (1968)

AN ACT To prescribe penalties for certain acts of violence or intimidation, and for other purposes.

Be it enacted by the Senate and House of Representatives of the United States of America in Congress assembled,

TITLE II—RIGHTS OF INDIANS
DEFINITIONS
SEC. 201.

For purposes of this title, the term—
(1) "Indian tribe" means any tribe, band, or other group of Indians subject to the jurisdiction of the United States and recognized as possessing powers of self-government;
(2) "powers of self-government" means and includes all governmental powers possessed by an Indian tribe, executive, legislative, and judicial, and all offices, bodies, and tribunals by and through which they are executed, including courts of Indian offenses; and
(3) "Indian court" means any Indian tribal court or court of Indian offense.

INDIAN RIGHTS
SEC. 202.

No Indian tribe in exercising powers of self-government shall—
(1) make or enforce any law prohibiting the free exercise of religion, or abridging the freedom of speech, or of the press,

or the right of the people peaceably to assemble and to petition for a redress of grievances;

(2) violate the right of the people to be secure in their persons, houses, papers, and effects against unreasonable search and seizures, nor issue warrants, but upon probable cause, supported by oath or affirmation, and particularly describing the place to be searched and the person or thing to be seized;

(3) subject any person for the same offense to be twice put in jeopardy;

(4) compel any person in any criminal case to be a witness against himself;

(5) take any private property for a public use without just compensation;

(6) deny to any person in a criminal proceeding the right to a speedy and public trial, to be informed of the nature and cause of the accusation, to be confronted with the witnesses against him, to have compulsory process for obtaining witnesses in his favor, and at his own expense to have the assistance of counsel for his defense;

(7) require excessive bail, impose excessive fines, inflict cruel and unusual punishments, and in no event impose for conviction of any one offense any penalty or punishment greater than imprisonment for a term of six months or a fine of $500, or both;

(8) deny to any person within its jurisdiction the equal protection of its laws or deprive any person of liberty or property without due process of law;

(9) pass any bill of attainder or ex post facto law; or

(10) deny to any person accused of an offense punishable by imprisonment the right, upon request, to a trial by jury of not less than six persons.

HABEAS CORPUS
SEC. 203.

The privilege of the writ of habeas corpus shall be available to any person, in a court of the United States, to test the legality of his detention by order of an Indian tribe.

TITLE III—MODEL CODE GOVERNING COURTS OF INDIAN
SEC. 301.

The Secretary of the Interior is authorized and directed to recommend to the Congress, on or before July 1, 1968, a model code to govern the administration of justice by courts of Indian offenses on Indian reservations

TITLE IV—JURISDICTION OVER CRIMINAL AND CIVIL ACTIONS
ASSUMPTION BY STATE
SEC. 401.

(a) The consent of the United States is hereby given to any State not having jurisdiction over criminal offenses committed by or against Indians in the areas of Indian country situated within such State to assume, with the consent of the Indian tribe occupying the particular Indian country or part thereof which could be affected by such assumption, such measure of jurisdiction over any or all of such offenses committed within such Indian country or any part thereof as may be determined by such State to the same extent that such State has jurisdiction over any such offense committed elsewhere within the State, and the criminal laws of such State shall have the same force and effect within such Indian country or part thereof as they have elsewhere within that State . . . .

(b) Nothing in this section shall authorize the alienation, encumbrance, or taxation of any real or personal property, including water rights, belonging to any Indian or any Indian tribe, band, or community that is held in trust by the United States or is subject to a restriction against alienation imposed by the United States; or shall authorize regulation of the use of such property in a manner inconsistent with any Federal treaty, agreement, or statute or with any regulation made pursuant thereto; or shall deprive any Indian or any Indian tribe, band, or community of any right, privilege, or immunity afforded under

Federal treaty, agreement, or statute with respect to hunting, trapping, or fishing or the control, licensing, or regulation thereof.

ASSUMPTION BY STATE OF CIVIL JURISDICTION
SEC. 402.

(a)   The consent of the United States is hereby given to any State not having jurisdiction over civil causes of action between Indians or to which Indians are parties which arise in the areas of Indian country situated within such State to assume, with the consent of the tribe occupying the particular Indian country or part thereof which would be affected by such assumption, such measure of jurisdiction over any or all such civil causes of action arising within such Indian country or any part thereof as may be determined by such State to the same extent that such State has jurisdiction over other civil causes of action, and those civil laws of such State that are of general application to private persons or private property shall have the same force and effect within such Indian country or part thereof as they have elsewhere within that State . . . .

SPECIAL ELECTION
SEC. 406.

State jurisdiction acquired pursuant to this title with respect to criminal offenses or civil causes of action, or with respect to both, shall be applicable in Indian country only where the enrolled Indians within the affected area of such Indian country accept such jurisdiction by a majority vote of the adult Indians voting at a special election held for that purpose. The Secretary of the Interior shall call such special election under such rules and regulations as he may prescribe, when requested to do so by the tribal council or other governing body, or by 20 per centum of such enrolled adults . . . .

Alcatraz Proclamation: A Proclamation from the Indians of All Tribes (1969)

To the Great White Father and All His People—We, the native Americans, re-claim the land known as Alcatraz Island in the name of all American Indians by right of discovery.

We wish to be fair and honorable in our dealings with the Caucasian inhabitants of this land, and hereby offer the following treaty:

We will purchase said Alcatraz Island for twenty-four dollars ($24) in glass beads and red cloth, a precedent set by the white man's purchase of a similar island about 300 years ago. We know that $24 in trade goods for these 16 acres is more than was paid when Manhattan Island was sold, but we know that land values have risen over the years. Our offer of $1.24 an acre is greater than the 47 cents an acre the white men are now paying the California Indians for their land.

We will give to the inhabitants of this island a portion of the land for their own to be held in trust . . . by the bureau of Caucasian Affairs to hold in perpetuity—for as long as the sun shall rise and the rivers go down to the sea. We will further guide the inhabitants in the proper way of living. We will offer them our religion, our education, our life-ways, in order to help them achieve our level of civilization and thus raise them and all their white brothers up from their savage and unhappy state. We offer this treaty in good faith and wish to be fair and honorable in our dealings with all white men.

We feel that this so-called Alcatraz Island is more than suitable for an Indian reservation, as determined by the white man's own standards. By this we mean that this place most resembles Indians reservations in that:

1. It is isolated from modern facilities, and without adequate means of transportation.
2. It has no fresh running water.
3. It has inadequate sanitation facilities.
4. There are no oil or mineral rights.
5. There is no industry and so unemployment is very great.
6. There are no health care facilities.
7. The soil is rocky and non-productive, and the land does not support game.
8. There are no educational facilities.
9. The population has always exceeded the land base.
10. The population has always been held as prisoners and kept dependent upon others.

Further, it would be fitting and symbolic that ships from all over the world, entering the Golden Gate, would first see Indian land, and thus be

reminded of the true history of this nation. This tiny island would be a symbol of the great lands once ruled by free and noble Indians.

What use will we make of this land?

Since the San Francisco Indian Center burned down, there is no place for Indians to assemble and carry on tribal life here in the white man's city. Therefore, we plan to develop on this island several Indian institutions:

1. A Center for Native American Studies which will educate them to the skills and knowledge relevant to improve the lives and spirits of Indian peoples. . . .
2. An American Indian Spiritual Center which will practice our ancient tribal religious and sacred healing ceremonies. . . .
3. An Indian Center of Ecology which will train and support our young people in scientific research and practice to restore our lands and waters to their pure and natural state. . . .
4. A Great Indian Training School will be developed to teach our people how to make a living in the world, improve our standard of living, and to end hunger and unemployment among all our people. . . .

Some of the present buildings will be taken over to develop an American Indian Museum which will depict our native food & other cultural contributions we have given to the world. Another part of the museum will present some of the things the white man has given to the Indians in return for the land and life he took: disease, alcohol, poverty and cultural decimation (As symbolized by old tin cans, barbed wire, rubber tires, plastic containers, etc.). . . .

In the name of all Indians, therefore, we re-claim this island for our Indian nations. . . .

Alaska Native Claims Settlement Act (1971)

For purposes of this chapter, the term—

. . .

(c) "Native Village" means any tribe, band, clan, group, village, community, or association in Alaska listed in sections 1610 and 1615 of this title, or which meets the requirements of this chapter, and which the Secretary determines was, on the 1970 census enumeration date (as shown by the census or other evidence satisfactory to the Secretary, who shall make findings of fact in each instance), composed of twenty-five or more Natives;

(d) "Native group" means any tribe, band, clan, village, community, or village association of Natives in Alaska composed of less than twenty-five Natives, who comprise a majority of the residents of the locality;

. . .

(g) "Regional Corporation" means an Alaska Native Regional Corporation established under the laws of the State of Alaska in accordance with the provisions of this chapter;

. . .

(j) "Village Corporation" means an Alaska Native Village Corporation organized under the laws of the State of Alaska as a business for profit or nonprofit corporation to hold, invest, manage and/or distribute lands, property, funds, and other rights and assets for and on behalf of a Native village in accordance with the terms of this chapter.[1]

. . .

SEC. 7. [43 U.S.C. 1606] (a) For purposes of this Act, the State of Alaska shall be divided by the Secretary within one year after the date of enactment at [2] this Act into twelve geographic regions, with each region composed as far as practicable of Natives having a common heritage and sharing common interests. In the absence of good cause shown to the contrary, such regions shall approximate the areas covered by the operations of the following existing Native associations:

(1) Arctic Slope Native Association (Barrow, Point Hope);
(2) Bering Straits Association (Seward Peninsula, Unalakleet, Saint Lawrence Island);
(3) Northwest Alaska Native Association (Kotzebue);
(4) Association of Village Council Presidents (southwest coast, all villages in the Bethel area, including all villages on the Lower Yukon River and the Lower Kuskokwim River);
(5) Tanana Chiefs' Conference (Koyukuk, Middle and Upper Yukon Rivers, Upper Kuskokwim, Tanana River);
(6) Cook Inlet Association (Kenai, Tyonek, Eklutna, Iliamna);

(7) Bristol Bay Native Association (Dillingham, Upper Alaska Peninsula);

(8) Aleut League (Aleutian Islands, Pribilof Islands and that part of the Alaska Peninsula which is in the Aleut League);

(9) Chugach Native Association (Cordova, Tatitlek, Port Graham, English Bay, Valdez, and Seward);

(10) Tlingit-Haida Central Council (southeastern Alaska, including Metlakatla);

(11) Kodiak Area Native Association (all villages on and around Kodiak Island); and

(12) Copper River Native Association (Copper Center, Glennallen, Chitina, Mentasta).

Any dispute over the boundaries of a region or regions shall be resolved by a board of arbitrators consisting of one person selected by each of the Native associations involved, and an additional one or two persons, whichever is needed to make an odd number of arbitrators, such additional person or persons to be selected by the arbitrators selected by the Native associations involved.

(h) (1) Rights and Restrictions.—

(A) Except as otherwise expressly provided in this Act, Settlement Common Stock of a Regional Corporation shall—

. . .

(i)   carry a right to vote in elections for the board of directors and on such other questions as properly may be presented to shareholders;

(ii) permit the holder to receive dividends or other distributions from the corporation; and

(iii) vest in the holder all rights of a shareholder in a business corporation organized under the laws of the State.

(B) Except as otherwise provided in this subsection, Settlement Common Stock, inchoate rights thereto, and rights to dividends or distributions declared with respect thereto shall not be—

(i)   sold;

(ii) pledged;

(iii) subjected to a lien or judgment execution;

(iv) assigned in present or future;

(v)   treated as an asset under—

(I)   title 11 of the United States Code or any successor statute,

(II) any other insolvency or moratorium law, or

(III) other laws generally affecting creditors' rights; or

(vi) otherwise alienated.

(C) Notwithstanding the restrictions set forth in subparagraph (B), Settlement Common Stock may be transferred to a Native or a descendant of a Native—

(i)   pursuant to a court decree of separation, divorce, or child support;

(ii) by a holder who is a member of a professional organization, association, or board that limits his or her ability to practice his or her profession because he or she holds Settlement Common Stock; or

(iii) as an inter vivos gift from a holder to his or her child, grandchild, great-grandchild, niece, nephew, or (if the holder has reached the age of majority as defined by the laws of the State of Alaska) brother or sister, notwithstanding an adoption, relinquishment, or termination of parental rights that may have altered or severed the legal relationship between the gift donor and recipient.

(2) Inheritance of Settlement Common Stock.—

(A) Upon the death of a holder of Settlement Common Stock, ownership of such stock [unless canceled in accordance with subsection (g)(1)(B)(iii)] shall be transferred in accordance with the lawful will of such holder or pursuant to applicable laws of intestate succession. If the holder fails to dispose of his or her stock by will and has no heirs under applicable laws of intestate succession, the stock shall escheat to the issuing Regional Corporation and be canceled.

(B) The issuing Regional Corporation shall have the right to purchase at fair value Settlement Common Stock transferred pursuant to applicable laws of intestate succession to a person not a Native or a

descendant of a Native after the date of the enactment of the Alaska Native Claims Settlement Act Amendments of 1987 if—

    (i) the corporation—

        (I)   amends its articles of incorporation to authorize such purchases, and

        (II) gives the person receiving such stock written notice of its intent to purchase within ninety days after the date that the corporation either determines the decedent's heirs in accordance with the laws of the State or receives notice that such heirs have been determined, whichever later occurs; and

    (ii) the person receiving such stock fails to transfer the stock pursuant to paragraph (1)(C)(iii) within sixty days after receiving such written notice.

  (C) Settlement Common Stock of a Regional Corporation—

    (i)   transferred by will or pursuant to applicable laws of intestate succession after the date of the enactment[3] of the Alaska Native Claims Settlement Act Amendments of 1987, or

    (ii) transferred by any means prior to the date of the enactment of the Alaska Native Claims Settlement Act Amendments of 1987, to a person not a Native or a descendant of a Native shall not carry voting rights. If at a later date such stock is lawfully transferred to a Native or a descendant of a Native, voting rights shall be automatically restored.

(3) Replacement Common Stock.—

  (A) On the date on which alienability restrictions terminate in accordance with the provisions of section 37, all Settlement Common Stock previously issued by a Regional Corporation shall be deemed canceled, and shares of Replacement Common Stock of the appropriate class shall be issued to each shareholder, share for share, subject only to subparagraph (B) and to such restrictions consistent with this Act as may be provided by the articles of incorporation of the corporation or in agreements between the corporation and individual shareholders.

    (i)   Replacement Common Stock issued in exchange for Settlement Common Stock issued subject to the restriction authorized by subsection (g)(1)(B)(iii) shall bear a legend indicating that the stock will eventually be canceled in accordance with the requirements of that subsection.

    (ii) Prior to the termination of alienability restrictions, the board of directors of the corporation shall approve a resolution to provide that each share of Settlement Common Stock carrying the right to share in distributions made to shareholders pursuant to subsections (j) and (m) shall be exchanged either for—

        (I)   a share of Replacement Common Stock that carries such right, or

        (II) a share of Replacement Common Stock that does not carry such right together with a separate, non-voting security that represents only such right.

    (iii) Replacement Common Stock issued in exchange for a class of Settlement Common Stock carrying greater per share voting power than Settlement Common Stock issued pursuant to subsections (g)(1)(A) and (g)(1)(B) shall carry such voting power and be subject to such other terms as may be provided in the amendment to the articles of incorporation authorizing the issuance of such class of Settlement Common Stock.

  (C) The articles of incorporation of the Regional Corporation shall be deemed amended to authorize the issuance of Replacement Common Stock and the security described in subparagraph (B)(ii)(II).

(D) Prior to the date on which alienability restrictions terminate, a Regional Corporation may amend its articles of incorporation to impose upon Replacement Common Stock one or more of the following—

    (i) a restriction denying voting rights to any holder of Replacement Common Stock who is not a Native or a descendant of a Native;

    (ii) a restriction granting the Regional Corporation, or the Regional Corporation and members of the shareholder's immediate family who are Natives or descendants of Natives, the first right to purchase, on reasonable terms, the Replacement Common Stock of the shareholder prior to the sale or transfer of such stock (other than a transfer by will or intestate succession) to any other party, including a transfer in satisfaction of a lien, writ of attachment, judgment execution, pledge, or other encumbrance; and

    (iii) any other term, restriction, limitation, or provision authorized by the laws of the State.

(E) Replacement Common Stock shall not be subjected to a lien or judgment execution based upon any asserted or unasserted legal obligation of the original recipient arising prior to the issuance of such stock.

. . .

SEC. 8. [43 U.S.C. 1607]

(c) Applicability of Section 7.—The provisions of subsections (g), (h) (other than paragraph (H), and (o) of section 7 shall apply in all respects to Village Corporations, Urban Corporations, and Group Corporations.

. . .

[Internal Reference.—SSAct §1613(a) cites the Alaska Native Claims Settlement Act.]

[1] As in original. Probably should be a colon.
[2] As in original. Probably should be "of."
[3] February 3, 1988.

American Indian Movement: Three-Point Program (1973)

On February 28, 1973, several hundred Oglala Lakota Sioux, supported by organizers from the American Indian Movement (AIM), stormed the Wounded Knee hamlet on the Pine Ridge Reservation in South Dakota and took hostages to call attention to the U.S. government's poor treatment of Native Americans. The reservation had been the site of the 1890 Wounded Knee Massacre, during which U.S. Army troops had killed at least 150 Sioux. The Wounded Knee siege in 1973 lasted for more than two months. After it ended in a tentative truce, the AIM released a three-point program, an excerpt of which follows, outlining the group's goals.

Point 1. A Senate Treaty Commission should examine the 371 treaties the U.S. has made (and broken) with Indians. All treaty rights should be enforced.

The land rights involved here for reservations are very large. The 1972 "Trail" [of Broken Treaties] proposal called, at a minimum, for restoration to Indian control of at least 110 million acres of land. Presently, the federal government holds "in trust" about 40 million tribal acres (much of it used for mineral, park, and other interests), with an additional 10 million acres held "in trust" for individual tribal members. Much of this land is leased out, advantageously to white interests. On Pine Ridge Reservation (South Dakota), Indian range land is leased for 80 cents an acre; this land is exactly like land owned by whites, which brings $15 an acre.

One response to the efforts to enforce the rights of this treaty (re. the 1868 Sioux/U.S. treaty) has been a government "offer" to settle a 50-year-old claim based on it. The U.S. National Indian Claims Commission finds about $102 million (or $2000 per person for about 60,000 Sioux) a fair settlement for 7.5 million acres of land, including the Homestake Mine, largest gold producing mine in the Western Hemisphere, and the sacred Paha Sapa, the beautiful Black Hills. However, old habits of cheating Indians die hard. By the time the U.S. government finished taking deductions for "money spent on the Sioux," only about $4 million is left. We don't want little bits of cash; we want a land base which is ours by right and could support meaningful lives. . . .

We need a Treaty Commission, and it should get to work quickly. The sort of litigation which goes on forever is all too familiar. . . . From Washington to New York, there have been many such incidents and

cases; it should not be necessary for Indians to go to court to win rights they (supposedly) already have by treaty.

Point 2. Repeal the Indian Reorganization Act of 1934 (Wheeler-Howard Act); it has been a major weapon used in robbing Indians of their land, settling white-controlled governments on many reservations, and establishing tribal constitutions which offer no real protection against sale and wholesale lease-out of tribal lands.

Point 3. Remove the Bureau of Indian Affairs from the Department of the Interior, restructure it as an independent agency, controlled by and accountable to, Indian people; audit the BIA records and make reparations for the many crooked land deals; cancel BIA-sanctioned non-Indian leasing of Indian land.

The BIA should never have been located in the Department of the Interior. (Maybe that's better than its original location, the Department of War, but not much.) The Department of the Interior serves oil, mineral, lands trusts, transportation, shipping, wood forestry, and energy interests; these usually conflict with Indian rights.

The BIA has a long history of corruption and mismanagement of our affairs. A tough, independent audit of BIA books and land rent records should be supported by all. Forced land sales and lease rentals arranged by the BIA should be examined, with returns and reparations made.

Pine Ridge data show part of the reason why this needs to be done. As of 1969, the federal government was spending, through BIA, about $8040 a year per family, to "help the Oglala Sioux out of poverty." But median family income from all sources (employment, land rental, and federal) was only $1910 per family, supporting many children and old people. Where did the rest of it go? The fact that there was about one well-paid bureaucrat per family gives part of the answer; kickbacks and corruption give the other part. All Indians would benefit if this inept and corrupt agency were accountable to us. . . .

This Three Point Program provides a strategy for a nationally coordinated attack on powerful financial and political interests, which have used the U.S. government to take advantage of Native Americans for more than a century. It will require strong commitment and wide support to win against these interests. Indian rights of sovereignty, self-government, and a decent means of living in accordance with traditions and beliefs will not come easily.

Without massive public pressure, the government will simply continue its present treatment of Indians, a continuing shame to all, and a continuing profit source to a few.

Boldt Decision (1974)

Officially titled United States vs. Washington *(1974), the "Boldt Decision" established a system by which Native Americans were allowed up to 50 percent of the salmon, and other fish returning to the waters of fishing sites guaranteed them by treaties signed during the 1850s.*

UNITED STATES of America, Plaintiff, Quinault Tribe of Indians on its own behalf and on behalf of the Queets Band of Indians, et al., Intervenor-Plaintiffs, v. STATE OF WASHINGTON, Defendant, Thor C. Tollefson, Director, Washington State Department of Fisheries, et al., Intervenor-Defendants
Civ. No. 9213
UNITED STATES DISTRICT COURT FOR THE WESTERN DISTRICT OF WASHINGTON, TACOMA DIVISION
384 F. Supp. 312; 1974 U.S. Dist. LEXIS 12291
February 12, 1974 . . .
STATEMENT OF THE CASE
GEORGE H. BOLDT, Senior District Judge.

In September, 1970 the United States, on its own behalf and as trustee for several Western Washington Indian Tribes, later joined as intervenor plaintiffs by additional tribes, filed the complaint initiating this action against the State of Washington. Shortly later the State Department of Fisheries (Fisheries) and the State Game Commission (Game), their respective directors, and the Washington Reef Net Owners Association (Reef Net Owners) were included as defendants. By state statute Fisheries is charged with exercising regulatory authority over fishing for all anadromous food fish. Regulation of anadromous steelhead trout is vested in Game. Plaintiffs seek a declaratory judgment pursuant to 28 U.S.C. §§ 2201 and 2202 concerning off reservation treaty right fishing within the case area by plaintiff tribes, which long has been and now is in controversy, and for injunctive relief to provide enforcement of those fishing rights as they previously have been or herein may be judicially determined. The case area is that portion of the State of Washington west of the Cascade Mountains and north of the Columbia River drainage

area, and includes the American portion of the Puget Sound watershed, the watersheds of the Olympic Peninsula north of the Grays Harbor watershed, and the offshore waters adjacent to those areas. . . .

More than a century of frequent and often violent controversy between Indians and non-Indians over treaty right fishing has resulted in deep distrust and animosity on both sides. This has been inflamed by provocative, sometimes illegal, conduct of extremists on both sides and by irresponsible demonstrations instigated by non-resident opportunists. . . .

The ultimate objective of this decision is to determine every issue of fact and law presented and, at long last, thereby finally settle, either in this decision or on appeal thereof, as many as possible of the divisive problems of treaty right fishing which for so long have plagued all of the citizens of this area, and still do.

I. ESTABLISHED BASIC FACTS AND LAW . . .

The "Constitution . . . of the United States . . . and all Treaties made, or which shall be made, under the Authority of the United States, shall be the supreme Law of the Land; and the Judges in every State shall be bound thereby, any Thing in the Constitution or Laws of any State to the Contrary notwithstanding." . . .

3. The United States Supreme Court in Missouri (252 U.S. p. 434, 40 S. Ct. p. 384) stated:

"Valid treaties of course 'are as binding within the territorial limits of the States as they are elsewhere throughout the dominion of the United States.' *Baldwin v. Franks*, 120 U.S. 678, 683, 7 S. Ct. 656, 30 L. Ed. 766."

4. Each of the basic fact and law issues in this case must be considered and decided in accordance with the treaty language reserving fishing rights to the plaintiff tribes, interpreted in the spirit and manner directed in the above quoted language of the United States Supreme Court. Each treaty in this case contains a provision substantially identical to that in the Medicine Creek treaty: "The right of taking fish, at all usual and accustomed grounds and stations, is further secured to said Indians, in common with all citizens of the territory, and of erecting temporary houses for the purpose of curing, . . ."

5. "The right to resort to the [usual and accustomed] fishing places in controversy was a part of larger rights possessed by the Indians, upon the exercise of which there was not a shadow of impediment, and which were not much less necessary to the existence of the Indians than the atmosphere they breathed. . . . [The] treaty was not a grant of rights to the Indians but a grant of right from them—a reservation of those not granted."

"And surely it was within the competency of the Nation to secure to the Indians such a remnant of the great rights they possessed as 'taking fish at all usual and accustomed places.'" . . .

6. ". . . [The] [treaty] negotiations were with the tribe. They reserved rights, however, to every individual Indian, as though named therein. . . . And the right was intended to be continuing against the United States and its grantees as well as against the State and its grantees." That those rights are also reserved to the descendants of treaty Indians, without limitation in time, excepting as Congress may determine, has been recognized and applied by the United States Supreme Court from the first to the latest decision of that court involving Indian treaty fishing rights. . . .

7. An exclusive right of fishing was reserved by the tribes within the area and boundary waters of their reservations, wherein tribal members might make their homes if they chose to do so. The tribes also reserved the right to off reservation fishing "at all usual and accustomed grounds and stations" and agreed that "all citizens of the territory" might fish at the same places "in common with" tribal members. The tribes and their members cannot rescind that agreement or limit non-Indian fishing pursuant to the agreement. However, off reservation fishing by other citizens and residents of the state is not a right but merely a privilege which may be granted, limited or withdrawn by the state as the interests of the state or the exercise of treaty fishing rights may require. . . .

III. STATE REGULATION OF OFF RESERVATION TREATY RIGHT FISHING

There is neither mention nor slightest intimation in the treaties themselves, in any of the treaty negotiation records or in any other credible evidence, that the Indians who represented the tribes in the making of the treaties, at that time or any time afterward, understood or intended that the fishing rights reserved by the tribes as recorded in the above quoted language would, or ever could, authorize the "citizens of the territory" or their successors, either individually or through their territorial or state government, to qualify, restrict or in any way interfere with the full exercise of those rights. All of the evidence is overwhelmingly to the contrary, particularly in the vivid showing in the record that the treaty Indians pleaded for and insisted upon retain-

ing the exercise of those rights as essential to their survival. They were given unqualified assurance of that by Governor Stevens himself without any suggestion that the Indians' exercise of those rights might some day, without authorization of Congress, be subjected to regulation by non-Indian citizens through their territorial or state government. . . .

These measures and others make plain the intent and philosophy of Congress to increase rather than diminish or limit the exercise of tribal self-government.

The right to fish for all species available in the waters from which, for so many ages, their ancestors derived most of their subsistence is the single most highly cherished interest and concern of the present members of plaintiff tribes, with rare exceptions even among tribal members who personally do not fish or derive therefrom any substantial amount of their subsistence. The right to fish, as reserved in the treaties of plaintiff tribes, certainly is the treaty provision most frequently in controversy and litigation involving all of the tribes and numerous of their individual members for many years past.

The philosophy of Congress referred to above and the evidence in this case as a whole clearly indicate to this court that the time has now arrived, and this case presents an appropriate opportunity, to take a step toward applying congressional philosophy to Indian treaty right fishing in a way that will not be inconsistent with Puyallup-I and Puyallup-II and also will provide ample security for the interest and purposes of conservation. . . .

CONCLUSIONS OF LAW . . .

17. Admission of the State of Washington into the Union upon an equal footing with the original states had no effect upon the treaty rights of the Plaintiff tribes. Such admission imposed upon the State, equally with other states, the obligation to observe and carry out the provisions of treaties of the United States. . . .

DECLARATORY JUDGMENT AND DECREE . . .

B.   Treaty Fishing Rights

10.   Each of the plaintiff tribes listed below is a Treaty Tribe. The list given below is a declaration only as to those 14 Indian entities which have been represented on the plaintiff side in this case. A Treaty Tribe occupies the status of a party to one or more of the Stevens treaties and therefore holds

for the benefit of its members a reserved right to harvest anadromous fish at all usual and accustomed places outside reservation boundaries, in common with others:

Hoh Tribe of Indians;
Lummi Indian Tribe;
Makah Indian Tribe;
Muckleshoot Indian Tribe;
Nisqually Indian Community of the
    Nisqually Reservation;
Puyallup Tribe of the Puyallup
    Reservation;
Quileute Indian Tribe;
Quinault Tribe of Indians;
Sauk-Suiattle Indian Tribe;
Skokomish Indian Tribe;
Squaxin Island Tribe of Indians;
Stillaguamish Tribe of Indians;
Upper Skagit River Tribe;
Confederated Tribes and Bands of the
    Yakima Indian Nation

11.   The right of a Treaty Tribe to harvest anadromous fish outside reservation boundaries arises from a provision which appears in each of the Stevens treaties and which, with immaterial variations, states: The right of taking fish, at all usual and accustomed grounds and stations, is further secured to said Indians, in common with all citizens of the Territory. . . .

12.   It is the responsibility of all citizens to see that the terms of the Stevens treaties are carried out, so far as possible, in accordance with the meaning they were understood to have by the tribal representatives at the councils, and in a spirit which generously recognizes the full obligation of this nation to protect the interests of a dependent people. . . .

15.   The treaty-secured rights to resort to the usual and accustomed places to fish were a part of larger rights possessed by the treating Indians, upon the exercise of which there was not a shadow of impediment, and which were not much less necessary to their existence than the atmosphere they breathed. The treaty was not a grant of rights to the treating Indians, but a grant of rights from them, and a reservation of those not granted. In the Stevens treaties, such reservations

were not of particular parcels of land, and could not be expressed in deeds, as dealings between private individuals. The reservations were in large areas of territory, and the negotiations were with the tribes. The treaties reserved rights, however, to every individual Indian, as though described therein. There was an exclusive right of fishing reserved within certain boundaries. There was a right outside of those boundaries reserved for exercise "in common with citizens of the Territory."

16. The Stevens treaties do not reserve to the Treaty Tribes any specific manner, method or purpose of taking fish; nor do the treaties prohibit any specific manner, method or purpose. Just as non-Indians may continue to take advantage of improvements in fishing techniques, the Treaty Tribes may, in exercising their rights to take anadromous fish, utilize improvements in traditional fishing methods, such for example as nylon nets and steel hooks.

17. The exercise of a Treaty Tribe's right to take anadromous fish outside of reservation boundaries is limited only by geographical extent of the usual and accustomed places, the limits of the harvestable stock and the number of fish which non-treaty fishermen shall have an opportunity to catch, as provided in the Decision of the Court.

18. Because the right of each Treaty Tribe to take anadromous fish arises from a treaty with the United States, that right is preserved and protected under the supreme law of the land, does not depend on State law, is distinct from rights or privileges held by others, and may not be qualified by any action of the State.

19. The treaty phrase "in common with" does not secure any treaty right or privilege to anyone other than the Treaty Tribes, nor does that phrase qualify any Indian's treaty right to fish, except as provided in the Decision of the Court.

20. Except for tribes now or hereafter entitled to self-regulation of tribal fishing, as provided in the Decision of the Court, the right of a Treaty Tribe to take anadromous fish may be regulated by an appropriate exercise of State power. To be appropriate, such regulation must:

   a. Not discriminate against the Treaty Tribe's reserved right to fish;

   b. Meet appropriate standards of substantive and procedural due process; and

   c. Be shown by the State to be both reasonable and necessary to preserve and maintain the resource. When State law or regulations affect the volume of anadromous fish available for harvest by a Treaty Tribe at usual and accustomed places, such regulations must be designed so as to carry out the purposes of the treaty provision securing to the Tribe the right to take fish.

21. If any person shows identification, as provided in the Decision of the Court, that he is exercising the fishing rights of a Treaty Tribe and if he is fishing in a usual and accustomed place, he is protected under federal law against any State action which affects the time, place, manner, purpose or volume of his harvest of anadromous fish, unless the State has previously established that such action is an appropriate exercise of its power.

22. The application of currently effective laws and regulations of the State of Washington specified in the Conclusions of Law which affect the time, place, manner and volume of off-reservation harvest of anadromous fish by Treaty Tribes is unlawful for the reasons also stated in the Conclusions of Law . . . .

Therefore, it is hereby Ordered, adjudged and decreed that the State of Washington; Thor C. Tollefson, Director, Washington State Department of Fisheries; Carl Crouse, Director, Washington Department of Game; The Washington State Game Commission; the Washington Reef Net Owners Association, their agents, officers, employees, successors in interest; and all persons acting in concert or

participation with any of them
("defendants") are permanently
enjoined and restrained to obey, to
respect and to comply with all rulings of
this court in its Final Decision #I and
with each provision of this injunction,
subject only to such modifications as
may be approved as a part of an interim
program.

1. Defendants shall:
   a. fully and fairly recognize each of
      the plaintiff tribes as a tribe
      holding all rights described and
      declared as to it in Final Decision
      #I and accord to each the tribal
      rights and powers recognized as
      to it in that decision;
   b. fully observe and to the best of
      their ability carry out the
      provisions and purposes of the
      treaties cited in paragraph 1 of
      the Findings of Fact;
   c. conform their regulatory action
      and enforcement to each and all
      of the standards set forth in Final
      Decision #I;
   d. recognize the fishing rights in the
      case area of any treaty tribe not a
      party to this case to the full extent
      declared in Final Decision #I as to
      the plaintiff tribes and perform all
      acts and duties set forth in this
      injunction with respect to such
      additional treaty tribe upon the
      agreement of defendants or
      determination by the court that
      the tribe is a treaty tribe.

2. Defendants shall not interfere with or
   regulate or attempt to regulate the
   treaty right fishing of members of the
   Yakima Indian Nation or Quinault
   Tribe or any other treaty tribe during
   any period for which said tribe has
   been or is hereafter determined
   pursuant to Final Decision #I to be
   entitled to self-regulate such fishing
   by its members without any state
   regulation thereof; provided however
   that monitoring by the state as stated
   as a condition for self-regulation may
   be exercised by the state and in case
   of a threat to the resource, the

defendants may apply to the court
for the exercise of regulatory
authority;

3. Defendants shall not interfere with or
   regulate or attempt to regulate the
   treaty right fishing of members of
   any treaty tribe during any period
   not covered by paragraph 2 above as
   to such tribe unless the state first
   shows to the satisfaction of such tribe
   or this court that such regulation
   conforms to the requirements of Final
   Decision #I and this injunction. . . .

11. The state defendants shall not adopt
    regulations or enforce any statutes or
    regulations affecting the volume of
    anadromous fish available for harvest
    by a treaty tribe at usual and
    accustomed places unless such
    regulations are designed so as to
    carry out the purposes of the treaty
    provisions securing to the tribe the
    right to take fish.

12. Except as otherwise provided by
    paragraph 19 hereof, the state
    defendants shall not adopt or enforce
    any regulations that affect the harvest
    by the tribe on future runs unless
    there first has been a full, fair and
    public consideration and
    determination in accordance with the
    requirements of the Washington
    Administrative Procedures Act and
    regulations under it.

13. The state defendants shall not
    regulate or restrain the exercise of
    treaty fishing rights of plaintiff tribes
    and their members by use of a state
    statute or regulation of broad
    applicability instead of one specific
    as to time, place, species and gear.

14. The state defendants shall not adopt
    or enforce any regulation which
    effectively limits the harvest by treaty
    tribes on future runs unless the
    state's regulatory scheme provides an
    opportunity for treaty tribes and
    their members to take, at their off-
    reservation usual and accustomed
    fishing places, by reasonable means
    feasible to them, an equal share of the
    harvestable number of each species

of fish that may be taken by all fishermen; provided that for the present time defendants shall not be required to achieve mathematical precision in so allocating the fish;

Provided further that in order to approach more nearly the principle of equal sharing, the fish which Indian treaty fishermen shall have an opportunity to catch shall include not only an equal share of the total number of fish of any species which are within the regulatory jurisdiction of the State of Washington but shall also include an additional amount or quantity of
fish which shall be determined by agreement of the parties or by approval of this court, to reflect the substantially disproportionate numbers of fish, many of which might otherwise be available for harvest by Indian treaty right fishermen, caught by non-treaty fishermen in marine areas closely adjacent to, but beyond the territorial waters of the state, or outside the jurisdiction of the state although within Washington waters; . . .

21. Defendants shall in no manner limit, restrict or inhibit the time, place, manner, volume or purpose of the disposition by a member of a plaintiff tribe of fish harvested according to his rights and the rights and powers of his tribe, as declared and adjudged in Final Decision #I, or interfere with any person purchasing, attempting to purchase, transporting, receiving for shipment, processing or reselling, fish taken pursuant to the exercise of such rights.

. . .

INTERIM PLAN AND STAY ORDER PENDING FINAL DECISION ON APPEAL

The court having considered the need for an interim plan and having considered the interim proposal, now hereby orders that the following interim plan shall be in effect and shall be binding upon all parties to this litigation except as to tribes determined

to be self-regulating. In making this order the court does so reserving jurisdiction to make further modifications if the court deems them necessary and further orders a stay of portions of the injunction, final decision No. 1 and the decree of February 12, 1974.

The court now, therefore, orders, adjudges and decrees:

(1) Effective June 1, 1974, all off-reservation fishing areas in the case area are closed to Indian treaty fishing except to the extent that tribes adopt and file with the court and the defendants tribal regulations for the fishing activities of their members and specifying the areas to be opened to fishing by tribal members. Indians who engage in fishing activities not in accordance with those tribal regulations shall be subject to the same provisions of the state law as non-Indians engaging in fishing activities. . . .

Indian Self-Determination and Education Assistance Act (1975)

Be it enacted by the Senate and House of Representatives of the United States of America in Congress assembled, (25 U.S.C. 450 note) That this Act may be cited as the "Indian Self-Determination and Education Assistance Act".

CONGRESSIONAL FINDINGS SEC. 2. 25 U.S.C. 450 (a) The Congress, after careful review of the Federal Government's historical and special legal relationship with, and resulting responsibilities to, American Indian people, finds that—(1) the prolonged Federal domination of Indian service programs has served to retard rather than enhance the progress of Indian people and their communities by depriving Indians of the full opportunity to develop leadership skills crucial to the realization of self-government, and has denied to the Indian people an effective voice in the planning and implementation of programs for the benefit of Indians which are responsive to the true needs of Indian communities; and (2) the Indian people will never surrender their desire to control their relationships both among themselves and with non-Indian governments, organizations, and persons.

(b) The Congress further finds that—(1) true self-determination in any society of people is dependent upon an educational process which will insure the development of qualified people to fulfill meaningful leadership roles; (2) the Federal responsibility for and assistance to education of Indian children

has not effected the desired level of educational achievement or created the diverse opportunities and personal satisfaction which education can and should provide; and (3) parental and community control of the educational process is of crucial importance to the Indian people.

DECLARATION OF POLICY SEC. 3. 25 U.S.C. 450a (a) The Congress hereby recognizes the obligation of the United States to respond to the strong expression of the Indian people for self-determination by assuring maximum Indian participation in the direction of educational as well as other Federal services to Indian communities so as to render such services more responsive to the needs and desires of those communities.

(b) The Congress declares its commitment to the maintenance of the Federal Government's unique and continuing relationship with, and responsibility to, individual Indian tribes and to the Indian people as a whole through the establishment of a meaningful Indian self-determination policy which will permit an orderly transition from the Federal domination of programs for, and services to, Indians to effective and meaningful participation by the Indian people in the planning, conduct, and administration of those programs and services. In accordance with this policy, the United States is committed to supporting and assisting Indian tribes in the development of strong and stable tribal governments, capable of administering quality programs and developing the economies of their respective communities.

(c) The Congress declares that a major national goal of the United States is to provide the quantity and quality of educational services and opportunities which will permit Indian children to compete and excel in the life areas of their choice, and to achieve the measure of self-determination essential to their social and economic well-being. . . .

WAGE AND LABOR STANDARDS . . .

(b) Any contract, subcontract, grant, or subgrant pursuant to this Act, the Act of April 16, 1934 (48 Stat. 596), as amended, or any other Act authorizing Federal contracts with or grants to Indian organizations or for the benefit of Indians, shall require that to the greatest extent feasible—

(1) preferences and opportunities for training and employment in connection with the administration of such contracts or grants shall be given to Indians; and

(2) preference in the award of subcontracts and subgrants in connection with the administration of such contracts or grants shall be given to Indian organizations and to Indian-owned economic enterprises as defined in section 3 of the Indian Financing Act of 1974 (88 Stat. 77).

(c) Notwithstanding subsections (a) and (b), with respect to any self-determination contract, or portion of a self-determination contract, that is intended to benefit one tribe, the tribal employment or contract preference laws adopted by such tribe shall govern with respect to the administration of the contract or portion of the contract. . . .

American Indian Religious Freedom Act

Enacted on August 11, 1978, the American Indian Religious Freedom Act offers safeguards for Native Americans' traditional religious practices and religions. After the U.S. Supreme Court ruled in Department of Human Services of Oregon v. Smith *(1990), and* Oregon v. Black *(1988) that this law did not allow Native Americans to use the illegal drug peyote in their religious services, Congress amended the act in 1994 to extend such protection.*

Resolved by the Senate and House of Representatives of the United States of America in Congress assembled,

That henceforth it shall be the policy of the United States to protect and preserve for American Indians their inherent fight of freedom to believe, express and exercise the traditional religions of the American Indian, Eskimo, Aleut, and Native Hawaiians, including but not limited to access to sites, use and possession of sacred objects, and the freedom to worship through ceremonials and traditional rites.

An Act to emend the American Indian Religious Freedom Act to provide for the traditional use of peyote by Indians for religious purposes, and for other purposes.

Be it enacted by the Senate and House of Representatives of the United States of America in Congress assembled,

SECTION 1. SHORT TITLE. This Act may be cited as the "American Indian Religious Freedom Act Amendments of 1994."

SECTION 2. TRADITIONAL INDIAN RELIGIOUS USE OF THE PEYOTE SACRAMENT. The Act of August 11, 1978 (42 U.S.C. 1996), commonly referred to as the "American Indian Religious Free-

dom Act," is amended by adding at the end thereof the following new section:

SECTION 3.

a. The Congress finds and declares that

1. for many Indian people, the traditional ceremonial use of the peyote cactus as a religious sacrament has for centuries been integral to a way of life, and significant in perpetuating Indian tribes and cultures;

2. since 1965, this ceremonial use of peyote by Indians has been protected by Federal regulation;

3. while at least 28 States have enacted laws which are similar to, or are in conformance with, the Federal regulation which protects the ceremonial use of peyote by Indian religious practitioners, 22 States have not done so, and this lack of uniformity has created hardship for Indian people who participate in such religious ceremonies;

4. the Supreme Court of the United States, in the case of *Employment Division v. Smith*, 494 U.S. 872 (1990), held that the First Amendment does not protect Indian practitioners who use peyote in Indian religious ceremonies, and also raised uncertainty whether this religious practice would be protected under the compelling State interest standard; and

5. the lack of adequate and clear legal protection for the religious use of peyote by Indians may serve to stigmatize and marginalize Indian tribes and cultures, and increase the risk that they will be exposed to discriminatory treatment.

b. 1. Notwithstanding any other provision of law, the use, possession, or transportation of peyote by an Indian for bona fide traditional ceremonial purposes in connection with the practice of a traditional Indian religion is lawful, and shall not be prohibited by the United States or any State. No Indian shall be penalized or discriminated against on the basis of such use, possession or transportation, including, but not limited to, denial of otherwise applicable benefits under public assistance programs.

2. This section does not prohibit such reasonable regulation and registration by the Drug Enforcement Administration of those persons who cultivate, harvest, or distribute peyote as may be consistent with the purposes of this Act.

3. This section does not prohibit application of the provisions of section 481.111 of Vernon's Texas Health and Safety Code Annotated, in effect on the date of enactment of this section, insofar as those provisions pertain to the cultivation, harvest, and distribution of peyote.

4. Nothing in this section shall prohibit any Federal department or agency, in carrying out its statutory responsibilities and functions, from promulgating regulations establishing reasonable limitations on the use or ingestion of peyote prior to or during the performance of duties by sworn law enforcement officers or personnel directly involved in public transportation or any other safety-sensitive positions where the performance of such duties may be adversely affected by such use or ingestion. Such regulations shall be adopted only after consultation with representatives of traditional Indian religions for which the sacramental use of peyote is integral to their practice. Any regulation promulgated pursuant to this section shall be subject to the balancing test set forth in section 3 of the Religious Freedom Restoration Act (Public Law 103–141; 42 U.S.C.2000bb–1).

5. This section shall not be construed as requiring prison authorities to permit, nor shall it be construed to prohibit prison authorities from

permitting, access to peyote by Indians while incarcerated within Federal or State prison facilities.

6. Subject to the provisions of the Religious Freedom Restoration Act (Public Law 103–141; 42 U.S.C. 2000bb–1), this section shall not be construed to prohibit States from enacting or enforcing reasonable traffic safety laws or regulations.

7. Subject to the provisions of the Religious Freedom Restoration Act (Public Law 103–141; 42 USC 2000bb–1), this section does not prohibit the Secretary of Defense from promulgating regulations establishing reasonable limitations on the use, possession, transportation, or distribution of peyote to promote military readiness, safety, or compliance with international law or laws of other countries. Such regulations shall be adopted only after consultation with representatives of traditional Indian religions for which the sacramental use of peyote is integral to their practice.

c. For purposes of this section,
1. the term 'Indian' means a member of an Indian tribe;
2. the term 'Indian tribe' means any tribe, band, nation, pueblo, or other organized group or community of Indians, including any Alaska Native village (as defined in, or established pursuant to, the Alaska Native Claims Settlement Act (43 U.S.C. 1601 et seq.), which is recognized as eligible for the special programs and services provide by the United States to Indians because of their status as Indians;
3. the term 'Indian religion' means any religion, A. which is practiced by Indians; and B. the origin and interpretation of which is from within a traditional Indian culture or community; and
4. the term 'State' means any State of the United States and any political subdivision thereof.

d. Nothing in this section shall be construed as abrogating, diminishing, or otherwise affecting,
1. the inherent rights of any Indian tribe;
2. the rights, express or implicit, of any Indian tribe which exist under treaties, Executive orders, and laws of the United States;
3. the inherent right of Indians to practice their religions; and
4. the right of Indians to practice their religions under any Federal or State law.

Oliphant v. Suquamish Indian Tribe (1978)

Criminal proceedings were brought in the Suquamish Indian Provisional Court against two non-Indian residents of the Port Madison Reservation. Both petitioners applied for a writ of habeas corpus to the United States District Court for the Western District of Washington, arguing that the tribal court does not have criminal jurisdiction over non-Indians. In separate proceedings, the District Court denied the petitions. The Court of Appeals for the Ninth Circuit (544 F.2d 1007) affirmed in one case, and the other petitioner's appeal was pending before the Court of Appeals. Upon granting certiorari, the Supreme Court, Mr. Justice Rehnquist, held that Indian tribal courts do not have inherent criminal jurisdiction to try and to punish non-Indians, and hence may not assume such jurisdiction unless specifically authorized to do so by Congress . . . .

Respondents do not contend that their exercise of criminal jurisdiction over non-Indians stems from affirmative congressional authorization or treaty provision. Instead, respondents urge that such jurisdiction flows automatically from the "Tribe's retained inherent powers of government over the Port Madison Indian Reservation." Seizing on language in our opinions describing Indian tribes as "quasi-sovereign entities," see, e.g., *Morton v. Mancari*, 417 U.S. 535, 554, 94 S.Ct. 2474, 2484, 41 L.Ed.2d 290 (1974), the Court of Appeals agreed and held that Indian tribes, "though conquered and dependent, retain those powers of autonomous states that

are neither inconsistent with their status nor expressly terminated by Congress." According to the Court of Appeals, criminal jurisdiction over anyone committing an offense on the reservation is a "sine qua non" of such powers. . . .

While in isolation the Treaty of Point Elliott, 12 Stat. 927 (1855), would appear to be silent as to tribal criminal jurisdiction over non-Indians, the addition of historical perspective casts substantial doubt upon the existence of such jurisdiction. In the Ninth Article, for example, the Suquamish "acknowledge their dependence on the government of the United States." As Mr. Chief Justice Marshall explained in *Worcester v. Georgia*, 6 Pet. 515, 551–552, 554, 8 L.Ed. 483 (1832), such an acknowledgment is not a mere abstract recognition of the United States' sovereignty. "The Indian nations were, from their situation, necessarily dependent on [the United States] . . . for their protection from lawless and injurious intrusions into their country." Id., at 555. By acknowledging their dependence on the United States, in the Treaty of Point Elliott, the Suquamish were in all probability recognizing that the United States would arrest and try non-Indian intruders who came within their Reservation. Other provisions of the Treaty also point to the absence of tribal jurisdiction. Thus the Tribe "agree [s] not to shelter or conceal offenders against the laws of the United States, but to deliver them up to the authorities for trial." Read in conjunction with 18 U.S.C. §1152, which extends federal enclave law to non-Indian offenses on Indian reservations, this provision implies that the Suquamish are to promptly deliver up any non-Indian offender, rather than try and punish him themselves.

By themselves, these treaty provisions would probably not be sufficient to remove criminal jurisdiction over non-Indians if the Tribe otherwise retained such jurisdiction. But an examination of our earlier precedents satisfies us that, even ignoring treaty provisions and congressional policy, Indians do not have criminal jurisdiction over non-Indians absent affirmative delegation of such power by Congress. Indian tribes do retain elements of "quasi-sovereign" authority after ceding their lands to the United States and announcing their dependence on the Federal Government. See *Cherokee Nation v. Georgia*, 5 Pet. 1, 15, 8 L.Ed. 25 (1831). But the tribes' retained powers are not such that they are limited only by specific restrictions in treaties or congressional enactments. As the Court of Appeals recog-

nized Indian tribes are prohibited from exercising both those powers of autonomous states that are expressly terminated by Congress and those powers *inconsistent with their status. Oliphant v. Schlie*, 544 F.2d, at 1009

Indian reservations are "a part of the territory of the United States." *United States v. Rogers*, 4 How. 567, 571, 11 L.Ed. 1105 (1846). Indian tribes "hold and occupy [the reservations] with the assent of the United States, and under their authority." Id., at 572. Upon incorporation into the territory of the United States, the Indian tribes thereby come under the territorial sovereignty of the United States and their exercise of separate power is constrained so as not to conflict with the interests of this overriding sovereignty. "[T]heir rights to complete sovereignty, as independent nations, [are] necessarily diminished." *Johnson v. M'Intosh*, 8 Wheat. 543, 574, 5 L.Ed. 681 (1823). . . .

In summary, respondents' position ignores that "Indians are within the geographical limits of the United States. The soil and people within these limits are under the political control of the Government of the United States, or of the States of the Union. There exists in the broad domain of sovereignty but these two. There may be cities, counties, and other organized bodies with limited legislative functions, but they . . . exist in subordination to one or the other of these." *United States v. Kagama*, 118 U.S. 375, 379, 6 S.Ct. 1109, 1111, 30 L.Ed. 228 (1886).

We recognize that some Indian tribal court systems have become increasingly sophisticated and resemble in many respects their state counterparts. We also acknowledge that with the passage of the Indian Civil Rights Act of 1968, which extends certain basic procedural rights to anyone tried in Indian tribal court, many of the dangers that might have accompanied the exercise by tribal courts of criminal jurisdiction over non-Indians only a few decades ago have disappeared. Finally, we are not unaware of the prevalence of non-Indian crime on today's reservations which the tribes forcefully argue requires the ability to try non-Indians. But these are considerations for Congress to weigh in deciding whether Indian tribes should finally be authorized to try non-Indians. They have little relevance to the principles which lead us to conclude that Indian tribes do not have inherent jurisdiction to try and to punish non-Indians. The judgments below are therefore

Reversed.

California v. Cabazon Band of Mission Indians (1987)

Justice White (for the Court):

The Cabazon and Morongo Bands of Mission Indians, federally recognized Indian Tribes, occupy reservations in Riverside County, California. [Footnote 1. . . . The Cabazon Band has 25 enrolled members and the Morongo Band . . . approximately 730. . . . Each Band, pursuant to an ordinance approved by the [U.S.] Secretary of the Interior, conducts bingo games on its reservation. The Cabazon Band has also opened a card club at which draw poker and other card games are played. The games are open to the public and are played predominantly by non-Indians coming onto the reservations. The games are a major source of employment for tribal members, and the profits are the Tribes' sole source of income. The State of California seeks to apply to the two Tribes [a California Penal Code provision that] . . . does not entirely prohibit the playing of bingo but permits it [only] when the games are operated and staffed by members of designated charitable organizations who may not be paid for their services. Profits must be kept in special accounts and used only for charitable purposes; prizes may not exceed $250 per game. Asserting that the bingo games on the two reservations violated each of these restrictions, California insisted that the Tribes comply with state law. Riverside County also sought to apply its local [o]rdinance . . . regulating bingo, as well as its [o]rdinance . . . prohibiting the playing of draw poker and the other card games. . . .

[The Ninth Circuit U.S. Court of Appeals], applying what it thought to be the civil/criminal dichotomy [of] Bryan[,] . . . [has drawn] a distinction between state "criminal/prohibitory" laws and state "civil/regulatory" laws: [I]f the intent of a state law is generally to prohibit certain conduct, it falls within Public Law 280's grant of criminal jurisdiction, but if the state law generally permits the conduct at issue, subject to regulation, it must be classified as civil/regulatory and Public Law 280 does not authorize its enforcement on an Indian reservation. The shorthand test is whether the conduct at issue violates the State's public policy. Inquiring into the nature of [the California bingo statute], the Court of Appeals held that it was regulatory rather than prohibitory. . . .

We are persuaded that the prohibitory/regulatory distinction is consistent with Bryan's construc-

tion of Public Law 280. It is not a bright-line rule [and] . . . an argument of some weight may be made that the bingo statute is prohibitory rather than regulatory. But . . . we are reluctant to disagree with [the Court of Appeals'] view of the nature and intent of the state law at issue here. . . .

. . . This case . . . involves a state burden on tribal Indians in the context of their dealings with non-Indians since the question is whether the State may prevent the Tribes from making available high stakes bingo games to non-Indians coming from outside the reservations. . . . [S]tate authority . . . "is preempted . . . if it interferes . . . with federal and tribal interests reflected in federal law, unless the state interests at stake are sufficient to justify the assertion of state authority." [*New Mexico v. Mescalero Apache Tribe* 1983, 333–334] The inquiry is to proceed in light of traditional notions of Indian sovereignty and the congressional goal of Indian self-government, including its "overriding goal" of encouraging tribal self-sufficiency and economic development. [*Mescalero* 1983, 334–335]

These are important federal interests. They were reaffirmed by [President Ronald Reagan's] 1983 Statement on Indian Policy. More specifically, the Department of the Interior, which has the primary responsibility for carrying out the Federal Government's trust obligations to Indian tribes, [and also the Department of Health and Human Services and the Department of Housing and Urban Development,] ha[ve] sought to implement these policies by promoting tribal bingo enterprises. . . .

These policies and actions, which demonstrate the Government's approval and active promotion of tribal bingo enterprises, are of particular relevance in this case. The Cabazon and Morongo Reservations contain no natural resources which can be exploited. The tribal games at present provide the sole source of revenues for the operation of the tribal governments and the provision of tribal services. They are also the major sources of employment on the reservations. Self-determination and economic development are not within reach if the Tribes cannot raise revenues and provide employment for their members. The Tribes' interests obviously parallel the federal interests. . . .

The [other] interest asserted by the State to justify the imposition of its bingo laws on the Tribes is in preventing the infiltration of the tribal games by organized crime. To the extent that the State seeks to prevent any and all bingo games from being played

on tribal lands while permitting regulated, off-reservation games, this asserted interest is irrelevant. . . . The State insists that the high stakes offered at tribal games are attractive to organized crime, whereas the controlled games authorized under California law are not. This is surely a legitimate concern, but we are unconvinced that it is sufficient. . . . California does not allege any present criminal involvement in the Cabazon and Morongo enterprises. . . . [F]ar from any action being taken [by the Federal Government] evidencing this concern[,] . . . the prevailing federal policy continues to support these tribal enterprises, including those of the Tribes involved in this case.

We conclude that the State's interest in preventing the infiltration of the tribal bingo enterprises by organized crime does not justify state regulation of [those] enterprises in light of the compelling federal and tribal interests supporting them . .

Native American Graves Protection and Repatriation Act (1990)

SEC. 3. OWNERSHIP.

  (a) NATIVE AMERICAN HUMAN REMAINS AND OBJECTS—The ownership or control of Native American cultural items which are excavated or discovered on Federal or tribal lands after the date of enactment of this Act shall be (with priority given in the order listed)—

    (1) in the case of Native American human remains and associated funerary objects, in the lineal descendants of the Native American; or

    (2) in any case in which such lineal descendants cannot be ascertained, and in the case of unassociated funerary objects, sacred objects, and objects of cultural patrimony—

(A) in the Indian tribe or Native Hawaiian organization on whose tribal land such objects or remains were discovered;

(B) in the Indian tribe or Native Hawaiian organization which has the closest cultural affiliation with such remains or objects and which, upon notice, states a claim for such remains or objects; or

(C) if the cultural affiliation of the objects cannot be reasonably ascertained and if the objects were discovered on Federal land that is recognized by a final judgment of the Indian Claims Commission or the United States Court of Claims as the aboriginal land of some Indian tribe—

    (1) in the Indian tribe that is recognized as aboriginally occupying the area in which the objects were discovered, if upon notice, such tribe states a claim for such remains or objects, or

    (2) if it can be shown by a preponderance of the evidence that a different tribe has a stronger cultural relationship with the remains or objects than the tribe or organization specified in paragraph (1), in the Indian tribe that has the strongest demonstrated relationship, if upon notice, such tribe states a claim for such remains or objects.

  (b) UNCLAIMED NATIVE AMERICAN HUMAN REMAINS AND OBJECTS—Native American cultural items not claimed under subsection (a) shall be disposed of in accordance with regulations promulgated by the Secretary in consultation with the review committee established under section 8, Native American groups, representatives of museums and the scientific community.

  (c) INTENTIONAL EXCAVATION AND REMOVAL OF NATIVE AMERICAN HUMAN REMAINS AND OBJECTS—The intentional removal from or excavation of Native American cultural items from Federal or tribal lands for purposes of discovery, study, or removal of such items is permitted only if—

    (1) such items are excavated or removed pursuant to a permit issued under section 4 of the Archaeological Resources Protection Act of 1979 (93 Stat. 721; 16 U.S.C. 470aa et seq.) which shall be consistent with this Act;

    (2) such items are excavated or removed after consultation with or, in the case of tribal lands, consent of the

appropriate (if any) Indian tribe or Native Hawaiian organization;

(3) the ownership and right of control of the disposition of such items shall be as provided in subsections (a) and (b); and

(4) proof of consultation or consent under paragraph (2) is shown.

(d) INADVERTENT DISCOVERY OF NATIVE AMERICAN REMAINS AND OBJECTS—(1) Any person who knows, or has reason to know, that such person has discovered Native American cultural items on Federal or tribal lands after the date of enactment of this Act shall notify, in writing, the Secretary of the Department, or head of any other agency or instrumentality of the United States, having primary management authority with respect to Federal lands and the appropriate Indian tribe or Native Hawaiian organization with respect to tribal lands, if known or readily ascertainable, and, in the case of lands that have been selected by an Alaska Native Corporation or group organized pursuant to the Alaska Native Claims Settlement Act of 1971, the appropriate corporation or group. If the discovery occurred in connection with an activity, including (but not limited to) construction, mining, logging, and agriculture, the person shall cease the activity in the area of the discovery, make a reasonable effort to protect the items discovered before resuming such activity, and provide notice under this subsection. Following the notification under this subsection, and upon certification by the Secretary of the department or the head of any agency or instrumentality of the United States or the appropriate Indian tribe or Native Hawaiian organization that notification has been received, the activity may resume after 30 days of such certification. . . .

SEC. 4. ILLEGAL TRAFFICKING.

(a) Chapter 53 of title 18, United States Code, is amended by adding at the end thereof the following new section: Sec. 1170.

Illegal Trafficking in Native American Human Remains and Cultural Items

(b) Whoever knowingly sells, purchases, uses for profit, or transports for sale or profit, the human remains of a Native American without the right of possession to those remains as provided in the Native American Graves Protection and Repatriation Act shall be fined in accordance with this title, or imprisoned not more than 12 months, or both, and in the case of a second or subsequent violation, be fined in accordance with this title, or imprisoned not more than 5 years, or both.

TABLE OF CONTENTS—The table of contents for chapter 53 of title 18, United States Code, is amended by adding at the end thereof the following new item: 1170. Illegal Trafficking in Native American Human Remains and Cultural Items.

SEC. 5. INVENTORY FOR HUMAN REMAINS AND ASSOCIATED FUNERARY OBJECTS.

(a) IN GENERAL—Each Federal agency and each museum which has possession or control over holdings or collections of Native American human remains and associated funerary objects shall compile an inventory of such items and, to the extent possible based on information possessed by such museum or Federal agency, identify the geographical and cultural affiliation of such item . . . .

SEC. 6. SUMMARY FOR UNASSOCIATED FUNERARY OBJECTS, SACRED OBJECTS, AND CULTURAL PATRIMONY.

(a) IN GENERAL—Each Federal agency or museum which has possession or control over holdings or collections of Native American unassociated funerary objects, sacred objects, or objects of cultural patrimony shall provide a written summary of such objects based upon available information held by such agency or museum. The summary shall describe the scope of the collection, kinds of objects included, reference to geographical location, means and period of acquisition and cultural affiliation, where readily ascertainable.

. . .

Native American Languages Act (1990)

The Congress finds that

(1)   the status of the cultures and languages of Native Americans is unique and the United States has the responsibility to act together with Native Americans to ensure the survival of these unique cultures and languages;

(2)   special status is accorded Native Americans in the United States, a status that recognizes distinct cultural and political rights, including the right to continue separate identities;

(3)   the traditional languages of Native Americans are an integral part of their cultures and identities and form the basic medium for the transmission, and thus survival, of Native American cultures, literatures, histories, religions, political institutions, and values;

. . .

(5)   there is a lack of clear, comprehensive, and consistent Federal policy on treatment of Native American languages which has often resulted in acts of suppression and extermination of Native American languages and cultures;

(6)   there is convincing evidence that student achievement and performance, community and school pride, and educational opportunity is clearly and directly tied to respect for, and support of, the first language of the child or student;

(7)   it is clearly in the interests of the United States, individual States, and territories to encourage the full academic and human potential achievements of all students and citizens and to take steps to realize these ends;

(8)   acts of suppression and extermination directed against Native American languages and cultures are in conflict with the United States policy of self-determination for Native Americans;

(9)   languages are the means of communication for the full range of human experiences and are critical to the survival of cultural and political integrity of any people; and

(10)   language provides a direct and powerful means of promoting international communication by people who share languages.

Sec. 2902.—Definitions

For purposes of this chapter

(1)   The term "Native American" means an Indian, Native Hawaiian, or Native American Pacific Islander.

(2)   The term "Indian" has the meaning given to such term under section 7881(4) of title 20.

(3)   The term "Native Hawaiian" has the meaning given to such term by section 7912(1) of title 20.

(4)   The term "Native American Pacific Islander" means any descendent of the aboriginal people of any island in the Pacific Ocean that is a territory or possession of the United States.

(5)   The terms "Indian tribe" and "tribal organization" have the respective meaning given to each of such terms under section 450b of this title.

(6)   The term "Native American language" means the historical, traditional languages spoken by Native Americans.

(7)   The term "traditional leaders" includes Native Americans who have special expertise in Native American culture and Native American languages.

(8)   The term "Indian reservation" has the same meaning given to the term "reservation" under section 1452 of this title.

Sec. 2903.—Declaration of policy

It is the policy of the United States to

(1)   preserve, protect, and promote the rights and freedom of Native Americans to use, practice, and develop Native American languages;

(2)   allow exceptions to teacher certification requirements for Federal programs, and programs funded in whole or in part by the Federal Government, for instruction in Native American languages when such teacher certification requirements hinder the employment of qualified teachers who teach in Native American languages, and to encourage State and territorial governments to make similar exceptions;

(3) encourage and support the use of Native American languages as a medium of instruction in order to encourage and support
- (A) Native American language survival,
- (B) educational opportunity,
- (C) increased student success and performance,
- (D) increased student awareness and knowledge of their culture and history, and
- (E) increased student and community pride;

(4) encourage State and local education programs to work with Native American parents, educators, Indian tribes, and other Native American governing bodies in the implementation of programs to put this policy into effect;

(5) recognize the right of Indian tribes and other Native American governing bodies to use the Native American languages as a medium of instruction in all schools funded by the Secretary of the Interior;

(6) fully recognize the inherent right of Indian tribes and other Native American governing bodies, States, territories, and possessions of the United States to take action on, and give official status to, their Native American languages for the purpose of conducting their own business;

(7) support the granting of comparable proficiency achieved through course work in a Native American language the same academic credit as comparable proficiency achieved through course work in a foreign language, with recognition of such Native American language proficiency by institutions of higher education as fulfilling foreign language entrance or degree requirements; and

(8) encourage all institutions of elementary, secondary and higher education, where appropriate, to include Native American languages in the curriculum in the same manner as foreign languages and to grant proficiency in Native American languages the same full academic credit as proficiency in foreign languages.

Sec. 2904.—No restrictions

The right of Native Americans to express themselves through the use of Native American languages shall not be restricted in any public proceeding, including publicly supported education programs.

Sec. 2905.—Evaluations

(a) The President shall direct the heads of the various Federal departments, agencies, and instrumentalities to

(1) evaluate their policies and procedures in consultation with Indian tribes and other Native American governing bodies as well as traditional leaders and educators in order to determine and implement changes needed to bring the policies and procedures into compliance with the provisions of this chapter;

(2) give the greatest effect possible in making such evaluations, absent a clear specific Federal statutory requirement to the contrary, to the policies and procedures which will give the broadest effect to the provisions of this chapter; and

(3) evaluate the laws which they administer and make recommendations to the President on amendments needed to bring such laws into compliance with the provisions of this chapter.

(b) By no later than the date that is 1 year after October 30, 1990, the President shall submit to the Congress a report containing recommendations for amendments to Federal laws that are needed to bring such laws into compliance with the provisions of this chapter.

Sec. 2906.—Use of English

Nothing in this chapter shall be construed as precluding the use of Federal funds to teach English to Native Americans.

United States of America v. Robert Lawrence Boyll (1991)

There is a genius to our Constitution. Its genius is that it speaks to the freedoms of the individual. It is this genius that brings the present matter before the Court. More specifically, this matter concerns a free-

dom that was a natural idea whose genesis was in the Plymouth Charter, and finds its present form in the First Amendment to the United States Constitution—the freedom of religion.

The Government's "war on drugs" has become a wildfire that threatens to consume those fundamental rights of the individual deliberately enshrined in our Constitution. Ironically, as we celebrate the 200th anniversary of the Bill of Rights, the tattered Fourth Amendment right to be free from unreasonable searches and seizures and the now frail Fifth Amendment right against self-incrimination or deprivation of liberty without due process have fallen as casualties in this "war on drugs." It was naive of this Court to hope that this erosion of constitutional protections would stop at the Fourth and Fifth Amendments. But today, the "war" targets one of the most deeply held fundamental rights— the First Amendment right to freely exercise one's religion . . . .

The issue presented is the recurring conflict between the Native American Church members' right to freely exercise their religion through the ceremonial use of peyote and the Government's efforts to eradicate illegal drugs. To the Government, peyote is a dangerous hallucinogen. To Robert Boyll, peyote is both a sacrament and a deity essential to his religion. But this matter concerns competing interests far greater than those relating to this small, spineless cactus having psychedelic properties. It draws forth a troublesome constitutional conflict which arises from fundamentally different perspectives of peyote.

In its "war" to free our society of the devastating effects of drugs, the Government slights its duty to observe the fundamental freedom of individuals to practice the religion of their choice, regardless of race. Simply put, the Court is faced with the quintessential constitutional conflict between an inalienable right upon which this country was founded and the response by the Government to the swelling political passions of the day. In this fray, the Court is compelled to halt this menacing attack on our constitutional freedoms. . . .

The following will constitute the Court's findings of fact and conclusions of law.

The peyote plant is a small, spineless cactus having psychedelic properties and the experience of eating it is central to the Peyote Religion. Unlike traditional religions which have sacramental symbols such as bread and wine, peyote is more than a sacrament to members of the Native American Church.

Peyote is, itself, considered a deity which cannot be owned by any individual. . . .

The peyote ceremony is unique and the very cornerstone of the Peyote Religion. . . . Although one branch of the Native American Church, the Native American Church of North America, is known to restrict membership to Native Americans, most other branches of the Native American Church do not. As a result, non-Indian members are accepted within the Native American Church. . . .

Since attending his first ceremony of the Native American Church at Taos, New Mexico, in 1981, Mr. Boyll has been, and continues to be, an active member of the Native American Church. As the uncontradicted evidence in this case shows, the history of the Native American Church attests to the fact that non-Indian worshipers have always been, and continue to be, active and sincere members of the Native American Church.

Since the use of peyote by Native American Church members is the very essence of their religious beliefs, the proposed racially restrictive reading of 21 C.F.R. § 1307.31 would have the sure effect of imposing a racial exclusion to membership in the Native American Church itself. To exclude individuals of a particular race from being members of a recognized religious faith is offensive to the very heart of the First Amendment. See *Waltz v. Tax Comm'n of New York*, 397 U.S. 664, 668–69 (1970) (the First Amendment's Establishment Clause ensures that governmental interference with religion will be not tolerated). In fact, there can be no more excessive entanglement of Government with religion than the Government's attempt to impose a racial restriction to membership in a religious organization. . . .

An examination of the record as to the nature of peyote and its role in the religion practiced by defendants as [Indian and non-Indian] members of the Native American Church . . . compels the conclusion that the [racially restrictive] prohibition most seriously infringes upon the observance of the religion. . . .

The record thus establishes that the [indictment for] . . . the use of peyote results in a virtual inhibition of the practice of defendants' religion. . . .

Additionally, the Court finds that Mr. Boyll's trip to Mexico to obtain peyote is an integral part of the Peyote Religion practiced by the Native American Church. Such a substantial infringement necessarily triggers further First Amendment scrutiny. . . .

First, the United States has failed to present any evidence of a compelling interest to justify its actions in the present case. "In the absence of evidence, we cannot simply assume that the psychedelic is so baneful that its use must be prohibited to a group of [non-Indian] members but poses no equal threat when used by [Indian] members of the Native American Church." *Peyote Way Church of God*, 742 F.2d at 201. In fact, in light of the absence of factual support and the scarcity of legal support for the United States' opposition to Defendant's motions to dismiss, this Court cannot help but believe that the present prosecution is, at best, an overreaction driven by political passions or, at worst, influenced by religious and racial insensitivity, if not outright hostility. . . .

Congress has articulated an unequivocal federal policy protecting the right of the Native American Church and its members to worship, possess and use peyote in bona fide religious ceremonies. This policy arises out of our country's recognition of the importance of individual freedom. For, the right to free religious expression embodies a precious heritage of our history. In a mass society, which presses at every point toward conformity, the protection of a self-expression, however unique, of the individual and the group become ever more important. . . .

Individual freedom, whether it be freedom of religion, expression or association, has been particularly important to maintaining the culturally diverse character of New Mexico. Here, we celebrate the right of the individual to revel in the passions of the spirit. The survival of this right owes much to the protection afforded by the First Amendment, which has allowed New Mexico's distinct cultures to learn mutual respect for each other's jealously-guarded customs and traditions. Diversity is New Mexico's enchantment.

For the reasons set out in this Memorandum Opinion and Order, the Court holds that, pursuant to 21 C.F.R. § 1307.31 (1990), the classification of peyote as a Schedule I controlled substance, see 21 U.S.C. §812(c), Schedule I (c)(12), does not apply to the importation, possession or use of peyote for bona fide ceremonial use by members of the Native American Church, regardless of race.

Wherefore,

It is ordered, adjudged and decreed that Defendant Robert Boyll's motions to dismiss the indictment be and hereby are granted.

Dated at Albuquerque the—of September, 1991.

Chief Judge

Nunavut Land Claims Agreement Act (1993)

An Act respecting an Agreement between the Inuit of the Nunavut Settlement Area and Her Majesty the Queen in right of Canada.

WHEREAS the Inuit of the Nunavut Settlement Area have asserted an aboriginal title to that Area based on their traditional and current use and occupation of the lands, waters and land-fast ice therein in accordance with their own customs and usages;

WHEREAS the Constitution Act, 1982 recognizes and affirms the existing aboriginal and treaty rights of the aboriginal peoples of Canada;

WHEREAS Her Majesty the Queen in right of Canada and the Inuit of the Nunavut Settlement Area have negotiated an Agreement based on and reflecting the following objectives:

to provide for certainty and clarity of rights to ownership and use of lands and resources and of rights for Inuit to participate in decision-making concerning the use, management and conservation of land, water and resources, including the offshore,

to provide Inuit with wildlife harvesting rights and rights to participate in decision-making concerning wildlife harvesting,

to provide Inuit with financial compensation and means of participating in economic opportunities,

to encourage self-reliance and the cultural and social well-being of Inuit;

WHEREAS Her Majesty the Queen in right of Canada and the Inuit of the Nunavut Settlement Area, through their duly mandated representatives, have entered into the Agreement through which Inuit shall receive defined rights and benefits in exchange for the surrender of certain claims, rights, title and interests, based on their assertion of an aboriginal title;

WHEREAS the Agreement provides that it will be a land claims agreement within the meaning of section 35 of the Constitution Act, 1982;

WHEREAS the Inuit of the Nunavut Settlement Area have ratified the Agreement in accordance with the provisions of the Agreement;

AND WHEREAS the ratification by Her Majesty under Article 36 of the Agreement requires the enactment by Parliament of a statute ratifying the Agreement;

NOW, THEREFORE, Her Majesty, by and with the advice and consent of the Senate and House of Commons of Canada, enacts as follows:

SHORT TITLE

1. This Act may be cited as the Nunavut Land Claims Agreement Act.

INTERPRETATION

2. In this Act,

"Agreement" means the land claims agreement between the Inuit of the Nunavut Settlement Area and Her Majesty the Queen in right of Canada, signed on May 25, 1993, and tabled in the House of Commons for the Minister of Indian Affairs and Northern Development on May 26, 1993, and includes any amendments to that agreement made pursuant to the agreement; "Nunavut Settlement Area" means the area described in section 3.1.1 of the Agreement.

HER MAJESTY

3. This Act is binding on Her Majesty in right of Canada or a province.

AGREEMENT

4. (1) The Agreement is hereby ratified, given effect and declared valid.

(2) For greater certainty, the Agreement is binding on all persons and bodies that are not parties to the Agreement.

(3) For greater certainty, any person or body on which the Agreement confers a right, privilege, benefit or power or imposes a duty or liability may exercise the right, privilege, benefit or power, shall perform the duty or is subject to the liability, to the extent provided for by the Agreement.

5. The rights and benefits of the Inuit of the Nunavut Settlement Area under the Agreement do not merge in this Act or any other law.

6. (1) In the event of an inconsistency or conflict between the Agreement and any law, including this Act, the Agreement prevails to the extent of the inconsistency or conflict.

(2) In the event of an inconsistency or conflict between this Act and any other law, this Act prevails to the extent of the inconsistency or conflict.

7. The Minister of Indian Affairs and Northern Development shall cause a certified copy of the Agreement and any amendments to the Agreement to be deposited in

(a) the Library and Archives of Canada;

(b) the library of the Department of Indian Affairs and Northern Development that is situated in the National Capital Region;

(c) the legislative library of the territorial government that has jurisdiction over the Nunavut Settlement Area; and

(d) such other places as the Minister considers advisable.

1993, c. 29, s. 7; 2004, c. 11, s. 34.

8. The Governor in Council may make such orders and regulations as are necessary for the purpose of carrying out any of the provisions of the Agreement.

APPROPRIATION

9. There shall be paid out of the Consolidated Revenue Fund the sums required to meet the monetary obligations of Her Majesty under Articles 25 and 29 of the Agreement that arise after the coming into force of this Act.

NUNAVUT WILDLIFE MANAGEMENT BOARD

10. (1) The Nunavut Wildlife Management Board established by the Agreement is hereby constituted as a corporation and, as such, the Board has, for the purposes of carrying out its functions under the Agreement, the capacity, rights, powers and privileges of a natural person.

(2) The Nunavut Wildlife Management Board is not an agent of Her Majesty in right of Canada.

11. The head office of the Nunavut Wildlife Management Board shall be in Iqaluit or in such other place in the Nunavut Settlement Area as the Governor in Council may designate.

12. The remuneration of the members of the Nunavut Wildlife Management Board shall be set by the Governor in Council.

COMING INTO FORCE

*13. This Act shall come into force on December 31, 1993 or such earlier date as may be fixed by order of the Governor in Council.

[Note: Act in force July 9, 1993]

Bureau of Indian Affairs: Establishing the Existence of an Indian Tribe

Section 2. Purpose.

The purpose of this part is to establish a departmental procedure and policy for acknowledging that certain American Indian groups exist as tribes. Acknowledgment of tribal existence by the Department is a prerequisite to the protection, services, and benefits of the Federal government available to Indian tribes by virtue of their status as tribes. Acknowledgment shall also mean that the tribe is entitled to the immunities and privileges available to other federally acknowledged Indian tribes by virtue of their government-to-government relationship with the United States as well as the responsibilities, powers, limitations and obligations of such tribes. Acknowledgment shall subject the Indian tribe to the same authority of Congress and the United States to which other federally acknowledged tribes are subjected. . . .

Section 7. Mandatory criteria for Federal acknowledgment.

The mandatory criteria are:

(a) The petitioner has been identified as an American Indian entity on a substantially continuous basis since 1900. Evidence that the group's character as an Indian entity has from time to time been denied shall not be considered to be conclusive evidence that this criterion has not been met. Evidence to be relied upon in determining a group's Indian identity may include one or a combination of the following, as well as other evidence of identification by other than the petitioner itself or its members.

   (1) Identification as an Indian entity by Federal authorities.

   (2) Relationships with State governments based on identification of the group as Indian.

   (3) Dealings with a county, parish, or other local government in a relationship based on the group's Indian identity.

   (4) Identification as an Indian entity by anthropologists, historians, and/or other scholars.

   (5) Identification as an Indian entity in newspapers and books.

   (6) Identification as an Indian entity in relationships with Indian tribes or with national, regional, or state Indian organizations.

(b) A predominant portion of the petitioning group comprises a distinct community and has existed as a community from historical times until the present.

   (1) This criterion may be demonstrated by some combination of the following evidence and/or other evidence that the petitioner meets the definition of community set forth in Section 1:

      (i) Significant rates of marriage within the group, and/or, as may be culturally required, patterned out-marriages with other Indian populations.

      (ii) Significant social relationships connecting individual members.

      (iii) Significant rates of informal social interaction which exist broadly among the members of a group.

      (iv) A significant degree of shared or cooperative labor or other economic activity among the membership.

      (v) Evidence of strong patterns of discrimination or other social distinctions by non-members.

      (vi) Shared sacred or secular ritual activity encompassing most of the group.

      (vii) Cultural patterns shared among a significant portion of the group that are different from those of the non-Indian populations with whom it interacts. These patterns must function as more than a symbolic identification of the group as Indian. They may include, but are not limited to, language, kinship organization, or religious beliefs and practices.

      (viii) The persistence of a named, collective Indian identity continuously over a period of more than 50 years, notwithstanding changes in name.

      (ix) A demonstration of historical political influence under the criterion in Section 7(c) shall be evidence for demonstrating historical community.

(2) A petitioner shall be considered to have provided sufficient evidence of community at a given point in time if evidence is provided to demonstrate any one of the following:

   (i) More than 50 percent of the members reside in a geographical area exclusively or almost exclusively composed of members of the group, and the balance of the group maintains consistent interaction with some members of the community;

   (ii) At least 50 percent of the marriages in the group are between members of the group;

   (iii) At least 50 percent of the group members maintain distinct cultural patterns such as, but not limited to, language, kinship organization, or religious beliefs and practices;

   (iv) There are distinct community social institutions encompassing most of the members, such as kinship organizations, formal or informal economic cooperation, or religious organizations; or

   (v) The group has met the criterion in Section 7(c) using evidence described in Section 7(c)(2).

(c) The petitioner has maintained political influence or authority over its members as an autonomous entity from historical times until the present.

  (1) This criterion may be demonstrated by some combination of the evidence listed below and/or by other evidence that the petitioner meets the definition of political influence or authority in Section 1.

   (i) The group is able to mobilize significant numbers of members and significant resources from its members for group purposes.

   (ii) Most of the membership considers issues acted upon or actions taken by group leaders or governing bodies to be of importance.

   (iii) There is widespread knowledge, communication and involvement in political processes by most of the group's members.

   (iv) The group meets the criterion in Section 7(b) at more than a minimal level.

   (v) There are internal conflicts which show controversy over valued group goals, properties, policies, processes and/or decisions.

  (2) A petitioning group shall be considered to have provided sufficient evidence to demonstrate the exercise of political influence or authority at a given point in time by demonstrating that group leaders and/or other mechanisms exist or existed which:

   (i) Allocate group resources such as land, residence rights and the like on a consistent basis.

   (ii) Settle disputes between members or subgroups by mediation or other means on a regular basis;

   (iii) Exert strong influence on the behavior of individual members, such as the establishment or maintenance of norms and the enforcement of sanctions to direct or control behavior;

   (iv) Organize or influence economic subsistence activities among the members, including shared or cooperative labor.

  (3) A group that has met the requirements in paragraph 83.7(b)(2) at a given point in time shall be considered to have provided sufficient evidence to meet this criterion at that point in time.

(d) A copy of the group's present governing document including its membership criteria. In the absence of a written document, the petitioner must provide a statement describing in full its membership criteria and current governing procedures.

(e) The petitioner's membership consists of individuals who descend from a historical Indian tribe or from historical Indian tribes which combined and functioned as a single autonomous political entity.

  (1) Evidence acceptable to the Secretary which can be used for this purpose includes but is not limited to:

(i)   Rolls prepared by the Secretary on a descendancy basis for purposes of distributing claims money, providing allotments, or other purposes;

(ii)   State, Federal, or other official records or evidence identifying present members or ancestors of present members as being descendants of a historical tribe or tribes that combined and functioned as a single autonomous political entity.

(iii)   Church, school, and other similar enrollment records identifying present members or ancestors of present members as being descendants of a historical tribe or tribes that combined and functioned as a single autonomous political entity.

(iv)   Affidavits of recognition by tribal elders, leaders, or the tribal governing body identifying present members or ancestors of present members as being descendants of a historical tribe or tribes that combined and functioned as a single autonomous political entity.

(v)   Other records or evidence identifying present members or ancestors of present members as being descendants of a historical tribe or tribes that combined and functioned as a single autonomous political entity.

(2)   The petitioner must provide an official membership list, separately certified by the group's governing body, of all known current members of the group. This list must include each member's full name (including maiden name), date of birth, and current residential address. The petitioner must also provide a copy of each available former list of members based on the group's own defined criteria, as well as a statement describing the circumstances surrounding the preparation of the current list and, insofar as possible, the circumstances surrounding the preparation of former lists.

(f)   The membership of the petitioning group is composed principally of persons who are not members of any acknowledged North American Indian tribe. However, under certain conditions a petitioning group may be acknowledged even if its membership is composed principally of persons whose names have appeared on rolls of, or who have been otherwise associated with, an acknowledged Indian tribe. The conditions are that the group must establish that it has functioned throughout history until the present as a separate and autonomous Indian tribal entity, that its members do not maintain a bilateral political relationship with the acknowledged tribe, and that its members have provided written confirmation of their membership in the petitioning group.

(g)   Neither the petitioner nor its members are the subject of congressional legislation that has expressly terminated or forbidden the Federal relationship. . . .

Section 10. Processing of the documented petition.

(a)   Upon receipt of a documented petition, the Assistant Secretary shall cause a review to be conducted to determine whether the petitioner is entitled to be acknowledged as an Indian tribe. The review shall include consideration of the documented petition and the factual statements contained therein. The Assistant Secretary may also initiate other research for any purpose relative to analyzing the documented petition and obtaining additional information about the petitioner's status. The Assistant Secretary may likewise consider any evidence which may be submitted by interested parties or informed parties. . . .

Section 12. Implementation of decisions.

(a)   Upon final determination that the petitioner exists as an Indian tribe, it shall be considered eligible for the services and benefits from the Federal government that are available to other federally recognized tribes. The newly acknowledged tribe shall be considered a historic tribe and shall be entitled to the privileges and immunities

available to other federally recognized historic tribes by virtue of their government-to-government relationship with the United States. It shall also have the responsibilities and obligations of such tribes. Newly acknowledged Indian tribes shall likewise be subject to the same authority of Congress and the United States as are other federally acknowledged tribes. . . .

Navajo–Hopi Land Dispute Settlement Act of 1996

To provide for the settlement of the Navajo-Hopi land dispute, and for other purposes . . .

The Congress finds that—

(1) it is in the public interest for the Tribe, Navajos residing on the Hopi Partitioned Lands, and the United States to reach a peaceful resolution of the longstanding disagreements between the parties under the Act commonly known as the "Navajo-Hopi Land Settlement Act of 1974" (Public Law 93–531; 25 U.S.C. 640d et seq.);

(2) it is in the best interest of the Tribe and the United States that there be a fair and final settlement of certain issues remaining in connection with the Navajo-Hopi Land Settlement Act of 1974, including the full and final settlement of the multiple claims that the Tribe has against the United States;

(3) this Act, together with the Settlement Agreement executed on December 14, 1995, and the Accommodation Agreement (as incorporated by the Settlement Agreement), provide the authority for the Tribe to enter agreements with eligible Navajo families in order for those families to remain residents of the Hopi Partitioned Lands for a period of 75 years, subject to the terms and conditions of the Accommodation Agreement;

(4) the United States acknowledges and respects—

(A) the sincerity of the traditional beliefs of the members of the Tribe and the Navajo families residing on the Hopi Partitioned Lands; and

(B) the importance that the respective traditional beliefs of the members of the

Tribe and Navajo families have with respect to the culture and way of life of those members and families;

(5) this Act, the Settlement Agreement, and the Accommodation Agreement provide for the mutual respect and protection of the traditional religious beliefs and practices of the Tribe and the Navajo families residing on the Hopi Partitioned Lands;

(6) the Tribe is encouraged to work with the Navajo families residing on the Hopi Partitioned Lands to address their concerns regarding the establishment of family or individual burial plots for deceased family members who have resided on the Hopi Partitioned Lands; and

(7) neither the Navajo Nation nor the Navajo families residing upon Hopi Partitioned Lands were parties to or signers of the Settlement Agreement between the United States and the Hopi Tribe . . . .

Sec. 4. Ratification of Settlement Agreement.

The United States approves, ratifies, and confirms the Settlement Agreement.

Sec. 5. Conditions for Lands Taken into Trust.

The Secretary shall take such action as may be necessary to ensure that the following conditions are met prior to taking lands into trust for the benefit of the Tribe pursuant to the Settlement Agreement:

(1) Selection of lands taken into trust.—

(A) Primary area.—In accordance with section 7(a) of the Settlement Agreement, the primary area within which lands acquired by the Tribe may be taken into trust by the Secretary for the benefit of the Tribe under the Settlement Agreement shall be located in northern Arizona.

(B) Requirements for lands taken into trust in the primary area.—Lands taken into trust in the primary area referred to in subparagraph (A) shall be—

(i) land that is used substantially for ranching, agriculture, or another similar use; and

(ii) to the extent feasible, in contiguous parcels.

(2) Acquisition of lands.—Before taking any land into trust for the benefit of the Tribe under this section, the Secretary shall ensure that—

(A) at least 85 percent of the eligible Navajo heads of household (as determined under the Settlement Agreement) have entered into an accommodation or have chosen to relocate and are eligible for relocation assistance (as determined under the Settlement Agreement . . .)

Sec. 9. 75-Year Leasing Authority.

The first section of the Act of August 9, 1955 (69 Stat. 539, chapter 615; 25 U.S.C. 415) is amended by adding at the end the following new subsections:

(c) Leases Involving the Hopi Tribe and the Hopi Partitioned Lands Accommodation Agreement.— Notwithstanding subsection (a), a lease of land by the Hopi Tribe to Navajo Indians on the Hopi Partitioned Lands may be for a term of 75 years, and may be extended at the conclusion of the term of the lease . . . .

Sec. 12. Water Rights.

(a) In General.—

(1) Water rights.—Subject to the other provisions of this section, newly acquired trust lands shall have only the following water rights:

(A) The right to the reasonable use of groundwater pumped from such lands.

(B) All rights to the use of surface water on such lands existing under State law on the date of acquisition, with the priority date of such right under State law.

(C) The right to make any further beneficial use on such lands which is unappropriated on the date each parcel of newly acquired trust lands is taken into trust. The priority date for the right shall be the date the lands are taken into trust.

(2) Rights not subject to forfeiture or abandonment.—The Tribe's water rights for newly acquired trust lands shall not be subject to forfeiture or abandonment arising from events occurring after the date the lands are taken into trust.

Delgamuukw v. British Columbia (1997)

Delgamuukw, also known as Earl Muldoe, suing on his own behalf and on behalf of all the members of the Houses of Delgamuukw and Haaxw (and others suing on their own behalf and on behalf of thirty-eight Gitksan Houses and twelve Wet'suwet'en Houses as shown in Schedule 1) Appellants/ Respondents on the cross-appeal

v.

Her Majesty The Queen in Right of

the Province of British Columbia Respondent/ Appellant on the cross-appeal

and

The Attorney General of Canada Respondent

and

The First Nations Summit,

the Musqueam Nation et al. (as shown in Schedule 2),

the Westbank First Nation,

the B.C. Cattlemen's Association et al. (as shown in Schedule 3),

Skeena Cellulose Inc.,

Alcan Aluminum Ltd. Interveners

ON APPEAL FROM THE COURT OF APPEAL FOR BRITISH COLUMBIA

The appellants, all Gitksan or Wet'suwet'en hereditary chiefs, both individually and on behalf of their "Houses," claimed separate portions of 58,000 square kilometres in British Columbia. For the purpose of the claim, this area was divided into 133 individual territories, claimed by the 71 Houses. This represents all of the Wet'suwet'en people, and all but 12 of the Gitksan Houses. Their claim was originally for "ownership" of the territory and "jurisdiction" over it. (At this Court, this was transformed into, primarily, a claim for aboriginal title over the land in question.) British Columbia counterclaimed for a declaration that the appellants have no right or interest in and to the territory or alternatively, that the appellants' cause of action ought to be for compensation from the Government of Canada.

At trial, the appellants' claim was based on their historical use and "ownership" of one or more of the territories. In addition, the Gitksan Houses have an "adaawk" which is a collection of sacred oral tradition about their ancestors, histories and territories. The Wet'suwet'en each have a "kungax" which is a spiritual song or dance or performance which ties them to their land. Both of these were entered as evidence on behalf of the appellants. The most significant evidence of spiritual connection between the

Houses and their territory was a feast hall where the Gitksan and Wet'suwet'en people tell and retell their stories and identify their territories to remind themselves of the sacred connection that they have with their lands. The feast has a ceremonial purpose but is also used for making important decisions.

The trial judge did not accept the appellants' evidence of oral history of attachment to the land. He dismissed the action against Canada, dismissed the plaintiffs' claims for ownership and jurisdiction and for aboriginal rights in the territory, granted a declaration that the plaintiffs were entitled to use unoccupied or vacant land subject to the general law of the province, dismissed the claim for damages and dismissed the province's counterclaim. No order for costs was made. On appeal, the original claim was altered in two different ways. First, the claims for ownership and jurisdiction were replaced with claims for aboriginal title and self-government, respectively. Second, the individual claims by each House were amalgamated into two communal claims, one advanced on behalf of each nation. There were no formal amendments to the pleadings to this effect. The appeal was dismissed by a majority of the Court of Appeal.

The principal issues on the appeal, some of which raised a number of sub-issues, were as follows: (1) whether the pleadings precluded the Court from entertaining claims for aboriginal title and self-government; (2) what was the ability of this Court to interfere with the factual findings made by the trial judge; (3) what is the content of aboriginal title, how is it protected by s. 35(1) of the Constitution Act, 1982, and what is required for its proof; (4) whether the appellants made out a claim to self-government; and, (5) whether the province had the power to extinguish aboriginal rights after 1871, either under its own jurisdiction or through the operation of s. 88 of the Indian Act.

Held: The appeal should be allowed in part and the cross-appeal should be dismissed. . . .

The Ability of the Court to Interfere with the Trial Judge's Factual Findings. . . .The factual findings made at trial could not stand because the trial judge's treatment of the various kinds of oral histories did not satisfy the principles laid down in *R. v. Van der Peet.* The oral histories were used in an attempt to establish occupation and use of the disputed territory which is an essential requirement for aboriginal title. The trial judge refused to admit or gave no independent weight to these oral histories and then concluded that the appellants had not

demonstrated the requisite degree of occupation for "ownership." Had the oral histories been correctly assessed, the conclusions on these issues of fact might have been very different.

The Content of Aboriginal Title, How It Is Protected by s. 35(1) of the Constitution Act, 1982, and the Requirements Necessary to Prove It . . .

Aboriginal title encompasses the right to exclusive use and occupation of the land held pursuant to that title for a variety of purposes, which need not be aspects of those aboriginal practices, customs and traditions which are integral to distinctive aboriginal cultures. The protected uses must not be irreconcilable with the nature of the group's attachment to that land.

Aboriginal title is sui generis, and so distinguished from other proprietary interests, and characterized by several dimensions. It is inalienable and cannot be transferred, sold or surrendered to anyone other than the Crown. Another dimension of aboriginal title is its sources: its recognition by the Royal Proclamation of 1763 and the relationship between the common law which recognizes occupation as proof of possession and systems of aboriginal law pre-existing assertion of British sovereignty. Finally, aboriginal title is held communally.

The exclusive right to use the land is not restricted to the right to engage in activities which are aspects of aboriginal practices, customs and traditions integral to the claimant group's distinctive aboriginal culture. Canadian jurisprudence on aboriginal title frames the "right to occupy and possess" in broad terms and, significantly, is not qualified by the restriction that use be tied to practice, custom or tradition. The nature of the Indian interest in reserve land which has been found to be the same as the interest in tribal lands is very broad and incorporates present-day needs. Finally, aboriginal title encompasses mineral rights and lands held pursuant to aboriginal title should be capable of exploitation. Such a use is certainly not a traditional one.

The content of aboriginal title contains an inherent limit in that lands so held cannot be used in a manner that is irreconcilable with the nature of the claimants' attachment to those lands. This inherent limit arises because the relationship of an aboriginal community with its land should not be prevented from continuing into the future. Occupancy is determined by reference to the activities that have taken place on the land and the uses to which the land has been put by the particular group. If lands are so

occupied, there will exist a special bond between the group and the land in question such that the land will be part of the definition of the group's distinctive culture. Land held by virtue of aboriginal title may not be alienated because the land has an inherent and unique value in itself, which is enjoyed by the community with aboriginal title to it. The community cannot put the land to uses which would destroy that value. Finally, the importance of the continuity of the relationship between an aboriginal community and its land, and the non-economic or inherent value of that land, should not be taken to detract from the possibility of surrender to the Crown in exchange for valuable consideration. On the contrary, the idea of surrender reinforces the conclusion that aboriginal title is limited. If aboriginal peoples wish to use their lands in a way that aboriginal title does not permit, then they must surrender those lands and convert them into non-title lands to do so.

Aboriginal title at common law was recognized well before 1982 and is accordingly protected in its full form by s. 35(1). The constitutionalization of common law aboriginal rights, however, does not mean that those rights exhaust the content of s. 35(1). The existence of an aboriginal right at common law is sufficient, but not necessary, for the recognition and affirmation of that right by s. 35(1).

Constitutionally recognized aboriginal rights fall along a spectrum with respect to their degree of connection with the land. At the one end are those aboriginal rights which are practices, customs and traditions integral to the distinctive aboriginal culture of the group claiming the right but where the use and occupation of the land where the activity is taking place is not sufficient to support a claim of title to the land. In the middle are activities which, out of necessity, take place on land and indeed, might be intimately related to a particular piece of land. Although an aboriginal group may not be able to demonstrate title to the land, it may nevertheless have a site-specific right to engage in a particular activity. At the other end of the spectrum is aboriginal title itself which confers more than the right to engage in site-specific activities which are aspects of the practices, customs and traditions of distinctive aboriginal cultures. Site-specific rights can be made out even if title cannot. Because aboriginal rights can vary with respect to their degree of connection with the land, some aboriginal groups may be unable to make out a claim to title, but will nevertheless pos-

sess aboriginal rights that are recognized and affirmed by s. 35(1), including site-specific rights to engage in particular activities.

Aboriginal title is a right to the land itself. That land may be used, subject to the inherent limitations of aboriginal title, for a variety of activities, none of which need be individually protected as aboriginal rights under s. 35(1). Those activities are parasitic on the underlying title. Section 35(1), since its purpose is to reconcile the prior presence of aboriginal peoples with the assertion of Crown sovereignty, must recognize and affirm both aspects of that prior presence—first, the occupation of land, and second, the prior social organization and distinctive cultures of aboriginal peoples on that land.

The test for the identification of aboriginal rights to engage in particular activities and the test for the identification of aboriginal title, although broadly similar, are distinct in two ways. First, under the test for aboriginal title, the requirement that the land be integral to the distinctive culture of the claimants is subsumed by the requirement of occupancy. Second, whereas the time for the identification of aboriginal rights is the time of first contact, the time for the identification of aboriginal title is the time at which the Crown asserted sovereignty over the land.

In order to establish a claim to aboriginal title, the aboriginal group asserting the claim must establish that it occupied the lands in question at the time at which the Crown asserted sovereignty over the land subject to the title. In the context of aboriginal title, sovereignty is the appropriate time period to consider for several reasons. First, from a theoretical standpoint, aboriginal title arises out of prior occupation of the land by aboriginal peoples and out of the relationship between the common law and pre-existing systems of aboriginal law. Aboriginal title is a burden on the Crown's underlying title. The Crown, however, did not gain this title until it asserted sovereignty and it makes no sense to speak of a burden on the underlying title before that title existed. Aboriginal title crystallized at the time sovereignty was asserted. Second, aboriginal title does not raise the problem of distinguishing between distinctive, integral aboriginal practices, customs and traditions and those influenced or introduced by European contact. Under common law, the act of occupation or possession is sufficient to ground aboriginal title and it is not necessary to prove that the land was a distinctive or integral part of the aboriginal society before the

arrival of Europeans. Finally, the date of sovereignty is more certain than the date of first contact. . . .

If present occupation is relied on as proof of occupation pre-sovereignty, there must be a continuity between present and pre-sovereignty occupation. Since conclusive evidence of pre-sovereignty occupation may be difficult, an aboriginal community may provide evidence of present occupation as proof of pre-sovereignty occupation in support of a claim to aboriginal title. An unbroken chain of continuity need not be established between present and prior occupation. The fact that the nature of occupation has changed would not ordinarily preclude a claim for aboriginal title, as long as a substantial connection between the people and the land is maintained. The only limitation on this principle might be that the land not be used in ways which are inconsistent with continued use by future generations of aboriginals.

At sovereignty, occupation must have been exclusive. This requirement flows from the definition of aboriginal title itself, which is defined in terms of the right to exclusive use and occupation of land. The test must take into account the context of the aboriginal society at the time of sovereignty. The requirement of exclusive occupancy and the possibility of joint title can be reconciled by recognizing that joint title can arise from shared exclusivity. As well, shared, non-exclusive aboriginal rights short of aboriginal title but tied to the land and permitting a number of uses can be established if exclusivity cannot be proved. The common law should develop to recognize aboriginal rights as they were recognized by either de facto practice or by aboriginal systems of governance. . . .

C. What is the content of aboriginal title, how is it protected by s. 35(1) of the Constitution Act, 1982, and what is required for its proof? . . .

(d) Aboriginal Title under s. 35(1) of the Constitution Act, 1982

Aboriginal title at common law is protected in its full form by s. 35(1). This conclusion flows from the express language of s. 35(1) itself, which states in full: "[t]he existing aboriginal and treaty rights of the aboriginal peoples of Canada are hereby recognized and affirmed". On a plain reading of the provision,

s. 35(1) did not create aboriginal rights; rather, it accorded constitutional status to those rights which were "existing" in 1982. The provision, at the very least, constitutionalized those rights which aboriginal peoples possessed at common law, since those rights existed at the time s. 35(1) came into force. Since aboriginal title was a common law right whose existence was recognized well before 1982 (e.g., Calder, supra), s. 35(1) has constitutionalized it in its full form . . . .

VI. Conclusion and Disposition

For the reasons I have given above, I would allow the appeal in part, and dismiss the cross-appeal. Reluctantly, I would also order a new trial.

I conclude with two observations. The first is that many aboriginal nations with territorial claims that overlap with those of the appellants did not intervene in this appeal, and do not appear to have done so at trial. This is unfortunate, because determinations of aboriginal title for the Gitksan and Wet'suwet'en will undoubtedly affect their claims as well. This is particularly so because aboriginal title encompasses an exclusive right to the use and occupation of land, i.e., to the exclusion of both non-aboriginals and members of other aboriginal nations. It may, therefore, be advisable if those aboriginal nations intervened in any new litigation.

Finally, this litigation has been both long and expensive, not only in economic but in human terms as well. By ordering a new trial, I do not necessarily encourage the parties to proceed to litigation and to settle their dispute through the courts . . . Sparrow, at p. 1105, s. 35(1) "provides a solid constitutional base upon which subsequent negotiations can take place." Those negotiations should also include other aboriginal nations which have a stake in the territory claimed. Moreover, the Crown is under a moral, if not a legal, duty to enter into and conduct those negotiations in good faith. Ultimately, it is through negotiated settlements, with good faith and give and take on all sides, reinforced by the judgments of this Court, that we will achieve what I stated in *Van der Peet*, supra, at para. 31, to be a basic purpose of s. 35(1)—"the reconciliation of the pre-existence of aboriginal societies with the sovereignty of the Crown." Let us face it, we are all here to stay . . ."

Index

Note: Page locators in **boldface** type indicate the location of a main encyclopedia entry.